Harnessing MicroStation

DEDICATION

HATS OFF!

bhuvana
avinash
kavitha

dorothy
zachary

mary
leah
john

Harnessing MicroStation

· · · · · · · · · · · · · · · · · · · ·

Version 5

G.V. Krishnan

Robert A. Rhea

James E. Taylor

Delmar
Publishers Inc.™

I(T)P™

NOTICE TO THE READER

Cover credit: Michael Speke

Delmar staff:
  Publisher: Michael McDermott
  Associate Editor: Pamela Graul
  Project Development Editor: Mary Beth Ray
  Production Coordinator: Andrew Crouth
  Art and Design Coordinator: Lisa Bower

For information, address
Delmar Publishers Inc.
3 Columbia Circle, Box 15015
Albany, New York 12212-5015

Printed in the United States of America
Published simultaneously in Canada
by Nelson Canada,
a division of The Thomson Corporation

10 9 8 7 6 5 4 3 2 1 XXX 00 99 98 97 96 95 94

Library of Congress Cataloging-in-Publication Data

Krishnan, G. V.
    Harnessing MicroStation, version 5/G.V. Krishnan, Robert A.
  Rhea, James E. Taylor.
      p. cm.
    Includes index.
    ISBN 0-8273-6452-0
    1. MicroStation. 2. Computer graphics. I. Rhea, Robert A.
  II. Taylor, James E. III. Title.
  T385.K74 1993   93–33108
  620'.0042'02855369—dc20   CIP

CONTENTS

●

INTRODUCTION

Harnessing MicroStation gives you the necessary skills to get going with a very powerful CAD program—MicroStation Version 5. We have created a comprehensive book providing information, references, instructions, and exercises for people of varied skill levels, disciplines, and requirements for applying this powerful design/drafting software. The book opens with an overview of all aspects of MicroStation so that the reader can get a good feeling of how CAD works as a whole. Readers immediately gain a broad range of knowledge of the elementary CAD concepts necessary to complete a simple design. We do not believe the user should be asked to wade through all components of every command or concept the first time that command or concept is introduced. Therefore, we have set up the early chapters so that fundamentals are covered and practiced extensively to better prepare them for the more advanced topics covered later in the book.

Harnessing MicroStation is intended to be both a classroom text and a desk reference. If you are already a user of MicroStation Version 3.3 or Version 4, you will see an in-depth explanation provided in the corresponding chapters for all the new features for MicroStation Version 5. Features introduced in MicroStation Version 5 give personal computer-based CADD even greater depth and breadth.

Chapter 1—Overview The beginning of this chapter describes the hardware you need to get started with MicroStation. The balance of this chapter explains how to start MicroStation, the salient features of dialog and settings boxes, and an overview of all aspects of MicroStation, including an explanation of conventions used in this book. At the end of the chapter, the enhancements to MicroStation Version 5 are listed for reference.

Chapters 2 through 5—Fundamentals Introduces all the basic element placement and manipulation commands needed to draw a moderately intricate design. All commands are accompanied by examples. Ample exercises are designed to give students the chance to test their level of skill and understanding.

Chapter 6—Plotting Introduces the features related to plotting.

Chapter 7—Cells and Cell Libraries Introduces the powerful set of tools available in MicroStation for creating and placing symbols, called cells, and storing them in Cell Libraries. The tools permit you to group elements under a user-determined name and perform certain manipulation commands on the group as though they were a single element.

Chapter 8—Patterning Introduces the set of tools available in MicroStation to place repeating patterns to fill regions in a design for various purposes.

Chapter 9—Reference Files One of the most powerful time-saving features of MicroStation is its ability to view other design files while you are working in your current design file. MicroStation lets you display the contents of up to 255 other design files (although the default is set to 32 design files) while working in your current design file. This function is in the form of reference files. This chapter introduces all the powerful tools that are available to manipulate reference files.

Chapter 10—Special Features MicroStation provides some special features that are less often used than the commands described in Chapters 1 through 9, but provide added power and versatility. This chapter introduces several such features.

Chapter 11—Customizing MicroStation Introduces several facets of Customizing MicroStation such as creating multi-line definition, custom line styles, workspace, function key menus, and installing fonts.

Chapter 12—User Commands Introduces one of the powerful features of MicroStation—the MicroStation User Command Language.

Chapter 13—3D Design and Rendering This chapter provides an overview of the tools and specific commands available for 3D design.

In addition, **appendices** are included that provide valuable information to the user such as the MicroStation Command Window pull-down menu layout and palettes, tablet menu, list of key-in commands, list of alternate key-ins, primitive commands, element types, and list of available seed files.

A sequence suitable for learning, ample exercises, examples, and review questions, and thorough coverage of the MicroStation program should make *Harnessing MicroStation* a must for multiple courses in MicroStation, as well as self-learners, everyday operators on the job, and aspiring customizers.

ACKNOWLEDGMENTS:

This book was a team effort. We are very grateful to many people who worked very hard to help create this book. We are especially grateful to the following individuals at Delmar Publishers whose efforts made it possible to complete the project on time: Mr. Mike McDermott, Publisher; Ms. Mary Beth Ray, Project Development Editor; Ms. Pamela Graul, Associate Editor; Mr. Andrew Crouth, Production Coordinator. And a special thanks to Mr. Larry O'Brien. In addition, we wish to thank Intergraph Corporation and Bentley Systems, Inc. for providing the software in a timely fashion to complete the project.

And, last but not least, we appreciate the contributions made by Anthony G. Kendrick to chapters 11 and 12.

1

OVERVIEW

INTRODUCTION

The beginning of this chapter describes the hardware you need to get started with Micro-Station. If you need to set up the MicroStation program on the computer and you are not familiar with the computer operating system (files, drives, directories, operating system commands, etc.), you may wish to review the Appendix C DOS and File Handling, refer to the Installation Guide that comes with the program, and/or consult the dealer from whom you purchased MicroStation. Once the computer is set up, you will have at your disposal a versatile design and drafting tool that continues to grow in power with each new version.

The balance of this chapter explains how to start MicroStation and gives an overview of the screen layout, the salient features of dialog and settings boxes, and all of MicroStation features. Detailed explanations and examples are provided for the concepts and commands throughout the chapters that follow.

At the end of the chapter, a list of enhancements is provided for MicroStation Version 5. If you are already a user of MicroStation Version 4, check the list to see the new and improved features in version 5. Throughout the book you will see that an in-depth explanation is provided in the corresponding chapters for all the new features of MicroStation Version 5. Features introduced in MicroStation Version 5 give personal computer-based CADD even greater depth and breadth. Following are the four important goals that were met in enhancing the MicroStation Version 5:

■ Improved ease of use.
■ Increased productivity.
■ Enhancement of visualization tools.
■ Read/Write files in industry-accepted formats.

HARDWARE CONFIGURATION

The configuration of your system is a combination of the hardware and software you have assembled to create your system. Countless PC configurations are available. The goal for a new computer user should be to assemble a PC workstation that will not block future software and hardware upgrades.

To use MicroStation, your computer system must meet certain requirements. The PC must have:

Processors: 80386SX, 80386, 80486SX, 80486, or Pentium processor.

Math coprocessor: Required only for 80386SX and 80486SX processors (80386, 80486, and Pentium processors have a built-in coprocessor).

Memory: Minimum of 4 megabytes of random access memory (RAM). One megabyte contains 640K of conventional memory.

Drives: A hard disk with at least 40 megabyte (MB) capacity and 1.2MB 5¼″ floppy drive or 1.44MB 3½″ floppy drive.

A video monitor and supported display adapter.

A graphic input device (mouse or digitizing tablet)

DOS version 3.1 or better.

Plotters and printers.

Processors Select the one that best suits your work load. The faster and more powerful the processor, the better MicroStation performs. Thus, the processor of choice is generally the most technologically advanced one currently available. With the availability of fast 80486 base systems under $2,000, a good platform for MicroStation can be attained from a number of sources. Several manufacturers of RISC processors are introducing PC compatible systems that can now run most DOS applications.

Memory To run MicroStation, your computer must be equipped with at least 4 MB of RAM (random access memory). Depending on your MicroStation application 8 MB of RAM or more may be required for optimal performance. If you are going to be using MicroStation in Windows 3.1, you may require 12 to 16 MB for the same level of performance. The availability of low-cost RAM has made this an easy upgrade for most MicroStation users.

Hard Drives The hard disk is the personal computer's primary data storage device. A hard disk with at least 40 MB capacity is required, but a larger capacity is advised. The hard disk accesses data at a rate of 12 milliseconds to 80 milliseconds. High performance is 30 milliseconds or faster, while 80 milliseconds is considered slow. Obviously, the faster the hard-disk drive, the more productive you will be with MicroStation.

Video Adapter and Display As with any graphics program for PC CAD systems, MicroStation requires a video adapter capable of displaying graphics information. A video adapter is a printed circuit board that plugs into the central processing unit (CPU) and generates signals to drive a monitor. MicroStation supports a number of display options, ranging from low-priced monochrome setups to high resolution color units. Some of the video display controllers can be used in combination, giving a two-screen display.

Input Devices MicroStation supports several input device configurations. Data may be entered through the keyboard, a mouse, or a digitizing tablet with a cursor.

The keyboard is one of the primary input methods. It can be used to enter commands and responses.

A mouse is used with the keyboard as a tracking device to move the cross hairs on the screen. MicroStation supports a two-button mouse, and a three-button mouse (see Figure 1–1). As you move your pointing device around on a mouse pad or other suitable surface, the cursor will mimic your movements on the screen. It may be in the form of cross hairs when you are being prompted to select a point. Each of the buttons in the mouse is programmed to serve specific functions in MicroStation. See Table 1–1 for the specific functions that are programmed for the two- and three-button mice:

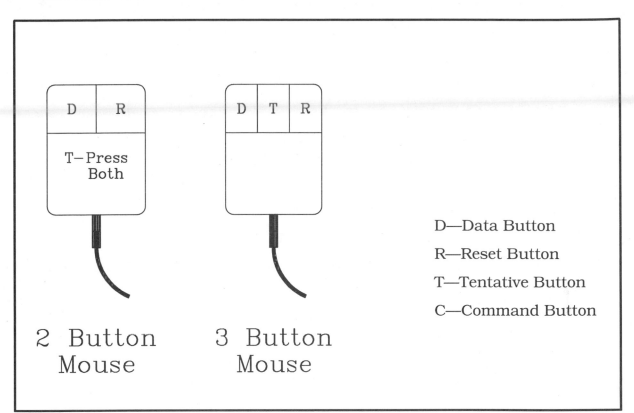

FIGURE 1–1   Pointing Device—Two-button mouse and Three-button mouse.

Table 1–1.

FUNCTION	TWO-BUTTON MOUSE	THREE-BUTTON MOUSE
Data button	left (first)	left (first)
Reset button	right (second)	right (third)
Tentative button	left and right simultaneously	center (second)

A digitizer is literally an electronic drawing board. An internal wiring system forms a grid of fine mesh, which corresponds to the coordinate points on the screen. The digitizer is used with a puck. When the user moves the puck across the digitizer, cross hairs follow on the screen. The number of buttons found on a cursor depends on the manufacturer. A puck usually has four buttons, as shown in Figure 1–2; each of the buttons on the puck is programmed to serve specific functions in MicroStation. If there are more than four buttons on the puck, the first four are pre-programmed. For example, when you place a line, the points are selected by pressing the designated data button in two locations. Although the user's attention is focused on the screen, the points are actually selected on the coordinates of the tablet. The coordinates from the tablet are then transmitted to the computer, which draws the image of a line on your screen.

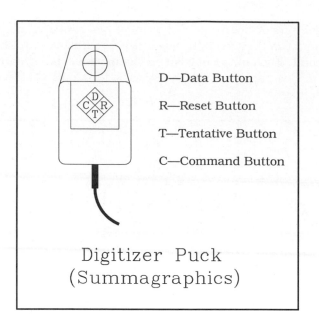

D—Data Button

R—Reset Button

T—Tentative Button

C—Command Button

Digitizer Puck
(Summagraphics)

FIGURE 1–2 Pointing Device—Digitizer Puck.

Another advantage of a tablet is the ability to use a tablet menu for command selection. Menus have graphic representations of the commands and are taped to the digitizing tablet's surface. The menu is attached or activated with the key-in **AM=** followed by that menu's specific name. See Appendix B for a detailed explanation of the menu attachment. The commands are chosen by placing the puck's cross hairs over the block that represents the command you want to use and pressing the designated command button. Another powerful feature of the tablet (not related to entering commands) is that it allows you to lay a map or other picture on the tablet and trace over it with the puck. See Table 1–2 for the specific functions that are programmed for the four-button puck:

Table 1–2.

FUNCTION	FOUR-BUTTON PUCK
Data button	Top (yellow)
Reset button	Right (green)
Tentative button	Bottom (blue)
Command button	Left (white)

Detailed explanations of the functions are explained later in the chapter.

GETTING STARTED

To get started with MicroStation, call up the USTATION batch file by typing USTATION at the DOS prompt and press [ENTER].

    C:\> **USTATION** [ENTER]

This causes the MicroStation Manager dialog box to be displayed on your screen, as shown in Figure 1–3.

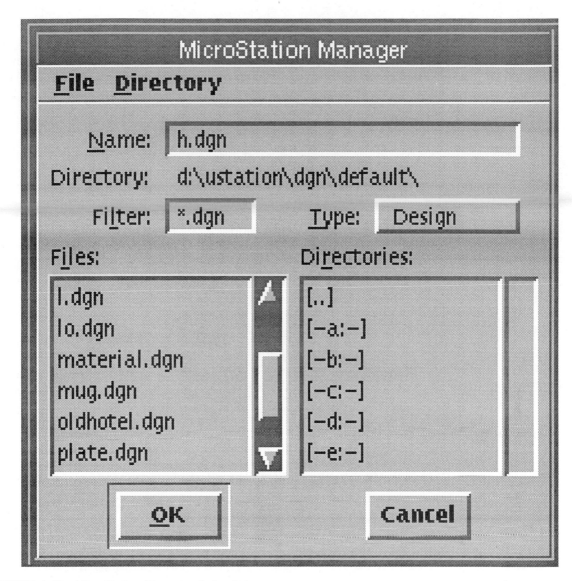

FIGURE 1-3   MicroStation Manager dialog box.

> **NOTE:** Unless certain DOS paths and systems configurations are properly set up, you should not initiate the MicroStation program from a directory other than the one that the MicroStation files are in.

Before we start a new design file, let's discuss the important features of dialog and settings boxes.

USING DIALOG AND SETTINGS BOXES

A dialog box is a special type of window displayed by MicroStation. Dialog boxes were designed to permit the user to perform many actions easily within MicroStation. Dialog boxes force MicroStation to stop and focus on what is happening in that dialog box only. You cannot do anything else in MicroStation until you close the dialog box. The MicroStation Manager is a good example of this type of dialog box.

In addition to dialog boxes, MicroStation provides setting boxes. Several settings boxes can be left on the screen while you work in other areas of MicroStation. For instance, the Lock Toggles settings box (see Figure 1–4) can be left open as long as you need. When it is left open, you can turn the locks on and off as you need and at the same time interact with other dialog boxes. To close the settings box, double-click the (–) symbol located on the top left corner of the settings box.

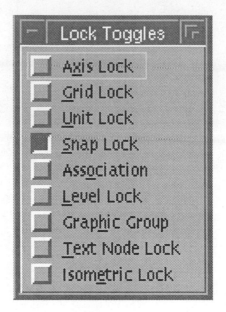

FIGURE 1–4   Lock Toggles settings box.

When you move the cursor on to a dialog/settings box, the cursor changes to a pointer. You can use the arrow keys on your keyboard to make selections, but it is much easier to use your pointing device. Another way to make selections is to use keyboard equivalents.

Title Bar and Menu Bar Item   MicroStation displays the title of the dialog and settings boxes in the Title Bar as shown in Figure 1–5. Below the Title Bar, MicroStation displays any available pull-down menus in the menu bar, as shown in Figure 1–5. In this case, two pull-down menus are available, File and Directory. Selecting from the list is a simple matter of moving the cursor down until the desired item is highlighted, then pressing the designated pick (data) button on the pointing device. If a menu item has an arrow to the right, it has a cascading sub-menu, as shown in Figure 1–6. To display the sub-menu, just click on the menu title. Menu items that include ellipses (...) display dialog boxes. To select these, just pick the menu item.

Label Item   MicroStation displays the text (display only) to label the different parts of the dialog box/settings box as shown in Figure 1–7.

Edit Field   An edit field is an area that accepts one line of text entry. It normally is used to specify a name such as a filename including the drive and/or directory path or level name. Edit fields often are used as an alternative to selecting from a list of names when the desired name is not displayed in the list box. Once the correct text is keyed in, enter it by pressing ENTER.

Moving the pointer into the edit box causes the text cursor to appear in a manner similar to the cursor in a word processor. If necessary, the text cursor, in combination with special editing keys, can be used to facilitate changes to the text. You can see the text cursor and the pointer at the same time, making it possible to click the pointer on a character in the edit field and relocate the text cursor to

MicroStation Manager

File   Directory

Name: first.dgh

Directory: d:\ustation\dgn\default\

Filter: *.dgn   Type: Design

Files: Directories:

first.dgn   [..]
h.dgn   [-a:-]
l.dgn   [-b:-]
lo.dgn   [-c:-]
material.dgn   [-d:-]
mug.dgn   [-e:-]

OK   **Cancel**

FIGURE 1–5   MicroStation Manager dialog box showing the Title bar and pull-down menus.

MicroStation Command Window – first.dgn, NOT SERIALIZED

File Edit Element   Settings View Palettes Snaps User   Help

Locks=SN   **Tool Settings**   LV=1,WT=0,LC=SOL,CO=0,TP=KeyPt
Element Selection
(1) uSTN>   **Groups**   ▷   **Select**
                                                        Edit
                            Active Angle
                            Active Scale
                            Auxiliary Coordinates
                            Cells
                            Colors   ▷
                            Coordinate Readout
                            Database
                            Digitizing
                            Grid
                            Level Names...
                            Level Symbology...
                            Locks   ▷
                            Rendering   ▷
                            Tag Sets
                            Working Units...

                            Precision Input

FIGURE 1–6   MicroStation Command Window displaying cascading sub-menu for the Groups in the settings pull-down menu.

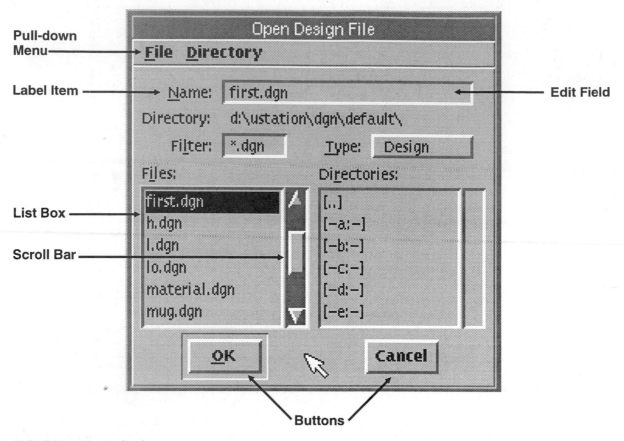

FIGURE 1–7 Dialog box.

that character. You can select a group of characters in the edit box to manipulate, for instance, or to delete by highlighting the characters. This is accomplished by holding down the designated pick button on your pointing device and dragging left or right. You can also use the right and left arrows on the keyboard to move the cursor right or left, respectively, across text without affecting the text.

List Boxes and Scroll Bars List boxes make it easy to view, select, and enter a name from a list of existing items such as filenames (see Figure 1–7). Use the pointer to highlight the desired selection. The item, when clicked, will appear in the edit box. You may accept this item by clicking OK or by double-clicking on the item. List boxes are accompanied by scroll bars to facilitate moving long lists up and down in the list box. When you point and hold onto the slider box, you can move it up and down to cause the list to scroll. Using the up/down arrows cause the list to scroll up or down one item at a time.

Buttons Actions are initiated immediately when one of the various buttons is clicked (OK or Cancel, for example). If a button (such as the OK button in Figure 1–7) is surrounded by a heavy line, it is the default button and pressing [ENTER] is the same as clicking that button. Buttons with action that is not acceptable will be disabled; they will appear grayed out. Buttons with ellipses (...) will cause that action's own dialog box (sub-dialog) to appear.

Toggle Buttons A button that indicates an ON or OFF setting, it is also called a Check Box or Toggle Button. For instance, in Figure 1–8, Axis, Grid, and Snap locks are set to ON and the remaining locks are set to OFF.

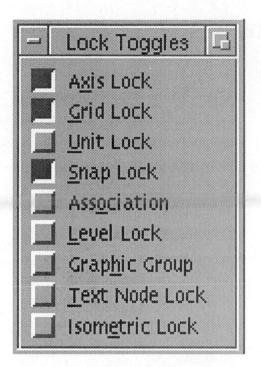

FIGURE 1–8 Toggle buttons.

Option Button A list of items is displayed when you click on the option button menu and only one item may be selected from the list as shown in Figure 1–9.

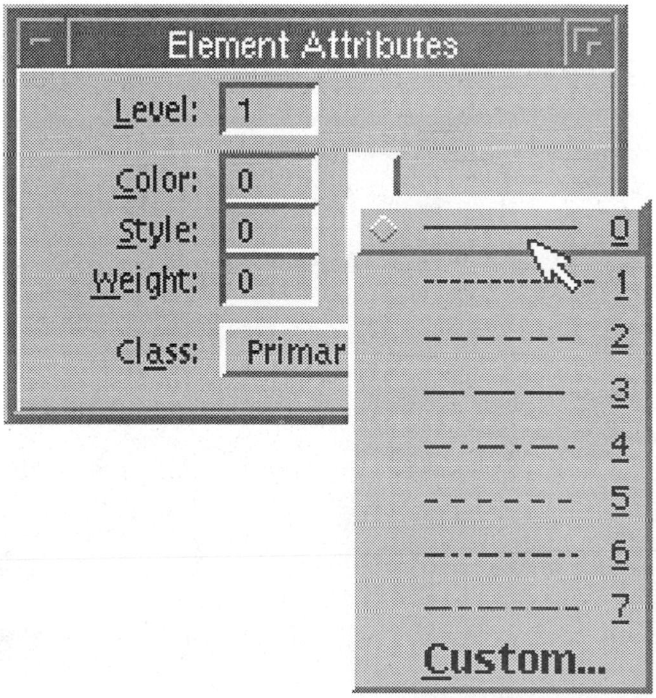

FIGURE 1–9 Option button menu.

Let's get on to the business of starting a new design file in MicroStation.

BEGINNING A NEW DESIGN

To begin a new design, select the New... command from the File pull-down menu as shown in Figure 1–10.

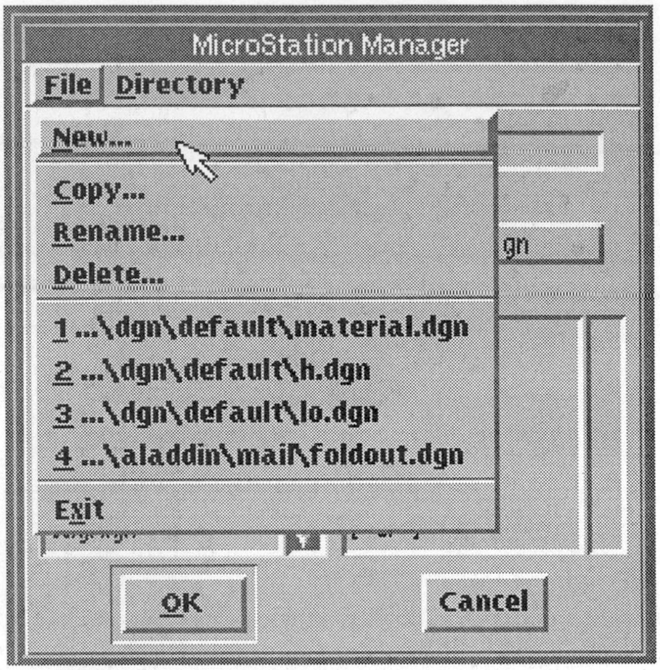

FIGURE 1–10   Invoking the New... command from the File pull-down menu.

The Create Design File dialog box opens as shown in Figure 1–11.

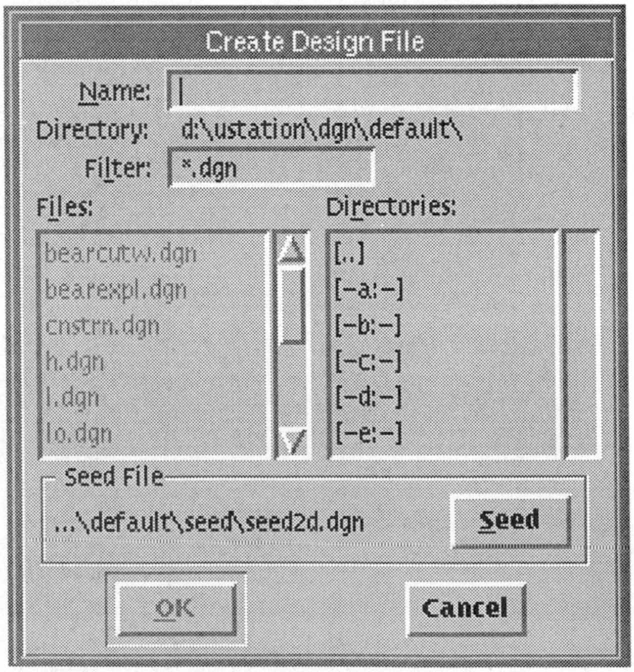

FIGURE 1–11   Create Design File dialog box.

Select the appropriate seed file (more about this in the section on seed files), enter a name for your new design in the Name edit field, and click OK. The Create Design File dialog box is closed and control is passed to MicroStation Manager. MicroStation by default highlights the name of the file you just created in the Files list box. To open the new design file, click the OK button and your screen will look similar to the one shown in Figure 1–12.

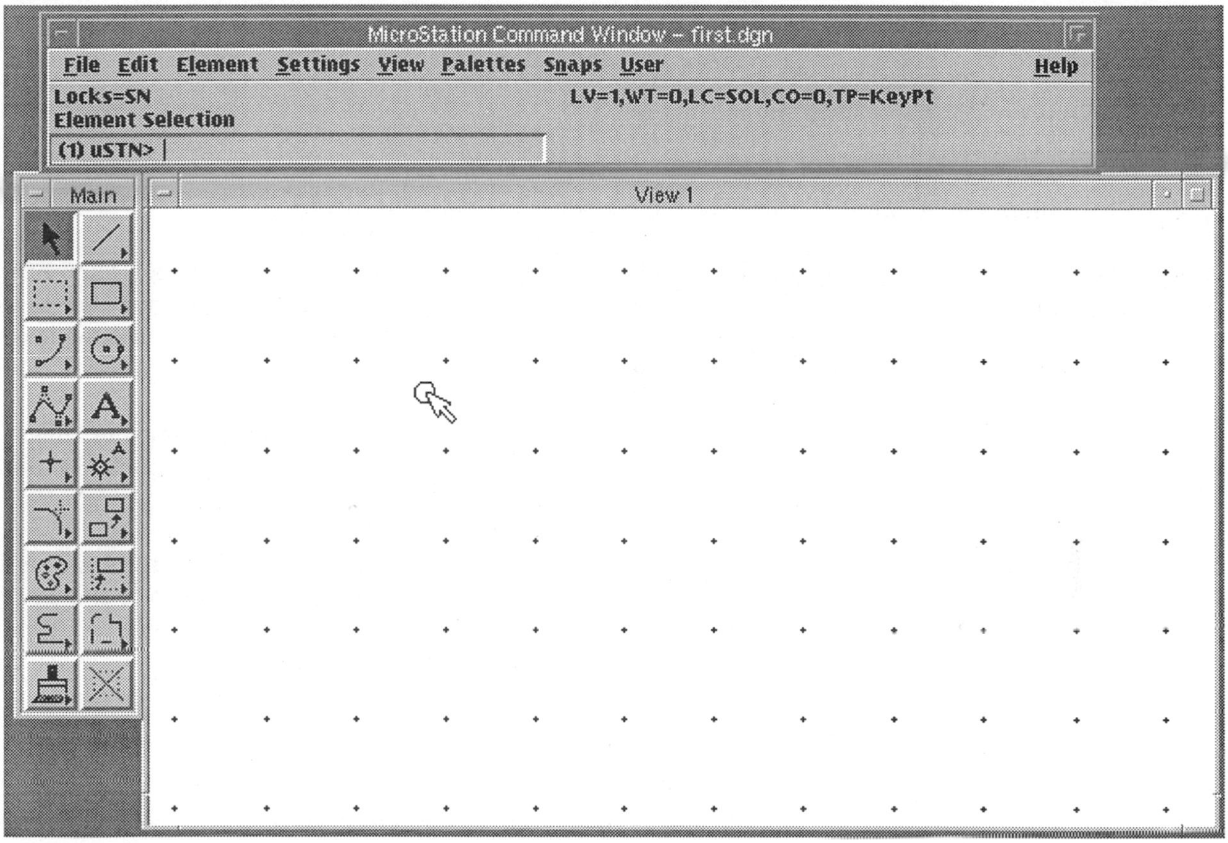

FIGURE 1–12   MicroStation Command Window and View display.

NOTE: If the design filename you key-in is the same as the name of an existing file name, MicroStation displays an Alert Box asking if you want to replace the existing file. Click OK to replace, or Cancel to reissue a new filename.

Filenames

The name you enter in the Name edit field will be the name of the file in which information about the design is stored. It must satisfy the requirements for filenames as specified by the particular operating system your computer uses. DOS and UNIX are the two most common operating systems.

Filenames in DOS   In PC-DOS™ and MS-DOS™ each design is a file with a "file specification." The file specification, or file spec, is the full name of the file. The file specification consists of a name and an extension. For example, in the file specification, FLOOR.DGN, FLOOR is the filename and .DGN is the extension. Filenames are from one to eight characters and extensions can be a maximum of three characters. Names and extensions are separated by a period. Names may be made up of combinations of uppercase or lowercase letters, numbers, the underscore (_), the hyphen (-), and the dollar sign ($). DOS converts all of the characters to uppercase. No blank spaces are allowed in the name. Valid examples include:

> floor-1.dgn
> lab1.dgn
> $345-p.dgn
> PART_NO5.wrk

Examples of improper key names include:

> *test.dgn   asterisk not a valid character
> nametoolong.dgn   name too long, more than eight characters

When MicroStation prompts for a design name, just type in the filename and MicroStation will append the extension .DGN by default. For instance, if you respond to the design name as FLOOR1, then MicroStation will create a file with the file spec FLOOR1.DGN. If you need to provide a different extension, key-in the extension with the filename.

As you progress through the lessons, note how various functions ask for names of files. If Micro-Station performs the file processing, it usually adds the proper default extension. If you use DOS, you should include the extension.

The Path   If you want to create a new design file or edit a design file that is on a drive and/or directory other than the current drive/directory, you must furnish what is called the path to the design file as part of the file specification you enter. Specifying a path requires that you use the correct pathfinder symbols, colon (:) and/or backslash (\). The drive with a letter name (usually A through E) is identified as such by a colon, and slashes enclose the name of the directory where the design file is (or will be) located. Examples of path/key name combinations are as follows:

> a:proj1   the file proj1 in working directory on drive A
> b:\spec\elev   the file elev is in \spec directory on drive B
> \buil\john   the file john in \buil directory
> ACME\doors   the file doors in working directory's ACME sub-directory
> ..\PIT\flange   the file flange in parent directory's PIT sub-directory

> **NOTE:** Instead of specifying the path as part of the design file name, select the appropriate drive and directory from the list box and then select the design file from file list box. MicroStation Manager displays the current drive and path in the dialog box just below Name edit field.

Seed Files

Each time you use MicroStation's Create New File utility, a copy is made of an existing "prototype" or "seed" file. If necessary, you can customize the seed file. In other words, you can control the initial "makeup" of the file. To do so, open an existing seed file, make the necessary changes in the settings of the parameters, and place elements such as title block, etc. Whenever you start a new design file, make sure to copy the appropriate seed file.

MicroStation programs come with several seed files. See Appendix J for a list of seed files and default working units. Depending on the discipline, use an appropriate seed file. For instance, if you plan to work on an architecture floor plan, then use the architecture seed file (SDARCH2D.DGN). When you open the Create Design file, MicroStation displays the name of the default seed file as shown in Figure 1–13. If necessary, you can change the default seed file by clicking the seed button. MicroStation displays a list of seed files available as shown in Figure 1–14. Select the one you want to use from the list and click OK button.

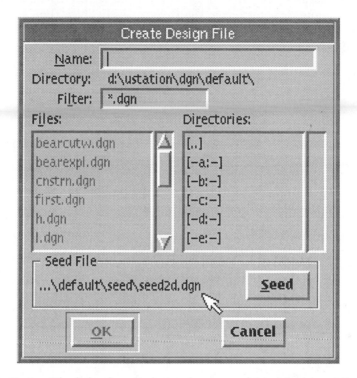

FIGURE 1–13   Create Design File dialog box displaying the name of the default seed file.

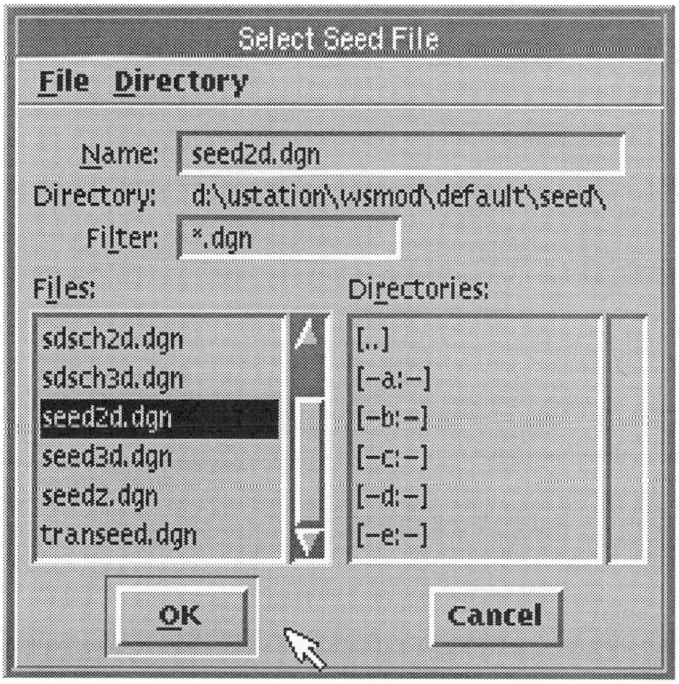

FIGURE 1–14   Select Seed File dialog box.

OPENING AN EXISTING DESIGN

Whenever you want to open an existing design in MicroStation, simply click the name of the file in the Files list box item of the MicroStation Manager dialog box, then click the OK button or double-click the name of the file. If the design file is not in the current directory, change to the appropriate drive and directory from the Directories list box, then select the appropriate design file. In addition, MicroStation displays the names (including the path) of the last four design files opened in the File pull-down menu as shown in Figure 1–15. If you need to open one of the four design files, click on the file name and MicroStation displays the design file.

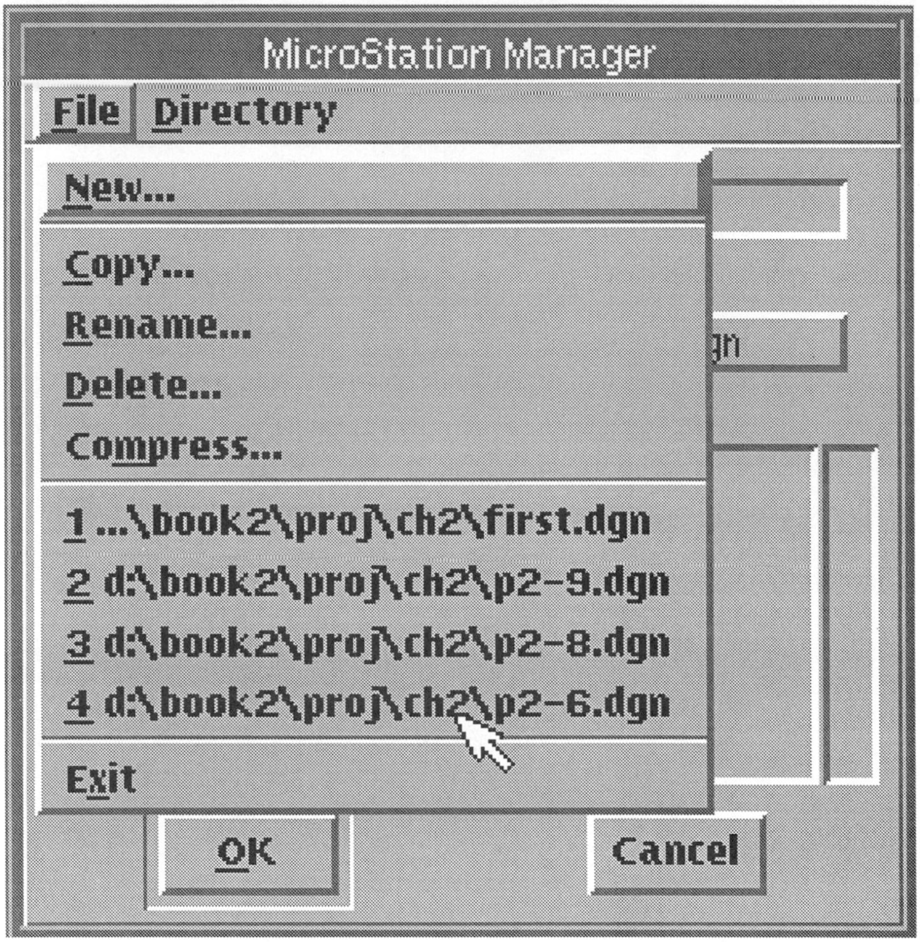

FIGURE 1–15 File pull-down menu from the MicroStation Manager displaying the names of the last four design files opened.

NOTE: You can also create a new design file or open an existing design file by selecting the New... and Open... commands respectively from the File pull-down menu located in the MicroStation Command Window.

MICROSTATION COMMAND WINDOW

When you first get into MicroStation, you will see one or more views and MicroStation Command Window, as shown in Figure 1–16.

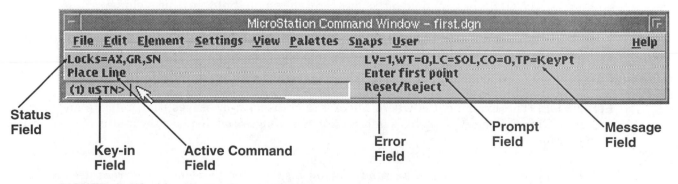

FIGURE 1–16 MicroStation Command Window and View windows.

The MicroStation Command Window is the heart and soul of MicroStation, and it is the "Command Center" much like the dashboard of a car. The Command Window is movable and it is the only window you cannot close. It has a set of pull-down menus. The Command Window is divided into six fields, as shown in Figure 1–17, that keep you aware of MicroStation's internal activity. The fields tell you what MicroStation is currently doing and when an operation is complete, and it will help you along by supplying cues or prompts to complete a command. It is very important to keep track of what is going on in the program by keeping an eye on the six fields:

FIGURE 1–17 MicroStation Command Window.

Status Field The Status field is where MicroStation answers a query and displays the status of the locks, such as the grid, snap, axis, etc.

Message Field The Message field is where MicroStation displays the values of your most basic element parameters, such as the active color, line weight, line code, and so forth.

Active Command Field The Active Command field is where MicroStation displays the name of the last command you selected (the active command). You may continue using the command as long as it is displayed in this field. A command continues to be displayed in this field until a new command is selected, or, in a few cases, when the Reset button is pressed.

Prompt Field The Prompt field is where MicroStation displays messages that tell you what to do next. Several key words appear in this field. The key words indicate which buttons on the pointing device are appropriate for the active command. As you gain experience with MicroStation, the key words will become familiar and easy to use.

> **NOTE:** The Prompt field messages are shown in *italics* in this volume at appropriate places.

Key-in Field The Key-in field (uSTN>) is where MicroStation displays the keyboard input. Whatever you type on the keyboard is displayed in this field. Of special interest is the time-saving feature of this field. It allows the last 20 commands entered to be recalled by pressing the up and down arrow keys on the keyboard. The prompt (uSTN>) may change from time to time, depending upon the active command. For instance, while placing a Circle with Radius option, the uSTN> prompt is replaced with RADIUS: to tell the user to input the radius for the circle to be drawn.

> **NOTE:** The prompt changes only when you key-in the command instead of selecting from the menu. If you invoke the command from the menu, appropriate prompts appear in the dialog or settings box.

> **NOTE:** Key-in field messages are shown in **bold** in this volume at appropriate places.

Error Field The Error field is where MicroStation displays messages that indicate an error has occurred. This field most often gives informational messages and displays the status of an operation being performed.

In addition, the MicroStation Command Window displays the name of the current design you are working in, as shown in Figure 1–17.

PULL-DOWN MENUS AND PALETTES

As explained earlier, the Command Window has a set of pull-down menus, as shown in Figure 1–17. Several palettes and dialog and setting boxes are available from the pull-down menus. To select one of the pull-down menus, click on the name of the pull-down menu, and MicroStation displays the list of options available. Selecting from the list is a simple matter of moving the cursor down until the desired item is highlighted and then pressing the Data button on the pointing device. If a menu item has an arrow to the right, it has a cascading sub-menu. To display the sub-menu, click on the name of the sub-menu and the cascading sub-menu will be displayed. Menu items that include ellipses (...) display dialog boxes. When a dialog box is displayed, no other action is allowed until that dialog box is dismissed or closed.

The Palettes pull-down menu displays the list of palettes available in MicroStation. To select one of the available palettes, just click on the name of the palette and it will be displayed on the screen. You can place the palette anywhere on the screen by dragging with your pointing device. There is no limit to the number of palettes that can be displayed on the screen. If you are working with two monitors, you can drag the palette to the second monitor. You can close the palette by double-clicking the (–) symbol located on the top left corner of the palette. When you open the palette, it is displayed at the same location where it was previously open.

The most important palette is the Main palette. To access the Main palette, click on the Main under the Palettes pull-down menu, as shown in Figure 1–18. The Main palette is displayed, as shown in Figure 1–19. Most drawing tools are selected from the Main palette and its sub-palettes. Consider always leaving the Main palette open while drawing. The palette with an arrow pointing right indicates the availability of the sub-palette, as shown in Figure 1–19. To access one of the sub-palettes press and hold on the sub-palette, drag it to anywhere on the screen, and release it. Then select the appropriate command options from the sub-palette. Figure 1–20 shows the Lines sub-palette taken out from the Main palette.

FIGURE 1–18   Invoking the Main palette from the Palettes pull-down menu.

FIGURE 1–19 Main palette.

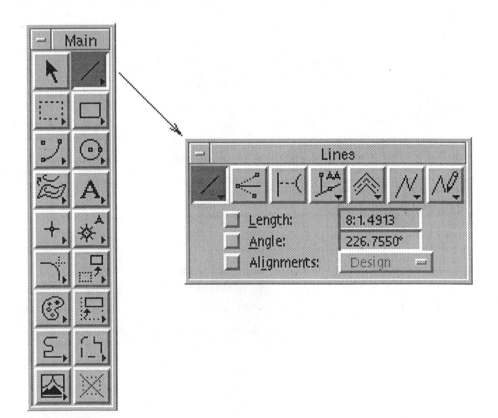

FIGURE 1–20 Lines sub-palette taken out from the Main palette.

See the pull-out MicroStation menu layout for the MicroStation pull-down menu, palettes, and dialog and settings boxes in the back of this book.

SETTINGS BOXES

The settings boxes allow you to define how a design is displayed and how elements in the design are placed, scaled, dimensioned, etc. As mentioned earlier, you can open more than one settings box and change settings as necessary. For example, the Active Scale settings box shown in Figure 1–21 has controls to adjust the settings that determine how elements are scaled. Most settings boxes are opened from the pull-down Settings menu. You can close the settings box by double-clicking the (–) symbol located at the top left corner or clicking the push buttons at the top right of the settings box.

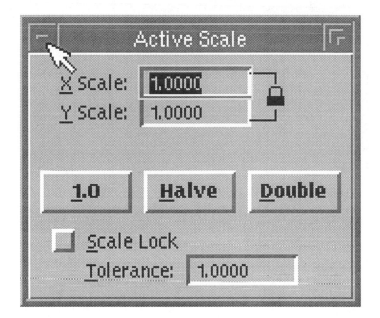

FIGURE 1–21   Scale settings box.

VIEW WINDOWS

MicroStation displays the elements you draw in the view windows. The portion of the design displayed within a view window is referred to as a view. Within this part of the screen, all of the various commands you enter will construct your design. As you progress, you can ZOOM IN and ZOOM OUT to control the design's display. A view typically shows a portion of the design, but may show in its entirety, as in Figure 1–22.

Eight views can be open (ON) at the same time and all views are active. This lets you begin an operation in one view and complete it in another. You can move a view window by pressing and holding the cursor on the Title Bar and dragging it to anywhere on the screen. You can close the view window by double-clicking the (–) symbol located at the top left corner of the window. You can resize the display window by clicking and dragging on its surrounding border, and shrink and expand the window by clicking the push buttons located at the top right corner of the window. Detailed explanations of the Display (View) commands are provided in chapters 2 through 6.

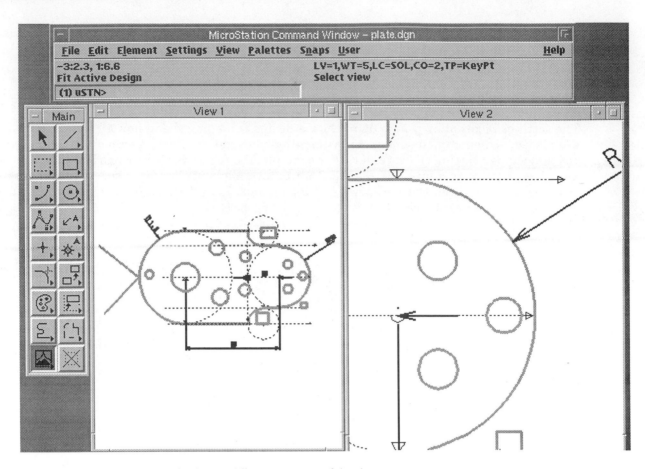

FIGURE 1–22 Two views displaying different portions of the design.

INPUT METHODS

Input method refers to the manner in which you tell MicroStation what command to use and how to operate the command. As mentioned earlier, the two most popular input devices used are the mouse and the digitizing tablet in addition to the keyboard.

Keyboard

To enter a command from the keyboard, simply key-in (type) the command name at the "uSTN>" prompt, then press ⟦ENTER⟧. Key-in is the name given to the function of providing information via the keyboard to MicroStation. MicroStation key-in language is much like plain English. For example, keying in the PLACE LINE selects the line command, DELETE ELEMENT selects the delete command, and so on. See Appendix D for a list of the key-in commands available in MicroStation.

Pointing Devices

As mentioned earlier, MicroStation supports a two-button mouse, three-button mouse, and a digitizer. Depending on your needs and hardware, select one of the three pointing devices.

Detailed explanations of the functions that are programmed to the pointing device buttons (mouse and digitizing tablet puck) are as follows:

Data Button (or Pick button) This is the most-used button on the mouse/puck. The Data button is used to:

> Select command from pull-down menus and palettes.

> Define location points in the design plane.

> Identify elements that are to be manipulated.

In addition, it is used to accept tentative points, and generally tell the computer "yes" (accept) whenever it is prompted to do so. The Data button is also referred as the Identify button or Accept button.

Reset Button The Reset button is used to stop the current operation and reset MicroStation to the beginning of the current command sequence. For instance, when you are in the Place Line command, a series of lines can be drawn by using the Data button. When you are ready to stop the sequence, press the Reset button. MicroStation will stop the current operation and reset the Line sequence to the beginning. In addition, the Reset button is also used to reject a prompt, and generally to tell the computer "no" (reject) whenever it is prompted to do so. The reset button is also referred as the Reject button.

Tentative Button The tentative point is one of MicroStation's most powerful features. The Tentative button is used to place a tentative (temporary) point on the screen. Once you are happy with the location of the point, accept it with the Data button. In other words, the tentative point lets you try a couple of places before actually selecting the final resting point for the data point. The Tentative button also can snap to elements at specific locations; for instance, the center and four quadrants of the circle, when the Snap lock is turned to ON. For a detailed explanation, see Chapter 2.

Command Button The Command button is only available on digitizer tablet puck and is used to choose commands from the tablet menu. To do so, look down on the tablet menu, and place the puck cross hairs in the box that represents the command you want to activate, then press the Command button. The corresponding command will appear in the active command field of the Command Window.

See Table 1–1 (page 1–3) and Table 1–2 (page 1–4) for the specific functions that are programmed for the two- and three-button mouse and four-button digitizer puck.

Cursor Menu

MicroStation Version 5 introduces a cursor menu that can be made to appear at the location of the cursor by pressing the designated button on your pointing device. Two cursor menus are available, one for View Control commands and other one for Snap Mode options.

To invoke the View Control Commands (Figure 1–23), press ⌗SHIFT + Reset button. The menu includes all the available commands for controlling the display of the design.

To invoke the Snap Mode options (Figure 1–24), press ⌗SHIFT + Tentative button. The menu includes all the available snap mode options. The reason for the snap mode options being in such ready access will become evident when you learn the significance of these functions.

FIGURE 1–23   Cursor menu ([SHIFT] + Reset button)—View Control commands.

FIGURE 1–24   Cursor menu ([SHIFT] + Tentative button)—Snap Mode options.

THE DESIGN PLANE

In conventional drafting, the drawing is normally done to a certain scale, such as ¼″ = 1′-0″ or 1″ = 1′-0″. But in MicroStation, you draw full scale: All lines, circles, and other elements are drawn and measured as full size. For example, if a part is 150 feet long, it is drawn as 150 feet actual size. When you are ready to plot the part, MicroStation scales the design to fit a given sheet size.

Whenever you start a new two-dimensional design, you get a design plane—the electronic equivalent of a sheet of paper on a drafting table. The two-dimensional design planc is a large, flat plane covered with an invisible matrix grid consisting of 4,294,967,296 (2^{32}) by 4,294,967,296 (2^{32}) coordinate intersections along the X and Y axis. The distance between two adjutant points is one positional unit or unit of resolution (UOR). The center of the design plane (2,147,483,648 by 2,147,483,648) is the global origin and assigned coordinates (0,0) as shown in Figure 1–25. Any point to the right of the global origin has a positive X valuc; any point to the left has a negative X value. Any point above the global origin has a positive Y value; any point below has a negative Y value.

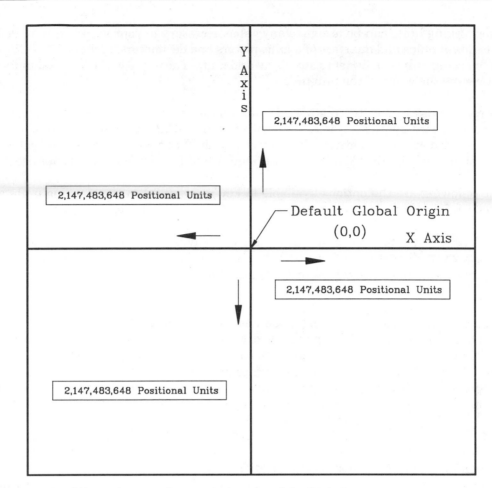

FIGURE 1-25   X and Y coordinates indicating the location of the Global origin.

If necessary, you can change the location or coordinates of the global origin. For example, an architect may want all coordinates to be positive in value, therefore sets the global origin at the left bottom corner of the design plane.

WORKING UNITS

As mentioned earlier, a design plane is divided into positional units (2^{32} by 2^{32}), but, at the same time, you can draw in "real world" units such as feet and inches, or meters and centimeters. These real world units are called Working Units.

Working units are composed of Master or Major units (MU), Sub-units (SU) and working resolution or Positional Units (PU). The Master unit is the largest unit that is being used in the design. The fractional parts of a Master unit are called Sub-units. The number of positional units per sub-unit is the working resolution. Working resolution determines both the precision with which elements are drawn and the working area of the design plane.

For example, you can draw a building floor plan specifying feet as Master units, inches as Sub-units (12 parts make one Master unit), and 1,600 positional units per Sub-unit. Adjacent data points can be entered as close as 1/1600 of an inch on a design plane stretching 223,696 feet (4,294,967,296 ÷ 1600 × 12) in each dimension. Enough room for a whole city!

The working units can be assigned any value necessary to your work. You can define working area in terms of miles and quarters of a mile, meters and decimeters, inches and tenths of an inch, and so on. Working units can be set to any real world units. The number of positional units that are specified determine the value of the Sub-units.

When you wish to specify a distance, radius, and so on, it is based on the working units. MicroStation has a standard syntax for doing this with the MU:SU:PU format. Each one of the three positions represents a value in relation to its respective unit. Whenever you key-in the value, make sure to use the colon (:) to separate Major units, Sub-units, and Positional units. Do *not* use semicolon (;).

The following are the options available to key-in 3⅛ ft when the working units are set as feet for Major units, inches for Sub-units, and 1,600 Positional units per Sub-unit:

3.125	(In terms of feet, one need not specify SU and PU as they are 0)
3:1.25	(In terms of feet and inches, one need not specify PU)
3:1:200	(In terms of feet, inches, positional units)
0:37.25	(In terms of inches)

Whenever you start a new design, you need not set the working units if you used the appropriate seed file to create the new design file. To draw an architectural floor plan, you copy SDARCH2D.DGN (architectural seed file); then MicroStation sets the working units to feet, inches, and 8,000 positional units. See Appendix J for a list of seed files and default working units available with MicroStation Version 5. If necessary, you can make changes to the current working units, by invoking the Working Units... command from the Settings pull-down menu. The Working Units dialog box is displayed, similar to the one shown in Figure 1–26. Enter the appropriate unit names under the Master units edit box and Sub-units edit box. Enter the number of Sub-units per Master unit in the edit box provided under the Resolution column. You can also change the number of positional units per Sub-unit under the Resolution column. MicroStation will display the total working area at the bottom of the settings box. Click the OK button to close the dialog box. MicroStation will display an Alert dialog box similar to the one shown in Figure 1–27. Click OK button to continue if you really want to make the changes.

FIGURE 1–26 Working Units dialog box.

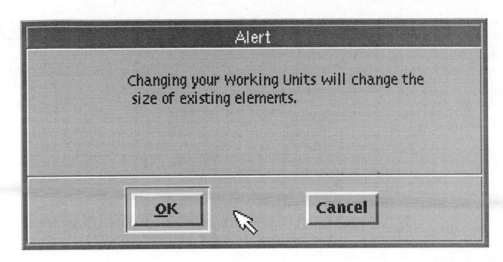

FIGURE 1–27 Alert dialog box.

Set the appropriate working units before you start drawing. Do not change the working units when you have already placed elements in the design. Changing the working units changes the size of existing elements.

SAVING CHANGES AND EXITING THE DESIGN FILE

Before we discuss how to place elements in the design file, let's talk about how to save the current design file. MicroStation saves all elements in your design file as you draw them. There is no separate SAVE command. You may get out of your design file without doing the proper exit procedure and still not lose any work. Even if there is a power failure during a design session, you will get most of the design file back without significant damage. If necessary, you can save the current design file to a different name by invoking the SAVE AS... command located under the File pull-down menu.

As mentioned earlier, MicroStation automatically saves everything you draw. However, it does not save design and view settings. Design settings affect the appearance of your design in the view windows. You may have the color set to red so that everything you are currently drawing is red. View settings are the view window setup you are currently using. For example, you may have view 1 zoomed in close to see greater detail in a section of the design and view 2 displaying the complete design.

To save your design and view settings before you exit from MicroStation, select the Save Settings option from the File pull-down menu (see Figure 1–28). Make it a practice to save settings before you exit from MicroStation. If you forget to save settings, you will have to spend time adjusting the design and view settings to match what you had in place the last time you worked on the design.

To exit the MicroStation design session and return to the operating system, invoke the EXIT command from the File pull-down menu. To exit the current design and return to the MicroStation Manager window, invoke the CLOSE command from the File pull-down menu.

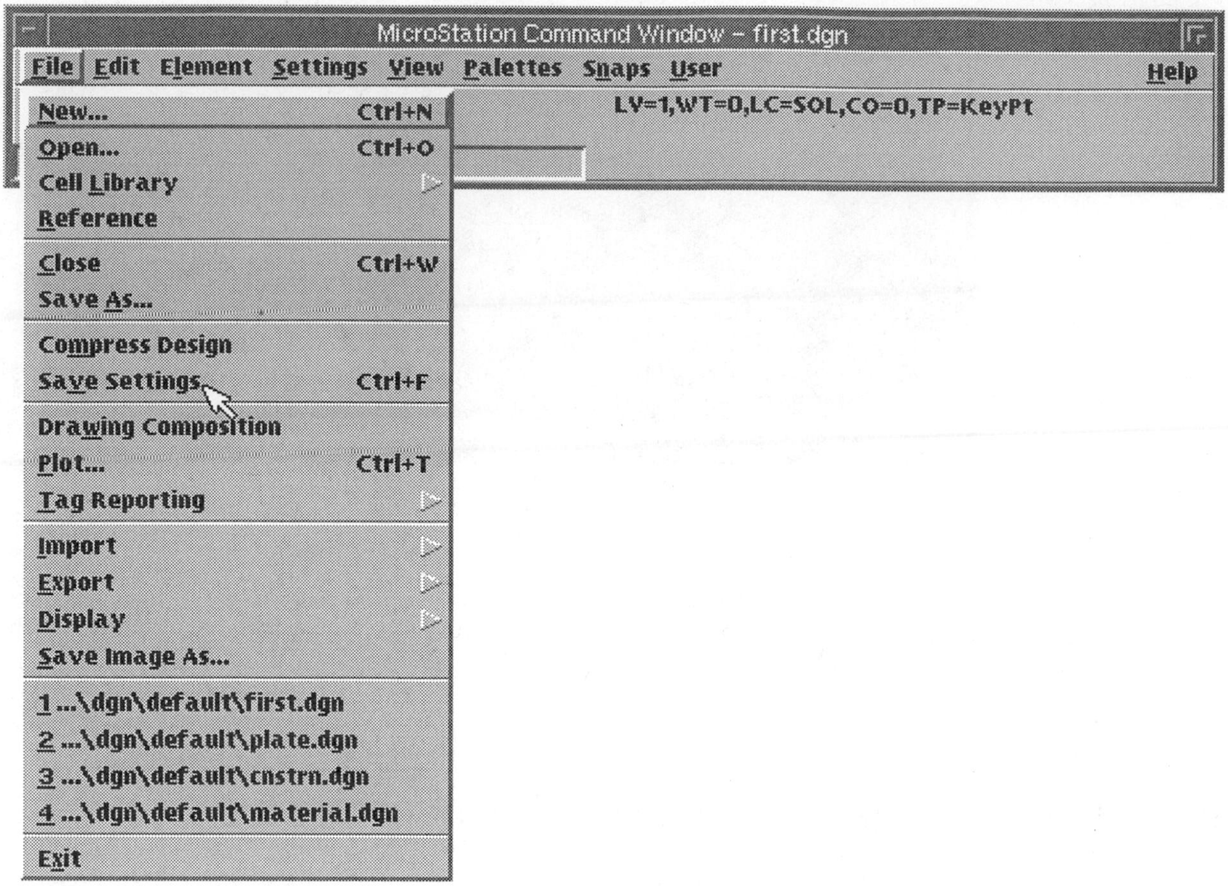

FIGURE 1–28 Invoking the Save Settings command from the File pull-down menu.

GETTING HELP

When you are in a design file, MicroStation provides on-line help facility available from the Help pull-down menu in the MicroStation Command Window (see Figure 1–29). On-line help is provided through the Help window, by specific topics, by searching for a text string within help topic names or help articles, and by browsing key-ins.

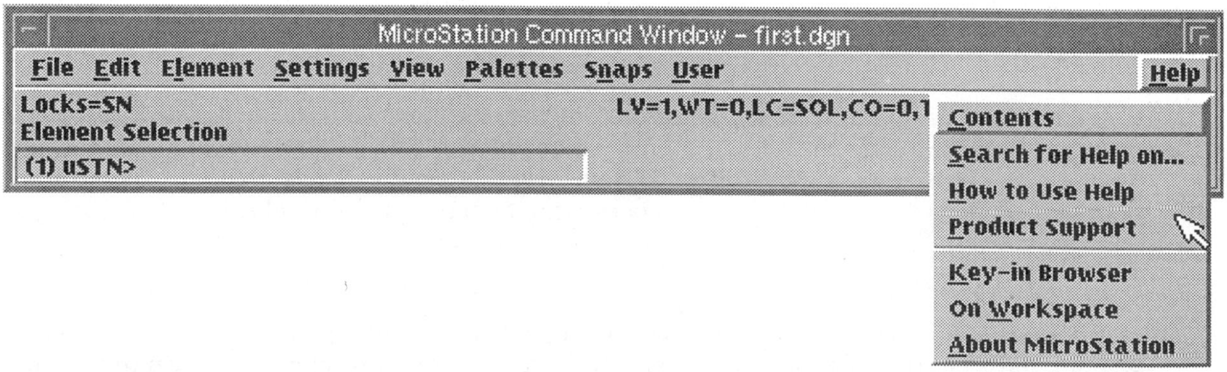

FIGURE 1–29 Help pull-down menu in the MicroStation Command Window.

The Help Pull-Down Menu

Contents The Contents window lists the top level topics as shown in Figure 1–30. To see a list of more specific subtopics related to a topic in the list, select the topic. MicroStation displays a list of sub-topics, and by selecting a sub-topic, MicroStation displays the available help information on that topic. In addition, you can also search for a text string by clicking the Search button and MicroStation will display the Search settings box. Key-in the text string and click the Search button, and MicroStation will display the help available on the text string.

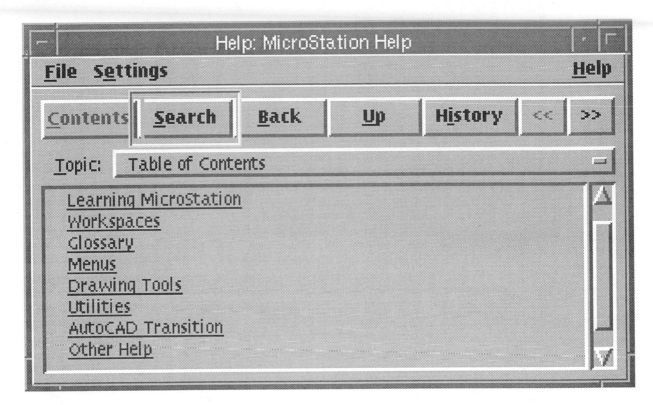

FIGURE 1–30   Help Contents window.

The MicroStation Help window also has a Topic option menu displaying the current topic's parent, its parent's topic, and so on, up to the Contents. Selecting any one of the topics moves you "up" to that level in the help document. You can also display the help file's previous and next article by clicking the Previous (<<) and Next (>>).

Search for Help On... Opens the Search settings box as shown in Figure 1–31, which is used to search for a text string in the open help file. The In option menu allows you select one of the two options. The Current Document selection searches the entire help file. The Subtopics of Current Topic selection restricts the search to sub-topics of the topic displayed in the Help window. If you set the toggle button to ON for Match Case, then searching is case-sensitive: the text matches the capitalization of the specified text in the Help file. If you set the toggle button to ON for Whole Words Only, then MicroStation finds only topics that contain character sequences that exactly match the specified text in the Help file. And if you set the toggle button to ON for Topics Only, then only article titles are searched.

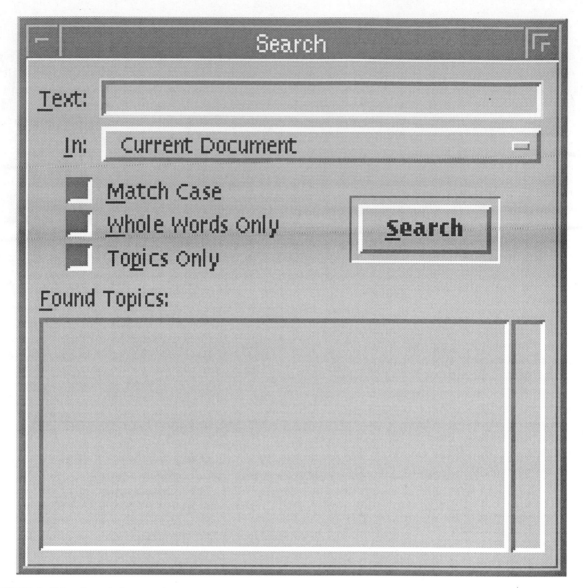

FIGURE 1-31 Search Settings box.

Click the Search button to begin searching for the specified text string. Topics that contain or match the specified text are displayed in the Found Topics list box. Select the name of the topic from the Found Topics list box, and MicroStation displays the article on that topic in the Help window.

Using Help Opens the Help window that provides instructions for using on-line help.

Product Support Displays information about contacting MicroStation technical support.

Key-in Browser Opens the Key-in Browser settings box similar to the one shown in Figure 1–32. The settings box is used to browse, construct, and submit key-ins. Each list box corresponds to a keyword level in the hierarchical MicroStation key-in language. The leftmost column contains the keywords of the top level. By selecting the keyword from the leftmost column, MicroStation displays the subordinate second-level keywords. Repeat keyword selection in this manner until the desired key-in is constructed. Click Key-in button to display at the Command field of the MicroStation Command Window.

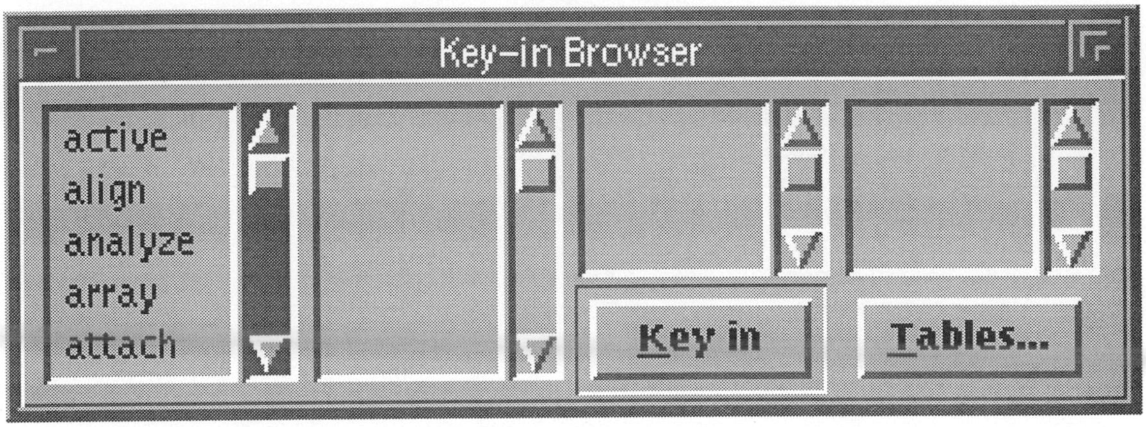

FIGURE 1–32 Key-in Browser settings box.

Workspace Opens the Workspace window as shown in Figure 1–33. MicroStation displays the following information in the Workspace window:

  User Configuration filename.
  Project Configuration filename.
  User Interface selection.
  User Preferences filename.

In addition, you can also get help on Workspace by clicking the Help button.

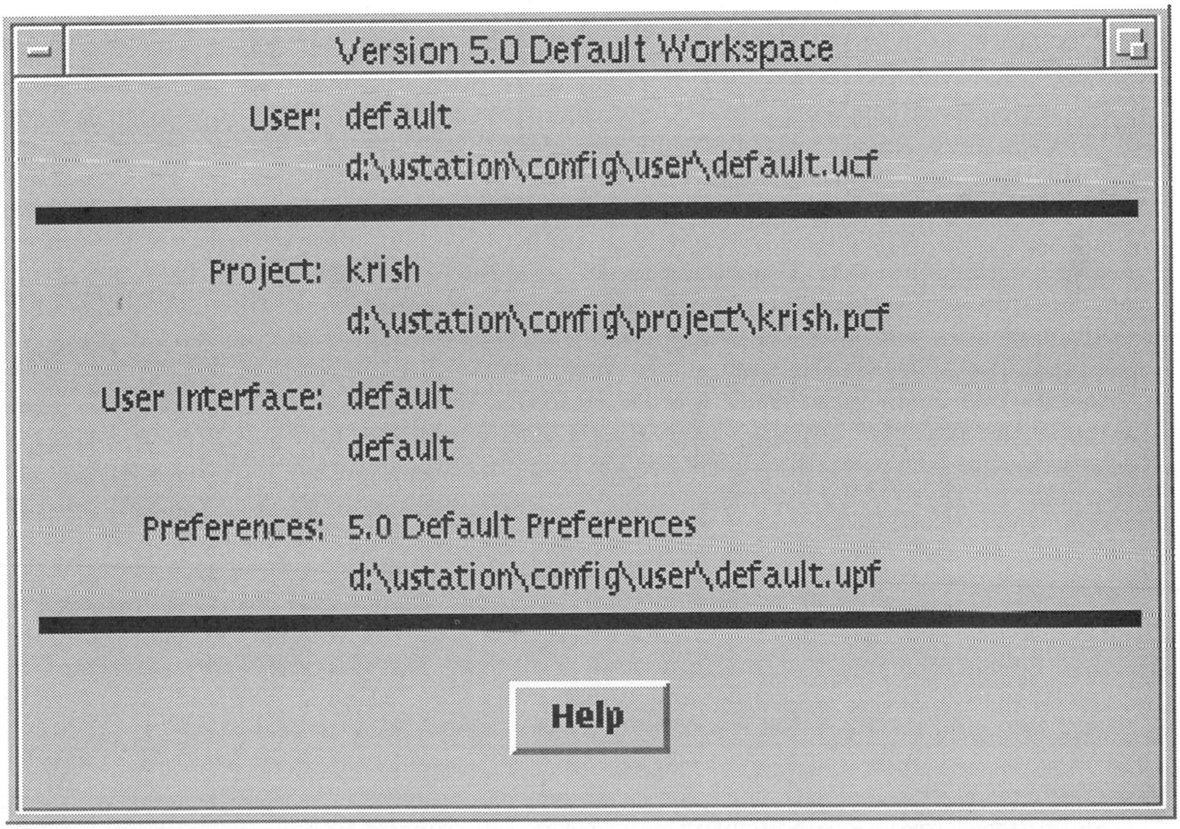

FIGURE 1–33 Workspace window.

About MicroStation Opens a window in which the following information is displayed:

> MicroStation version number.
> Active design file name.
> Name of attached cell library, if any.
> MicroStation font library name.
> Element cache size and usage.
> MicroStation serial number.
> Registered user name.
> User's organization.
> MicroStation license number.

DRAWING AIDS

MicroStation provides four different tools (locks) to make your drafting and design easier. The tools include GRID, SNAP, UNIT, and AXIS. The following are brief explanations of these tools; a more detailed explanation is provided in chapters 2, 3, and 4.

MicroStation supports a visual design and accuracy tool called the Grid. This is a matrix of grid points that cover the entire design plane. This feature helps you get a sense of the drawing elements sizes and their relationships. MicroStation displays two types of grid system. The first is the Grid Reference, which appears on your screen as crosses, and is set to a distance equivalent to Master Units (MU) by default. The second is the Grid Unit, which appears as a dot on the screen and is set to a distance equivalent to Sub units (SU) by default. If necessary, you can change the spacing for Grid Reference and Grid Unit and toggle the Grid Lock ON/OFF to snap the elements to the nearest grid point.

A very powerful feature in MicroStation is the Snap Lock in conjunction with the tentative point. It permits you to specify a specific point on an existing element. For instance, you can place the cursor near the end point of a line, and click tentative point (when the Snap Lock is set to ON) to snap to the end point of the line. For example, draw a line starting at point 0,0 for a distance of 5 units and at an angle of 45 degrees. If you wish to use the end point of that first line for some other purpose (e.g., to place the center of a circle without using the tentative point), you have to stop and calculate its coordinate. To calculate, you may have to use a calculator, key-in the numbers, and hope that you did not make a mistake in the reading, typing, or method of calculation. Also, you are limiting yourself to the accuracy of the number of significant figures on your calculator. By using the tentative point when the Snap Keypoint mode is set to ON, you can place the cursor near the end of the line, press the Tentative button, accept it with the Data button, and have that end point used as the response to the prompt. In addition to snapping to element keypoints, several other snap modes are available. There is, for example, a snap mode that finds the center of certain type of elements, and one that finds the intersection of two elements.

The Axis Lock, when set to ON, limits the selectable point to one at a right angle to the last point. This means you can turn the Axis Lock to ON if you want the new point to be displaced from the base point along an orthogonal line (horizontal or vertical). It restricts the rubber-band line and the new point accordingly. Instead of drawing orthogonally, you can change the angle anywhere from 0 to 90 degrees and limit the selectable point to the fixed angle from the last point.

The Unit Lock, when set to ON, forces all data points to the nearest increment in the unit roundoff definition. This lock, along with the unit roundoff value, may be used instead of the Grid Lock if something other than the current grid setting is desired. If necessary, you can set the unit roundoff definition to half the value of Grid Unit spacing, and turn ON the Unit lock. By this, you can snap to the grid unit dot as well as the invisible nearest unit increment dot.

Detailed explanations of all of the drawing aids are provided in chapters 2 through 4.

PLACING ELEMENTS

MicroStation gives you ample methods for placing elements in your design file. It also provides you with many ways to generate each element type in your drawing. It is important to keep in mind that the examples in this text of how to generate the various lines, circles, arcs, and other types of elements are not always the only methods available. You are invited, even challenged, to find other more expedient methods to perform tasks demonstrated in the exercises. You can also progress at a better rate if you try to learn as much as possible and as soon as possible about the descriptive properties of the individual elements. When you become familiar with how MicroStation creates, manipulates, and stores the data that describe the elements, you will be able to create drawings more effectively.

See Table 1–3 for a brief description of the placement commands available in MicroStation. Detailed explanations of these placement commands are provided in chapters 2 through 6.

Table 1–3. Element Placement Commands

ELEMENT TYPE	DESCRIPTION
LINES	Drawn by specifying a start and end point. They can be constrained at a specific angle of rotation or a fixed length.
LINE STRINGS, SHAPES, CURVES, AND MULTI-LINES	Allows you to place multi-segmented elements, and, in the case of Multi-lines, multiple parallel lines.
BLOCKS AND POLYGONS	Allows you to place multi-sided closed shapes, such as blocks and irregular shapes.
CIRCLES, ARCS, AND ELLIPSES	Several commands are provided for placing circles, arcs, ellipses, and partial ellipses.
B-SPLINE CURVES	Several methods of constructing closed and open B-spline curves are provided.
3D-SPECIFIC ELEMENTS	3D elements, such as cones, can be placed in 3D designs.
PATTERNING	Either system-generated or user-created pattern, that fill in a specified drawing area.

ELEMENT MANIPULATION COMMANDS

To manipulate an element is to make a change to one of its existing characteristics. There are several options open to a user among the manipulation commands offered by MicroStation. These commands offered by MicroStation make it easy to correct or revise a design. The experienced CAD operator will often create an element in anticipation of using a particular manipulation command. For instance, if you wish to draw two parallel lines of equal length, you can place one line and then use the Copy Parallel command to create the second line. If you wish to create an array of radial lines similar to spokes on a wheel, you need only place one line, and then generate the other spokes with the one manipulation command called Array. Some manipulation commands are specific to certain elements. The commands presented here manipulate one element at a time.

See Table 1–4 for a brief description of the element manipulation commands available in Micro-Station. Detailed explanations of these placement commands are provided in chapters 2 through 5.

Table 1–4. Element Manipulation Commands

MANIPULATION	DESCRIPTION
MOVE	Moves a selected element from its present location to a new location without changing its orientation or size in the design.
MOVE PARALLEL	Moves a selected element parallel to current location at either a keyed-in distance or through a specified point.
COPY	Copies an element at the specified displacment without changing its orientation or size, leaving the original intact.
COPY PARALLEL	Used for constructing an element parallel to another element at either a keyed-in distance or through a specified point.
ROTATE	Rotates an element, or a copy of an element, by specified rotation angle or by a graphically defined angle.
MIRROR	Creates a mirror image of the original element or a copy of the original element.
DELETE	Deletes an element or part of a selected element.
SCALE	Increases or decreases the size of a selected element or a copy of the selected element.
ARRAY	Used to make multiple copies of a selected element in a rectangular or circular (polar) pattern; each resulting element can be manipulated independently.
MODIFY	Allows you to change the geometric shape of an element.
CHANGE	Changes selected attributes of an element.
FILLET	Used for connecting lines, arcs, or circles by means of a smoothly fitted arc of a specified radius.
CHAMFER	Used to trim two intersection lines a specified distance from the intersection and connect the trimmed ends with a new line segment.
TRIM	Trims an element at a cutting plane.
MULTI-LINE JOINTS	Cleans up the intersections of multi-line elements.
CREATE COMPLEX	Combines separate elements into complex shape or string.
DROP	Breaks complex elements into simple elements.
UNDO/REDO	UNDO is used for backing up step-by-step to any earlier point in an editing session. REDO will undo the UNDO.

FENCE MANIPULATION COMMANDS

The fence manipulation commands provide manipulation for groups of elements as do the element manipulation commands listed above. To use fence manipulation commands, first place a fence around the elements to be manipulated, then select the command to provide the required manipulation.

Through the use of the powerful fence manipulation commands, and other grouping commands, you need never draw anything twice.

See Table 1–5 for a brief description of the fence manipulation commands available in MicroStation. Detailed explanations of these placement commands are provided in Chapter 4.

Table 1–5. Fence Manipulation Commands

COMMAND	DESCRIPTION
PLACE FENCE	Places a rectangular (block) or multi-sided (shape) fence around the elements you need to manipulate.
FENCE MOVE	Allows you to move the fence itself (not the elements in the fence) to a new location.
FENCE MODIFY	Allows you to modify the geometric shape of the previously placed fence.
FENCE LOCK MODES	Allows you to limit the manipulation to selected elements only. The locks include inside, overlap, clip, void, void-overlap, and void clip.
FENCE CONTENTS COMMANDS	Provides fence equivalents of each of the element manipulation commands to manipulate all elements contained in the fence.
FENCE STRETCH	Stretches linear elements that overlap the fence boundaries.

LEVELS

MicroStation offers a means of grouping elements in a design similar to the manual drafter drawing groups of objects on separate transparent sheets superimposed in a single stack. The concept is provided in terms of Levels. You can place various portions or groups of your design elements to different levels. MicroStation provides 63 levels in each design file, and you can place elements on any of the levels. These levels allow you to separate different parts of your design, then view only the part or parts you are currently working on. There is only one Active level. The Active level could be compared to the manual drafter's top sheet on the stack of transparencies.

Table 1–6 describes the commands available for manipulating the level structure. These commands are available as fields in settings boxes or as key-in commands. Levels are discussed in Chapter 3.

Table 1–6. Level Structure Commands

FEATURE	DESCRIPTION
ACTIVE LEVEL	Determines placement of level elements.
LEVEL ON	Allows you to select what levels you wish to see in each view window.
LEVEL OFF	Allows you to select what levels should not be displayed in each view window.
LEVEL LOCK	Allows you to limit element manipulation to only those elements on the active level.

TEXT PLACEMENT

MicroStation provides a suit of commands for placing text strings in your design. These commands allow you to quickly place text describing the components of your design and general instructional text. Once placed, text can be manipulated using any of the previously listed element and fence manipulation commands. Text Placement commands are discussed in detail in chapters 2 and 5.

CELLS AND CELL LIBRARIES

Cells are like symbols on a template. They allow you to quickly place standard symbols in your design, promote standardization, and greatly reduce the need to draw anything more than one time. Cells are stored in cell libraries that can be attached to your design. Once the library is attached, copies of cells can be placed in your design using any one of several cell placement commands. After placing the cells, they can be manipulated like any other element.

Table 1–7 briefly describes the cell and cell library features. Cells are discussed in detail in Chapter 7.

Table 1–7. Cell and Cell Library Features

FEATURE	DESCRIPTION
CREATE OR ATTACH CELL LIBRARY	Allows you to create your own cell library file or attach an existing one to your design.
PREVIEW CELLS	A settings box allows you to preview the cells in the attached library and perform other cell housekeeping functions.
ACTIVE CELL	Allows you to select the cell you want to place at origin points, as line terminators
PLACE CELLS	Provides commands for placing cells at an origin point, as line terminators, and in groups.
CREATE CELL	Allows you to create a cell from a group of selected elements in your design.
DELETE CELL	Allows you to delete obsolete and incorrectly drawn cells from the cell library.
RENAME CELL	Allows you to change the name used to identify a cell in the attached cell library.
TAGS	Allows you to assign non-graphical information to a cell or an element.

REFERENCE FILES

MicroStation has a feature that lets you display or view the contents of the number of design files (maximum, 132) while working in your current design file. This function can be accomplished by using an external reference file. When a design is externally referenced, the user can view and snap to the referenced design from the current design. If necessary, you can copy the element(s) from the reference file to your current design file. A set of commands is provided specifically to manipulate reference files, such as Rotate, Scale, Mirror, Move, and so forth. All the manipulations performed on an external reference file will not affect the original design file because a reference file is only an image.

When you attach a design file as an external reference file, it is permanently attached until it is detached. When you open a design file, MicroStation reloads all the external reference files; thus, each external design file reflects the latest state of the referenced design file. Table 1–8 briefly lists the reference file commands. See Chapter 9 for a detailed explanation of the external reference file.

Table 1–8. Reference File Commands

COMMAND	DESCRIPTION
ATTACH REFERENCE FILE	Allows you to refer to other design files from your design.
DISPLAY	Allows you to turn on and off the display of reference files.
SNAP AND LOCATE	Allows you to control the ability to identify elements in the attached reference files.
MOVE	Moves a reference file to a new position in the design.
ROTATE	Rotates your view of a reference file.
SCALE	Increases or decreases the size of your view of a reference file in relation to your design file.
MIRROR	Allows you to display a mirror image of the reference file in your design file.
LEVELS ON AND OFF	Allows you to turn on or off the display of selected levels in the reference file.
CLIP	Allows you to fence part of a reference file, then clip off your view of that part of the reference file outside (or inside) the fence.
DETACH	Detaches a reference file from your design file.

DIMENSION PLACEMENT

MicroStation provides a comprehensive set of commands and settings for placing dimensions on your design. A great variety of discipline-related conventions are accommodated. Dimensions can be associated with the element they dimension, so that a change in the size of the element automatically changes the dimension. Table 1–9 briefly describes the available dimensioning commands. See Chapters 2 through 5 for a detailed explanation of all the related commands for dimensioning.

Table 1–9. Dimension Placement

COMMAND	DESCRIPTION
DIMENSION SETUP	A set of settings boxes provides control over the way dimensions appear in your design.
LINEAR	Set of dimensioning commands to place linear dimensioning.
ANGULAR	Set of dimensioning commands to place angular dimensioning.
RADIAL	Set of dimensioning commands to place radius or diameter dimensioning of circles, ellipses, and arcs.
ELEMENT DIMENSION	Places a dimension (linear, angular, or radial), depending on the type of element identified.
ORDINATE	Places ordinate dimensions.
LABEL	Labels a line with its length and angle of rotation.

PLOTTING

Plotting is the process of placing a scaled "snapshot" of all or part of your design in a separate plot file, then sending that plot file to a plotting device to create a hard copy on paper or other "hard" media. Plotting can be done on a pen plotter, electrostatic plotter, or a printer with graphics capability at various scale factors. MicroStation calculates the largest possible plot scale by default, or you can override MicroStation's scale factor by keying the appropriate scale factor. See Chapter 6 for a detailed explanation for plotting.

SPECIAL FEATURES

In addition to the features listed above, MicroStation includes several useful features. Table 1–10 briefly describes the special features. They are discussed in detail in Chapter 10.

Table 1–10.   Special Features

COMMAND	DESCRIPTION
GRAPHIC GROUPS	Allows you to permanently group elements so that when the graphic group lock is on, all elements in the group are manipulated as if they are one element.
SELECTION BY TYPE	Allows you to designate a criteria for selecting elements based on their geometric configuration or position in the design plane.
LEVEL SYMBOLOGY	Allows you to define the level display symbology for each of the 63 levels.
RECORD AND LISTEN	Allows you to record and play back a series of actions in MicroStation.
IMPORT/EXPORT	Allows you to import designs that were created in other CAD formats, and to export to various formats.
SAVE AND REPLAY IMAGES	Allows you to save screen images and to display such images.
GLOSSARY	Allows you to maintain a glossary of command terms, and to place text from the glossary into your design.

ENHANCEMENTS IN MICROSTATION VERSION 5

Following are the enhancements that were added to MicroStation Version 5:

- Improved Ease of Use
  - □ GUI Toggle—Motif or OS specific
  - □ Pull-down mens stick when opened
  - □ Combines semi-redundant commands
  - □ File pull-down menu displays last four files open in MicroStation. Just click on the name to open one of them.
- Open designs created in other CAD formats from the MicroStation Manager and the Open dialog box.
- Open a plot preview window to see the way the plot is going to appear on paper.

- Dynamic alignment adds a new dimension to dynamic update by showing temporary dashed lines that indicate the relationship to the element you are placing to other elements.
- Create custom-line styles or use MicroStation's default set of custom-line styles.
- All Fence commands are in the Main palette and there is no Fence palette.
- Switch manipulation commands between element and fence contents manipulations using a toggle button in the sub-palettes.
- The new Select By settings box allows you to create a selection criteria to help find and select elements for manipulation.
- Variations of the same type of commands no longer have separate icons. Example: There is one Place Text icon that includes an options menu from which you can select the method of text placement (at origin, fitted, etc.).
- The class (such as Solid or Hole) for placing elements is available from an options menu in each sub-palette that contains element placement commands.
- Most of the element construction commands have been replaced by a new set of snap modes. For instance, Bisector snap mode replaces the Construct Bisector command.
- The new snap modes are available from the Full Locks settings box, a Snaps pull-down menu, and a Snaps palette.
- Fonts settings box available from Text settings box.
- Fonts you can use—MicroStation, AutoCAD, PostScript, and True Type.
- Replace Text option available to search and replace text.
- Create a glossary of standard text in a separate file, then build text strings by selecting from the glossary.
- In addition to matching text attributes, you can now match element attributes, multi-line definitions, dimension settings, pattern attributes, and curve settings.
- A settings box for opening and closing views is available from the View pull-down menu.
- The Color option in the Edit pull-down menu opens settings boxes in which you can select one of ten colors for highlighting elements and for displaying the drawing pointer.
- Create and open cell libraries from Cells settings box.
- Attach multiple cell libraries to all design files by using the MS_CELLLIST configuration variable.
- Store non-graphic information with elements and cells as Tags.
- Associative hatching and patterning.
- 2D Boolean Operations—Quickly modify, measure, and hatch multiple 2D shapes with integrated Boolean operations.
- Create custom workspaces to optimize MicroStation for handling a specific type of design; e.g., Architectural designs.
- Complete Surface Modeler.
- Advanced Rendering.
- Help Systems—Similar to Windows Help; Re-sizeable, Hypertext, and Embedded Graphics.

CONCLUSION

This chapter is designed to give you a quick overview of MicroStation. For a detailed explanation of all the MicroStation commands and new features of Version 5, refer to the corresponding chapters.

2

FUNDAMENTALS I

This chapter introduces some of the basic MicroStation commands that can be used to complete a simple drawing. It has fundamental problems that are "grist for the mill" for lessons in creating and manipulating elements and dimensioning. The basic elements that will be introduced are Line, Block, Shape, and Linear Dimensioning. These can be created by using certain commands from the palettes and pull-down menu(s). Also introduced are several different drawing tools to make your drafting and design layout quicker, easier, and more accurate. When you learn how to access and use the commands, how to find your way around the screen, and how MicroStation makes use of coordinate geometry, you can apply these skills to the chapters containing more advanced drawings and projects.

After completing this chapter, you will be able to:

- Place lines, line strings, blocks, and shapes.
- Drop line strings and delete commands.
- Display commands—zoom in, zoom out, window area, and fit.
- Manipulate text placement—text parameters and placing text by origin.
- Use drawing aids—Grid, Snap, and Axis locks.
- Set linear dimensioning.

GETTING STARTED

The primary drawing element is the line. A series of connected straight line segments can be drawn by invoking the Place Line command, then selecting the proper sequence of data points. Micro-Station will connect these points with a series of lines. It uses the ending point of one line as the starting point of the next, continuing to prompt you for each subsequent ending point. To terminate the Line command press Reset or select another command. Even though a series of lines is drawn using a single Line command, each line is a separate element as if it had been drawn with a separate Line command.

You can specify the data points using your pointing device (mouse or puck) or you can key-in 2D (x,y) coordinates. If you key-in 3D (x,y,x) coordinates, MicroStation ignores the Z coordinate unless you created the design file from a 3D seed file. This chapter and subsequent ones are concerned only with 2D points. Chapter 13 discusses 3D concepts and nonzero elevations in detail.

MicroStation provides four sets of Line commands (Place Line, Place Line String, Place Multi-line, and Place Stream Line String) with several options. The commands are located in the Lines palette invoked from the Main palette as shown in Figure 2–1.

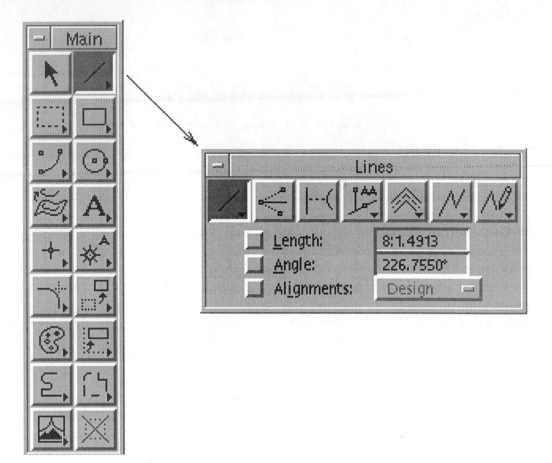

FIGURE 2–1 Lines sub-palette invoked from the Main palette.

Place Line

To draw a line, invoke the Place Line command by clicking the Place Line icon from the Lines sub-palette (see Figure 2–2), or key-in at the uSTN> field **place line** (or **pla li**) and press [ENTER]. MicroStation prompts:

Enter first point (Place a data point to define the starting point of the line.)

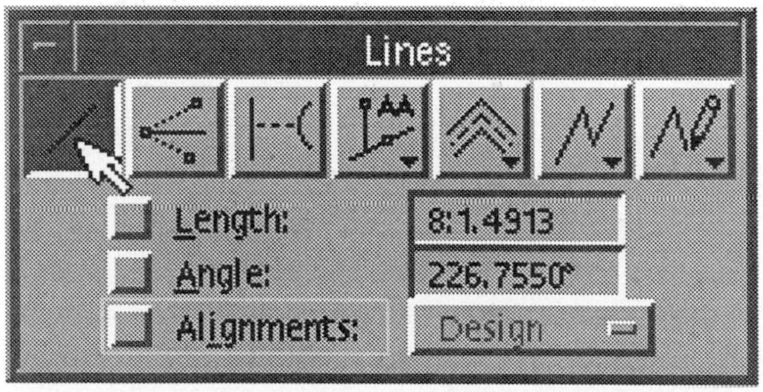

FIGURE 2–2   Invoking the Place Line command from the Lines sub-palette.

The first point of the first element in a drawing normally establishes where all of the other elements must be placed. It is like the cornerstone of a building. Careful thought should go into locating the first point.

> **NOTE:** After you place the first data point a dynamic image of the line will drag with the screen pointer.

You can specify the first point by providing a data point by using your pointing device (mouse or puck) or by precision input (more on this later). After specifying the first point, MicroStation prompts:

Enter end point (Place a data point to define the end point of the line.)

In addition to the first point being the cornerstone, the direction of the first element is also critical to where all other points of other elements are located with respect to each other.

You can specify the end of the line by providing a data point by using your pointing device (mouse or puck) or by precision input. MicroStation will repeat the prompt:

Enter end point:

Place a data point or by precision input to continue. To save time, the Place Line command remains active and prompts for a new *end point* after each point you specify. When you have finished placing a series of lines, press Reset or invoke another command to terminate the Place Line command.

As mentioned earlier, when placing data points with your pointing device to draw a series of lines, a rubber band line is displayed between the starting point and the cross hairs. This helps you to see where the resulting line will go. In Figure 2–3 the dotted lines represent previous cursor positions. To specify the end point of the line, click the Data button. You can continue to place lines with the Place Line command until you press Reset or select another command.

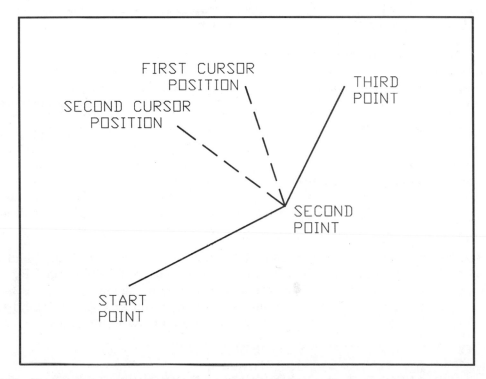

FIGURE 2–3   Placing data points with the cursor rather than with coordinates.

Place Line to a Specified Length To place a line to a specified length, click the Place Line icon in the Lines palette and turn ON the toggle button for Length in the sub-palette. Key-in the distance in MU:SU:PU in the Length edit field. The prompts are similar to Place Line command and you can place any number of line segments of specified length.

Place Line at an Angle To place a line to a specified angle, click the Place Line icon in the Lines palette and turn ON the toggle button for Angle in the sub-palette. Key-in the angle in the Angle edit field. The prompts are similar to Place Line command and you can place any number of line segments of specified angle.

Alignment To place lines aligned to temporary lines, click the Place Line icon in the Lines palette and turn ON the toggle button for Alignment in the sub-palette. Dynamic alignment enhances in placing elements by displaying temporary alignment lines that lie along vectors from alignment vectors. As you move the pointer, temporary lines indicate alignment with alignment points. Alignment points include data points entered when placing elements and tentative points snapped to elements. Each successive data point defines the origin of a temporary rectangular coordinate system. As you move the pointer, the dynamically displayed element highlights in red when it is co-linear (or within the Locate Tolerance of co-linearity) with the defined axis. The temporary lines lets you snap precisely to a variety of significant points that are not located on any elements.

Precision Input

MicroStation allows you to draw an object at its true size and then make the border, title block, and other non-object associated features fit the object. The completed combination is reduced (or increased) to fit the plotted sheet size you require when you plot.

Drawing a not-to-scale schematic does not take advantage of MicroStation's full graphics and computing potential. But even though the symbols and distances between them have no relationship to any real-life dimensions, the sheet size, text size, line widths, and other visible characteristics of the drawing must be considered to give your schematic the readability you desire. Some planning, including sizing, needs to be applied to all drawings.

When MicroStation prompts for the location of a point, in addition to providing the data point with your pointing device, you can use three precision input commands that allow you to place data points precisely. Each of the commands allows you to key-in by coordinates, which include absolute rectangular coordinates, relative rectangular coordinates, and relative polar coordinates.

The rectangular coordinates system is based on specifying a point's location by giving its distances from two intersecting perpendicular axes in two-dimensional (2D) points or from three intersecting perpendicular planes for three-dimensional (3D) points. Each data point is measured along the X axis (horizontal) and Y axis (vertical) for two-dimensional design and X axis, Y axis, and Z axis (toward or away from the viewer) for three-dimensional design. The intersection of the axes, called the origin (XY=0,0,0), divides the coordinates into four quadrants for two-dimensional design as shown in Figure 2–4.

Absolute Rectangular Coordinates Points are located by Absolute Rectangular Coordinates at an exact X,Y intersection on the design plane in relation to the Global Origin. By default, the Global Origin is located at the center of the design plane, as shown in Figure 2–5. The horizontal distance increases in the positive X direction from origin, and the vertical distance increases in the positive Y direction from origin. To enter an absolute coordinate, key-in:

    XY=<X COORDINATE>,<Y COORDINATE> ⌨
    or
    POINT ABSOLUTE <X COORDINATE>,<Y COORDINATE> ⌨

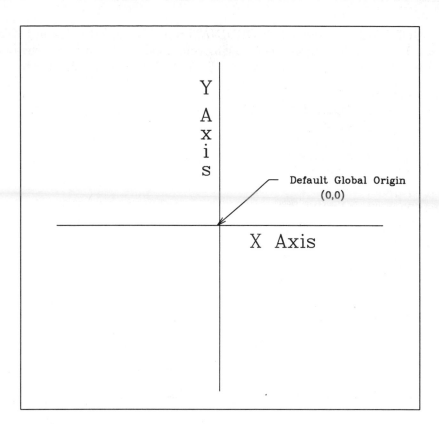

FIGURE 2–4 Two-dimensional coordinate system.

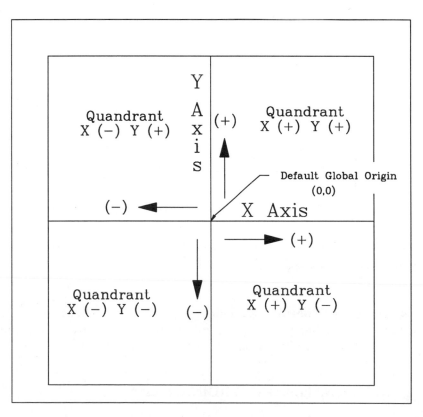

FIGURE 2–5 Showing Global Origin in a two-dimensional design.

The <X COORDINATE> and <Y COORDINATE> are the coordinates in MU:SU:PU in relation to the Global Origin. For example, the following command sequence shows the placement of connected lines by Place Line command, as shown in Figure 2–6 using absolute coordinates (see Figure 2–7):

Enter first point   **XY=2,2** ⏎
Enter end point   **XY=2,4** ⏎
Enter end point   **XY=4,6** ⏎
Enter end point   **XY=6,6** ⏎
Enter end point   **XY=6,8** ⏎
Enter end point   **XY=7,9** ⏎
Enter end point   **XY=9,9** ⏎
Enter end point   **XY=10,8** ⏎
Enter end point   **XY=10,5** ⏎
Enter end point   **XY=12,3** ⏎
Enter end point   **XY=12,2** ⏎
Enter end point   **XY=2,2** ⏎
Enter end point   (Reset or select another command)

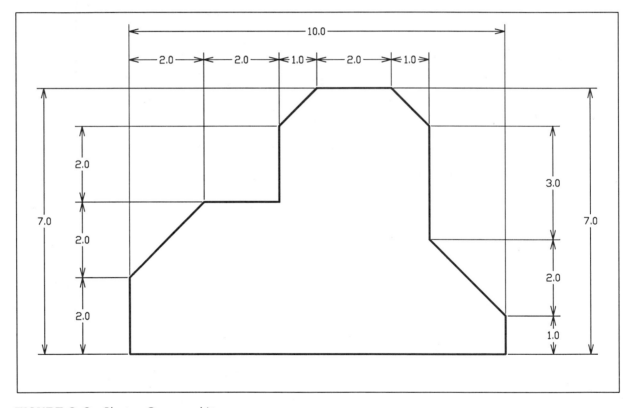

FIGURE 2–6   Placing Connected Lines.

Relative Rectangular Coordinates Points are located by Relative Rectangular Coordinates in relation to the last specified position or point in MU:SU:PU, rather than the origin. This is similar to specifying a point as an offset from the last point you entered. To enter a Relative Rectangular Coordinate, key-in:

DL=<X COORDINATE>,<Y COORDINATE> ⏎
or
POINT DELTA <X COORDINATE>,<Y COORDINATE> ⏎

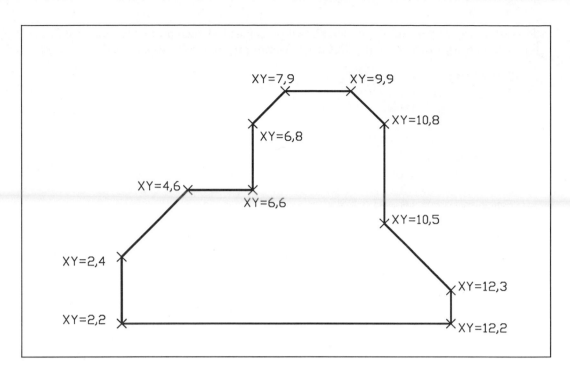

FIGURE 2–7 Placing Connected Lines Using Absolute Coordinates.

The <X COORDINATE> and <Y COORDINATE> are the coordinates in relation to the last specified position or point. For example, if the last point specified was XY=4,4, key-in

   DL=5,4

is equivalent to specifying the Absolute Rectangular Coordinates XY=9,8 (see Figure 2–8).

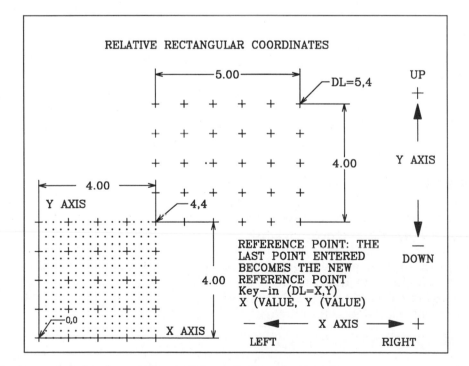

FIGURE 2–8 An example for placing a line by Relative Rectangular Coordinates.

The following command sequence shows placement of the connected lines by Place Line command, as shown in Figure 2–6, using Relative Rectangular Coordinates (see Figure 2–9):

Enter first point **XY=2,2** ⏎
Enter end point **DL=0,2** ⏎
Enter end point **DL=2,2** ⏎
Enter end point **DL=2,0** ⏎
Enter end point **DL=0,2** ⏎
Enter end point **DL=1,1** ⏎
Enter end point **DL=2,0** ⏎
Enter end point **DL=1,–1** ⏎
Enter end point **DL=0,–3** ⏎
Enter end point **DL=2,–2** ⏎
Enter end point **DL=0,–1** ⏎
Enter end point **XY=2,2** ⏎
Enter end point (Reset or select another command)

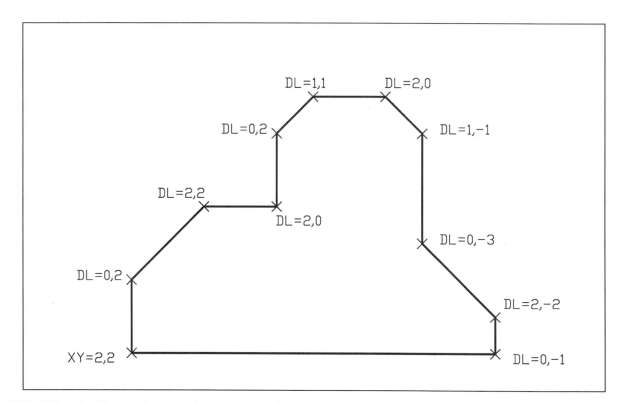

FIGURE 2–9   Placing Connected Lines Using Relative Rectangular Coordinates.

Relative Polar Coordinates   Relative Polar Coordinates are based on a distance from a fixed point at a given angle. In MicroStation, a Relative Polar Coordinate is determined by distance and angle measured from the previous data point. By default, the angle is measured in a counterclockwise direction relative to the positive X axis. It is important to remember that points located using Relative Polar Coordinates are always positioned relative to the previous point, not the Global Origin (0,0). To enter a Relative Rectangular Coordinate, key-in:

DI=<DISTANCE>,<ANGLE> ⏎
or
POINT DISTANCE <DISTANCE>,<ANGLE> ⏎

The <DISTANCE> and <ANGLE> are specified in relation to the last specified position or point. The distance is specified in current working units (MU:SU:PU), and the direction is specified as an angle in degrees relative to the X-axis. For example, to specify a point at a distance of 6.4 Master units from the previous point and at an angle of 39 degrees relative to the positive X axis (see Figure 2–10), key-in:

DI=6.4,39

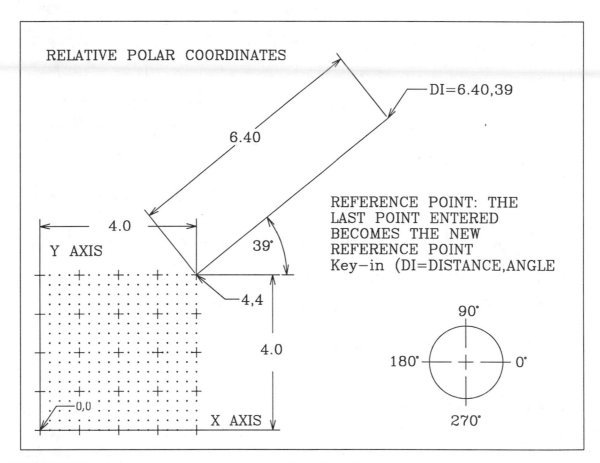

FIGURE 2–10   An example for placing a line by Relative Polar Coordinates.

The following command sequence shows placement of connected lines by Place Line command, as shown in Figure 2–6, using a combination of rectangular and polar coordinates (see Figure 2–11).

Enter first point **XY=2,2** ⏎
Enter end point **DI=2,90** ⏎
Enter end point **DI=2.8284,45** ⏎
Enter end point **DI=2,0** ⏎
Enter end point **DI=2,90** ⏎
Enter end point **DI=1.4142,315** ⏎
Enter end point **DI=2,90** ⏎
Enter end point **DI=1.4142,315** ⏎
Enter end point **DI=3,270** ⏎
Enter end point **DI=2.8284,315** ⏎
Enter end point **DI=1,270** ⏎
Enter end point **XY=2,2** ⏎
Enter end point (Reset or select another command)

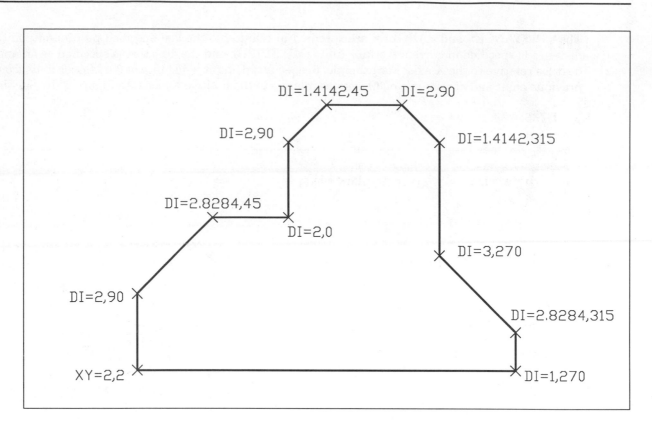

FIGURE 2–11 Placing Connected Lines Using Relative Polar Coordinates.

See Figure 2–12 for review of the coordinate systems.

Precision Input Settings Box

The Precision Input Setting Box continuously displays coordinates (absolute and relative), distances, and angles, and provides a means for precise input of data points. Select the Precision Input option from the Settings pull-down menu, as shown in Figure 2–13, to display the Precision Input Setting Box, as shown in Figure 2–14.

Clicking a label button (for example, Distance) causes the value in the associated field to stop changing as the pointer is moved. This is useful for constraining data point entry. Constraining continues, even if new values are keyed in, until a data point is entered or button(s) are clicked again.

Shift-clicking (hold the **SHIFT** key and click the data button at the same time) a label button locks the associated field and the constraining continues even after a data point is entered. This is useful for using the same value (for example, distance and/or angle) more than once. To unlock a field, click the associated label button.

When no constraints are set, the fields reflect the current position of the pointer. This is very useful whenever you need to know the location of the pointer in relation to Global Origin. Instead of using the key-in commands (XY, DL, and DI) to place data points by precision input, you can key-in the coordinates in the Precision Input settings box. Enter absolute coordinates in the X and Y edit fields, relative coordinates in the DX and DY fields or polar coordinates in the Distance and Angle edit field and click the Apply button.

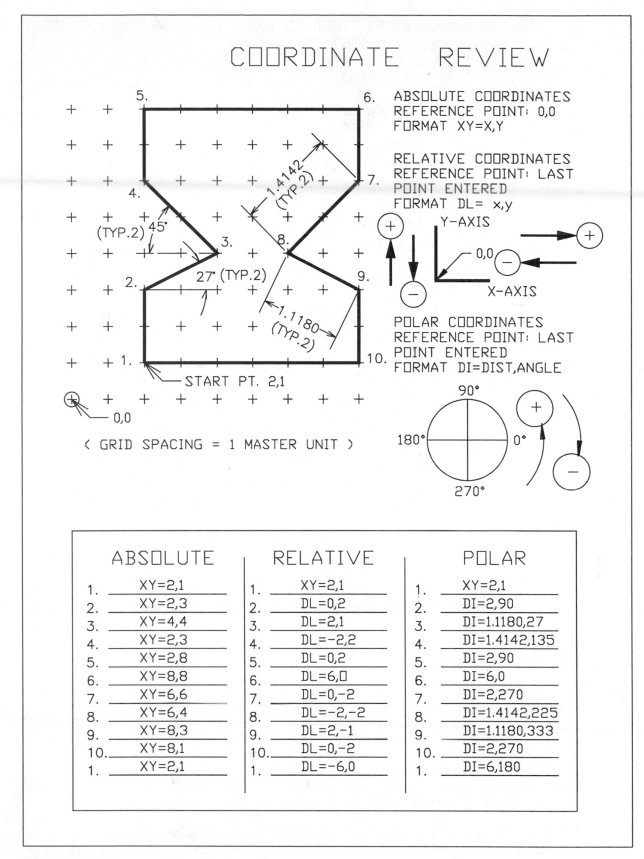

COORDINATE REVIEW

ABSOLUTE COORDINATES
REFERENCE POINT: 0,0
FORMAT XY=X,Y

RELATIVE COORDINATES
REFERENCE POINT: LAST
POINT ENTERED
FORMAT DL= x,y

POLAR COORDINATES
REFERENCE POINT: LAST
POINT ENTERED
FORMAT DI=DIST,ANGLE

(GRID SPACING = 1 MASTER UNIT)

START PT. 2,1

ABSOLUTE		RELATIVE		POLAR	
1.	XY=2,1	1.	XY=2,1	1.	XY=2,1
2.	XY=2,3	2.	DL=0,2	2.	DI=2,90
3.	XY=4,4	3.	DL=2,1	3.	DI=1.1180,27
4.	XY=2,3	4.	DL=-2,2	4.	DI=1.4142,135
5.	XY=2,8	5.	DL=0,2	5.	DI=2,90
6.	XY=8,8	6.	DL=6,0	6.	DI=6,0
7.	XY=6,6	7.	DL=0,-2	7.	DI=2,270
8.	XY=6,4	8.	DL=-2,-2	8.	DI=1.4142,225
9.	XY=8,3	9.	DL=2,-1	9.	DI=1.1180,333
10.	XY=8,1	10.	DL=0,-2	10.	DI=2,270
1.	XY=2,1	1.	DL=-6,0	1.	DI=6,180

FIGURE 2–12   Review of the Coordinate Systems.

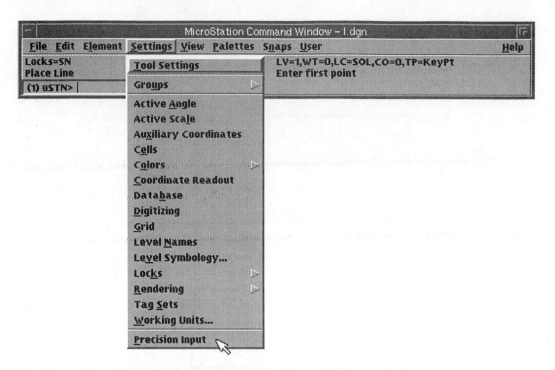

FIGURE 2-13 Invoking the Precision Input settings box from the Settings pull-down menu.

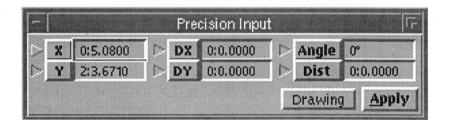

FIGURE 2-14 Precision Input settings box.

> **NOTE:** To place lines with different line styles (line types) and line weights (thickness), refer to Chapter 3.

PLACE LINE STRING

Place Line String is similar to Place Line command except that all segments drawn in one sequence form a single element containing a number of coordinate pairs known as vertices. Element manipulation commands such as Move, Copy, and Delete manipulate line string as one element. If necessary, you can make a line string into individual elements using the Drop String command (explained later in this chapter).

Line strings are created by entering data points or keying-in successive coordinates with a final Reset or invoke another placement command to terminate the line string.

To draw a line string, invoke the Place Line String command by clicking the Place Line String icon from the Lines sub-palette (see Figure 2–15), or key-in at the uSTN> field **place line string** (or **pla ls**) and press . MicroStation prompts:

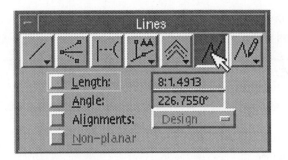

FIGURE 2-15   Invoking the Place Line String command from the Lines sub-palette.

Enter first point (Place a data point as shown in Figure 2–16 indicated by P1 to define the starting point of the line string.)

> **NOTE:** After you place the first data point, a dynamic image of the line segment drags with the screen pointer.

You can specify the first point by providing a data point using your pointing device (mouse or puck) or using precision input. After specifying the first point, MicroStation prompts:

Enter end point (Place a data point as shown in Figure 2–16 indicated by P2 to define the end point of the line segment.)

You can specify the end of the line segment by providing a data point using your pointing device (mouse or puck) or using precision input. MicroStation will repeat the prompt:

Enter end point (Place a data point as shown in Figure 2–16 indicated by P3 to define the end point of the line segment.)

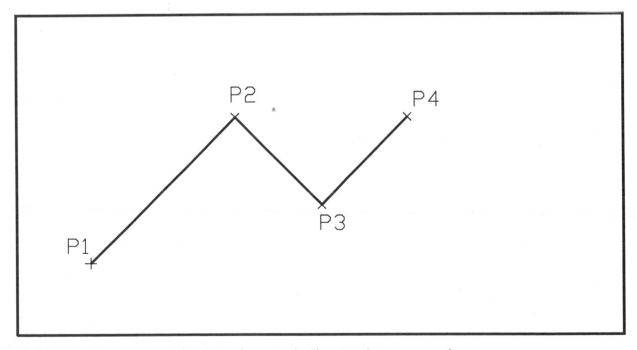

FIGURE 2-16   An example for placing line string by Place Line String command.

Place a data point or use precision input to continue. When you have finished placing the series of line segments, press Reset button to terminate the Place Line String command.

> **NOTE:** To place lines with different line styles (line types) and line weights (thickness), refer to Chapter 3.

DROP LINE STRING

The Drop String command causes line strings to separate into a series of connected individual line elements that can be manipulated as individual elements. Once a line string is dropped, it behaves as if it has been drawn with a Place Line command. Invoke the Drop Line String command by clicking the Drop Line String icon from the Drop sub-palette (see Figure 2–17) or key-in at the uSTN> field, **drop string** (or **dr s**) and press [ENTER]. MicroStation prompts:

Identify Element (Identify the line string to be dropped.)
Accept/Reject (Select next input) (Place a data point to Accept or Reject button to reject it.)

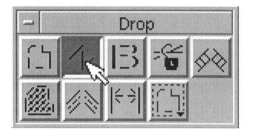

FIGURE 2–17   Invoking the Drop String command from the Drop sub-palette.

You can also identify another line string to drop with the second data point.

EXERCISES

Exercise 2-1

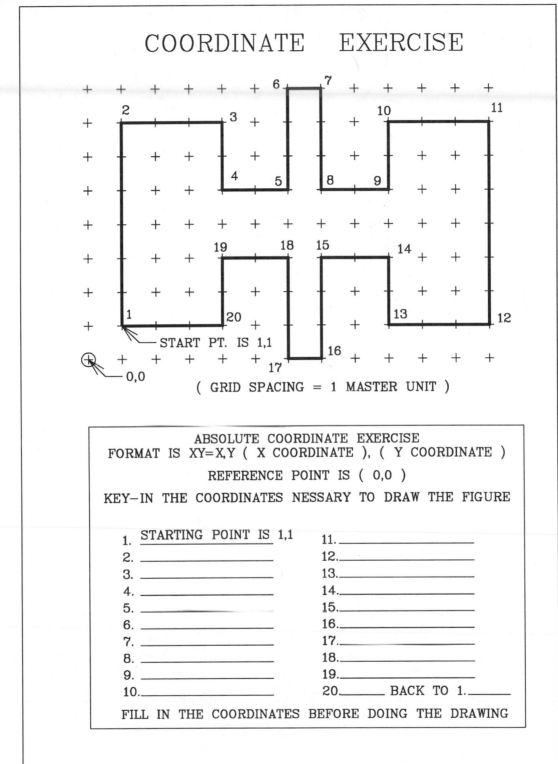

COORDINATE EXERCISE

(GRID SPACING = 1 MASTER UNIT)

ABSOLUTE COORDINATE EXERCISE
FORMAT IS XY=X,Y (X COORDINATE), (Y COORDINATE)

REFERENCE POINT IS (0,0)

KEY-IN THE COORDINATES NESSARY TO DRAW THE FIGURE

1. __STARTING POINT IS__ 1,1   11._____
2. _____   12._____
3. _____   13._____
4. _____   14._____
5. _____   15._____
6. _____   16._____
7. _____   17._____
8. _____   18._____
9. _____   19._____
10._____   20._____ BACK TO 1._____

FILL IN THE COORDINATES BEFORE DOING THE DRAWING

Exercise 2–2

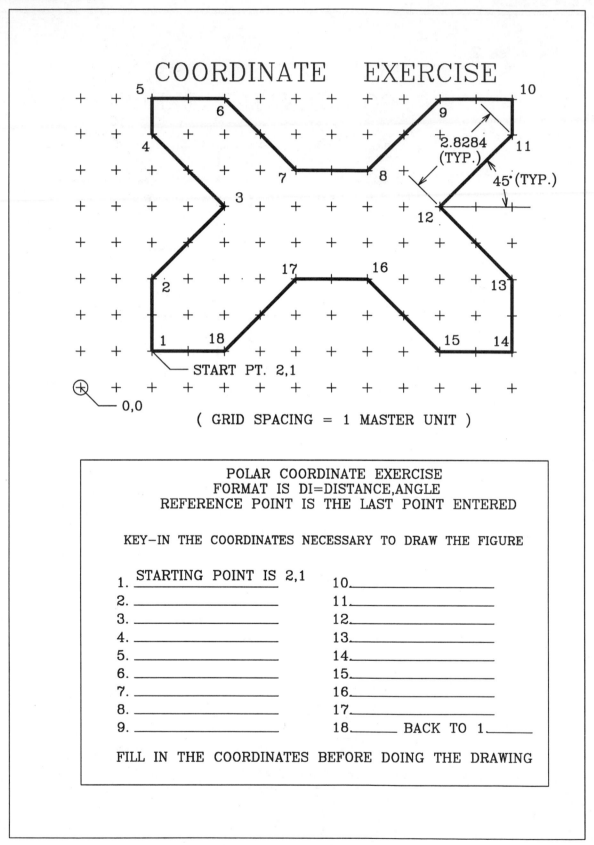

COORDINATE EXERCISE

(GRID SPACING = 1 MASTER UNIT)

POLAR COORDINATE EXERCISE
FORMAT IS DI=DISTANCE,ANGLE
REFERENCE POINT IS THE LAST POINT ENTERED

KEY-IN THE COORDINATES NECESSARY TO DRAW THE FIGURE

1. STARTING POINT IS 2,1
2. _____
3. _____
4. _____
5. _____
6. _____
7. _____
8. _____
9. _____

10. _____
11. _____
12. _____
13. _____
14. _____
15. _____
16. _____
17. _____
18. _____ BACK TO 1 _____

FILL IN THE COORDINATES BEFORE DOING THE DRAWING

Exercise 2–3

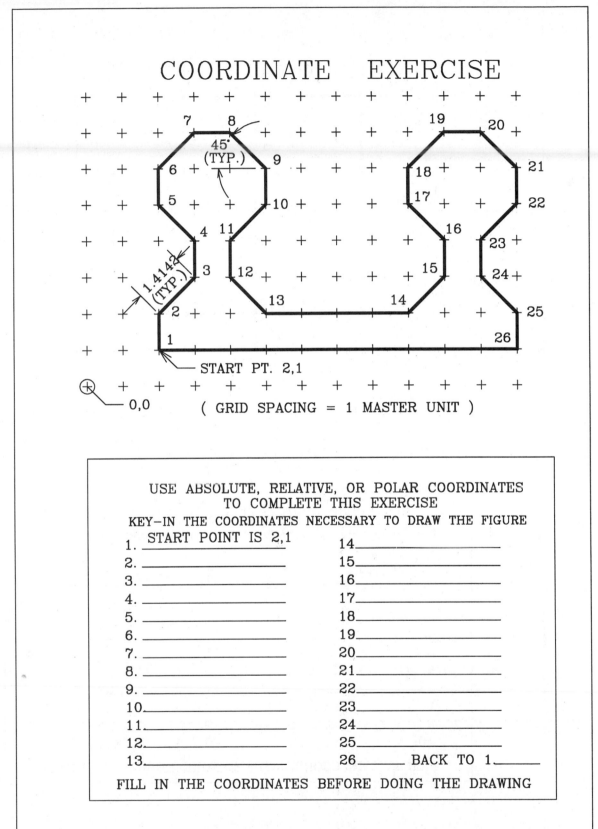

COORDINATE   EXERCISE

START PT. 2,1

0,0   (GRID SPACING = 1 MASTER UNIT)

USE ABSOLUTE, RELATIVE, OR POLAR COORDINATES
TO COMPLETE THIS EXERCISE
KEY-IN THE COORDINATES NECESSARY TO DRAW THE FIGURE

1. _START POINT IS 2,1_   14._____
2. _____   15._____
3. _____   16._____
4. _____   17._____
5. _____   18._____
6. _____   19._____
7. _____   20._____
8. _____   21._____
9. _____   22._____
10._____   23._____
11._____   24._____
12._____   25._____
13._____   26._____ BACK TO 1._____

FILL IN THE COORDINATES BEFORE DOING THE DRAWING

Exercise 2–4

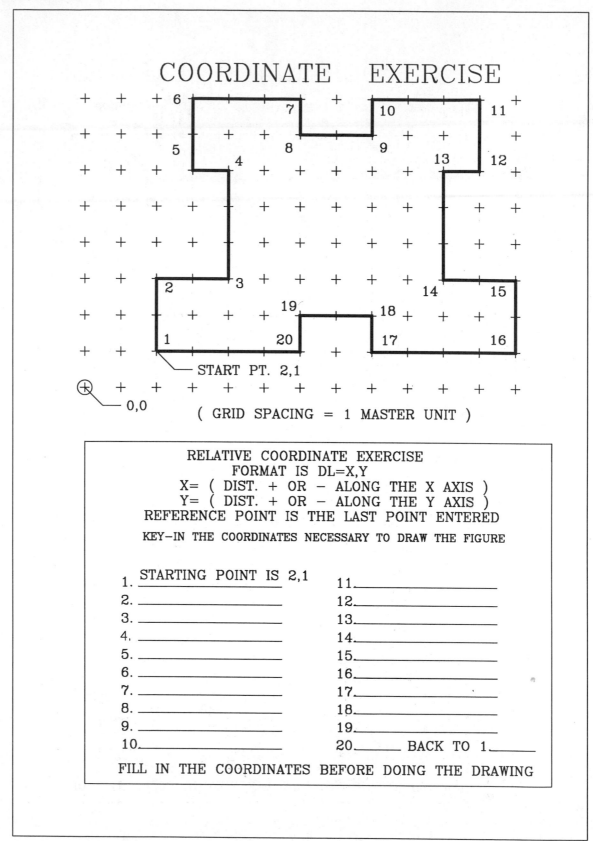

COORDINATE EXERCISE

(GRID SPACING = 1 MASTER UNIT)

RELATIVE COORDINATE EXERCISE
FORMAT IS DL=X,Y
X= (DIST. + OR − ALONG THE X AXIS)
Y= (DIST. + OR − ALONG THE Y AXIS)
REFERENCE POINT IS THE LAST POINT ENTERED

KEY-IN THE COORDINATES NECESSARY TO DRAW THE FIGURE

1. STARTING POINT IS 2,1 _____   11. _____
2. _____   12. _____
3. _____   13. _____
4. _____   14. _____
5. _____   15. _____
6. _____   16. _____
7. _____   17. _____
8. _____   18. _____
9. _____   19. _____
10. _____   20. _____ BACK TO 1 _____

FILL IN THE COORDINATES BEFORE DOING THE DRAWING

Exercises 2–5 through 2–7

Use Precision Key-ins (XY= , DL= , and/or DI=) to draw the figures.

> **NOTE:** Use SDMECH2.DGN seed file to create the design files. Do not add the dimensions at this time.

Exercise 2–5

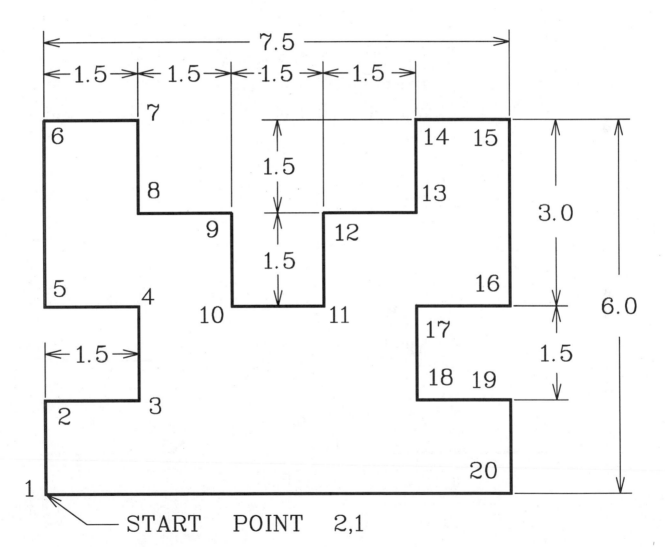

START   POINT   2,1

Exercise 2–6

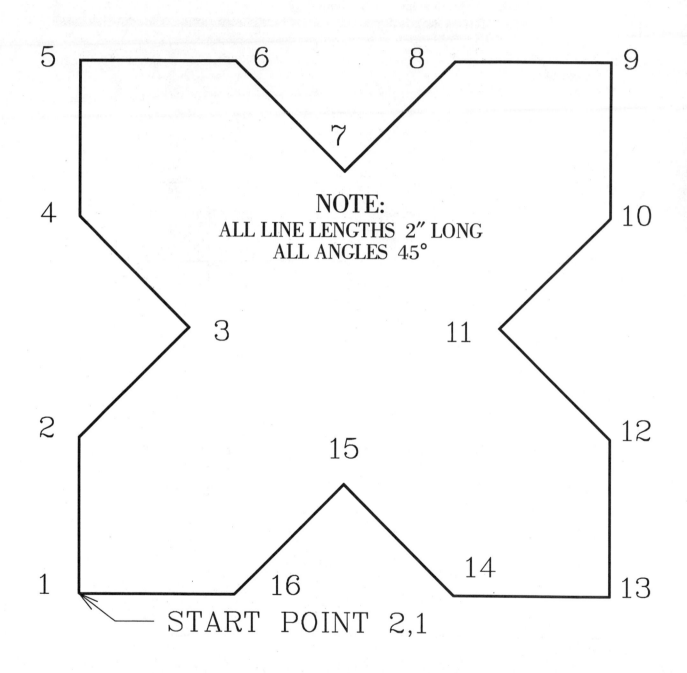

NOTE:
ALL LINE LENGTHS 2″ LONG
ALL ANGLES 45°

START POINT 2,1

Exercise 2–7

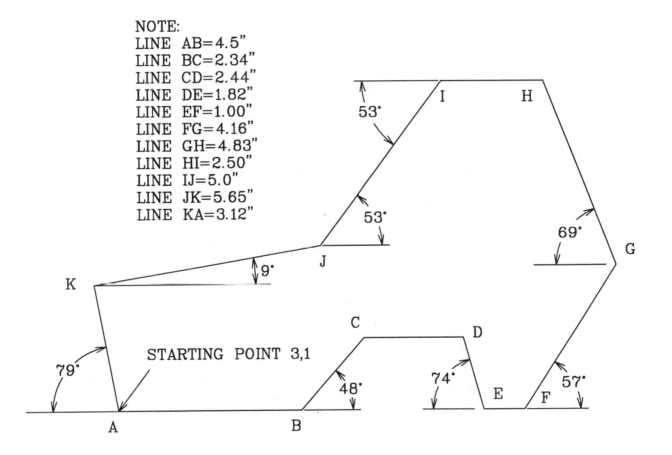

NOTE:
LINE AB=4.5"
LINE BC=2.34"
LINE CD=2.44"
LINE DE=1.82"
LINE EF=1.00"
LINE FG=4.16"
LINE GH=4.83"
LINE HI=2.50"
LINE IJ=5.0"
LINE JK=5.65"
LINE KA=3.12"

STARTING POINT 3,1

PLACE BLOCK

The Place Block command allows you to place a rectangular block by selecting two points that define the diagonal corners of the shape. Place the two diagonal corners by placing data points using your pointing device or by keying in 2D coordinates. The first data point defines the first corner of the block and second data point entered diagonally from the first defines the opposite corner of the block.

To draw a rectangular block, invoke the Place Block command by clicking the Place Block icon from the Polygons sub-palette and selecting Orthogonal from the Method option menu, as shown in Figure 2–18, or key-in at the uSTN> field, **place block orthogonal** (or **pla bl o**) and press [ENTER]. MicroStation prompts:

> *Enter first point* (Place a data point or key-in the coordinates to define the start point of the block.)
> *Enter opposite corner* (Place a data point or key-in coordinates to define the opposite corner of the block.)

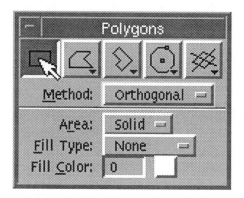

FIGURE 2–18 Invoking the Place Block command from the Polygons sub-palette.

Similar to line string, a block is also a single element. Element manipulation commands such as Move, Copy, and Delete manipulate a block as one entity. If necessary, you can make a block into individual line elements by using the Drop Line String command.

For example, the following command sequence shows placement of a 3 Master units by 5 Master units block using Place Block command (see Figure 2–19).

> *Place first point* (Place a data point as shown in Figure 2–19.)
> *Place opposite corner* **DL=3,5** [ENTER]

Place Block Rotated

The Place Block Rotated command allows you to place a rectangular block at an angle that is defined by the first two data points. The first data point defines the first corner of the block and the point the block rotates around. The second data point defines the angle of the block, and the third data point entered diagonally from the first defines the opposite corner of the block.

To draw a rectangular block at an angle, invoke the Place Block command by clicking the Place Block icon from the Polygons sub-palette and selecting Rotated from the Method option menu, as shown in Figure 2–20, or key-in at the uSTN> field **place block rotated** (or **pla bl r**) and press [ENTER]. MicroStation prompts:

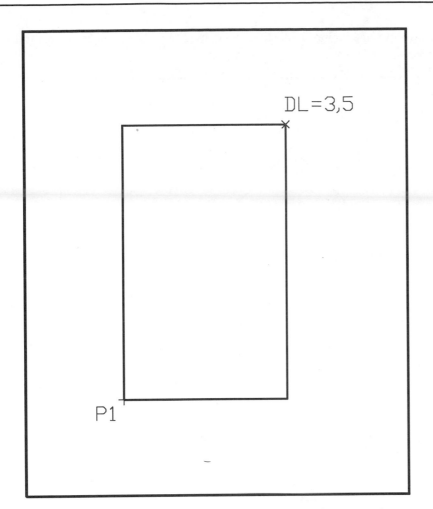

FIGURE 2–19   Placing 3 by 5 block using Place Block command.

Enter first base point (Place a data point or key-in coordinates to define the start point of the block.)

Enter second base point (Place a data point or key-in coordinates to define the angle of the block.)

Enter opposite corner (Place a data point or key-in coordinates to define the opposite corner of the block.)

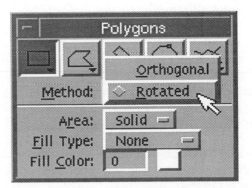

FIGURE 2–20   Invoking the Place Block Rotated command from the Polygons sub-palette by selecting the Rotated option from the Method option menu.

See Figure 2–21 for an example of placing a block rotated by Place Block Rotated command by providing three data points.

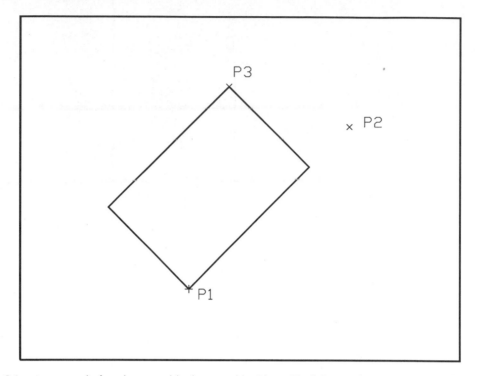

FIGURE 2-21   An example for placing a block rotated by Place Block Rotated command.

Similar to line string, block rotated is also a single element. Element manipulation commands such as Move, Copy, and Delete manipulate the block as one entity. If necessary, you can make the block into individual line elements using the Drop Line String command.

> **NOTE:** Area and Fill type options are explained in Chapter 8 on Patterning.

PLACE SHAPE

The Place Shape command allows you to place a multi-sided shape defined by a series of data points (3 to 100) that indicate the vertices of the polygon. To complete the polygon shape, the last data point should be placed on top of the starting point. You can specify the starting point and subsequent points by absolute or relative coordinates or by using your pointing device.

To draw a polygon shape, invoke the Place Shape command by clicking the Place Shape icon from the Polygons sub-palette, as shown in Figure 2–22 or key-in at the uSTN> field **place shape** (or **pla s**) and press ⏎. MicroStation prompts:

Enter first point (Place a data point or key-in coordinates to define the starting point of the shape.)
Enter end point (Place a data point or key-in coordinates to define the vertex.)

Continue placing data points. To complete the polygon shape, place the last data point on top of the starting point or click the Close Element button located in the sub-palette, as shown in Figure 2–22.

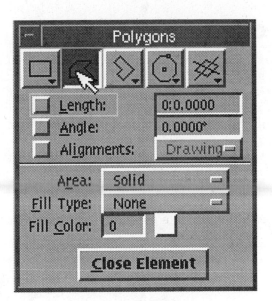

FIGURE 2-22   Invoking the Place Shape command from the Polygons sub-palette.

See Figure 2-23 for an example of placing a closed shape by Place Shape command by providing six data points.

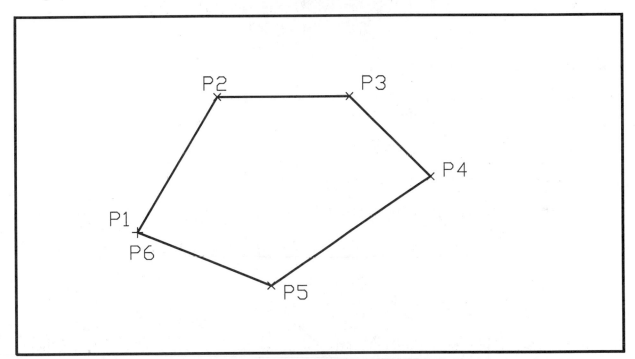

FIGURE 2-23   An example for placing a closed shape by Place Shape command.

Similar to the line string, a shape is also a single element. Element manipulation commands such as Move, Copy, and Delete manipulate the shape as one entity. If necessary, you can make the shape into individual line elements using the Drop Line String command.

> **NOTE:** Area and Fill type options are explained in Chapter 8 on Patterning.

Place Shape Orthogonal

The Place Shape Orthogonal command allows you to create a multi-sided shape that has adjacent sides at right angles. As with Place Block Rotated, the first two points define the vertices of the orthogonal shape. The additional points define the corners of the shape. To complete the polygon shape, the last data point should be placed on top of the starting point. You can specify the starting point and subsequent points by absolute or relative coordinates or by using your pointing device.

To draw an orthogonal shape, invoke the Place Shape Orthogonal command by clicking the Place Shape Orthogonal icon from the Polygons sub-palette as shown in Figure 2–24, or key-in at the uSTN> field **place shape orthogonal** (or **pla s o**) and press ⏎. MicroStation prompts:

> *Enter shape vertex* (Place a data point or key-in coordinates to define the starting point of the shape.)

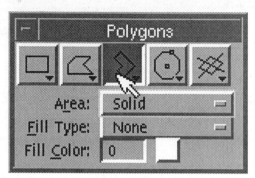

FIGURE 2–24 Invoking the Place Shape Orthogonal from the Polygons sub-palette.

MicroStation prompts for additional shape vertices. Continue placing data points. To complete the polygon shape, the last data point should be placed on top of the starting point.

Similar to the line string, shape orthogonal is also a single element. Element manipulation commands such as Move, Copy, and Delete manipulate the shape orthogonal as one entity. If necessary, you can make the shape into individual line elements using the Drop Line String command.

See Figure 2–25 for an example of placing an orthogonal shape by Place Shape Orthogonal command by providing nine data points.

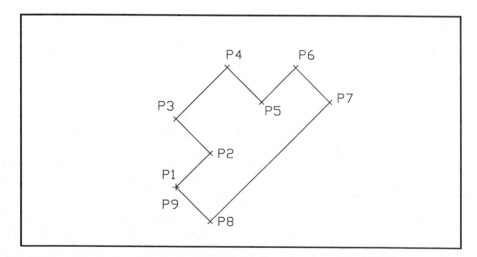

FIGURE 2–25 An example for placing an orthogonal shape by Place Shape Orthogonal.

> **NOTE:** Area and Fill type options are explained in Chapter 8 on Patterning.

DELETING ELEMENTS

MicroStation not only allows you to draw easily, it also allows you to manipulate the elements you have drawn. Of the many manipulation commands available, the Delete Element command probably will be the one you use most often. Everyone makes mistakes, but MicroStation makes it easy to delete them.

To delete an element, invoke the Delete Element command by clicking the Delete Element icon located in the Main Palette as shown in Figure 2–26, or key-in at the uSTN> field **delete element** (or **del**) and press ⏎. MicroStation prompts:

> *Delete element* (Identify the element to delete with the Data button; MicroStation highlights the element.)
> *Accept/Reject (select next input)* (Accept with a data point or identify another element to delete and the element selected with first data point will disappear.)

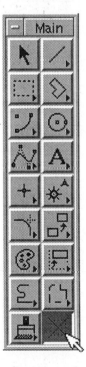

FIGURE 2–26 Invoking the Delete command in the Main palette.

If you change your mind about deleting an element, press the Reject button. If you need to delete additional elements, identify one after another and accept them. The only way to get out of the Delete Element command is to invoke another command.

> **NOTE:** Delete Element command deletes only one element at a time. If you need to delete a group of elements, use Fence Delete command, explained in Chapter 4.

EXERCISES

Exercises 2–8 through 2–11

Use Precision Key-ins (XY= , DL= , and/or DI=) to draw the figures.

> **NOTE:** Use SDMECH2.DGN seed file to create the design files. Do not add the dimensions at this time.

Exercise 2–8

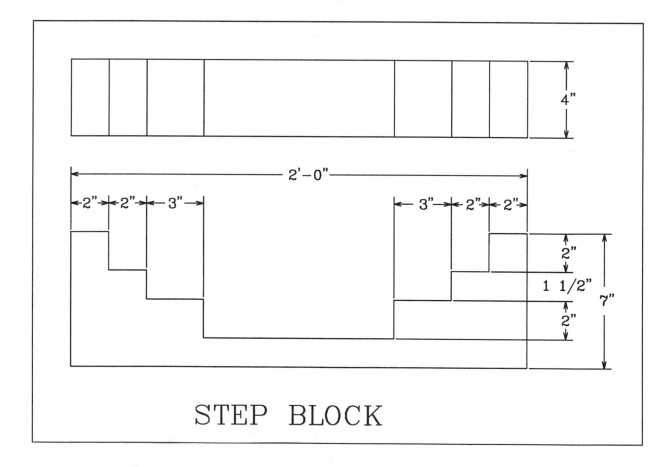

STEP BLOCK

Exercise 2-9

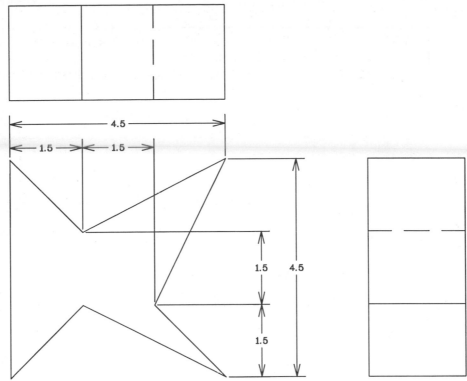

Exercise 2-10

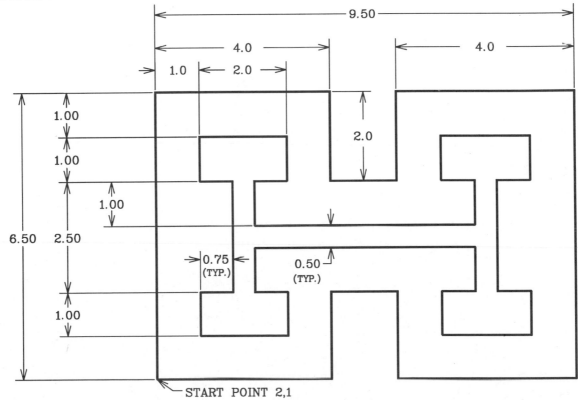

Exercise 2–11

NOTE: Use SDARCH2.DGN seed file to create the design files. Do not add the dimensions at this time.

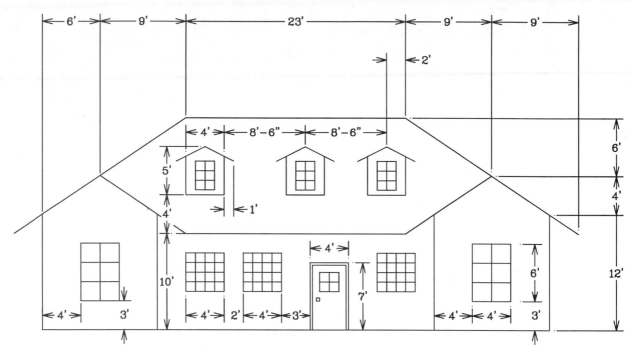

HOUSE 1 DRAWING

DISPLAY COMMANDS

There are many ways to view a drawing in MicroStation. Using the display commands you can select the portion of the drawing to be displayed. By letting you see your drawing in different ways, MicroStation gives you the means to draw more quickly, easily, and accurately.

The commands explained in this section are utility commands; they make your job easier and help you to draw more accurately.

Controlling the Amount of Display

The amount of information that can be displayed in a view can be controlled in a way similar to using a zoom lens on a camera. You can increase or decrease the viewing area, although the actual size of the object remains constant. As you increase the visible size of an object, you view a smaller area of the drawing in greater detail. As you decrease the visible size of an object, you view a larger area. This ability provides the means for greater accuracy and detail.

MicroStation provides you with three commands (Zoom In, Zoom Out, Window Area) that control the amount of information that can be displayed on the screen view. Let's look at each one of them.

Zoom In The Zoom In command increases the visible size of objects, allowing you to view a smaller area of the drawing in greater detail. The default scale factor is 2. In other words, each entity appears twice as large as it does relative to the current view.

To increase the size of visible objects, invoke the Zoom In command by clicking the Zoom In icon located in the View Control sub-palette, as shown in Figure 2–27, or key-in at the uSTN> field **zoom in** (or **zo i**) and press ⏎. MicroStation prompts:

> *Select point to zoom about* (Place a data button to zoom about.)

FIGURE 2–27   Invoking the Zoom In command from the View Control sub-palette.

The data point that you define will become the center of the new window with the increased magnification (see Figures 2–28a and b). You may continue defining data points to magnify further, or invoke a new command.

> **NOTE:** To specify other than the default zoom factor of 2, key-in the Zoom In command followed by a scale factor at the uSTN> field. When you select the Zoom In command from the View Control sub-palette, you cannot specify the scale factor; it will remain 2 (the default scale).

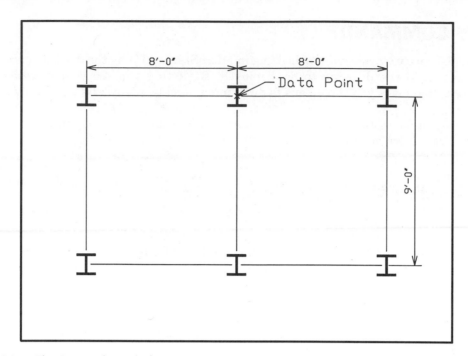

FIGURE 2–28a The Design shown before Zoom In command is invoked.

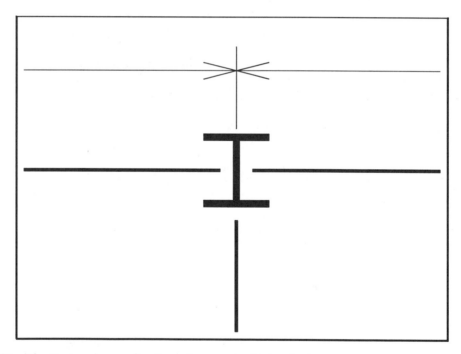

FIGURE 2–28b The Design shown after Zoom In command is invoked.

Zoom Out The Zoom Out command decreases the visible size of objects, allowing you to view a larger area of the drawing. The default scale factor is 2. In other words, each entity appears half the size relative to the current view.

To decrease the size of visible objects, invoke the Zoom Out command by clicking the Zoom Out icon located in the View Control Sub-palette, as shown in Figure 2–29, or key-in at the uSTN> field **zoom out** (or **zo o**) and press [ENTER]. MicroStation prompts:

Select point to zoom about (Place a data button to zoom about.)

FIGURE 2–29   Invoking the Zoom Out command from the View Control sub-palette.

The data point that you define will become the center of the new window with the decreased magnification (see Figure 2–30a and b). You may continue defining data points to magnify further, or invoke a new command.

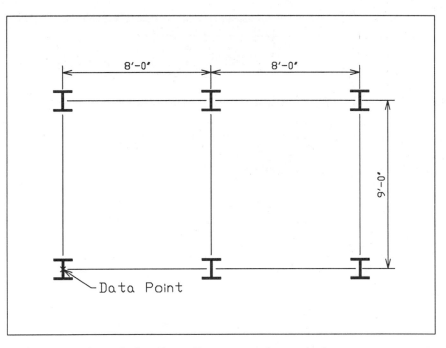

FIGURE 2–30a   The Design shown before Zoom Out command is invoked.

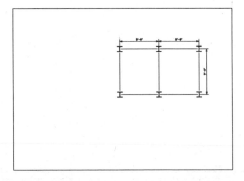

FIGURE 2–30b   The Design shown after Zoom Out command is invoked.

> **NOTE:** To specify other than the default zoom factor of 2, key-in the Zoom Out command followed by a scale factor at the uSTN> field. When you select the Zoom Out command from the View Control sub-palette, you cannot specify the scale factor; it will remain 2 (the default scale).

Window Area Window area allows you to specify an area of the design you wish to magnify by placing two opposite corner points of a rectangular window. The center of the area selected becomes the new display center, and the area inside the window is enlarged to fill the display as completely as possible.

To magnify a specific area of the drawing, invoke the Window Area command by clicking the Window Area icon located in the View Control Sub-Palette, as shown in Figure 2–31, or key-in at the uSTN> field **window area** (or **wi a**) and press [ENTER]. MicroStation prompts:

> *Select window origin* (Place a data point or key-in coordinates.)
> *Select window corner* (Place a data point or key-in coordinates.)
> *Select View* (Place a data point anywhere in the view where you want to display the design.)

FIGURE 2–31   Invoking the Window Area command from the View Control sub-palette.

At this point the contents of the box will update in the view you have selected (see Figure 2–32a and b). You may continue using this command by defining another area and displaying in the view, or you may select a new command.

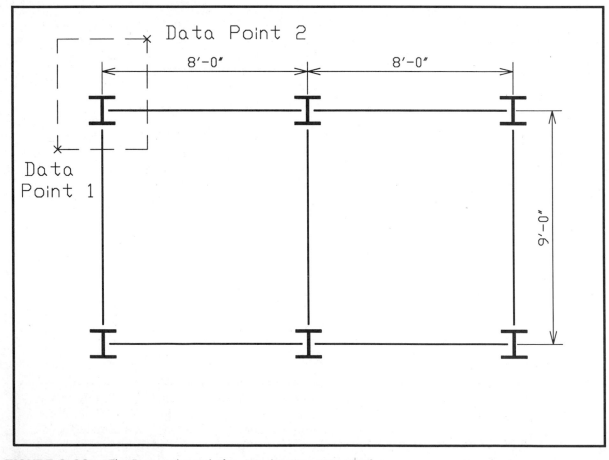

FIGURE 2–32a   The Design shown before Window Area is invoked.

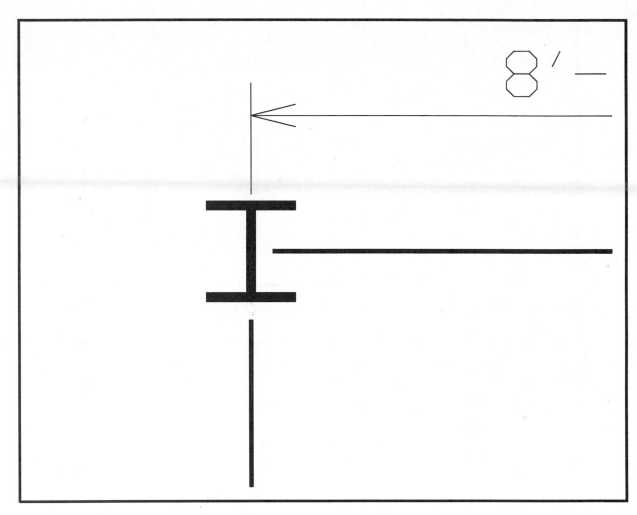

FIGURE 2–32b   The Design shown after Window Area is invoked.

Fit Active Design

The Fit command lets you see the entire design. In a plan view, it zooms to show the entire design drawn on the design plane.

To display the entire design drawn in the design plane, invoke the Fit Active Design command by clicking the Fit Active Design icon located in the View Control sub-Palette, as shown in Figure 2–33, or key-in at the uSTN> field **fit active design** (or **fit**) and press [ENTER]. MicroStation prompts:

Select view (Place a data point anywhere in the view to display the design.)

FIGURE 2–33   Invoking the Fit Active Design command from the View Control sub-palette.

At this point, the view will update showing all elements on the design plane (see Figure 2–34a and b).

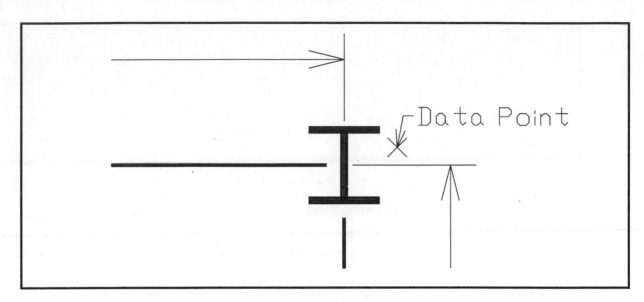

FIGURE 2–34a   The Design shown before Fit Active Design is invoked.

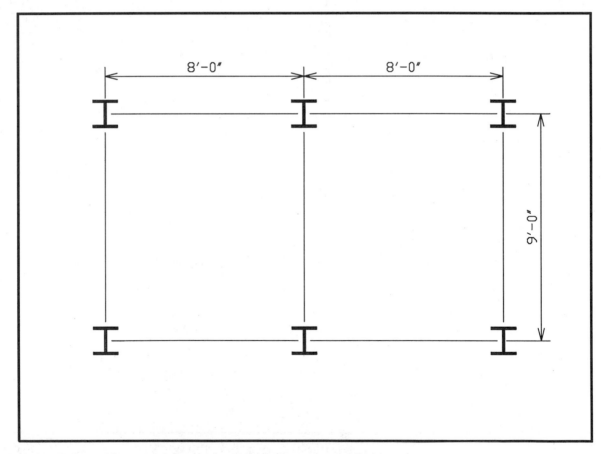

FIGURE 2–34b   The Design shown after Fit Active Design is invoked.

NOTE: If you ever get lost in your drawing, just invoke the Fit Active Design to return to the entire drawing.

Panning

Panning lets you view a different portion of the design in the current view, without changing the magnification. You can move your viewing area to see details that are currently off-screen. Imagine that you are looking at your design through the display window and that you can slide the design left, right, up, and down without moving the window.

To pan in a view, hold the [SHIFT] key and press the Data button, (the pointer location becomes the anchor point for panning) and drag the pointer in the direction to pan. When panning begins, the [SHIFT] key can be released. You can drag the pointer in any direction. Release the Data button to terminate the panning. The panning speed increases as the pointer is dragged farther away from the anchor point.

In addition, you can also pan by keying in the command at the uSTN> field, **Move** <Down/Left/Right/Up> followed by a factor. MicroStation prompts:

Select view(s) (Place a data point anywhere in the view(s).)

Update

The Update command tells the computer to redraw the on-screen image. You can use this command whenever you see an incomplete image of your drawing. If you delete an object on the display, there may be gaps in the outline of other elements it crossed or grid dots that do not show up after deleting. If you update the display, the grid dots will be refreshed and all elements will be repainted.

To update the view, invoke the Update View command by clicking the Update View icon located in the View Control sub-palette, as shown in Figure 2–35, or key-in at the uSTN> field **update view** (or **up vi**) and press [ENTER]. MicroStation prompts:

Select view (Place a data point anywhere in the view to update the view.)

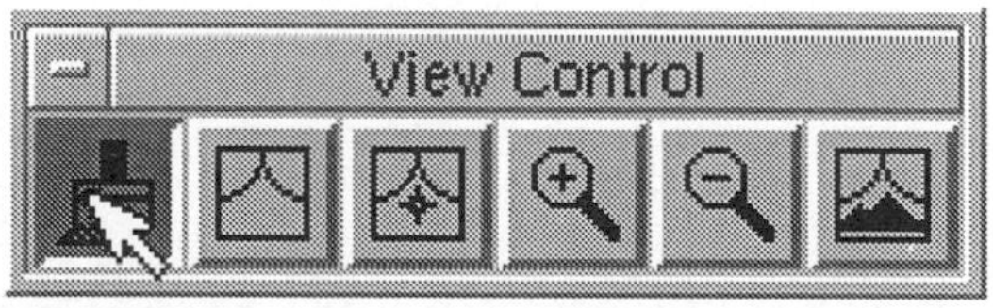

FIGURE 2–35   Invoking the Update command from the View Control sub-palette.

At this point, the selected view is updated. The additional options of the Update command located in the View pull-down menu are explained in Chapter 4.

TEXT PLACEMENT

You have learned how to draw the geometric shapes that make up your design. Now it is time to learn how to annotate your design. When you draw on paper, adding descriptions of the design components and the necessary shop and fabrication notes is a time-consuming, tedious process. MicroStation provides several text placement commands and tools that greatly reduce the time and tedium of text placement.

The text placement procedure includes setting up the text parameters (size, line spacing, style, etc.), selecting a placement command, typing your text, and then placing it in the design. Each string of text you place is a single element to which all of the element and fence contents manipulation commands can be applied.

> **NOTE:** If you do not know how to type, you can place text quickly and easily after a period of learning the keyboard and developing typing skills. If you create designs that require a lot of text entry, it may be worth your time to learn to type with all ten fingers. There are several computer programs that can help you teach yourself to type, and almost all colleges offer typing classes. If you do not have time to learn proper typing, there is no need to worry—many "two-finger" typists productively place text in their designs.

Text Parameters

Before you can place text in your design, you have to make sure the text parameters, such as font, text size, line spacing, justification, etc., are set up appropriately. You can do so by invoking the Text settings box similar to the one shown in Figure 2–36 selecting Text from the Element pull-down menu. All settings come with certain defaults, which you can change if necessary. Following are the parameters that can be changed in the Text settings box:

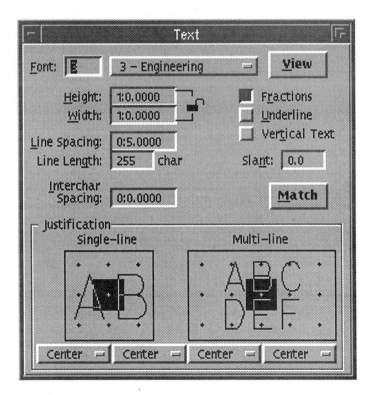

FIGURE 2-36 Text Settings box.

Font Before you start placing text you must decide what style (font) you want to use. Do you want fancy text, italic text, block text, or some other font? Text fonts are identified by numbers, and MicroStation can support up to 255 different fonts. To find out what fonts are loaded in your copy of MicroStation click the View button in the Text Attributes settings box. MicroStation displays the Fonts settings box listing the available fonts (see Figure 2–37).

The top half of the Fonts settings box lists all fonts loaded in MicroStation. Each line in the list area describes one font. Use the scroll bar to view all of the available fonts.

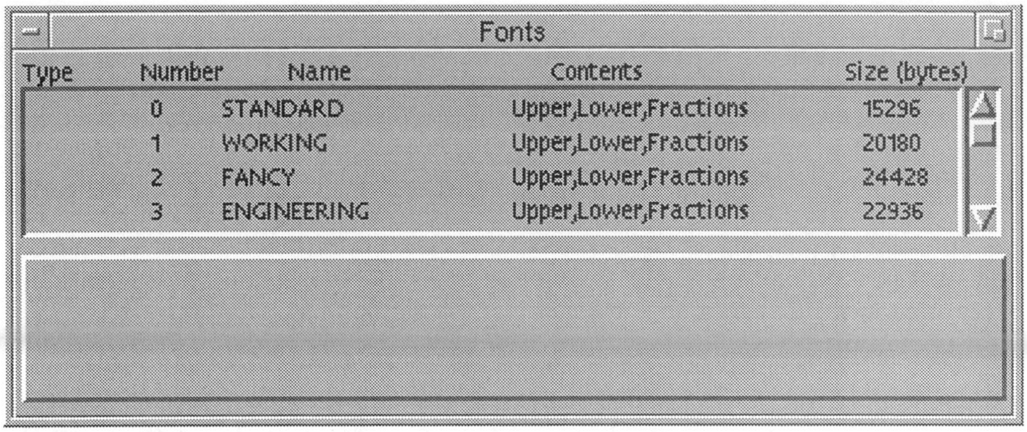

FIGURE 2–37   Fonts Settings box.

To see what a font looks like, click on the font's description line. An example of the font you click on appears in the bottom half of the settings box. Figure 2–38 shows an example of a font that provides upper and lowercase letters, numbers, and single-character fractions. Some fonts do not contain lowercase letters, and some do not contain single-character fractions. If a font does not include one type of character, that type will not show up in the font example. The font description in the upper half of the Fonts setting box also tells you what types of characters the font contains.

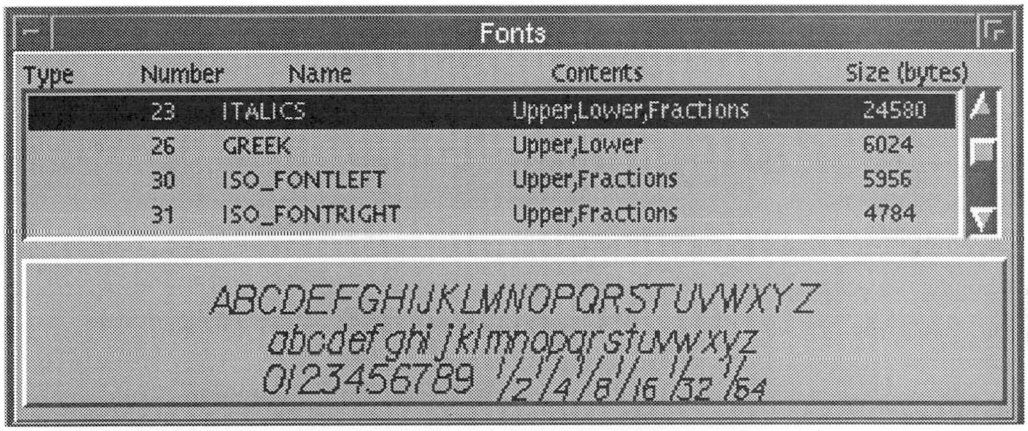

FIGURE 2–38   Displaying an example font in the Fonts Setting box.

A few fonts provide symbols rather than letters and numbers. When you select a symbol font, the letters you type provide symbols rather than the letters. For example, the font 102 contains the upper and lowercase letters that provide different symbols (such as arrowheads) rather than the letters.

To select a font, click on the font's description. MicroStation displays an example in the lower half of the Fonts settings box. Click in the lower half of the window. The selected font becomes the active font. You also can select the font by key-in at the uSTN> field, **FT=<#>** and press [ENTER]. The selected font becomes the active font.

After you select a font number, MicroStation displays your selection in the Status field of the Command Window. The font number you select remains the active font until you select another font number or exit MicroStation. To keep the font number active for the next time you edit the design, select Save Settings from the File pull-down menu.

Text Size After you have selected a text font, you must tell MicroStation what size you want the text to be. Text size consists of the height and width specified in working units (MU:SU:PU).

If you are drawing an unscaled schematic, or if you are going to plot your design full size, selecting a text size is simple—just enter the size you want your text to be when you plot it.

If you are drawing a design that must be scaled to be plotted, selecting a text size is a little more complicated. As mentioned earlier, you draw objects in MicroStation full size (real world size), and tell MicroStation what scale to use when it plots the design to paper. MicroStation scales down everything in the design to fit the paper you use for plotting, including the text. Therefore you must scale up your text by the inverse of the plot scale, so it will be the correct size when you plot.

For example, if you are creating a design that will be plotted at 1″=10′, and you want your text size to be .1 in., your text size in the design must be 1 ft (if 1 in. of plotter paper equals 10 ft, then .1 in. of plotter paper equals 1 ft).

Let's put that into a formula:

Text height in design = (design units ÷ plotter units) × plotted text size

Now let's try the formula for providing ⅛ in text when we plot at ⅛″=1′. Our design units are 1 ft, our plotter units are ⅛ in., and we want our plotted text size to be ⅛ in. The formula, (1′ ÷ ⅛″ × ⅛″) says we need to place 1 ft. text size in the design.

To specify the text size, first invoke the Text Settings box, click in the Text Height field and key-in your text height (see Figure 2–39), and press either ⏎ or ⭾ to go to the Width edit field. Key-in the text width and press either ⏎ or ⭾.

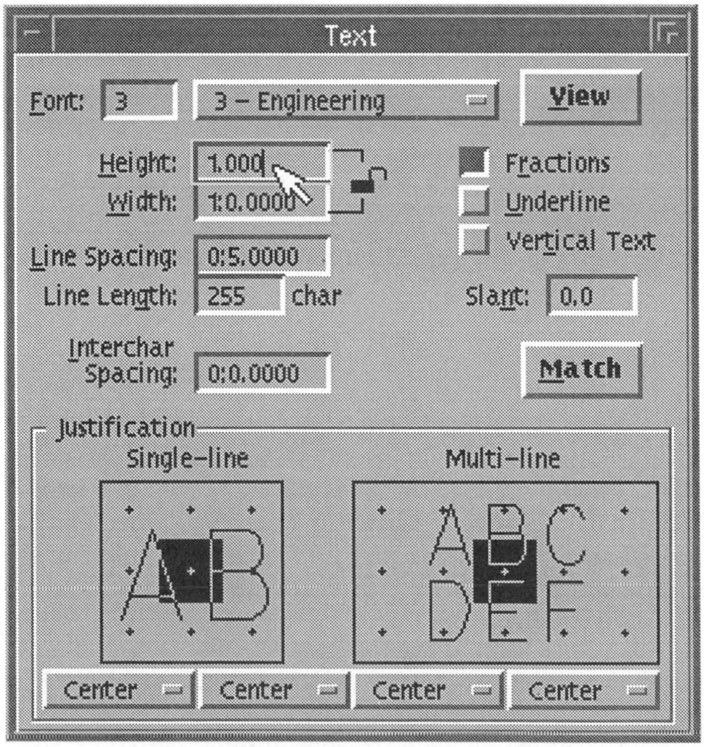

FIGURE 2–39 Cursor in the Text Height edit field in the Text Settings box.

There is a small lock symbol to the right of the text height and width fields (see Figure 2–39). If you want your text height and width to be equal, click on the lock symbol to close the lock. When the lock is closed you can key-in a value in either of the size fields and the other will automatically be set to equal what you type. If the lock is open, you must enter each field separately.

You can also key-in the text size at the uSTN> field in the Command Window by using one or more of the following key-ins:

TX=<size>   (to set both the text height and width with one command)
TH=<size>   (to set only the text height)
TW=<size>   (to set only the text width)

In each key-in command replace <size> with the text size (in working units) and press [ENTER].

Once you set the text size, it remains active until you change it or exit MicroStation. Save Settings from the File pull-down menu saves the settings for the next time you load your design file in MicroStation.

Underline and Vertical Text To place a text with a line below the text as shown in Figure 2–40, turn on the toggle button for Underline in the Text settings box. Similarly, to place text vertical as shown in Figure 2–40, turn on the toggle button for Vertical text in the Text settings box.

Slant To place a text at an angle as shown in Figure 2–40, key-in the slant angle in the Slant edit field in the Text Attributes settings box. The slant angle can be anywhere from –89 degrees to 89 degrees.

FIGURE 2–40   Examples for placing text with a line below the text, vertical text and slant text.

Text Spacing and Line Length When you place text it becomes one element in your design. While you are typing the text, you can press [ENTER] to create multi-line text that is treated as one element. If you plan to enter multi-line text, you must tell MicroStation how much space to leave between the text lines and the maximum number of characters you want on one line.

There are no firm rules for setting the line spacing, but if you set it to a value less than half the text height, the lines may appear too close when plotted.

For the majority of text work, the maximum number of characters per line is not important, just leave it set at the default value of 255 characters (the maximum it can be). If you try to type more characters in one line of text than the maximum allows, you will be wrapped to a new line at the maximum number of characters. (It wraps even if you are in the middle of a word.)

To specify the line spacing and maximum number of characters, first invoke the Text Settings box, click in the Line Spacing field and key-in your line spacing in working units (MU:SU:PU), and press either [ENTER] or [TAB] to go to the Line Length edit field. Key-in the maximum number of characters per line in the Line Length field and press either [ENTER] or [TAB].

You can also key-in the Line Spacing and Line Length at the uSTN> field in the Command Window by using the following key-ins:

> **LS=<space>** (to set space between lines)
> **LL=<charc>** (to set the maximum characters per line)

Replace <space> with the line spacing in working units, replace <charc> with the maximum number of characters per line and press [ENTER].

Once you set the Line Spacing and Line Length these settings remain active until you change them or exit MicroStation. Save Settings from the File pull-down menu saves the settings for the next time you load your design file in MicroStation.

Inter-Character Spacing When you place a text along an element, MicroStation places each character in the text as a separate text element. To specify the spacing between two characters, key-in the value in MU:SU:PU in the Inter-Char spacing edit field in the Text Attributes settings box. See the section on Place Text Along an Element for additional explanation.

Setting the Justification To place the text you typed in, first you have to define a data point in your design. Before you do so, you have to tell MicroStation where to place the text in relation to that data point. That relationship is called the justification. The Text settings box provides an excellent visual aid to setting up the justification (see Figure 2–41).

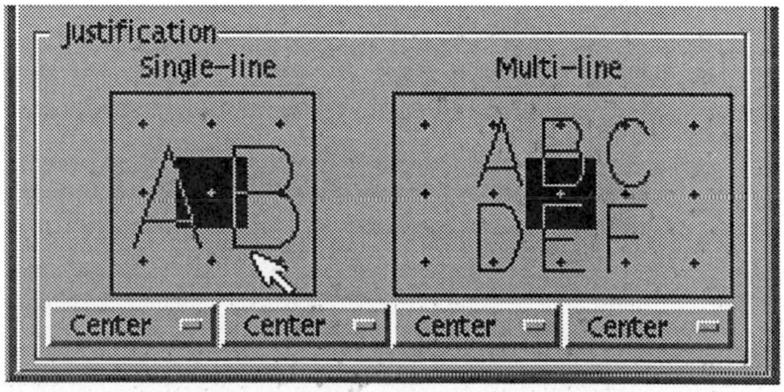

FIGURE 2–41 Text settings box showing the justification options.

In the window are two pictures of large text over a grid or dots. The text is shown using the currently active font. The dark square in each picture shows the relation of the Data button to the text. The Text String picture on the left defines the justification when you place a single line of text. The Multi-line Text picture defines the justification when you place text that is longer than one line.

To set the justification, click on one of the grid points in the justification pictures, or select the justification from the sets of option menus below the pictures. Once set, the justification remains active until you change it or exit MicroStation. Select Save Settings from the File pull-down menu to save the active justification for the next editing session.

The multi-line text justification also determines which side of the text will be smooth. Additional options available for justification in the multi-line text picture are Left Margin and Right Margin. These two justifications use the line length setting that was discussed earlier. When you use a Left Margin justification, the right edge of the multi-string text is placed equivalent to the number of characters of Line Length from the data point. If a Right Margin justification is used, the left edge of the multi-string text is placed equivalent to the number of characters of Line Length from the data point.

> **NOTE:** A common mistake of inexperienced MicroStation users (and occasionally experienced users) is forgetting that the outside settings set the multi-line text justification to margin. They click those thinking they are selecting left or right justification. If the line length is set to 255 characters, the results can be startling when the text is placed.

Setting Angle Set the appropriate active angle to place the text string at an angle. This can be set by key-in **AA=<angle>** at uSTN> field. The default Active Angle is 0 degrees. You can also set the active angle by invoking the Active Angle settings box from the Settings pull-down menu.

Setting Color, Weight, and Level Set the appropriate color, weight, and level to place the text. This can be set by invoking the Attributes settings box from the Element pull-down menu. (See Chapter 3 section on setting up the element attributes.)

Text View Attributes There is one last thing to check before you start placing text in your design file. Make sure the Text view attribute is set to ON. This can be done by invoking the View Attributes from the View pull-down menu.

If the Text view attribute is set to ON, all text that is placed in the design will appear in the view. If it is set to OFF, all text disappears from the view. Updates may be completed faster when no text is displayed, but you must be careful not to use the space occupied by the text.

If the Fast Font view attribute is set to ON, all text is displayed as font 127, regardless of the font that was used to place it. Font 127 is a simple font that may update faster than other fonts. Text size is affected by font. If you turn Fast Font to ON, the text may appear to take up more room than it does when its true font is used.

If the Text Nodes view attribute is set to ON, you will see a cross and number placed at the data point of multi-line text strings. For the majority of your work, keep this attribute set to OFF.

Detailed explanation is provided for View Attributes in Chapter 4 and Text Nodes in Chapter 5.

Place Text

You finally have all the text parameters set up and you are ready to place text.

- The Place Text at Origin command places text at the data point you define.
- The Place Fitted Text command scales the text to fill the space between two data points.
- The Place Text Above Element command places text above a line you have identified.
- The Place Text Below Element command places text below a line you have identified.
- The Place Text on Element command places the text on the identified line and removes the portion of the line where the text is placed.
- The Place Text Along Element command places text along a curved element.
- The Place Note command places text at the end of a line and arrowhead.

Each of these commands can be selected from the Text sub-palette that is available from the Main palette (see Figure 2–42).

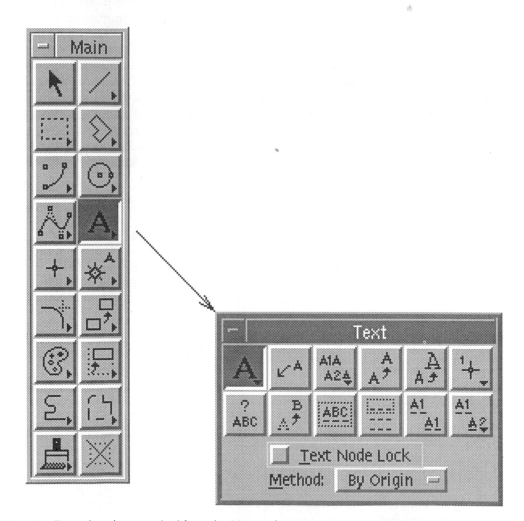

FIGURE 2–42   Text sub-palette invoked from the Main palette.

When you select one of the seven text placement commands, the Text Editor box will be displayed as shown in Figure 2–43. This box provides a place to type the text and some helpful text editing commands.

FIGURE 2–43 Text editor.

If necessary you can resize the Text Editor box so you can see more of what you are typing. Point to the box border, press the data button, and drag it to the new size.

To type text in the box, place the screen cursor in the box and click the data button. When you see a text cursor similar to the cursor in a word processor you may start typing.

For multi-line text press ⏎ at the place where you want the new line to start and continue typing. If you do not press ⏎, the text will wrap to a new line when you reach the right end of the Text Editor box, but all the text will be on one line when you place it in your design. You can place multi-line text only when you press ⏎.

The key-ins described in Table 2–1 position the text cursor within the text in the Text Editor box.

Table 2–1. Positioning the Text Cursor

PRESS:	TO MOVE THE TEXT CURSOR:
←	Left one character.
→	Right one character.
CTRL + ←	Left one word.
CTRL + →	Right one word.
Home key	To the beginning of the current text line.
End key	To the end of the current text line.
↑	Up to the previous line of text.
↓	Down to the next line of text.
PG↑	Straight up into the first text line.
PG↓	Straight down into the last text line.
CTRL +**Home** key	Up to the beginning of the first text line.
CTRL +**End** key	Down to the end of the last text line.

The key-ins described in Table 2–2 delete characters from the text in the Text Editor box.

Table 2–2. Keys That Delete Text

PRESS:	TO DELETE:
Back Space	Character to the left of the text cursor.
DEL	Character to the right of the text cursor.
SHIFT+**Back Space**	All characters from the text cursor to the beginning of the word.
ALT + **DEL**	All characters from the text cursor to the end of the word.
CTRL+**Back Space**	All characters from the text cursor to the beginning of the current line.
CTRL + **DEL**	All characters from the text cursor to the end of the current line.
Reset button in Text Editor box	All characters in the Text Editor box.

The Key-ins described in Table 2–3 select, or deselect, text in the Text Editor box. Selected text is shown with a dark background. Selected text can be moved, copied, or deleted.

Table 2–3. Selecting Text With Key-Ins

PRESS:	TO SELECT:
SHIFT + **←**	The character to the left of the text cursor, or, if the character was already selected, deselect it.
SHIFT + **→**	The character to the right of the text cursor, or, if the character was already selected, deselect it.
CTRL + **SHIFT** + **←**	The characters from the text cursor to the left end of a word, or, if the characters were already selected, deselect them.
CTRL + **SHIFT** + **→**	The characters from the text cursor to the right end of a word, or, if the characters were already selected, deselect them.
CTRL + **A**	Select all text in the Text Editor box.
← or **→** key	Deselect all previously selected text.

The pointing device actions described in Table 2–4 select, or deselect, text in the Text Editor box.

Table 2–4. Selecting Text With the Pointing Device

POINTING DEVICE ACTION:	RESULT:
Press Data button and drag screen cursor across the text.	All text you drag across is selected.
Double-click the Data button.	The word the cursor is in is selected.
Hold down **SHIFT**+Data button and drag across the text	Add more text to the text already selected.
Click Data button in an area where there is no text.	Deselects all previously selected text.

The actions required to replace, delete, and copy previously selected text are shown in Table 2–5.

Table 2–5. Replacing, Deleting, and Copying Selected Text

ACTION:	RESULT:
Start typing characters.	Selected text is replaced with the text you type.
Click **Back Space** key	All selected text is deleted.
Click **DEL** key	All selected text is deleted.
Click **CTRL**+**Insert** keys	Selected text is copied to a buffer.
Click **SHIFT**+**Insert** keys	Paste previously copied or deleted text at text cursor position.

In this section, Place Text by Origin is explained. The remaining text placement commands are explained in Chapter 5.

Place Text by Origin The Place Text command places the text at the data point you define using the active text parameters (font, size, line spacing, line length, and justification), active color, active line weight, and active angle.

You also can place multi-line text by pressing **ENTER** while typing the text in the Text Editor box. Remember that there are separate justification fields for text strings (all the text in one line) and multi-line text in the Text settings box.

To place text by origin, click on the Place Text icon in the Text sub-palette and select By Origin from the Method options menu (see Fig. 2–44). The Text Editor box opens and MicroStation prompts:

> *Enter Text* (If the Text Editor box does not already contain the text you want to place, click in the box and type the text. Place a data point in the design to indicate the text justification point.)
> *Enter more chars or position text* (Continue placing copies of the text in the design, change the text in the Text Editor box before continuing, or select another command.)

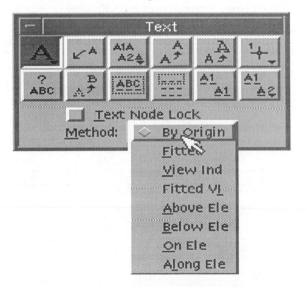

FIGURE 2–44 Invoking the Place Text command by Origin from the Text sub-palette.

Each copy of the text you place becomes a single element that can be manipulated like any other type of element. The only key point in a text string or multi-line element is the placement point. As you place the text you can change any of the text or element attributes.

EXERCISES

Exercises 2–12 through 2–13

Draw the schematic diagram with annotations by using appropriate grid spacing.

> *NOTE:* Use SDMECH2.DGN seed file to create the design files.
> *HINT:*   Set GU=.25, GR=4, TX=.25, and LS=.125

Exercise 2–12

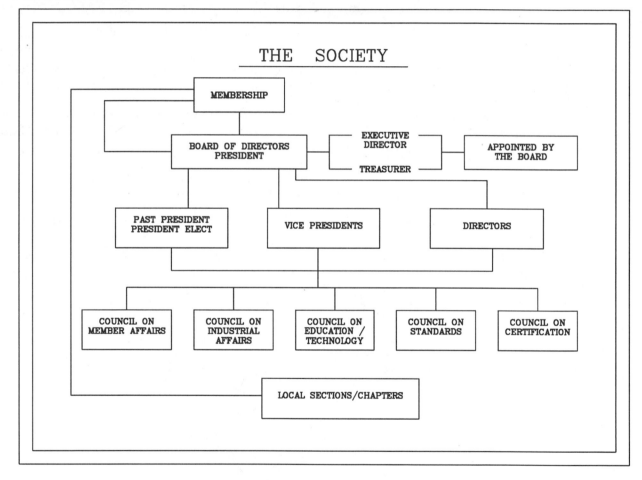

Exercise 2–13

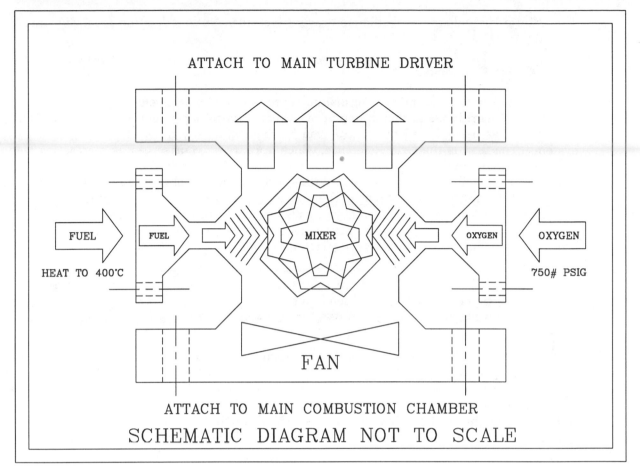

ATTACH TO MAIN TURBINE DRIVER

FUEL

FUEL

MIXER

OXYGEN

OXYGEN

HEAT TO 400°C

750# PSIG

FAN

ATTACH TO MAIN COMBUSTION CHAMBER

SCHEMATIC DIAGRAM NOT TO SCALE

DRAWING AIDS

MicroStation provides several different drawing tools to make your drafting and design layout easier.

The Grid System

Grids are a visual tool for measuring distances precisely and placing elements accurately. MicroStation displays a grid system that is similar to a sheet of graph paper. You can turn the Grid display to ON or OFF as needed, and the spacing can be changed at any time. There are two types of grid systems. The first is the Grid Reference, which appears on your screen as a cross; by default the spacing between crosses is set to one Master Unit (MU). The second is the Grid Unit (GU), which appears as a dot on the screen; by default the spacing between dots is set to one Sub-Unit (SU). The grid is just a drawing tool, not part of the drawing; it is used for visual reference only and is never plotted. Grids serve two purposes; they provide a visual indication of distances and, with Grid lock set to ON, they force all data points to start and end on a grid point. This is useful for keeping lines straight, ensuring that distances are exact and making sure all elements meet.

> **NOTE:** MicroStation overrides the Grid lock when you key-in the location of a point by precision input.

Grid Display The Grid display (visual) can be turned ON or OFF. If it is set to ON, then you can see the Grid display on the screen. MicroStation, by default displays a maximum of 90 dots and 46 crosses. You may not see any crosses or dots if you zoom out farther away. When it is set to OFF, the grid is not displayed. You can change the status of the Grid display from the View Attributes setting box. To change the status, invoke the View Attributes settings box by selecting View Attributes from the View pull-down menu. The resulting settings box is similar to the one shown in Figure 2–45.

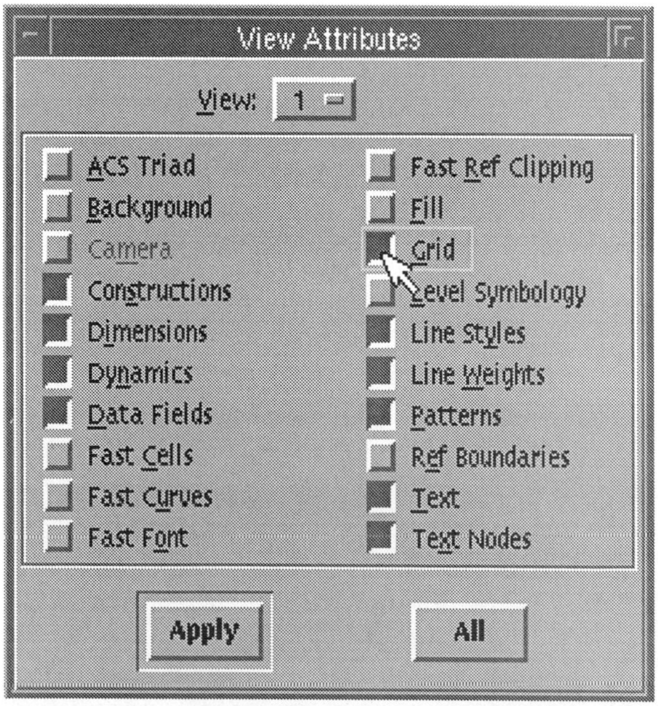

FIGURE 2–45 View Attributes Settnigs box with cursor position on Grid toggle.

Make any necessary change to Grid Display in the view attributes settings box. If the button is depressed and has a dark center, the attribute is ON. If the button appears to be sticking out, the attribute is OFF. If you only want the attribute change applied to a specific view, pick the number of the view you want in the View Number (default current working view) options menu at the top of the settings box, then click the Apply button. If you want to turn ON the Grid display on all the open views, click the ALL button. (For a detailed explanation of Views and View Attributes settings box, see Chapter 4.)

Grid Spacing   You will notice when the grid display is turned ON that it consists of a series of evenly spaced dots and crosses. The grid consists of a matrix of dots with the reference crosses falling at equally spaced intervals. The spacing between both the grid dots and the reference crosses may be changed at any time to suit your drawing needs. When you begin the drawing the reference crosses default to reflect the Master units and the grid dots are spaced to reflect the sub-units.

The Grid settings can be adjusted by invoking the Grid settings box from the Settings pull-down menu in the MicroStation Command Window, as shown in Figure 2–46. The Grid settings box, similar to the one shown in Figure 2–47, is displayed. In the settings box two edit fields are provided, one for Master/Grid unit, the other one for Reference Grid. The Master/Grid unit defines the distance between the grid units (dots) and is specified in terms of MU:SU:PU. By default, this is set for one sub-unit. If necessary, you can override the default spacing by keying-in in the edit field in terms of MU:SU:PU.

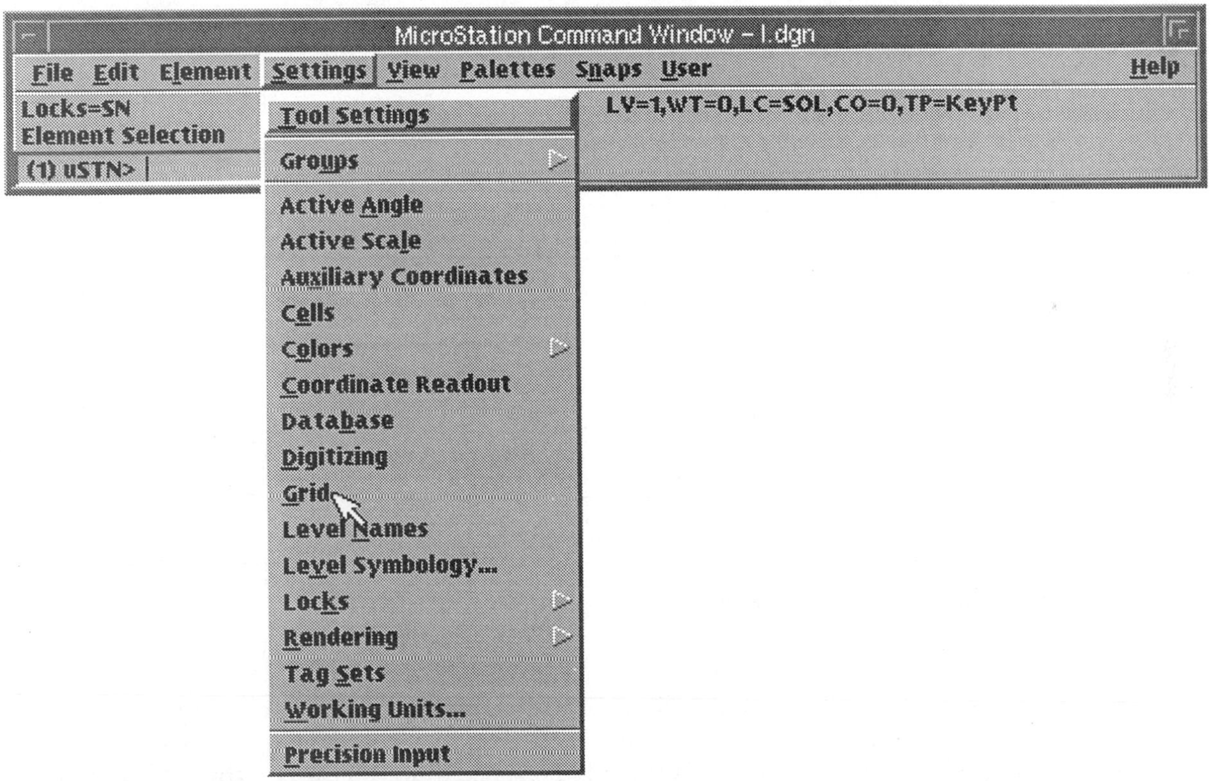

FIGURE 2–46   Invoking the Grid settings box from the Settings pull-down menu.

The Grid Reference is set to define the number (integer) of grid units between the grid reference (crosses). For example, let's say the Master/Grid unit is set up to .125 inches and you would like to have the distance between the Crossing be 0.5 inch. Then the Grid Reference has to be set to 4 (0.5"/.125"), as shown in Figure 2–47.

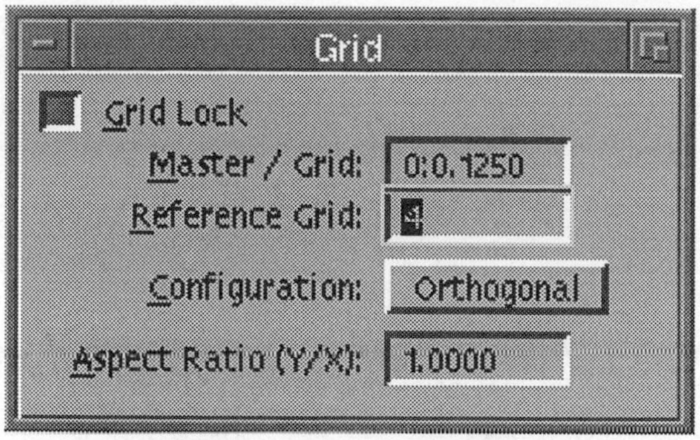

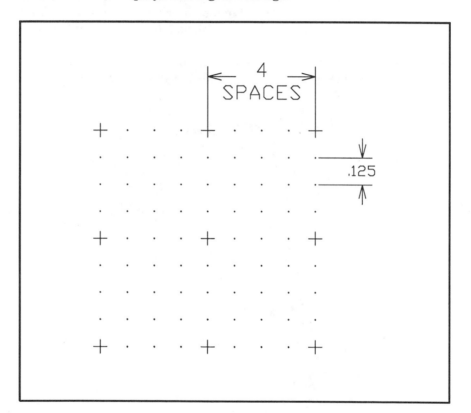

FIGURE 2-47 Grid Settings box.

Figure 2–48 shows the screen display for the grid settings.

FIGURE 2-48 Screen display for the grid settings.

You can also set the Master/Grid unit and Grid Reference by key-in at the uSTN> field. To set the Master/Grid unit, key-in at the uSTN> field, **GU**=<distance>, and press ⏎. <distance> has to be specified in MU:SU:PU. To set the Grid Reference, key-in at the uSTN> field, **GR**=<integer number>, and press ⏎. <integer number> is the number of grid units between the grid reference (crosses). To keep the grid settings in effect for future editing sessions for the current design file, select Save Settings from the File pull-down menu.

Grid Lock The Grid lock can be set to ON or OFF. When it is set to ON, MicroStation forces all the data points to the grid marks. You cannot place a data point in between the grid dots. By setting the Grid lock to ON, you can enter points quickly, letting MicroStation ensure that they are placed precisely. You can always override grid lock by keying-in absolute or relative coordinate points.

When grid lock is set to ON, you can identify the elements that were drawn on the grid. To identify an element that is not on the grid, simply set the Grid lock to OFF and try again.

The Grid lock can be turned ON or OFF (toggle) from the Grid Settings box. If the button is depressed and has a dark center, the Grid lock is ON. If the button appears to be sticking out, the Grid lock is OFF. You can also toggle the Grid lock from the Toggle Settings box, as shown in Figure 2–49, invoked from the Settings pull-down menu. To keep the grid settings (lock status) in effect for future editing sessions for the current design file, select Save Settings from the File pull-down menu.

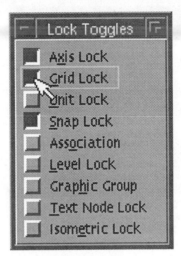

FIGURE 2–49   Locks Toggles Settings box.

> **NOTE:** The Grid lock is effective regardless of the status of the grid display. It still locks to grid points, even if you cannot see the grid.

Configuration MicroStation provides you three choices; Orthogonal, Isometric, and Offset to control the orientation of the Grid display. The selection can be made from the Grid Settings box under the Configuration options menu. The Orthogonal option aligns the grid points orthogonally (default option). The Isometric option aligns the grid points isometrically. The Offset option offsets the rows by half the distance between horizontal grid points.

Aspect Ratio (Y/X) The Aspect Ratio edit field in the Grid Settings box allows you to set the ratio of vertical (Y) Grid points to horizontal (X) grid points. The default is set 1.000.

Tentative Snapping

Tentative snapping is a way of previewing a data point before it is actually entered in the drawing. Once the tentative point is placed in your design plane, a large cross appears to identify the tentative point. In addition, MicroStation displays the absolute coordinates of the point selected in the Status of the Command Window. A tentative point is placed by clicking the designated tentative button on your pointing device. For example, for a three-button mouse, click the middle button to place the tentative point; for a two-button mouse, press both buttons simultaneously to place a tentative point. If this is the point you wish to select, click the Accept button (same as the Data button) to confirm it. If, however, this is not the point you wish to select, move the cursor and click the tentative button again. This process of selecting another tentative point rejects the last tentative point and selects a new one highlighted by the large cross. Once you accept the tentative point with the Accept button, the large cross disappears. You may cancel the tentative point by clicking the Reset button. When the Snap lock is set to ON, you can place a tentative point at a specific point on an element depending on the snap mode selected. For example, if you set the snap mode called Center and turn ON the snap lock, the tentative button snaps to the center of circles, blocks, lines, and segments of line strings. A tentative point can be placed while executing any MicroStation command which requests a point, such as Line, Circle, Arc, Move, Copy, etc. The snap lock can be turned ON or OFF (toggle) from Locks (Full and Toggle) settings box as shown in Figure 2–50.

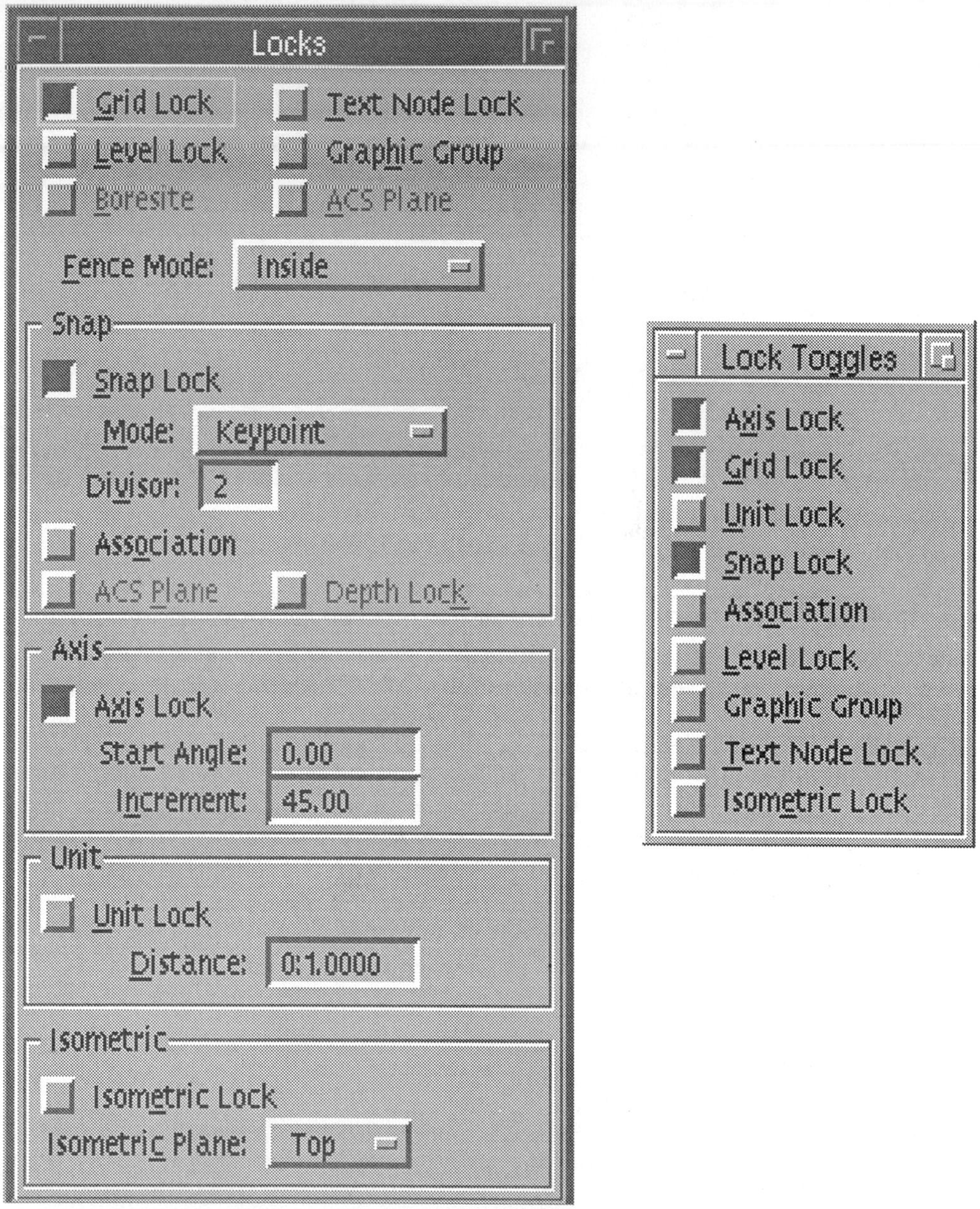

FIGURE 2–50 Locks Toggles Settings box (Full and Toggle).

Selecting a Snap Mode You can select an active (default) snap mode that always stays in effect, and, when you occasionally need a different one, you can select an override snap mode that only applies to the next tentative point. Save the active mode for future editing sessions by selecting the Save Settings option from the File pull-down menu.

Three menus are available in which you can select the snap mode you want.

1. Select the active (default) snap mode by opening the Full Locks setting box from the Locks option in the Settings pull-down menu. After the box opens, click on the Mode options menu and select the mode you want to be your active one (see Figure 2–51).

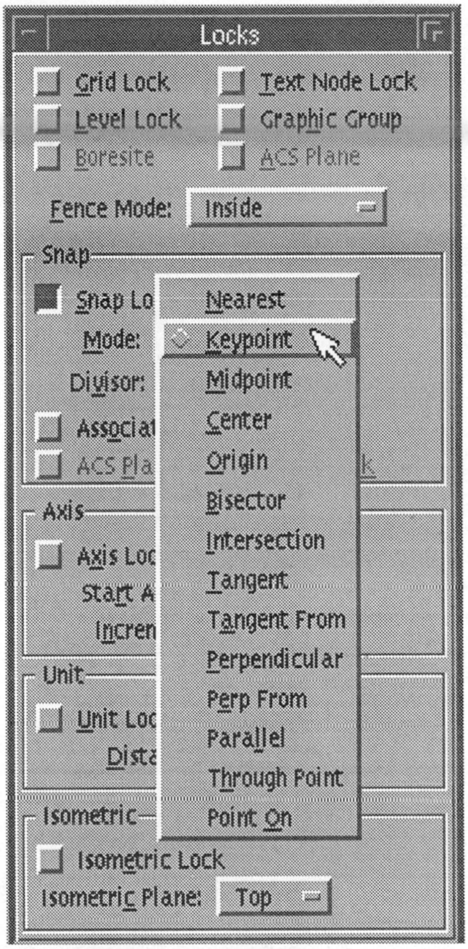

FIGURE 2–51   Locks Full Settings box displaying the option menu for the Snap.

2. Pull down the Snaps menu from the Command Window (see Figure 2–52), then:
    - Select the active (default) snap mode by holding down the [SHIFT] key while you select one of the snap modes.
    - Select a temporary override snap mode by clicking on the snap mode from the menu.

> **NOTE:** The number of snap modes included in the Snaps pull-down menu varies. It shows only the snap modes that are available for the active placement or manipulation command. Some commands do not allow all snap modes. The Snaps pull-down menu is the only one that lets you know which modes are available. The other two methods always show all possible snap modes.

3. Select a temporary override snap mode by opening the Snap Mode palette (see Figure 2–53) from the Snaps pull-down menu available from the Command Window.

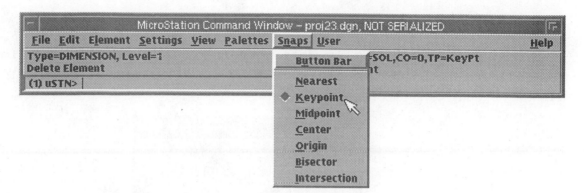

FIGURE 2–52 Snaps pull-down menu.

FIGURE 2–53 Snaps palette.

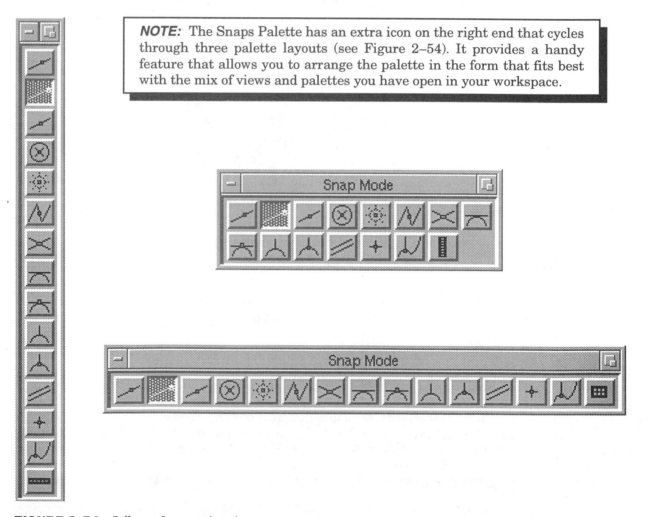

NOTE: The Snaps Palette has an extra icon on the right end that cycles through three palette layouts (see Figure 2–54). It provides a handy feature that allows you to arrange the palette in the form that fits best with the mix of views and palettes you have open in your workspace.

FIGURE 2–54 Different Snaps palette layout.

Following are the snap modes available in MicroStation:

Nearest	Snaps to a point on an element nearest to the cross hairs.
Keypoint	Snaps to predefined keypoints on elements.
Midpoint	Snaps to the midpoint of an element or segment of a complex element.
Center	Snaps to the center of an arc, circle or block.
Origin	Snaps to the center of an arc, circle, origin of the text, or cell.
Bisector	Sets the snap mode to bisect an element, snap point varies with different types of elements.
Intersection	Snaps to the intersection of two elements.
Tangent	Forces the element to be tangent to a non-linear element (such as a circle, ellipse, or arc).
Tangent From	Forces the element you are placing to be tangent to an existing non-linear element at the point where you place the tentative point.
Perpendicular	Forces the element to be perpendicular to an existing element. The actual perpendicular point depends on the way the element is placed.
Perpendicular From	Forces the element to be perpendicular to an existing element at the point where you place the tentative point.
Parallel	Forces the line or segment of the line string to be parallel to a linear element.
Through Point	Snaps to element keypoints and defines a point for the element being placed to pass through.
On Point	Snaps to the nearest element (after you have entered the first point of element placement) and constrains the next data point to lie on a closed element or anywhere on a linear element's line.

Snap Mode Status There are two ways to check on which snap mode is in effect at the moment. The message field normally shows the active or override snap mode that will be applied to the next tentative point. In the Snaps pull-down menu, if no override snap mode is selected, a diamond appears to the left of the active snap mode. If an override mode has been selected, a square appears to the left of the active mode and a diamond appears to the left of the current override mode (see Figure 2–55).

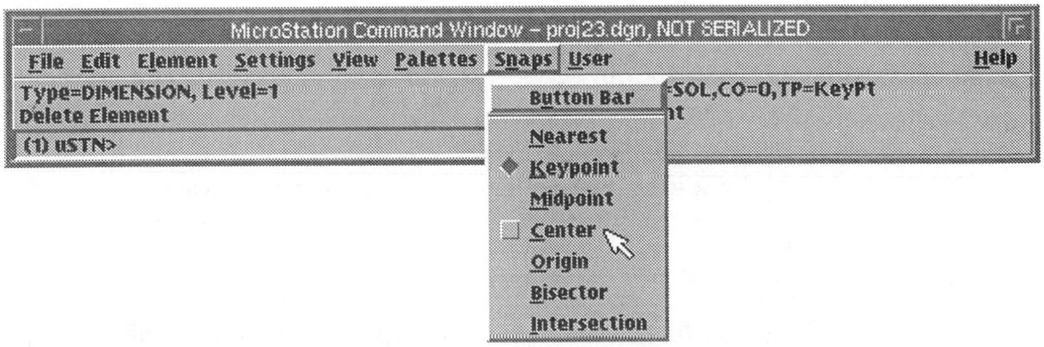

FIGURE 2-55 Displaying the different modes in the Snaps pull-down menu.

How to Use the Tentative Button To use the Tentative button in placing and manipulating elements:

1. Select the placement or manipulation command you want to use.
2. Select the snap mode you want to use (modes are described later).
3. Point to the element you want to snap to and click the Tentative button.
4. Click the Data button to accept the tentative point.
5. Continue using snap modes and tentative points as necessary to complete the placement or manipulation.

If you want to start a line in the exact center of a block, select Place Line, set the snap mode to Center, then click the Tentative button on the block. The block is highlighted and a large tentative cross appears at the exact center of the block. Place a data point to start the line at the block center (see Figure 2–56).

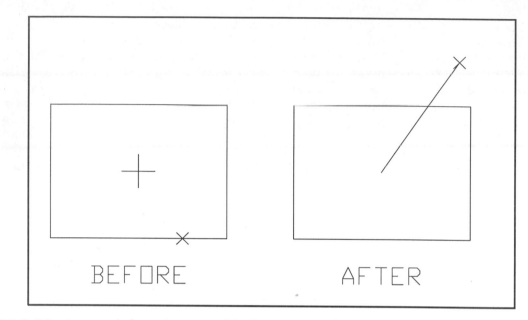

FIGURE 2–56   An example for a placement of the Tentative point.

Keep in mind the following points when you use the tentative button:

- You can only snap to elements when Snap lock is ON. Snap lock is turned on in the Full Locks or Toggle Locks settings boxes. Both setting boxes are available from the Locks option in the Settings pull-down menu.

- If grid lock is ON, and the element you are trying to snap to is placed between grid points, the Tentative button may always snap to grid points rather than the element you want. If that happens, turn OFF Grid Lock in either the Full Locks or Toggle Locks settings boxes.

- When the tentative button snaps to an element, the element is highlighted and the tentative cross appears at the snap to point. If the cross appears on the snap point, but the element is not highlighted, you did not snap to the element; you may have snapped to a grid point close to the point you wanted.

- When you press the Tentative button, MicroStation starts searching for elements in the area immediately around the screen pointer. It selects elements in the order they were placed in the design. If the element it finds is not the one you want, just click the tentative button again and the next element is found; there is no need to move the screen pointer location or press Reset. If the tentative button cycles through all elements in the area without finding the one you want, move the screen pointer closer to the element and press the tentative button again. For example: You placed a block, then placed a line starting very near one corner of the block. You need to snap to the end of the line for the next command, but the tentative point snaps to the corner of the block. Just click the tentative button again and it should snap to the end of the line. If the second snap also does not find the end of the line, move the screen pointer a little closer to it and snap again.

- You do not have to place the screen pointer exactly on the point of the element you want to snap to, just near it. In fact, to lessen the chance of snapping to the wrong element, it is best to move back along the element away from other elements.

Tentative Snapping (Nearest, Keypoint, Midpoint)

In this section, snap modes Keypoint, Nearest, and Midpoint are explained. The remaining modes are explained in later chapters.

Keypoint Mode Keypoint mode allows tentative points to snap to predefined keypoints on elements. For a line, it is the end points of the line; for a circle, it is the center and four quadrants; for a block it is the four corners and so on. See Figure 2–57 for snap points for various element types. To snap to a key point on an element, position the cursor close to the key point (make sure the snap lock is turned ON and keypoint mode is selected), and click the Tentative button. The tentative cross appears on the element's key point and the element highlights. If the tentative cross appears but the element does not highlight, you have not found the element's snap point. Press the Tentative button until the snap point is located, then press the Accept button.

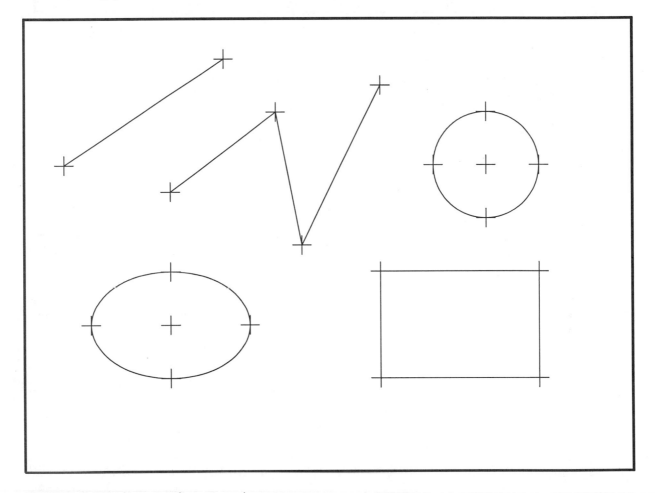

FIGURE 2–57 Keypoints for various element types.

Keypoint Snap Divisor The Keypoint snap divisor works with the keypoint snap mode and allows you to select additional snap points on an element by defining a value that divides the element into a specific number of divisions or parts. For example, setting the keypoint snap divisor to five divides an element into five equal divisions. Figure 2–58 shows the keypoint snaps for different keypoint snap divisor values. The keypoint snap divisor can be set in the Locks settings box (Full) by keying the value in the Divisor edit field. You can also set the value by key-in at the uSTN> field, **KY**=<number of divisors> and press ⏎ENTER.

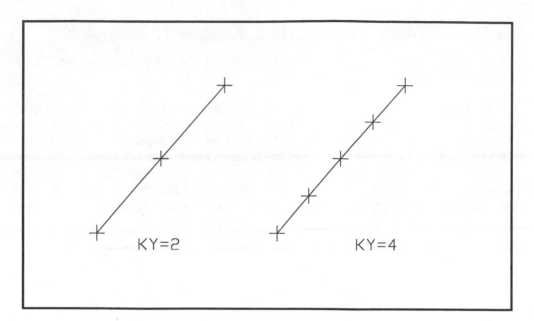

FIGURE 2–58 Examples for various keypoint snap divisor.

Nearest Mode The Nearest mode when active will place tentative points on any point of an element that is closest to the cursor. This rule remains the same among all element types, except as applied to text where the project point is the justification point. With the nearest mode you are always certain that you may locate any point on any type of element. To pick a specific point on an element, position the cursor close to the point you want to select, ensure that the snap lock is set to ON and the nearest mode is selected from the Mode option menu. Press the Tentative button, and the tentative cross will appear at the closest point on the element as the element highlights. If the tentative cross appears but the element does not highlight, then you have not found the element. Press the Tentative button until a point is located and press the Accept button.

Midpoint Mode The Midpoint mode when active will place tentative points at the midpoint of an element or segment of a complex element (see Figure 2–59). The point position varies with different types of elements.

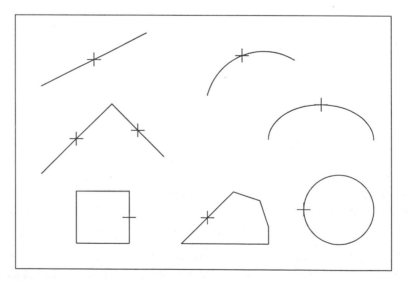

FIGURE 2–59 Midpoint for various element types.

It bisects a line, arc, or partial ellipse.
It bisects the selected segment of a line string, block, multi-sided shape, or regular polygon.
It snaps to the 180 degree (9 o'clock) position of a circle and an ellipse.

Axis Lock

Axis Lock (AX) forces each data point to lie at an angle (or multiples of that angle) from the previous data point. You can key-in the axis start angle and axis increment angle in the edit boxes provided in the Lock settings box as shown in Figure 2–60. The Axis Start Angle is relative to the X-Axis, and successive points are limited to the Axis Increment angle. For example; whenever you want to draw lines horizontal or vertical, key-in an axis start angle of 0 degrees and an axis increment angle of 90 degrees, and turn ON axis lock. Axis Start Angle and Axis Increment are only in effect when the Axis Lock is turned ON.

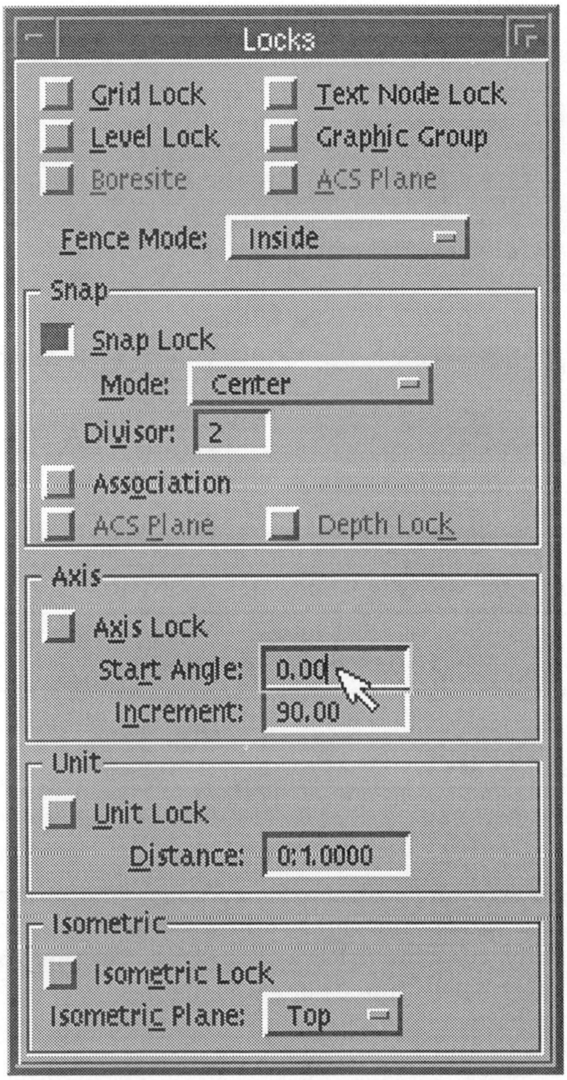

FIGURE 2–60   Locks Full Settings box with the cursor positioned in the Axis Start Angle edit field.

The remaining locks are explained in later chapters.

DIMENSIONING

MicroStation's dimensioning features provide an excellent way to add dimensional information such as lengths, widths, angles, tolerances, and clearances to your drawing.

Dimensioning of any drawing is generally one of the last steps in manual drawing; however, it does not need to be the last step in your MicroStation drawing. If you place the dimensions and find out later they must be changed because the size of the objects they are related to have changed, MicroStation allows you to stretch or extend the objects and have the dimensions automatically change to the new size. MicroStation provides three basic types of dimensions: Linear, Angular, and Radial Dimensioning. Figure 2–61 shows examples of these three basic types of dimensions.

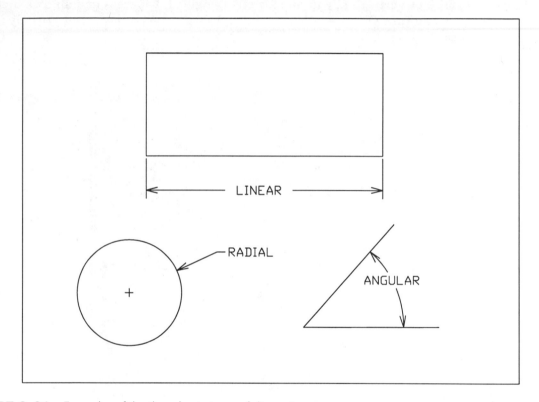

FIGURE 2–61 Examples of the three basic types of dimensions.

Dimensioning Terminology

The following terms are commonly used in the MicroStation dimensioning procedures.

Dimension Line This is a line with markers at each end (arrows, dots, ticks, etc.). The dimensioning text is located along this line; you may place it above the line or in a break in the dimension line. Usually, the dimension line is inside the measured area. If there is insufficient space, MicroStation places the dimensions and draws two short lines outside the measured area with arrows pointing inward.

Extension Lines The extension lines (also called witness lines) are the lines that extend from the object to the dimension line. Extension lines normally are drawn perpendicular to the dimension line. Several options that are associated with this element will be reviewed later in this chapter. Also, you can suppress one or both of the extension lines.

Arrows The arrows are placed at one or both ends depending on the type of dimension line placed. MicroStation allows you to place arrows, tick marks, or arbitrary symbols of your own choosing. You can also adjust the size of any of these three symbols.

Dimension Text This is a text string that usually indicates the actual measurement. You can accept the default measurement computed automatically by MicroStation, or change it by supplying your own text.

Figure 2–62 shows the different components of a typical dimension.

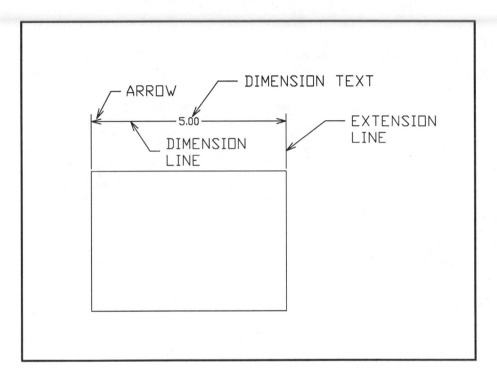

FIGURE 2–62   Different components of a typical dimension.

Leader The leader line is a line from text to an object on the drawing, as shown in Figure 2–63. For some dimensioning, the text may not fit next to the object it describes, hence, it is customary to place the text nearby and draw a leader from it to the object.

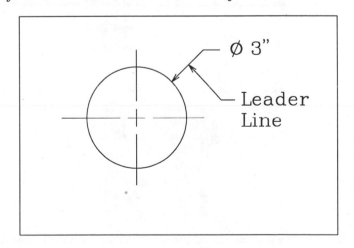

FIGURE 2–63   Example for placing a leader line.

Associative Dimension

Dimensions can be placed either as Associative dimension or normal (non-associative) dimension. Associative dimensioning links dimension elements to the objects dimensioned. An association point does not have its own coordinates, but is positioned by the coordinates of the point it is associated with. When you use manipulation commands (such as Stretch) to modify the object, MicroStation modifies the dimension text automatically to reflect the change. It also draws the dimension entity to its new location, size, and rotation. If you want to edit individual components of a dimension, you can drop the dimension using the Drop dimension command (see Chapter 3) to separate an associative dimension into its individual simpler objects.

To place associative dimension, the Associative lock must be set to ON. This can be set to ON from the Lock Settings Box or from the Linear Dimensions palette as shown in Figure 2–64. If you place a dimension when the Associative lock is OFF, then the dimension will not associate with the object dimensioned, and if the object is modified, the dimension is not changed.

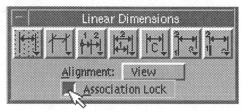

FIGURE 2–64 Displaying a toggle for Association Lock in the Linear Dimensions sub-palette.

Placing associative dimension can significantly reduce the size of a design file that has many dimensions, since a dimension element is usually smaller than the corresponding individual elements.

Dimension Settings

An architectural design is not dimensioned in the same way a mechanical design is dimensioned. MicroStation allows you to adjust the dimension settings to suit your particular needs. You then are able to save these settings in a style library so this does not have to be repeated over and over again.

Invoke the Placement dimension settings box from Dimension menu located in the Element pull-down menu as shown in Figure 2–65. The Placement dimension settings box is displayed similar to

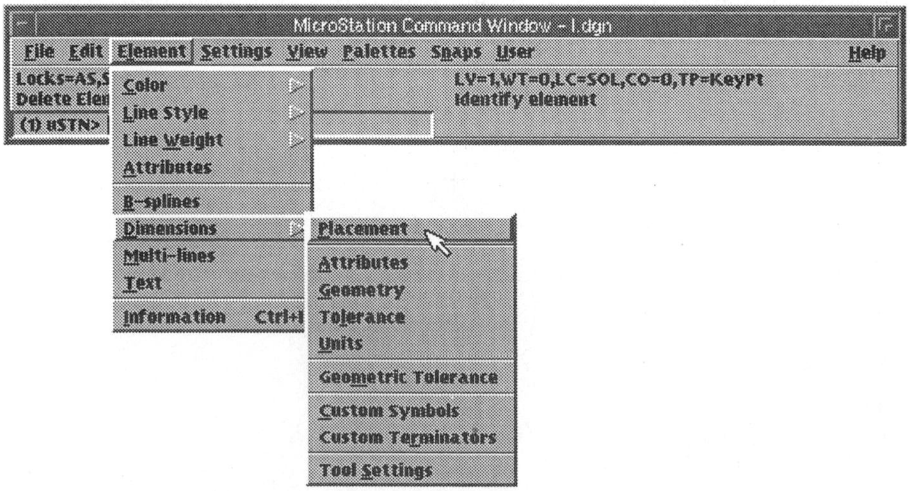

FIGURE 2–65 Invoking the Dimension Placement Settings box from the Dimensions menu located in the Element pull-down menu.

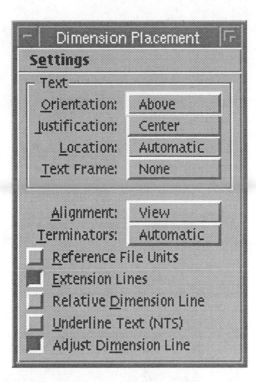

FIGURE 2–66   Dimension Placement Settings box.

the one shown in Figure 2–66. MicroStation lists names of the settings boxes available in the Settings pull-down menu of the Dimension Placement setting box as shown in Figure 2–67. In this chapter, Dimension Placement and Units settings box are introduced to get you started with Linear dimensioning. The remaining setting boxes are explained in later chapters.

FIGURE 2–67   Lists of the Settings box available in the Settings pull-down menu Dimension Placement Settings box.

Dimension Placement The Dimension Placement setting box can be divided into two sections as shown in Figure 2–68. The first part deals with the dimension text placement and the second deals with dimension element placement.

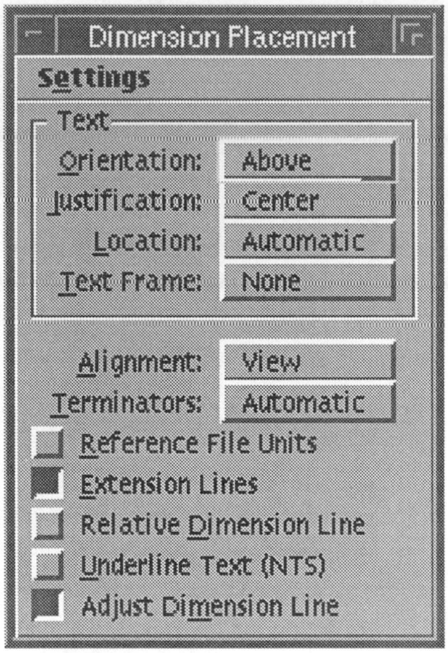

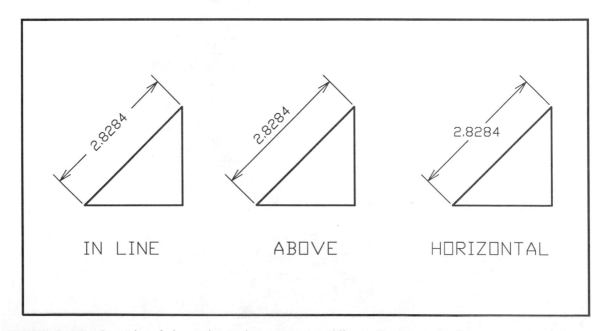

FIGURE 2–68   Dimension Placement Settings box.

The Orientation field sets the orientation of dimension text relative to the dimension line. In Line, Above and Horizontal are the options available from the option menu. The In Line option places text on the line, the Above option places the text above the dimension line, and the Horizontal option places the text horizontal to the dimension line (see Figure 2–69).

FIGURE 2–69   Examples of placing linear dimensioning in different Orientation modes.

The Justification field sets the justification of dimension text. Left, Center and Right are the options available from the options menu. Figure 2–70 shows examples of three different justification setting.

> **NOTE:** The justification field setting applies only when the Automatic text placement mode is selected.

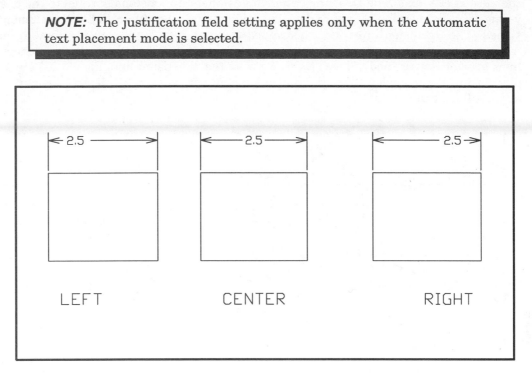

FIGURE 2–70   Examples of placing linear dimensioning in different Justification modes.

The Location field controls the location of dimension text. Automatic, Semi-Automatic, and Manual are the options available from the options menu. Automatic places the dimension according to the justification setting. Semi-automatic places the dimension according to the justification setting if the text fits between the extension lines. If the text does not fit, you can position the text anywhere in the design. Manual option allows you to place the text anywhere in the design without regard to the justification setting.

The Text frame controls the framing of dimension text. None, Box, and Capsule are the options available from the options menu. Figure 2–71 shows the examples of placing dimension with text frame (Box and Capsule). Box frame is used to designate a reference dimension, and capsule is typically used to designate a dimension for quality control.

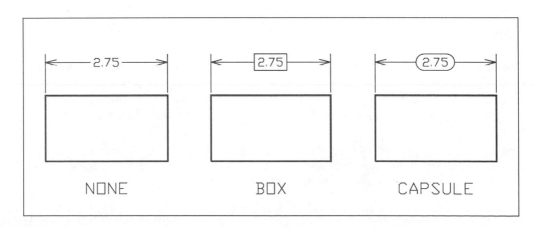

FIGURE 2–71   Examples of placing linear dimensioning in different Text frame modes.

The Alignment controls the orientation of Linear dimensions. View, Drawing, True, and Arbitrary are the options available from the options menu. The View option aligns linear dimensions parallel to the view x- or y-axis. The Drawing option aligns linear dimensions parallel to the design plane x- or y-axis. The True option aligns linear dimensions to be placed parallel to the element being dimensioned. The extension lines are constrained to be at right angles to the dimension line, and the Arbitrary option places linear dimensions parallel to the element being dimensioned. The extension lines are not constrained to be at right angles to the dimension line. Figure 2–72 shows examples of placing linear dimension with different alignment controls. In 2D design view and drawing alignment will look the same.

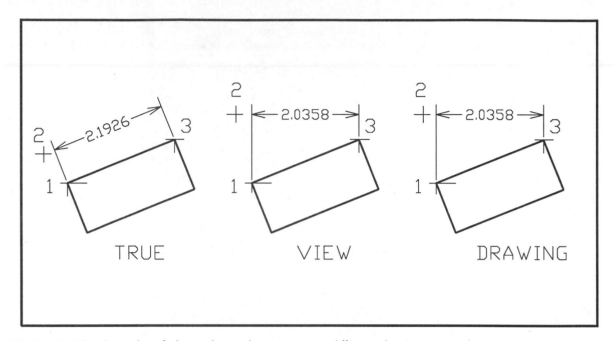

FIGURE 2–72 Examples of placing linear dimensioning in different alignment controls.

The Terminators field controls the placement of the terminators such as arrows, tick marks, etc. Automatic, Inside, Outside, and Reversed are the options available from the options menu. Figure 2–73 shows examples of placing linear dimension with different terminator options.

The Reference file units toggle allows MicroStation to dimension reference file elements using the working units defined in the reference. If it is set to ON, the dimensions are computed in the units of the reference file to dimension the reference file elements. If it is set to OFF, MicroStation uses the working units of the current design. (See Chapter 9 for Reference Files.)

The extension line toggle enables and disables the placement of extension lines. If it is set to ON, extension lines (also called witness lines) are placed, and if it is set to OFF, extension lines are not placed. You can also use the Tool settings box (selected from the Settings from the Dimension Placement setting box) to disable the placement of individual extension lines.

The Relative dimension lock toggle is used when modifying dimension elements. If it is set to ON, the length of extension lines remains the same. If it is set to OFF, the location of the dimension line is constant, and the extension line is allowed to vary in length.

The Underline text toggle is used to underline the dimension text. If it is set to ON, the dimension text is underlined.

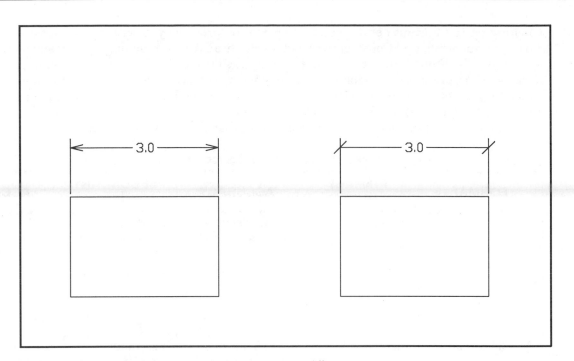

FIGURE 2-73   Examples of placing linear dimensioning in different Terminators.

Units The Units setting box (see Figure 2–74) is invoked from the Settings pull-down of the Dimension Placement settings box. In addition to selecting the dimension text length format, which is very important, you can also select the primary and secondary units, angle format, and the scale factor from Units setting box.

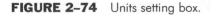

FIGURE 2-74   Units setting box.

Clicking on the Format option menu, MicroStation provides you with two options: AEC (Architectural, Engineering, and Construction) and Mechanical. AEC option place dimensions in units of feet and inches for English dimensions and millimeters for metric dimensions. Mechanical option place dimensions in units of inches for English dimensions and millimeters for metric dimensions. To place Secondary units, turn on the toggle button for Show Secondary Units and select appropriate Units, Accuracy, and Key-in label in the label edit field. See Table 2–6 for the available Primary and Secondary unit options including accuracy for AEC and Mechanical formats.

Table 2-6. Primary and Secondary Unit Options

FORMAT	PRIMARY UNITS	ACCURACY	SECONDARY UNITS	ACCURACY
AEC	Feet	1 to 8 decimal places and ½ to 1/64	Millimeters, Centimeters, and Meters	1 to 8 decimal places
	Meters	1 to 8 decimal places	Inches, Feet	1 to 8 decimal places and ½ to 1/64
MECHANICAL	Inches	1 to 8 decimal places and ½ to 1/64	Millimeters, Centimeters, and Meters	1 to 8 decimal places
	Millimeters	1 to 8 decimal places	Feet, Inches	1 to 8 decimal places and ½ to 1/64

Figure 2–75 shows examples of placing linear dimension with AEC and Mechanical format options.

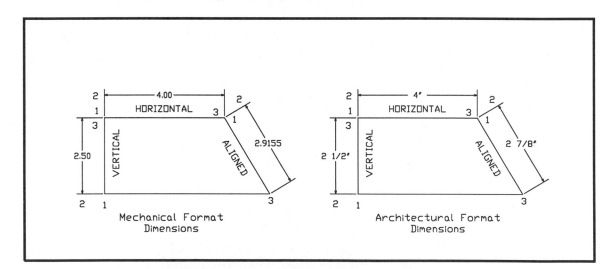

FIGURE 2–75 Examples of placing linear dimensioning with AEC and Mechanical formats.

> **NOTE:** For AEC dimensioning purposes, sub-units must represent inches or millimeters and sub-units per master unit setting is ignored. For Mechanical dimensioning purposes, master units must represent inches or millimeters.

The Angle Format contains controls that are used to specify the format for angular dimension text expressed as degrees. The unit under Angle Format has two options, Degrees and Length. The degrees options allows you to dimension arcs in degrees with an option to display in decimal form or degrees, minutes, and seconds (DD^MM'SS") anywhere from one to four decimal places. The length option allows you to dimension arc in working units.

If the Show Leading Zero toggle is set to ON, MicroStation places the dimension text with a zero followed by the dimension text if the dimension is less than 1.0.

If the Show Trailing Zeros toggle is set to ON, MicroStation places the dimension text filled with zeros, if necessary, to the number of decimal places specified by the English or Metric setting.

If the Use Comma for Decimal toggle is turned ON, MicroStation places a comma instead of decimal points in dimension text to conform to European standards.

The Scale Factor edit field sets the scale factor to dimension length. For example, if is set to 2.0000, then all the linear dimension will be shown twice the size of the actual length.

Linear Dimensions

Linear dimensioning is the basic type of dimensioning used by MicroStation. It measures the straight-line distance from one point to another. The linear dimensioning commands are provided in the Linear Dimensions palette (see Figure 2–76) invoked from Dimension menu located in the Palettes pull-down menu.

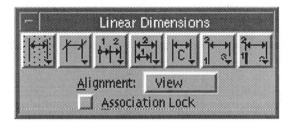

FIGURE 2–76 Linear Dimensions sub-palette.

MicroStation provides three types of linear dimensioning, Dimension size (Arrows, Strokes, or Custom), Dimension Location, and Dimension Location (stacked). The Dimension size with strokes or custom commands work the same as the Dimension size with arrows command. They are provided to maintain the compatibility with earlier versions of MicroStation. Having three commands lets you place linear size dimensions with different terminator types without having to set the terminators in the Dimension Tool settings box. You can also select the Alignment options and toggle the association lock from the Linear Dimensions sub-palette.

Dimension Size with Arrows To start placing Linear dimensioning with Arrows, click the Dimension size arrow icon from the Linear Dimensions sub-palette (see Figure 2–77), or

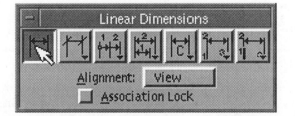

FIGURE 2–77 Invoking the Linear dimensioning with Arrows command from the Linear Dimensions sub-palette.

key-in at the uSTN> field, **dimension size arrow** (or **dim si a**) and press ENTER. Micro-Station prompts:

Select start of dimension (Place a data point to define the origin, see Figure 2–78.)

Define length of Extension line (Place a data point to define length of extension line, see Figure 2–78.)

Select dimension end point (Place a data point to define the end point of the dimension, see Figure 2–78.)

Press (Return) to edit the dimension end point (Optional—press ENTER if necessary to edit dimension text. Dimension text editor opens to let you make changes to the dimension text.)

Select Dimension end point (Continue placing data point to continue linear dimensioning in the same direction and/or press Reset button to change the direction or press Reset button twice to start all over again.)

> **NOTE:** Make sure to use tentative keypoint when placing data points for the start and end point of dimension.

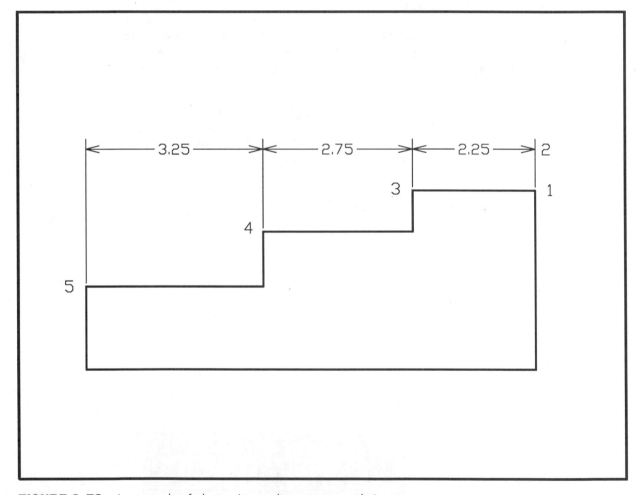

FIGURE 2–78 An example of placing Linear dimensioning with Arrows.

After you press the Reset button, you can continue the linear dimension from the last data point in a different direction (turn the corner). Press Reset button one more time to start linear dimension all over again from a different location.

Dimension Size With Strokes To start placing Linear dimensioning with Strokes, click the Dimension size strokes icon from the Linear Dimensions sub-palette (see Figure 2–79), or key-in at the uSTN> field, **dimension size strokes** (or **dim si s**) and press ⏎. The Dimension size with strokes command works identically to the Dimension size with arrows command, except instead of placing arrows at the end of the dimension line, MicroStation places strokes as shown in Figure 2–80.

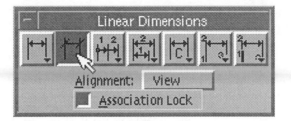

FIGURE 2–79   Invoking the Linear dimensioning with Strokes command from the Linear Dimensions sub-palette.

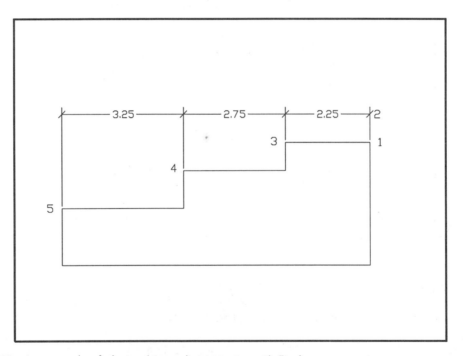

FIGURE 2–80   An example of placing Linear dimensioning with Strokes.

Dimension Size (Custom) To start placing Linear dimensioning (custom), click the Dimension size (custom) icon from the Linear Dimensions sub-palette (see Figure 2–81). The Dimension size command works identically to the Dimension size with arrows command. This command is provided to keep the compatibility with previous versions of MicroStation.

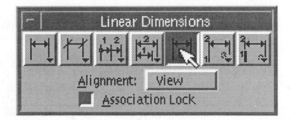

FIGURE 2–81   Invoking the Linear dimensioning (Custom) command from the Linear Dimensions sub-palette.

Dimension Location The Dimension Location command is used to dimension linear distance from an origin (datum) as shown in Figure 2–82. The dimensions are placed in line (chain). All dimensions are measured on an element originating from a common surface, center line, or centerplane. The Dimension Location command is commonly used in mechanical drafting.

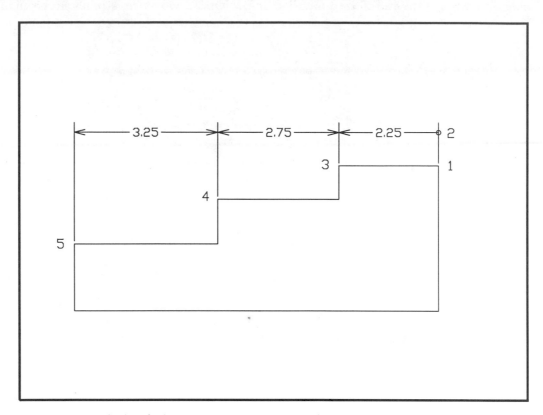

FIGURE 2–82 An example of placing Linear dimensioning from an Origin (datum) by Dimension Location command.

To start placing linear dimensioning by Dimension Location, click the Dimension Location icon from the Linear Dimensions sub-palette (see Figure 2–83), or key-in at the uSTN> field, **dimension location single** (or **dim lo**) and press [ENTER]. MicroStation prompts:

Select start of dimension (Place a data point to define the origin.)
Define length of Extension line (Place a data point to define length of extension line.)
Select dimension end point (Place a data point to define the endpoint of the dimension.)
Press (Return) to edit the dimension end point (Optional—press [ENTER] if necessary to edit dimension text. Dimension text editor opens to let you make changes to the dimension text.)
Select Dimension end point (Continue placing data point to continue linear dimensioning and/or press Reset button.)

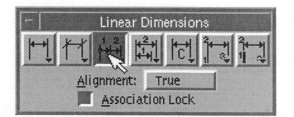

FIGURE 2–83 Invoking the Dimension Location command from the Linear Dimensions sub-palette.

After you press the Reset button, you can continue linear dimension from the last data point in a different direction (turn the corner). If not, press Reset button one more time, and then start linear dimension all over again from a different location.

Dimension Location (Stacked) The Dimension Location (stacked) command is used to dimension linear distance from an origin (datum) as shown in Figure 2–84. The dimensions are stacked. All dimensions are measured on an element originating from a common surface, center line, or center-plane. The Dimension Location command is commonly used in mechanical drafting because all dimensions are independent, even though they are taken from a common datum. MicroStation automatically spaces and places the extension lines, dimension lines, arrowheads, and dimension text. The stack offset distance is set in the Dimension Geometry settings box.

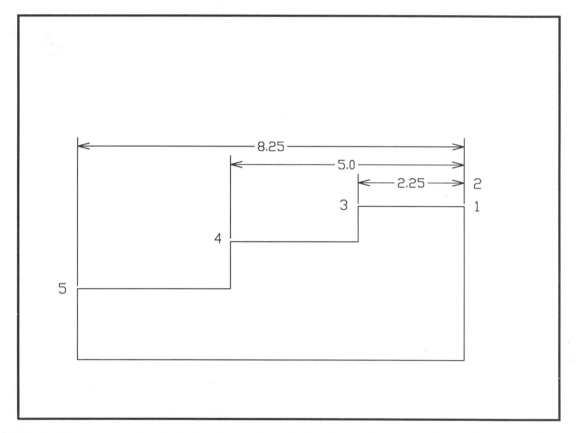

FIGURE 2–84 An example of placing Linear dimensioning (stacked) from an Origin (datum) by Dimension Location (stacked) command.

To start placing linear dimensioning by Dimension Location (Stacked), click the Dimension Location (Stacked) icon from the Linear Dimensions sub-palette (see Figure 2–85), or key-in at the uSTN> field, **dimension location stacked** (or **dim lo st**) and press ⌨. MicroStation prompts:

> *Select start of dimension* (Place a data point to define the origin.)
> *Define length of Extension line* (Place a data point to define length of extension line.)
> *Select dimension end point* (Place a data point to define the endpoint of the dimension.)
> *Press (Return) to edit the dimension end point* (Optional—press ⌨ if necessary to edit dimension text. Dimension text editor opens to let you make changes to the dimension text.)
> *Select Dimension end point* (Continue placing data point to continue linear dimensioning and press Reset button.)

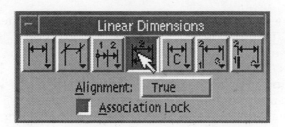

FIGURE 2–85 Invoking the Dimension Location (stacked) command from the Linear Dimensions sub-palette.

After you press the Reset button, you can continue linear dimension from the last data point in a different direction (turn the corner). If not, press Reset button one more time, and then start linear dimension (stacked) all over again from a different location.

EXERCISES

Exercises 2–14 through 2–18

Use Precision Key-ins (XY= , DL= , and/or DI=) and appropriate grid spacing to draw the figures. Add dimensions.

Exercise 2–14

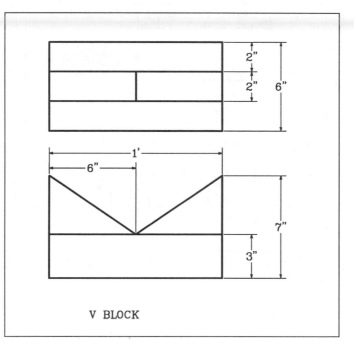

V BLOCK

Exercise 2–15

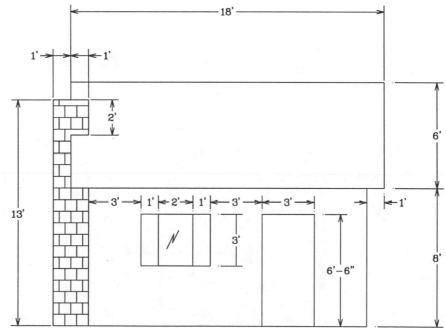

Exercise 2–16

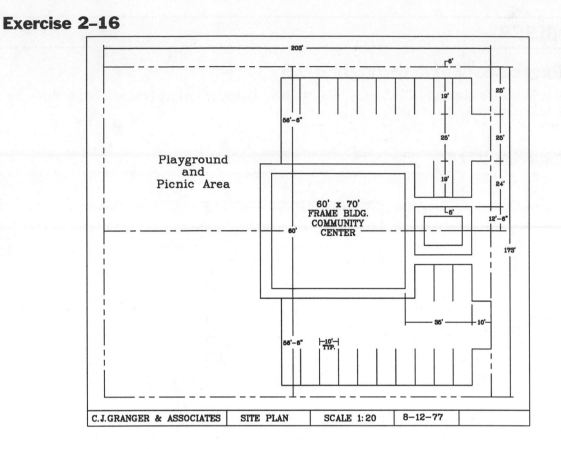

| C.J.GRANGER & ASSOCIATES | SITE PLAN | SCALE 1:20 | 8–12–77 | |

Exercise 2–17

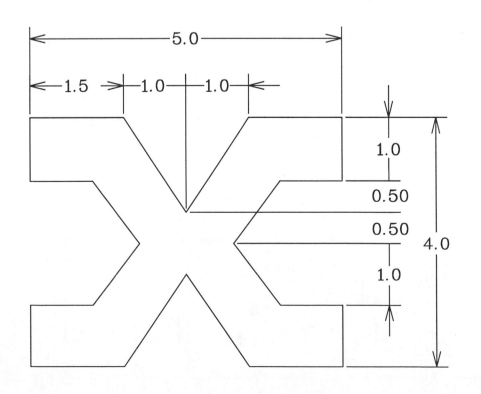

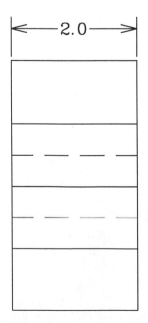

Exercise 2–18

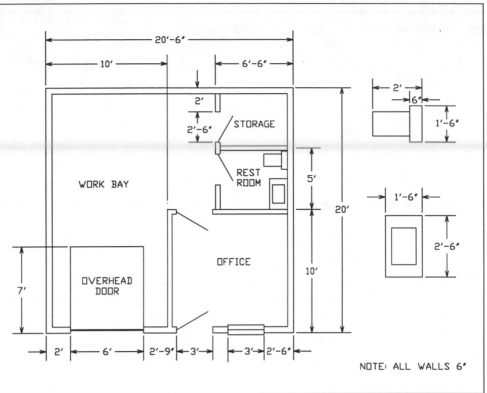

Exercises 2–19 through 2–25

Add dimensions to the drawing exercises completed earlier in the chapter (see Exercises 2–5 through 2–11).

REVIEW QUESTIONS

Write your answers in the spaces provided:

1. How many possible positions (positional units) are there in the X & Y directions of a 2D design file?

   _____

2. Define Master Units:

   _____

   _____

3. Define Sub Units:

   _____

   _____

4. Define Positional Units:

   _____

   _____

5. What is the difference between using a Place Line command and Place Line String command?

   _____

   _____

6. Name the command that will make individual elements from a Line String.

   _____

7. Explain briefly the differences between the Absolute Rectangular coordinates and Relative Rectangular coordinates precision key-ins.

   _____

   _____

8. Name the three key-ins that are used in precision input for Absolute Rectangular coordinates, Relative Rectangular coordinates, and Polar Relative coordinates.

   _____

   _____

9. Explain briefly the difference between the ZOOM IN and ZOOM OUT commands.

   _____

   _____

10. Which command will get you closer to a portion of your design by a factor of two?

   _____

11. Name the command that will Rebuild, Refresh, or Update your views.

   _____

12. When MicroStation displays the information regarding the size of an element or coordinates, it does so in the following format:

    _____:_____:_____

13. Panning lets you view _____

    _____ .

14. To pan in a view, hold the [CTRL] key and press the _____ button.

15. Text settings box is invoked from the _____ pull-down menu.

16. Name three text parameters that can be changed from the Text settings box.

    _____

17. You can change the current font by keying in _____ .

18. List the two key-ins that are used to change the Text height and Text width.

    _____

19. To place a text string with a line below the text, turn on the toggle button for _____

    in the _____ settings box.

20. The slant angle to place text can be anywhere from _____ degrees to _____ degrees.

21. Name the text parameter that controls the distance between two lines of text in placing multi-line text.

    _____

22. With the current working units set to MU=1 in., SU=4 qt., and PU=1000 how would you set your text size to 1/8th of an inch?

    _____

23. In a design file, the working units are setup as inches, eights, and 1600 positional units per eighth, what distance does 1:6:600 represent?

    _____

24. In a design file, the working units are setup as feet, inches, and 1600 positional units per inch, what working units expression is equivalent to 4'-0.3200"?

    _____

25. If a design is to be plotted at 1/2 inch equals 1 foot scale, what should be the text size in the design to plot at 1/8 inch? (Note: Working units are set to feet, inches, and 1600 positional units per inch.)

    _____

26. What is the purpose of the Grid lock?

    _____

27. The _____ settings box allows you to control the display of the grid.

28. The Master/Grid unit defines the distance between the _____

    and specified in terms of _____:_____:_____ .

29. The Grid Reference is set to define the _____ .

30. The key-in GR= sets the _____ .

31. The key-in GU= sets the _____ .

32. If the button is depressed and has a dark center for the Grid Lock toggle in the Locks settings box, then the Grid Lock is _____ .

33. To keep the grid settings in effect for future editing sessions for the current design file, invoke the _____ command.

34. The Aspect Ratio edit field in the Grid settings box allows you to set the _____ _____ .

35. Name the three menu options that are available to select the snap mode.

_____

36. Name four snap modes available in MicroStation.

_____

37. Keypoint mode allows tentative points to snap to _____ .

38. The keypoint snap divisor settings allows you to _____ .

39. The Midpoint mode snaps to the _____ position of a circle and an ellipse.

40. The Axis Lock forces each data point _____ .

41. The Dimension Line is a _____ .

42. The Extension lines are the _____ .

43. The Leader line is a _____ .

44. Associative Dimensioning links _____ .

45. To place associative dimension, the Association Lock must be _____ .

46. The three options available for orientation of dimension text relative to the dimension line are _____ .

47. The justification field setting for dimension text applies only when the _____ mode is selected.

48. MicroStation provides two options for dimension text length format, and they include _____ .

49. The three types of linear dimensioning available in MicroStation are _____ _____ .

50. The linear dimensioning commands are provided in the _____ palette.

PROJECT EXERCISE

The concepts introduced in chapters 1 and 2 provide you with a foundation of CAD knowledge and skills necessary to start creating simple designs. You can now apply these concepts to produce a complete drawing in step-by-step fashion, as shown in Figure P2–1.

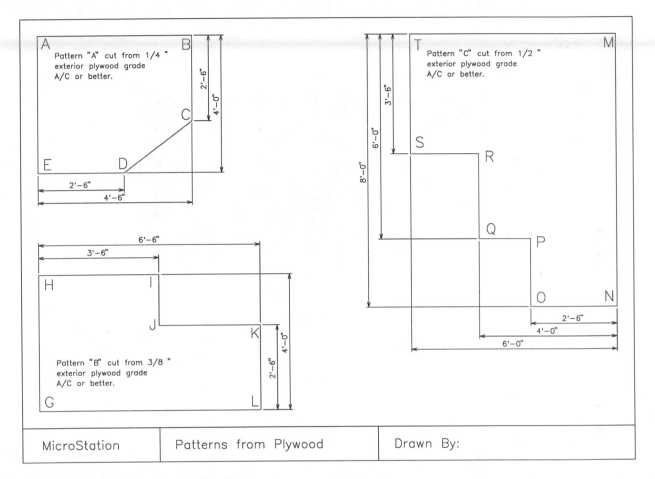

FIGURE P2–1 Completed Project Design.

> **NOTE:** The step-by-step instructions for this project are designed to provide practice in the concepts presented in chapters 1 and 2. It is not necessarily the most efficient way to draw the design.

The concepts that are used in this project include:

- Creating a new design file
- Drawing setup—working units and grid
- Display commands—Zoom In, Zoom Out, Window Area, Fit
- Placement commands—Line, Block, Text
- Linear Dimensioning

GETTING STARTED

STEP 1: Invoke Ustation batch file to start MicroStation program.

*C:\\>***USTATION** ⏎

STEP 2: Create a new design file named CH2.DGN using the SEED2D.DGN seed file from the MicroStation Manager Dialog Box if you just started MicroStation, or from the New option in the File pull-down menu of the MicroStation Command Window.

STEP 3: Open the Working Units dialog box from the Settings pull-down menu and set up your working units for feet and inches, as shown in Figure P2–2.

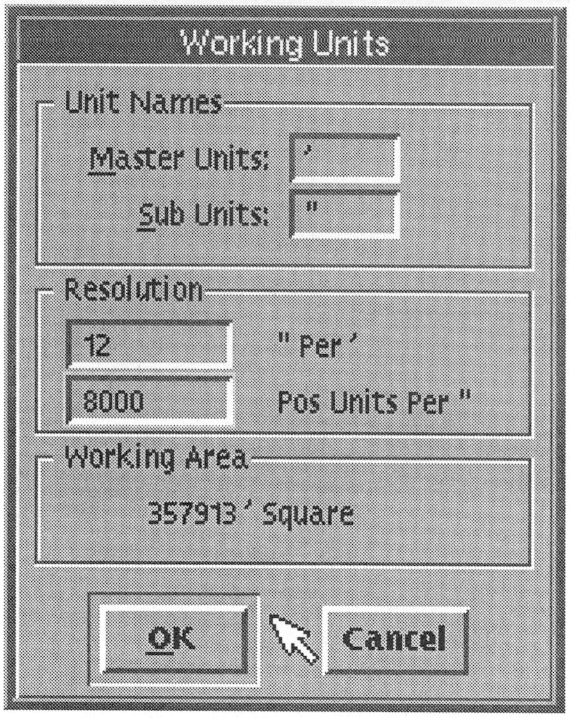

FIGURE P2–2 Working Units Dialog Box.

STEP 4: Open the Grid settings box from the Settings pull-down menu and set the grid unit to :6 units, grid reference to 2, and set the Grid lock to ON as shown in Figure P2–3.

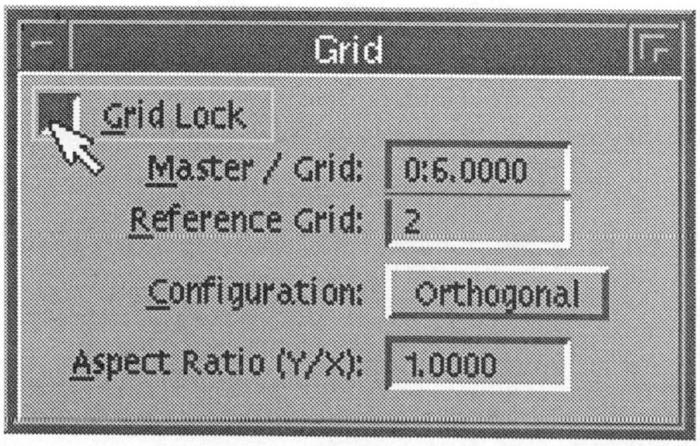

FIGURE P2–3 Grid Settings Box.

STEP 5: Open the Full Locks settings box from the Settings pull-down menu. Set the Snap toggle button to ON and select keypoint from the Snap Mode options menu.

STEP 6: Open the View Attributes settings box from the View pull-down menu. Set the Text Node toggle button to OFF as shown in Figure P2–4 and click Apply button. Close the View Attributes settings box.

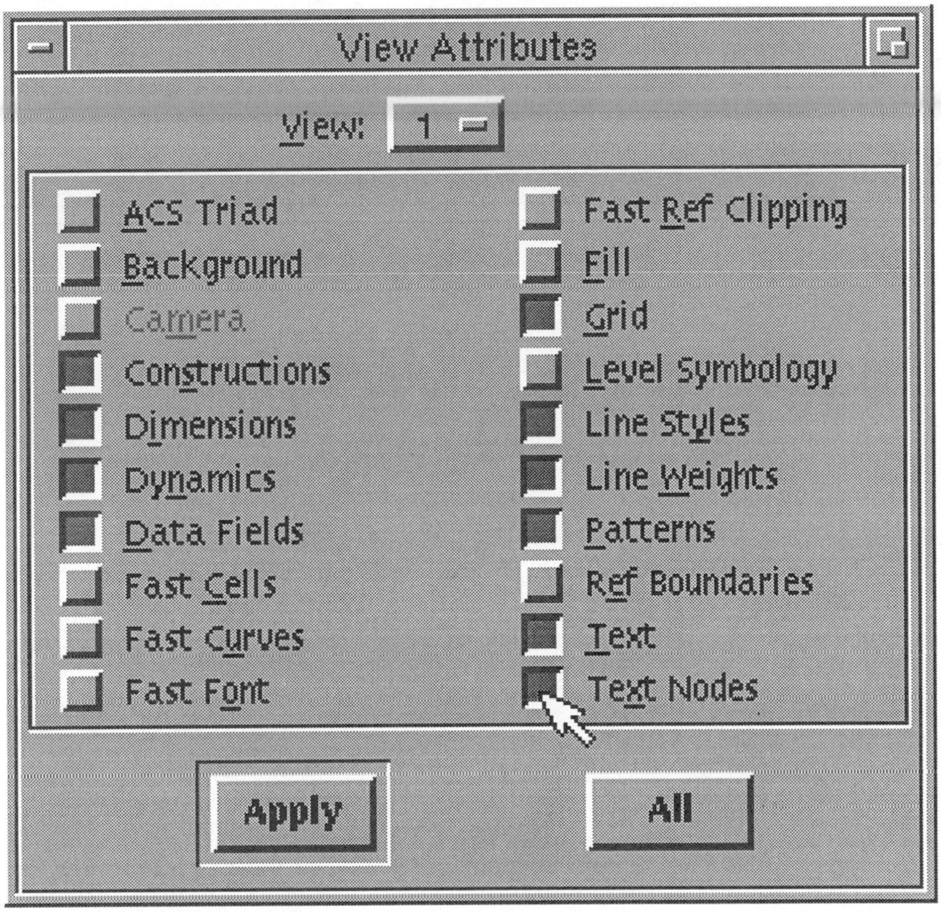

FIGURE P2–4 View Attributes Settings Box.

> **NOTE:** Text Nodes are introduced in Chapter 5. All we need to do now is make sure that the text node display is set to OFF.

STEP 7: Open the Tool Settings Box from the Settings pull-down menu.

> **NOTE:** Having tool settings box open allows you to make command parameter settings without having to "rip-off" the palette from the Main palette that contains the command you are using.

STEP 8: Invoke Save Settings command from the File pull-down menu to save the settings.

STEP 9: Invoke the place block command from the Main palette to draw a border (18′ by 13′). MicroStation prompts:

> *Enter first point* (Key-in **xy=0,0** at uSTN> field and press [ENTER].)
> *Enter opposite point* (Key-in **xy=18,13** at uSTN> field and press [ENTER].)

STEP 10: Invoke the Fit command and place a data point anywhere in the view. You will see the border as shown in Figure P2–5.

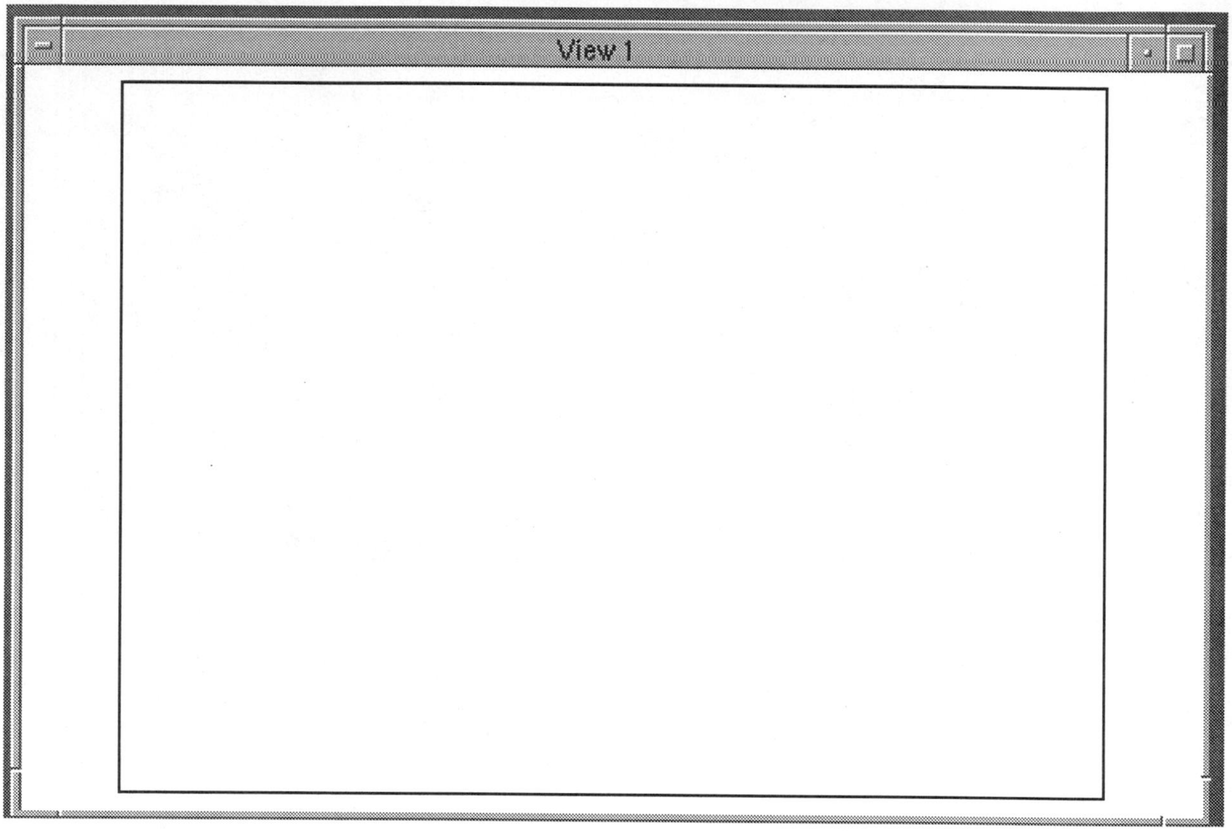

FIGURE P2–5 Border for the Project Design.

Draw Pattern A by Keying the Coordinates

Create pattern A (the upper left one in the design) by keying the coordinates. Figure P2–6 shows the figure with letters added to aid in drawing the shape.

> **NOTE:** Other input methods work just as well, but we are going to practice by keying the coordinates.

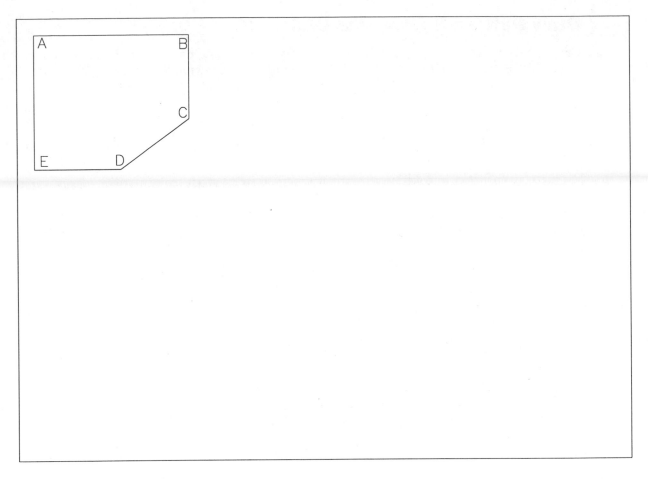

FIGURE P2–6   Pattern A.

STEP 11:   Invoke the Place Line command from the Main palette. Make sure in the Tool Settings Box the length and angle constraints are set to OFF, as shown in Figure P2–7. Micro-Station prompts:

Enter first point (Key-in **XY=0:6,12:6** for point A and press [ENTER].)
Enter end point (Key-in **DL=4:6,0** for point B and press [ENTER].)
Enter end point (Key-in **DL=0,-2:6** for point C and press [ENTER].)
Enter end point (Key-in **DL=-2,-1:6** for point D and press [ENTER].)
Enter end point (Key-in **DL=-2:6,0** for point E and press [ENTER].)
Enter end point (Key-in **DL=0,4** for point A and press [ENTER].)
Enter end point (Press the Reset button.)

FIGURE P2–7   Tool Settings Box displaying the status of the Place Line command constraints.

Draw Pattern B Using the Grid

Create pattern B (the lower left one in the design) by placing data points by snapping to the grid. Figure P2–8 shows the figure with letters added to aid in drawing the shape.

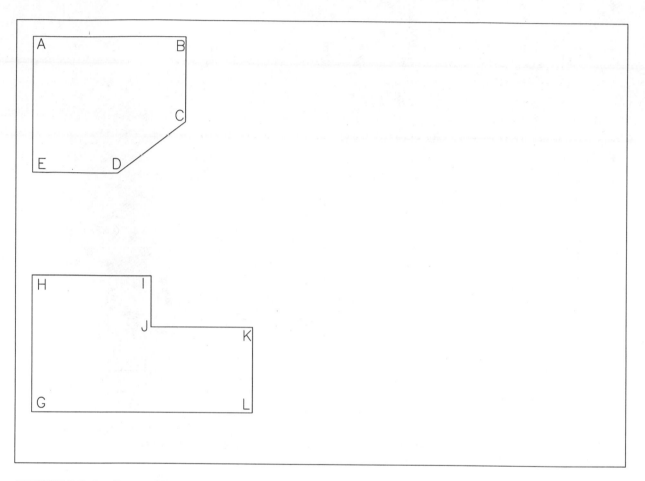

FIGURE P2–8 Pattern B.

STEP 12: If you cannot see the grid units (dots), zoom in until you can see an area just large enough display to draw the pattern B.

STEP 13: Invoke the Place Line command from the Main palette. Make sure the length and angle constraints are set to OFF in the Tool Settings Box. MicroStation prompts:

> *First data point* (Key-in **XY=.5,1.5** for point G, and press ⏎.)
> *Enter end point* (Place a data point for point H, 4 feet vertically up (8 grid dots) from the last data point.)
> *Enter end point* (Place a data point for point I, 3.5 feet horizontally to the right of the last data point (7 grid dots).)
> *Enter end point* (Place a data point for point J, 1.5 feet vertically down (3 grid dots) from the previous data point.)
> *Enter end point* (Place a data point for point K, 3 feet horizontally to the right of the last data point (6 grid dots).)

Enter end point (Place a data point for point L, 2.5 feet vertically down (5 grid dots) from the previous data point.)

Enter end point (Place a data point for point G, 6.5 feet horizontally to the left of the previous data point (13 grid dots).)

Enter end point (Click the Reset button.)

STEP 14: If you zoomed in before drawing pattern B, invoke the fit command and place a data point anywhere in the view to display all of the design.

Draw Pattern C Using Placement Constraints

Create pattern C by placing data points using the placement constraints provided with the Place Line command. Figure P2–9 shows the figure with letters added to aid in drawing the shape.

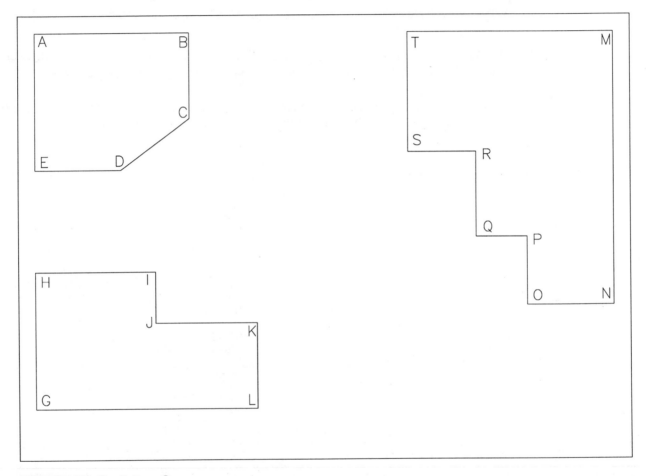

FIGURE P2–9   Pattern C.

STEP 15: If the Tool Settings Box is not already open, open it from the Settings pull-down menu.

STEP 16: If Place Line is already active, click the Reset button to make sure it is ready to start a new line. If it is not active, invoke the place line command.

STEP 17: In the Tool Settings Box, turn ON the toggle buttons for Length and Angle constraints (see Figure P2–10).

FIGURE P2–10 Tool Settings Box displaying the status of the Place Line command constraints.

> **NOTE:** The title bar of the Tool Settings Box displays the name of the currently active placement or manipulation command (in this case Place Line command).

STEP 18: To place the line from point M to N, key-in 8 in the Length edit field and press [TAB] key. Key-in 270 in the Angle edit field and press [TAB] key. MicroStation prompts:

> *Enter first point* (Place a data point by keying the absolute coordinates **xy=17:6,12:6** for point M at the uSTN> field of the MicroStation Command Window and press [ENTER].)

STEP 19: To draw the line from point N to O, set the constraints to Length and Angle to 2:6 and 180 respectively. MicroStation prompts:

> *Enter first point* (Tentative snap to the end of the previous line, point N and click the Data button to accept it.)

Complete the object by placing additional data points by keying appropriate values in the Length and Angle edit fields and snapping to end point of the previous line.

LINE	LENGTH	ANGLE
O-P	2	90
P-Q	1:6	180
Q-R	2:6	90
R-S	2	180
S-T	3:6	90
T-M	6	0

STEP 20: Turn off the Length and Angle constraint toggle buttons in the Tool Settings Box.

Place Text in Each Pattern

Place the descriptive text in each of the three patterns, as shown in Figure P2–11.

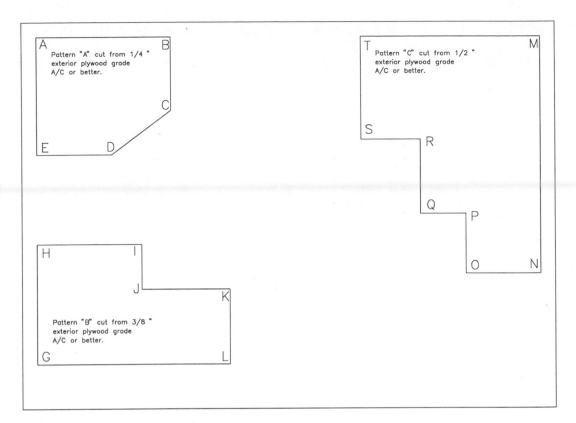

FIGURE P2–11 Design displaying descriptive text.

STEP 21: Open the Text settings box from the Element pull-down menu. Set the font to the Engineering font (3), the text height and width to 0:1.5, the line spacing to 0:1.5, and the line length to 255. Set the Multi-line Text justification to top left (see Figure P2–12).

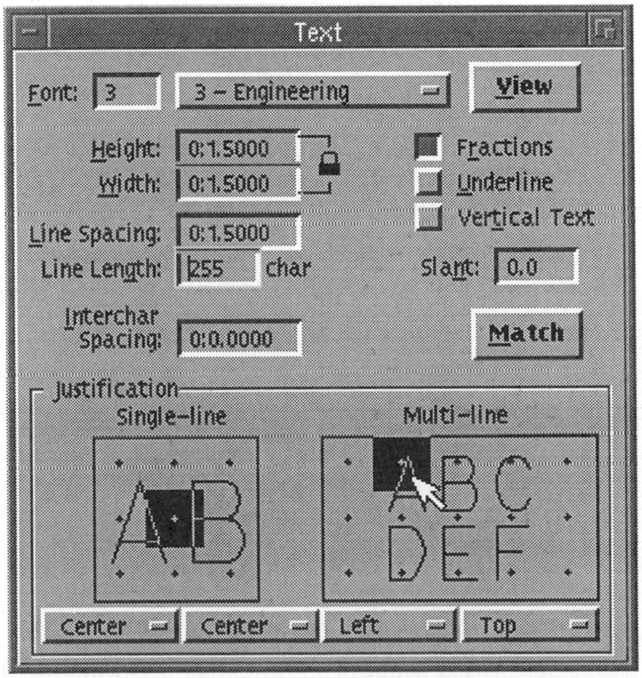

FIGURE P2–12 Text Settings Box.

STEP 22:   Select Save Settings from the File pull-down menu to save the settings.

STEP 23:   Invoke the Place Text command from the Main palette, and select By Origin from the Method options menu in the Tool Settings Box.

STEP 24:   In the Text Editor box, type the descriptive text for pattern A (refer to Figure P2–11), then place a data point in the upper left corner of pattern A to place the text.

> **NOTE:** When typing the text make sure to press ⌨ key at the end of each line of text.

Place additional text in Patterns B and C as shown in Figure P2–11.

Placing Dimensions for Each Pattern

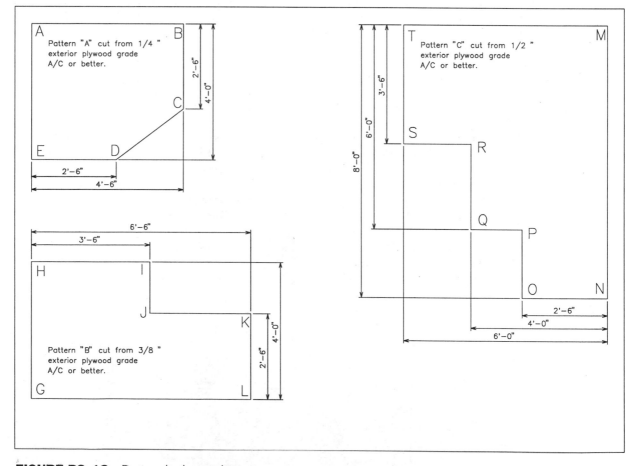

FIGURE P2–13   Design displaying dimensions.

STEP 25:   Open the Units settings box from the Dimensions sub-menu of the Element Pull-down menu. Select AEC format from the Format Option menu and leave the remaining option selections to the default selection. Close the settings box.

STEP 26: Select the Linear Dimension sub-palette from the Dimensioning sub-menu of the Palettes pull-down menu. Invoke the Dimension Location (Stacked) command from the Linear Dimensions sub-palette as shown in Figure P2–14. MicroStation prompts:

Select start of dimension (Place a data point on Point B.)
Define length of extension line (Move the screen pointer horizontally one grid unit to the right and click the Data button.)
Select dimension end point (Place a data point on Point C.)
Select dimension end point (Place a data point on Point D.)
Select dimension end point (Click the Reset button.)
Define length of extension line (Click the Reset button.)
Select start of dimension (Place a data point on Point E.)
Define length of extension line (Move the screen pointer vertically down one grid unit and click the Data button.)
Select dimension end point (Place a data point on Point D.)
Select dimension endpoint (Place a data point on Point C.)
Select dimension endpoint (Click the Reset button.)
Define length of extension line (Click the Reset button.)

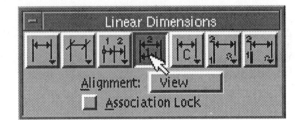

FIGURE P2–14 Invoking Dimension Location (Stacked) command from the Linear Dimension sub-palette.

STEP 27: Use Figure P2–15 as a guide to dimension pattern B.

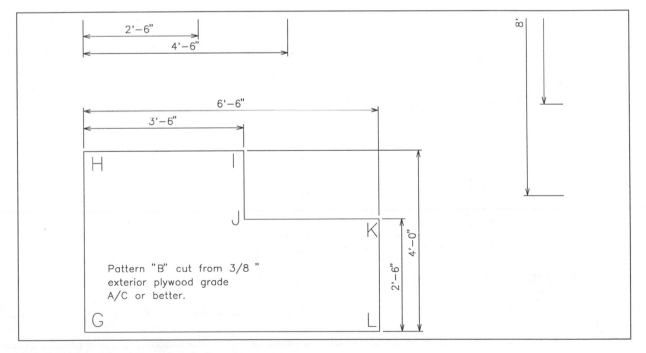

FIGURE P2–15 Pattern B with dimensions.

STEP 28: Use Figure P2–16 as a guide to dimension pattern C.

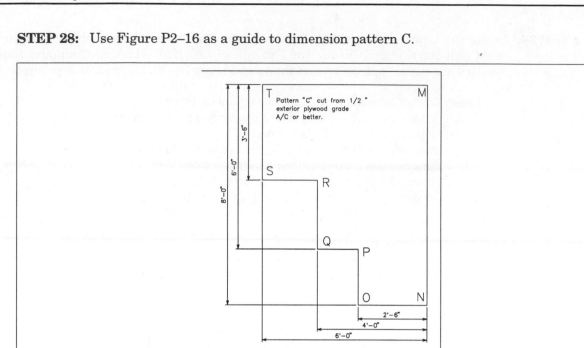

FIGURE P2–16 Pattern C with dimensions.

STEP 29: Invoke the Fit command to display the design.

STEP 30: Create a title as shown in Figure P2–17.

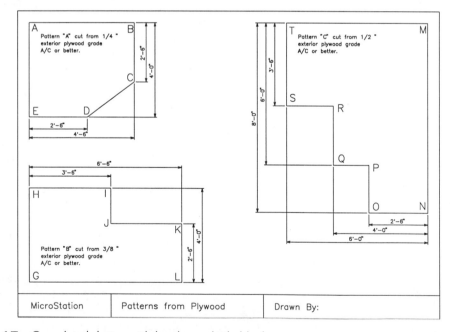

FIGURE P2–17 Completed design with border and title block.

STEP 31: Invoke Save Settings command from the File pull-down menu to save the settings.

Congratulations. You just successfully applied several MicroStation concepts in creating a simple design.

3

FUNDAMENTALS II

. . . .

After completing this chapter, you will be able to:

- Place circles, arcs, ellipses, polygons, curves, and multi-lines.
- Manipulate elements using the commands Fillet, Chamfer, Trim, Move, Copy, Array, Rotate, Spin, Scale, and Mirror.
- Control and view levels.
- Set element symbology.
- Match element attributes.
- Undo and redo commands.
- Dimension Attributes.
- Dimension radii, diameters, and angles.

PLACEMENT COMMANDS

In this chapter, seven additional placement commands are explained—the Circle, Arc, Polygon, Ellipse, Curve (Place Point Curve and Place Curve Stream), and Multi-line commands—in addition to the placement commands explained in Chapter 2.

Place Circle

MicroStation offers several methods for drawing circles. These include Place Circle by Center, Place Circle Edge, and Place Circle by Diameter. The commands are located in the Circles & Ellipses sub-palette invoked from the Main palette as shown in Figure 3–1.

Place Circle Center If you wish to draw a circle by specifying Center Point and a point on the circle, invoke the Place Circle Center command by clicking the Place Circle Center icon from the Circles & Ellipses sub-palette (see Figure 3–2), or key-in in at the uSTN> field **place circle center** (or **pla ci**) and press ⏎. MicroStation prompts:

Identify Center Point (Place a data point or key-in coordinates to define the center of the circle.)

> **NOTE:** After you place the first data point, a dynamic image of the circle drags with the screen pointer.

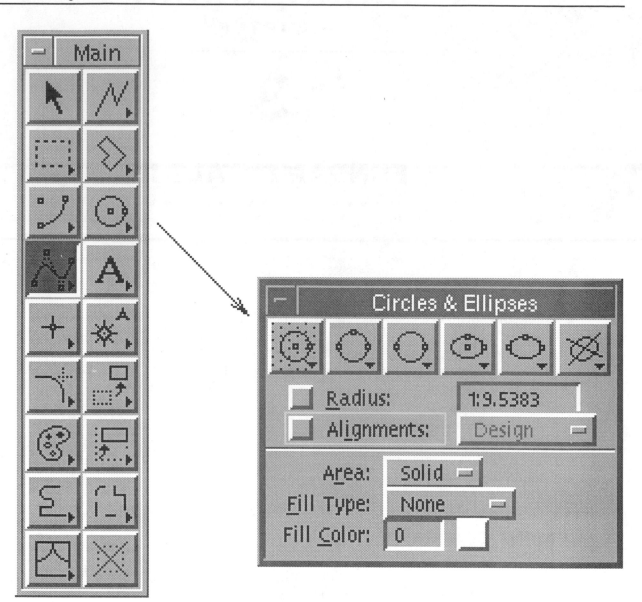

FIGURE 3–1   Invoking the Circles and Ellipses sub-palette from the Main palette.

FIGURE 3–2   Invoking the Place Circle Center command from the Circles and Ellipses sub-palette.

You can specify the center point by providing a data point using your pointing device (mouse or puck) or precision input. After specifying the center point, MicroStation prompts:

Identify Point on Circle (Place a data point or key-in coordinate to define the edge of the circle.)

You can specify the point on the circle by providing a data point using your pointing device (mouse or puck) or by precision input. To save time, Place Circle Center remains active and prompts for a new center point. When you are finished placing circles, invoke another command to terminate the Place Circle Center command.

For example, the following command sequence shows placement of a circle by Place Circle Center command (see Figure 3–3).

Identify Center Point: **XY=2,2** [ENTER]
Identify Point on Circle: **DL=1,0** [ENTER]

In the last example, MicroStation used the distance between the center point and the point given on the circle for the radius of the circle.

You can also place a Circle by Center by key-in Radius. To do so, click the Place Circle by Center icon and turn on the toggle button for Radius in the palette. Key-in the Radius in the Radius edit field and press [ENTER] or [TAB]. When the desired radius is entered using the MU:SU:PU format, a circle of that radius appears on the screen cursor. You will then be asked to identify the center point of the circle. Position your cursor where you want the center of the circle to be and place a data point. Continue placing circles having the same radius, or press the Reset button to allow you to change the radius of the circle. If you do not wish to continue placing circles, invoke another command to terminate the Place Circle by Center command.

Place Circle by Edge If you wish to draw a circle by specifying three known points on the circle, invoke the Place Circle by Edge command by clicking the Place Circle by Edge icon from the Circles & Ellipses sub-palette (see Figure 3–4), or key-in at the uSTN> field **place circle edge** (or **pla ci e**), and press [ENTER]. MicroStation prompts:

Identify Point on Circle (Place a data point or key-in coordinates to locate the first circle edge point.)
Identify Point on Circle (Place a data point or key-in coordinates to locate the second edge point.)
Identify Point on Circle (Place a data point or key-in coordinates to locate the third edge point.)

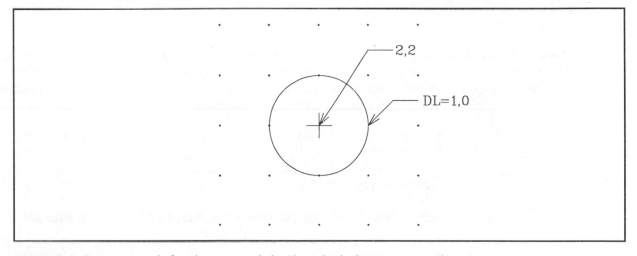

FIGURE 3–3   An example for placing a circle by Place Circle Center command.

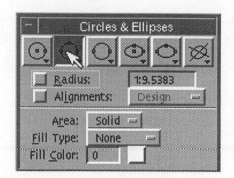

FIGURE 3–4 Invoking the Place Circle Edge command from the Circles and Ellipses sub-palette.

The following command sequence shows an example of placing a circle using Place Circle by Edge (see Figure 3–5).

Identify Point on Circle: **XY= 2,3** [ENTER]
Identify Point on Circle: **XY= 3,2** [ENTER]
Identify Point on Circle: **XY= 2,1** [ENTER]

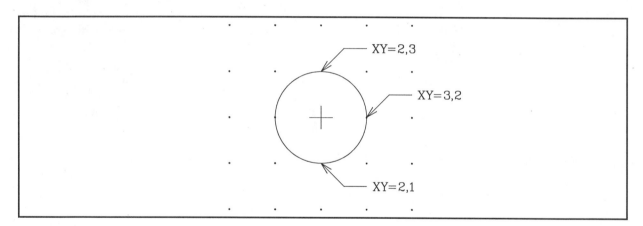

FIGURE 3–5 An example for placing a circle by Place Circle Edge command.

You can also place a Circle by Edge by key-in Radius. To do so, click the Place Circle by Edge icon and turn on the toggle button for Radius in the sub-palette. Key-in the Radius in the Radius edit field and press [ENTER] or [TAB]. When the desired radius is entered using the MU:SU:PU format, MicroStation prompts for two data points, instead of three, to place a circle by edge.

Place Circle Diameter If you wish to place a circle by specifying the two end points of one of its diameters, select the Place Circle Diameter command by clicking the Place Circle Diameter icon from the Circles & Ellipses sub-palette (see Figure 3–6), or key-in at the uSTN> field **place circle diameter** (or **pla ci d**) and press [ENTER]. MicroStation prompts:

Enter first point on diameter (Place a data point or key-in the coordinates to locate the first end point of one of its diameters.)

> **NOTE:** After you place the first data point a dynamic image of the circle drags with the screen pointer.

Enter second point on diameter (Place a data point or key-in the coordinates to locate the second end point of one of its diameters.)

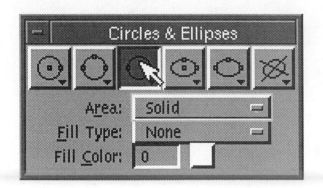

FIGURE 3–6   Invoking the Place Circle Diameter command from the Circles and Ellipses sub-palette.

The following command sequence shows an example of placing a circle by using the Place Circle Diameter command (see Figure 3–7).

Enter first point on diameter: **XY=1,2** ⏎
Enter second point on diameter: **XY=3,2** ⏎

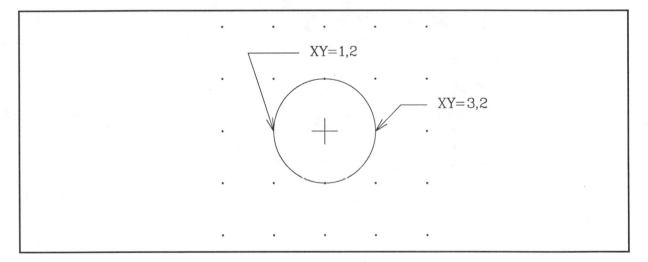

FIGURE 3–7   An example for placing a circle by Place Circle Diameter command.

Place Arc

MicroStation offers several ways for drawing arcs. The commands related to arc placement are located in the Arcs sub-palette invoked from the Main palette as shown in Figure 3–8.

Place Arc Center   The Place Arc Center command is used to place an arc defined by three points: the center point, the first arc end point, and the second arc end point. To draw an arc using the Place Arc Center command, invoke the command by clicking the Place Arc Center icon from the Arcs sub-palette (see Figure 3–9), or key-in at the uSTN> field **place arc center** (or **pla a c**) and press ⏎. MicroStation prompts:

Identify Arc Center (Place a data point or key-in coordinates to define the arc center point.)
Identify First Arc End point (Place a data point or key-in coordinates to define the first end point.)
Identify Second Arc End point (Place a data point or key-in coordinates to define the other end point.)

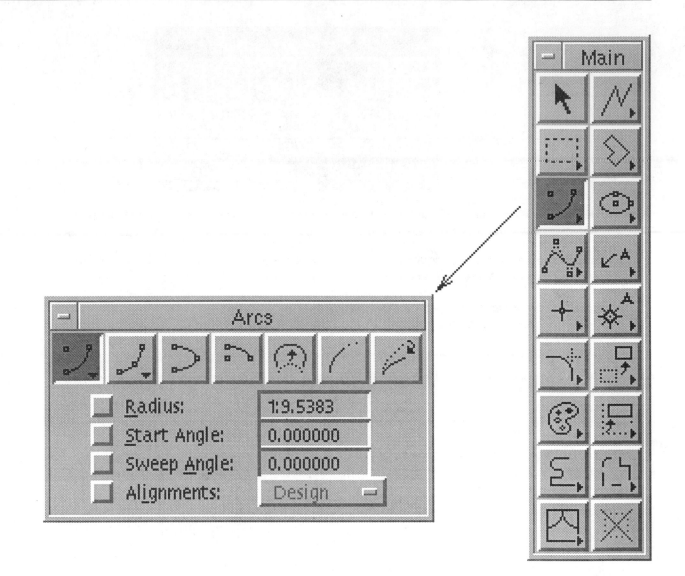

FIGURE 3–8 Invoking the Arcs sub-palette from Main palette.

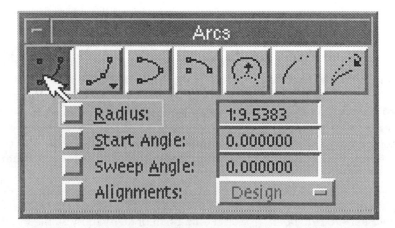

FIGURE 3–9 Invoking the Place Arc Center command from the Circles and Ellipses sub-palette.

The following command sequence shows an example of placing an arc with the Place Arc Center command (see Figure 3–10).

> *Identify Arc Center:* **xy=2,3** ⏎
> *Identify First Arc End Point:* **DL=-1,0** ⏎
> *Identify Second Arc End Point:* **DL=1,1** ⏎

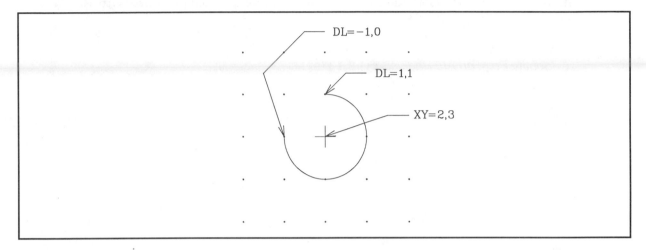

FIGURE 3–10   An example for placing an Arc by Place Arc Center command.

You can also place an Arc by Center by key-in Radius (constrain). To do so, click the Place Arc by Center icon and turn ON the toggle button for Radius in the Arcs sub-palette. Key-in the Radius in MU:SU:PU in the Radius edit field and press ⏎ or ⇥. The prompts are similar to Arc by Center command, except the First Arc End Point and Second Arc End Point defines starting and ending direction of the arc.

Similarly, you can also constrain the Start Angle and Sweep Angle by keying in appropriate angles in the edit fields respectively. MicroStation prompts depends on the number of constraints turned ON. For example, if Radius and Start Angle are pre-set, MicroStation prompts for the Center point of the Arc and the Sweep Angle. If Radius, Start Angle, and Sweep Angle are pre-set, MicroStation prompts only for the center of the Arc.

Place Arc Edge   The Place Arc Edge command is used to place an arc by identifying three points on the arc. To draw an arc, invoke the Place Arc Edge command by clicking the Place Arc Edge icon from the Arc sub-palette (see Figure 3–11), or key-in at the uSTN> field **place arc edge** (or **pla a**) and press ⏎. MicroStation prompts:

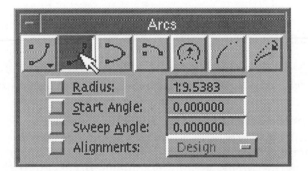

FIGURE 3–11   Invoking the Place Arc Edge command from the Circles and Ellipses sub-palette.

Identify First Arc End Point (Place a data point or key-in the coordinates to define the arc end point.)
Identify Point on Arc Radius (Place a data point or key-in coordinates to define another point on the arc radius.)
Identify Second Arc End Point (Place a data point or key-in coordinates to define the second arc end point.)

The following command sequence shows an example of placing an arc with the Place Arc Edge command (see Figure 3–12).

Identify First Arc End Point: **xy=1,2** ⏎
Identify Point on Arc Radius: **xy=2,1** ⏎
Identify Second Arc End Point: **xy=3,2** ⏎

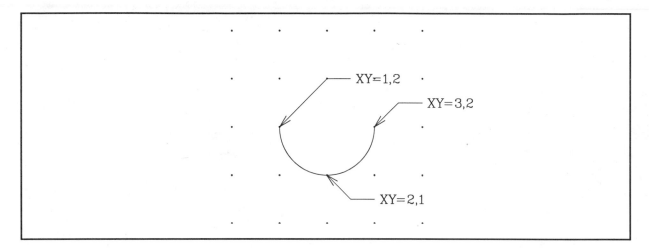

FIGURE 3–12   An example for placing an Arc by Place Arc Edge command.

You can also place an Arc by Edge by key-in Radius (constrain). To do so, click the Place Arc by Edge icon and turn ON the toggle button for Radius in the Arcs sub-palette. Key-in the Radius in MU:SU:PU in the Radius edit field and press ⏎ or TAB. The prompts are similar to Arc by Edge command, except the First Arc End Point and Second Arc End Point defines the starting and ending direction of the arc. Similarly, you can also constrain the Start Angle and Sweep Angle by keying in the appropriate angles in the edit fields respectively. MicroStation prompts depends on the number of constraints turned ON. For example, if the Radius and Start Angle are pre-set, MicroStation prompts you to Identify First Arc End Point and Identity Second Arc End Point. If Radius, Start Angle, and Sweep Angle are pre-set, MicroStation prompts you to Identify First Arc End Point.

Place Ellipse

MicroStation offers several ways to draw ellipses. The commands related to ellipse placement are located in the Circles & Ellipses sub-palette invoked from the Main palette as shown in Figure 3–13.

Place Ellipse Center and Edge The Place Ellipse Center and Edge command is used to place an ellipse when you need to precisely position the center point and one end of the major axis. To place an ellipse invoke the Place Ellipse Center and Edge command by clicking the Place Ellipse Center and Edge icon from the Circles & Ellipses sub-palette (see Figure 3–14), or key-in at the uSTN> field **place ellipse center constrained** (or **pla e c**) and press ⏎. MicroStation prompts:

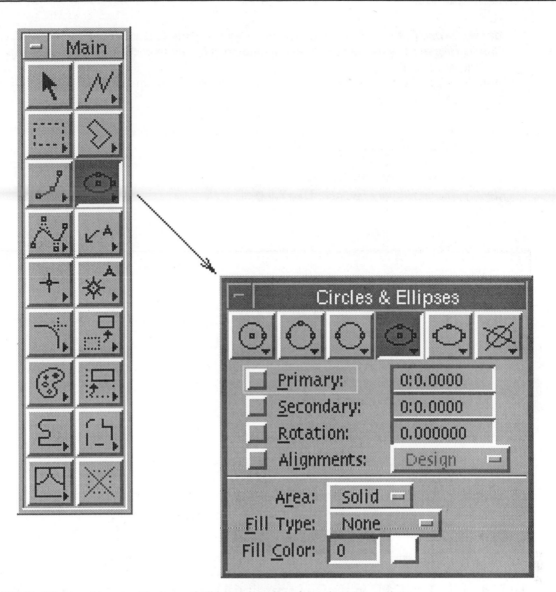

FIGURE 3–13   Invoking the Circles and Ellipse sub-palette from the Main palette.

FIGURE 3–14   Invoking the Place Ellipse Center and Edge command from the Circles and Ellipse sub-palette.

Identify Ellipse Center (Place a data point or key-in coordinates to define the center of the ellipse.)
Identify Ellipse Primary Radius (Place a data point or key-in coordinates to define the end of the primary axis.)
Identify Ellipse Secondary Radius (Place a data point or key-in coordinates to define the end of the secondary axis.)

The following command sequence shows an example of placing an ellipse with the Place Ellipse by Center and Edge command (see Figure 3–15).

Identify Ellipse Center: **xy=3,2** [ENTER]
Identity Ellipse Primary Radius: **DL=2,0** [ENTER]
Identify Ellipse Secondary Radius: **XY=3,3** [ENTER]

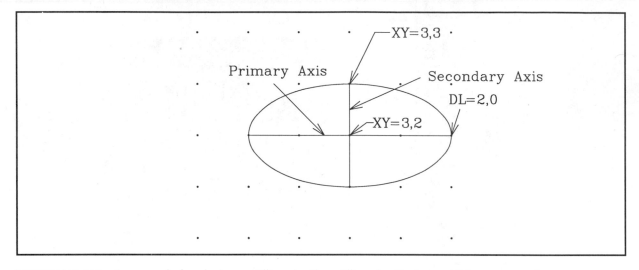

FIGURE 3–15   An example for placing an Ellipse by Place Ellipse by Center and Edge command.

You can also place an Ellipse by keying in the Primary Radius (constrain). To do so, click the Place Ellipse by Center and Edge icon and turn ON the toggle button for Primary in the sub-palette. Key-in the Radius in MU:SU:PU in the Primary edit field and press [ENTER] or [TAB]. MicroStation prompts to identify the Ellipse Center and the Secondary Ellipse Radius. Similarly, you can also constrain the Secondary Radius and Rotation by keying in the appropriate edit fields. MicroStation prompts depends on the number of constraints turned ON. For example, if the Primary and Secondary Radius are pre-set, MicroStation prompts you to Identify the Center and Rotation points. If the Primary Radius, Secondary Radius and Rotation are pre-set, MicroStation prompts you to identify the ellipse center point.

Place Ellipse by Edge Points   The Place Ellipse by Edge Points command should be used when it becomes necessary to precisely place both ends of the primary axis (major axis). To place an ellipse using the Place Ellipse by Edge Points command, invoke the command by clicking the Place Ellipse by Edge Points icon from the Circles & Ellipses sub-palette (see Figure 3–16), or key-in at the uSTN> field **place ellipse edge** (or **pla e e**), and press [ENTER]. MicroStation prompts:

Identify Point on Ellipse (Place a data point or key-in coordinates to locate one end of the primary axis.)
Identify Point on Ellipse (Place a data point or key-in coordinates to locate other end of the primary axis.)
Identify Point on Ellipse (Place a data point or key-in to locate one end of the secondary axis.)

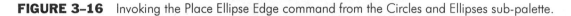

FIGURE 3–16   Invoking the Place Ellipse Edge command from the Circles and Ellipses sub-palette.

The following command sequence shows an example of placing an ellipse with the Place Ellipse by Edge Points command (see Figure 3–17).

Identify Point on Ellipse: **xy=1,2** ⏎
Identity Point on Ellipse: **dl=4,0** ⏎
Identity Point on Ellipse: **xy=3,3** ⏎

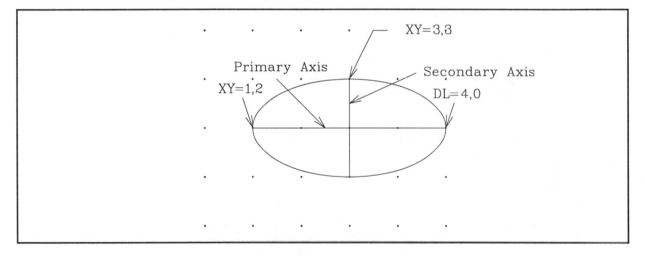

FIGURE 3–17   An example for placing an Ellipse by Place Ellipse by Edge Points command.

You can also place an Ellipse by keying in the Primary Radius (constrain). To do so, click the Place Ellipse by Edge Points icon and turn ON the toggle button for Primary in the sub-palette. Key-in the Radius in MU:SU:PU in the Primary edit field and press ⏎ or ⇥. MicroStation prompts you to identify three data points and places an ellipse constraint using the keyed-in primary axis radius. Similarly, you can also constrain the Secondary Radius and Rotation by keying in appropriate edit fields. MicroStation prompts depends on the number of constraints turned ON. For example, if the Primary and Secondary Radius are pre-set, MicroStation prompts for two data points. If Primary Radius, Secondary Radius, and Rotation are pre-set, MicroStation prompts to identify any point on the ellipse.

> **NOTE:** Similar to placing arcs, you can also place half and quarter ellipses. The commands are located in Arcs sub-palette.

Place Polygon

You can place regular 2D polygons (all edges are equal length, and equal angles at each vertex) with the Place Polygon command. The maximum number of sides is limited to 100. MicroStation provides three methods for placing regular polygons. The listing of the methods is provided under the Method option menu in the sub-palette.

To place a polygon, click on the Place Polygon icon in the Polygons sub-palette invoked from the Main palette (as shown in Figure 3–18), and select the Method you want to use to place the polygon.

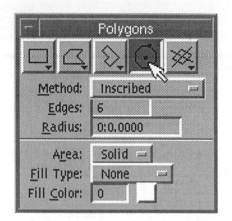

FIGURE 3–18 Invoking the Place Polygon command from the Polygons sub-palette.

The Inscribed option places a polygon of equal length for all sides inscribed inside an imaginary circle (see Figure 3–19) having the same diameter as the distance across opposite polygon corners. The number of sides and the radius of the inscribing circle are keyed in the edit field. The radius can also be defined graphically if the Radius field is set to 0. MicroStation prompts:

Enter point on axis (Place a data point or key-in coordinates to define the center of the polygon.)

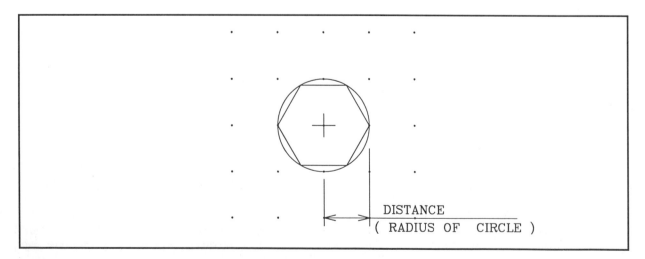

FIGURE 3–19 An example displaying a polygon inscribed inside an imaginary circle.

If the radius is set to 0, MicroStation prompts for two data points, one for the center of the imaginary circle, and one for location on the circumference of the imaginary circle. For example, the following command sequence shows the placement of an inscribed polygon using the Place Polygon command when the radius is set for 2.00 and the number of sides is equal to 6 (see Figure 3-20).

Enter point on axis: **xy=3,3**

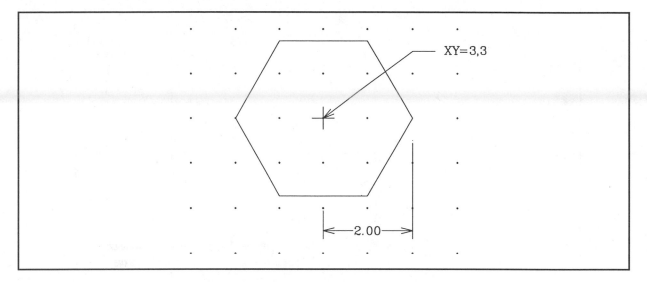

FIGURE 3–20   An example for placing a polygon by Place Polygon command when inscribed option is selected.

The Circumscribed option places a polygon circumscribed outside an imaginary circle having the same diameter as the distance across the polygon sides (see Figure 3–21). If the Radius is keyed in, the midpoint of one side is placed to the center's right. The number of sides and the radius of the inscribing circle is keyed in the edit field. The radius can also be defined graphically, if the Radius field is set to 0. MicroStation prompts:

Enter point on axis (Place a data point or key-in coordinates to define the center of the polygon.)

If the radius is set to 0, MicroStation prompts for two data points, one for the center of the imaginary circle and one for location on the circumference of the imaginary circle.

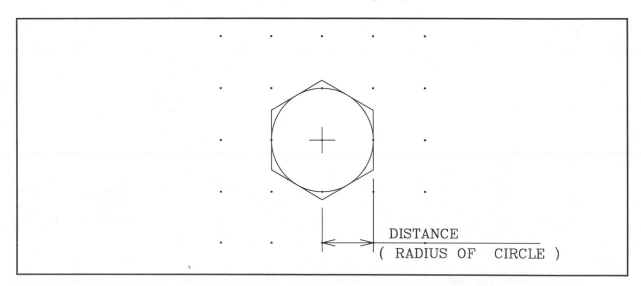

FIGURE 3–21   An example displaying a polygon outside a circle.

See Figure 3–22 for an example of placing a polygon, using the Place Polygon Circumscribed command.

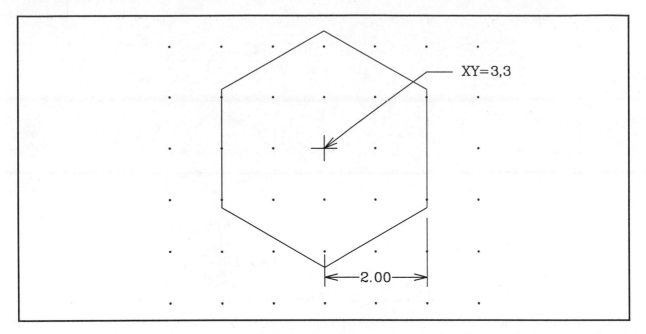

FIGURE 3–22 An example for placing a polygon by Place Polygon command when Circumscribed option is selected.

The Edge option allows you to place a polygon by defining one edge graphically (see Figure 3–23). Key-in the number of sides in the # of Edges edit field. MicroStation prompts:

Enter first edge point (Place a data point or key-in coordinates to define the vertex of the edge.)
Enter next (CCW) edge point (Place a data point or key-in coordinates to define the second edge point.)

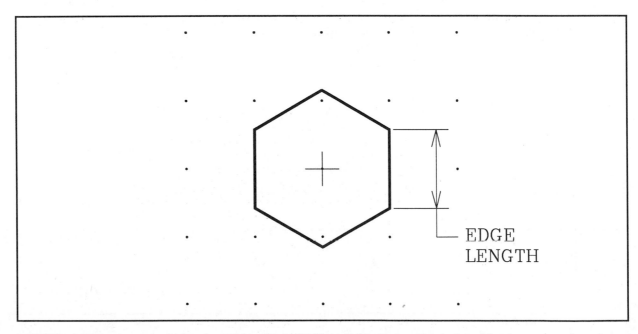

FIGURE 3–23 An example for placing a polygon by Place Polygon command when Edge option is selected.

Place Point Curve

The Place Point Curve command is used to place a 2D (single plane) curve element. This is accomplished by defining a series of data points the curve passes through. This command is similar to placing line string, except the vertices for a curve are smooth rather than sharp. A curve element can have 3 to 97 vertices. If more than 97 vertices are selected, MicroStation creates a complex chain consisting of one or more curved elements.

To draw a curved element using the Place Point Curve command, invoke the command by clicking the Place Point Curve icon in the Curves sub-palette (see Figure 3–24), or key-in at the uSTN> field **place curve point** (or **pla cu**) and press ⏎. MicroStation prompts:

> *Enter start point* (Place a data point or key-in coordinates to define the starting point of the curve.)
> *Enter next point or Reset to finish* (Place a data point or key-in coordinates to define the next vertex.)

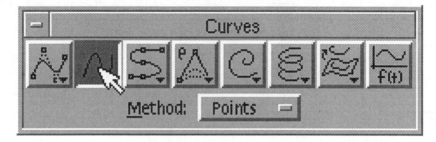

FIGURE 3–24   Invoking the Place Point Curve command from the Curves sub-palette.

At least three points are required to describe a curved element. Once you are through defining curve data points and/or key-in coordinates, press the Reset button to terminate the command sequence. See Figure 3–25 for an example of placing a curve by Place Point Curve command by providing five data points.

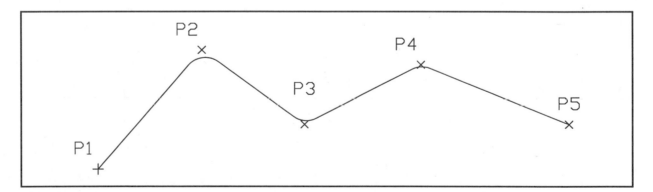

FIGURE 3–25   An example for placing a curve by Place Point Curve command.

Place Curve Stream

The Place Stream Curve command is used to place a curve stream that follows the movement of your cursor. As you move your input device, MicroStation records data points based on stream settings—active stream delta, active stream tolerance, active stream angle, and active stream area. A stream curve element can have 3 to 97 vertices. If more than 97 vertices are defined, MicroStation automatically creates a complex chain consisting of one or more curve elements.

To place a curve stream using the Place Curve Stream command, invoke the command by clicking the Place Point Curve in the Curves sub-palette and select Stream option from the Method option menu (see Figure 3–26), or key-in at the uSTN> field **place curve stream** (or **pla cu st**) and press [ENTER]. MicroStation prompts:

Enter first point in curve string (Place a data point to define the starting point of the curve stream.)
Enter point or RESET to complete (Move your cursor to define the curve stream. When you are finished, press the Reset button to complete the curve stream.)

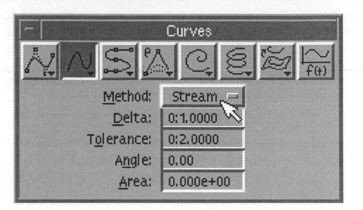

FIGURE 3–26 Invoking the Place Curve Stream command from the Curves sub-palette.

See Figure 3–27, for an example of placing a curve stream by Place Curve Stream command.

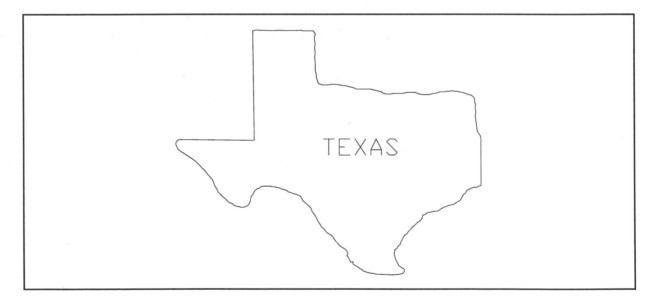

FIGURE 3–27 An example for placing a curve Stream by Place Curve Stream command.

Place Multi-Line

The Multi-Line command allows you to place up to 16 separate lines of various line styles, weights, and colors with a single command. The Multi-Line command is similar to the Line String command in that all the lines are placed as one continous element. To edit them separately you must use the Drop Multi-Line command.

You can create a customized version of a multi-line with as many as 16 separate lines of various line styles, weights, and colors and save the definition to a style file. Then you can use the Multi-line definition to place Multi-lines in any design file. Detailed explanation is provided in Chapter 11 for creating a Multi-line defintion.

To place a Multi-line, invoke the Place Multi-line command by clicking the Place Multi-Line icon from the Lines sub-palette, or key-in at the uSTN> field **place multi-line** and press 【ENTER】. MicroStation prompts are similar to Place Line String command.

MicroStation has a set of tools to edit Multi-lines called Multi-line Joints. See Chapter 5 for a detailed explnation about using Multi-line Joint command.

ELEMENT MODIFICATION

MicroStation not only allows you to place elements easily, but also allows you to modify them as needed. This section discusses three important commands that will make your job easier. The commands includes Fillet, Chamfer, and Trim.

Placing Fillet

The Place Fillet command joins two lines, adjacent segments of a line string, arcs, or circles with an arc of a specified radius. MicroStation provides three methods by which you can control the removal (truncation) of extension lines when placing the fillet.

- The None option (No Modify) feature places the fillet radius but does not modify the selected elements.
- The Both option (Modify) feature places the fillet radius and modifies both the selected elements.
- The First option (Single) feature places the fillet radius and modifies the first element selected.

See Figure 3–28 for an example of placing a fillet for all the three option methods.

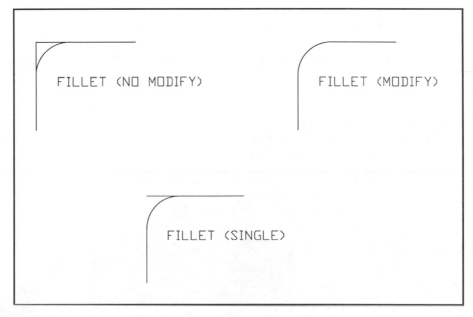

FIGURE 3–28   Examples of placing fillet by three different option methods.

To place a fillet using the Place Fillet command, invoke the command by clicking the Place Fillet icon from the Fillets sub-palette (see Figure 3–29), select (Both, First, or None) from the Truncate option menu and key-in the fillet radius in the Radius edit field. MicroStation prompts:

Select first segment (Identify the first element.)
Select second segment (Identify the second element.)
Accept-initiate construction (Click the Accept button to accept the placement of fillet or click the Reject button to reject the placement of fillet.)

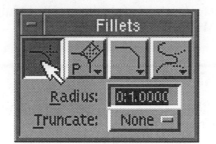

FIGURE 3–29 Invoking the Place Fillet command from the Fillets sub-palette.

Alternate Method You can place a fillet by keying in the command at the uSTN> prompt. To place a fillet with no modification, key-in **fillet no modify** and press [ENTER]. To place a fillet with modification for both selected elements, key-in **fillet modify** and press [ENTER]. And to place a fillet with a single element modification, key-in **fillet single** and press [ENTER]. The prompts are identical to those explained earlier.

Placing Chamfer

The Chamfer command is very similar to the Place Fillet command, but it allows you to draw an angled corner instead of an arc. The size of the chamfer is determined by its distance from the corner. If it is to be a 45-degree chamfer, the two distances have to be the same. The Chamfer command can be used to construct a chamfer between two lines or between adjacent segments of a line string. Key-in the two distances in the edit fields provided in the sub-palette.

To construct a chamfer using the Place Chamfer command, invoke the command by clicking the Chamfer icon from the Fillets sub-palette (see Figure 3–30) and keying in the distances in the edit field (Distance 1 and Distance 2) in MU:SU:PU. MicroStation prompts:

Select first chamfer segment (Place a data point to identify the first line or segment.)
Select second chamfer segment (Place a data point to identify the second line or segment.)

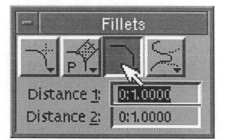

FIGURE 3–30 Invoking the Place Chamfer command from the Fillets sub-palette.

Click the Accept button to accept the placement of chamfer or click the Reject button to reject the placement of chamfer. For example, the following command sequence shows placement of a chamfer.

> *Select first chamfer segment* (Identify line p1, Figure 3–31.)
> *Select second chamfer segment* (Identify line p2, Figure 3–31.)

Click the Accept button.

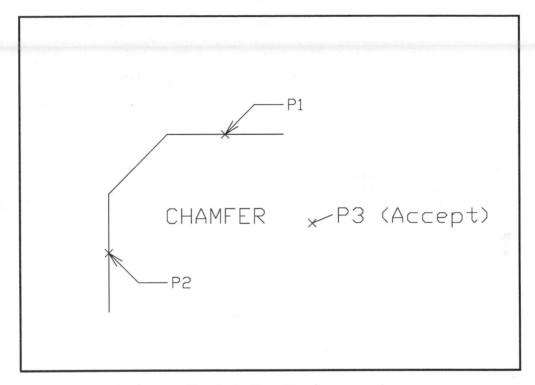

FIGURE 3–31   *An example of placing Chamfer by Place Chamfer command.*

Alternate Method You can also start the Chamfer command by keying in at the uSTN> field, **chamfer** (or **cham**) and pressing [ENTER]. When you use the key-in method, MicroStation will prompt you to type each chamfer distance in the uSTN> field.

Trim

The Trim command changes the end point(s) of lines, circles, and arcs. It will remove the portion of the object(s) that extends past the cutting element (edge). Any line, line segment, circle, or arc can be selected as a cutting element.

The Trim command is invoked by clicking the Trim icon from the Modify Element sub-palette (see Figure 3–32), or key-in at the uSTN> field **trim**, and press [ENTER]. MicroStation prompts:

> *Select Cutting Element* (Identify the element to define as the cutting element.)
> *Accept, Identify Trim Element/Reject* (Identify the element to trim.)
> *Accept, Identify Trim Element/Reject* (Identify additional elements to trim.)

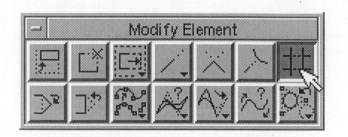

FIGURE 3–32 Invoking the Trim command from the Modify Element sub-palette.

Once you are through identifying elements, click the Accept button to accept the last element selected for trimming. Click the Reset button to start the trimming operation all over again. For example, the following command sequence shows how to use the Trim command to trim the two lines (see Figure 3–33).

Select Cutting Element (Identify the cutting element.)
Accept, Identify Trim Element/Reject (Identify the line.)
Accept, Identify Trim Element/Reject (Identify the line.)
Accept, Identify Trim Element/Reject (Click the Accept button.)
Accept, Identify Trim Element/Reject (Click the Reset button to terminate the command.)

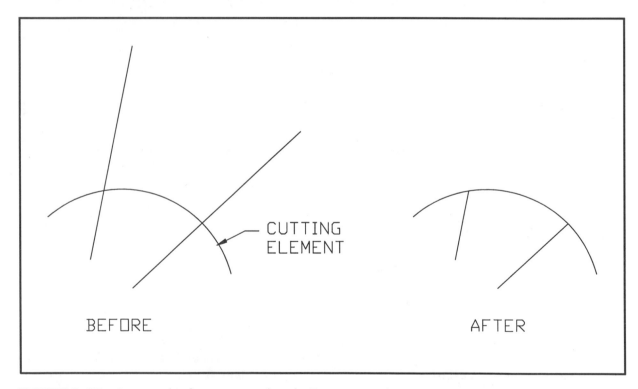

FIGURE 3–33 An example of trimming two lines by Trim command.

Delete Part of Element

The Delete Part of Element (Partial Delete) command allows you to delete part of an element. In the case of a line, line string, multi-line, curve, or arc, you can remove part of the element, and the element is divided into two elements of the same type. A partially deleted ellipse or circle becomes an arc, and a shape becomes a line string.

To partially delete an element, click the Delete Part of Element icon from the Modify Element sub-palette (see Figure 3–34), or key-in at the uSTN> field, **delete partial** (**del p**) and press [ENTER]. MicroStation prompts:

Select start point for partial delete (Identify the element where you want to start deleting partially.)
Select end point for partial delete (Place a data point or key-in coordinates for end point for partial delete.)

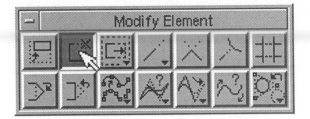

FIGURE 3–34   Invoking the Delete Part of Element command from the Modify Element sub-palette.

If you identify a closed element (circle, shape, or ellipse) for the first data point, MicroStation prompts for the direction of partial delete before it prompts for end point. The direction can be either counterclockwise or clockwise. See Figure 3–35 for examples of the delete partial command.

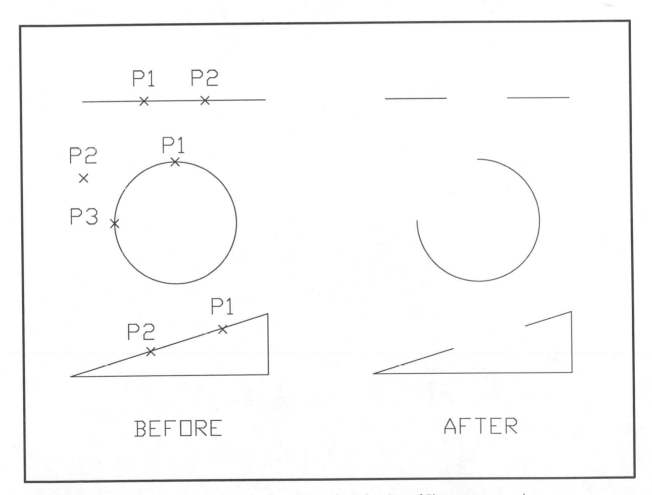

FIGURE 3–35   Examples of deleting part of an element by Delete Part of Element command.

EXERCISES

Exercises 3–1 through 3–5

Use Precision Key-ins (XY= , DL= , and/or DI=) and appropriate grid spacing to draw the figures.

Exercise 3–1

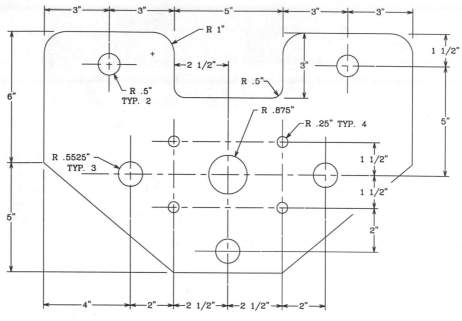

CRANE PULLY PLATE

Exercise 3–2

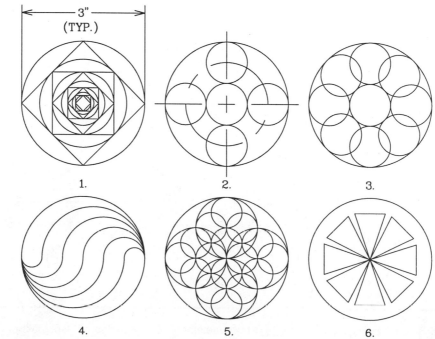

1. 2. 3.

4. 5. 6.

Exercise 3–3

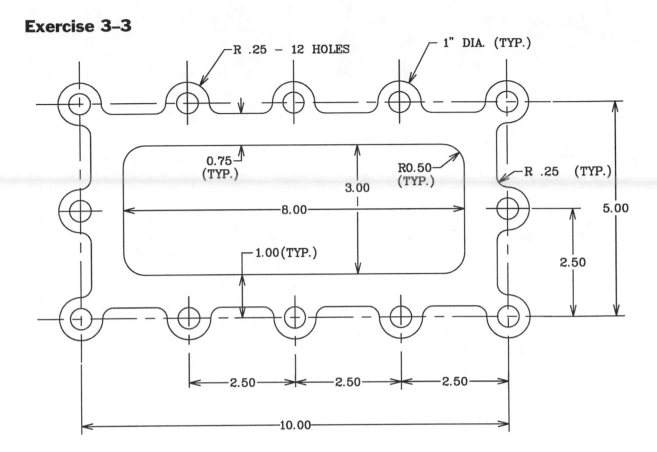

R .25 – 12 HOLES

1" DIA. (TYP.)

0.75 (TYP.)

R0.50 (TYP.)

R .25 (TYP.)

3.00

8.00

1.00 (TYP.)

5.00

2.50

2.50 2.50 2.50

10.00

Exercise 3–4

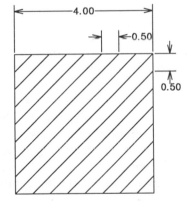

4.00

0.50

0.50

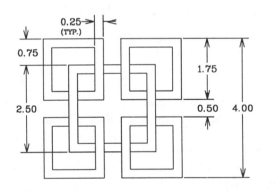

0.25 (TYP.)

0.75

2.50

1.75

0.50

4.00

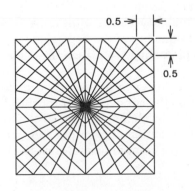

0.5

0.5

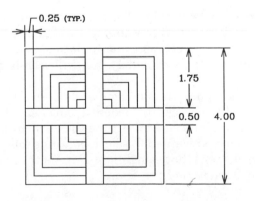

0.25 (TYP.)

1.75

0.50

4.00

Exercise 3–5

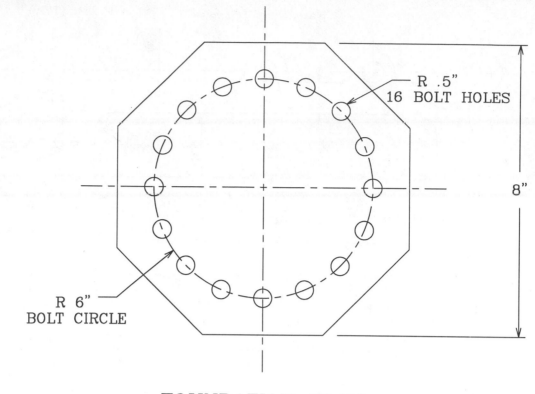

R .5"
16 BOLT HOLES

8"

R 6"
BOLT CIRCLE

FOUNDATION PLAN

ELEMENT MANIPULATION

MicroStation not only allows you to draw entities easily, but also allows easy manipulation and modification of the objects you have drawn. To manipulate or modify an entity is to make a change to one of its existing characteristics.

MicroStation offers two main categories of manipulation commands: single element manipulation and multi-element manipulations. Single element manipulation commands allow you to manipulate one element at a time, and multi-element manipulation commands manipulate groups of elements. This is done with Element Selection commands and Fence manipulation commands. This section discusses element manipulation commands. Multi-element manipulation commands are described in Chapter 4.

After mastering the element manipulation commands and learning when and how to apply them, you will start to really appreciate the power and capability of MicroStation. You can draw one element, then use the element manipulation commands to quickly make copies, saving you from having to draw each one separately. You will soon begin to plan ahead to utilize these powerful commands.

All the manipulation commands described here require you to identify the element to be manipulated, then accept it. To identify an element, position the cursor until it touches the element and click the Data button. At this time the element highlights by changing color. If the highlighted element is the one you wanted to select, continue following the command prompts shown in the prompt field. If the element that is highlighted is not the one you want to manipulate, click the Reject button to reject the element and try again.

> **NOTE:** Be sure to check the status of your lock settings before you begin to modify your drawing. A good rule to follow is to turn OFF all of the locks that are not being used with the exception of the snap lock. It is very frustrating to try and select an element that does not lie on the grid when the grid lock is turned ON. The cursor bounces around from grid dot to grid dot, and it may be impossible to identify an element if it is not on the grid. It is a simple matter to quickly toggle the grid lock OFF, identify the object, and then toggle the grid lock back ON again, if needed.

Move Element

The Move Element command allows you to move an element from its present location to a new location without changing its orientation or size. The data point you enter to identify the element you want to move also becomes the (base) point on the element to which the cursor is attached. Select this point with care, and use the tentative snap if you need to snap to the element at a precise location (with appropriate snap mode selected). Once you have moved the element to an appropriate location, click the Reset button to terminate the command sequence. After clicking the Reset button, you can select another element to move or invoke another command to continue working on your design file.

To move an element using the Move Element command, invoke the command by clicking the Move Element icon from the Manipulate Element sub-palette (see Figure 3–36) or key-in at the uSTN> field **move** and press [ENTER]. MicroStation prompts:

Identify element (Identify an element to move.)
Accept/Reject (Select next input) (Reposition the element to its new location by providing data point or key-in coordinates.)
Accept/Reject (Select next input) (If necessary move it to another location by providing data point or key-in coordinates and/or click Reset button to terminate the command sequence.)

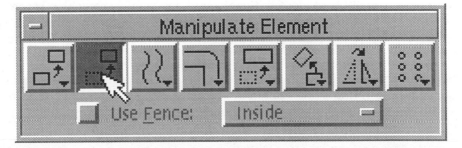

FIGURE 3–36 Invoking the Move Element command from the Manipulate Element sub-palette.

For example, the following command sequence shows how to move a line to the center of a circle using the Move Element command (see Figure 3–37).

Identify element (Identify line by tentative snapping to the end point of the line and accept.)
Accept/Reject (Select next input) (Tentative snap to the center of the circle and accept.)
Accept/Reject (Select next input) (Click the Reset button.)

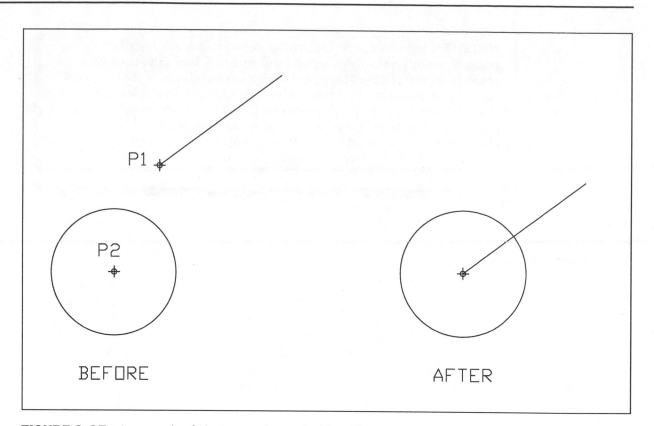

FIGURE 3–37 An example of Moving an element by Move Element command.

Copy Element

The Copy Element command is similar to the Move command, but it places a copy of the element at the specified displacement, leaving the original element intact. The copy is oriented and scaled the same as the original. You can make as many copies of the original as needed. Each resulting copy is completely independent of the original and can be manipulated and modified like any other element. The data point you enter to identify the element you want to copy also becomes the (base) point on the element to which the cursor is attached. Select this point with care, and use the tentative snap if you need to snap to the element at a precise location (with appropriate snap mode selected).

You can place any number of copies in your design file. Once you are through placing copies, click the Reset button to terminate the command sequence. If necessary, you can select another element to copy or invoke another command to continue working on your design file.

To copy an element using the Copy Element command, invoke the command by clicking the Copy Element icon from the Manipulate Element sub-palette (see Figure 3–38) or key-in at the uSTN> field **copy** and press [ENTER]. MicroStation prompts:

> *Identify element* (Identify an element to copy.)
> *Accept/Reject (Select next input)* (Provide the location of the copy by a data point or key-in coordinates.)
> *Accept/Reject (Select next input)* (If necessary, copy to another location by providing a data point or by keying in coordinates and/or click Reset button to terminate the command sequence.)

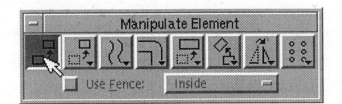

FIGURE 3–38   Invoking the Copy Element command from the Manipulate Element sub-palette.

For example, the following command sequence shows how to copy an element using the Copy Element command (see Figure 3–39).

Identify element (Identify line by tentative snapping to the end point of the line and accept.)
Accept/Reject (Select next input) (Tentative snap to the center of the circle and accept.)
Accept/Reject (Select next input) (Click the Reset button.)

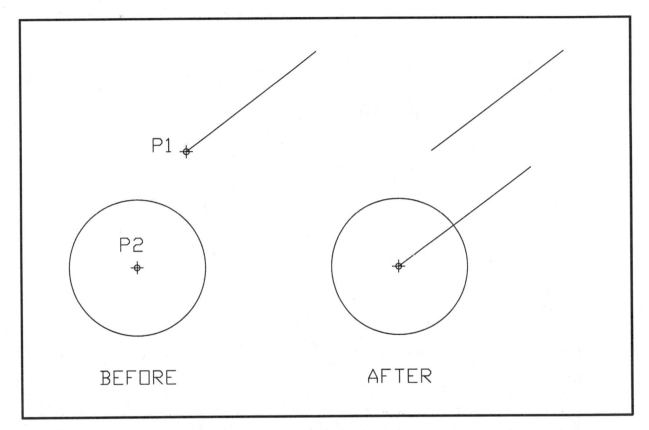

FIGURE 3–39   An example of Copying an element by Copy Element command.

Move and Copy Parallel

The Move Parallel command is used to move an element (such as a line, line string, multi-line, circles, curve, arc, ellipse, shape, complex chain, or complex shape) parallel to the original location of the element. The distance may be keyed in or defined by a data point.

To move an element parallel to its original location, invoke the Move Parallel Distance command by clicking the Move Parallel icon from the Manipulate Element sub-palette (see Figure 3–40). Micro-Station prompts:

Identify element (Identify an element to move parallel.)
Accept/Reject (Select next input) (Reposition the element to its new location by providing data
   point or key-in coordinates.)
Accept/Reject (Select next input) (If necessary move it to another location by providing a data
   point or key-in coordinates, and/or click Reset button to terminate the command sequence.)

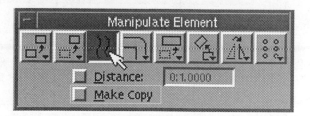

FIGURE 3–40   Invoking the Move Parallel Distance command from the Manipulate Element sub-palette.

For example, the following command sequence shows moving an element parallel to its original
location using the Move Parallel Distance command (see Figure 3–41).

Identify element (Identify the line.)
Accept/Reject (Select next input) (Place a data point to move the element parallel to the original
   location.)
Accept/Reject (Select next input) (Click the Reset button.)

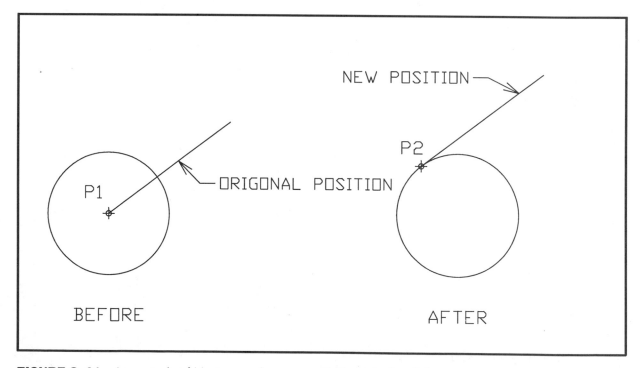

FIGURE 3–41   An example of Moving an element parallel by Move Parallel Distance command.

You can also move an element parallel by keying in distance. To do so, click the Move Parallel icon in
the manipulate sub-palette and turn ON the toggle button for Distance in the sub-palette. Key-in the
parallel distance in MU:SU:PU in the Distance edit field and press ENTER or TAB. The prompts are
similar to Move Parallel command, and you can move the element parallel to either side of the
original location.

Instead of moving the original element parallel, you can make a copy and then move the copy parallel to the original location of the element. To do so, click the Move Parallel icon in the manipulate sub-palette and turn ON the toggle button for Make Copy. The prompts are similar to Move Parallel command, and you can place the copy of the element parallel to either side of the original location.

Alternate Method You can move or copy an element parallel by keying in the command at the uSTN> prompt. To move an element parallel, key-in **move parallel distance** (or **mov p**) and press ⏎. To move an element parallel by key-in distance, key-in **move parallel keyin** (or **mov p v**) and press ⏎. To copy an element parallel, key-in **copy parallel distance** (or **copy p**) and press ⏎. To copy an element parallel by key-in distance, key-in **copy parallel keyin** (or **cop k**) and press ⏎.

OFFSET ELEMENT

The Offset Element command lets you copy or move elements to make them parallel to one another. This command also lets you define the corner type of strings, curves, and shapes. The Offset command is similar to Move Parallel and Copy Parallel commands, except that Offset command is a one time command. Once the element is offset, you must identify the element all over again to offset. And the Offset command manipulates the B-Spline curve itself, rather than the control polygon.

To Offset an element parallel to its original location, invoke the Offset command by clicking the Offset command from the Manipulate Element sub-palette or key-in at uSTN> field, **construct curve offset** and press ⏎. MicroStation prompts:

> *Identify element* (Identify an element to offset.)
> *Locate Corresponding point (key-in/Data)* (Reposition the element to its new location by provid-
>   ing data point or key-in coordinates.)
> *Identify element* (Identify same/another element or invoke another command.)

You can also offset an element parallel to its original location by keying in the distance. To do so, click the Offset command icon in the Manipulate Element sub-palette and turn ON the toggle button for Distance in the sub-palette. Key-in the parallel distance in MU:SU:PU in the Distance edit field and press ⏎ or ⭾. The prompts are similar to Offset command, and can offset the element to either side of the original distance.

Instead of moving the original element parallel, you can make a copy and then move the copy parallel to the original location of the element. To do so, click the Offset command icon in the Manipulate Element sub-palette and turn ON the toggle button for Make Copy. The prompts are similar to Offset command, and you can place the copy of the element parallel to either side of the original location.

The Cusp option menu controls the vertices condition on line strings, curves, complex elements, and shapes. The options are:

Round—makes the radius a function of the offset distance. The Tolerance must be set to a non-zero value with this option.

Corner—results in no modification of the basic corner geometry.

Scale Original and Copy

The Scale command lets you increase or decrease the size of an existing element. If necessary, you can have a different scale factor for the X and Y axes. To enlarge an element, enter a scale factor greater than 1. For instance, a scale factor of 3 makes the selected element three times larger. To shrink an element, use a scale factor between 0 and 1. Do not give a negative scale factor. For instance, a scale factor of 0.75 shrinks the selected element to three-quarters of its current size.

MicroStation provides three methods for setting the active scale factor:

- Invoke the Active Scale settings box from the Settings pull-down menu. The Active Scale settings box displayed is similar to the one shown in Figure 3–42. Enter scale factors in the X Scale and Y Scale edit fields respectively. There is a small lock symbol to the right of the X Scale and Y Scale edit field. If you want your scale factor for X and Y axes to be equal, click on the lock symbol to close the lock. When the lock is closed you can key-in a value in either of the edit fields and the other field is automatically set equal to what you key-in. If the lock is open, you can set separately the scale factors for the X and Y axes. You can also set the scale factor by clicking the 1.0, Halve, or Double buttons.

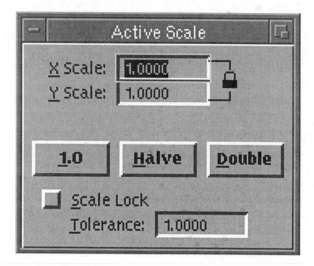

FIGURE 3–42 Active Scale Settings box.

- Set the active scale factor by key-in at the uSTN> field. This is done by keying in **AS=<scale factor>**. The <scale factor> can be any value greater than zero. The **AS** key-in sets scale equally for both the X and Y axes. If you need to set different scale factors for X and Y axes, key-in **XS=<scale factor>** for the X axis and **YS=<scale factor>** for the Y axes.

- Set the active scale factor in the edit field provided in the Manipulate sub-palette. To do so, click the Scale Element icon, and MicroStation displays two edit fields in the sub-palette for the X and Y scale factors respectively. Key-in the appropriate scale factors in the edit fields.

To scale an element, invoke the Scale Element command by clicking the Scale Element icon from the Manipulate Element sub-palette (see Figure 3–43). MicroStation prompts:

> *Identify element* (Identify the element to scale.)
> *Accept/Reject (Select next input)* (Click the data point or key-in coordinates to place the scaled element.)
> *Accept/Reject (Select next input)* (If necessary, scale it again by providing a data point or key-in coordinates, and/or click Reset button to terminate the command sequence.)

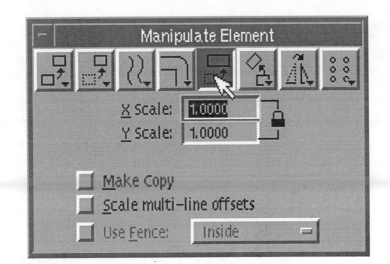

FIGURE 3–43 Invoking the Scale Element command from the Manipulate Element sub-palette.

The following command sequence shows an example of using the Scale Element command to scale a circle to half its present size (see Figure 3–44).

> *Identify element* (Identify the circle by tentative snapping to the center of the circle and accept.)
> *Accept/Reject (Select next input)* (Tentative snap to the center of the circle and accept.)
> *Accept/Reject (Select next input)* (Click the Reset button.)

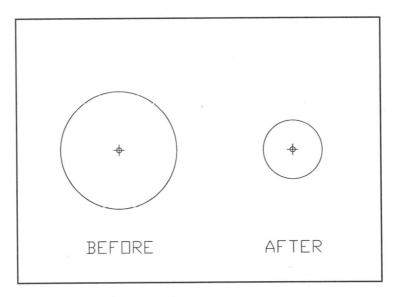

FIGURE 3–44 An example of Scaling an element by Scale Element command.

Instead of scaling the original element, you can make a copy and then scale the copy. To do so, click the Scale Element icon in the manipulate sub-palette and turn ON the toggle button for Make Copy. The prompts are similar to Scale Element command, and you can move the copy of the scaled element to another location.

Alternate Method You can scale original/copy of an element by keying in the command at the uSTN> prompt. To scale an original element, key-in **scale original** (or **sc**) and press [ENTER]. To scale a copy of an element, key-in **scale copy** (or **sc c**) and press [ENTER].

Spin Original and Copy

The Spin command changes the orientation of an existing element by rotating it graphically about a specified pivot point. Design changes often require that an element be rotated.

To change the orientation of an element, invoke the Spin command by clicking the Spin Element icon from the Manipulate Elements sub-palette (see Figure 3–45). MicroStation prompts:

Identify element (Identify the element; see Figure 3–46 data point P1.)
Accept (define pivot point)/Reject (Place a data point about which the element will be rotated; see Figure 3–46 data point P2.)
Rotation angle (Place a data point to define the angle of rotation; see Figure 3–46 data point P3.)
Rotation angle (If necessary, rotate it again by providing data point and/or click Reset button to terminate the command sequence.)

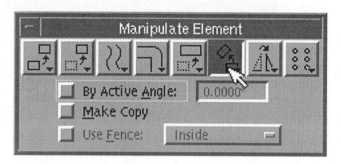

FIGURE 3–45   Invoking the Spin Element command from the Manipulate Element sub-palette.

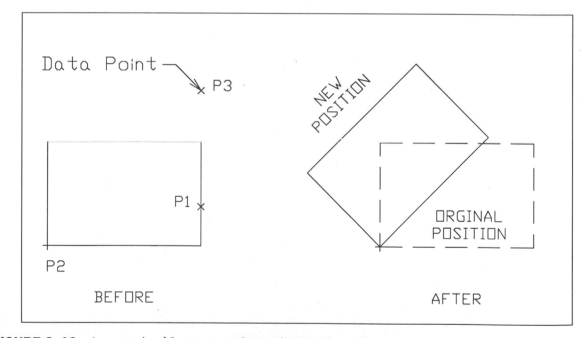

FIGURE 3–46   An example of Spinning an element by Spin Element command.

> **NOTE:** The actual "angle" of rotation is calculated by the angle between the point you used to select the element, the pivot point, and the third data point.

You can also change the orientation of an existing element by specifying the rotation angle (active angle) instead of graphically spinning the element. MicroStation provides three alternative methods by which you can set the active angle.

■ Invoke the Active Angle settings box from the Settings pull-down menu. The Active Angle settings box is displayed similar to the one shown in Figure 3–47. The Active Angle settings box gives you a variety of ways to set the active angle. The conventional way is to key-in the angle in edit field provided in the settings box. An alternative method is to hold and drag the "clock face" pointer dial with the Data button and drag to any angle position. The angle is measured in the counterclockwise direction from the horizontal location (3 o'clock) to the selected point. The Angle Lock and Angle roundoff field allow you to limit the change in degrees to the roundoff value. For example, if the lock is ON and the roundoff value is set to 10, dragging the pointer changes the active angle in 10-degree increments.

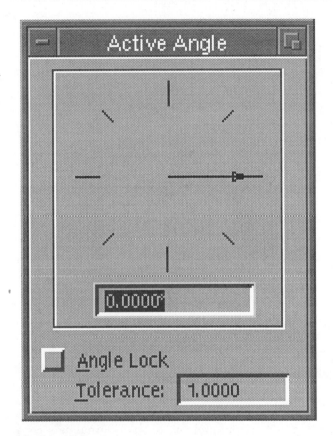

FIGURE 3–47 Active Angle Settings box.

■ Set the active angle by key-in at the uSTN> field by keying in **AA=<rotatation angle>**. The <rotation angle> can be any value between 0 and 360 degrees in both the positive (counterclockwise) and negative (counterclockwise) direction.

■ Set the active angle in the edit field provided in the Manipulate sub-palette. To do so, click Spin Element icon, turn on the toggle button By Active Angle, key-in the rotation angle in the By Active Angle edit field, and press ⟨ENTER⟩ or ⟨TAB⟩.

To rotate an element, invoke the Spin command by clicking the Spin Element icon from the Manipulate Element sub-palette, turn ON the toggle button for Active Angle. MicroStation prompts:

Identify element (Identify the element.)

Accept/Reject (Select next input) (Click the data point or key-in coordinates to place the rotated element.)

Accept/Reject (Select next input) (If necessary, rotate it again providing a data point or key-in coordinates and/or click Reset button to terminate the command sequence.)

Instead of spinning/rotating the original element, you can make a copy and spin or rotate the copy. To do so, click the Spin Element icon in the manipulate sub-palette and turn ON the toggle button for Make Copy. The prompts are similar to Spin/Rotate Element command, and you can move the copy of the spin or rotated element to another location.

See Figure 3–48 for an example in rotating and copying an element.

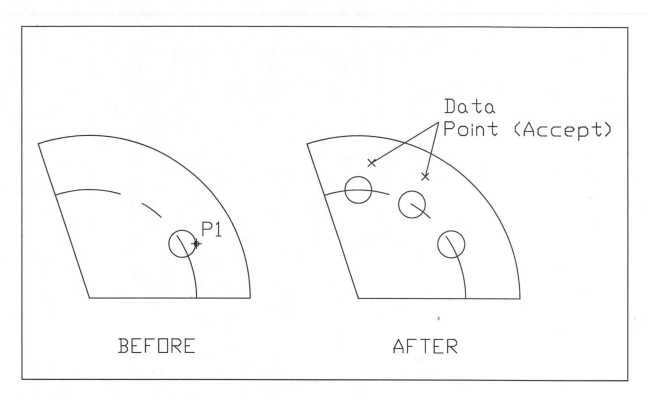

FIGURE 3–48 An example of Rotating and Copying an element.

Alternate Method You can spin and rotate the original or a copy of an element by keying in the command at the uSTN> prompt. To spin an original element, key-in **spin original** (or **sp**) and press [ENTER]. To spin a copy of an element, key-in **spin copy** (or **sp c**) and press [ENTER]. To rotate an original element, key-in **rotate original** (or **ro**) and press [ENTER]. To rotate a copy of an element, key-in **rotate copy** (or **ro c**) and press [ENTER].

Mirror Original and Copy

The Mirror command is used to create a mirror image (backward) of an element. MicroStation provides three different methods by which you can mirror an element. Two of the methods are along the X and Y axes, and the third method is along a defined line (see Figure 3–49).

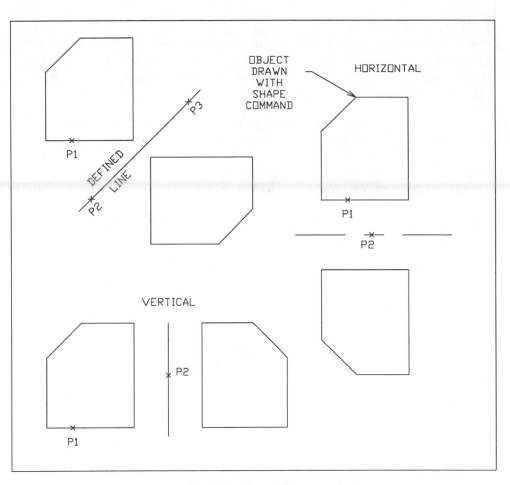

FIGURE 3–49   Examples of mirroring an element by three different methods.

To place a mirror image of an element, invoke the Mirror Element command by clicking the Mirror Element icon from the Manipulate Element sub-palette. Select one of the three methods (Vertical Horizontal, or Line) from the Mirror About option menu located in the Manipulate sub-palette (see Figure 3–50). MicroStation prompts:

Identify element (Identify the element to mirror.)
Accept/Reject (Select next input) (Click the data point or key-in coordinates to place the mirror image of the element.)
Accept/Reject (Select next input) (If necessary, mirror it again by providing a data point or key-in coordinates, or click Reset button to terminate the command sequence.)

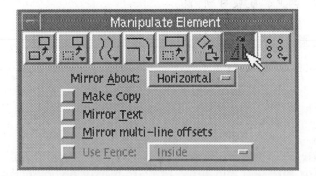

FIGURE 3–50   Invoking the Mirror Element command from the Manipulate Element sub-palette.

Instead of mirroring the original element, you can make a copy and then mirror the copy. To do so, click the Mirror Element icon in the manipulate sub-palette and turn ON the toggle button for Make Copy. The prompts are similar to Mirror Element command, and you can move the copy of the Mirrored element to another location. To mirror the text element, make sure the toggle button is set to ON for Mirror Text.

The following command sequence shows an example of using the Mirror Element command when the Mirror About Line is selected (see Figure 3–51).

Identify element (Identify the shape; see Figure 3–51 data point P1.)
Enter 1st point on mirrorline (or Reject) (Place a data point as shown in Figure 3–51 data point P2.)
Enter 2nd point on mirrorline (Place a data point as shown in Figure 3–51 data point P3.)
Enter 2nd point on mirrorline (Click the Reset button.)

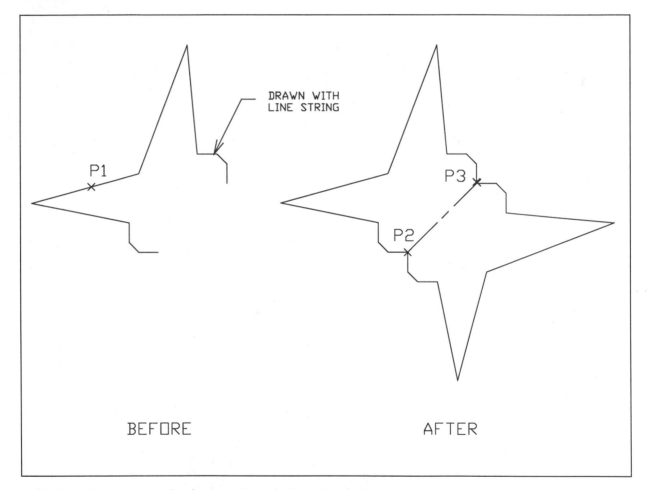

FIGURE 3–51 An example of mirroring an element when the Mirror About Line method is selected.

Alternate Method You can Mirror original/copy of an element by keying in the command at the uSTN> prompt. To Mirror an original element along an X axis, key-in **mirror original horizontal** (or **mir**) and press ⏎. To Mirror an original element along a y axis, key-in **mirror original vertical** (or **mir o v**)and press ⏎. To Mirror an original element along a line, key-in **mirror original line** (or **mir o l**) and press ⏎. To Mirror a copy of an element along an X axis, key-in **mirror copy horizontal** (or **mir c**) and press ⏎. To Mirror a copy of an element along a Y axis, key-in **mirror copy vertical** (or **mir c v**) and press ⏎. To Mirror a copy of an element along a line, key-in **mirror copy line** (or **mir c l**) and press ⏎.

Array

The Array command is used to make multiple copies of a selected element in either rectangular or polar arrays. In a rectangular array, place copies in rows and columns by specifying the number of rows, the number of columns, and the spacing between rows and columns (row and column spacing may differ). The whole rectangular array can be rotated to a selected angle. In the polar array, place copies in a circular fashion by specifying the number of copies, the angle between two adjacent copies (delta angle), and whether or not the element will be rotated as it is copied.

To make multiple copies of an element, invoke the command by clicking the Construct Array icon from the Manipulate sub-palette (see Figure 3–52), and select one of the two Array types from the Array Type option menu.

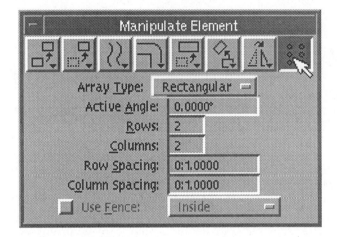

FIGURE 3–52   Invoking the Construct Array Element command from the Manipulate Element sub-palette.

Rectangular Array The rectangular array places copies in rows and columns. Key-in the number of rows and columns in the Rows and Columns edit fields in the Manipulate sub-palette respectively. In addition, you have to specify the distance between the rows and columns in MU:SU:PU. This is done by keying in the Row Spacing and Column Spacing edit fields respectively. If you need to rotate the rectangular array, key-in the active angle in the Active Angle edit field. Once you set all the necessary parameters, MicroStation prompts:

Identify element (Identify the element.)
Accept/Reject (Select next input) (Click the Accept button to place copies or the Reject button to disregard the selection.)

> **NOTE:** Any combination of a whole number of rows and columns may be entered (except both 1 row and 1 column, which would not create any copies). MicroStation includes the original element in the number you enter. A positive distance for the column and row spacing causes the elements to array toward the right and upward. A negative distance for the column and row spacing causes the elements to array toward the left and downward.

The following command sequence shows an example of using the Construct Array command to place rectangular array when the number of rows and columns are set to 6 and 8 respectively, row distance to 1.5 Major Units and column distance to 2.75 Major units (see Figure 3–53).

Identify element (Identify the shape.)
Accept/Reject (Select next input) (Click the Accept button to place the copies.)

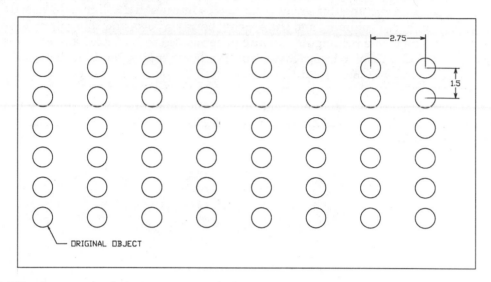

FIGURE 3–53 An example of placing a rectangular array.

Polar Array The polar array places copies in a circular fashion. Key-in the number of items in the Items edit field in the Manipulate sub-palette, and specify the angle between adjacent items in the Delta Angle edit field. To rotate the elements as they are copied, toggle the Rotate button to ON. Figure 3–54 shows the difference between rotating and not rotating the elements as they are copied. Once you set all the necessary parameters, MicroStation prompts:

Identify element (Identify the element.)
Accept, select center/Reject (Specify the center point of the array by Data button or key-in coordinates, or click Reject button to disregard the selection.)

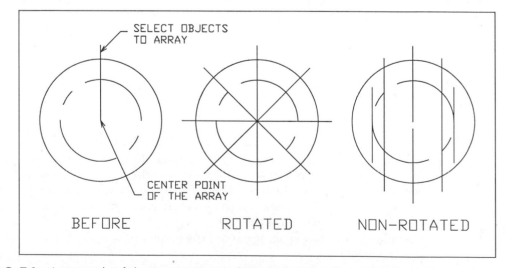

FIGURE 3–54 An example of showing rotating and not rotating the elements as they are copied.

> **NOTE:** Key-in a whole number for the number of items to be copied, and MicroStation includes the original element in the number of array items. In other words, if you request 7 items, your array will consist of the original element and 6 copies.

The following command sequence shows an example (see Figure 3–55) of using the Construct Array command to place a polar array when the number of items is set to 8 and the delta angle to 45 degrees. MicroStation prompts:

Identify element (Identify the shape.)
Accept, select center/Reject (Place a tentative point at the center of the circle and accept it.)

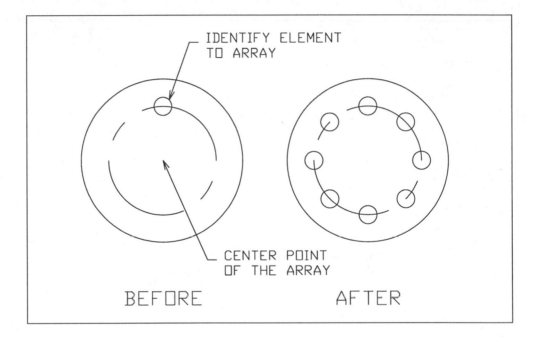

FIGURE 3–55 An example of placing a polar array.

ELEMENT ATTRIBUTES

There are four important attributes associated with placement of elements. The attributes includes level, color, weight, and line code.

Levels

MicroStation offers a way to group elements on levels in a manner similar to a designer drawing different parts of a design on separate transparent sheets. By stacking the transparent sheets one on top of another, the designer can see the complete drawing, but can only draw on the top sheet. If the designer only wants to show a customer part of the design, he or she can remove from the stack the sheets that contain the parts of the design the customer does not need to see.

MicroStation provides the same functionality as the transparent sheets by providing you with 63 levels in each design file. For example, an architectural design in MicroStation might have the walls on one level, the dimensions on another level, electrical information on still another level, and so on.

Separating parts of the design by level allows designers to turn on only the part they need to work on and plot parts of the design separately.

You can only draw on one level at a time (the active level), and you can turn ON or OFF the display of levels in selected views. Elements on levels that are not displayed disappear from the view, but they are still in the design file. The same coordinate system and zoom factors apply to all levels. Levels are identified by numbers (1 through 63), and the message field in the Command Window displays the number of the active level with LV=<level number> (see Figure 3–56).

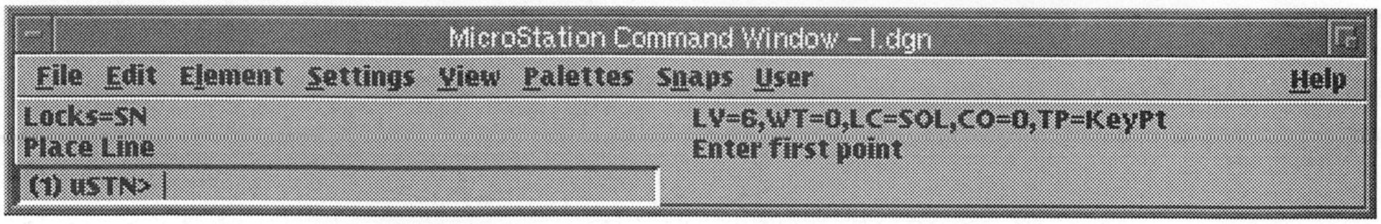

MicroStation Command Window – l.dgn	
File Edit Element Settings View Palettes Snaps User	Help
Locks=SN	LV=6,WT=0,LC=SOL,CO=0,TP=KeyPt
Place Line	Enter first point
(1) uSTN>	

FIGURE 3–56 MicroStation Command Window.

When you manipulate an element, the resulting manipulation takes place on the same level the element was placed on. For instance, a copy of an element goes on the same level as the original element, regardless of what level is currently active. The Change Element Attributes command moves elements to different levels (discussed later).

Controlling the Levels The View Levels Settings Box allows you to set the active level and turn level display ON and OFF. To open the View Levels settings box, pull down the View menu in the MicroStation Command Window and select the Levels option (see Figure 3–57), or key-in the

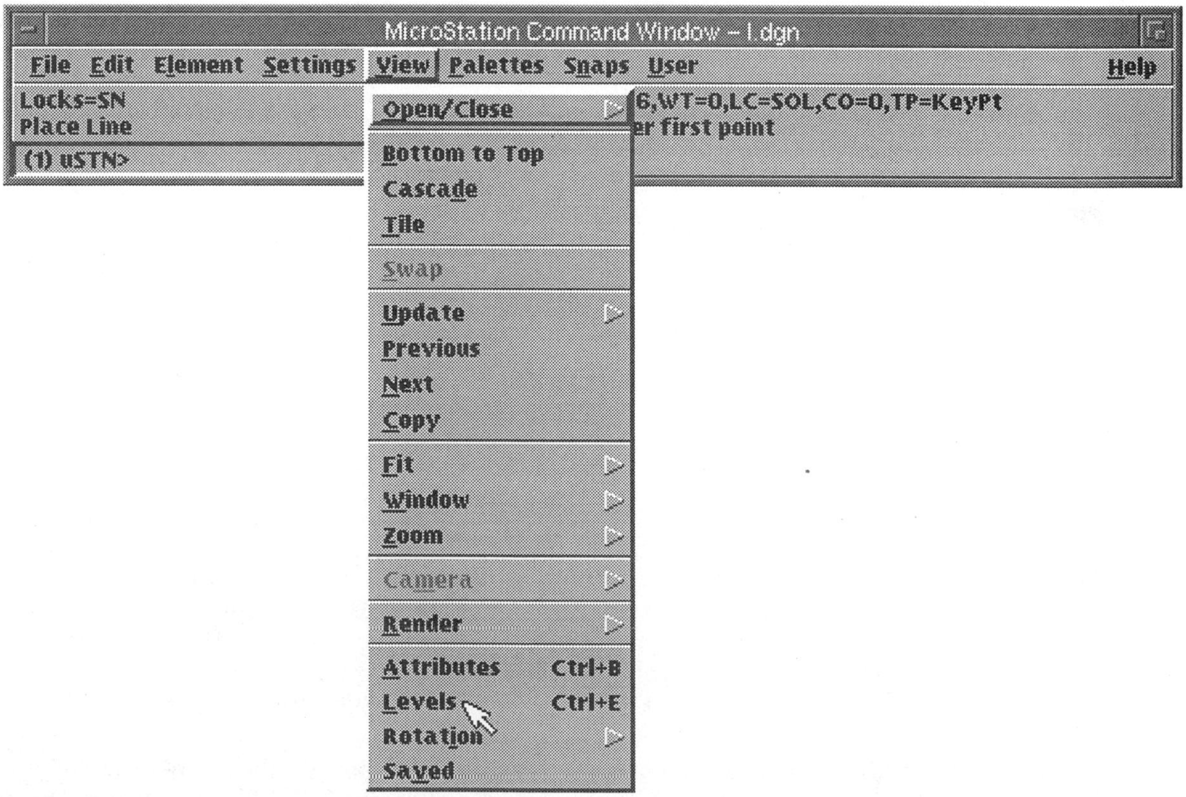

MicroStation Command Window – l.dgn	
File Edit Element Settings View Palettes Snaps User	Help
Locks=SN	6,WT=0,LC=SOL,CO=0,TP=KeyPt
Place Line	er first point
(1) uSTN>	

Open/Close ▷
Bottom to Top
Cascade
Tile
Swap
Update ▷
Previous
Next
Copy
Fit ▷
Window ▷
Zoom ▷
Camera ▷
Render ▷
Attributes   Ctrl+B
Levels   Ctrl+E
Rotation ▷
Saved

FIGURE 3–57 Invoking the Levels Settings box from the View pull-down menu of the MicroStation Command Window.

uSTN> field **selector level** and press ⌨. MicroStation displays a View Levels settings box similar to the Figure 3–58.

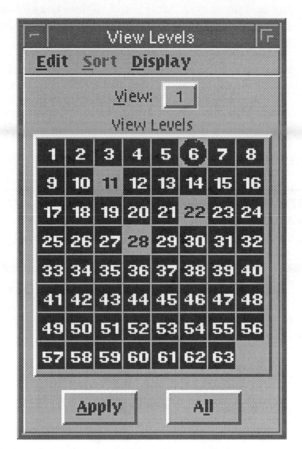

FIGURE 3–58   View Levels Settings box.

The settings box shows the number of each of the 63 total levels. The display of level numbers with a black background is turned ON, and the display of level numbers with a gray background is turned OFF. The View Number options menu at the top of the settings box displays the number of the view the level display settings apply to. The View Number menu also allows you to change the number of the view displayed in the settings box (see Chapter 4 for a discussion on View setting).

The level number with a black circle around it is the current active level (the level all new elements are placed on). The active level applies to all views.

To change the active level, double-click the level number you want to make it active. Click once on a level number to toggle its display status between ON and OFF. To change the display status of a group of level numbers, drag the screen cursor across them while holding down the Data button on your pointing device.

NOTE: Display of the active level cannot be turned OFF.

The Apply button applies the current level display settings (ON or OFF) to the selected view and applies the active level to all views. The All button applies the current level display settings (ON or OFF) and the active level to all views.

Alternate Method You can turn ON and OFF the display of levels, and set the active level using key-ins. To turn OFF levels, key-in **of=** <level numbers> and press ⏎. To turn ON levels, key-in **on=** <level numbers> and press ⏎. After you complete the key-in, click the Data button somewhere in the view where you want the level display changed. For each key-in, replace <level numbers> with the level number, or numbers you want to turn OFF or ON.

For example, key-in **of=**3–6,8,23–29,45, press ⏎, then select a view. In the selected view, MicroStation turns off levels 3 through 6, level 8, levels 23 through 29, and level 45.

To set the active level, key-in **lv=** <level number> and press ⏎. Replace <level number> with the number of the level you want to make it active.

For example, key-in **lv=**10 and press ⏎. All elements drawn after this key-in are placed on level 10.

> **NOTE:** The active level and the level display settings for each view remain in effect until you change them or exit from MicroStation. To keep them in effect for the next editing session, select Save Settings from the File pull-down menu.

Keeping Up With the Levels Keeping up with what level everything is on can be confusing. To help overcome the confusion, MicroStation provides a level symbology table. Use the table to specify unique combinations of display color, weight, and style for each level. When level symbology is turned ON, all elements display using the symbology assigned to the level the elements are placed on, rather than their true symbology. Chapter 10 describes the level symbology table in detail. In addition, MicroStation allows you to assign a name to a level. For detailed explanation, see Chapter 11 on customizing MicroStation.

Element Color

The color for an element is very helpful in enabling you to differentiate between the many elements on your design, especially when all the levels are displayed at one time. Before you place an element with a specific color, you have to select the active color. To do so, select the Color command from the Element pull-down menu. MicroStation displays a color palette with 256 colors or shades of colors as shown in Figure 3–59. The actual colors shown depend on your monitor, graphics card, and what colors are defined in MicroStation's color table. Click on a color in the color palette to make it the active color. MicroStation displays in the message field of the MicroStation Command Window the current active color with **CO=** <color number>.

If you are using the default color table, MicroStation displays the name of the color for the first seven colors. Those colors and their numbers are:

COLOR:	NUMBERS:
White	0
Blue	1
Green	2
Red	3
Yellow	4
Violet	5
Orange	6

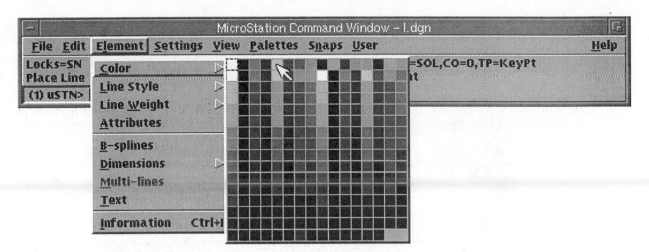

FIGURE 3-59   Color palette displayed when Color command is selected from the Element pull-down menu of the MicroStation Command Window.

Alternate Method You can set the active color by keying in the command at the uSTN> field. To do so, key-in **co=** <color name or number> and press ⏎. If you want one of the first seven colors, key-in the name of the color or the color number. If you want any other color, you must key-in the color number. The color number can be anywhere from 0 to 255.

> **NOTE:** Setting up the active color does not affect elements that are already in the design plane, unless the Change Element Attributes command (explained later in this chapter) is used.

To keep the active color in effect for future editing sessions for the current design file, select Save Settings from the File pull-down menu.

Element Line Style

Similar to color, MicroStation allows you to place elements with a specific line style (or line type). By default, MicroStation provides you with eight line styles (called internal line styles) as shown in Figure 3-60. In addition, MicroStation comes with numerous custom-made line styles. If necessary, you can change the custom-made line styles, or add new ones. A detailed explanation for creating and modifying the custom-made line styles is explained in Chapter 11.

Before you place an element with a specific line style, you have to make that line style an active line style. To do so, select the Line Style command from the Element pull-down menu, and MicroStation displays eight available line styles. Click on the picture of the line style to declare it the active line style. MicroStation displays in the message field of the MicroStation Command Window the current active line style with **LC=**<name of the line style>.

If you need to use one of the custom line styles, select Edit from the Line Style sub-menu, and MicroStation displays Line Style Settings box as shown in Figure 3-61. Select one of the available line styles from the list.

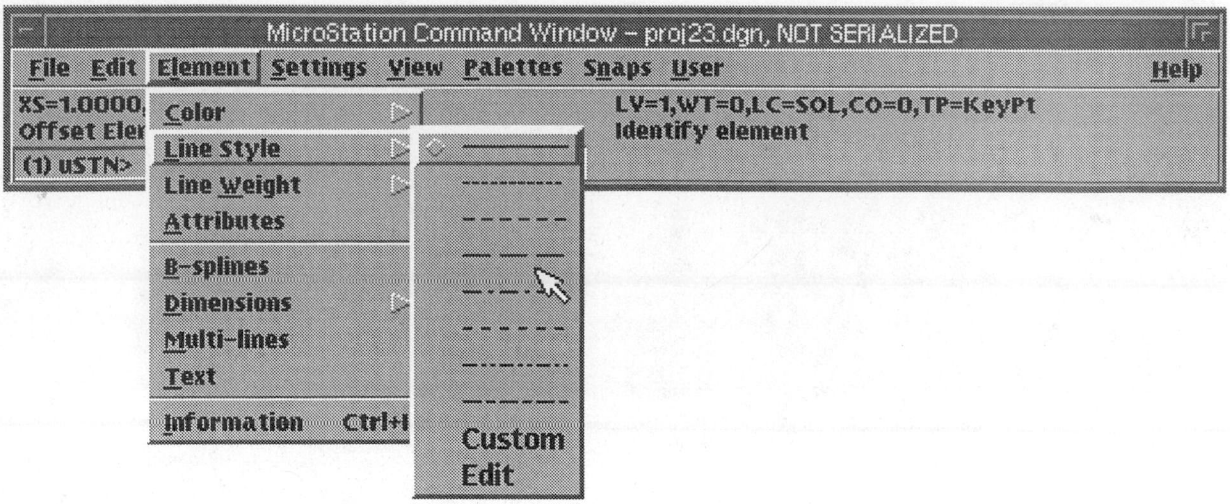

FIGURE 3–60   Listing of the available standard Line style.

Alternate Method You can set the active line style by keying in the command at the uSTN> field. To do so, key-in **lc=**<line style name or number> and press ENTER.

> **NOTE:** Selecting a new active line style does not affect elements that already exist in the design plane, unless the Change Element Attributes command (explained later in the chapter) is used.

To keep the active line style in effect for future editing sessions for the current design file, select Save Settings from the File pull-down menu.

Element Weight

In MicroStation Weight refers to the width of the element. There are 32 line weights (numbered from 0 to 31) to choose from, which is comparable to 32 different technical pens.

FIGURE 3–61   Listing of the customized line style.

In drafting, the color, style, and even the weight (width) of the lines used to create elements in the design contribute to the "readability" or understanding of the design. For example, in a piping arrangement drawing the line weight (width) used to place the pipe is the widest of all lines on the drawing to make the pipe stand out from the equipment, foundations, and supports.

Before you place an element with a specific weight, set that weight as an active line weight. To do so, select the Line Weight command from the Element pull-down menu, and MicroStation displays 16 (0 to 15) available line weights as shown in Figure 3–62. Select one of the available 16 line weights. Use the key-in command (described later) to set the active line weight to a value greater than 15. MicroStation displays the current active weight in the message field of the MicroStation Command Window with **WT=<weight number>**.

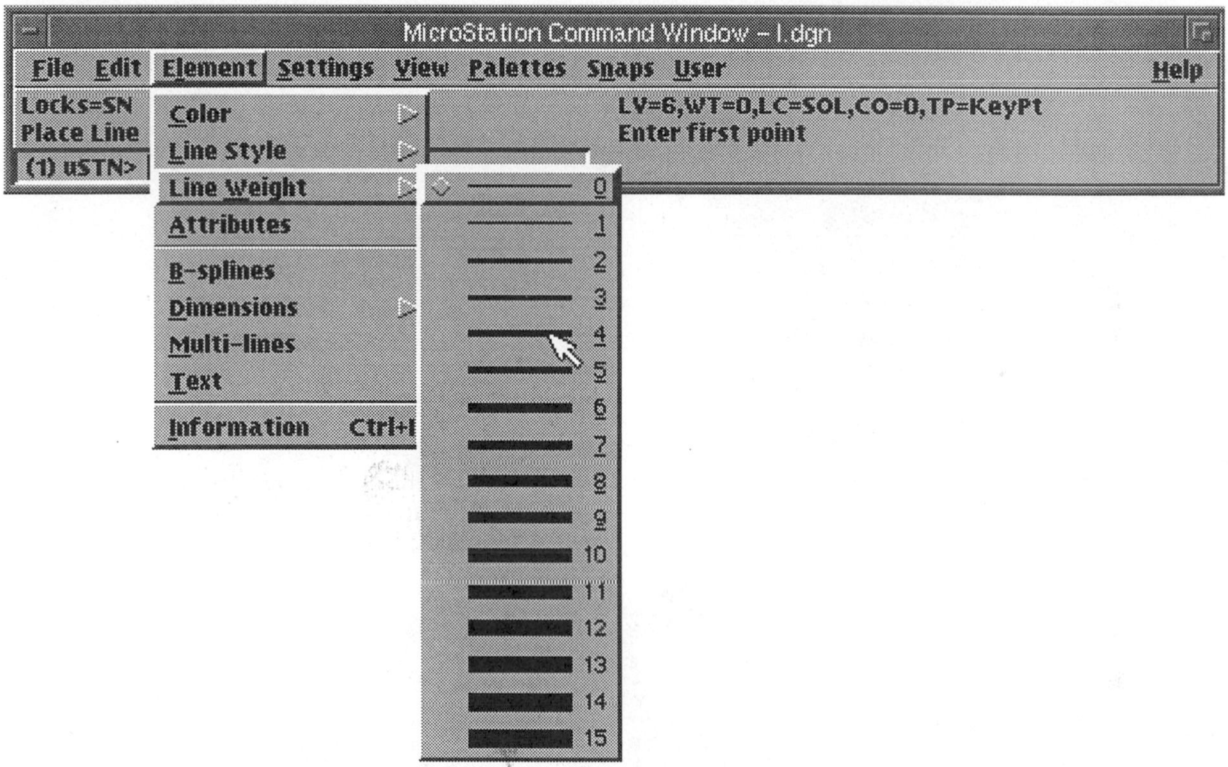

FIGURE 3–62   Listing of the available line weights from the pull-down menu.

Alternate Method   You can set the active line weight by keying in the command at the uSTN> field. To do so, key-in **wt=<line weight number>** and press [ENTER].

> **NOTE:** Setting up the active line weight does not affect elements that already exist on the design plane, unless the Change Element Attributes command (explained later in the chapter) is used.

To keep the active line weight in effect for future editing sessions for the current design file, select Save Settings from the File pull-down menu.

Element Attribute Settings Box

The Element Attributes settings box lets you control the attributes of elements, such as level, color, line style, and line weight. Instead of using four different commands (level, color, line style, and line weight) to set up the attributes, use the Element Attributes setting box to do the same in one place. If you need to change the element parameters often, using the settings box is faster than using the individual options from the Element pull-down menu.

Invoke the Element Attributes settings box by selecting Attributes from the Element pull-down menu in the MicroStation Command Window, as shown in Figure 3–63. The Element Attributes settings box similar to the one shown in Figure 3–64, is displayed.

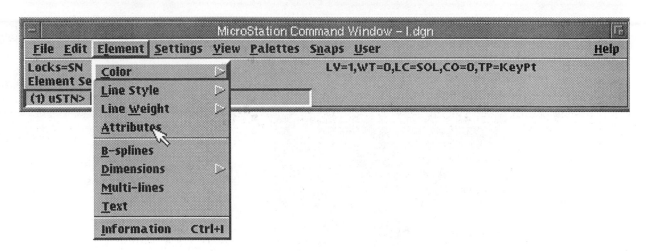

FIGURE 3–63 Invoking the Element Attributes Settings box from the Element pull-down menu.

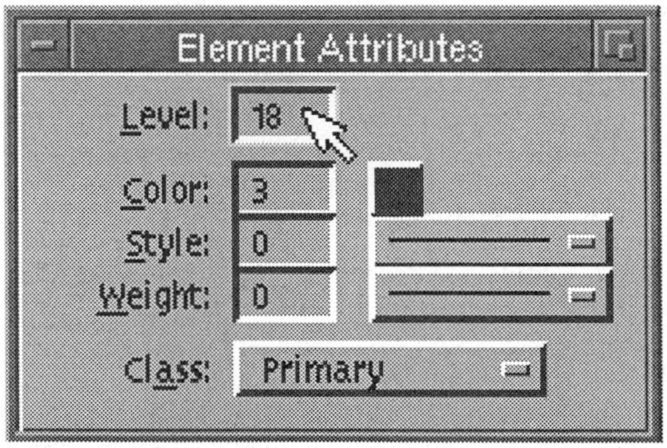

FIGURE 3–64 Element Attributes Settings box.

The Level edit field allows you to set the active level by keying in the level number and press [ENTER] or [TAB].

The Color edit field allows you to set the current active color by keying in a numerical value in the Color edit field and pressing [ENTER], or by choosing a color, without regard for numerical values, from the color palette. To open the color palette, which represents the active color table, click the colored button located next to the Color edit field and select the appropriate color from the palette.

The Style edit field allows you to set the current active line style by keying in a numerical value in the Style edit field and pressing [ENTER], or by choosing a line style, without regard for numerical values, from the option menu located next to the Style edit field.

The Weight edit field allows you to set the current active line weight by keying in a numerical value in the Weight edit field and pressing [ENTER], or by choosing a line weight, without regard for numerical values, from the option menu located next to the Weight edit field.

The Class option menu specifies the class of an element upon placement. Two options are available, Primary and Construction. Primary (default option) elements are the elements that comprise the design. Construction elements are placed in the design plane, then used as an aid to placing the primary elements. You create geometric constructions with fundamental entities such as lines, circles, and arcs to generate intersections, endpoints, centers, points of tangency, midpoints, and other useful data that might take a manual drafter considerable time to calculate or hand-measure on the board. From these you can create primary elements using intersections or other data generated from the construction elements. When the design is complete, display of the construction elements can be turned OFF from the View Attributes settings box (see Chapter 4).

> **NOTE:** If construction elements are displayed in a plotted view, they also plot. Turn them OFF before creating a plot of the finished drawing.

Changing Element Attributes—Change Symbology

The Change Element Attribute command is used to change an element to the active element attributes (level, color, line style, line weight, and class). To change an attribute of an existing element, invoke the Change Element Attribute command by clicking the Change Element Attribute icon from the Change sub-palette (see Figure 3–65). Then change one or more of the attributes by keying in the edit field provided in the sub-palette (or from one of the attribute options in the Element pull-down menu). MicroStation prompts:

Identify element (Identify the element.)
Accept/Reject (Select next input) (Click the Data button and, if desired, identify another element
    to change the attributes.)

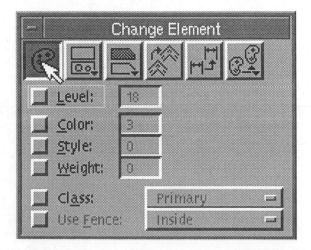

FIGURE 3–65 Invoking the Change Element Attribute command from the Change sub-palette.

Match Element Attributes

In addition to being able to change the attributes of an element to the active settings, the Match Element Attributes command allows you to change the active attributes (level, color, style, and weight) to those that were in effect when an existing element was created. The command provides a quick way to return to placing elements with the same attributes as elements you placed earlier in the design.

The Match Element Attribute command is available in the Match palette that can be opened from the Palettes pull-down menu in the Command Window (see Figure 3–66). Click the Match Element command icon in the Match palette (see Figure 3–67). MicroStation prompts:

> *Select element* (Identify the element whose attributes you want to match.)
> *Accept/Reject (Select next input)* (Click the data button a second time to initiate setting the active attributes to the selected element, or click the Reset button to reject the element.)

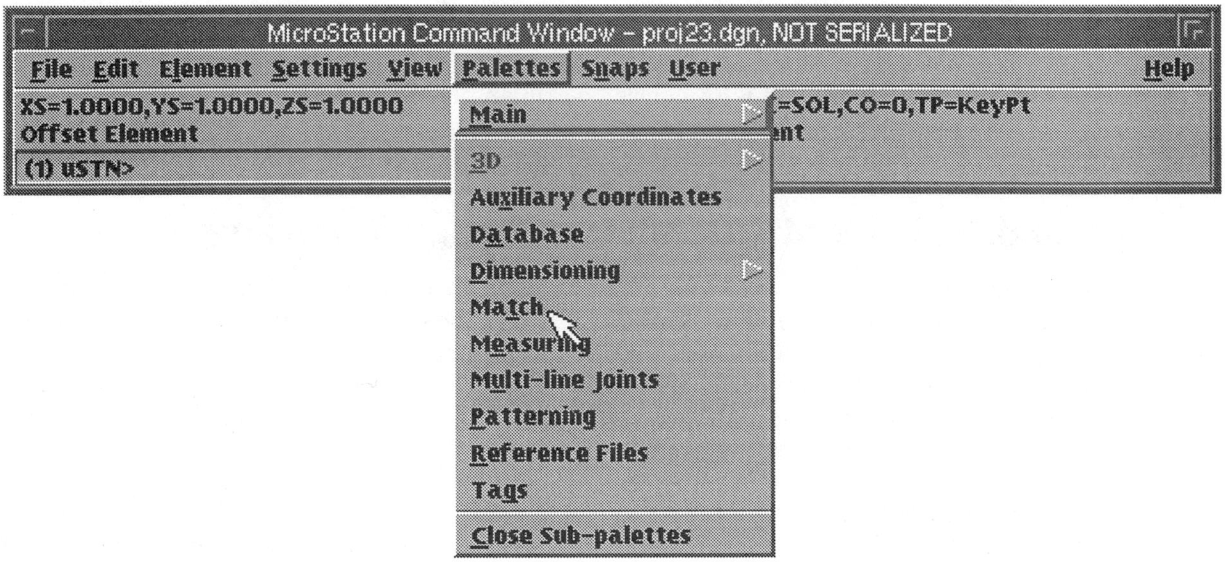

FIGURE 3–66 Invoking the Match palette from the Palettes pull-down menu.

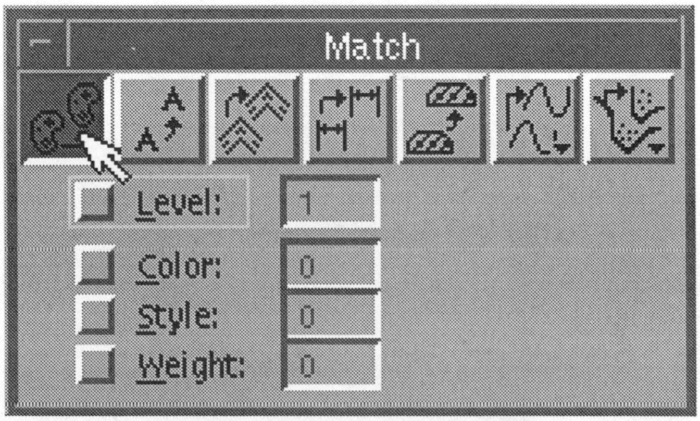

FIGURE 3–67 Invoking the Match Element command from the Match palette.

After the second data point, the active settings match those of the selected element. The settings are displayed in fields in the Match palette (see Figure 3–67). If you want to override any of the matched attributes, change them in these fields.

TENTATIVE SNAPPING

In Chapter 2 you were introduced to Tentative Snapping and 3 of the 14 snap modes. In this chapter, 5 additional snap modes are explained.

Center Mode Snap causes tentative points to snap to the center of the space in the design occupied by an element (such as circle, block, and arc); see Figure 3–68.

Intersection Mode Snap causes tentative points to snap to the intersection of two elements. To find the intersection, snap to one of the intersecting elements. One or both of the elements may

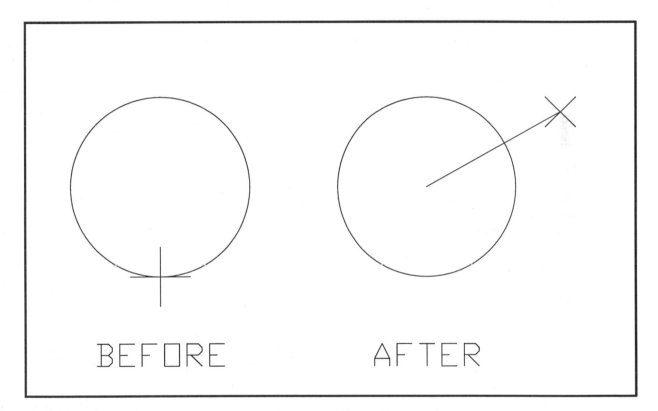

FIGURE 3–68   An example for snapping to the center of the circle.

appear dashed while they are highlighted, but they return to normal appearance when you complete the command.

If the elements do not actually intersect, the tentative cross appears at the intersection of an imaginary extension of the two elements. If the two elements cannot be extended to an intersection, the message "Elements do not intersect" appears in the Error field of the Command Window, and a tentative cross is not placed (see Figure 3–69).

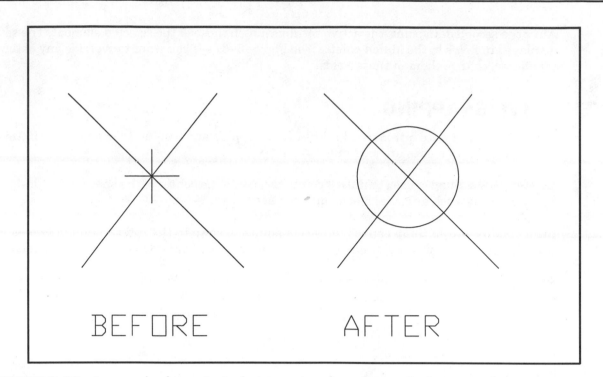

FIGURE 3–69   An example of snapping to the intersection of two elements in placing a circle.

Through Point Mode Snap causes tentative points to define a point on an existing element through which the element you are placing must pass. If you are placing a line or line string, the next data point accepts only the through-point tentative snap. The data point after the tentative snap is the end point of the line or line string. For all other element types, the acceptance point is one of the element placement points (see Figure 3–70).

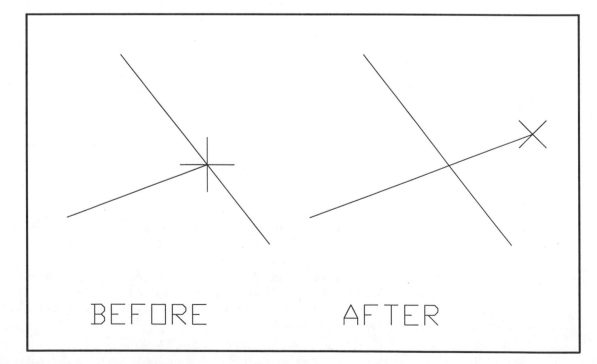

FIGURE 3–70   An example of snapping to a through point.

Tangent Snap Mode forces the element you are creating to be tangent to a non-linear element (such as a circle, ellipse, or arc). The actual point of tangency varies, depending on how you place the element (see Figure 3–71).

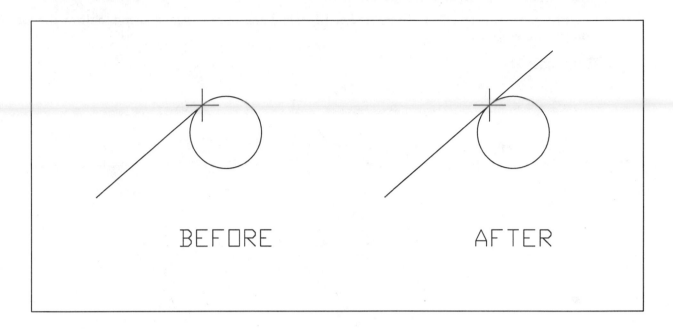

BEFORE   AFTER

FIGURE 3–71   An example of snapping to a tangent point.

Tangent Point Snap Mode forces the element you are placing to be tangent to an existing non-linear element (such as a circle, ellipse, or arc) at the point where you placed the tentative point (see Figure 3–72).

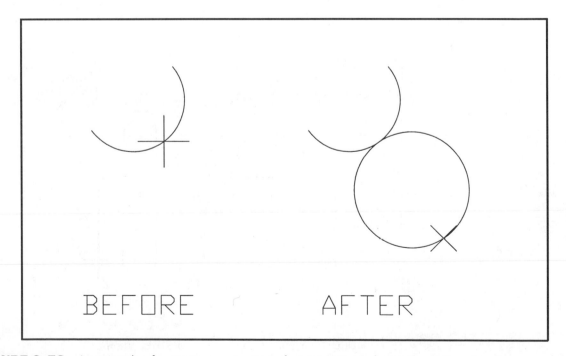

BEFORE   AFTER

FIGURE 3–72   An example of snapping to a tangent of an existing non-linear element.

EXERCISES

Exercises 3–6 through 3–12

Use Precision Key-ins (XY= , DL= , and/or DI=) and appropriate grid spacing to draw the figures. Add the dimensions.

Exercise 3–6

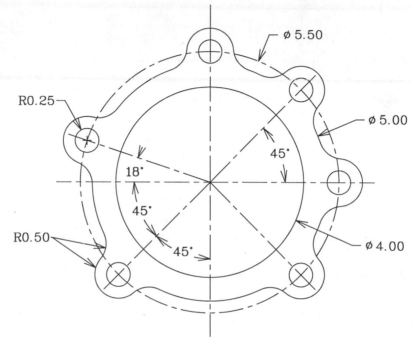

Exercise 3–7

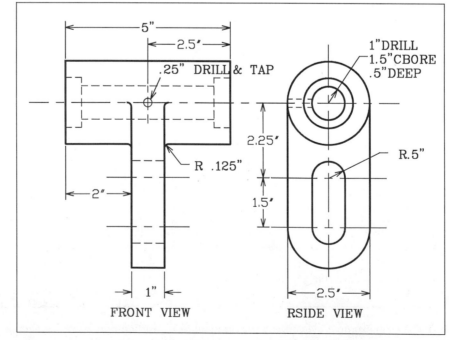

Exercise 3–8

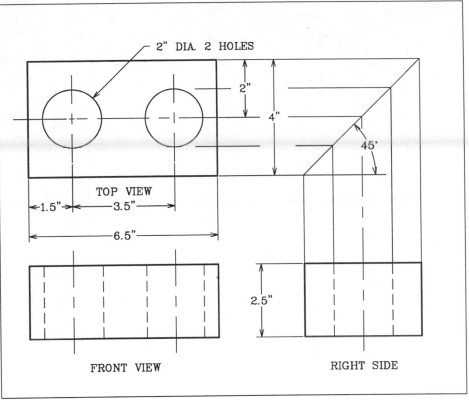

2" DIA. 2 HOLES

2"

4"

45°

TOP VIEW

←1.5"→←——3.5"——→

←————6.5"————→

2.5"

FRONT VIEW

RIGHT SIDE

Exercise 3–9

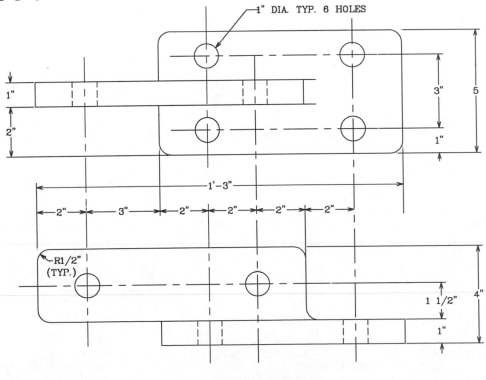

1" DIA. TYP. 6 HOLES

1"

2"

3"

1"

5

1'–3"

←2"→←—3"—→←2"→←2"→←2"→←2"→

R1/2"
(TYP.)

1 1/2"

1"

4"

BEAM CLAMP

Exercise 3–10

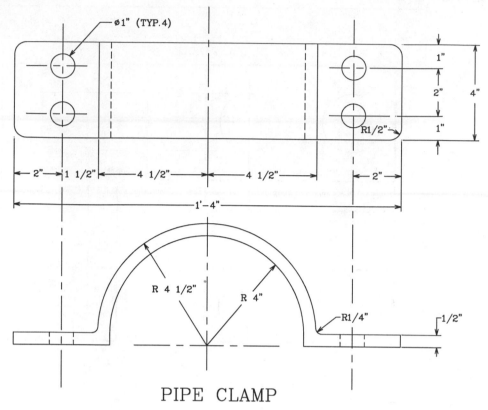

PIPE CLAMP

Exercise 3–11

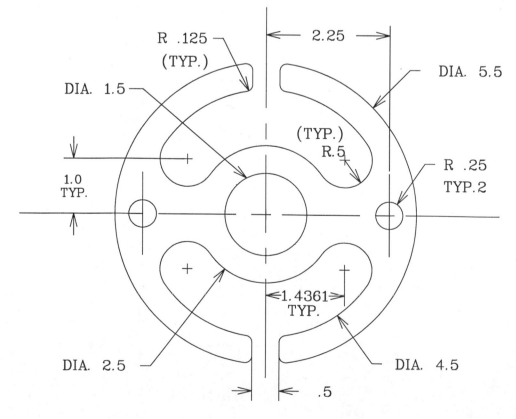

Exercise 3–12

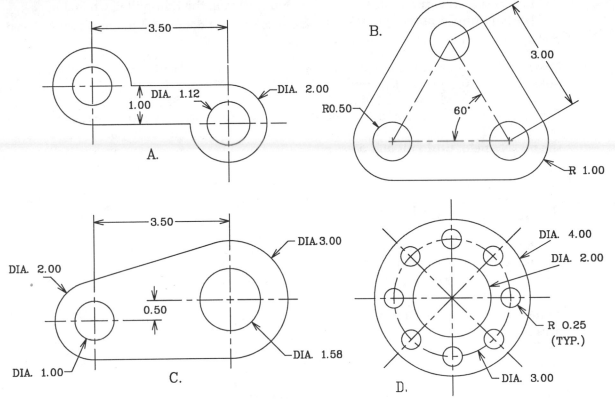

UNDO AND REDO

The Undo command undoes the effects of the previous command or group of commands, depending upon the option employed. The REDO command is a one-time reversal of the effects of the previous Undo. Commands can be undone because all steps required for each command you use are stored in an undo buffer in your computer's RAM. The undo command goes to that buffer to get the information necessary to put things back the way they were before the command was issued. The last command you did is the first one undone, the next-to-last command you did is the next one undone, and so on.

Undo Command

The Undo command permits you to select the last command or a marked group of prior commands for undoing. The Undo (action) option in the Edit pull-down menu negates the last drawing operation. MicroStation displays the name of the last command operation that was performed in the Edit pull-down menu in place of (action). When you select the command, MicroStation negates the last drawing operation.

You can also undo the last command by keying in at the uSTN> field, **undo** and pressing [ENTER]. If you know how many drawing commands you want to undo, key-in **undo n**, where **n** is the number of operations. For example, **undo 3** negates the last 3 previous operations.

Set Mark and Undo Mark If you are at a point in the editing session from which you want to experiment, but want to be able to undo the experiment, place a mark in the design before you start. To place a mark, invoke the Set Mark command from the Edit pull-down menu or key-in at the uSTN>

field, **mark** and press ⏎. Later, if you need to undo the experiment back to the mark, invoke the To Mark option from the Undo Other sub-menu located in the Edit pull-down menu, or key-in at the uSTN> field, **undo mark** and press ⏎. All commands done after the mark was placed, and the mark, are undone.

Undo All The Undo All command lets you negate all of the drawing operations recorded in the undo buffer. Before you invoke this command, think twice. MicroStation displays an alert box that will warn you that it will undo all of the drawing operations recorded in the undo buffer. If you are not sure, just cancel the command. To undo all the drawing operations recorded in the undo buffer, invoke the Undo All option from the Undo Other sub-menu located in the Edit pull-down menu or key-in at the uSTN> field, **undo all** and press ⏎.

Redo Command

The Redo command permits one reversal of a prior Undo command. It undoes the last undo. To undo the undo, the Redo command should be used immediately after using the Undo command. You can redo a series of negated operations by repeatedly choosing redo.

To redo an undo, select Redo from the Edit pull-down menu, or key-in in the uSTN> field, **redo** and press ⏎.

Things to Consider Before Undoing

Following are the points to consider before using the Undo and Redo commands:

- The undo buffer resides in your computer's RAM; it must be limited in size. If you have issued more commands than the buffer can hold, the oldest commands can no longer be undone. For example, if the buffer can hold only information for 100 commands, you can undo only the last 100 commands. Compressing the design (from the File pull-down menu) clears the undo buffer. No commands issued before the compress can be undone.
- Exiting from the design clears the undo buffer. Commands issued in a previous editing session cannot be undone.
- The undo commands back up through the undo buffer. They are not always the best way to clean up a problem. For example, if five commands ago you placed a circle you want to get rid of, undo forces you to undo the four commands issued after the circle placement to get to the circle. In this case, a better way to get rid of the circle is to use the Delete Element command.
- When you use one of the undo commands, you are undoing commands, not elements. If the command manipulated multiple elements, undo undoes the manipulation of all the elements. For example, the fence commands can manipulate hundreds of elements at one time. If you undo a fence contents delete command, you get back all the elements the fence deleted.

DIMENSION SETTINGS

In Chapter 2 a detailed explanation was provided for Dimension Placement and Units settings box to get you started with Linear Dimensioning. Let's look at three additional dimension settings, Dimension Attributes, Dimension Geometry, and Tolerance. The remaining Dimension setting boxes are explained in Chapter 4.

Dimension Attributes

The Dimension Attribute Settings box (invoked from the Settings pull-down menu of the Dimension Placement Settings box) controls the attributes of dimensions being placed in the design and is divided into five sections (see Figure 3–73). The five sections include Dimension Line, Extension Lines, Terminators, Dimension Text, and Level.

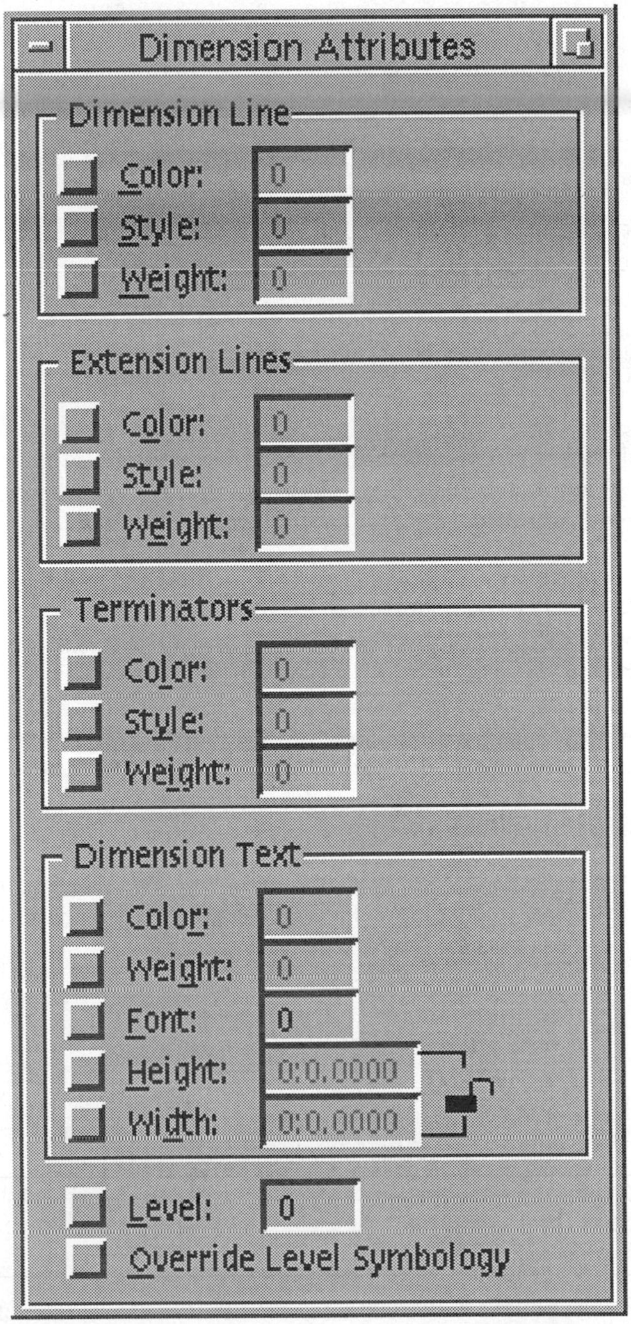

FIGURE 3–73   Dimension Attributes Settings box.

Dimension Line   The options under Dimension Line controls override the active element attributes for the dimension line. If a toggle button to the left of the control is turned ON, then dimension line is placed with the active attributes overriding the element attributes. Each of these controls is analogous to a control for setting attributes for an element from the Element pull-down menu.

Extension Lines The options under Extension Lines controls override the active element attributes for the extension lines. If a toggle button to the left of the control is turned ON, then extension lines are placed with the active attributes overriding the element attributes. For example, this allows you to use center line type for an extension line. Each of these controls is analogous to a control for setting attributes for an element from the Element pull-down menu.

Terminators The options under Terminators controls override the active element attributes for the terminators, such as arrowhead, tick marks, etc. If a toggle button to the left of the control is turned ON, then terminators are placed with the active attributes overriding the element attributes. Each of these controls is analogous to a control for setting an attribute for an element from the Element pull-down menu.

Dimension Text The options under Dimension Text controls override the active element attributes as well as the active text font, height, and width for the dimension text. If a toggle button to the left of the control is turned ON, then dimension text is placed with the active attributes overriding the element attributes. Each of these controls is analogous to a control for setting an attribute for an element and text from the Element pull-down menu.

Level The Level edit field allows you to key-in a level number independent of the active level to place dimensions. If the Level toggle button is turned OFF, then dimensions are placed on Active Level. To override the level symbology, turn ON the toggle button for override level symbology. (See Chapter 10 for detailed explanation for setting up level symbology table.)

> **NOTE:** If Extension Lines, Terminators, or Dimension Text overrides are set to ON, then the components are placed with the active Dimension attributes. And if the Dimension attributes are set to OFF, then the components are placed with the active element attributes.

Dimension Geometry

The Dimension Geometry settings box (invoked from the Settings pull-down menu of the Dimension Placement Settings box) control the settings related to extension lines, text margins, terminators, offsets, leaders, and center size (see Figure 3–74).

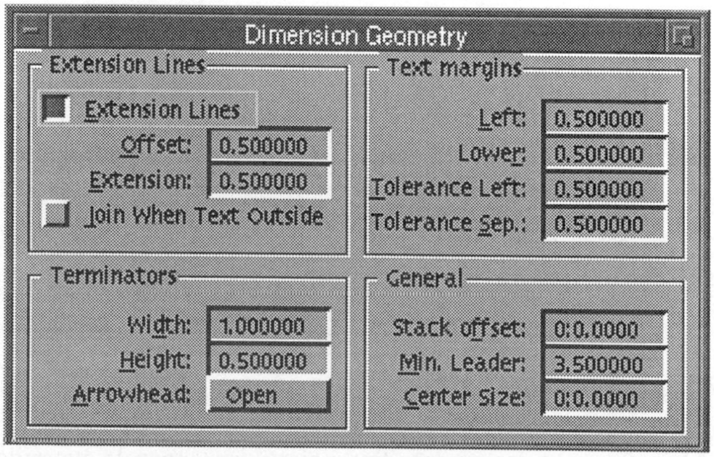

FIGURE 3–74 Dimension Geometry Settings box.

Extension Lines The Extension Lines controls the affect of the placement and appearance of extension lines. The toggle button for the extension lines is set to ON when you need to place the extension lines. If it is set to OFF, then extension lines are not placed. The Offset edit field controls the distance (MU:SU:PU) between the start of the extension line and the object line. The Extension edit field controls the distance (MU:SU:PU) that the extension line extends beyond the dimension line. The toggle button when it is set to ON to Join When Text Outside places a connecting line between extension lines and text placed outside extension lines. If it is set to OFF, no connecting line is placed.

Text Margins The Text Margin controls are used to set dimension text margins. The Left edit field sets the distance (MU:SU:PU) between leader line and text. The Lower edit field sets the distance (MU:SU:PU) between the dimension line and the bottom of text. The Tolerance Left edit field sets the distance (MU:SU:PU) between tolerance and text. And the Tolerance Separation edit field sets the distance (MU:SU:PU) between tolerance values.

Terminators The Terminator controls are used to set the appearance of the default dimension terminators. The Width and Height edit fields set the width and height of the terminator respectively. The Arrowhead option menu sets the appearance of the default arrowhead terminator. The options include Open, Closed, or Filled.

General The General option controls the Stack Offset spacing, Minimum Leader distance, and Center Size. The Stack Offset spacing is the distance between dimension lines in stacked dimensions. If it is set to zero (default), a reasonable value based on text size and orientation is computed. Set to a value other than zero for a constant spacing between dimension lines. The Minimum Leader distance controls the distance between the extension lines and text. The Center Size distance edit field sets the size of the center mark.

Tolerance

The Tolerance settings box (invoked from the Settings pull-down menu of the Dimension Placement Settings box) controls the generation of toleranced dimensions (see Figure 3–75).

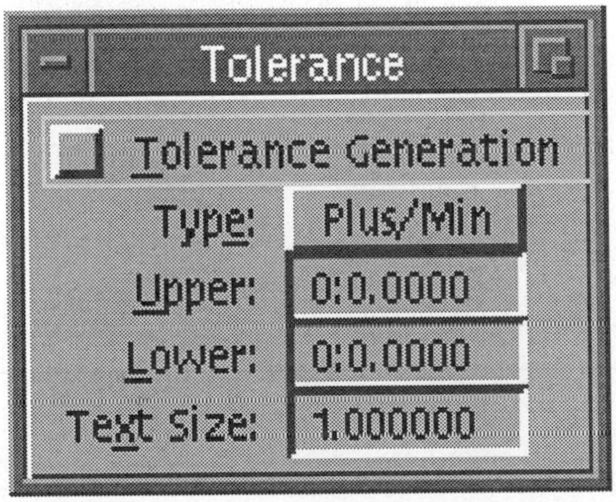

FIGURE 3–75 Tolerance Settings box.

Tolerance Generation If the Tolerance Generation toggle button is set to ON, or either Upper or Lower is set to a non-zero value, tolerances are generated. If it is OFF, or both Upper and Lower are set to zero, tolerances are not generated.

Type The Type options menu sets the tolerance type. The Plus/Minus option expresses the dimension in the upper and lower limits as positive and negative limits. The Limit option is expressed plus and minus the limits.

Upper The Upper edit field sets the upper tolerance limits, in MU:SU:PU.

Lower The Lower edit field sets the lower tolerance limits, in MU:SU:PU.

Text Size The Text Size edit field sets the tolerance text size, specified as a multiple of the dimension text Height and Width.

CIRCULAR DIMENSIONING

In Chapter 2 detailed explanation was provided for linear dimensioning involving straight line distances. The circular dimensions comprise the balance of the dimensioning command set—angular and Radial dimensioning includes dimensioning circles and arcs.

Features Common to Linear and Circular Dimensions

Items such as dimension lines, extension lines, arrows, dimension text, tolerances, limits, and alternate units are properties that are common to both linear and circular dimensioning. Some of the aspects of these terms that are particular to circular dimensioning are outlined in the following text and figures.

Dimension lines become dimension arcs for angular dimensions. The dimension arc has as its center the intersection of the two lines whose angle (between the two) you are measuring. The location of the arc is where you select, as shown in Figure 3–76.

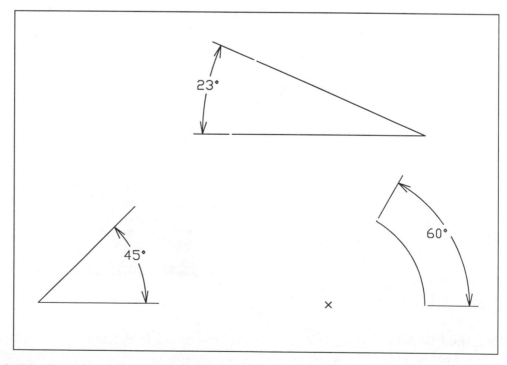

FIGURE 3–76 Examples of placing arc dimensioning.

In angular dimensioning, MicroStation provides radial extension lines. Diameter and radius dimensions may or may not add extension lines, as shown in Figure 3–77.

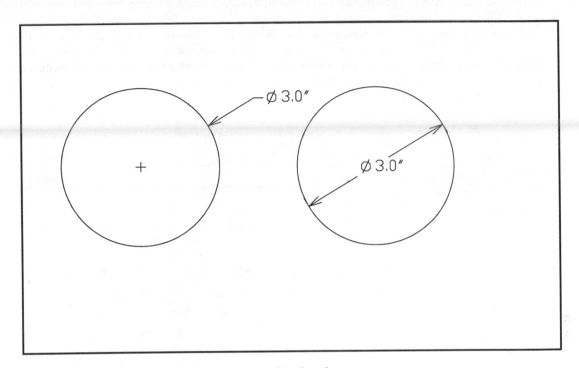

FIGURE 3–77 An example of placing Diameter and Radius dimensioning.

Dimension lines are straight for radius and diameter dimensions. The dimensions go toward or through the center of the circle or arc being dimensioned, as shown in Figure 3–78. The dimensions are also measured to a point or points on the circle or arc, unless you select the Dimension Diameter Parallel mode. Dimension text defaults to the setting for text height.

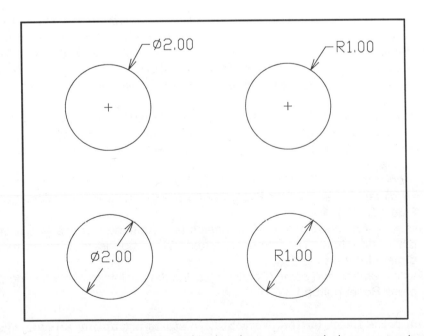

FIGURE 3–78 Examples of placing Diameter and Radius dimensioning with dimensioning lines being straight.

Angular Dimensioning

This feature provides commands to create dimensions of the angle between two non-parallel lines, using the conventions that conform to the dimension variable settings you have established. "Angle" is defined by *Webster's New Collegiate Dictionary* as "a measure of the amount of turning necessary to bring one line or plane into coincidence with or parallel to another." There are seven different methods for placing angular dimension available in Angular sub-palette, invoked from the Dimension menu located in the Palettes pull-down menu as shown in Figure 3–79.

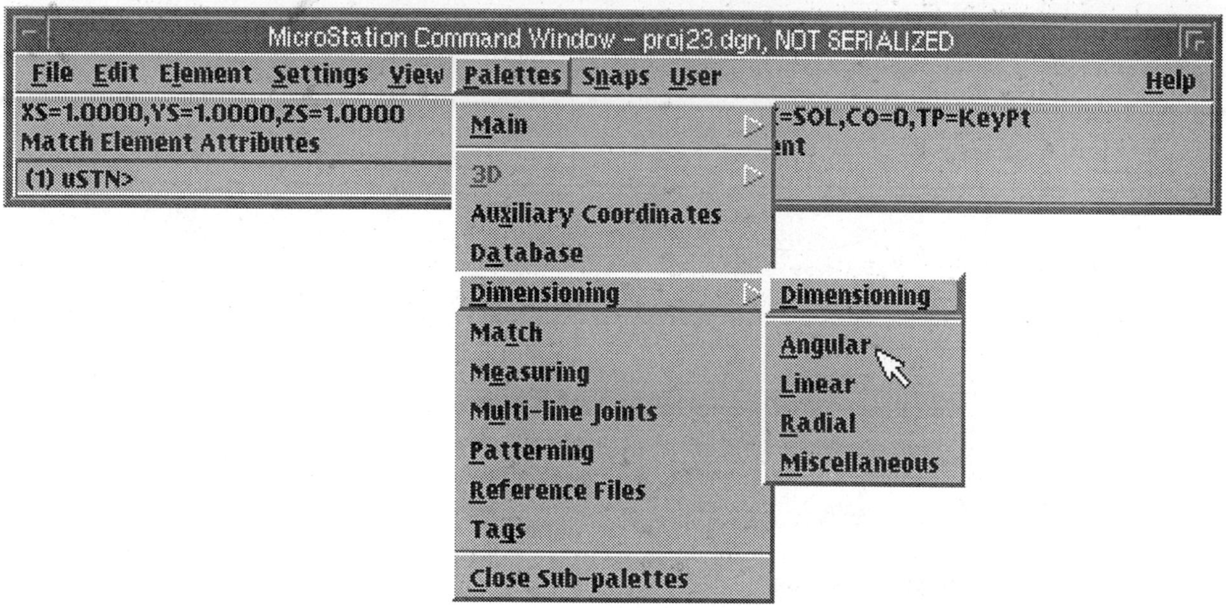

FIGURE 3–79 Invoking the Angular dimension sub-palette from the Palettes sub-palette.

Dimension Angle Size The Dimension Angle Size command is used to dimension angle. Each dimension is computed from the end point of the previous dimension, except the first one. To place angular dimensioning with dimension angle size, click the Dimension Angle Size icon from the Angular Dimensions sub-palette (see Figure 3–80), or key-in at the uSTN> field **dimension angle size** (or **dim ang siz**) and press ⏎. MicroStation prompts:

> *Select start of dimension* (Place a data point to define the origin; see Figure 3–81. The dimension is measured counterclockwise from this point.)
>
> *Define length of extension line* (Place a data point to define the length of the extension line; see Figure 3–81.)
>
> *Enter point on axis* (Place a data point to define the vertex of the angle; see Figure 3–81.)
>
> *Select dimension end point* (Place a data point to define the endpoint of the dimension; see Figure 3–81.)
>
> *Press ⏎ if necessary to edit dimension text* (optional—press ⏎ if necessary to edit the dimension text. The dimension text editor opens to let you make changes to the dimension text.)
>
> *Select dimension end point* (Continue placing data points to continue angular dimensioning and press Reset button.)

Once you press Reset button, MicroStation starts prompting all over again to place Dimension Angle Size.

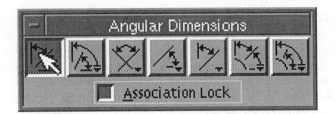

FIGURE 3–80   Invoking the Place Angular Dimensioning with Dimension angle size command from the Angular Dimensions sub-palette.

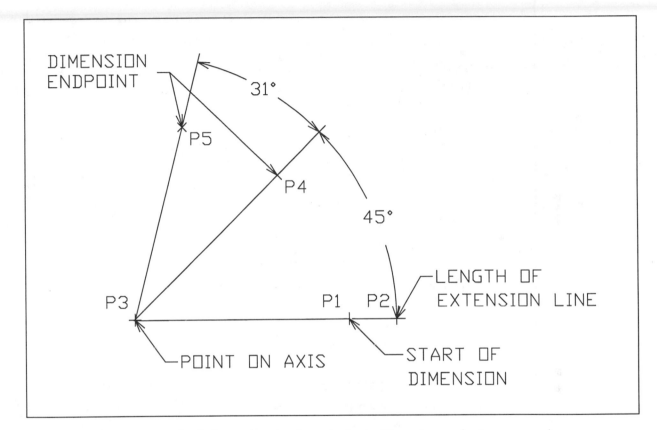

FIGURE 3–81   An example of placing Angular dimensioning by Dimension angle size command.

> **NOTE:** To associate the dimensions you place with the elements they dimension, turn ON the Association lock before you start dimensioning.

Dimension Angle Location   The Dimension Angle Location command is used to dimension angle(s) similar to Dimension Angle Size command. Here, each dimension is computed from the dimension origin (datum) as shown in Figure 3–82. To place angular dimensioning with dimension angle location, click the Dimension Angle Location icon from the Angular Dimensions sub-palette (see Figure 3–83), or key-in at the uSTN> field **dimension angle location** (or **dim ang loc**) and press [ENTER]. MicroStation prompts:

Select start of dimension (Place a data point to define the origin. The dimension is measured counterclockwise from this point.)

Define length of extension line (Place a data point to define the length of the extension line.)

Enter point on axis (Place a data point to define the vertex of the angle.)

Select dimension end point (Place a data point to define the end point of the dimension.)

Press ⏎ if necessary to edit dimension text (Optional—press ⏎ if necessary to edit dimension text. The Dimension text editor opens to let you make changes to the dimension text.)

Select dimension end point (Continue placing data points to continue angular dimensioning and press Reset button.)

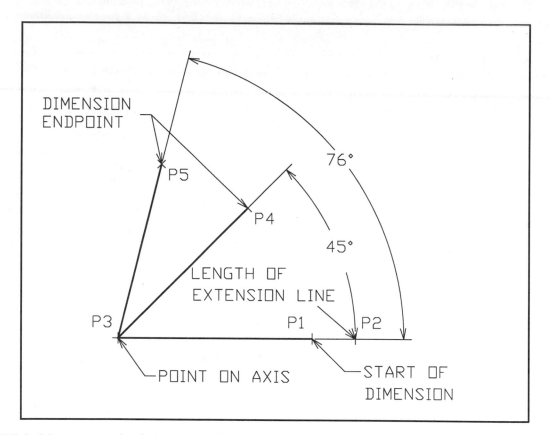

FIGURE 3–82 An example of placing Angular dimensioning by computed from the dimension origin (datum).

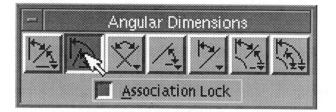

FIGURE 3–83 Invoking the Dimension Angle Location command from the Angular Dimensions sub-palette.

Once you press the Reset button, MicroStation starts prompting all over again to place Dimension Angle Location.

> **NOTE:** To associate the dimensions you place with the elements they dimension, turn ON the Association lock before you start dimensioning.

Dimension Angle Between Lines The Dimension Angle Between Lines command is used to dimension the angle between two lines, two segments of a line string, or two sides of a shape. To place angular dimensioning with dimension angle between lines, click the Dimension Angle Between Lines icon from the Angular Dimensions sub-palette (see Figure 3–84), or key-in at the uSTN> field **dimension angle lines** (or **dim ang lin**) and press [ENTER]. MicroStation prompts:

Select first line (Identify the first line or segment; see Figure 3–85.)
Select second line (Identify the second line or segment; see Figure 3–85.)
Accept/Reject (Select next input) (Place a data point to define the radius of the dimension or identify another line or segment to continue; see Figure 3–85.)

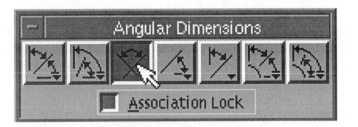

FIGURE 3–84 Invoking the Dimension Angle Between Lines command from the Angular Dimensions sub-palette.

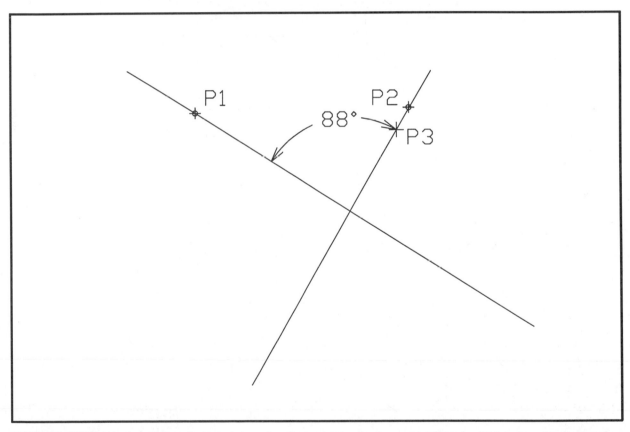

FIGURE 3–85 An example of placing Angular dimensioning between two lines by Dimension Angle Between Lines command.

Once you press Reset button, MicroStation will start prompting all over again to place Dimension Angle Between Lines.

> **NOTE:** To associate the dimensions you place with the elements they dimension, turn ON the Association lock before you start dimensioning.

Dimension Angle X-Axis The Dimension Angle X-Axis command is used to dimension the angle between a line, side of a shape, or segment of a line string and the view X-axis. To place angular dimensioning with dimension angle X-axis, click the Dimension Angle X-Axis icon from the Angular Dimensions sub-palette (see Figure 3–86), or key-in at the uSTN> field **dimension angle x-axis** (or **dim ang x-axis**) and press ⏎. MicroStation prompts:

Identify element (Identify the element; see Figure 3–87.)
Accept, define dimension axis (Place a Data point to specify the location and direction of the dimension.)

FIGURE 3–86 Invoking the Dimension Angle X-Axis command from the Angular Dimensions sub-palette.

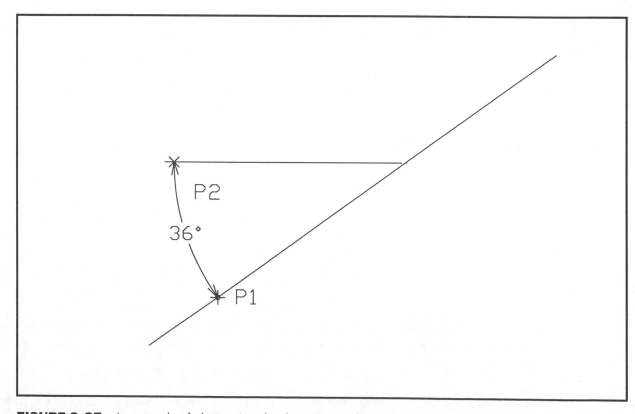

FIGURE 3–87 An example of placing Angular dimensioning from X-Axis by Dimension Angle X-Axis command.

Dimension Angle Y-Axis The Dimension Angle Y-Axis is used to dimension the angle between a line, side of a shape, or segment of a line string, and the view Y-axis. To place angular dimensioning with dimension angle Y-axis, click the Dimension Angle Y-Axis icon from the Angular Dimensions sub-palette (see Figure 3–88), or key-in at the uSTN> field **dimension angle y-axis** (or **dim ang y-axis**) and press [ENTER]. MicroStation prompts:

Identify element (Identify the element; see Figure 3–89.)
Accept, define dimension axis (Place a Data point to specify the location and direction of the dimension.)

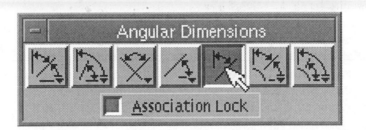

FIGURE 3–88   Invoking the Dimension Angle Y-Axis command from the Angular Dimensions sub-palette.

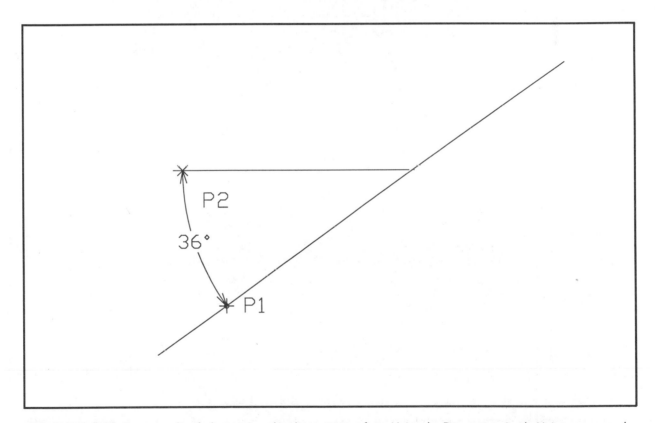

FIGURE 3–89   An example of placing Angular dimensioning from Y-Axis by Dimension Angle Y-Axis command.

NOTE: To associate the dimensions you place with the elements they dimension, turn ON the Association lock before you start dimensioning.

Dimension Arc Size The Dimension Arc Size command is used to dimension a circle or circular arc. Each dimension is computed from the end point of the previous dimension, except the first one, similar to Dimension Angle Size command. To place angular dimensioning with dimension arc size, click the Dimension Arc Size icon from the Angular Dimensions sub-palette (see Figure 3–90), or key-in at the uSTN> field **dimension arc size** (or **dim arc siz**) and press [ENTER]. MicroStation prompts:

Select start of dimension (Place a data point to define the origin; see Figure 3–91. The dimension is measured counterclockwise from this point.)

Define length of extension line (Place a data point to define the length of the extension line; see Figure 3–91.)

Select dimension end point (Place a data point to define the end point of the dimension; see Figure 3–91.)

Press [ENTER] *if necessary to edit dimension text* (Optional—press [ENTER] if necessary to edit dimension text. Dimension text editor opens to let you make changes to the dimension text.)

Select dimension end point (Continue placing data points to continue angular dimensioning and press Reset button.)

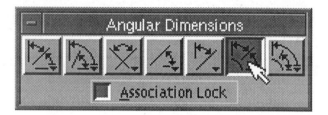

FIGURE 3–90 Invoking the Dimension Arc Size command in the Angular Dimensions sub-palette.

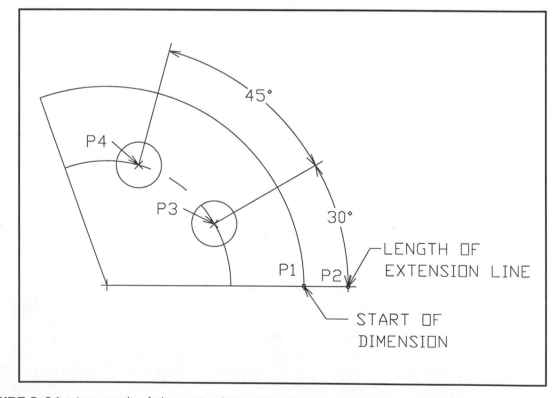

FIGURE 3–91 An example of placing Arc dimensioning by Dimension Arc Size command.

Once you press Reset button, MicroStation will start prompting all over again to place Dimension Arc Size.

> **NOTE:** To associate the dimensions you place with the elements they dimension, turn ON the Association lock before you start dimensioning.

Dimension Arc Location The Dimension Arc Location command is used to dimension a circle or circular arc. Here, each dimension is computed from the dimension origin (datum) as shown in Figure 3–92. To place angular dimensioning with dimension arc location, click the Dimension Arc Location icon from the Angular Dimensions sub-palette (see Figure 3–93), or key-in at the uSTN> field **dimension arc location** (or **dim arc loc**) and press [ENTER]. MicroStation prompts:

Select start of dimension (Place a data point to define the origin. The dimension is measured counterclockwise from this point.)
Define length of extension line (Place a data point to define the length of the extension line.)
Select dimension end point (Place a data point to define the endpoint of the dimension.)
Press [ENTER] if necessary to edit dimension text (Optional—press [ENTER] if necessary to edit dimension text. The Dimension text editor opens to let you make changes to the dimension text.)
Select dimension end point (Continue placing data points to continue angular dimensioning and press Reset button.)

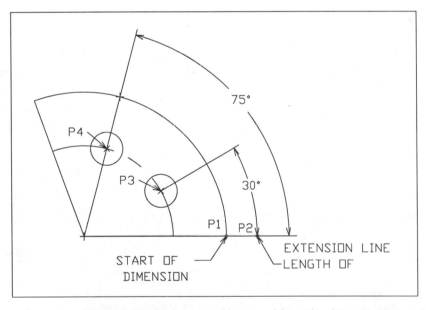

FIGURE 3–92   An example of placing Arc dimensioning computed from the dimension origin (datum).

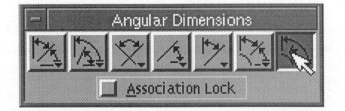

FIGURE 3–93   Invoking the Dimension Arc Location command from the Angular Dimensions sub-palette.

Once you press Reset button, MicroStation starts prompting all over again to place Dimension Arc Location.

> **NOTE:** To associate the dimensions you place with the elements they dimension, turn ON the Association lock before you start dimensioning.

Radial Dimensioning

This feature provides commands to create dimensions for the radius or diameter of a circle or arc and to place a center mark. There are five commands, in addition to the Place Center Mark command, that can be used to dimension a circle or arc:

Dimension Diameter
Dimension Diameter (Extended Leader)
Dimension Diameter Parallel
Dimension Radius
Dimension Radius (Extended Leader)
Dimension Center Mark

The radial dimensioning commands are provided in the Radial Dimensions palette invoked from the Dimension menu located in the Palettes pull-down menu as shown in Figure 3–94.

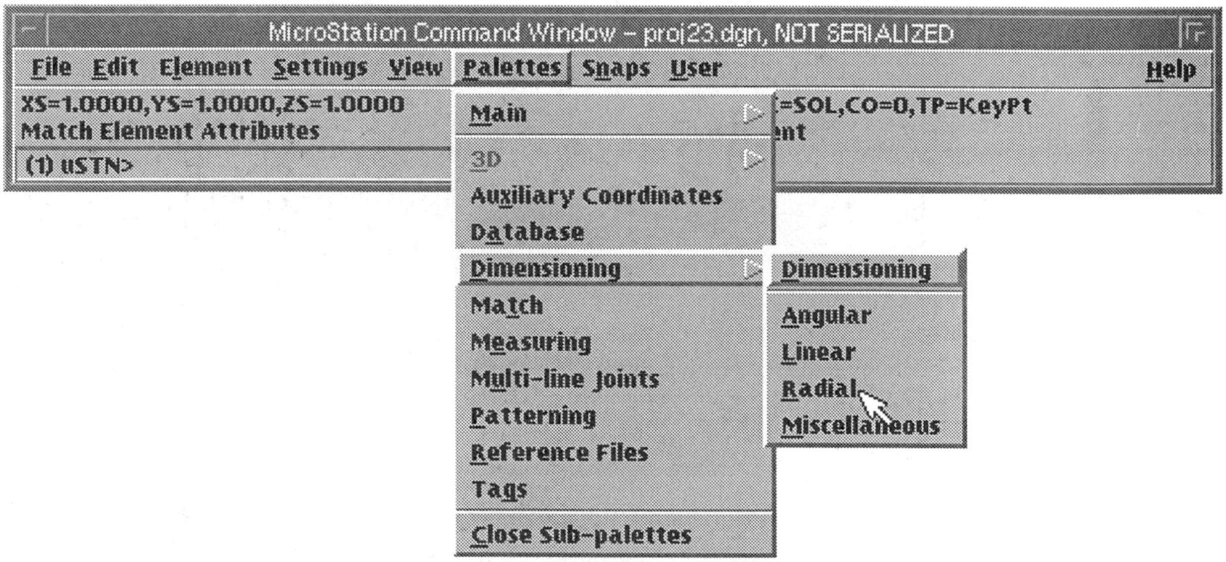

FIGURE 3–94 Invoking the Radial Dimensions sub-palette from the Palettes pull-down menu.

Dimension Diameter The Dimension Diameter command is used to dimension the diameter of a circle or a circular arc. To place radial dimensioning with dimension diameter, click the Dimension Diameter icon from the Radial Dimensions sub-palette (see Figure 3–95), or key-in at the uSTN> field **dimension diameter** (or **dim dia**) and press [ENTER]. MicroStation prompts:

Identify the element (Identify a circle or arc, as shown in Figure 3–96.)

Select dimension end point (Place a data point inside or outside the circle or arc to place the dimension line; see Figure 3–96.)

Press ⌨ENTER *if necessary to edit dimension text* (Optional—press ⌨ENTER if necessary to edit dimension text. The Dimension text editor opens to let you make changes to the dimension text.)

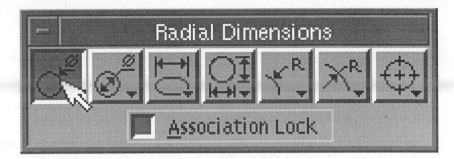

FIGURE 3–95   Invoking the Dimension Diameter command from the Radial Dimensions sub-palette.

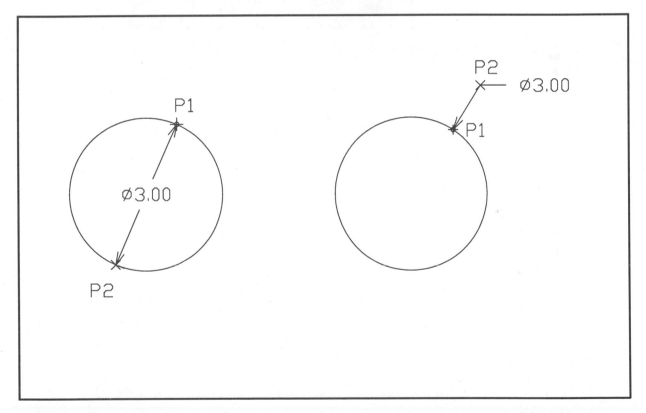

FIGURE 3–96   An example of placing diameter dimensioning by Dimension Diameter command.

Once you place a second Data point, MicroStation starts prompting all over again to place Dimension Diameter.

> **NOTE:** To associate the dimensions you place with the elements they dimension, turn ON the Association lock before you start dimensioning.

Dimension Diameter (Extended Leader) The Dimension Diameter (Extended Leader) command is identical to Dimension Diameter, except the leader line continues across the center of the circle with terminators that point outward. To place radial dimensioning with dimension diameter (extended leader), click the Dimension Diameter (Extended Leader) icon from the Radial Dimensions sub-palette (see Figure 3–97), or key-in at the uSTN> field **dimension diameter extended** (or **dim dia ext**) and press [ENTER]. MicroStation prompts:

Identify the element (Identify a circle or arc, as shown in Figure 3–98.)
Select dimension end point (Place a data point inside or outside the circle or arc to place the dimension line; see Figure 3–98.)
Press [ENTER] *if necessary to edit dimension text* (Optional—press [ENTER] if necessary to edit dimension text. The Dimension text editor opens to let you make changes to the dimension text.)

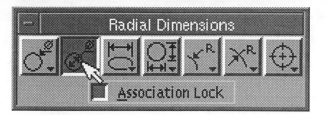

FIGURE 3–97 Invoking the Dimension Diameter (extended leader) command from the Radial Dimensions sub-palette.

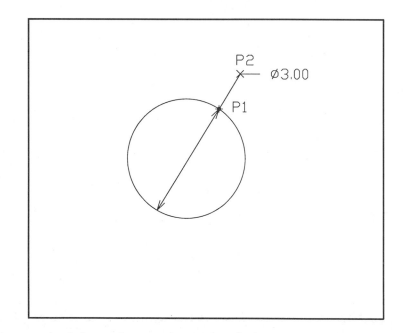

FIGURE 3–98 An example of placing diameter dimensioning by Dimension Diameter (extended leader) command.

Once you place a second Data point, MicroStation starts prompting all over again to place Dimension Diameter (Extended Leader).

> **NOTE:** To associate the dimensions you place with the elements they dimension, turn ON the Association lock before you start dimensioning.

Dimension Diameter Parallel The Dimension Diameter Parallel command is identical to Dimension Diameter, except the dimension is placed parallel to the circle or arc with extension lines placed tangent to the circle or arc as shown in Figure 3–99. To place dimension diameter parallel, click the Dimension Diameter Parallel icon from the Radial Dimensions sub-palette (see Figure 3–100), or key-in at the uSTN> field **dimension diameter parallel** (or **dim dia par**) and press <kbd>ENTER</kbd>. MicroStation prompts:

Identify the element (Identify a circle or arc, as shown in Figure 3–101.)
Select dimension end point (Place a data point inside or outside the circle or arc to place the dimension line; see Figure 3–101.)
Press <kbd>ENTER</kbd> *if necessary to edit dimension text* (Optional—press <kbd>ENTER</kbd> if necessary to edit dimension text. The Dimension text editor opens to let you make changes to the dimension text.)

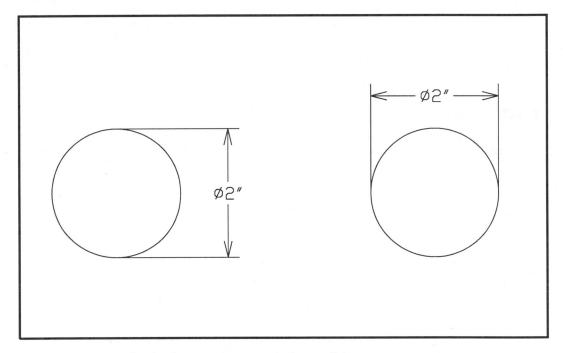

FIGURE 3–99 An example of a diameter dimensioning by parallel.

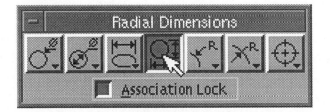

FIGURE 3–100 Invoking the Dimension Diameter Parallel from the Radial Dimensions sub-palette.

Once you place a second Data point, MicroStation starts prompting all over again to place Dimension Diameter Parallel.

NOTE: To associate the dimensions you place with the elements they dimension, turn ON the Association lock before you start dimensioning.

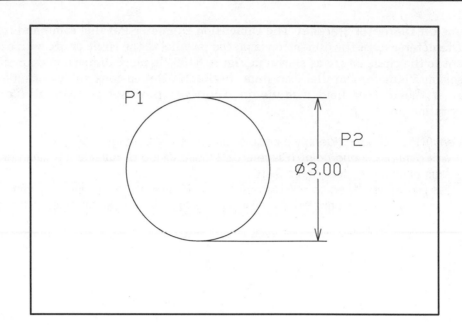

FIGURE 3–101 An example of placing diameter dimension parallel by Dimension Diameter parallel command.

Dimension Radius The Dimension Radius command is identical to Dimension Diameter, except the text is placed at the end of the dimension line indicating the radius for a circle or arc as shown in Figure 3–102. To place radial dimensioning with dimension radius, click the Dimension Radius icon from the Radial Dimensions sub-palette (see Figure 3–103), or key-in at the uSTN> field **dimension radius** (or **dim rad**) and press [ENTER]. MicroStation prompts:

> *Identify the element* (Identify a circle or arc, as shown in Figure 3–104.)
> *Select dimension end point* (Place a data point inside or outside the circle or arc to place the dimension line; see Figure 3–104.)
> *Press* [ENTER] *if necessary to edit dimension text* (Optional—press [ENTER] if necessary to edit dimension text. The Dimension text editor opens to let you make changes to the dimension text.)

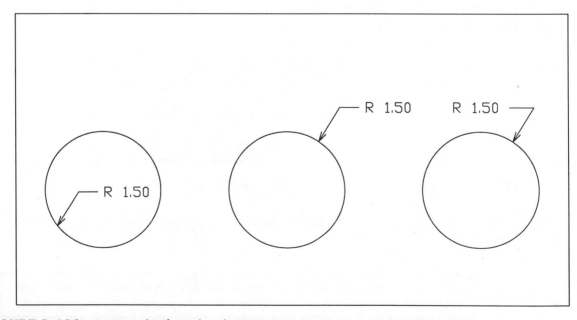

FIGURE 3–102 An example of a radius dimensioning.

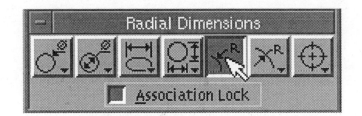

FIGURE 3-103   Invoking the Dimension Radius from the Radial Dimensions sub-palette.

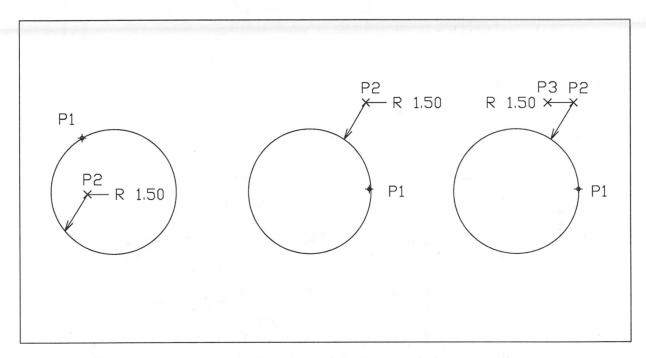

FIGURE 3-104   An example of placing radius dimension by Dimension Radius command.

Once you place a second Data point, MicroStation will start prompting all over again to place Dimension Radius.

> **NOTE:** To associate the dimensions you place with the elements they dimension, turn ON the Association lock before you start dimensioning.

Dimension Radius (Extended Leader)   The Dimension Radius (Extended Leader) command is identical to Dimension Diameter, except the leader line continues across the center of the circle with terminators that point outward indicating the radius of the arc or circle as shown in Figure 3-105. To place radial dimensioning with dimension radius (extended leader), click the Dimension Radius (Extended Leader) icon from the Radial Dimensions sub-palette (see Figure 3-106), or key-in at the uSTN> field **dimension radius extended** (or **dim rad ext**) and press [ENTER]. MicroStation prompts:

Identify the element (Identify a circle or arc.)
Select dimension end point (Place a data point inside or outside the circle or arc to place the dimension line.)
Press [ENTER] if necessary to edit dimension text (Optional—press [ENTER] if necessary to edit dimension text. The Dimension text editor opens to let you make changes to the dimension text.)

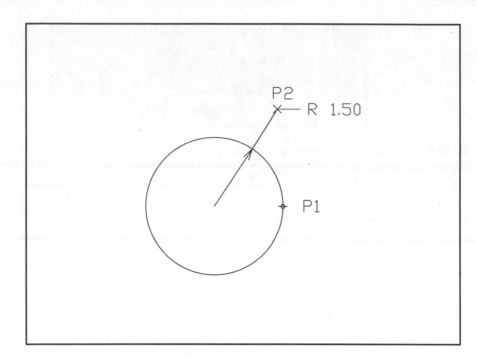

FIGURE 3–105 An example of a radius dimensioning extended leader.

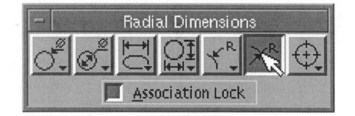

FIGURE 3–106 Invoking the Dimension Radius extended from the Radial Dimensions sub-palette.

Once you place a second Data point, MicroStation starts prompting all over again to place Dimension Radius (Extended Leader).

> **NOTE:** To associate the dimensions you place with the elements they dimension, turn ON the Association lock before you start dimensioning.

Place Center Mark The Place Center Mark command is used to place a center mark at the center of a circle or circular arc as shown in Figure 3–107. To place a center mark for a circle or arc, click the Place Center Mark icon from the Radial Dimensions sub-palette (see Figure 3–108), and, if necessary, key-in the Distance in the edit field for the size of the center mark or key-in at the uSTN> field **dimension center mark** (or **dim cen mar**) and press ⏎. MicroStation prompts:

Identify the element (Identify a circle or arc to place a center mark.)
Accept (next input) (Click the Accept button or identify another circle or arc to place the center mark.)

Once you place a second Data point, MicroStation starts prompting all over again to place Center Mark.

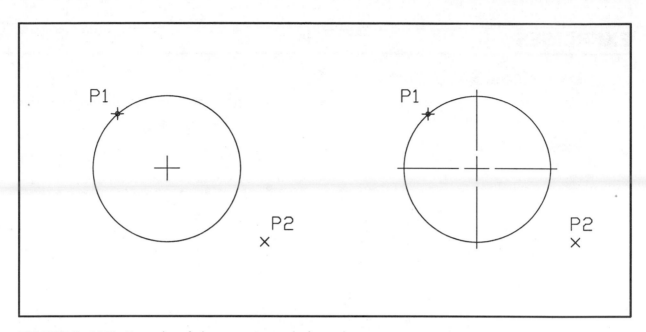

FIGURE 3–107   Examples of placing center marks for circles.

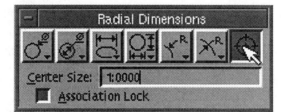

FIGURE 3–108   Invoking the Place Center Mark from the Radial Dimensions sub-palette.

> **_NOTE:_** To associate the dimensions you place with the elements they dimension, turn ON the Association lock before you start dimensioning.

EXERCISES

Exercises 3–13 through 3–21

Use Precision Key-ins (XY= , DL= , and/or DI=) and appropriate grid spacing to draw the figures. Add the dimensions.

Exercise 3–13

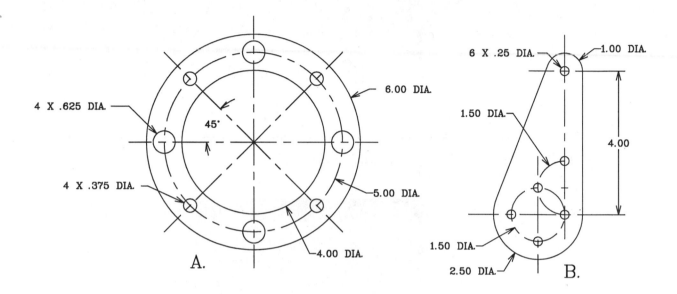

Exercise 3–14

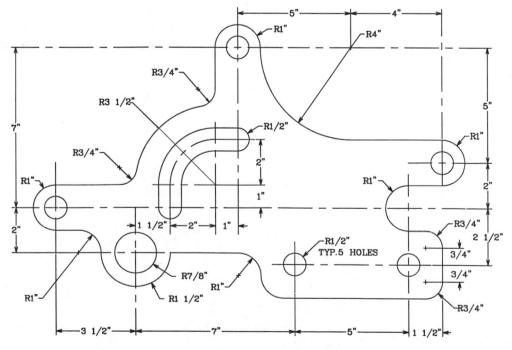

Exercise 3–15

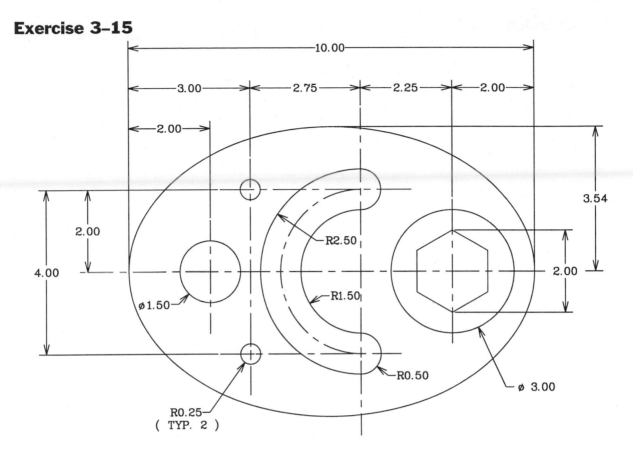

Exercise 3–16

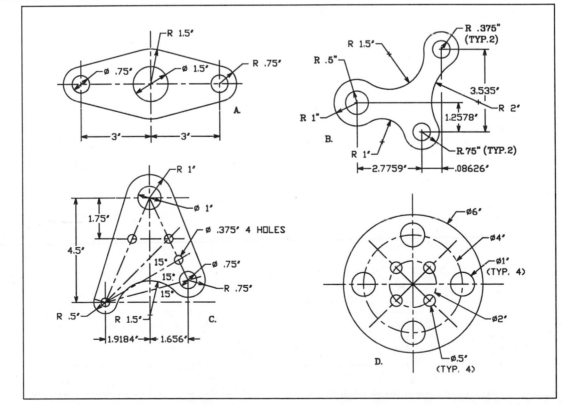

Exercise 3–17

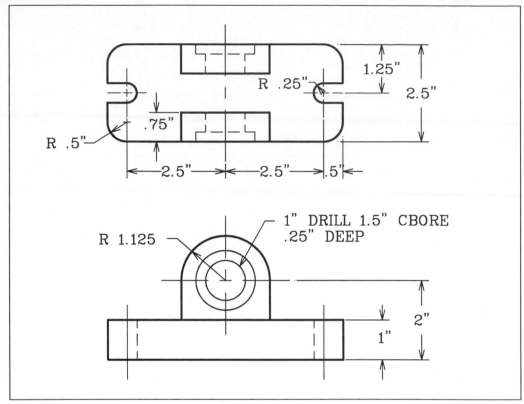

Exercise 3–18

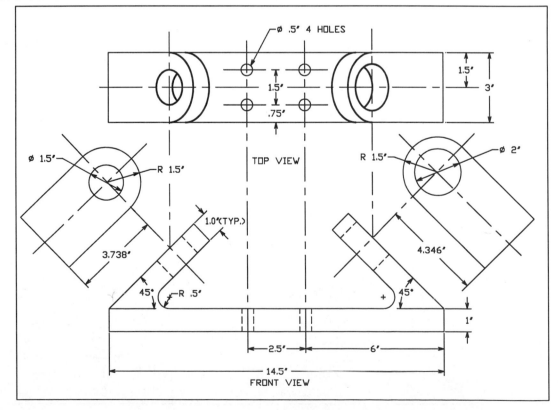

Exercise 3–19

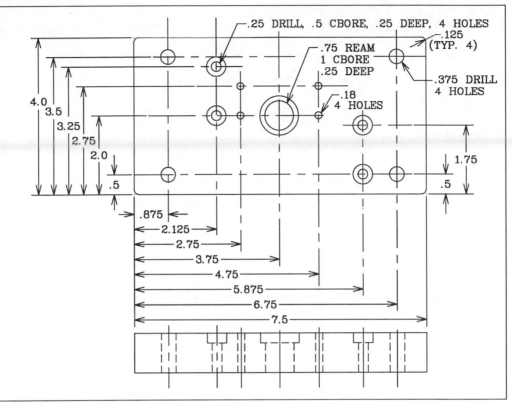

Exercise 3–20

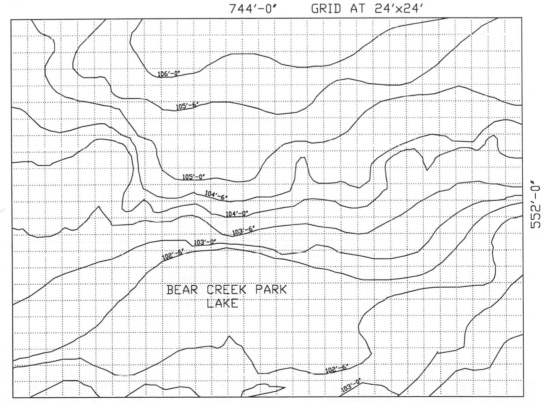

Exercise 3-21

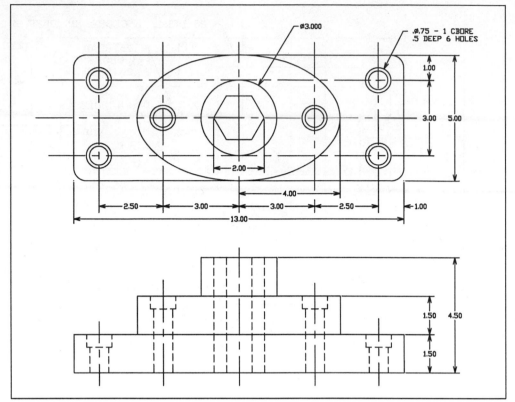

REVIEW QUESTIONS

Write your answers in the spaces provided:

1. Name the three methods by which you can place circles in MicroStation.
   _____

2. If you wish to draw a circle by specifying three known points on the circle, invoke the
   _____ command.

3. The commands related to placing Arcs are in the _____ sub-palette.

4. The Place Arc Edge command is used to place an arc by identifying _____ points on the arc.

5. The Place Polygon command is used to place polygons that can have a maximum of _____ sides.

6. The Place Point Curve command is used _____.

7. The Place Stream Curve command is used _____.

8. The Multi-line command allows you to place up to _____ separate lines of various
   _____ , _____ , and _____ with a single command.

9. The Place Fillet command joins two lines, adjacent segments of a line string, arcs, or circles with an _____ of a specified radius.

10. Name the three methods by which you can control the removal of extension lines when placing the fillet.
    _____

11. To place a fillet with no modification, the key-in command is _____.

12. The Chamfer command allows you to draw a _____ instead of an arc.

13. To place a chamfer, the key-in command is _____.

14. The purpose of the Trim command is _____.

15. What is the name of the command that will delete part of the element? _____.

16. Name the two categories of manipulation commands available in MicroStation.
    _____

17. The Copy command is similar to Move command, but it _____.

18. Name at least three element manipulation commands available in MicroStation.
    _____

19. To rotate an element, the key-in command is _____.

20. The Array command is used to make multiple copies of selected element in either
    _____ or _____ arrays.

21. List the four parameters you have to specify for a rectangular array.

    _____

    _____

22. List the four attributes associated with the placement of elements.

    _____

    _____

23. How many levels come with a new design file? _____

24. How many level(s) can be active at any time? _____

25. How many level(s) can you turn ON or OFF at any one time in a specific view? _____

26. What is the two letter key-in used to make a level active? _____

27. How many colors or shades of colors are available in the color palette? _____

28. What is the two letter key-in used to make a color active? _____

29. How many line styles (internal) are available in MicroStation? _____

30. What is the two letter key-in used to make a line style active? _____

31. In MicroStation, weight refers to _____ .

32. How many line weights are available in MicroStation? _____

33. What is the two letter key-in used to make an active weight? _____

34. Explain briefly the difference between Primary and Construction Class options available in MicroStation.

    _____

    _____

35. Explain briefly the functions of the Undo and Redo commands.

    _____

    _____

36. The two types of dimensioning included in the Circular dimensioning are _____ .

37. The Dimension Angle Size command is used to _____ .

38. The Dimension Angle X-Axis command is used to _____ .

39. The Place Center Mark command is used to _____ .

40. What snap lock is used to snap to center of a block? _____

41. Which command would you use to change an element's weight and color at the same time?

    _____

42. Which command will increase the size of an existing element? _____

43. What is the alternate key-in AA= used for? _____

44. How will you find out what is your current active angle? _____ .

45. What does the $ mean when paired with the Alternate Key-ins? _____ .

PROJECT EXERCISE

In this project you apply MicroStation concepts and skills discussed in chapters 1 through 3 to create the machine part step-by-step fashion, as shown in Figure P3–1.

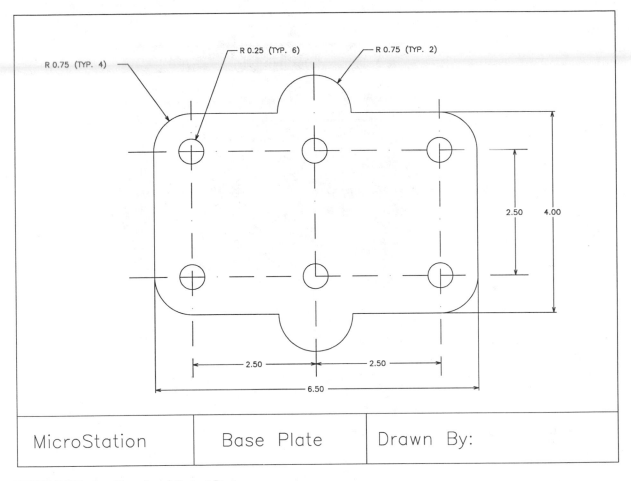

FIGURE P3–1   Completed Project Design.

> **NOTE:** The step-by-step instructions for this project are designed to provide practice in the concepts presented in chapters 1 through 3. It is not necessarily the most efficient way to draw the design.

The new concepts that are introduced in this project include:

- Placement commands—Line String, Arc, Circle
- Manipulation commands—Mirror, Copy Parallel, Fillet, Array
- Dimensioning—Linear and Radial

GETTING STARTED

STEP 1: Create a new design file named CH3.DGN using the SEED2D.DGN seed file from the MicroStation Manager dialog box if you just started MicroStation, or from the New option in the File pull-down menu of the MicroStation Command Window.

STEP 2: Set the design's working units as shown in Figure P3–2.

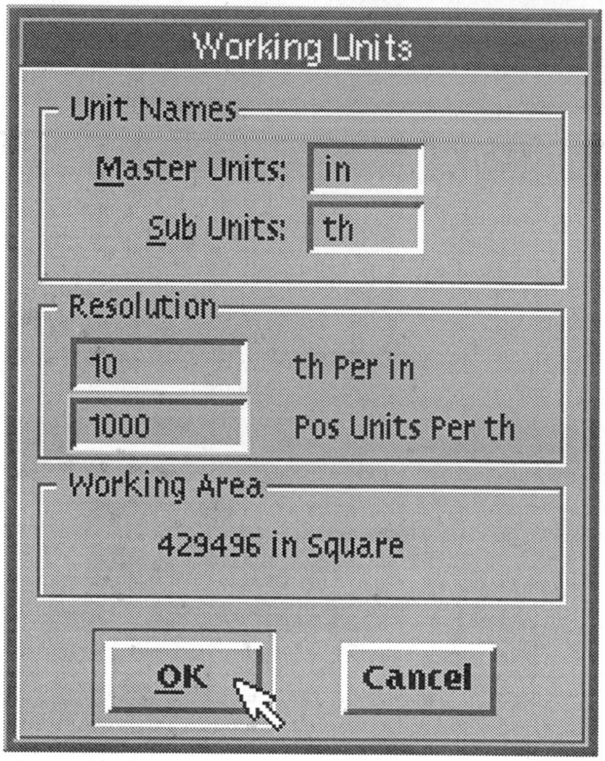

Working Units

┌ **Unit Names** ─────────────────
    Master Units: in
    Sub Units: th

┌ **Resolution** ─────────────────
    10   th Per in
    1000   Pos Units Per th

┌ **Working Area** ───────────────
    429496 in Square

    OK   **Cancel**

FIGURE P3–2 Working Units Dialog Box.

STEP 3: Open the Grid Settings box from the Settings pull-down menu and set the grid unit to .25, Grid Reference to 4 and set the Grid Lock to ON.

STEP 4: Open the Full Locks settings box from the Settings pull-down menu. Set the Snap toggle button to ON and select keypoint from the Snap Mode options menu.

STEP 5: If it is not already open, open the Tool Settings Box.

STEP 6: Invoke Save Settings command from the File pull-down menu to save the settings.

STEP 7: Invoke the place block command to place a 12″ wide by 9″ border with the lower left corner at coordinates 0,0.

STEP 8: Invoke the Fit command and place a data point anywhere in the view. You will see the border as shown in Figure P3–3.

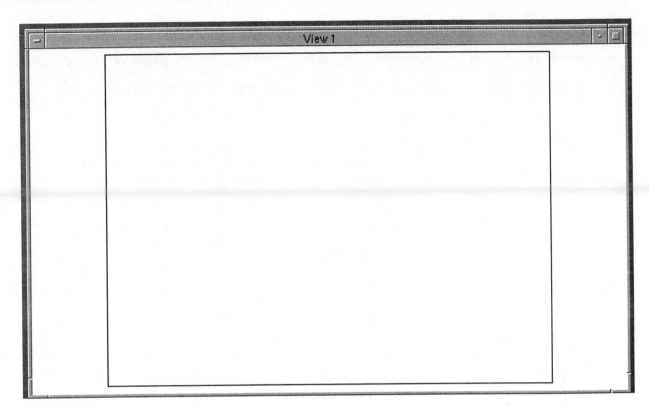

FIGURE P3–3   Border for the Project Design.

Creating a Layout for the Object

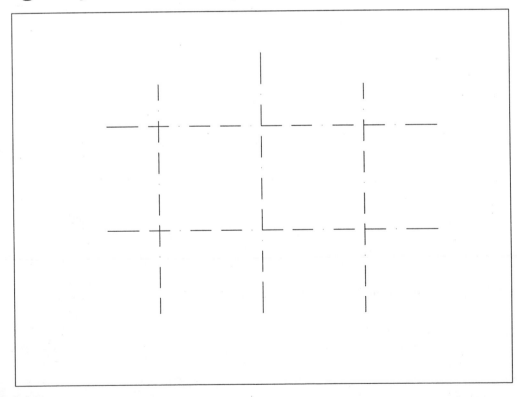

FIGURE P3–4   Design's center lines.

STEP 9: Set the active level to 2, color to blue, and the line style to 7.

STEP 10: Invoke Save Settings command from the File pull-down menu to save the settings.

STEP 11: Draw the top horizontal line 8″ to the right starting at x=2.25 and y=6.25.

STEP 12: Draw the left vertical line 5.5″ up from x=3.5 and y=1.75.

STEP 13: Invoke the Parallel command from the Manipulate Element sub-palette. In the Tool Settings box, set the toggle buttons to Make Copy and Distance to ON. Key-in the distance to 2.5 in the Distance edit field and press the ⌨ key. MicroStation prompts:

> *Identify an element* (Identify the horizontal line.)
> *Accept/Reject (Select next input)* (Place a data point below the horizontal line.)
> *Accept/Reject (Select next input)* (Click the Reset button.)
> *Identify an element* (Identify the vertical line.)
> *Accept/Reject (Select next input)* (Place a data point to the right of the vertical line.)
> *Accept/Reject (Select next input)* (Place another data point to the right of the vertical line.)
> *Accept/Reject (Select next input)* (Click the Reset button.)

STEP 14: Invoke the Extend Line command from the Modify sub-palette. In the Tool Settings box, set the Distance toggle button to ON. Key-in the distance to .75 in the Distance edit field and press the ⌨ key. MicroStation prompts:

> *Identify an element* (Identify the middle vertical line near its top end of the line.)
> *Accept/Reject (Select next input)* (Place a data point to accept it.)

Draw the Base Plate

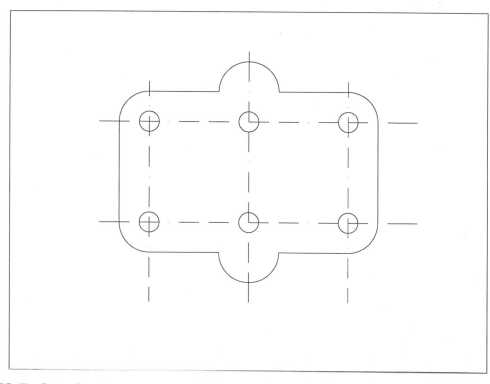

FIGURE P3–5 Base plate.

STEP 15: Set the active level to 5, color to red, line weight to 2, and the line style to 0.

STEP 16: Invoke Save Settings command from the File pull-down menu to save the settings.

STEP 17: Invoke the Line String command from the Main palette to draw the shape as shown in Figure P3–6. MicroStation prompts:

> *Enter first point* (Key-in **xy=5.25,3** and press ⏎.)
> *Enter end point* (Key-in **dl=-2.5,0** and press ⏎.)
> *Enter end point* (Key-in **dl=0,4** and press ⏎.)
> *Enter end point* (Key-in **dl=2.5,0** and press ⏎.)
> *Enter end point* (Click the Reset button.)

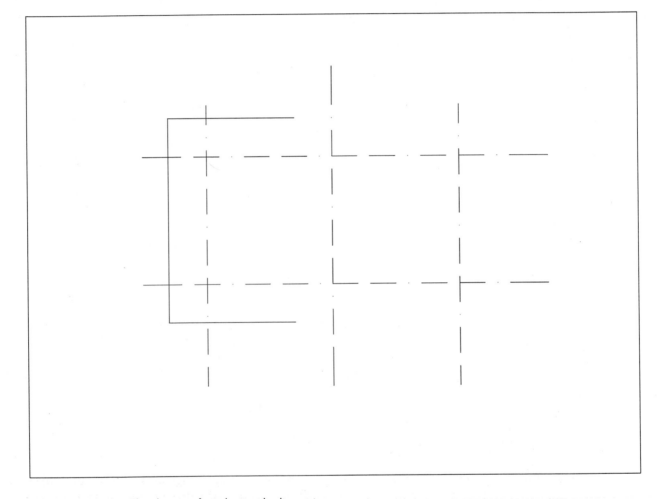

FIGURE P3–6   The design after placing the line string.

STEP 18: Invoke the Mirror command from the Manipulate Element sub-palette. In the tool settings box, set the Make Copy toggle button to ON and select Vertical from the Mirror About option menu. MicroStation prompts:

> *Identify the element* (Identify the line string.)
> *Accept/Reject (Select next input)* (Snap to the middle vertical line.)
> *Accept/Reject (Select next input)* (Click the Reset button.)

The result should be similar to Figure P3–7.

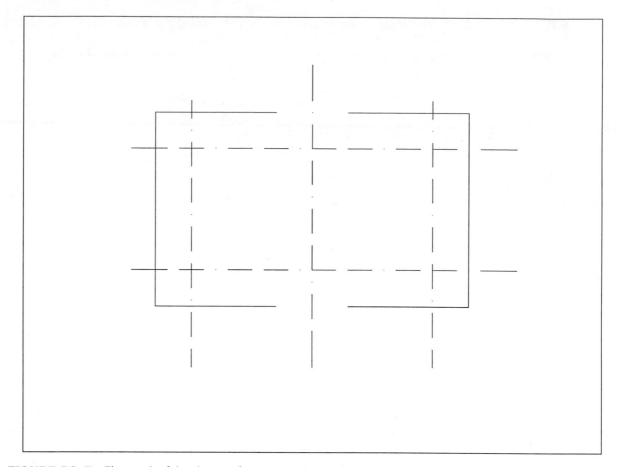

FIGURE P3–7   The result of the design after mirror copying the line string.

STEP 19:   Invoke the Place Arc by Center command from the Arc sub-palette. In the Tool Settings box, set the toggle buttons to Radius, Start Angle, and Sweep Angle constraints to ON. Key-in the radius to .75 in the Radius edit field, the start angle to 180 in the Start Angle edit field, and the sweep angle to 180 in the Sweep Angle edit field. MicroStation prompts:

> *Identify Arc Center* (Key-in **xy=6,3** and press [ENTER].)

The design should now be similar to Figure P3–8.

STEP 20:   Change the arc's Start Angle to 0, and the dynamic image of the arc should flip over. Drag the dynamic image of the arc until it lines up with the top ends of the two line strings and click the Data button. The design should now be similar to Figure P3–9.

STEP 21:   Invoke the Fillet command from the Fillets sub-palette to round off the four corners of the base plate. In the Tool Settings box, key-in .75 in the Radius edit field and select Both from the Truncate options menu. MicroStation prompts:

> *Select first segment* (Identify the top horizontal line close to the left corner.)
> *Select second segment* (Identify the left most vertical line.)
> *Accept-initial construction* (Place a data point to accept.)

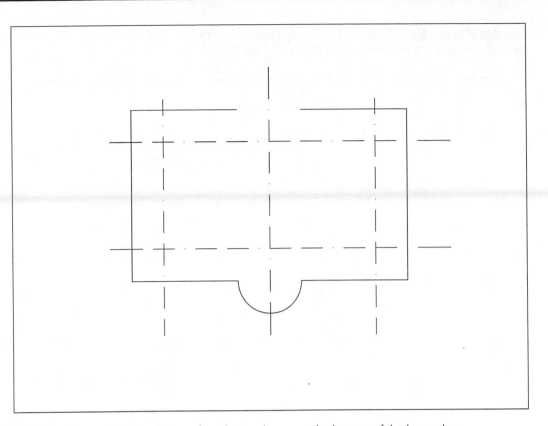

FIGURE P3–8   The result of the design after placing the arc at the bottom of the base plate.

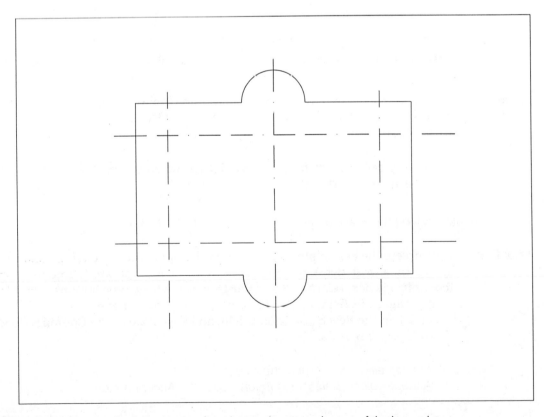

FIGURE P3–9   The result of the design after placing the arc at the top of the base plate.

Similarly place the fillets to remaining three corners with a fillet radius to .75. After the fillets are placed, the design should be similar to Figure P3–10.

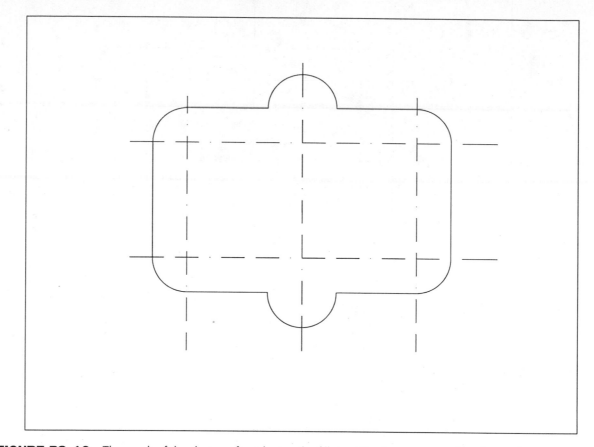

FIGURE P3–10 The result of the design after placing the fillets at the four corners of the base plate.

STEP 22: Invoke the place circle radius command from Circles and Ellipse sub-palette. In the Tool Settings box, set the Radius toggle button to ON, key-in .25 in the Radius edit field. MicroStation prompts:

> *Identify center point* (Key-in **xy=3.5,3.75** and press .)
> *Identify center point* (Click the Reset button.)

After placing the circle, the design should be similar to Figure P3–11.

STEP 23: To complete the base plate, place five additional ¼″ Radius circles in a rectangular array. Invoke the Construct Array command from the Manipulate Element sub-palette. In the Tool Settings box, select Rectangular from the Array Type options menu, key-in 0 in the Active Angle edit field, key-in 2 in the Rows edit field, key-in 3 in the Columns edit field, key-in 2.5 in the Row Spacing edit field, and key-in 2.5 in the Columns Spacing edit field. MicroStation prompts:

> *Identify element* (Identify the circle.)
> *Accept/Reject (Select next input)* (Click the Accept button.)

The design should now be similar to Figure P3–12.

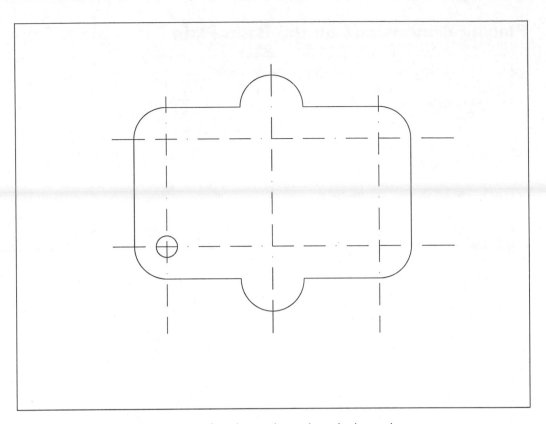

FIGURE P3–11   The result of the design after placing the circle in the base plate.

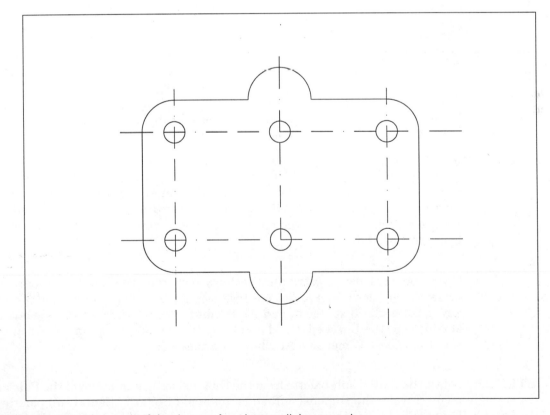

FIGURE P3–12   The result of the design after placing all the six circles.

Placing Dimensions on the Base Plate

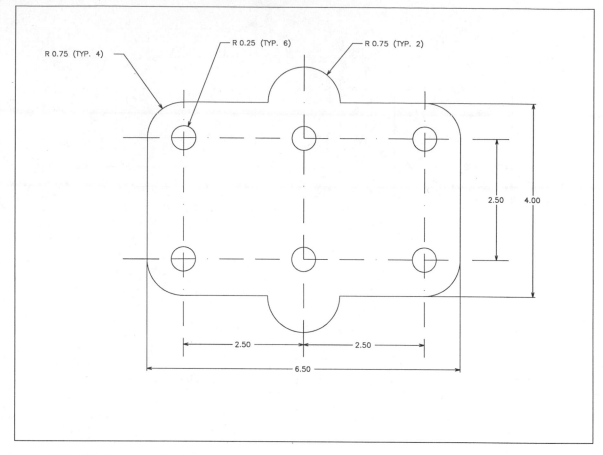

FIGURE P3–13 Design displaying dimensions.

STEP 24: Open Dimension Placement settings box from the Element pull-down menu. Select Horizontal from the Orientation option menu, Automatic from the Location option menu and set the Extension Lines toggle button to ON.

Open the Units settings box from the Dimensions sub-menu of the Element pull-down menu. Select Mechanical format from the Format options menu, set Accuracy (Primary) to two decimal places, and set the toggle buttons to Show Leading Zero and Show Trailing Zero to ON and leave the remaining option selection to the default selection. Close the Units settings box.

Open the Dimension Attributes settings box from the Dimensions sub-menu of the Element pull-down menu. Set the toggle buttons to Text Height and Width to ON and key-in 0.1 in the Text Height and Width edit fields. Set the Level toggle button to ON and key-in 10 in the Level edit field and leave the remaining option selection to the default selection. Close Dimension Attributes settings box.

STEP 25: Select the Radial sub-palette from the Dimensioning sub-menu of the Palettes pull-down menu. Invoke the Dimension Radius command from the Radial sub-palette as shown in Figure P3–14. Set the toggle button to Association to ON. MicroStation prompts:

Identify element (Identify the top left ¼″ circle radius.)
Press Return to edit dimension text
Select Dimension end point (Press [ENTER] key, Dimension edit dialog box appears
   similar to Figure P3–15, type (TYP. 6) next to the * and click OK.)
Press Return to edit dimension text
Select Dimension end point (Place a data point to place the dimension line.)
Identify element (Identify the top left arc that was drawn with the fillet command.)
Press Return to edit dimension text
Select Dimension end point (Press [ENTER] key, Dimension edit dialog box appears,
   type (TYP. 4) next to the * and click OK.)
Select Dimension end point (Place a data point to place the dimension line.)
Identify element (Identify the arc.)
Press Return to edit dimension text
Select Dimension end point (Press [ENTER] key, Dimension edit dialog box appears,
   type (TYP. 2) next to the * and click OK.)
Select Dimension end point (Place a data point to place the dimension line.)

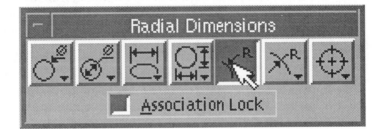

FIGURE P3–14 Invoking Dimension Radius command from the Radial Dimension sub-palette.

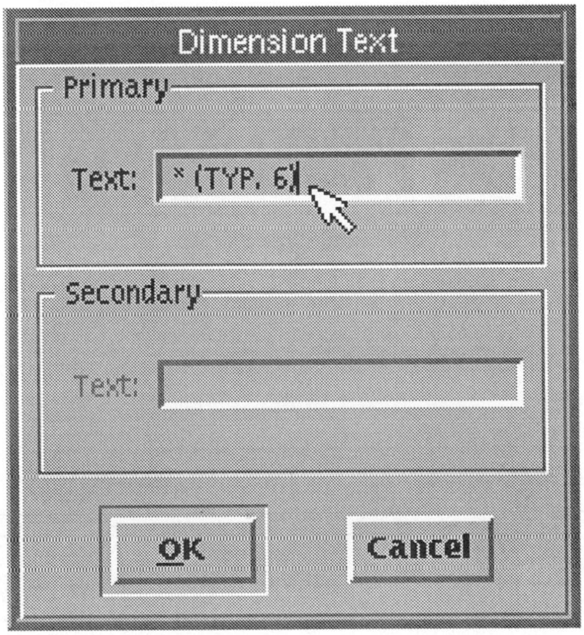

FIGURE P3–15 Dimension edit dialog box.

STEP 26: Select the Linear sub-palette from the Dimensioning sub-menu of the Palettes pull-down
menu. Invoke the Dimension Size with Arrows command from the Linear sub-palette as

shown in Figure P3–16. Place the 4″ dimension on the right side of the base plate and the 6.5″ dimension on the bottom of the base plate. Make each extension line approximately 2″ long.

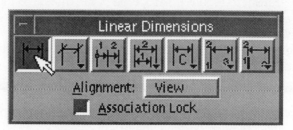

FIGURE P3–16 Invoking Dimension Size with Arrows from the Linear Dimension sub-palette.

STEP 27: In the Dimension Placement settings box, set the Extension lines toggle button to OFF.

STEP 28: Invoke the Dimension Size with Arrows command from the Linear sub-palette. Place the linear dimensions that use the center lines as the extension lines. Each time you are asked to define the length of the extension line, click about .25″ below the end of the center line where you started the dimension.

STEP 29: Create a title block as shown in Figure P3–17.

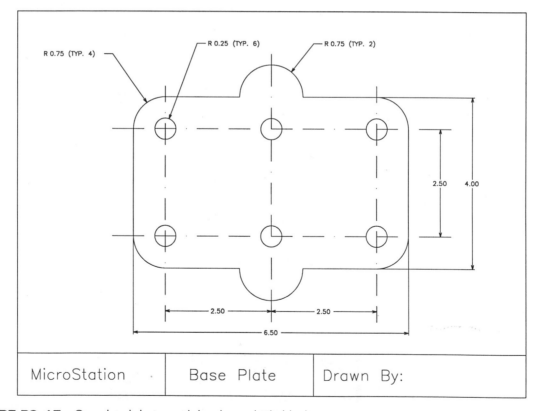

FIGURE P3–17 Completed design with border and title block.

STEP 30: Invoke Save Settings command from the File pull-down menu to save the settings.

STEP 31: If you are finished with MicroStation, exit the program.

CHAPTER

4

FUNDAMENTALS III

After completing this chapter, you will be able to:

- Select elements by element selection command and manipulate with element manipulation commands.
- Manipulate groups of elements using the fence commands.
- Manipulate views of the design.
- Take measurements in the design.
- Use the miscellaneous dimensioning commands.

ELEMENT SELECTION

While you were practicing the element manipulation commands described in the preceding chapters, did little squares occasionally appear on the corners of one of your elements? Did they make the commands act differently from the way the book said they would? The book was not wrong—you had accidentally turned on the Element Selection command.

Let's remove that confusion now by showing you how the Element Selection command can help you manipulate elements.

A New Way to Select Elements

In the previous chapters you first invoked an element manipulation command and then identified the element you wanted to manipulate. With the Element Selection command, you identify an element, or group of elements, first, then select a manipulation command and manipulate the previously selected elements. For example, instead of selecting the Copy command, identify the element(s) to be copied first and then select the Copy command to copy the selected element(s).

Selected elements are easily spotted because of the square "handles" that appear around the elements. See Figure 4–1 for examples of the handles on different element types.

To select the elements for manipulation, first invoke the Element Selection command by clicking the icon located in the Main palette, as shown in Figure 4–2. Once you select the Element Selection

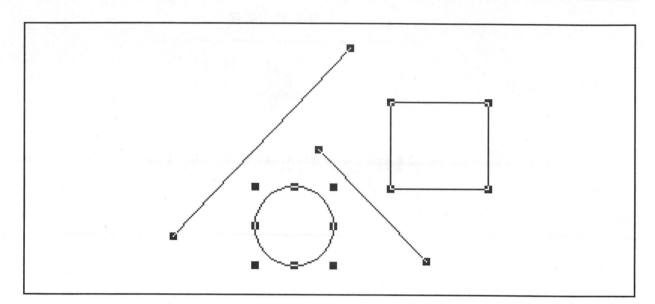

FIGURE 4–1   Examples of the handles on different element types.

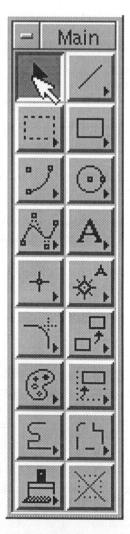

FIGURE 4–2   Invoking the Elememt Selection command from the Main palette.

command, the pointer changes to an arrow with a circle at the top similar to the one shown in Figure 4–3. There is no key-in for this command.

FIGURE 4–3   Element Selection pointer.

The following discussion presents several ways to use the selection tool to select elements.

- Select a single element by clicking the Data button on it.
- Select several elements by pressing and holding the Data button and dragging around the elements. As you drag, a dynamic rectangle outlines the area. When you release the data button, all elements completely inside the dynamic rectangle are selected.
- Add an additional element to the selection by clicking on the element while you hold down the [CTRL] key. If you do not hold down the [CTRL] key, the previous selection is de-selected and the current selection becomes active.
- Add several additional elements to the selection by holding down the [CTRL] key and the Data button and dragging around the additional elements.
- By invoking the Select All command (located in the Edit pull-down menu in the Command Window) you can select all the elements in the design file, regardless of whether they are visible (including the ones on the levels that are turned off).

To deselect elements, invoke the Element Selection command from the Main palette (if you have not already done so), then:

- To deselect one element, hold down the [CTRL] key and click on the element.
- To deselect all elements, click somewhere in the view where there is no element or select an element placement command.

Grouping of Selected Elements

You can consolidate selected elements into a group and manipulate them as a single element. You can have any number of groups, but you cannot name a group unless you create a cell (more about cell creation in Chapter 7). To create a group, first select the elements using the Element Selection command, then invoke the Group command (or [CTRL] + [G]) from the Edit pull-down menu located in the Command Window. Handles appear on a group's boundary instead of individual elements, as shown in Figure 4–4.

> **NOTE:** The Group command is dimmed in the pull-down menu if no elements are selected.

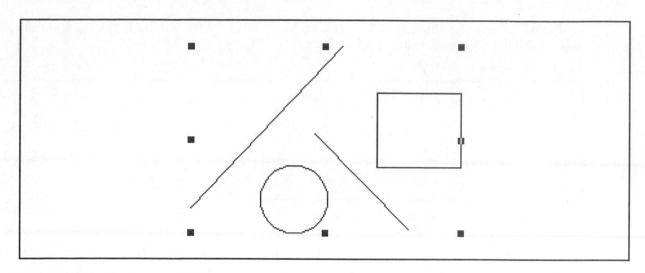

FIGURE 4–4   Handles on a group boundary.

Ungrouping the Group

You also can make a group into individual elements. Select the group using the Element Selection command, then invoke the Ungroup command (or [CTRL] + [U]) from the Edit pull-down menu located in the Command Window. Handles appear on individual elements instead of on a group's boundary. Each ungrouped element can be manipulated by itself.

> **NOTE:** The Ungroup command is dimmed in the pull-down menu if no elements are selected.

Locking the Selected Elements

Similar to grouping elements, you also can lock the selected elements. Locking is useful to prevent accidental element manipulation (including deleting the elements). If you try to manipulate a locked element, MicroStation beeps to alert you that the element is locked. Locked elements behave similarly to elements that are on a level that is locked (level lock). This feature is very helpful if you are working on a complicated design file and not wish to manipulate certain elements.

To lock the selected elements, first select the elements using the Element Selection command, then invoke the Lock command (or [CTRL] + [L]) from the Edit pull-down menu located in the Command Window. Grayed handles appear on a locked element's boundary when the element is selected. When you group a locked element with other unlocked elements, the whole group is locked.

> **NOTE:** The Lock command is dimmed in the pull-down menu if no elements are selected.

Unlocking the Selected Elements

As well as locking the elements, you can unlock the elements. Each unlocked element can be manipulated. To unlock the elements, select the elements using the Element Selection command, then invoke the Unlock command (or ⌨CTRL + ⌨M) from the Edit pull-down menu located in the Command Window.

> **NOTE:** The Unlock command is dimmed in the pull-down menu if no elements are selected.

Duplicating the Selected Elements

This feature allows you to duplicate each selected element and place the copy next to the corresponding original, as shown in Figure 4–5. There is no way to control the distance between the original and copy. To duplicate, select the elements using the Element Selection command, then invoke the Duplicate command (or ⌨CTRL + ⌨D) from the Edit pull-down menu located in the Command Window.

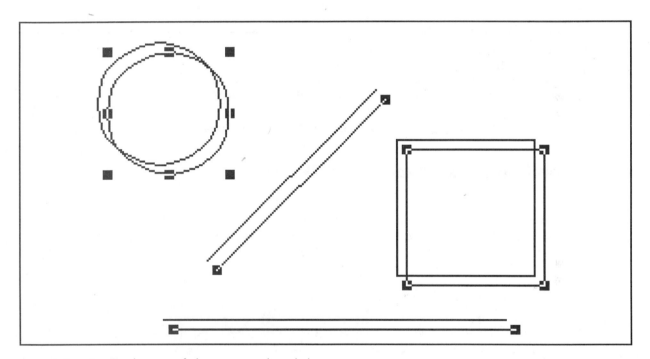

FIGURE 4–5   Duplication of elements on selected elements.

> **NOTE:** The Duplicate command is dimmed in the pull-down menu if no elements are selected.

Moving the Selected Elements

To move selected element(s), press and hold the data button anywhere on one of the selected elements (but not on the handle itself), then drag the selected element to the new location and release the data button. Dynamic update causes an image of the element to move with your screen pointer. All selected elements move to the new location. Figure 4–6 shows an example of moving selected elements.

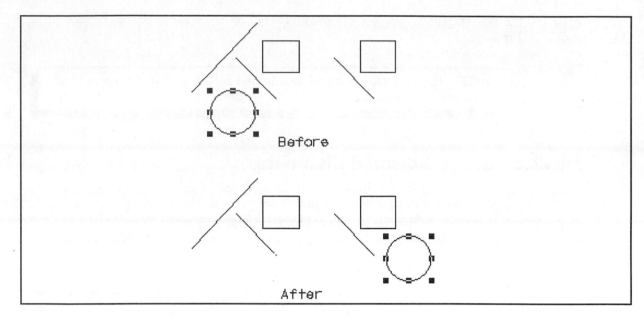

FIGURE 4–6 Moving an element with handle.

NOTE: You do not have to invoke the Move Element command to move the selected elements.

Modifying the Shape of an Element

You can modify the shape of an individual element by dragging one of its handles. Point to the handle of a selected element, then press and hold the Data button and drag the element to a new geometric shape. Only the element whose handle you selected is modified. Figure 4–7 shows how dragging an element handle changes various types of elements.

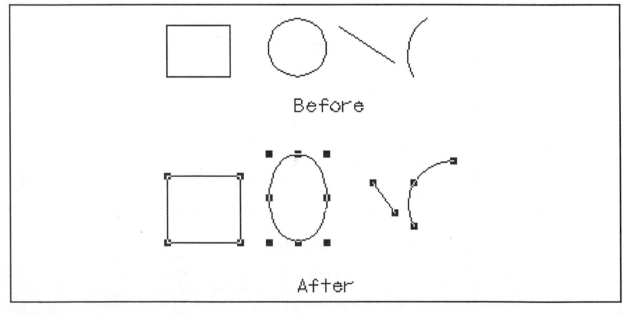

FIGURE 4–7 Modifying an element with handle.

Manipulation of Selected Elements

The element manipulation commands Array, Copy, Delete, Mirror, Move, Rotate, Scale, and Spin manipulate elements previously selected with the Element Selection command. They treat all elements with handles as if they were one element.

The handles already identify the elements to be manipulated, so each of these commands only requires you to indicate the manipulation to be performed. As always, read the prompts in the Command Window to find out what the command wants you to do. For example, to spin the selected element(s), place a data point to indicate the pivot point and another data point to indicate the angle of rotation (see Figure 4–8). You do not have to identify the element.

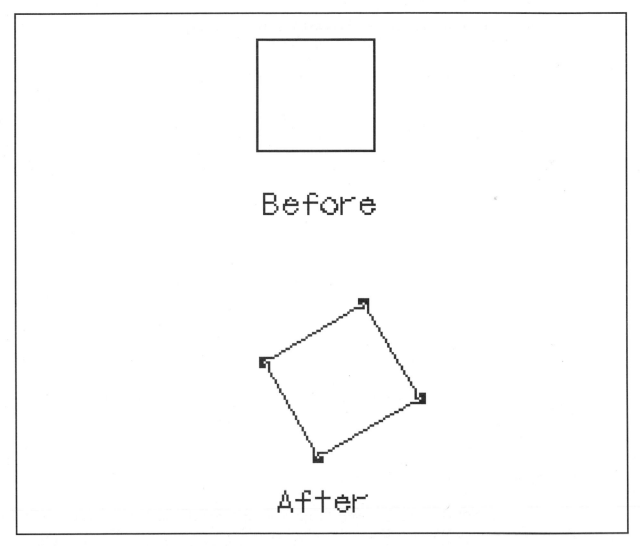

FIGURE 4–8   Spinning an element with handle.

> **NOTE:** Only the element manipulation commands discussed above work with elements that have handles. If you select any other manipulation or placement command, the handles disappear.

FENCE MANIPULATION

The fence manipulation commands provide another way to manipulate groups of elements. Before you can use the fence manipulation commands, you must place a fence around the elements and select the fence selection mode you want to use. After you have done that, you can use a set of fence content manipulation commands that are analogous to element manipulation commands.

Only one fence can be placed in your design plane at a time. If you place a second fence, the first fence disappears. The fence you place remains active until you remove it or close the design file.

Place a Fence

The fence can be a block defined by diagonally opposite data points or a shape defined by a series of vertex data points. See Figure 4–9 for examples of the two types of fences.

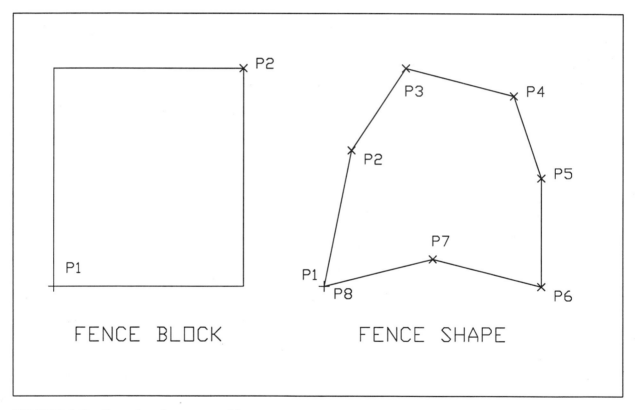

FIGURE 4–9 Examples of two types of fences.

The Place Fence Block and Place Fence Shape commands are available in the Fence palette that can be opened from the Main palette, as shown in Figure 4–10.

To place a fence block, invoke the Place Fence Block command by clicking the Place Fence Block icon in the Fence sub-palette (see Figure 4–11) or key-in at the uSTN> field **place fence block** (or **pla f**), and press ⏎. MicroStation prompts:

> *Enter first point* (Place a data point or key-in coordinates to define one corner of the fence block.)
> *Enter opposite corner* (Place a data point or key-in coordinates to define the diagonal opposite corner.)

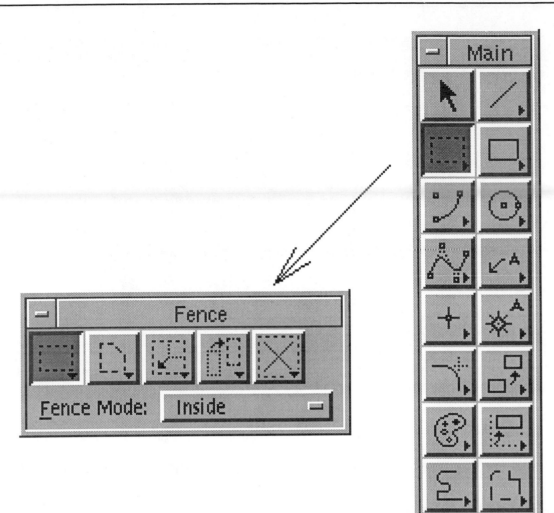

FIGURE 4–10   Invoking the Fence sub-palette from the Main palette.

FIGURE 4–11   Invoking Place Fence Block command from the Fence sub-palette.

NOTE: After you place the first data point, a dynamic image of the fence drags with the screen pointer.

To place a fence shape, invoke the Place Fence Shape command by clicking the Place Fence Shape icon in the Fence sub-palette (see Figure 4–12) or key-in at the uSTN> field **place fence shape** (or **pla f s**) and press [ENTER]. MicroStation prompts:

Enter fence points (Place data points to define each vertex of the fence. To close the fence, place a data point on top of the first data point or click on the Close Fence button from the Fence sub-palette.)

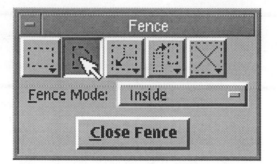

FIGURE 4–12   Invoking Place Fence Shape command from the Fence sub-palette.

As you place each vertex point, a dynamic image of the part of the fence shape you have defined appears on the screen.

> **NOTE:** To remove the fence, invoke either the Place Fence Block or Place Fence Shape command.

Modify a Fence

You have just finished placing a complicated fence shape and there, sitting outside the fence, is an element that should be inside the fence. No need to draw the fence again. The Modify Fence Vertex and the Move Fence Block/Shape commands can fix it. Figure 4–13 show examples of modifying a fence.

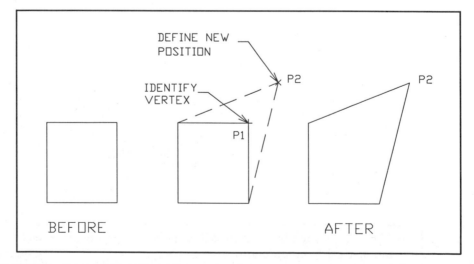

FIGURE 4–13   An example for modifying a fence.

To modify a fence's geometric shape, invoke the Modify Fence Vertex command by clicking the Modify Fence Vertex icon in the Fence sub-palette (see Figure 4–14) or key-in at the uSTN> field **modify fence** (or **mod f**) and press [ENTER]. MicroStation prompts:

Identify vertex (Select the fence on or near the vertex you want to move, drag the vertex to the new location, place a data point, then click the Reset button.)

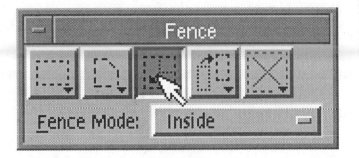

FIGURE 4–14 Invoking Modify fence command from the Fence sub-palette.

After you select the vertex to be moved, a dynamic image of the fence vertex follows the screen pointer. It continues following the screen pointer after you place a data button, unless you press the Reset button.

The command remains active after you press the Reset button, and if necessary, you can move another vertex.

To move a fence, invoke the Move Fence Block/Shape command by clicking the Move Fence Block/Shape icon in the Fence sub-palette (see Figure 4–15) or key-in at the uSTN> field **move fence** (or **mov f**) and press [ENTER]. MicroStation prompts:

Define origin (Place a data point anywhere in the design plane to start the move.)
Define distance (Place a data point to indicate where you want to move the fence.)

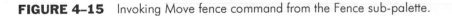

FIGURE 4–15 Invoking Move fence command from the Fence sub-palette.

After you place the first data point, a dynamic image of the fence follows the screen cursor. The fence is placed in the same relationship to the second data point as it was to the first data point.

> **NOTE:** The Move Fence Block/Shape command only moves the fence, not the contents of the fence. Do not confuse it with the Move Fence Contents command which moves the fence and its contents.

Remove a Fence

There is no separate command to remove a fence. To remove the fence, select either the Place Fence Block or Place Fence Shape command. As soon as you select either of these commands, the current fence disappears. After the fence has disappeared, select another command and continue your work.

> **NOTE:** Always remove the fence after you are finished with it. For example, if you accidentally select the Delete Fence Contents thinking you have selected the Delete Element command, you are going to delete the fence contents, not the element you select.

Set Fence Selection Mode

After you place the fence, the next step is to tell MicroStation what elements to include in fence manipulation. To do so, you have to select one of the six fence selection modes (locks). The Fence Selection modes options menu is available from the Locks settings box, fence sub-palette (see Figure 4–16), and all sub-palettes that contain fence manipulation commands.

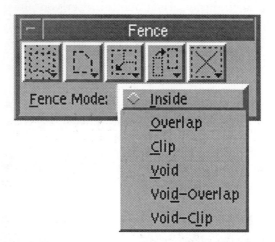

FIGURE 4–16   Displaying list of options available in the Fence Mode option menu.

The six fence mode selections are

Inside: Only the elements completely inside the fence are manipulated. For example, circles A, B, and D are deleted when the fence delete command is invoked at the time Inside fence lock is selected (see Figure 4–17a).

Overlap: Elements inside and overlapping the fence are manipulated. For example, circles A, B, C, D, and F, lines A and C are deleted when fence delete command is invoked at the time Overlap fence lock is selected (see Figure 4–17b).

Clip: Elements inside the fence and the portions of overlapping elements that are inside the fence are manipulated. For example, circles A, B, and D and parts of circles C, E, and F, lines A and C are deleted when fence delete command is invoked at the time Clip fence lock is selected (see Figure 4–17c).

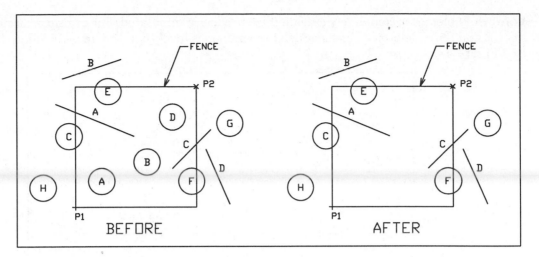

FIGURE 4–17a   Example showing before and after result when Inside fence mode is selected.

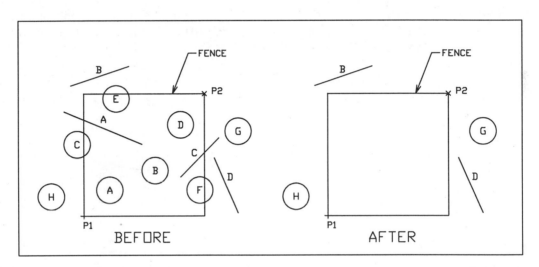

FIGURE 4–17b   Example showing before and after result when Overlap fence mode is selected.

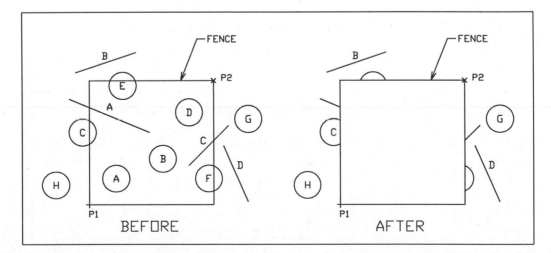

FIGURE 4–17c   Example showing before and after result when Clip fence mode is selected.

Void: Only elements completely outside the fence are manipulated. For example, circle G and H and lines B and D are deleted when fence delete command is invoked at the time Void fence lock is selected (see Figure 4–17d).

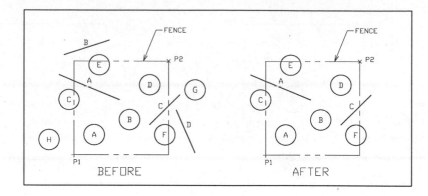

FIGURE 4–17d   Example showing before and after result when Void fence mode is selected.

Void-Overlap: Elements outside the fence and overlapping the fence are manipulated. For example, circles C, E, F, G, and H, and lines A, B, C, and D are deleted when fence delete command is invoked when Void-Overlap fence lock is selected (see Figure 4–17e).

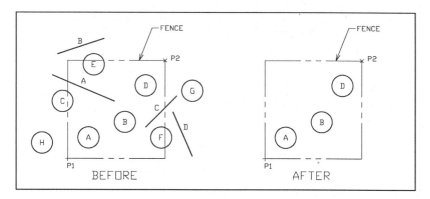

FIGURE 4–17e   Example showing before and after result when Void-Overlap fence mode is selected.

Void-clip: Elements outside the fence and the portions of overlapping elements that are outside the fence are manipulated. For example, circles G and H, lines B and D and parts of circles C, E, and F, lines A and C are deleted when fence delete command is invoked when Void-Clip fence lock is selected (see Figure 4–17f).

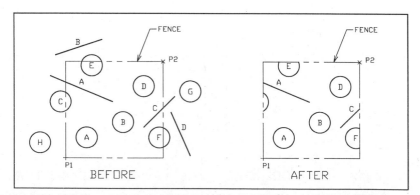

FIGURE 4–17f   Example showing before and after result when Void-Clip fence mode is selected.

Manipulating the Fence Contents

After you place your fence and select the appropriate fence selection mode, you are ready to use the fence contents manipulation commands. There is a fence contents manipulation equivalent for each of the element manipulation commands discussed in the previous chapters. The only difference is that you do not have to select the element to be manipulated—the fence does that for you.

The Copy, Move, Scale, Rotate, Mirror, and Array commands in the Manipulate Element sub-palette (available from the Main palette) can be switched between element manipulation and fence contents manipulation. The Use Fence button in the sub-palette determines which type of manipulation is done. If the button is set to ON, the fence contents are manipulated. If it is set to OFF, individual elements are manipulated. Similarly, the Change Element sub-palette also has a toggle button to switch between element and fence manipulation. Figure 4–18 shows the sub-palette with the button set to ON for the Copy command.

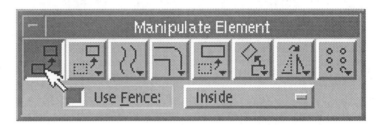

FIGURE 4–18   Sub-palette with toggle button set to ON for the Fence operation.

> **NOTE:** Use Fence button is dimmed when there is no fence placed in your design plane.

The Delete Fence Contents command is available in the Fence sub-palette, as shown in Figure 4–19.

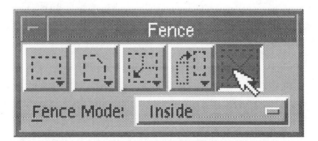

FIGURE 4–19   Invoking the Fence Delete command from the Fence sub-palette.

> **NOTE:** Manipulating fence contents on a large number of elements may overflow the undo buffer. If that happens, you will not be able to undo completely a fence contents manipulation you did in error. Before you start a fence contents manipulation, make sure you really want to do it.

Fence Stretch

The Fence Stretch command allows you to stretch the contents of a fence. There is no equivalent element manipulation command.

Fence Stretch ignores fence selection modes. The way it manipulates elements depends on their type and position. Line, Line String, Multi-line, Curve String, Shape, Polygon, Arc, and Cell (discussed in Chapter 7) elements that overlap the fence are stretched. Elements inside the fence are moved. Circle and ellipse elements that overlap the fence are ignored. Figure 4–20 shows an example of stretching elements.

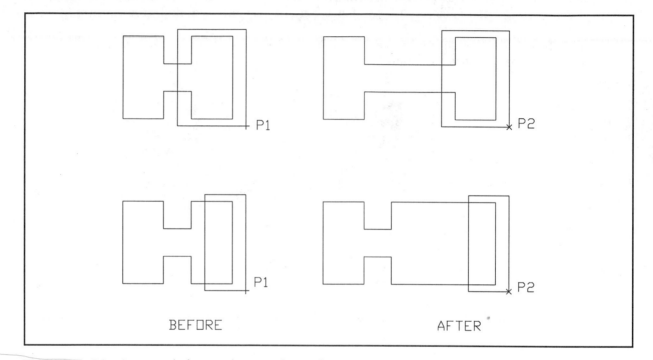

FIGURE 4–20   An example for stretching an element by a Fence.

To stretch a group of elements, place a fence that overlaps the elements you want to stretch, then invoke the Fence Stretch command by clicking the Fence Stretch icon from the Modify Element sub-palette (Figure 4–21), or key-in at the uSTN> field, **fence stretch** (or **fen st**) and press [ENTER]. MicroStation prompts:

Define origin (Place a data point anywhere in the design plane to start the stretch.)
Define distance (Place a data point to define the end and length of the stretch.)

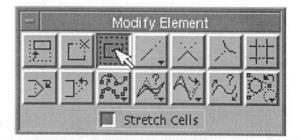

FIGURE 4–21   Invoking the Fence Stretch command from the Modify sub-palette.

VIEWS AND VIEW ATTRIBUTES

Thus far, you have been working in only one view at a time. If you need to look at a different part of the design, you used the view control commands (such as Zoom or Fit) to move to that part.

MicroStation actually provides eight views (or cameras) that let you work in different parts of your design at the same time. Each view is identified by its view number (1 to 8). The views are similar to having eight zoom lens cameras that can be pointed at different parts of your design. If you have a two-monitor workstation, you can open the views on either monitor.

Each view maintains a display of the current design independent of the display shown in other views. In one view you might display the entire drawing; in two other views you might be zoomed in close to widely separated design areas to show great detail (Figure 4–22). Any work you do in one view shows up immediately in all the other views that are looking at the same part of the design. You can draw and manipulate elements between views. For example, you might start a line placement in one view and complete it in another view.

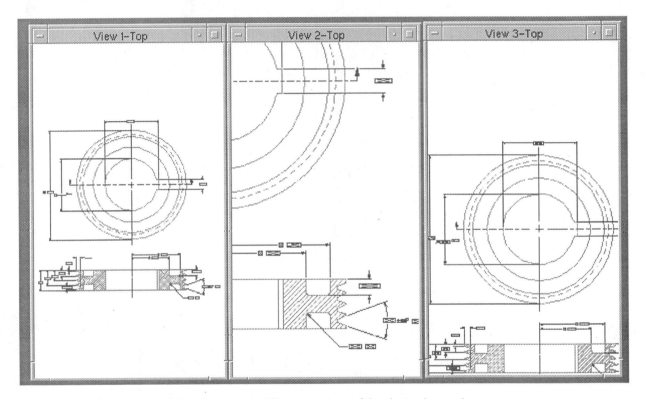

FIGURE 4–22   Displaying three views with different portions of the design being shown.

The view control commands you have already been introduced to (Zoom, Fit, Area, Center, and Update) work on any open view. Let's look now at the View commands that help you set up the eight views and additional commands that control what you see in a view.

Opening and Closing Views

Views are opened and closed from the View pull-down menu, the View open/close settings box, or by key-in.

To open or close a view from the View pull-down menu, select the Open/Close option, and in the sub-menu click on the toggle button for the number of the view you want to open or close (see Figure 4–23). If the view button appears to be pushed in (and has a dark center) the view is open. If the view button appears to be sticking out, the view is closed. You can also open/close views from the View open/close settings box as shown in Figure 4–24. To open Open/Close settings box select Dialog option from the Open/Close sub-menu.

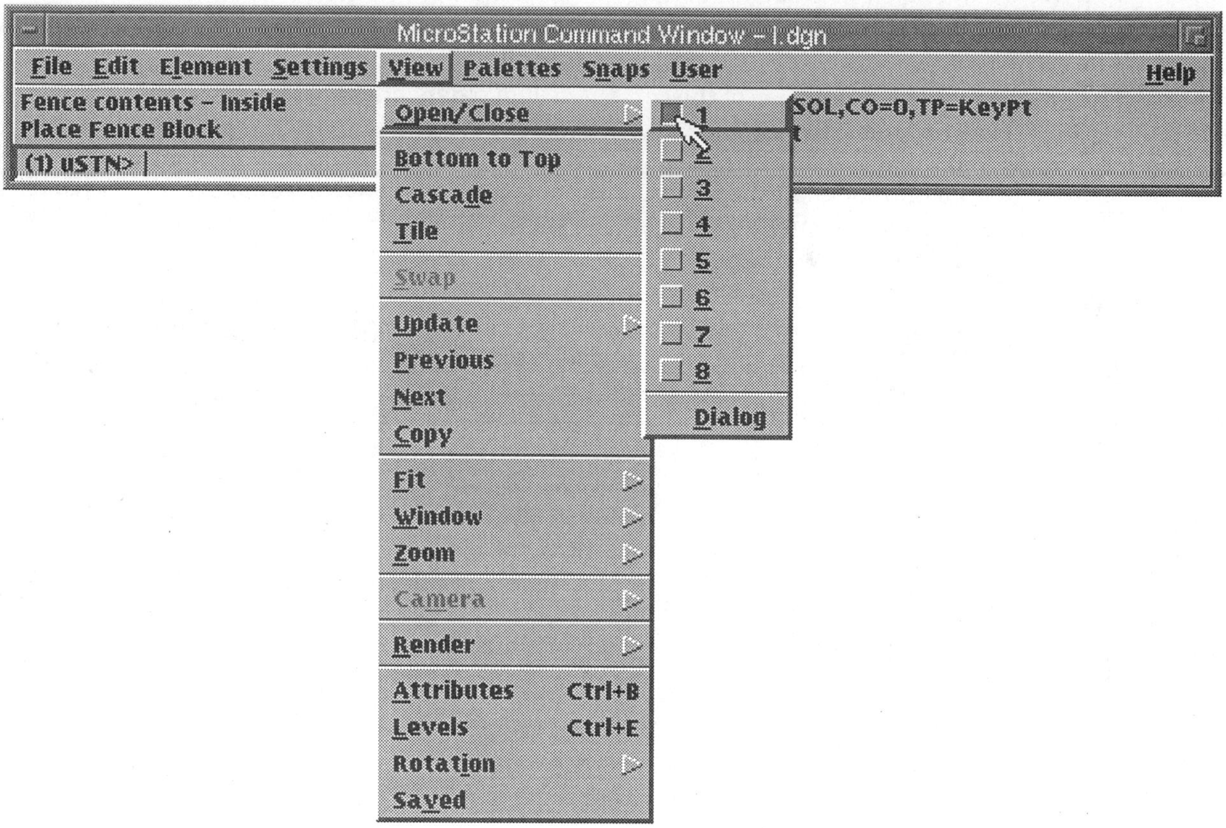

FIGURE 4–23 Invoking the Open/Close option of the views from the View pull-down menu of the MicroStation Command Window.

FIGURE 4–24 View Open/Close Settings box.

To open a view, key-in at the uSTN> field, **view on #**, and press [ENTER]. Replace the # sign with the number of the view you want to open. To close a view, key-in at the uSTN> field, **view off #,** and press [ENTER]. Replace the # sign with the number of the view you want to close. You can also close a view by double-clicking on its window menu button (–) located in the upper left corner of the window.

> **NOTE:** The views you open and close only apply to the current editing session. If you want your design file to have the same number of views open the next time you open the current design file, select Save Settings from the File pull-down menu.

Arranging Views

When you have several views open on one monitor at the same time, it can get a little messy. Three view commands are available from the View pull-down menu to help you deal with that mess. The commands are Bottom to Top, Cascade, and Tile (see Figure 4–25).

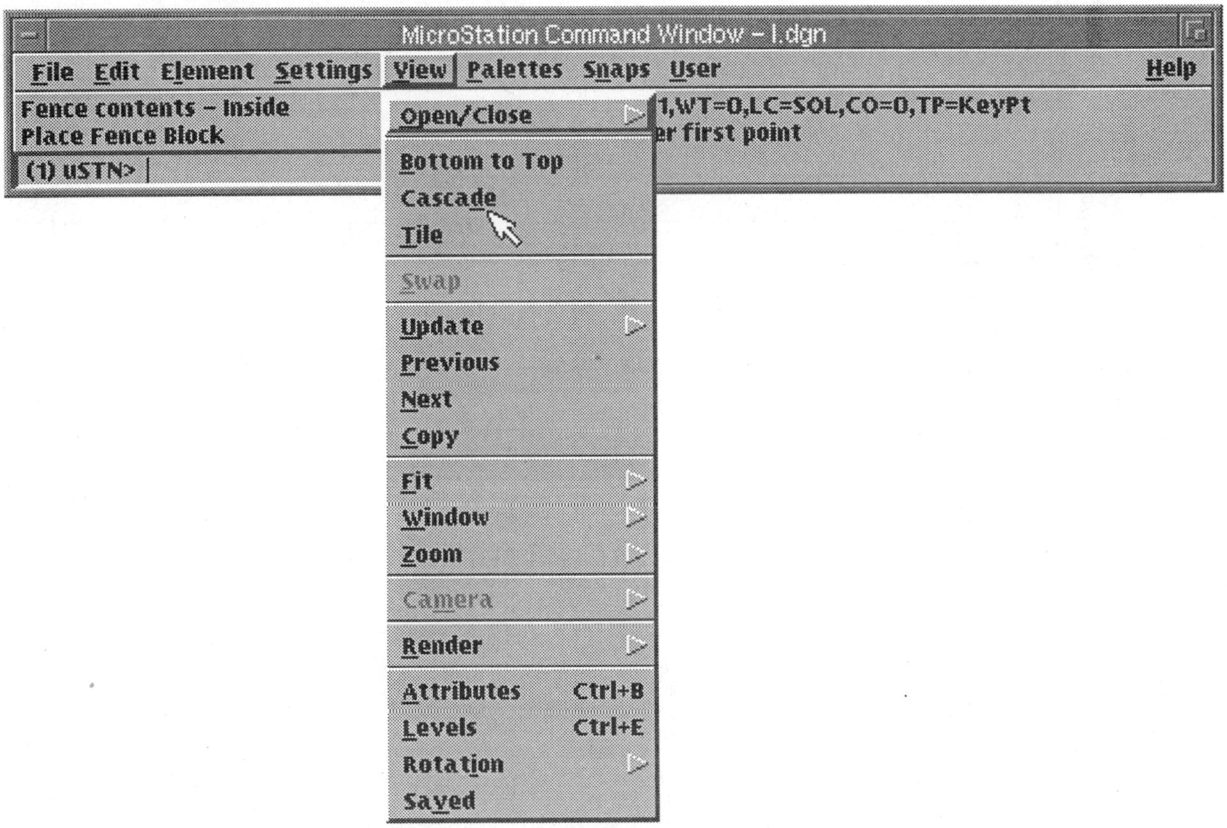

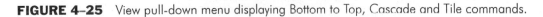

FIGURE 4–25   View pull-down menu displaying Bottom to Top, Cascade and Tile commands.

Bottom to Top To pop the bottom view in a stack of views to the top, invoke the Bottom to Top command from the View pull-down menu. Each time you select Bottom to Top, the bottom view in the stack pops to the top of the stack.

Cascade To arrange all open views in numerical order with the lowest view number on top and the Title Bars of the other views visible (see Figure 4–26), invoke the Cascade command located in the View pull-down menu. To work on a specific view, just click on the Title Bar and it will pop up to the top.

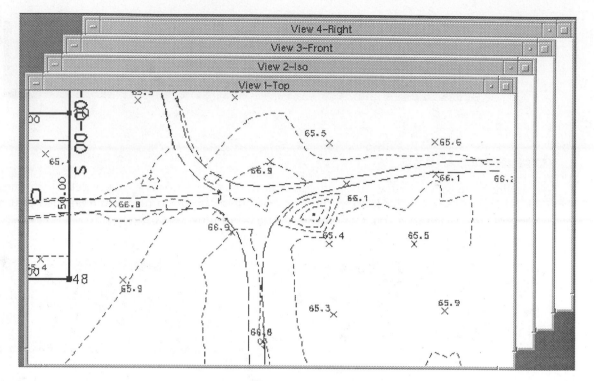

FIGURE 4–26 Displaying views by cascade.

Tile To arrange all open views (in each monitor, if you have two) side by side in a tiled fashion, invoke the Tile command from Views pull-down menu. As soon as you select Tile, the views re-arrange themselves in a tile pattern (see Figure 4–27).

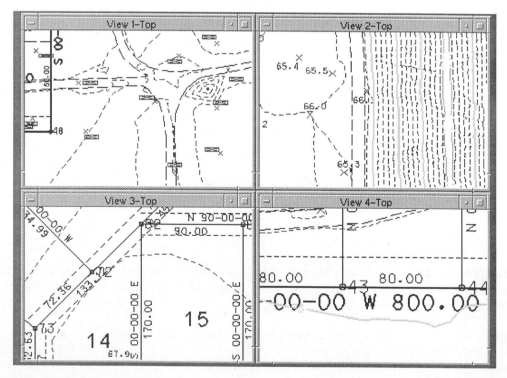

FIGURE 4–27 Displaying views by tile.

Arrange Individual Views In addition to the commands discussed above that arrange all views, MicroStation allows you to resize and move individual views. To change the size of a view, point to one of the view borders and watch for the screen pointer to change to a line with a small arrowhead on each end. When you get the two-headed line, press and hold the Data button, drag the border to the new position, and release the Data button. As you drag the border, a dynamic image of the border outline moves with the screen pointer. Grab the vertical or horizontal part of a view border to change the size in one direction only. Grab the corner of a view border to change the horizontal and vertical size at the same time.

To move a view to a new location in the MicroStation work space, point to the Title Bar at the top of the view and watch for the pointer to change to a cross with an arrowhead on all four cross ends. When you get the cross, press and hold the Data button, drag the window to the new position, and release the Data button. As you drag the window a dynamic image of the window's outline moves with the screen pointer.

> **NOTE:** The shape of the resize and move pointers described here are for a PC. The shape may be different in other platforms.

To maximize a view so it fills the MicroStation work space, click on the maximize button on the right end of the view's Title Bar (see Figure 4–28). Clicking on this button causes the view to increase in size until it fills the work space and covers all other open views.

To return a maximized view to the size it was before being maximized, click on the maximize button again. If the view was tiled before you expanded it, it will return to its tiled position. If the views were cascaded, it will be on the top of the stack when it goes back to its original size.

To minimize a view so that it takes up the minimum amount of space in the MicroStation work space, click on the minimize button (see Figure 4–28). Minimizing a view reduces it to the smallest size that can still display the view's complete Title Bar.

To return a minimized view to the size it was before being minimized, click on the Minimize button again. If the view was tiled before you minimized it, it goes back to its tiled position. If the views were cascaded, it will be on the top of the stack when it goes back to its original size.

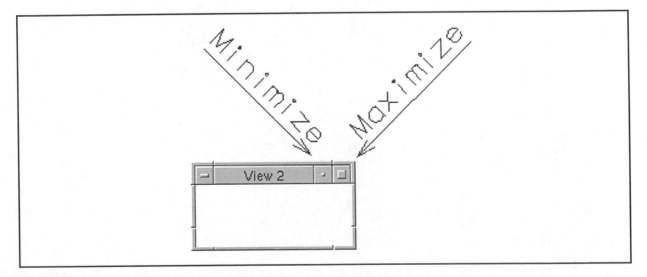

FIGURE 4–28   Displaying the location of the Maximize and Minimize buttons.

> **NOTE:** The way you arrange your views only applies to the current editing session. If you want your design file to have the same view arrangement the next time you load it in MicroStation, select Save Settings from the File pull-down menu.

Controlling What the View Sees

In Chapter 2 you were introduced to the six view control commands (Zoom In, Zoom Out, Window Area, Window Center, Fit, Update) available from the View Control sub-palette in the Main palette. This section explains additional options available from the View pull-down menu in the command window.

Update Options

As mentioned in Chapter 2, MicroStation does not always clean up the view properly after manipulations. Sometimes part of the grid will be missing and occasionally "ghosts" of elements are left on the screen after you move or delete them.

The View update commands repaint (redraw) views. They do not do anything to the elements in your design file, they just clean up the view. Following are the options available under the Update sub-menu in the View pull-down menu as shown in Figure 4–29:

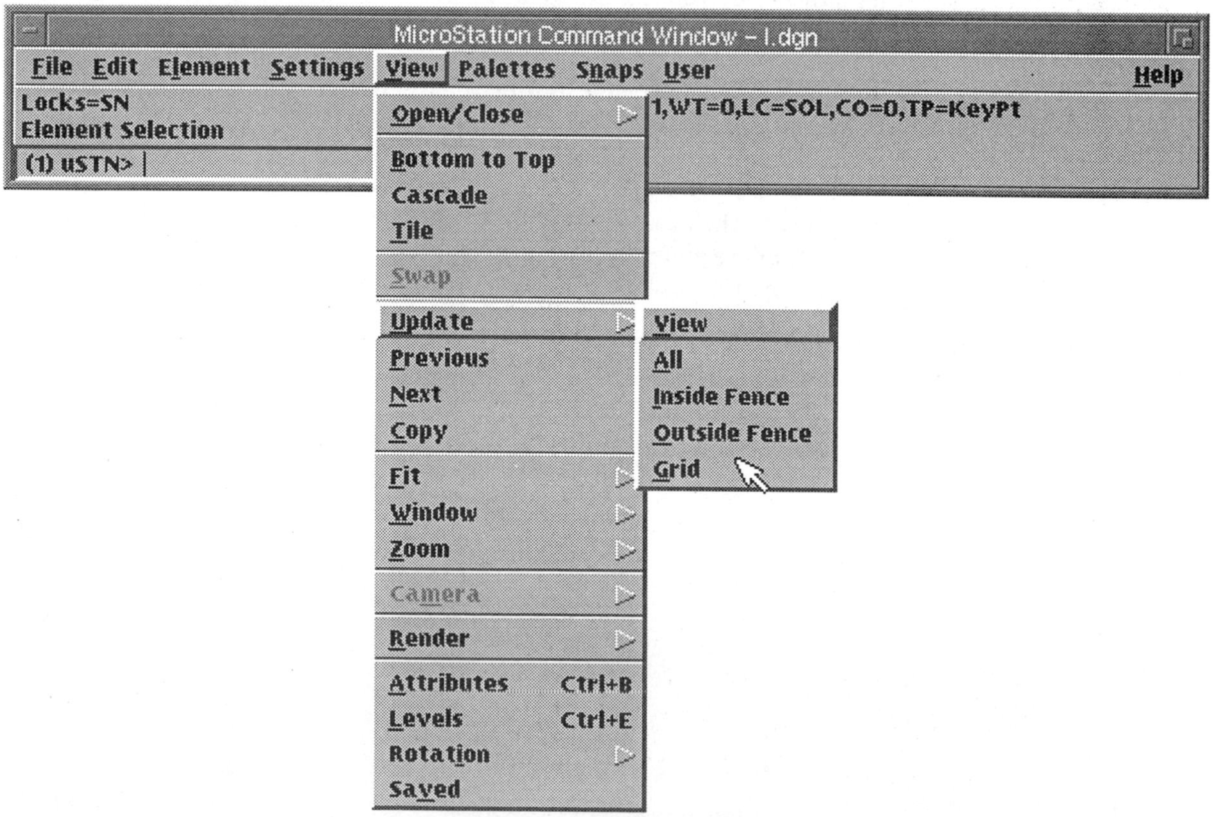

FIGURE 4–29 Displaying the Update sub-menu located in the View pull-down menu of the MicroStation Command Window.

The **View** update option is the same as the one in the View Control sub-palette. Select this option, then click the data button in the view you want updated.

The **All** update option updates all views (open or closed) as soon as you select it.

The **Inside Fence** update option updates only the area contained in a fence you placed previously. This is handy when you are working in a small area of a view that contains a lot of elements. You don't have to wait for the complete view to be updated. If no fence is defined, this option is grayed out and cannot be selected.

The **Outside Fence** update option updates only the area outside a fence you placed previously. If no fence is defined, this option is grayed out and cannot be selected.

The **Grid** update option updates only the grid in all views.

Negating View

The Previous command in the View sub-menu negates the last view control operation. This allows you to back up through the last eight view operations. For example, you might have used Window Area and a couple of window centers to get the view just the way you want it. You then do a fit and realize the view should have been left the way it was after the Window Area was done. Rather than having to do the Window Area procedure again, just use Previous three times to restore the view to the Window Area setup.

To restore previous views, invoke the Previous command from the View pull-down menu. MicroStation prompts:

> *Select view* (Click the Data button in the view you want to restore. You can click back through as many as eight previous view setups.)

If you clicked one too many times while using Previous to move backward through the previous view setups, use Next to move forward through those setups. The Next command restores the view setup negated by Previous.

To restore a negated view, invoke the Next command from the View sub-menu. MicroStation prompts:

> *Select view* (Click the data button in the view where you just used the Previous command. You can click back through each of the negated view setups.)

Copy View

The Copy option in the View sub-menu allows you to align a destination view in the same way as a source view. This is handy when you want to start out with all your views showing the same area of your design. To copy views, invoke the Copy from the View pull-down menu or key-in at the uSTN> field, **copy view** (or **copy vi**), and press [ENTER]. MicroStation prompts:

> *Select source view* (Click the data button in the view you want to copy.)
> *Select destination view(s)* (Click the data button in each view you want aligned the same as the source view.)

Each time you click in a destination view, that view is aligned to look exactly the same as the source view (see Figure 4–30).

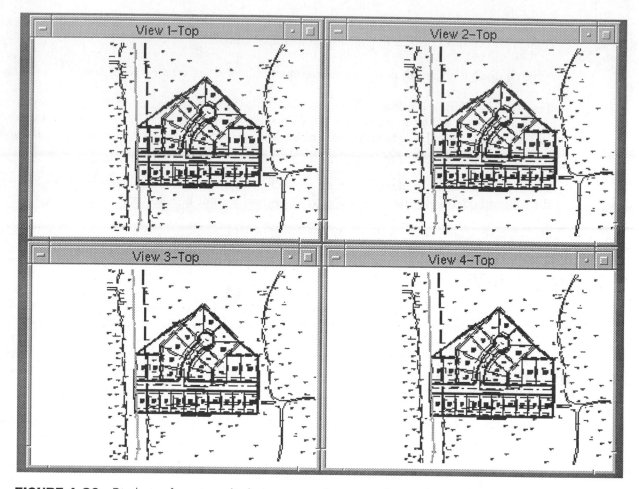

FIGURE 4–30 Displaying four views displaying same information after invoking the Copy View command.

Setting Up View Attributes

View attributes affect the display of certain types and classes of elements and certain drawing aids. For example, you can turn ON and OFF the display of the grid in the view you currently are working in. All the attributes you can control are listed in the View Attributes settings box.

To change view attributes, invoke the View Attributes settings box similar to the one shown in Figure 4–31 by selecting View Attributes from the View pull-down menu.

In the View Attributes settings box, set the attributes the way you want them by clicking on the attributes toggle button. If the button is depressed and has a dark center, the attribute is set to ON. If the button appears to be sticking out, the attribute is set to OFF. If you want to apply the attributes to all eight views, click on the All button at the bottom right of the window. If you want only the attributes applied to one view, pick the number of the view you want in the View Number options menu at the top of the settings box, then click the Apply button.

The View Number options menu allows you to select only views that are open. Closed views are grayed in the menu and cannot be selected. The All button will apply the attributes to all views, open or closed.

See Table 4–1 for brief explanations of the different display modes.

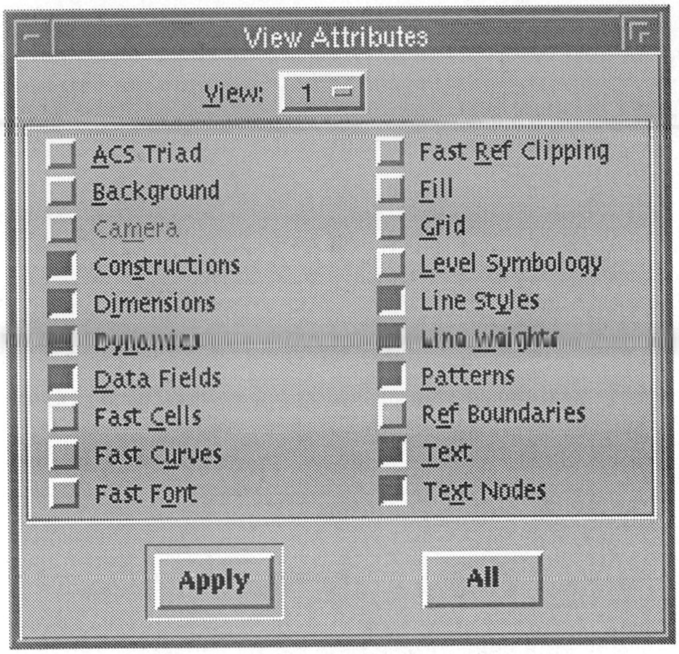

FIGURE 4–31 View Attributes Settings box.

> **NOTE:** The view attribute setting changes you make remain in effect until you change them again or exit MicroStation. To keep them in effect for future editing sessions, select Save Settings from the File pull-down menu.

Saving Views

If you regularly work in several specific areas of a design, MicroStation provides a way for you to return to those areas quickly by saving the view setup and attributes under a user-defined name. To return to one of those areas, you provide the saved view name, then click in the view you want set to have the saved view's setup. Let's look at how to save view information, how to recall views, and how to delete view setups when you no longer need them.

Save a View To save a view setup, first align a view to display the area of the design you want to save and set the view attributes you want to have in effect when you use the view. Invoke the Saved View settings box (see Figure 4–32) by selecting Saved from the View pull-down menu.

To save a view, first make sure the number of the view that contains the view setup is displayed in the View options menu in the Saved View settings box. Then key-in a Name and Description in the Name edit field and Description edit field, respectively. Saved view names can be from one to six characters long and can consist of any combination of letters, numbers, dashes (-), periods (.), and underscores (_). Try to make your view name descriptive (to the extent that six characters allow). Descriptions are optional and can be up to 27 characters long. Make it a habit to always use the description to explain what the saved view is set to. Your description will help other people who use your design file, and it will help you if you have not used the design file for a few weeks. Once you have provided name and optional description, click on the Save button. The view is saved, and the name and description appear in the Saved Views area of the Saved View settings box. The saved view is now a permanent part of your design file.

Table 4–1. Display Modes

MODE	DESCRIPTIONS
ACS Triad	Controls the display of the Auxiliary Coordinate System (ACS).
Background	Controls the display of the background image loaded with the Active Background command.
Camera	Controls the display of the view camera.
Constructions	Controls the display of the elements placed when the Construction Class mode was active. If it is set to ON, the construction elements are displayed.
Dimensions	Controls the display of the dimension elements. If it is set to ON, the dimension elements are displayed.
Dynamics	Controls the dynamic updating of the elements as they are placed in the design.
Data Fields	Controls the display of the Data Fields.
Fast Cells	If Fast Cells is set to ON, all cells are displayed with a box at the location of the cell. Turning Fast Cells ON can decrease view update time.
Fast Curves	If Fast Curves is set to ON, curve elements are displayed as line strings. Turning Fast Curves ON can decrease view update time.
Fast Font	If Fast Font is set to ON, all text elements are displayed in the fast font. Displaying with fast font can decrease view update time.
Fast Ref Clipping	If Fast Ref Clipping is set to ON, reference files are clipped to the largest block enclosing the clipping boundaries. Turning this ON can decrease view update time.
Fill	Controls the display of the closed elements. If it is set to ON, closed elements that have the fill attribute are displayed with color fill.
Grid	If Grid is set to ON, the grid is displayed.
Level Symbology	If Level Symbology is set to ON, the elements will be displayed according to the symbology table rather than element symbology.
Line Styles	If Line Styles is set to ON, elements are displayed with their line styles attribute. If OFF, elements are displayed with a continuous line style and can decrease view update time.
Line Weights	If Line Weights is set to ON, elements are displayed with their line weights attribute. If OFF, elements are displayed with a line weight of zero and can decrease view update time.
Patterns	If Patterns is set to ON, the pattern elements are displayed. If it is OFF, pattern elements are not displayed and can decrease view update time.
Ref Boundaries	If Ref Boundaries is set to ON, reference file clipping boundaries, represented by dashed polygons, are displayed.
Text	If Text is set to ON, text elements are displayed. If it is OFF, text is not displayed and can decrease view update time.
Text Nodes	If Text Nodes is set to ON, text nodes are displayed as small crosses with numeric identifiers.

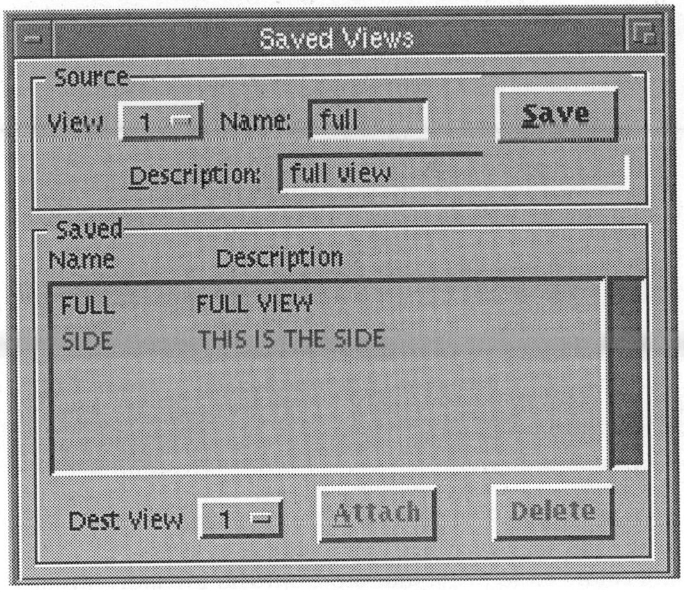

FIGURE 4–32 Saved View Settings box.

You also can save a view by keying in at the uSTN> field, **sv=<name>,<description>**, and pressing ⟨ENTER⟩. Replace <name> with the name you want to use for the saved view and <description> with a description of the saved view. MicroStation prompts:

   Select view (Click the Data button in the view that contains the set-up you want to save.)

Attach a Saved View To restore a saved view, invoke the Saved View settings box by selecting Saved from the View pull-down menu. Select the name of the view you want to restore from the list. Make sure the Dest View options menu (located at the bottom of the settings box) is displaying the number of the view you want to set the saved view to. Click the Attach button.

You also can restore a view by keying in at the uSTN> field, **vi=<name>**, and pressing ⟨ENTER⟩. Replace <name> with the name of the view to be restored. MicroStation prompts:

   Select view (Click the Data button in the view where you want to restore the view.)

Delete a Saved View To delete a saved view you no longer need, invoke the Saved View settings box by selecting Saved from the View pull-down menu. Select the name of the view you want to delete from the list. Click on the Delete button and the selected saved view is deleted.

You also can delete a view by keying in at the uSTN> field, **dv=<name>** and pressing ⟨ENTER⟩. Replace <name> with the name of the saved view to be deleted. The saved view is immediately deleted.

> **NOTE:** If you have the Saved Views settings box displayed and you key-in the **dv=<name>** to delete a saved view, the name and description of the deleted saved view may remain in the settings box Saved Views list, even though it has been deleted. To update the settings box, close and reopen it.

MEASURING COMMANDS

"I wonder if that line really is 12 feet long?" "What's the radius of that circle?" "I need the surface area of that foundation." MicroStation can answer these questions with the measuring commands.

The measurement commands do not do anything to your design. They just display distances, areas, and angles in the Message field of the Command Window (see Figure 4–33).

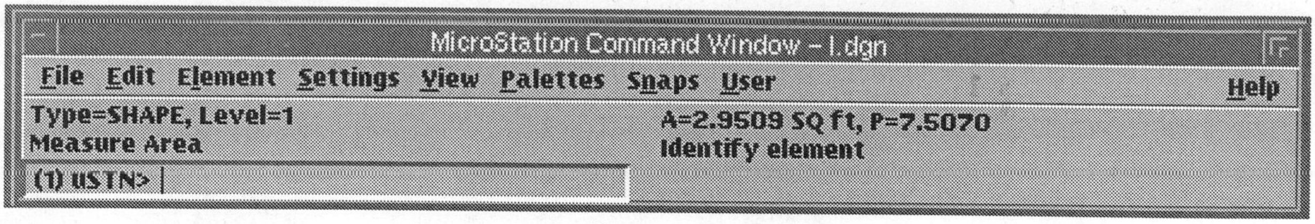

FIGURE 4–33 MicroStation Command Window displaying Measurement information in the Message field.

All measurement commands are available from the Measure palette shown in Figure 4–34, which can be opened from the Palettes pull-down menu.

FIGURE 4–34 Measuring Palette.

Measure Distances

MicroStation provides four distance measurement options. Distance options include measuring the distance between points you define, the distance along an element between points you define, the perpendicular distance from an element, and the minimum distance between two elements.

Measure Distance Between Points measures the cumulative straight-line distance from the first data point, through successive data points, to the last data point you define.

To measure the distance between points, click the Measure Distance icon from the Measure palette and select Between Points from the Distance options menu, as shown in Figure 4–35. MicroStation prompts:

> *Enter start point* (Place a data point where you want to start the measurement.)
> *Define distance to measure* (Place a data point to define the distance you want to measure and continue placing data points to define additional measurement segments.)

FIGURE 4–35 Invoking Measure Distance command when Between Points option is selected from the Distance option menu in the Measuring palette.

As you place each data point, the cumulative linear distance between points is displayed in the Message field of the Command Window. Once you are through placing data points, press the Reset button to start a new measurement.

Measure Distance Along Element measures the cumulative distance along an element from the data point that selects it through successive data points on the element to the last data point you define.

To measure the distance along an element, click the Measure Distance icon from the Measure palette and select Along Element from the Distance options menu, as shown in Figure 4–36. MicroStation prompts:

> *Identify element first point* (Place a data point where you want to start the measurement on the element.)
> *Enter end point* (Place a data point at the point on the element where you want to end the measurement.)
> *Measure more points/Reset to reselect* (Continue placing data points on the element to obtain a cumulative measurement from the first data point through the succeeding points, or press the Reset button to terminate the measurement.)

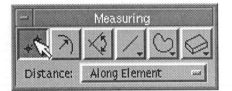

FIGURE 4–36 Invoking Measure Distance command when Along Element option is selected from the Distance option menu in the Measuring palette.

As you place each data point after the first one, the cumulative distance along the element is displayed in the Message field of the Command Window.

Measure Distance Perpendicular measures the perpendicular distance from a point you define to an element.

To measure the perpendicular distance, click the Measure Distance icon from the Measure palette and select Perpendicular from the Distance options menu, as shown in Figure 4–37. MicroStation prompts:

> *Enter first point* (Identify the element from which you want to measure the perpendicular distance.)
> *Enter end point* (Place a data point at the point from which you want to measure the perpendicular distance to the element.)
> *Measure more points/Reset to reselect* (Continue placing data points to obtain additional perpendicular measurements from the element, or press Reset to terminate the measurement.)

FIGURE 4–37 Invoking Measure Distance command when Perpendicular option is selected from the Distance option menu in the Measuring palette.

As you place each data point after identifying the element, a dashed line indicating the perpendicular distance appears in the design, and the perpendicular distance is displayed in the Message field of the Command Window. The dashed line is a temporary image that disappears when you update the view or select another command.

> **NOTE:** If you place the measurement end point beyond the end of a linear element (such as a line or box), the perpendicular is calculated from an imaginary extension of the measured element.

Measure Minimum Distance measures the minimum distance between two elements.

To measure the minimum distance between two elements, click the Measure Distance icon from the Measure palette and select Minimum Between from the Distance options menu, as shown in Figure 4–38. MicroStation prompts:

> *Identify first element* (Identify the first element.)
> *Accept, Identify second element/Reject* (Identify the second element.)
> *Accept, initiate min dist calculation* (Click the data button somewhere in the view to initiate the minimum distance calculation.)

FIGURE 4–38 Invoking Measure Distance command when Minimum Between option is selected from the Distance option menu in the Measuring palette.

After you place the third data point, a dashed line appears in the design to indicate where the minimum distance is, and the minimum distance is displayed in the Message field of the Command Window. The dashed line is a temporary image that disappears when you update the view or select another command.

Measure Radius

The Measure Radius command tells you the radius of arcs, circles, partial ellipses, and ellipses. To measure the radius, click the Measure Radius icon from the Measure palette (see Figure 4–39). MicroStation prompts:

> *Identify element* (Identify the element whose radius you want to measure.)
> *Accept/Reject (Select next input)* (Click the Data button again to accept the element. You also can identify another element to measure. Click the Reset button if you selected the wrong element with the first data point.)

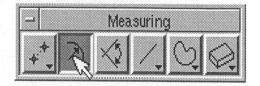

FIGURE 4–39 Invoking Measure Radius command in the Measuring palette.

After the second data point, the element's radius is displayed in the current working units, in the Message field of the Command Window. If the element you are measuring is an ellipse or partial ellipse, the major axis and minor axis radii are displayed.

Measure Angle Between Lines

The Measure Angle Between Lines command measures the minimum angle formed by two elements.

To measure an angle between two lines, click the Measure Angle Between Lines icon from the Measure palette (see Figure 4–40). MicroStation prompts:

> *Select first line* (Identify the first line from which the angle will be measured.)
> *Select second line* (Identify the second line.)
> *Accept/Reject (Select next input)* (Click the Data button to accept and initiate the measurement. You also can select the first line of another pair to measure with this data point. Click the Reset button if you selected wrong elements.)

FIGURE 4–40   Invoking Measure Angle Between Lines command in the Measuring palette.

After you accept the measurements, the angle between the two elements is displayed in the Message field of the Command Window.

Measure Length

The Measure Length command measures the total length of an open element or the length of the perimeter of a closed shape.

When you select Measure Length, a Tolerance (%) field appears in the Measure palette. Tolerance sets the maximum allowable percentage of the distance between the true curve and the approximation for measurement purposes. A low value produces a very accurate measurement but may take a long time to calculate. The default value is sufficient in most cases.

To measure the length of an element, click the Measure Length icon from the Measure palette (see Figure 4–41). MicroStation prompts:

> *Identify element* (Identify the element whose length you want to measure.)
> *Accept, Measure Elements(s)* (Click the data button anywhere in the design to initiate the measurement.)

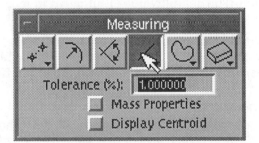

FIGURE 4–41   Invoking Measure Length command in the Measuring palette.

After the second data point, the total length of the element, or element perimeter, is displayed in the Message field of the Command Window.

You can use this command to measure the cumulative length of several elements by first using the Element Selection command to select all the elements that you want to include in the measurement. After selecting the elements, select Measure Length from the Measure palette, and the cumulative length of all selected elements appears in the Message field of the Command Window. In addition, you can turn the toggle switch to ON for Mass Properties, and MicroStation displays in a window the Mass Properties of the selected elements.

Measure Area

MicroStation provides seven ways to measure areas, which can be selected from the option menu when you select Area command from the Measure palette, as shown in Figure 4–42. Area options include measuring the area of a closed element; a fence; the intersection, union, or difference of two overlapping closed elements; a group of intersecting elements; or a group of points.

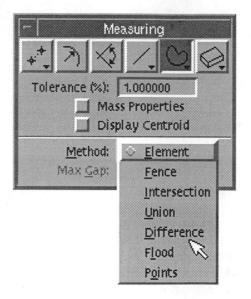

FIGURE 4–42   Listing all the available options from the Method option menu when Measure Area command is selected.

When you select the Measure Area command, a Tolerance (%) field appears in the Measure palette. Tolerance sets the maximum allowable percentage of the distance between the true curve and the approximation for area calculation purposes. A low value produces a very accurate area but may take a long time to calculate. The default value is sufficient in most cases.

Measure Area Element   This measures the area of a closed element, such as a circle, ellipse, shape, or block. To measure the area of a closed element, click the Measure Area icon from Measure sub-palette and select Element from the Method options menu. MicroStation prompts:

> *Identify element* (Identify the closed element.)
> *Accept, measure element(s)* (Click the data button anywhere in the view to initiate the area calculation. This data point can also select another closed element. Press the Reset button if you want to reject the selected element.)

After the second data point, the element's area and perimeter length are displayed in the Message field of the Command Window.

You can use this command to measure the cumulative area of several closed elements by first using the Element Selection command to select all the elements that you want to include in the area measurement. After selecting the elements, select Measure Area from the Measure palette, and the cumulative area of all selected elements then appears in the Message field of the Command Window.

Measure Area Fence This measures the area enclosed by a fence block or fence shape. To measure the area enclosed by a fence, click the Measure Area icon from the Measure palette and select Fence from the Method options menu. MicroStation displays the area of the fence in the Message field of the Command Window.

Measure Area Intersection, Union, or Difference These options measure areas formed by two intersecting closed elements. The intersection option allows you to determine the area that is common to two closed elements. The union option allows you to determine the area in such a way that there is no duplication between two closed elements. The difference option allows you to determine the area that is formed from a closed element after removing from it any area that it has in common with a second element.

To obtain the area of two intersecting closed elements, click Measure Area from the Measure palette, and select Intersection, Union, or Difference from the Mode options menu. MicroStation prompts:

> *Identify element* (Identify one of the two overlapping elements.)
> *Accept, identify second element/Reject* (Identify the second closed element, or click the Reset button to reject the first element.)
> *Accept, Measure Element(s)* (Click the Data button anywhere in the view to initiate the area calculation.)

After you select the second element, MicroStation displays an image of only the part of the two elements that is included in the type of area you select. After the third data point the elements reappear in their entirety, and MicroStation displays the area and perimeter length in the Message field of the Command Window.

Measure Area Flood This measures the area enclosed by a group of elements. The elements must either touch or overlap, and must enclose the area to be measured completely.

To measure the area enclosed by a group of elements, click Measure Area from the Measure palette, and select Flood from the Method options menu. MicroStation prompts:

> *Enter data point inside area* (Click the Data button inside the area enclosed by the elements.)

After you click the data button, a small spinner will appear in the Error field of the Command Window. The spinner spins to indicate that MicroStation is determining the area enclosed by the elements. As MicroStation traces the area, it highlights the elements. When the area has been determined, the spinner stops spinning and the area and perimeter length appear in the Message field of the Command Window.

> **NOTE:** Make sure the area you click inside is completely enclosed by connected elements. If it is not, MicroStation may spend a very long time trying to find an enclosed area using adjacent elements before it gives up and displays an error message in the Error field of the Command Window.

Measure Area Points This measures the area formed by a set of data points you enter. It assumes the perimeter of the area is formed by straight lines between the data points. An image of the area is displayed as you enter the data points. The image is temporary and disappears when you update the screen or select another command.

To measure the area enclosed by a group of data points, click Measure Area from the Measure palette, and select Points from the Method options menu. MicroStation prompts:

Enter shape vertex (Place data points to define the vertexes of the area to be measured. When the area is completely defined, click the Reset button.)

As you are entering data points, a closed dynamic image of the area appears on the screen. When you press Reset, the area and perimeter length appear in the Message field of the Command Window.

DIMENSION SETTINGS

In earlier chapters a detailed explanation was provided for Dimension Placement, Units settings box, Dimension Attributes, Dimension Geometry, and Tolerance. The remaining Dimension setting boxes (Geometric Tolerance, Custom Symbols, Custom Terminators, and Tool Settings) available in Micro-Station are explained in the following sections.

Geometric Tolerance

The Geometric Tolerance Settings box (invoked from the Settings pull-down menu of the Dimension Placement Settings box) is used to build feature control frames with geometric tolerance symbols (see Figure 4–43). The feature control frames are commonly used with the Place Note command. The Fonts pull-down menu available in the settings box allows you to select one of the two fonts. When a new font is chosen, the buttons reflect the availability of the symbols in the selected font. Whenever you want to add the symbols, click on the buttons as part of placing the text to the Place Note command.

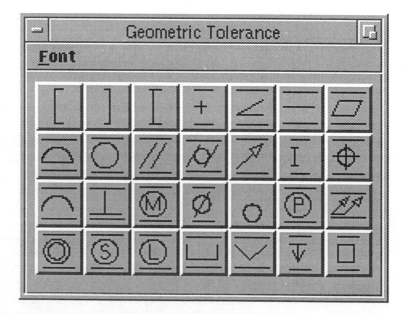

FIGURE 4–43 Geometric Tolerance Settings box.

> **NOTE:** The left ([ ) and right ( ]) brackets form the ends of compart-
> ments and the vertical line (|) separates compartments.

Custom Symbols

The Custom Symbols settings box (invoked from the Settings pull-down menu of the Dimension Placement Settings box) is used to specify symbols (characters from symbol fonts or cells) for Prefixes, Suffixes, and to override the diameter and plus-or-minus symbol, see Figure 4–44.

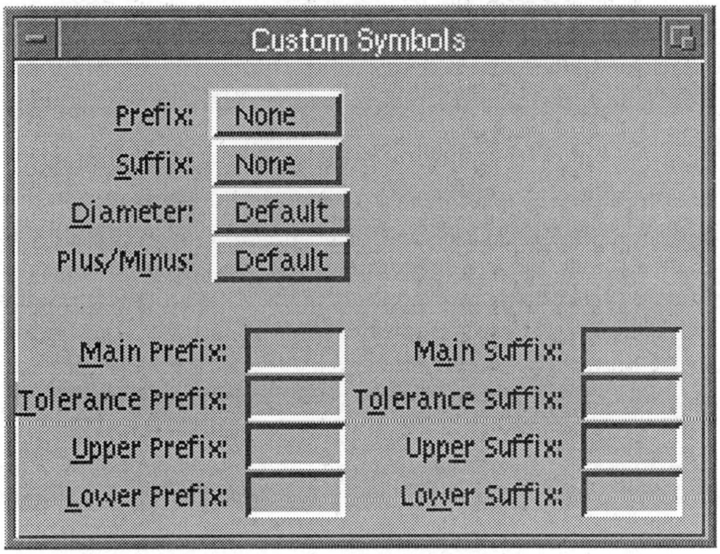

FIGURE 4–44   Custom Symbols settings box.

The Prefix option controls the specification of a custom Prefix symbol. The selected prefix symbol is placed preceding the dimension text. If None is selected (default) from the option menu then no prefix is added to the dimension. The symbol option allows you to select a specific character from a selected font. And the cell option allows you to key-in a name of a cell. The cell is placed as a shared cell (see Chapter 7 for a detailed explanation of cells).

The Suffix option controls the specification of a custom suffix symbol. The selected suffix symbol is placed following the dimension text. If None is selected (default) from the option menu then no suffix is added to the dimension. The symbol option allows you to select a specific character from a selected font. And the cell option allows you to key-in a name of a cell. The cell is placed as a shared cell (see Chapter 7 for a detailed explanation of cells).

The Diameter controls the specification of an alternate diameter symbol and allows you to select a specific character from a selected font.

The Plus/Minus controls the specification of an alternate Plus/Minus symbol and allows you to select a specific character from a selected font.

The lower half of the settings box contains fields for specifying additional single characters as dimension text prefixes and suffixes.

Custom Terminators

The Custom Terminators settings box (invoked from the Settings pull-down menu of the Dimension Placement Settings box) is used to alternate symbols (characters from symbol fonts or cells) for each of the four default dimension terminators (see Figure 4–45).

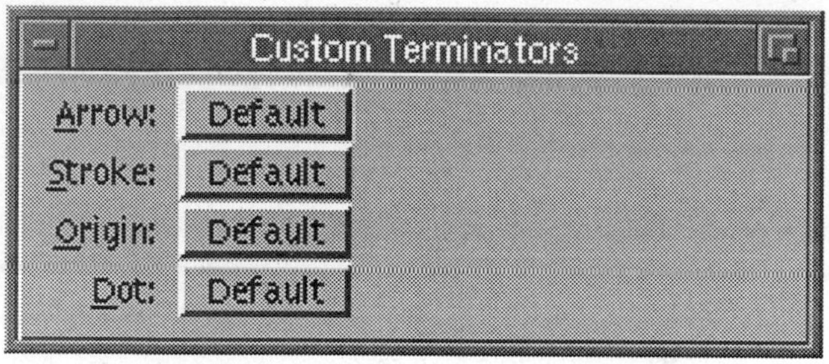

FIGURE 4–45 Custom Terminators settings box.

The Arrowhead controls the specification of an alternate to MicroStation's default arrowhead. If Default is selected from the option menu, then MicroStation places the default arrowhead. The symbol option places the character and font that are keyed in. The Cell option places whose cell name is keyed in. The cell is placed as a shared cell (see Chapter 7 for a detailed explanation of cells).

The Stroke controls the specification of an alternate to MicroStation's default stroke. If Default is selected from the option menu, then MicroStation places the default stroke. The symbol option places the character and font that are keyed in, and the Cell option places whose cell name is keyed in. The cell is placed as a shared cell (see Chapter 7 for a detailed explanation of cells).

Similarly the Origin and Dot controls the specification of an alternate to MicroStations default symbols. The option menu is identical to the Arrowhead and Stroke controls.

Tool Settings

The Tool Settings box (invoked from the Settings pull-down menu of the Dimension Placement Settings box) is used to control settings associated with individual dimensioning tools (see Figure 4–46). The tool settings allows you to set all the options (such as terminators, extension lines, prefix, suffix, and symbols), discussed earlier for individual dimensioning tools.

Once the necessary changes are made to the dimension settings box, then you can save them as a dimension style. Refer to Chapter 11 for a detailed explanation for creating a dimension style.

MATCH DIMENSION SETTINGS

The steps required to set up dimensioning involve several settings from various setting boxes and are rather time consuming. After setting everything up, it is all too easy to forget to make the changes permanent by using the Save Settings command. If you lose the dimension settings, but have placed dimension elements with appropriate settings in your design, the Match Dimension Settings can recover the settings by matching them to the settings in effect when the dimensions were placed.

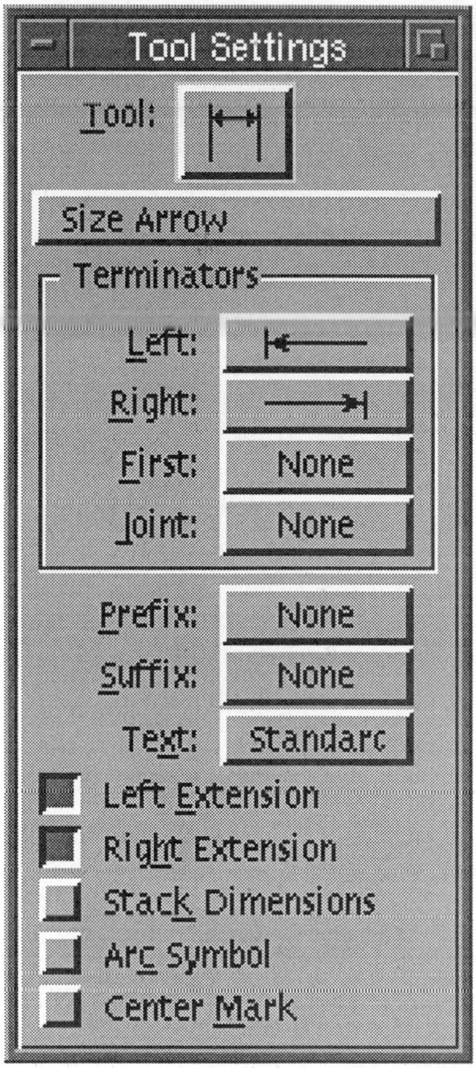

Tool Settings

Tool: |←→|

Size Arrow

┌─ Terminators ──────────┐

Left: |←——

Right: ——→|

First: None

Joint: None

Prefix: None

S**u**ffix: None

Te**x**t: Standard

☐ Left **E**xtension

■ Ri**g**ht Extension

☐ Stac**k** Dimensions

☐ Ar**c** Symbol

☐ Center **M**ark

FIGURE 4–46   Tool Settings box.

The Match Dimension Settings command is available in the Match palette that can be opened from the Palettes pull-down menu in the Command Window. To match the dimensioning setup, click the Match Dimension Settings icon in the Match palette (see Figure 4–47). MicroStation prompts:

Identify element (Identify the dimension element whose attributes you want to match.)
Accept/Reject (select next input) (Click the data button a second time to initiate setting the
    dimension settings to the selected element, or click the Reset button to reject the element.)

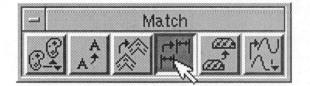

FIGURE 4–47   Invoking the Match Dimension Settings in the Match palette.

After the second data point, the dimension settings match those of the selected dimension element.

Miscellaneous Dimensioning

In chapters 2 and 3 you were introduced to the commands available in the Linear, Angular, and Radial dimensioning sub-palettes. Now let's learn to use the commands in the fourth and last dimensioning sub-palette, Misc Dimensions. It is available from the Dimensioning sub-menu in the Palettes pull-down menu or from the Dimensioning palette (see Figure 4–48).

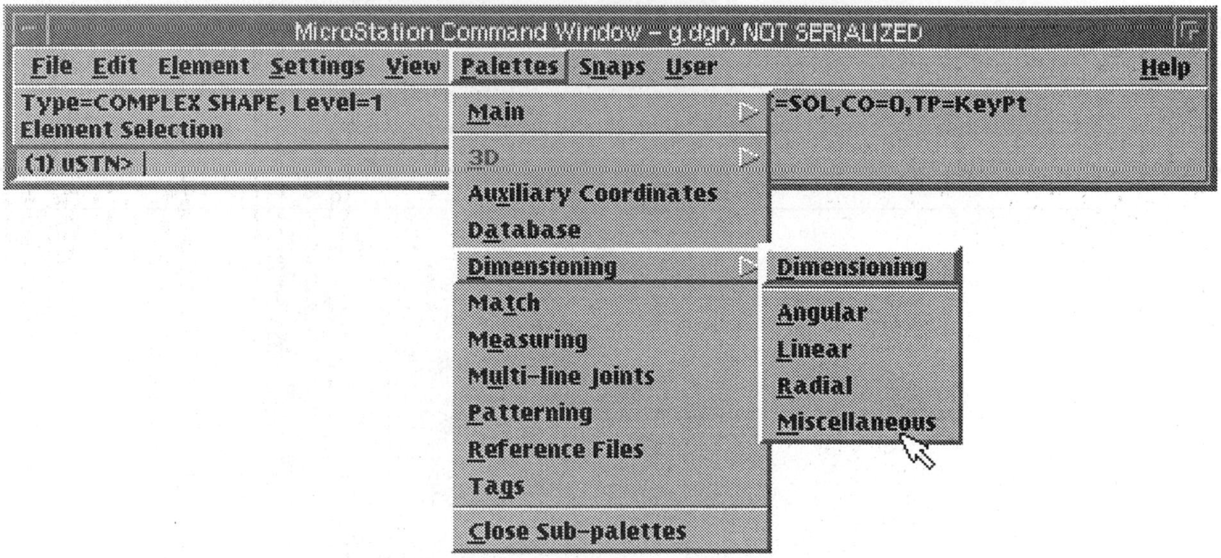

FIGURE 4–48 Invoking Miscellaneous Dimensioning sub-palette from the Palettes pull-down menu in the MicroStation Command Window.

Each of these commands is affected by the dimensioning setup that was discussed in Chapter 2. For example, you must decide if you want to place Mechanical (MEC) or Architectural, Engineering, and Construction (AEC) dimensions.

You must also choose, for each of these dimensioning commands, whether you want the dimension to be associated with the dimensioned element. You make the decision by clicking on the Association lock check button that appears in the Misc Dimensions sub-palette with each of the commands. When the button is depressed, association is ON.

If a dimension is associated with the element it dimensions, any changes to the element also affect the dimension. For example, if the length of the element is changed, the dimension is changed to show the new element length.

Dimension Element

The left-most command in the Misc Dimensions sub-palette, Dimension Element, provides a fast way to dimension an element. Simply identify the element and MicroStation selects the type of dimensioning command it thinks is best for dimensioning that type of element.

For line elements it selects one of the linear dimension commands for the length of the line. For line strings and shapes it selects one of the linear size dimension commands for the length of one segment of the element. For circles, arcs, and ellipses it selects one of the radial dimension commands.

When you invoke the Dimension Element command, the command name Dimension Element appears in the command field of the Command Window. As soon as you select an element, the name of the dimensioning command MicroStation intends to use appears in the command field. If you don't want to use the selected dimension command, press ⌨ENTER and MicroStation switches to another dimensioning command. Keep pressing ⌨ENTER until you find the command you want to use.

To use this command, click the Dimension Element icon from the Misc Dimensions sub-palette (see Figure 4–49), or key-in at the uSTN> field, **dimension element** (or **dim e**), and press ⌨ENTER. MicroStation prompts:

> *Select element to dimension* (Identify the element, or segment of the block or line string element, you want to dimension.)
> *Accept (Press RETURN to switch command)* (Place a data point to indicate where you want the dimension placed, or press ⌨ENTER as many times as necessary to find the dimensioning command you want to use and place a data point for the location of the dimension element.)

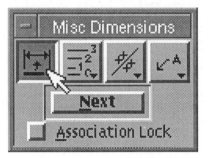

FIGURE 4–49   Invoking the Dimension Element command from the Miscellaneous Dimensioning sub-palette.

For most dimension commands, your second data point indicates the length and direction of the extension line. See Figure 4–50 for examples of placing the data points.

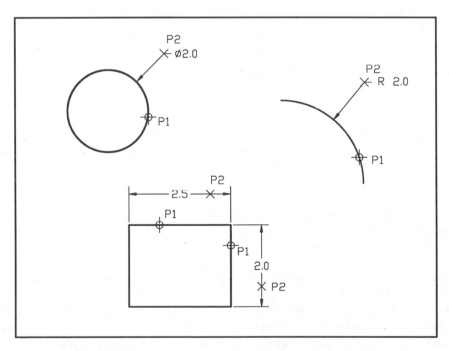

FIGURE 4–50   Examples of placing dimensioning by Dimension Element command.

Dimension Ordinate

Ordinate dimensioning is often used in mechanical drawings. It labels distances along an axis from a point of origin on the axis along which the distances are measured. See Figure 4–51 for examples of ordinate dimensions.

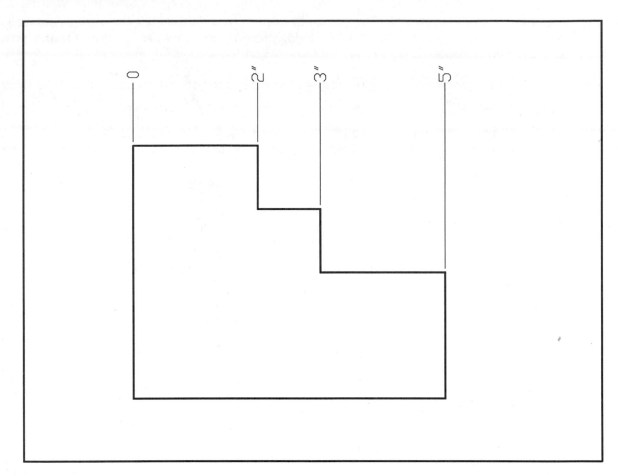

FIGURE 4–51   Examples for Ordinate Dimensioning.

When you select Dimension Ordinate from the Misc Dimensions sub-palette, the Alignment options menu appears in the sub-palette. Use it to select how you want to handle the axis along which the ordinates are placed. For a two-dimensional design, select either View or True. View axis forces the ordinate axis to be parallel to the x- or y-axis. True allows you to place the ordinate axis at any angle.

To start placing ordinate dimensions, click the Dimension Ordinate icon from the Misc Dimensions sub-palette (see Figure 4–52) or key-in at the uSTN> field, **dimension ordinate** (or **dim o**), and press ⏎. MicroStation prompts:

Select ordinate origin (Place a data point at the point where all ordinate labels are to be measured from.)
Select ordinate direction (Place a data point to indicate the rotation of the ordinate axis.)
Select dimension end point (Place a data point to indicate how long to make the extension line.)
Select start of dimension (Place data points at each place where you want an ordinate dimension placed. These points define the base of the extension line.)

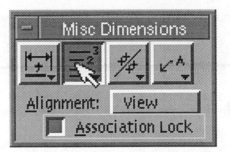

FIGURE 4–52   Invoking the Dimension Ordinate command from the Miscellaneous Dimensioning sub-palette.

When you finish placing ordinate dimensions, either press the Reset button to start a new one or select another command.

Label Line

The Label Line command places the line length above the line you select and the line rotation angle below the line. You can place a label on a line, line string, block, closed shape, or multi-line.

How it determines which side of the element is the top and what the angle of rotation is depends on how you drew it. The angle of the line or line segment, for example, is measured as a counterclockwise rotation from the first data point to the second. Use care in deciding how to draw elements you plan to label with the Label Line command, or you may not get the angle of rotation you expected. See Figure 4–53 for examples of line labels.

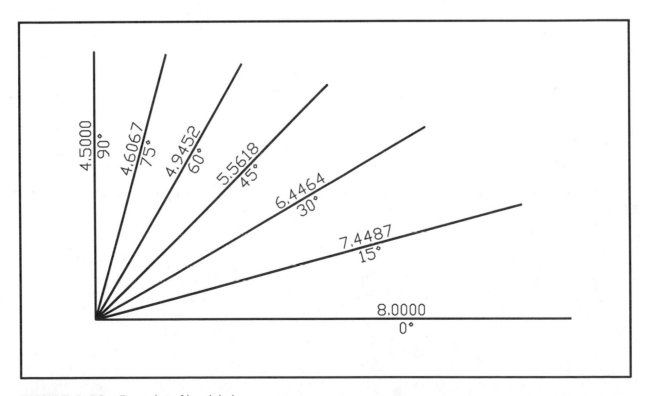

FIGURE 4–53   Examples of line labels.

Placing a label on a line or line segment requires two data points—the first identifies the element and the second causes the label to be placed. How these two data points determine label placement position depends on the current settings of the Dimension Placement Location and Justification Options (see Chapter 2).

If Location is set to Automatic or Semi-Auto, the first data point determines the location of the label, and the label's relation to that data point is determined by the Justification setting (left of the data point, centered on the data point, or right of the data point). As soon as you place the first data point to identify the element, an image of the label appears at the point where you identified the element.

If Location is set to Manual, the first data identifies the element, and an image of the label appears that follows the screen pointer along the line until you place the second data point.

To place a label on a line or line segment, click the Label Line icon from the Misc Dimensions sub-palette (see Figure 4–54) or key-in at the uSTN> field, **label line** (or **la**), and press ⏎. MicroStation prompts:

> *Identify element* (Identify the element on which you want to place the label.)
> *Accept/Reject (select next input)* (Place a second data point to place the label. If Location is set to Manual, this point also determines the location of the label on the line or line segment.)

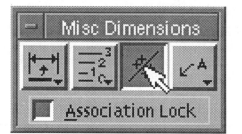

FIGURE 4–54 Invoking the Label Line command from the Miscellaneous Dimensioning sub-palette.

The second data point, in addition to causing the label to be placed, can select the next line or line segment on which you wish to place a label.

Place Note

The Place Note command is a hybrid of dimensioning and text placement. It allows you to enter text, then places the text on a pointer with an arrowhead. Note placement is discussed in Chapter 5.

EXERCISES

Exercises 4–1 through 4–3

Use precision key-ins and appropriate grid spacing to draw the objects. Use the Array (Rectangular and Polar) commands to your best advantage.

Exercise 4–1

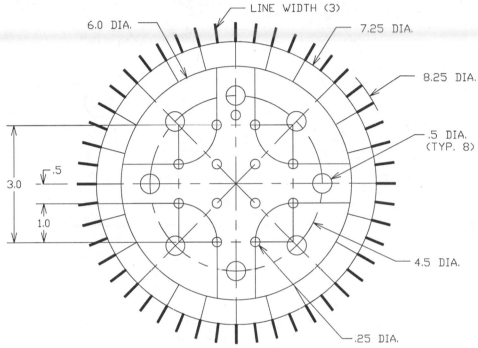

Exercise 4–2

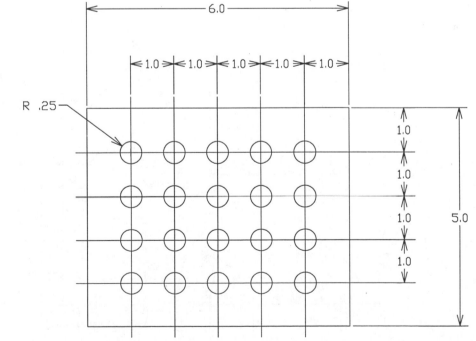

Exercise 4–3

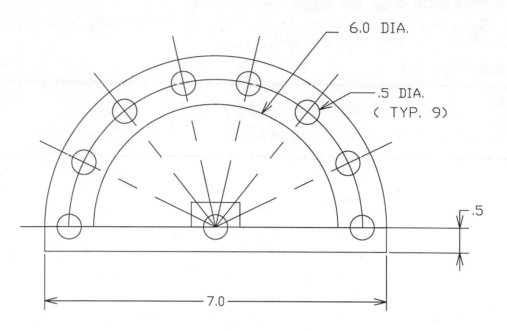

Exercise 4–4

Use precision key-ins and appropriate grid spacing to draw the object. Use the Array, copy parallel, and fence manipulation commands to your best advantage.

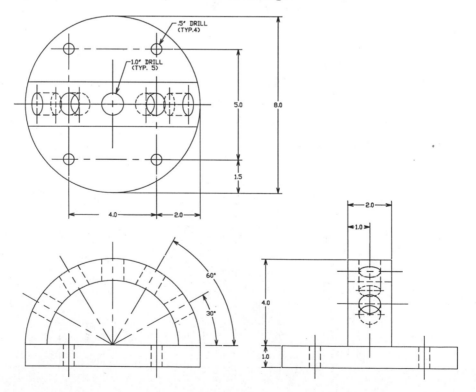

Exercises 4–5 through 4–7

Use Sdarch2d.dgn seed file to create the new design files. Use element selection and fence manipulation commands to your best advantage.

Exercise 4–5

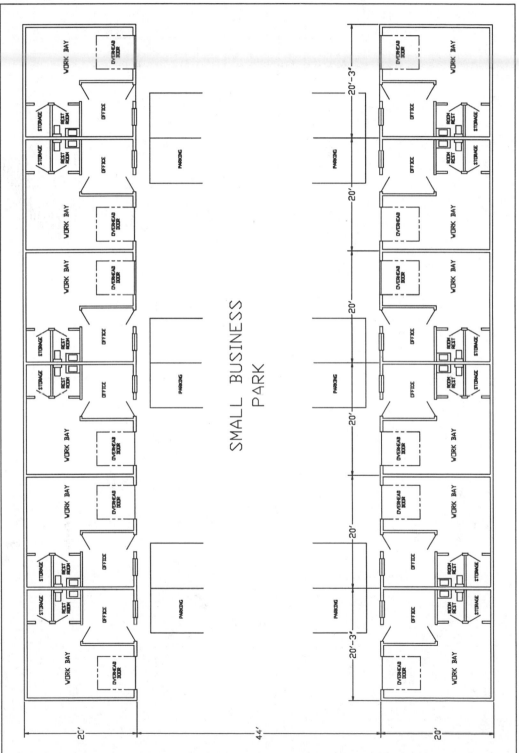

Exercise 4–6

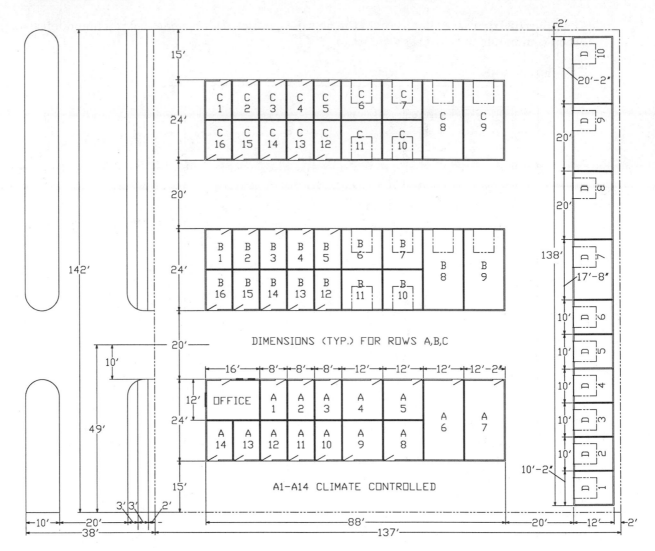

DIMENSIONS (TYP.) FOR ROWS A,B,C

A1–A14 CLIMATE CONTROLLED

Exercise 4–7

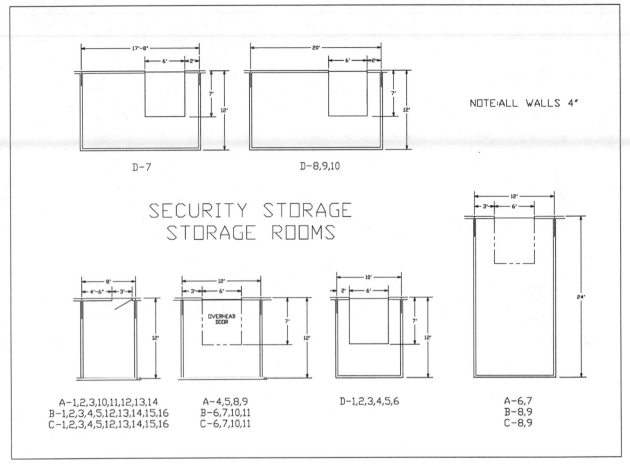

SECURITY STORAGE
STORAGE ROOMS

NOTE:ALL WALLS 4"

D-7

D-8,9,10

OVERHEAD DOOR

A-1,2,3,10,11,12,13,14
B-1,2,3,4,5,12,13,14,15,16
C-1,2,3,4,5,12,13,14,15,16

A-4,5,8,9
B-6,7,10,11
C-6,7,10,11

D-1,2,3,4,5,6

A-6,7
B-8,9
C-8,9

REVIEW QUESTIONS

Write your answers in the spaces provided:

1. To select several elements by Element Selection command hold the _____ button and _____ around the elements.

2. To deselect one element from a group of selected elements hold down the _____ key and click on the element.

3. Briefly explain the purpose of locking individual elements.

_____

_____

4. List the six fence selection modes available in MicroStation.

_____

_____

5. Explain briefly the difference between the Overlap and Void-Overlap mode.

_____

_____

6. How many views are available in MicroStation? _____

7. When MicroStation prompts you to Select View, which cursor button will you choose?

_____

8. List three most basic steps for operating a Fence.

_____

_____

9. Explain briefly the difference between Bottom to Top, Cascade, and Tile view commands.

_____

_____

10. List the options available to Update the views.

_____

_____

11. List five view attribute options available and its purpose in the View Attributes Settings box.

_____

_____

12. Explain briefly the benefits of saving views.

_____

_____

13. List the four measure distance options available in the Measure Distance command.

_____

_____

14. The Measure Radius command provides information of the elements such as _____

_____.

15. The Measure Angle Between Lines command measures the _____ angle formed by two elements.

16. List the seven area options available in the Measure Area command.

_____

_____

17. The Measure Area Flood option measures the area enclosed _____.

18. The Geometric Tolerance settings box is used to build _____.

19. Ordinate dimension is used to label _____.

20. The Label Line command places the _____ and _____.

5

FUNDAMENTALS IV

• • • • • • • • • • • • • • • • •

After completing this chapter, you will be able to:

- Place single-character natural fractions in text.
- Place text that is fitted between two data points.
- Place text above, below, or on a linear element.
- Place text along an element.
- Manipulate text elements.
- Place text nodes and data fields.
- Import text files.
- Extend lines.
- Modify vertices and arcs.
- Create complex shapes and chains.
- Modify multi-line joints.

PLACING TEXT

In Chapter 3 there was a detailed discussion about Text Attributes and placing Text by Origin. This chapter explores six additional methods of placing the text. Before we get to the additional text placement commands, let's discuss how to place fractions as part of the text.

Handling Fractions

Several of the font sets provide a one-character version of the commonly used natural fractions. For example, the fraction $\frac{1}{32}$ can be placed as one character rather than four, thus saving space in your design.

To place natural fractions in the one-character position, turn ON the Fractions toggle button located in the Text settings box (see Figure 5–1). If you want to keep fractions on for future editing sessions, select Save Settings from the File pull-down menu.

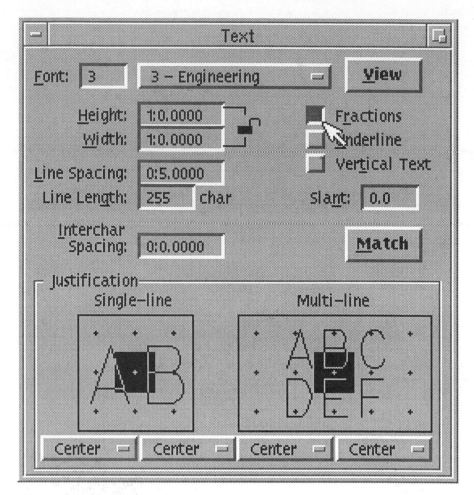

FIGURE 5–1 Setting the Fractions Toggle button from the Text settings box.

Here are few things to keep in mind about fractions:

- For a fraction to be placed in a single-character position, it must be pre-defined in the font. Not all possible fractions are pre-defined. If you type one that is not in the font, it is placed as a multiple-character fraction, regardless of the Fractions button setting.
- If you include a natural fraction in a string of text, there must be a space character before and after the fraction for it to be placed as a single-character fraction.
- Single-character fractions are slightly larger than non-fraction characters. Because of that they may overlap into the space between characters. You may have to insert an extra space character before and/or after the single-character fraction so that it does not appear to run into other characters.

Place Fitted Text

The Place Fitted Text command fits the text you type in the Text Editor box between two data points (see Figure 5–2). It ignores all text parameters except the active font and Text String Justification, and scales and rotates the text as necessary to fill the space between two data points. It places the fitted text at the active color and line weight. This command does not allow multi-line text. If you enter multi-line text, only the first line is placed.

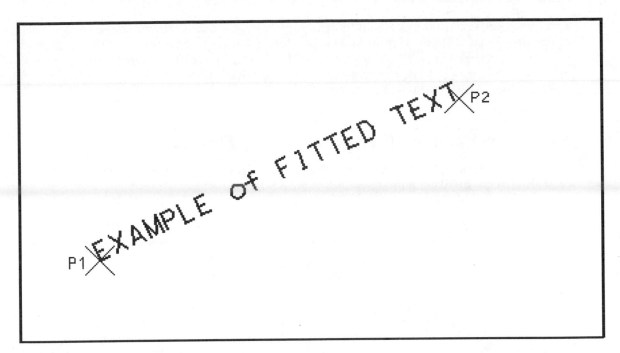

FIGURE 5–2   An example for placing a text between two data points by Place Fitted Text command.

To place fitted text, click the Place Text icon in the Text sub-palette, and select Fitted from the Method options menu (see Figure 5–3). The Text Editor box opens and MicroStation prompts:

Enter text (If the Text Editor box does not already contain the text you want to fit, click in the box and type your text. Place a data point in the design to indicate the text's starting point.)
Define end point of text (Place a data point in the design to indicate the text's ending point.)
Enter more chars or position text (Continue placing the same fitted text, edit the text in the Text Editor box before proceeding, or select another command.)

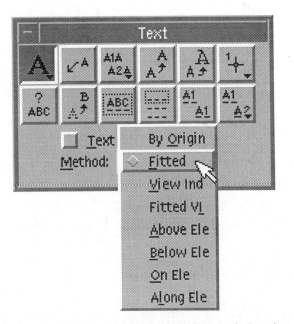

FIGURE 5–3   Clicking the Place Text icon in the Text sub-palette with Fitted option selected from the Method options menu.

After you place the first data point, a dynamic image of the text follows the screen cursor. Each copy of the fitted text you place becomes a single element that can be manipulated like any other type of element. The text's only keypoint is determined by the active Text String Justification that was in effect when it was placed. For example, if the justification was right bottom, the keypoint is the right-bottom corner of the text.

Place Text Above, Below, or On an Element

Three text placement options are available in MicroStation that place text above, below, or on a line, or segment of a line string or shape (see Figure 5–4).

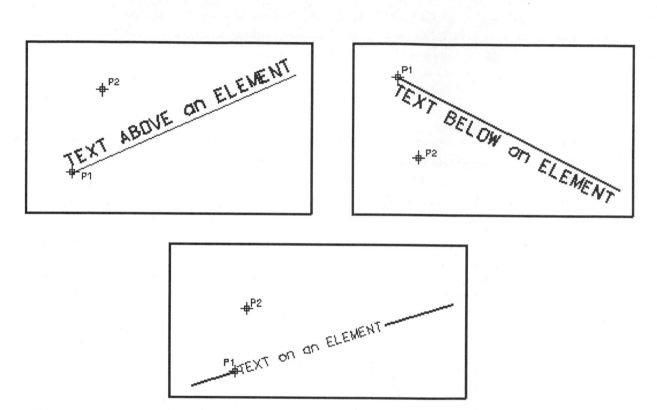

FIGURE 5–4   Examples of placing Text Above, Below, and On Line.

The text is placed above or below the element by a distance equal to the text Line Spacing attribute. When text is placed on an element, a hole is cut in the element and the text is placed in the hole (two lines or line-string elements result, and a shape is turned into a line string).

The relationship of the text to the data point that identifies the element is determined by the horizontal component of the Text String Justification (left of the data point, centered on the data point, or right of the data point). These commands do not allow multi-line text. If you enter multi-line text, only the first text line is used.

To place text above, below, or on a line or line segment, click on the Place Text icon in the Text sub-palette, and select the option (Above Ele, Below Ele, or On Ele) from the Method options menu (see Figure 5–5). The Text Editor box opens and MicroStation prompts:

Enter text (Type the text to be placed in the Text Editor box.)
Identify element (Click on the element in which the text is to be placed in relation to the point where the text is to be placed.)
Accept/Reject (Select next input) (Accept the element by clicking the data button, or click the Reset button to reject it.)

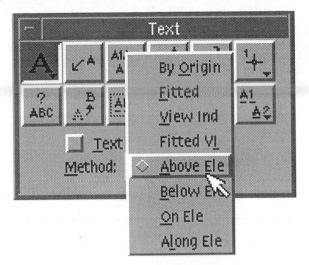

FIGURE 5–5 Clicking the Place Text icon in the Text sub-palette with Above Ele option selected from the Method options menu.

After the first data point, a dynamic image of the text appears at the location you selected, but the text is not actually placed until the second data point. Once placed, the text has no relationship to the element, and it is a single element that can be manipulated like any other type of element.

> **NOTE:** If the Text Editor box already contains text when you start the command to place text above, below, or on an element, the first Micro-Station prompt (*Enter text*) is skipped. You can either use the text or edit it, or replace it with new text. If the Text Editor box is empty when you select the element, the message "Enter characters first" appears in the error field of the Command Window, and the element is not selected.

Place Text Along an Element

You have seen how to place text above, below, and on linear elements. Now let's look at how to place text along an element such as a(n) arc, ellipse, circle, or curve-string (see Figure 5–6).

To make the text follow the curve of the element it is placed along, each character in the text is placed as a separate text element. To help compensate for a tight curve, this command allows you to specify how much space in working units you want to place between each character. If you do not provide the inter-character spacing, it is set equal to the current text width value. Fields are provided in the Text sub-palette for entering the inter-character spacing and line spacing (distance between the text and the element) when you select the Along Element placement option.

The relationship of the text to the data point that identifies the element is determined by the horizontal component of the Text String Justification. If, for example, you have a center justification, the text is centered about the data point that identifies the element.

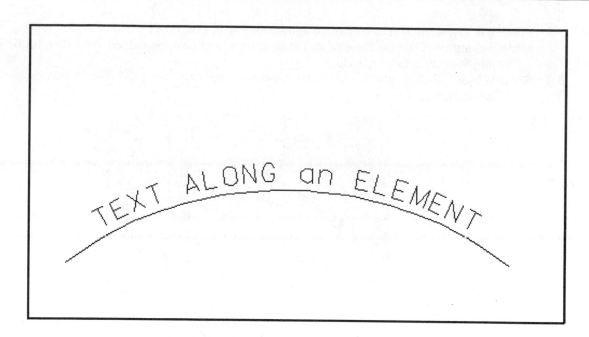

FIGURE 5–6 An example for placing a text along an element.

If you place your first data point on an element that does not allow all the text to fit, only the text that fits is placed. For example, if your text string is "Pipeway" and there is only room for three characters along the element where you place your first data point, the placed text will be "Pip."

In this command, the dynamic image of the text works differently from other commands. When you select the element along which you want to place text, two images of the text appear—one above the element and one below the element (see Figure 5–7). You select the image you want to keep by placing the screen pointer on the same side of the element as the image you want and clicking the data button. The text image on the opposite side of the element will disappear and you end up with text only on the side you select.

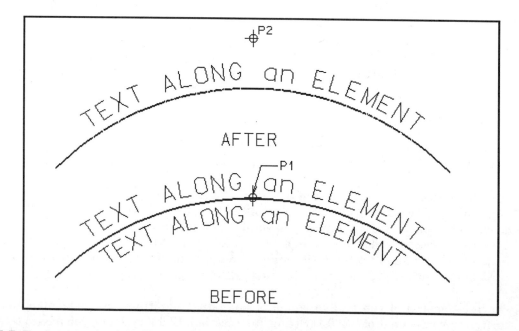

FIGURE 5–7 An example of displaying two images when text is placed along an element.

This command does not allow multi-line text. If you try to place multi-line text, it places only the first text line on the element you select. All additional text lines are ignored.

To place text along an element click on the Place Text icon in the Text sub-palette, select Along Ele from the Method options menu, and set the inter character spacing and line spacing in the fields provided in the sub-palette (see Figure 5–8). The Text Editor box opens and MicroStation prompts:

Enter text (Type the text you want to place in the Text Editor box.)
Identify element, text location (Click on the element at the point where you want the text placed.)
Accept/Select text above/below (Accept the element by clicking the Data button on the side of the element you want the text placed along, or reject it by clicking the Reset button.)

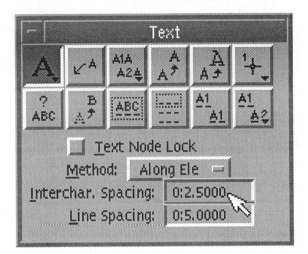

FIGURE 5–8 Displaying the availability of the edit fields when Place Text icon is selected with Along Ele option selected from the Method options menu.

When you identify the element, dynamic update provides two images of the text—one on each side of the element. Only the text on the side of the element you accept is actually placed.

> **NOTE:** If the Text Editor box already contains text when you start the command, the first MicroStation prompt (*Enter text*) is skipped. You can use the text, edit it, or replace it with new text.

> **NOTE:** If the Text Editor box is empty when you select the element, the message *Enter characters first* appears in the error field of the Command Window, and the element is not selected.

Place Note

The Place Note command is a hybrid of dimensioning and text placement. It places a line with an arrowhead as a pointer and places your text next to or at the end of the line, depending on the dimensioning placement setup (see Figure 5–9).

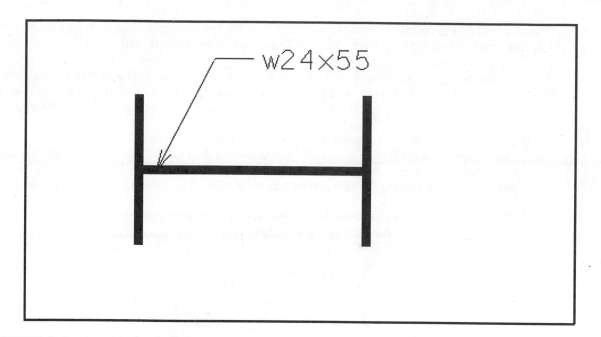

FIGURE 5–9 An example of placing text as a Note.

The text is placed using the current active settings for font and text size. If the dimensioning placement setup is for above, the line spacing parameter determines how far above the line the text is placed. The line, arrowhead, and text are all placed at the current active color and weight. The line and arrowhead also use the active style setting.

To place a note, click on the Place Note icon in the Text sub-palette (see Figure 5–10). The Text Editor box opens and MicroStation prompts:

> *Enter start point* (Type the note text in the Text Editor box, then place a data point to define the position of the arrowhead.)
> *Enter end point* (Place a data point to define the end of the note line and text placement point.)

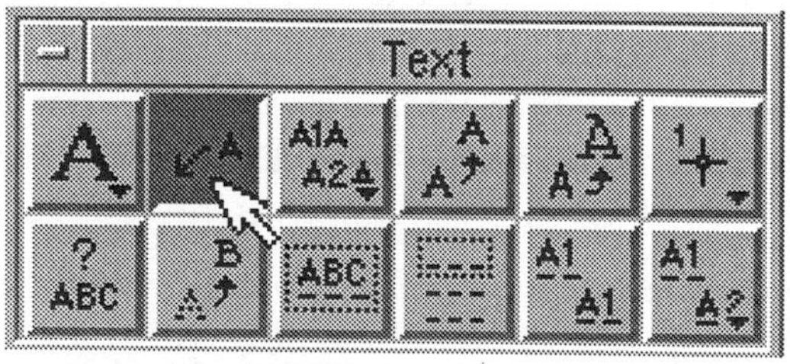

FIGURE 5–10 Clicking the Place Note icon from the Text sub-palette.

After you place the first data point, a dynamic image of the note line and text follows the screen cursor. The second data point completes placing the note.

NOTE: If there is no text in the Text Editor box when you place the note data points, the arrowhead and line are placed without text.

TEXT MANIPULATION

You have seen six ways to place text into your design. Now let's look at additional text commands that manipulate text after it has been placed. These commands include changing text content, changing attributes of text already placed in your design, and setting the current text attributes to the setting of existing text placed in your design.

Edit Text

If you type the way I do, there are going to be times when you discover a typing mistake in text that has already been placed. MicroStation provides the Edit Text command to allow you to change such mistakes. Unfortunately, MicroStation does not have a built-in spell checker, but third-party programs are available to check the spelling in your design file.

To edit text already placed in your design, click on the Edit Text icon in the Text sub-palette (see Figure 5–11). The Edit Text box opens and MicroStation prompts:

> *Identify text* (Identify the text element to be edited.)
> *Accept/Reject (Select next input)* (Click the data button again to place the text in the Text Editor box, or click the Reset button to reject the highlighted text element. This data point can also select the next text element for editing.)

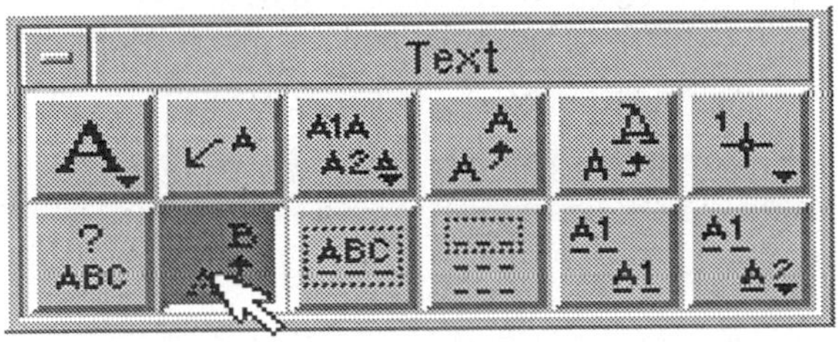

FIGURE 5–11   Clicking the Edit Text icon from the Text sub-palette.

After the text appears in the Text Editor box, make the required editing changes, then click the Text Editor box Accept button to update the text element. Refer to Chapter 2 for notes on using the Text Editor window.

Match Text Attributes

A common occurrence is the need to place additional text in a design that matches the text attributes of text already placed in the design. The Match Text Attributes command allows you to quickly match the active text attributes to the settings of existing text. It sets the font, text size, line spacing, and justification to the settings used to place the selected text.

To match the active attributes to an existing text, click the Match Text Attributes icon in the Text sub-palette (see Figure 5–12), MicroStation prompts:

> *Identify text element* (Identify the text element to be matched.)
> *Accept/Reject (Select next input)* (Click anywhere in the view to accept the text, or click the Reset button to reject it.)

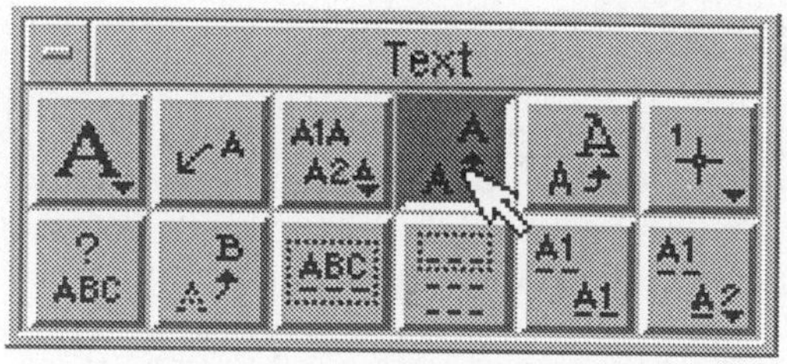

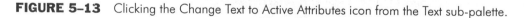

FIGURE 5–12 Clicking the Match Text Attributes icon from the Text sub-palette.

MicroStation displays the new active font, text size, and line spacing in the status field of the Command Window. To keep the settings in effect for the next time you open the design in MicroStation, select Save Settings from the File pull-down menu.

> **NOTE:** The Match Text command is also available as a button in the Text Attributes settings box.

Change Text to Active Attributes

If your design contains text that was placed using the wrong text attributes, the Change Text To Active Attributes command can update the attributes to the current setting. This command sets the selected text to the current active settings for font, text size, line spacing, and justification.

Before using this command, set the active text attributes to the values you want the text element to assume. Make the necessary changes in the Text Attributes settings box in the edit fields provided in the settings box.

To change existing text to the active text attributes, click the Change Text To Active Attributes icon in the Text sub-palette (see Figure 5–13). MicroStation prompts:

Identify text element (Identify the text element.)
Accept/Reject (Select next input) (Click anywhere in the view to accept the text, or click the Reset button to reject it. This data button can also select the next element to be changed.)

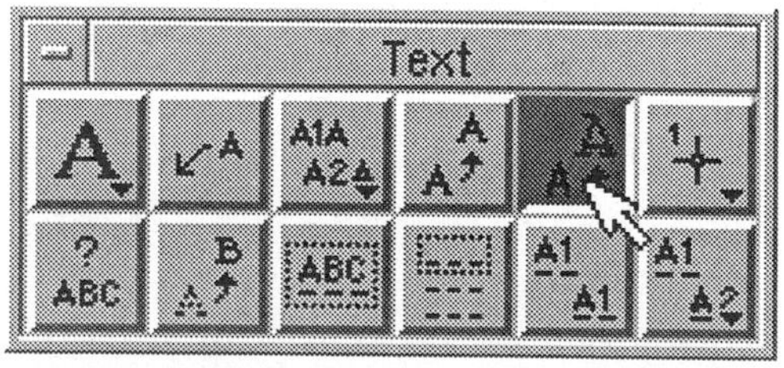

FIGURE 5–13 Clicking the Change Text to Active Attributes icon from the Text sub-palette.

> **NOTE:** The text position in the design changes if the current active justification is different from the justification that was in effect when the text was placed.

Copy and Increment Text

One of the more tedious jobs in drafting is annotating a series of objects with an incremented identification (such as P100, P101, P102, and so on). MicroStation provides a command to speed up the process. Place the identification text for the first object, then use the Copy and Increment Text command to place the additional object identifiers.

The default increment value (tag increment) is 1, but you can set it to any positive or negative number you want. For example, if your tag increment value is 10, each copy will increase by ten (P100, P110, P120, etc.). If your increment value is –10, each copy will be decreased by ten (P90, P80, P70, etc.). Set the increment value in the edit field provided in the Text sub-palette when you select the command, or key-in at the uSTN> field, **ti=#** and press ⏎. (Replace # with your tag increment value.)

The command cannot add digits to, or remove them from, the number it starts with. In other words, if you start with three digits, you cannot increment beyond 999, and you cannot decrement below 100. If you must continue beyond those limits, stop incrementing, use Place Text to place the next number in the series, and then start incrementing again.

Only the numeric part of a text string is incremented. It cannot increment letters. If the text string contains more than one set of numbers separated by non-numeric characters, it increments the set of numbers farthest to the right. For example, if you increment the text string P100-30, it only increments the number to the right of the dash (30). The 100 cannot be incremented.

To increment text, first place the text to be incremented, then click the Copy and Increment Text icon in the Text sub-palette (see Figure 5–14). If necessary, change the increment value to the amount you want to increment or decrement in the Tag Increment edit field. MicroStation prompts:

Identify element (Identify the text element to be copied.)
Accept/Reject (Select next input) (Place data points at each location where you want an incremented copy placed. To terminate in placing the current incrementing text copy, click the Reset button.)

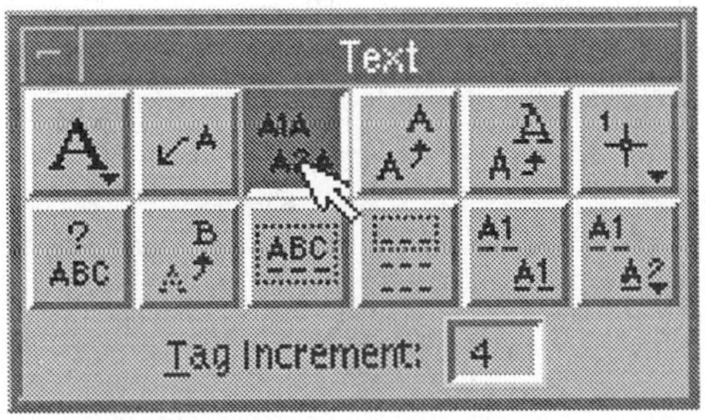

FIGURE 5–14   Clicking the Copy and Increment icon from the Text sub-palette.

Display Text Attributes

If you just want to see what text attribute settings were in effect when a text element was placed, use the Display Text Attributes command.

To see what text attribute settings were used to place a text element, click the Display Text Attributes icon in the Text sub-palette (see Figure 5–15). MicroStation prompts:

Identify text element (Identify the text element.)

FIGURE 5–15   Clicking the Display Text Attributes icon from the Text sub-palette.

When you select the text element, the text attributes and related information are displayed in the Status and Error fields of the Command Window.

If the element is a text string (one line of text), the status field displays the element type (Text) and the level on which it was placed. The Error field displays the text element's height, width, level, and font.

If the element is multi-line text, the status field displays the element type (Node) and the level on which it was placed. The error field displays the node number, characters per line, line spacing, level, and font. Multi-line text is placed as a Text Node.

TEXT NODES

Text Nodes provides a way for you to create text place holders (reservations) in a design file without actually placing any text. When you place the "empty" text nodes, they take on the current active text and element attributes. Later, when you add text to the nodes, the text takes on the attributes of the node, not the active attributes.

Text Nodes are most often used in MDL applications and user commands. For example, a title block application might find the title block in the border of your drawing, place text nodes in each title block field, and then guide you though filling in the text nodes. Use of such an application provides a standard title block layout and look for all designs.

Text Node View Attribute   MicroStation indicates the position of Text Nodes in your design with a cross and a number. The Text Node View Attribute allows you to turn ON or OFF the display of the cross and number in selected views. Figure 5–16 shows examples of the way empty text nodes and text nodes with text appear when the Text Node View attribute is set to ON.

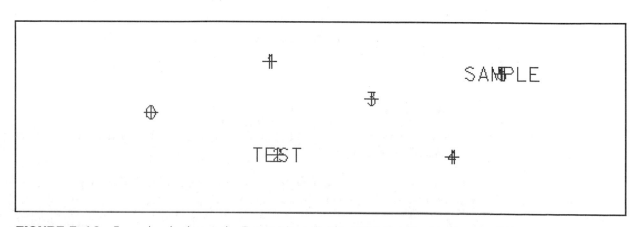

FIGURE 5–16   Examples displaying the Text Nodes with View Attributes Text node set to ON.

If the View Attributes is set to OFF, nothing appears to happen when you place empty nodes, so it is useful to have the attribute turned ON for the view you are working in. Use the View Attributes settings box to turn ON or OFF the Text Node view attribute (see Figure 5–17).

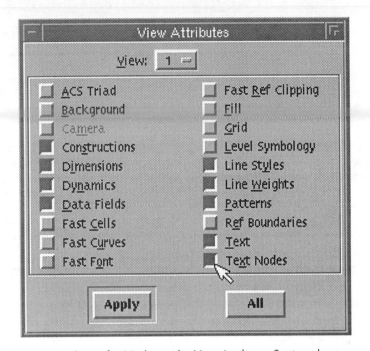

FIGURE 5–17   Setting the View Attributes for Nodes in the View Attributes Settings box.

> **NOTE:** If you plot a view in which the text node crosses and numbers are displayed, they also appear on the plot.

Text and Element Attributes   Select the element and text attributes for text nodes the same way you set them for placing text. When you place a text node, it takes on all the attribute settings except Text String Justification—text nodes use Multi-line Justification.

Placing Empty Text Nodes   The Place Text Node command places the node cross and node identification number, but does not place text on the node. The command prompts you to specify the node location with a data point and the rotation angle with either a data point or a reset. To place the node at the active angle, press the Reset button. To graphically define the rotation angle, place a second data point, and the rotation of an imaginary line from the first data point to the second data point defines the node angle.

To place an empty text node, click the Place Text Node icon in the Text sub-palette (see Figure 5–18), or key-in at the uSTN> field, **place node** (or **pla n**) and press ⏎. MicroStation prompts:

> *Enter text node origin* (Place a data point to indicate where you want the node to be placed in the design.)
> *Define angle or Reset for active angle* (Click the Reset button to assign the active angle to the node, or place a data point to define the rotation angle.)

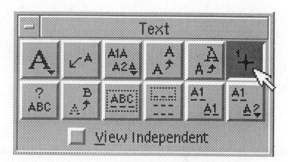

FIGURE 5–18 Clicking the Place Text Node icon from the Text sub-palette.

MicroStation does not provide a dynamic image of the node as you are placing it. Nothing appears until you place the second data point or press the Reset button. If the Text Node View attribute is set to OFF, the node is not displayed in the view after you place it.

> **NOTE:** When you select Place Text Node, a View Independent toggle button appears in the sub-palette. View Independent text is applicable to three dimensional designs.

Placing Text on Empty Text Nodes Before you place the text on the text node, set the Text Node Lock to ON. When the lock is set to ON, the Place Text command can only place text on an empty text node. When the lock is OFF, text cannot be placed on a node. The Text Node Lock is turned ON and OFF in either the Full or Toggle Lock settings box and Text sub-palette (see Figure 5–19). The lock is ON when its check button is depressed (shown dark).

FIGURE 5–19 Setting the Text Node Lock in the Lock settings box (Full and Toggle).

After setting the Text Node Lock to ON, click the Place Text icon in the Text sub-palette, or key-in at the uSTN> field, **place text** (or **pla tex**) and press ⏎. MicroStation prompts:

Enter text (Type the text, then click on the text node you want to place text on.)
Accept/Reject (Select next input) (Click the Data button to accept placing the text on the node, or click the Reset button to reject the selected node.)

> **NOTE:** After placing the first Data button, dynamic update highlights the selected node, but does not show the text on the node. You see the text only after placing the second Data button. The node cross is the justification point for the text. If, for example, you created the node with multi-line text justification set to center-center, text placed on the node is centered about the cross.

Placing Text Nodes in Cells If a cell was created with an empty text node as part of it, the text node is not part of the cell after you place a copy of the cell in your design. Cell manipulations do not affect the node and you can add text to the node. If a cell was created with a node that had text on it, the node remains part of the cell after you place a copy of it. Any manipulations you do to the cell affect the node too, and you cannot change the text in the node. See Chapter 7 for a detailed explanation on cells.

DATA FIELDS

Data fields provide another way to create place holders for text that will be filled in later. Like text nodes, data fields save the text and element attributes that were in effect when they were created, and, when you place text in them, the text takes on those attributes rather than the current active attributes.

Data fields provide some additional features that make them more versatile than text nodes. When you create a data field, you also specify the maximum number of characters allowed in the field. When you are ready to enter text in the data fields, several commands automate the process for you. For example, you can tell MicroStation to find all data fields in a view. Each time MicroStation finds one, you just type the text for the field and press [ENTER].

Data fields are often used to create "fill-in-the-blanks" design templates for things like standard specification sheets. Users can copy the template, then fill in the blanks. They are also useful in cells, because, unlike text nodes, empty data fields in a cell remain part of the cell and can be filled in after the cell is placed. For example, you might add data fields to process flow sheet symbol cells. See Chapter 7 for a discussion of cells.

How to Create Data Fields A data field is just an underscore, or contiguous string of underscores, in a text string or multi-line text element. Use any of the text placement commands to create data fields by typing underscores as all or part of the text. To type an underscore, press and hold the [SHIFT] key, then press the Dash (-) key for each underscore you need. For example; If you choose the Place Text command and type "Pump _ _ _" as the text, the three underscores after the word "Pump" are a data field that you can fill in later.

Each underscore, or set of contiguous underscores, that is separated by another character (including the [ENTER] key in multi-line text) is treated as a separate data field within the text element. Figure 5–20 shows examples of data fields in text elements.

> **NOTE:** In MicroStation the underscore is reserved by default as the Enter Data Field character. If necessary you can change the reserved character. See Chapter 11 for additional information.

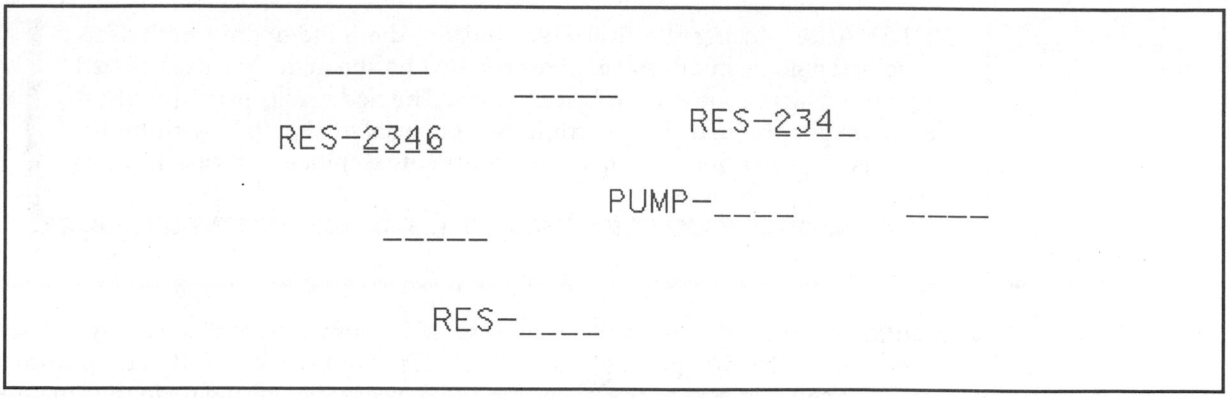

```
                        ‾‾‾‾
                              ‾‾‾‾‾                RES-234_
         RES-2346
                                      PUMP-____              ____
                        ‾‾‾‾‾

                        RES-____
```

FIGURE 5–20 Examples displaying the Enter Data Fields with View Attributes Data Field set to ON.

Data Fields View Attribute The display of the data field character (the underscore) can be turned ON and OFF for selected views using the View Attributes settings box that is available from the View pull-down menu (see Figure 5–21).

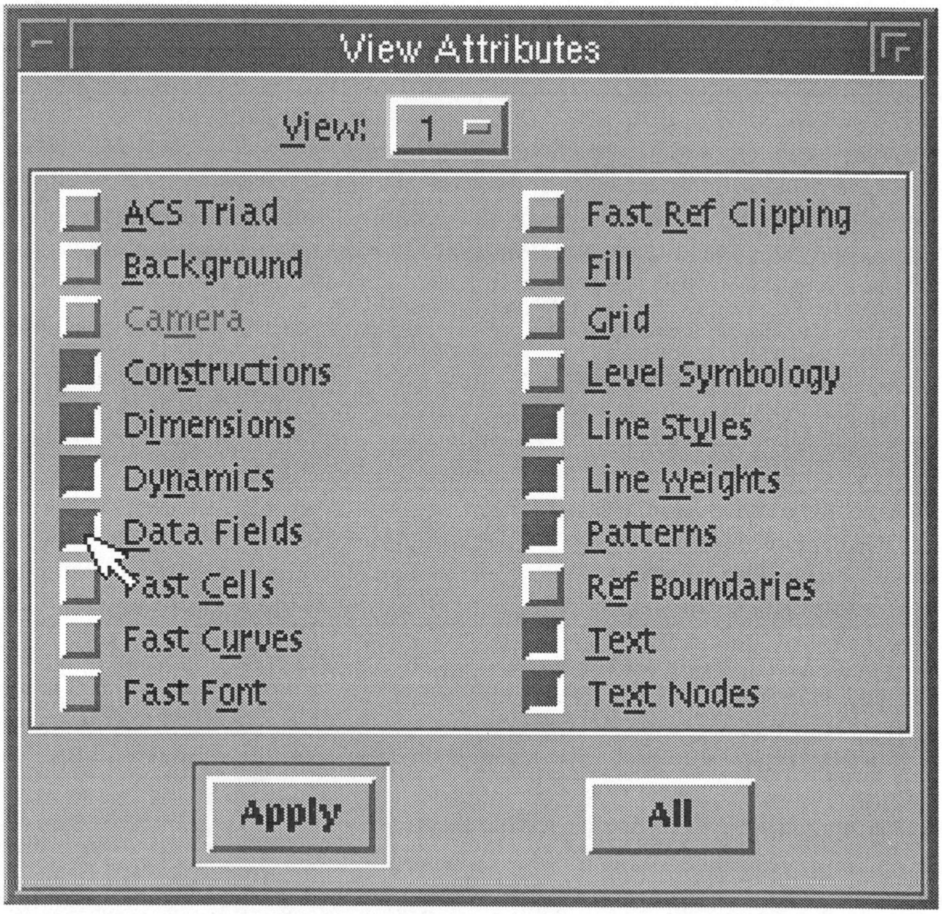

FIGURE 5–21 Setting the View Attributes for Enter Data in the View Attributes Settings box.

When the attribute is set to OFF, the data field underscores disappear from the view. Any text entered into a data field remains visible. When the View Attribute is set to ON, the data field underscores are visible, even when text has been entered in the field.

Data Fields Justification Data fields have their own justification settings. Don't confuse this justification with the text string and multi-line text justification settings. The data field justification applies only to the enter data field part of a text element when you place text in the field, and it is set after the text string containing the field is placed in the design. Three data field justifications are provided: left, center, and right.

Data Field Justification can only be set by key-ins (there is no option in the sub-palettes). To set the field justification to:

Left, key-in at the uSTN> field, **justify left** (or **ju l**) and press [ENTER].

Center, key-in at the uSTN> field, **justify center** (or **ju c**) and press [ENTER].

Right, key-in at the uSTN> field, **justify right** (or **ju r**) and press [ENTER].

In each case, MicroStation prompts:

Identify element (To set the justification, click the data button on each data field you want.)

Each field you select is highlighted and a box appears around the field underscores.

Fill In a Single Data Field Use the Fill In Single Enter Data Field command when you need to place text in a selected data field only. To do so, click the Fill In Single Enter_Data Field icon in the Text sub-palette (see Figure 5–22), or key-in at the uSTN> field **edit single** (or **ed s**) and press [ENTER]. MicroStation prompts:

Identify element (Click the data button on the field you want to fill in.)
Enter text or <CR> to fill in field (In the Text Editor box, type the text you want to place in the field, then press [ENTER].)

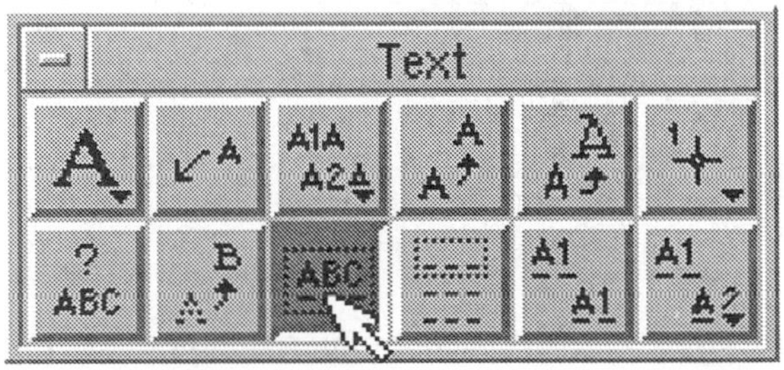

FIGURE 5–22 Clicking the File in Single Enter_Data Field icon from the Text sub-palette.

The selected field is highlighted after it is selected and a box appears around the underscores in the field. When [ENTER] is pressed, the text is placed in the selected field, and the box disappears. You are now ready to select another field for text entry.

With this command you can select a data field that already contains text and enter new text. The text you enter replaces all text currently in the data field.

> **NOTE:** Use this command to clear the text from a data field by pressing the **Space** and [ENTER].

Automatic Fill In Data Fields MicroStation provides a fast way to fill in all the data fields in a selected view. To do it, click the Auto Fill In Enter_Data Fields icon in the Text sub-palette (see Figure 5–23), or key-in at the uSTN> field, **edit auto** (or **ed au**) and press ⏎. MicroStation prompts:

> *Select view* (Click the data button anywhere in the view containing the fields you want to fill in, and MicroStation highlights one of the fields in the view.)
> *<CR> to fill in or DATA for next field* (In the Text Editor box, type the text you want to place in the highlighted field and press ⏎.)

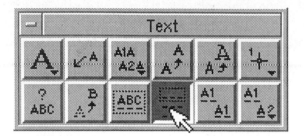

FIGURE 5–23 Clicking the Auto Fill In Enter_Data Fields icon from the Text sub-palette.

Each time you press ⏎, MicroStation finds the next data field, and waits for you to type the text for that field. This procedure continues until all fields are filled in, you select another command, or press the Reset button.

> **NOTE:** This command does not select data fields that already contain text. If all the data fields in the selected view already contain text, or if there are no fields in the view, an error message appears in the error field of the Command Window.

Copy Data Fields If you need to place the same text in several data fields, you can type the text in the first field using the Fill In Single Enter_Data Field command, then click the Copy Enter_Data Field icon in the Text sub-palette (see Figure 5–24), or key-in at the uSTN> field, **copy ed** (or **cop ed**) and press ⏎. MicroStation prompts:

> *Select enter data field to copy* (Click the data button on the data field that contains the text you want to copy to other fields.)
> *Select destination enter data field* (Click the data button on each field you want to place the text in.)

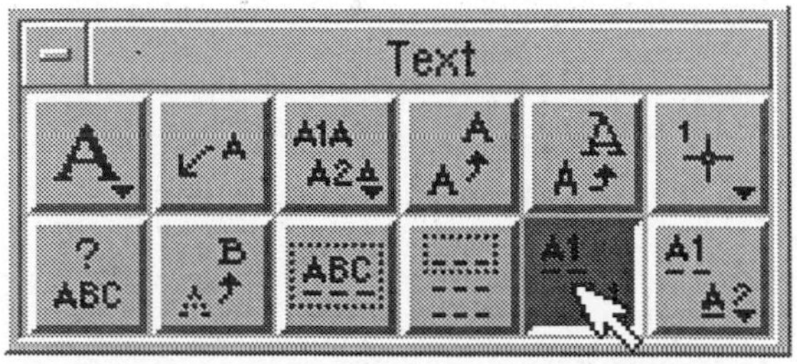

FIGURE 5–24 Clicking the Copy Enter_Data Field icon from the Text sub-palette.

The text is copied to the selected field as soon as you select it. When you have copied the text to all data fields, either select another command or click the Reset button. This command provides a quick way to clear several data fields. Use the Fill In Single Enter_Data Field command to place a space character in one of the fields to be cleared, then copy that space to the other fields. Placing a space character in a field clears it.

> **NOTE:** When you select the field containing the text to be copied, the text in that data field appears in the error field of the Command Window. This allows you to make sure you have the correct data field even when the view is zoomed so far out you cannot read the text in the design.

Copy and Increment Data Fields Need to place a sequential set of numbers in a group of data fields? The Copy and Increment Enter_Data Field can do it for you. You place the starting number in one of the fields, set the increment value you want to use, then use this command to copy and increment the number into the other data fields.

You can enter a positive number to increment the number as you copy, or a negative number to decrement as you copy. If you select the command from the sub-palette, you can set the increment value in the Tag Increment field that appears in the sub-palette. If you invoke the command by key-in at the uSTN> field in the Command Window, key-in the increment value by typing **TI=#** and press [ENTER]. Replace **#** with the positive or negative increment value.

Enter the starting number in a data field, then click the Copy and Increment Enter Data_Field icon in the Text sub-palette, and enter the increment value in the Tag Increment field (see Figure 5–25), or key-in at the uSTN> field, **increment ed** (or **incr e**) and press [ENTER]. MicroStation prompts:

Select enter data field to copy (Click the data button on the field containing the number to be copied and incremented.)
Select destination enter data field (Click the data button on each of the data fields to be copied and incremented.)

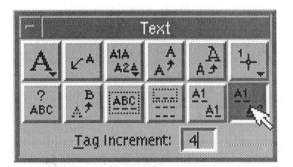

FIGURE 5–25   Clicking the Copy and Increment Enter Data_Field icon from the Text sub-palette.

> **NOTE:** When you select the field containing the number to be copied, or one of the fields to place the incremented copy in, the number appears in the error field of the Command Window. This allows you to track what you are doing even when the view is zoomed so far out you cannot read the number in the design.

This command cannot increase or decrease the number of digits in the number you start with. For example, if the starting number contains four digits you cannot decrement below 1000 or increment above 9999. If you must continue incrementing or decrementing beyond the number of digits you started with, use the Fill In Single Enter_Data Field command to enter the next number in the series, then start the Copy and Increment Enter_Data Field command again.

Edit Text in a Data Field In addition to using the commands described above to place and copy text in data fields, the Edit Text command (described earlier in this chapter) allows you to edit the text placed in data fields and the number of underscores in the data field.

When a text string that contains a data field is placed in the Text Editor box, the underscores are represented by spaces and a pair of angle brackets is placed on each end of the data field. To delete underscores from a data field, position the text cursor in the text in the Text Editor box and press the backspace delete key with insert mode on. To add underscores, type either spaces or underscores with insert mode on.

To place text in a field without changing the field length, make sure overstrike mode is on, position the text cursor in the field, and type your text. Do not type over the angle brackets.

To remove a data field from the text string in the Text Editor box, make sure insert mode is on, then delete the pairs of angle brackets that delimit the field and everything in between.

To insert a new data field into a text string, make sure insert mode is on, then position the text cursor at the point in the string where you want to start the insertion. Type a pair of left angle brackets (<<), the number of underscores you want in the field, and a pair of right angle brackets (>>).

TAGS

Tags provides another way to place or attach text (non-graphical) attributes to elements. If you delete or copy an element with attached tags, the tags are deleted or copied as well. Likewise, if you move an element with attached tags, the tags are also moved. You can also edit the tags and control the display of the tags. In addition, you can also extract data related to tags to an external file in a form that database handling programs can use.

Tags and Tag Sets

A tag definition includes several attributes, some are optional. The attributes are:

Tag Name—The tag name (maximum valid number of characters is 32) is the identifier of the tag definition and listed in the Tags list box.

Prompt—(optional) You can specify a string of characters (maximum valid number of characters is 32) that will prompt you to enter the appropriate value when you attach a tag to an element.

Type Option menu—Three options are available for tag data types: Character, Integer, or Real.

Variable Toggle—(optional) To prevent the tag value from being changed with the Edit Tags tool, set the Variable toggle button to OFF. If it set to ON, you can change the tag value with the Edit Tags tool.

Default Toggle—(optional) To use the default value and also prevent changing the tag by Edit Tags tool when the tag is attached, set the Default toggle button to ON.

Confirm Toggle—(optional) To display an alert box to confirm the value entered, set the Confirm toggle button to ON.

Default Tag Value edit field—(optional) Define the default tag value in the Default Tag Value edit field to attach the tag as the default value when the Default toggle button is set to ON.

Display Tag—(optional) To prevent the tag value from displaying with each element to which the tag is attached, set the Display Tag toggle button to OFF.

In addition to defining a tag, MicroStation allows you to provide a group name or tag set definition. Under a tag set definition you can define any number of tag definitions. Tags and Tag sets are analogous to the files and directories in the Dos Operating system.

Tag Set and Tag Definition The Tag Sets settings box allows you to define tag sets and tag definitions. To open the Tag Sets settings box, select the Settings pull-down menu in the MicroStation Command Window and select the Tag Sets option. MicroStation displays a Tag Sets settings box similar to the Figure 5–26.

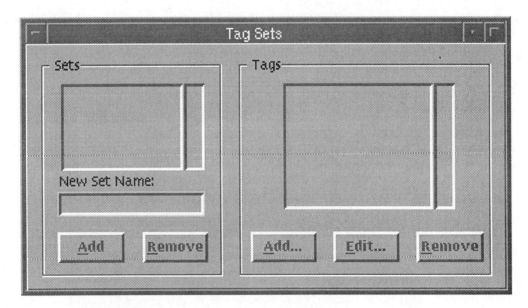

FIGURE 5–26   Tag Sets setting box.

To create a new Tag Set definition, key-in a tag set name in the New Set Name edit field and click the Add button. The new tag set name is displayed in the Sets list box.

Click the Remove button to delete the Tag set definition and all instances of the set's member tags in the design. MicroStation displays an alert box to confirm the request. If you are sure, click the OK button.

To create a Tag definition, first select the set to which the tag will be added in the Sets list box. Click the Add... button in the Tags section of the Settings box. The Define Tag dialog box opens similar to the Figure 5–27.

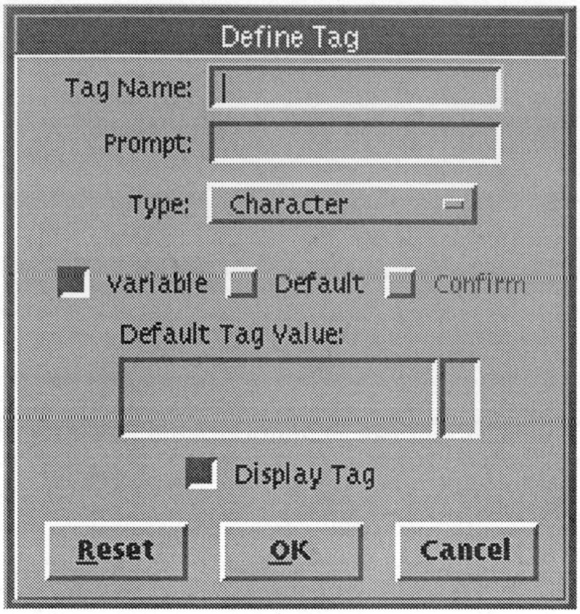

FIGURE 5–27 Define Tag dialog box.

Key-in the tag name in the Tag Name edit field (maximum valid number of characters is 32), and prompt in the Prompt edit field (maximum valid number of characters is 32). Select the Tag data type from the Type options menu. Set appropriate settings for Variable, Default, Confirm and Display Tag toggle buttons. If applicable, key-in the default tag value in the Default Tag Value edit field. Click the OK button and the tag is listed in the Tags list box.

There is no limit to the number of tags you can define for each tag set.

Editing a Tag Definition To edit a tag definition, first select the tag in the Tags list box and click the Edit... button. The Define Tag dialog box opens similar to the Figure 5–28.

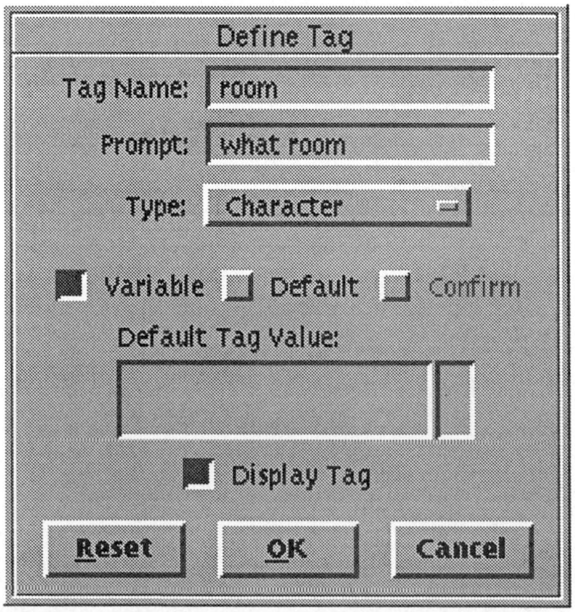

FIGURE 5–28 Editing a tag definition displays the Define Tag dialog box already created for the tag.

Make the necessary changes in the Define Tag dialog box and click OK button to keep the changes.

Click the Remove button to delete the Tag definition and all instances of the member tags in the design. MicroStation displays an alert box to confirm the request. If you are sure, click the OK button.

Attaching a Tag To attach a tag to an element, click the Attach Tag icon in the Tags palette (see Figure 5–29), or key-in at the uSTN> field, **attach tags** and press [ENTER]. MicroStation prompts:

Select Tag Set (Select the tag set from the Tag Sets list box.)
Select Tag to Attach (Select the tag definition from the Tags list box.)
Identify element (Identify the element to attach the tag definition.)
Accept/Reject (Select next input) (Click the Data button to accept the element or click the Reject button to reject the selected element.)

FIGURE 5–29 Invoking the Attach Tag command from the Tags palette.

If the value of the selected tag is variable and the tag is defined so that the default value is not automatically used, the Tag Value dialog box opens similar to the Figure 5–30. Key-in the value of the tag and if necessary, turn off the Display Tag to prevent the tag value from displaying. Click OK button to close the Tag Value dialog box.

FIGURE 5–30 The Tag Value dialog box.

If the tag is defined so that the keyed-in value must be confirmed, an alert box opens similar to Figure 5–31. To confirm the tag value, click the OK button.

FIGURE 5–31 Confirm Tag Value alert box.

Finally, MicroStation prompts:

> *Place Tag* (Place a data point to position the tag.)

The tag is placed according to the current Text attributes, such as Text size, slant angle, etc. Before you place a data point to position the tag, if necessary, you can change the text attributes.

Editing a Tag To edit a tag that is attached to an element, click the Edit Tags icon in the Tags palette (see Figure 5–32), or key-in at the uSTN> field, **edit tags** and press [ENTER]. MicroStation prompts:

> *Identify element* (Identify the element or the tag.)
> *Accept/Reject (Select next input)* (Click the Data button to accept the element—or tag—or click the Reject button to reject the selected element—or tag. If an element is selected, the Tag set box shows the names of sets containing tags attached to the selected element; otherwise, the Tag Value dialog box opens.)
> *Select Tag to edit* (In the Tag Sets box, select the set containing the desired tag and select the corresponding tag from the Tags list box.)

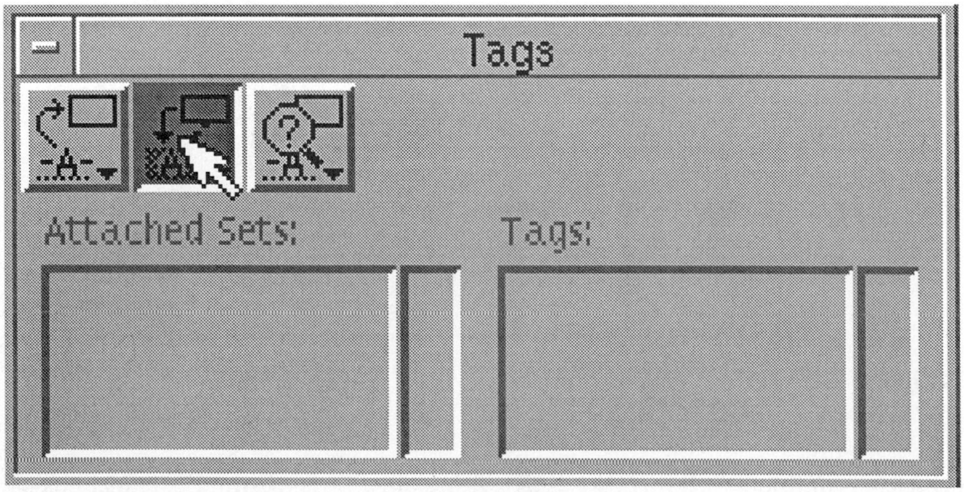

FIGURE 5–32 Invoking the Edit Tags command from the Tags palette.

MicroStation displays the Tag Value dialog box similar to the Figure 5–33. If the tag value is variable, key-in the new value. If necessary, turn OFF Display Tag toggle button to prevent the tag from displaying. Click the OK button to keep the changes.

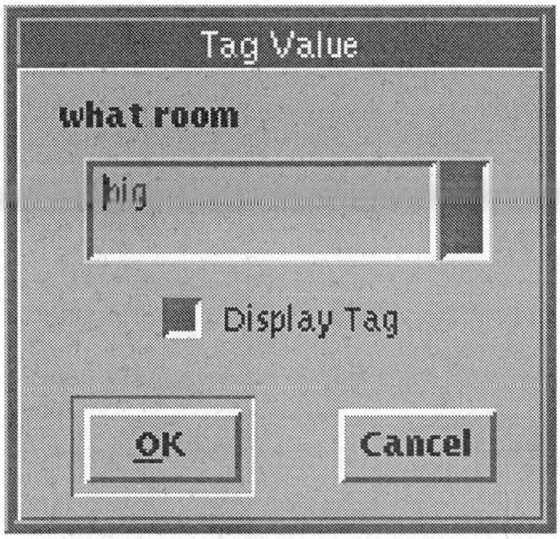

FIGURE 5–33   Displaying the Tag Value dialog box to edit a tag.

Reviewing a Tag To review a tag that is attached to an element, click the Review Tags icon in the Tags palette (see Figure 5–34), or key-in at the uSTN> field, **review tags** and press ⏎. Micro-Station prompts:

Identify element (Identify the element or the tag.)

Accept/Reject (Select next input) (Click the Data button to accept the element—or tag—or click the Reject button to reject the selected element—or tag. If an element is selected, the Tag set box shows the names of sets containing tags attached to the selected element; otherwise, the Tag Review dialog box opens.)

Select Tag to edit (In the Tag Sets box, select the set containing the desired tag and select the corresponding tag from the Tags list box.)

FIGURE 5–34   Invoking the Review Tags command from the Tags palette.

MicroStation displays the Tag Review dialog box similar to the Figure 5–35. The Tag Review dialog box displays the settings for the selected tag definition. You can not make any changes to the tag definition in the Tag Review dialog box. Click the OK button to close the Tag Review dialog box.

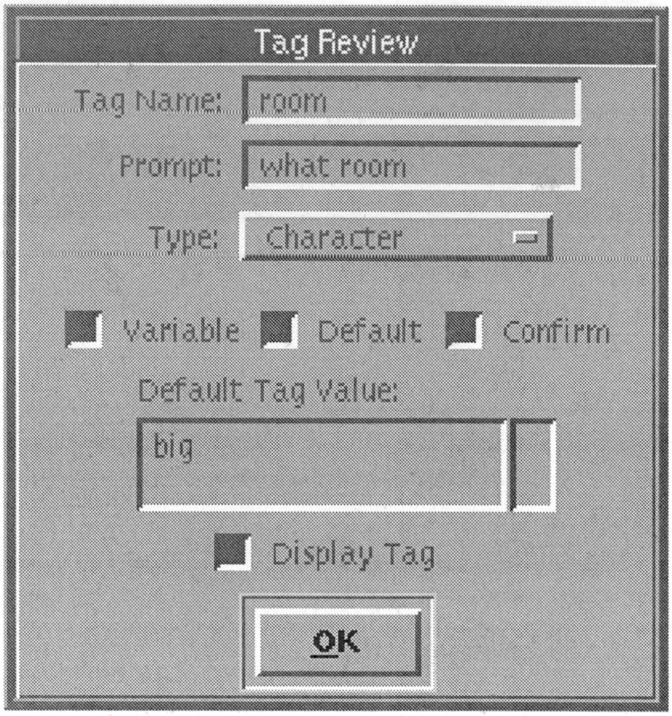

FIGURE 5–35   Displaying the Tag Review dialog box to review a tag that is attached to an element.

Reporting Tags

Extracting data from a drawing is one of the foremost innovations in CAD. Paper copies of drawings have long been used to communicate more than just how objects look. In addition to dimensions, drawings tell builders or fabricators what materials to use, quantities of objects to make, manufacture's names and models of parts in an assembly, coordinate locations of objects in a general area, and what types of finishes to apply to surfaces. But, until computers came into the picture, extracting data from manual drawings involved making lists (usually by hand) while studying the drawing, often checking off the data with a marker. With MicroStation, you can generate many different variations of reports on tags. Extracted data can be manipulated by a database application program. A listing of pipe, valves, and fittings in a piping system can be a data base if each item has essential data associated with it such as its size, flange rating, weight, material of manufacture, product that it handles, cost location within the system, and many others.

Extracting data is a two-step process, generating a tag report template file and a report file. The template file is saved in ASCII format specifing the tag set and its member tags plus any graphical element attributes on which to report. The report file generates a report on selected tags based on the template file.

Generating a template   To generate a template, invoke the Generate Template settings box by selecting the Tag Reporting sub-menu Generate Template from the File pull-down menu of the

MicroStation Command Window. MicroStation displays Generate Template settings box similar to Figure 5–36.

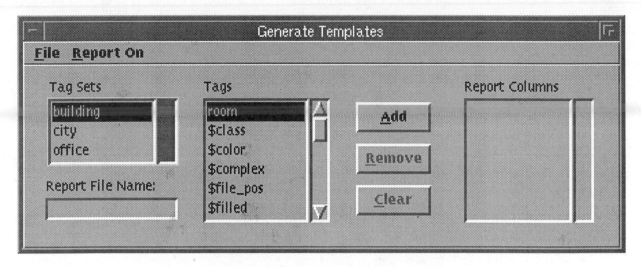

FIGURE 5–36   The Generate Templates settings box.

The Tag Sets lists sets defined in the current design file. To generate a template file, select the set that contains the tags on which to report. Select the tag from the tags lists and click Add button to add to the report list. If necessary, you can delete the tag selected in the Report columns box from the list by clicking Remove button. Similarly, click Clear button to remove the list of tags from the Report Columns list box. Key-in the name of the report file to be generated in the Report File Name edit field when the template file is used.

Select Tagged Elements option from the Report On pull-down menu to report on the only elements with attached tags.

Select All Elements option from the Report On pull-down menu to report on all elements regardless whether they have tags attached.

To save the current template file, invoke the Save Template dialog box by selecting Save... from the File pull-down of the Generate Template settings box. Key-in the name of the template file in the Name edit field and click the OK button. The default extension for the file name is .TMP.

Generating Reports   To generate a report, invoke the Generate Report dialog box by selecting the Tag Reporting sub menu Generate Report... from the File pull-down menu of the MicroStation Command Window. MicroStation displays Generate Report dialog box similar to Figure 5–37.

MicroStation lists the available template files from the default directory in the Files list box. To generate a report file, select the name of the template file from the Files list box and click the Add button. MicroStation places the template file in the Templates for Reports list box. You can place any number of template files in the Templates for Reports list box. After placing all the necessary template files in the Templates for Reports list box, click Done button to generate a report file for each template file. By default, MicroStation places the generated report files in the ustation\out\tag\ directory.

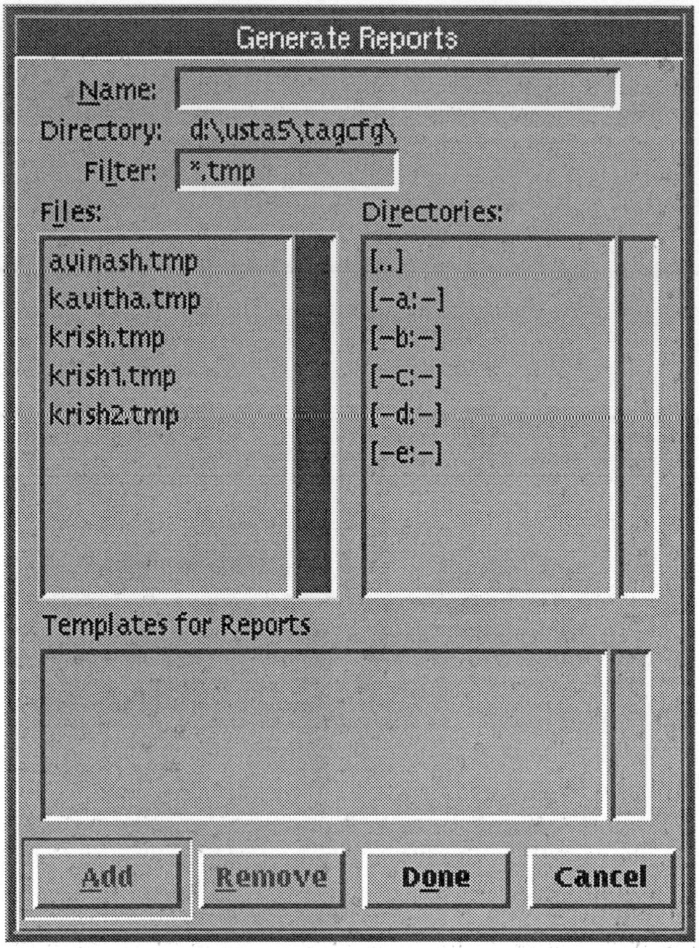

FIGURE 5–37 The Generate Reports dialog box.

IMPORTING TEXT

MicroStation provides powerful tools for placing short strings of text at various places in your design, but it can be tedious to enter a large amount of text using the Text Editor box. MicroStation provides a command to import text that was created in another program, such as a word processor.

The only requirement for creating your text outside of MicroStation is that the program you use must be able to save your text in an ASCII text file. For example, the Edit program that comes with MS DOS 5.0 or later saves the text as ASCII, and the MicroSoft Word for Windows program has a Save As option that allows you to save the file as ASCII text with line breaks.

If the imported text consists of more than 128 lines or more than 2,048 characters, the placement data point is the upper left corner of the text and each text line is placed as a separate text string. All lines of the imported text become part of a graphic group (discussed in Chapter 10). You will not see the text until you have defined the placement data point.

If the imported text consists of less than 128 lines and 2,048 characters, it is placed as one multi-line text element (a text node). The relation of the placement data point to the text is determined by the multi-line text justification setting. Dynamic update shows the text following the screen pointer until you define the placement data point.

To import a text file, invoke the Text... option from the Import command located in the File pull-down menu as shown in Figure 5–38. MicroStation displays the Import Text File dialog box similar to the one shown in Figure 5–39.

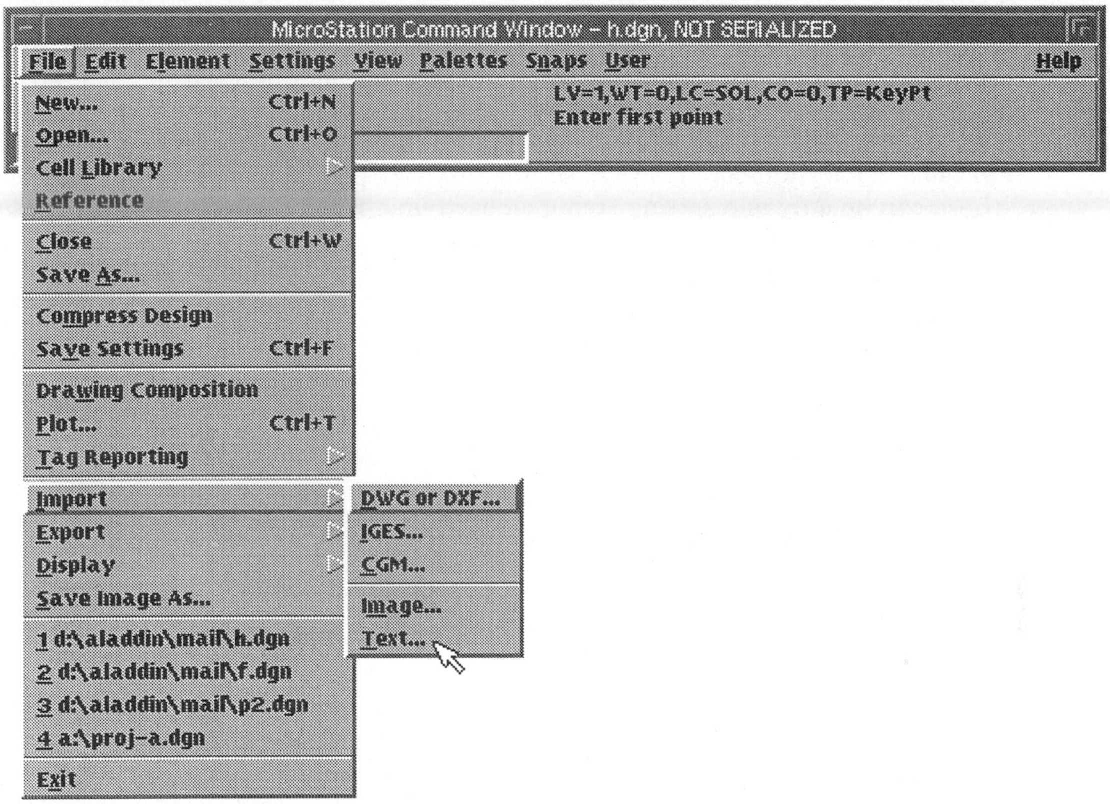

FIGURE 5–38   Displaying the Text... option in the Import sub-menu in the File pull-down menu.

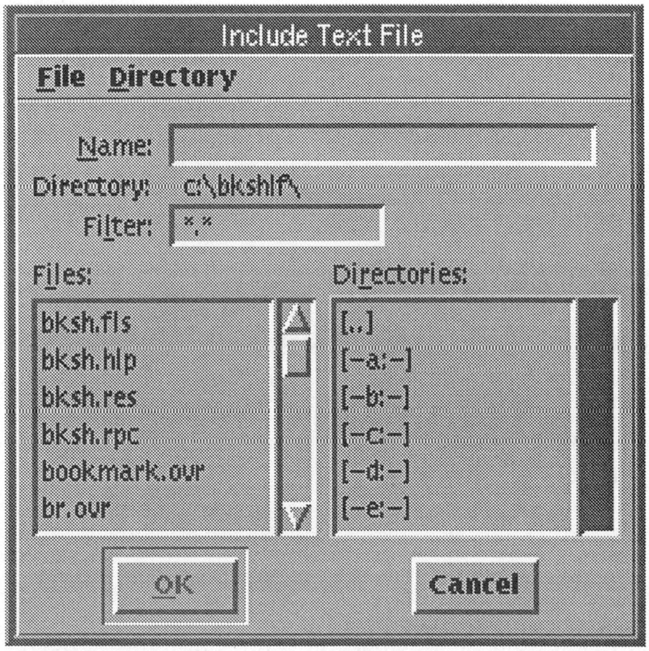

FIGURE 5–39   Import Text File Dialog Box.

You can also import text by keying in at the uSTN> field, **include** <file> and pressing ⏎. Replace <file> with the name of the file you want to import.

Handling Tabs MicroStation replaces all tab characters in the imported text with eight space characters. If you want a different number of spaces for each tab character, tell MicroStation how many you want before importing the text. To do so, key-in at the uSTN> field, **tb**=<space> and press ⏎. Replace <space> with the number of characters you want to place for each tab character.

Element Attributes The text file can also contain element attribute setting key-in strings (such as FT= to select a font number or TX= to set the text size). Each string must be preceded by a period, and there can be only one setting string on each line in the file. Figure 5–40 shows an example of a text file containing attribute setting key-in strings. Do not type text on the same line as a key-in string.

```
.FT=7
.TH=1:5
.TW=1
.CO=3
This text will be placed using font 7, text height 1:5, text width 1, and color 3.
.FT=0
.TX=:8
.CO=0
This text will be placed using font 0, text height and width :8, and color 9.
```

FIGURE 5–40 Example of Text file containing Attribute key-in strings.

Each time MicroStation encounters an attribute setting key-in in the text file it is importing, it makes that attribute the active setting and uses it for the text that follows.

Two additional commands can be included in the text file. Indent # causes MicroStation to indent each line the number of characters specified by #. The Newgg command causes MicroStation to end the current graphic group and place the text strings that follow in a separate graphic group. Newgg, of course, only applies to text files that contain more than 128 lines or 2,048 characters.

ELEMENT MODIFICATION—EXTENDING LINES

MicroStation allows you not only to place elements easily, but also allows you to modify them as needed. Three commands helpful for cleaning up and for modifying elements are available in MicroStation. The commands include Extend Line, Extend Two Elements To Intersection, and Extend Element To Intersection available from the Modify Element sub-palette that can be opened from the Main palette (see Figure 5–41).

Extend Line

The name Extend Line is a bit misleading. The command is used to extend or shorten a line, line string, or multi-line by a graphically defined length (with a data point) or by a keyed-in distance.

FIGURE 5–41   Invoking the Modify Element sub-palette from the Main palette.

To graphically extend a line, click the Extend Line icon in the Modify Element sub-palette, then turn OFF the Distance check button that appears in the sub-palette (see Figure 5–42), or key-in at the uSTN> field, **extend line** (or **ext l**) and press [ENTER]. MicroStation prompts:

> *Identify element* (Identify the element near the end to be extended or shortened.)
> *Accept or reject (Select next input)* (Drag the element to the new length and click the Data button
>   to accept, or click the Reject button to disregard the modification.)

The following command sequence shows an example (see Figure 5–43) of using the Extend Line command to extend a line.

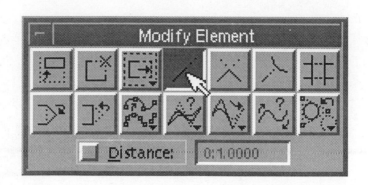

FIGURE 5–42   Clicking the Extend Line icon in the Modify Element sub-palette with Distance toggle button set to OFF.

Identify element (Identify the line.)
Accept or reject (Select next input) (Place a data point to extend the line.)

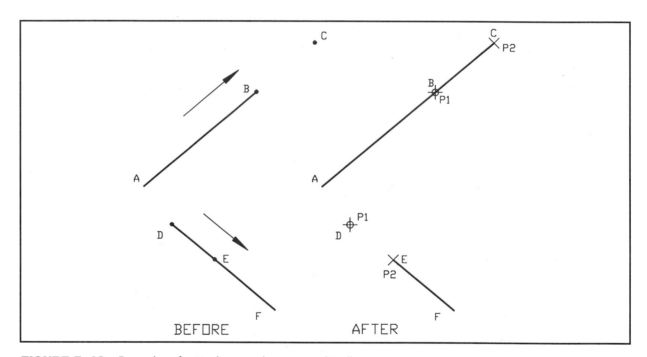

FIGURE 5–43   Examples of extending an element graphically.

To extend a line by key-in, click the Extend Line icon in the Modify Element sub-palette, turn ON the Distance toggle button (see Figure 5–44), key-in the Distance in the Distance edit field, and press ⟦ENTER⟧ or ⟦TAB⟧. Alternately, key-in at the uSTN> field, **extend line** (or **ext l k**) and press ⟦ENTER⟧. Then, if necessary, key-in at the uSTN> field the distance to extend or shorten. MicroStation prompts:

Identify element (Identify the element near the end to be extended or shortened.)
Accept or reject (Select next input) (Click again with the Data button anywhere in the design plane to accept the extension.)

> **NOTE:** A positive distance lengthens the selected element, and a negative distance shortens the element.

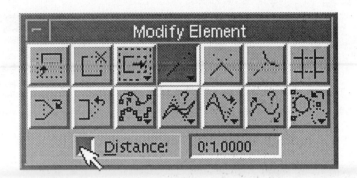

FIGURE 5–44   Clicking the Extend Line icon in the Modify Element sub-palette with Distance toggle button set to ON.

Extend Two Elements to Intersection

Two elements can be extended or shortened as necessary to create a clean intersection between the two. Elements that can be extended to a common intersection with each other are lines, line strings, arcs, half ellipses, and quarter ellipses. Figure 5–45 shows several examples of possible extensions to intersection.

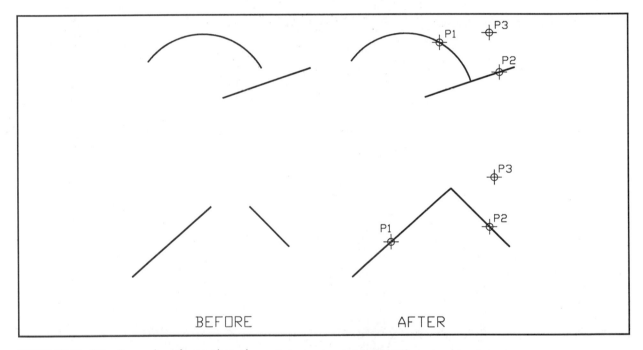

FIGURE 5–45   Examples of extending elements to a common intersection.

To extend two elements to their common intersection, click the Extend 2 Elements To Intersection icon in the Modify Element sub-palette (see Figure 5–46), or key-in at the uSTN> field, **extend element 2 (or ext e 2)** and press [ENTER]. MicroStation prompts:

> *Select first element for extension* (Identify one of the two elements.)
> *Select element for intersection* (Identify the second element.)
> *Accept/Initiate intersection* (Place a data point anywhere in the view to initiate the intersection.)

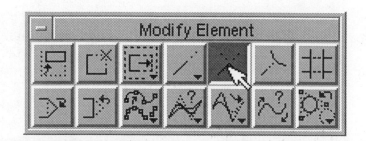

FIGURE 5–46 Clicking the Extend 2 Elements To Intersection icon from the Modify Element sub-palette.

Dynamic update shows the intersection as soon as you select the second element, but the intersection is not actually created until you accept it by clicking the Data button a third time.

> **NOTE:** If an element overlaps the intersection, select it on the part you want to keep. The part of the element beyond the intersection is deleted. If dynamic update shows the wrong part of the element deleted, click the Reset button to back up and try again.

Extend Element to Intersection

The Extend Element To Intersection command is used to change the end point of the selected line to extend to a selected line, line string, shape, circle, or arc. Elements that can be extended are lines, line strings, arcs, half ellipses, and quarter ellipses. Figure 5–47 shows several examples of possible extensions to intersection.

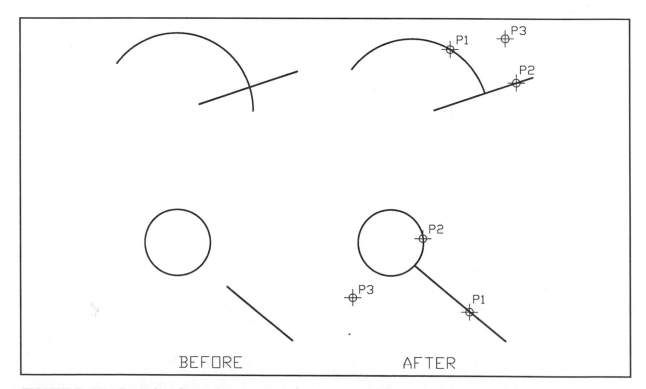

FIGURE 5–47 Examples of extending an element to an intersection.

To extend an element to its intersection with another element, click the Extend Element To Intersection icon in the Modify Element sub-palette (see Figure 5–48), or key-in at the uSTN> field, **extend element intersection** (or **ext e**) and press [ENTER]. MicroStation prompts:

> *Select first element for extension* (Identify the element to extend.)
> *Select element for intersection* (Identify the element to which the first element will be extended.)
> *Accept/Initiate intersection* (Place a data point anywhere in the view to initiate the intersection.)

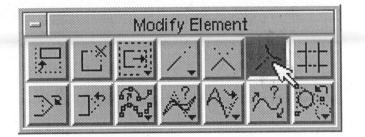

FIGURE 5–48   Clicking the Extend To Intersection icon from the Modify Element sub-palette.

Dynamic update shows the intersection as soon as you select the second element, but the intersection is not actually created until you accept it by clicking the Data button a third time.

> **NOTE:** If the element to be extended overlaps the intersection, select it on the part you want to keep. The part of the element beyond the intersection is deleted. If dynamic update shows the wrong part of the element deleted, click the Reset button to back up and try again.

ELEMENT MODIFICATION—MODIFYING VERTICES

Several commands allow you to modify the geometric shape of elements by moving, deleting, or inserting vertices. For example, you can change the size of a block by grabbing and moving one of the vertices of the block, or you can turn the block into a triangle by deleting one of the vertices.

Modify Element

The Modify Element command moves one vertex of a linear element, changes the radius of a circle or one axis of an ellipse, moves dimension text, or modifies the extension line length and position of a dimension element. Figure 5–49 shows examples of modifying elements.

To modify an element, click the Modify Element icon in the Modify Element sub-palette (see Figure 5–50), or key-in at the uSTN> field, **modify element** (or **mod**) and press [ENTER]. Micro-Station prompts:

> *Identify element* (Identify the element near the vertex you want to modify.)
> *Accept/Reject (Select next input)* (Move the screen pointer as necessary to modify the element and place a data point to complete the modification.)

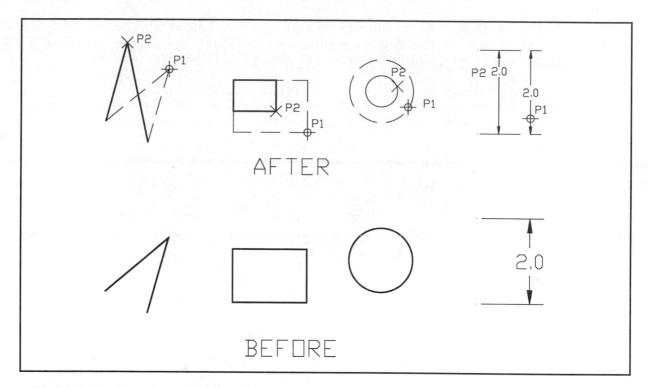

FIGURE 5-49 Examples of Modifying elements.

FIGURE 5-50 Clicking the Modify Element icon from the Modify Element sub-palette.

As you move the screen pointer, a dynamic image of the element moves with it. The element remains selected until you click the Reset button or select another command.

Delete Vertex

The Delete Vertex command removes a vertex from a shape, line string, or curve string. Figure 5–51 shows an example of deleting a vertex from a line string.

To delete a vertex from an element, click the Delete Vertex icon in the Modify Element sub-palette (see Figure 5–52), or key-in at the uSTN> field, **delete vertex** (or **del ver**) and press [ENTER]. MicroStation prompts:

Identify element (Identify the element near the vertex you want to delete.)
Accept/Reject (Select next input) (Click the Data button to accept the deleted vertex, or click the Reject button to disregard the modification.)

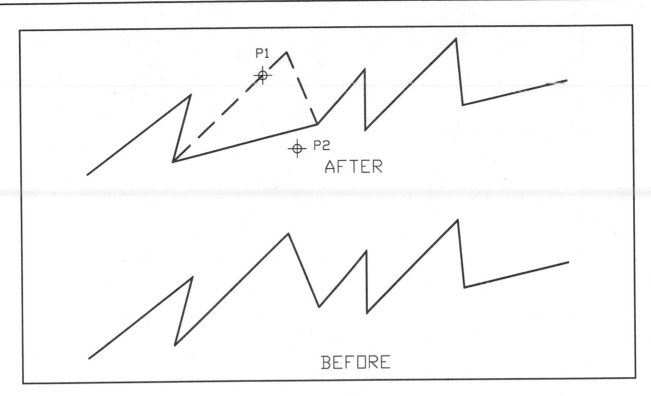

FIGURE 5–51   Examples of deleting a vertex into various elements.

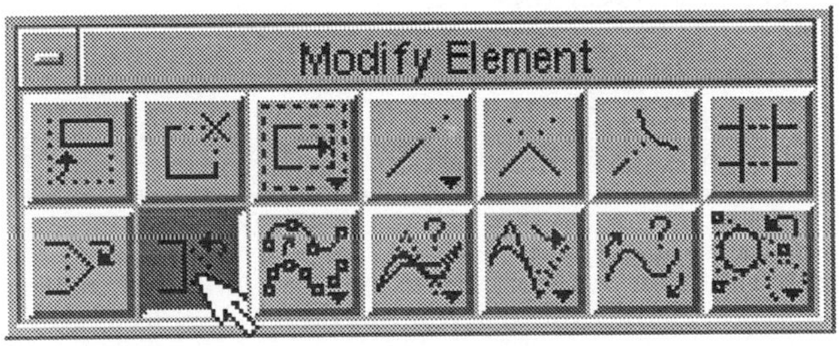

FIGURE 5–52   Clicking the Delete Vertex icon from the Modify Element sub-palette.

When you select the vertex to delete, dynamic update shows the element without the vertex, but it is not actually removed until the second data point. The second data point can also select another vertex to delete.

> **NOTE:** If the element has only the minimum number of vertices required to define that type of element, you cannot delete a vertex from it. The command indicates it is deleting the vertex, but nothing is deleted. For example, a minimum of three vertices is required to define a shape.

Insert Vertex

The Insert Vertex command inserts a new vertex into a shape, line string, or curve string. Figure 5–53 shows an example of inserting a vertex for a line string.

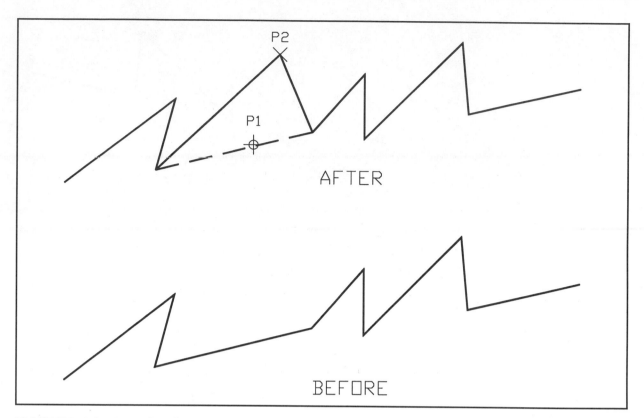

FIGURE 5-53 Examples of inserting a vertex.

To insert a vertex into an element, click the Insert Vertex icon in the Modify Element sub-palette (see Figure 5-54), or key-in at the uSTN> field, **insert vertex** (or **ins**) and press [ENTER]. Micro-Station prompts:

> *Identify element* (Identify the element at the point where you want the vertex inserted.)
> *Accept/Reject (Select next input)* (Drag the new vertex to where you want it in the design plane and click the Data button to insert it, or click the Reset button to reject your selection.)

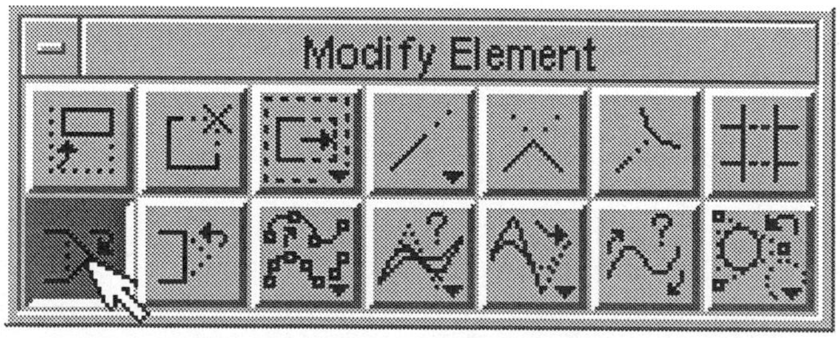

FIGURE 5-54 Clicking the Insert Vertex icon from the Modify Element sub-palette.

When you select the element at the point where you want the new vertex inserted, a dynamic image of the new vertex follows the screen pointer until you place the second data point where you want the vertex located. The second data point causes the new vertex to be inserted and dynamic update continues dragging the new vertices. Click the Reset button or select another MicroStation command once you are through with the modification.

ELEMENT MODIFICATION—MODIFYING ARCS

After you place an arc, you can modify its radius, sweep angle, and axis. The commands are available in Arcs sub-palette, or you can key-in the commands at the uSTN> field.

Modify Arc Radius

The Modify Arc Radius command changes the length of the radius of the selected arc. Figure 5–55 shows examples of modifying an arc radius.

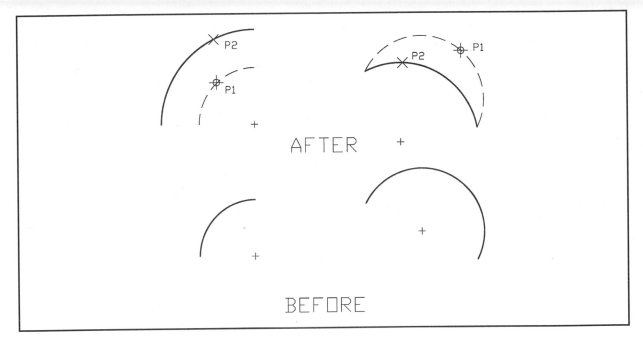

FIGURE 5–55   Examples of modifying an arc radius.

To modify an arc radius, click the Modify Arc Radius icon in the Arcs sub-palette (see Figure 5–56), or key-in at the uSTN> field, **modify arc radius** (or **mod ar r**) and press [ENTER]. Micro-Station prompts:

> *Identify element* (Identify the arc to modify.)
> *Accept/Reject (Select next input)* (Drag the arc to where you want it in the design plane and click the Data button to place it, or click the Reset button to reject your modification.)

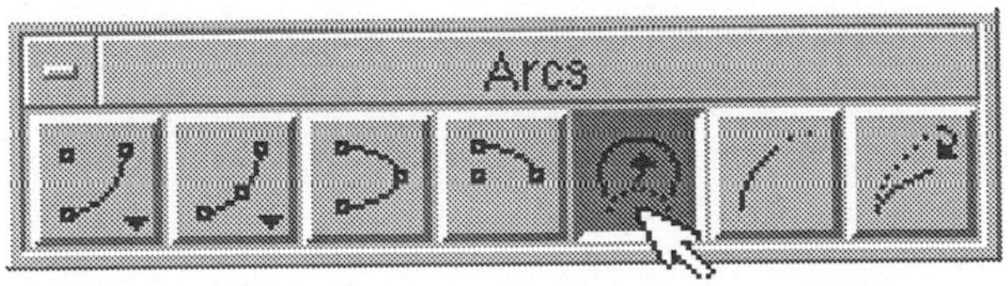

FIGURE 5–56   Clicking the Modify Arc Radius icon from the Arcs sub-palette.

Dynamic update shows the arc following the screen pointer after you select the arc. The arc is actually modified after you place the second data point, after which dynamic update continues to drag the arc. Click the Reset button or select another MicroStation command once you are through modification.

Modify Arc Angle

The Modify Arc Angle command increases or decreases the sweep angle of the selected arc. Figure 5–57 shows examples of modifying an arc angle.

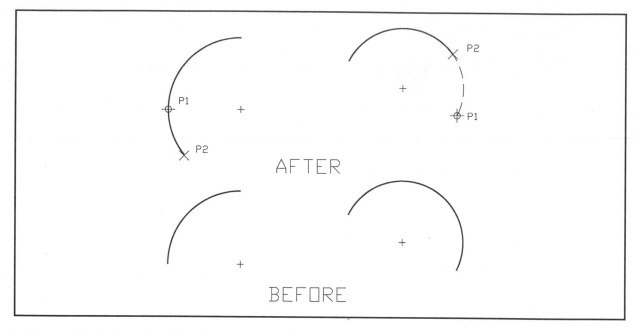

FIGURE 5–57 Examples of modifying an arc angle.

To modify an arc angle, click the Modify Arc Angle icon in the Arcs sub-palette (see Figure 5–58), or key-in at the uSTN> field, **modify arc angle** (or **mod ar an**) and press ⏎. MicroStation prompts:

> *Identify element* (Identify the arc near the end whose sweep angle you want to change.)
> *Accept/Reject (Select next input)* (Drag the end of the arc to where you want it in the design plane and click the Data button to place it, or click the Reset button to reject your modification.)

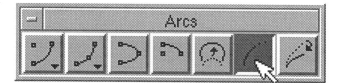

FIGURE 5–58 Clicking the Modify Arc Angle icon from the Arcs sub-palette.

Dynamic update shows the arc following the screen pointer after you select the arc. The arc sweep angle is actually modified after you place the second data point, after which dynamic update continues to drag the arc. Click the Reset button or select another MicroStation command once you are through with the modification.

> **NOTE:** If you drag the sweep angle around until the arc appears to be a circle, it is still an arc. Arcs that look like circles can be confusing later when using commands like patterning. If the arc should have been a circle, place a circle and delete the arc.

Modify Arc Axis

The Modify Arc Axis command modifies the axis of the selected arc. Figure 5–59 shows an example of modifying an arc axis.

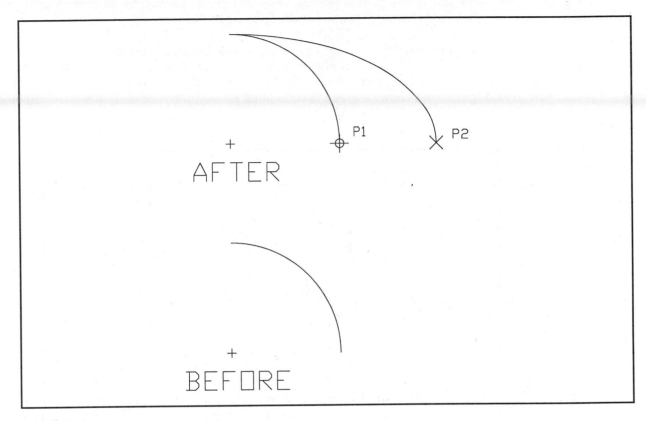

FIGURE 5–59   Examples of modifying an arc axis.

To modify an arc axis, click the Modify Arc Axis icon from the Arcs sub-palette (see Figure 5–60), or key-in at the uSTN> field, **modify arc axis** (or **mod ar ax**) and press [ENTER]. MicroStation prompts:

> *Identify element* (Identify the arc.)
> *Accept/Reject (Select next input)* (Drag the arc to where you want it in the design plane and click the Data button to place it, or click the Reset button to reject your modification.)

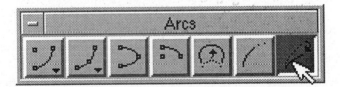

FIGURE 5–60   Clicking the Modify Arc Axis icon from the Arcs sub-palette.

Dynamic update shows the arc following the screen pointer after you select the arc. The arc is actually modified after you place the second data point, after which dynamic update continues to drag the arc. Click the Reset button or select another MicroStation command once you are through with the modification.

CREATING COMPLEX SHAPES AND CHAINS

The Create Complex Shape and Chain commands turn groups of elements into one complex element. A complex shape is a closed element (you could say it holds water), and a complex chain is an open element (the water can flow out between the two ends of the chain). The element manipulation commands treat the elements in a complex groupings as one element.

When you create a complex chain or shape from separate elements, the elements take on the current active element attributes (all the available settings in the Element Attributes settings box), and any gaps between the elements are closed. You can key-in Maximum allowable gap in the Max Gap edit field. Figure 5–61 shows a group of individual elements before and after being turned into a complex shape.

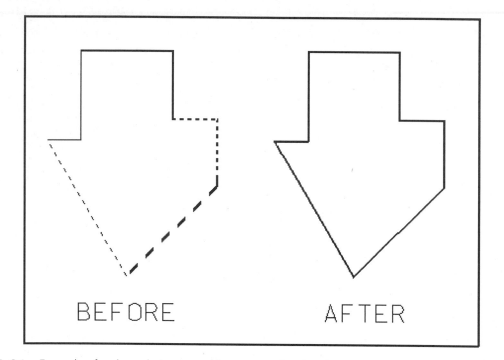

FIGURE 5–61   Example of a shape being turned into a complex shape.

You can create a complex shape or chain manually by selecting each element to be included, or automatically by letting MicroStation find each element. If you want the elements that make up the complex shape or chain to be individual elements again, you can drop them by using the Drop Complex command (the dropped elements keep the parameters of the complex shape).

A quick way to check to see if you really created a complex group from the elements is to apply one of the element manipulation commands to it. If the elements are complex, dynamic update shows an image of all elements following the screen pointer, and the element type in the Command Window status field tells you it is either a Complex Chain or Complex Shape.

> **NOTE:** It is easy to make a mistake in creating complex chains and shapes, and only experience will make you competent. If you goof while creating a complex chain or shape, undo it and try again. Do not give up—you will get the hang of it!

Manually Create a Complex Chain

When you manually create a complex chain you must select and accept, in order, each of the elements to be included in the chain. Any gaps between the elements are closed and the complex chain takes on the current active element attributes.

To manually create a complex chain, click the Create Chain icon in the Chain sub-palette, then select Manual from the Method options menu in the same sub-palette (see Figure 5–62). If necessary key-in Maximum Gap in the Max Gap edit field, or key-in at the uSTN> field, **create chain manual** (or **cre ch**) and press ⏎. MicroStation prompts:

Identify element (Click the Data button on the first element to be in the chain.)

Accept/Reject (Identify next element) (Point to the next element to be in the chain and click the Data button again. Continue selecting elements in order until all elements are selected. When all elements have been selected, click the Data button one more time anywhere in the view to accept the last element.)

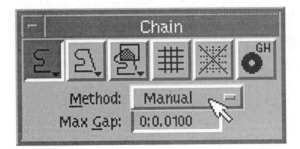

FIGURE 5–62   Clicking the Create Chain icon in the Chain sub-palette when Manual option is selected in the Method options menu.

After you click the last data point, the message *Element not found* appears in the error field of the Command Window, and the chain is completed. Figure 5–63 provides an example of manually creating a complex chain.

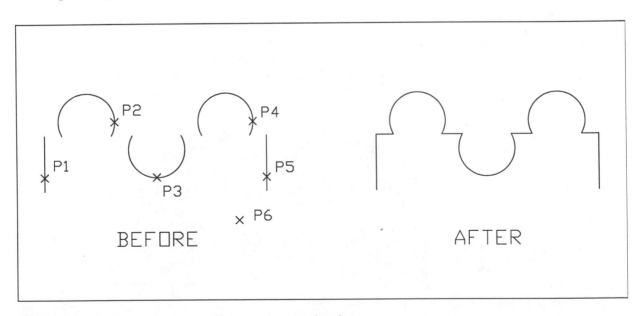

FIGURE 5–63   Example of manually creating a complex chain.

> **NOTE:** Sometimes when you update the view, the lines closing the gaps between elements in the complex chain may disappear. They are still there—update the view again, and they should reappear.

Automatically Create a Complex Chain

To automatically create a complex chain, start the process by selecting and accepting the first element in the chain. After that MicroStation finds and highlights more elements in series, and you must accept or reject each one.

The automatic version of the command also allows you to specify a search tolerance that tells MicroStation how far away, in working units, from the end of the previous element it can search for another element. If the tolerance is set to zero, the next element must touch the last selected one before MicroStation finds it.

If there are two or more possible elements at a junction, MicroStation tells you that there is a fork in the path and selects one of the possible elements. You can either accept or reject the element and have MicroStation highlight another possible element in the fork.

> **NOTE:** If the complex chain contains many elements, and there are not very many forks, the automatic method is probably faster than the manual method. If there are many fork points, manually creating the chain may go faster.

To automatically create a complex chain, click the Create Chain icon in the Chain sub-palette, select Automatic from the Method options menu, and, if necessary, enter the maximum allowed space between elements in the Max Gap edit field (see Figure 5–64). As an alternate, you can key-in at the uSTN> field, **create chain automatic** (or **cre ch a**) and press [ENTER]. Then, if necessary, key-in at the uSTN> field, the maximum allowed space (tolerance) between elements. MicroStation prompts:

Identify element (Identify the first element to be in the chain.)
Accept/Reject (Identify next element) (Move the screen pointer in the direction you want the search to go and click the Data button to accept the first element, or click the reset button to reject it and start over.)

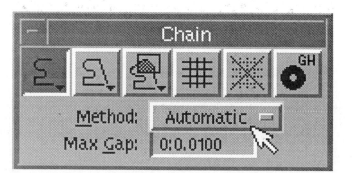

FIGURE 5–64   Clicking the Create Chain icon in the Chain sub-palette when Automatic option is selected from the Method options menu.

If there are no forks in the path from the previous element, MicroStation prompts:

Accept chain element (Click the Data button to accept the element and continue the search, or press the Reset button to complete the chain with the previous element.)

If there is a fork in the path from the previous element, MicroStation prompts:

Fork—Accept/Reject path (To accept the fork element MicroStation picked, click the Data button. Click the Reset button to cause MicroStation to drop the current element and select another fork element.)

The process continues until MicroStation cannot find another element to add, or until you reject a selection when there is no fork in the path. You cannot end a search at a fork point. Figure 5–65 shows an example of creating a complex chain automatically.

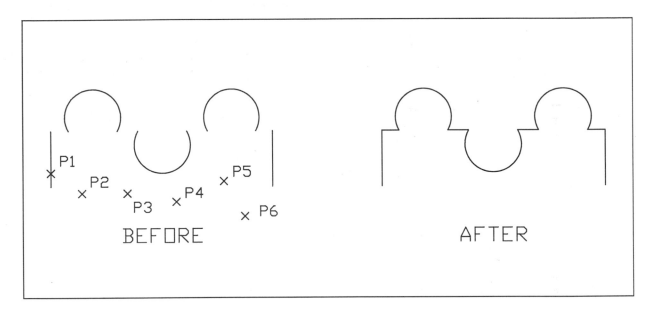

FIGURE 5–65   Example of automatically creating a complex chain.

If you end the chain by clicking the Data button anywhere in the view, the message Element not found appears in the error field of the Command Window and the chain is completed.

Manually Create a Complex Shape

To manually create a complex shape you must select and accept, in order, each of the elements to be included in the shape. Any gaps between the elements are closed, and the complex chain takes on the current active element attributes.

To manually create a complex shape, click the Create Shape icon in the Chain sub-palette, then select Manual from the Method options menu in the sub-palette (see Figure 5–66). If necessary key-in Maximum Gap in the Max Gap edit field, or key-in at the uSTN> field, **create shape manual** (or **cre s**) and press ENTER. MicroStation prompts:

Identify element (Click the Data button on the first element to be in the shape.)

Accept/Reject (Identify next element) (Point to the next element to be in the shape, and click the Data button again. Continue selecting elements in order until all elements are selected. When all elements have been selected, accept the last element by clicking the Data button anywhere in the view, then click the Reset button to close the shape.)

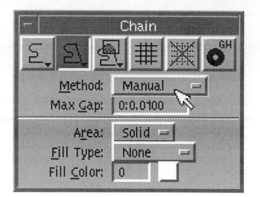

FIGURE 5–66   Clicking the Create Shape icon in the Chain sub-palette when Manual option is selected from the Method options menu.

After you click the data button anywhere in the view, the message *Element not found* appears in the error field of the Command Window. When you click the reset button, the shape is closed. Figure 5–67 provides an example of manually creating a complex chain.

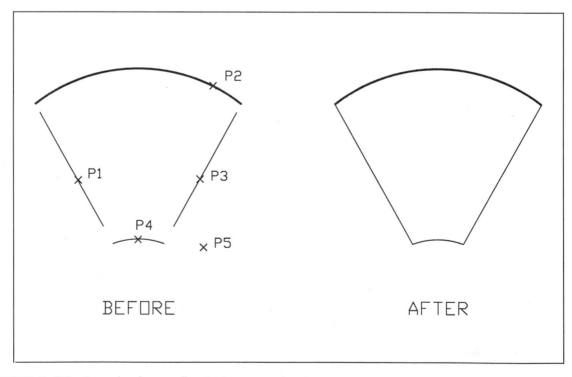

FIGURE 5–67   Example of manually creating a complex shape.

If the end of the last element is touching the start of the first element, you can click the Data button back on top of the first element to close the shape without clicking the Reset button.

Automatically Create a Complex Shape

To automatically create a complex shape, start the process by selecting and accepting the first element in the shape. After that MicroStation finds and highlights more elements in series, and you must accept or reject each one.

If there are two or more possible elements at a junction, MicroStation tells you there is a fork in the path and picks one of the possible elements. You can either accept or reject the element and have MicroStation highlight another possible element.

The automatic version of the command also allows you to specify a search tolerance that tells MicroStation how far away, in working units, from the end of the previous element it can search for another element. If the tolerance is set to zero, the next element must touch the last selected one before MicroStation finds it.

> **NOTE:** If the complex shape contains many elements, and there are not very many forks, the automatic is probably faster than the manual method. If there are many fork points, manually creating the shape may go faster.

To automatically create a complex shape, click the Create Shape icon in the Chain sub-palette, select Automatic from the Method options menu, and, if necessary, enter the maximum allowed space between elements in the Max Gap edit field (see Figure 5–68). Alternately, you can key-in at the uSTN> field, **create shape automatic** (or **cre s a**) and press ⏎. Then, if necessary, key-in at the uSTN> field the maximum allowed space between elements. MicroStation prompts:

Identify element (Identify the first element to be in the shape.)
Accept/Reject (Identify next element) (Move the screen pointer in the direction you want the
search to go, and click the Data button to accept the first element, or click the reset button to
reject it and start over.)

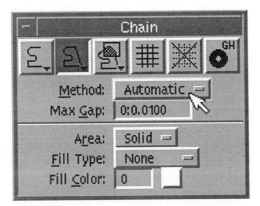

FIGURE 5–68 Clicking the Create Shape icon in the Chain sub-palette when Automatic option is selected from the Method options menu.

If there are no forks in the path from the previous element, MicroStation prompts:

Accept shape element (Click the Data button to accept the element and continue the search, or
press the Reset button to complete the shape with the previous element.)

If there is a fork in the path from the previous element, MicroStation prompts:

> *Fork—Accept/Reject path* (To accept the fork element MicroStation selected, click the Data button. Click the Reset button to cause MicroStation to drop the current element and select another fork element.)

The process continues until MicroStation cannot find another element to add, or until you reject a selection when there is no fork in the path. You cannot end a search at a fork point. If you press the Reset button when another element is highlighted, that element is not used in the shape. Figure 5–69 shows an example of automatically creating a complex shape.

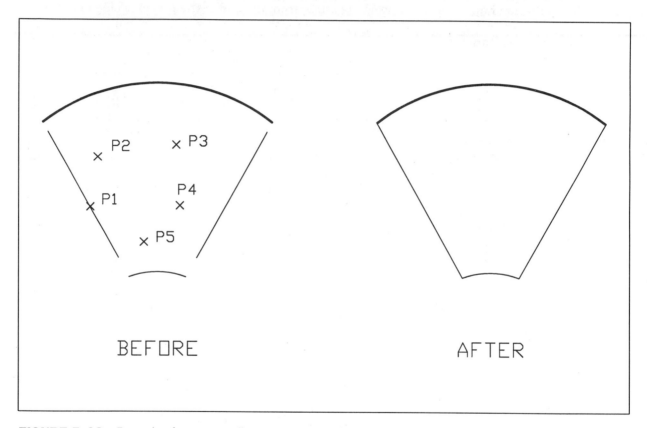

FIGURE 5–69   Example of automatically creating a complex shape.

If you end the chain by clicking the Data button anywhere in the view, the message *Element not found* appears in the error field of the Command Window and the chain is completed.

Create Region

The Create Region is used to create a complex shape similar to Complex Shape commands. You can create a complex shape from either of the following:

- The union, intersection, or difference between two or more closed elements.
- A region bounded by elements that have endpoints that are closed together by the Maximum Gap.

To create a complex shape, click the Create Region icon in the Chain sub-palette, then select one of the options available from the Method option menu.

The Intersection option allows you to create a region from a composite area formed from the area that is common to two closed elements.

The Union option allows you to create a region from a composite area formed in such a way that there is no duplication between two closed elements. The total resulting area can be equal to or less than the sum of the areas in the original closed elements.

The Difference option allows you to create a region from a closed element after removing from it any area that it has in common with a second element.

The Flood option allows you to create a region made up of one or more elements. MicroStation prompts you to pick a point inside the closed area. When you place the first data point inside the area, MicroStation searches for the elements that enclose the area and highlights pieces of the elements as it finds them.

If you wish to keep the original elements, set the Keep Original toggle button to ON. Micro-Station prompts:

Identify element (Click the Data button on the element.)
Accept/Reject (Select next input) (Click the Data button to accept the element.)
Identify additional/Reset to complete (Identify additional elements or click the Reset button to terminate the sequence.)

DROPPING COMPLEX CHAINS AND SHAPES

If you want to return the elements in a complex chain or shape to individual elements, you can drop their complex status. The Drop Complex Status command drops an individual complex group. The Fence Drop Complex Status drops all complex groups within the boundary of a fence.

Dropped complex elements return to being individual elements, but they keep the element parameters (color, weight, etc.).

Drop a Complex Chain or Shape

To drop an individual complex chain or shape, click Drop Complex Status from the Drop sub-palette (see Figure 5–70), or key-in at the uSTN> field, **drop complex** (or **dr**) and press [ENTER]. MicroStation prompts:

Identify element (Identify the complex element you want to drop.)
Accept/Reject (Select next input) (Click the Accept button to drop the complex element back to individual elements. At the same time, you can also select another complex element to drop.)

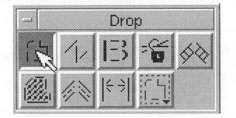

FIGURE 5–70   Clicking the Drop Complex Status from the Drop sub-palette.

Drop Several Complex Chains or Shapes

The Drop Complex Status Of Fence Contents command breaks all the complex elements enclosed in a fence into separate elements. Before you invoke the command, place a fence that encloses all the complex elements you want to drop and select the fence lock you want to use. Click the Drop Complex Status Of Fence Contents icon from the Drop sub-palette (see Figure 5–71), or key-in at the uSTN> field, **fence drop complex** (or **fen dr**) and press [ENTER]. MicroStation prompts:

> *Accept/Reject fence contents* (Click the Data button anywhere in the view to drop the complex elements.)

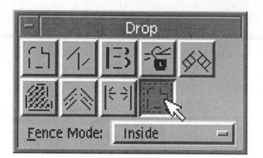

FIGURE 5–71   Clicking the Drop Complex Status of Fence Contents icon from the Drop sub-palette.

All complex elements enclosed in the fence are broken into separate elements.

MODIFYING MULTI-LINES

Chapter 3 introduced you to placing multi-line elements. The multi-line joint commands help you modify the intersections of two multi-lines or cut holes in the lines of one multi-line. The commands are available in the Multi-line Joints palette that is opened from the Palettes pull-down menu (see Figure 5–72).

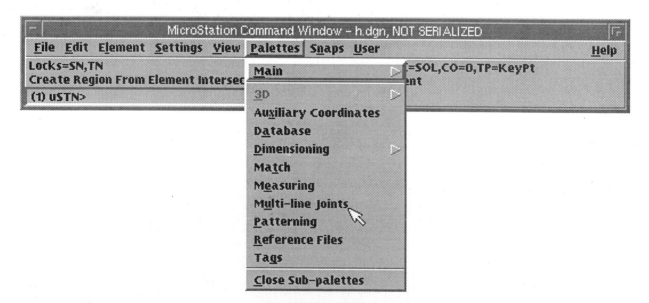

FIGURE 5–72   Invoking Multi-line Joints Palette from the Palettes pull-down menu.

Closed Cross Joint

The Closed Cross Joint command cuts all lines that make up the second multi-line you select at the point where it crosses the first multi-line, as shown in Figure 5–73. To invoke the command, click the Closed Cross Joint icon in the Multi-line Joints sub-palette (see Figure 5–74), Micro-Station prompts:

Identify element (Identify one of the intersecting multi-lines.)
Identify element (Identify the second intersecting multi-line.)
Identify element (Click the Data button anywhere in the view to initiate cleaning up the intersection.)

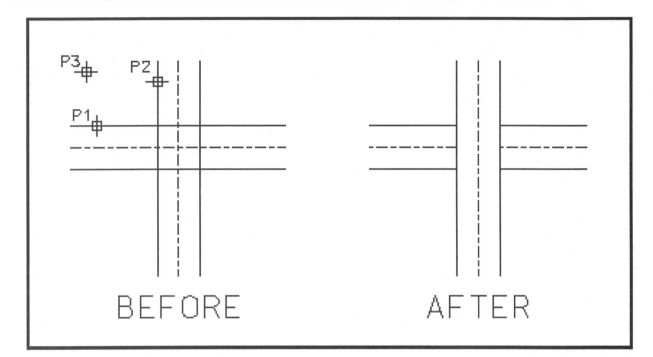

FIGURE 5–73 Example of using a Closed Cross Joint command.

> **NOTE:** For each Multi-Line Joint command, dynamic update shows the intersection cleaned up after the second data point, but it does not become permanent until you provide the third data point.

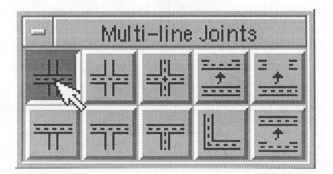

FIGURE 5–74 Clicking the Closed Cross Joint icon from the Multi-line Joints palette.

Open Cross Joint

The Open Cross Joint command cuts all lines that make up the first multi-line you select and cuts only the outside line of the second multi-line, as shown in Figure 5–75. To invoke the command, click the Open Cross Joint icon in the Multi-line Joints sub-palette (see Figure 5–76).

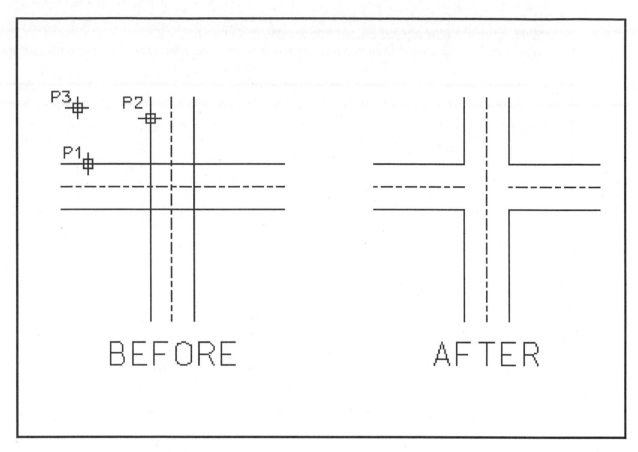

FIGURE 5–75   Example of using an Open Cross Joint command.

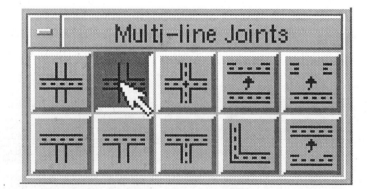

FIGURE 5–76   Clicking the Open Cross Joint icon from the Multi-line Joints palette.

The prompts are identical to the Closed Cross Joint command.

Merged Cross Joint

The Merged Cross Joint command cuts all lines that make up each of the intersecting multi-line you select, except the center lines, as shown in Figure 5–77. If there are no center lines, all lines in each multi-line are cut. To invoke the command, click the Merged Cross Joint icon in the Multi-line Joints sub-palette (see Figure 5–78).

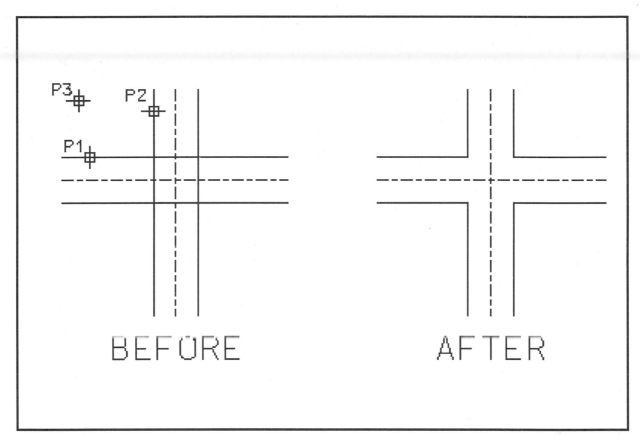

FIGURE 5–77   Example of using a Merged Cross Joint command.

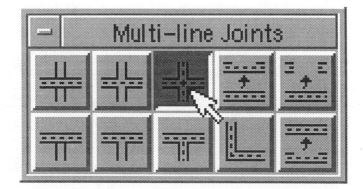

FIGURE 5–78   Clicking the Merged Cross Joint icon from the Multi-line Joints palette.

The prompts are identical to the Closed Cross Joint command.

Closed Tee Joint

The Closed Tee Joint command extends or shortens the first multi-line you identify to its intersection with the second multi-line. The first multi-line ends at the near side of the intersecting multi-line, which is left intact, as shown in Figure 5–79. To invoke the command, click the Closed Tee Joint icon in the Multi-line Joints sub-palette (see Figure 5–80).

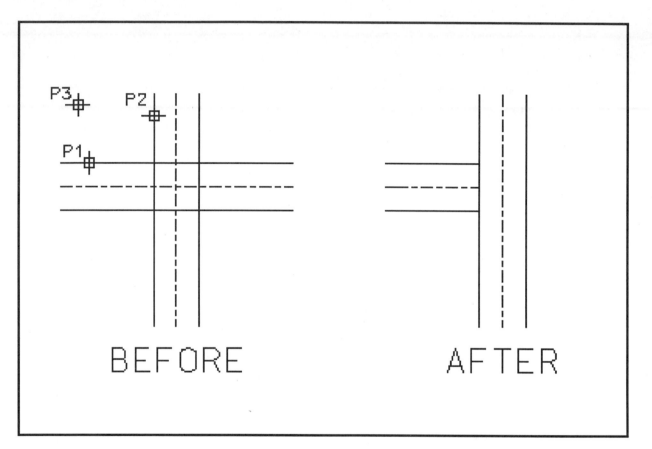

FIGURE 5–79 Example of using a Closed Tee Joint command.

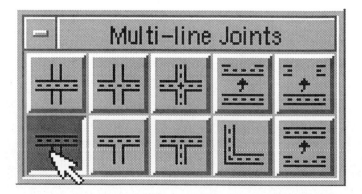

FIGURE 5–80 Clicking the Closed Tee Joint icon from the Multi-line Joints palette.

The prompts are identical to the Closed Cross Joint command.

Open Tee Joint

The Open Tee Joint command is similar to the closed Tee Joint command, except it leaves an open end at intersecting mutli line, as shown in Figure 5 81. To invoke the command, click the Open Tee Joint icon in the Multi-line Joints sub-palette (see Figure 5–82).

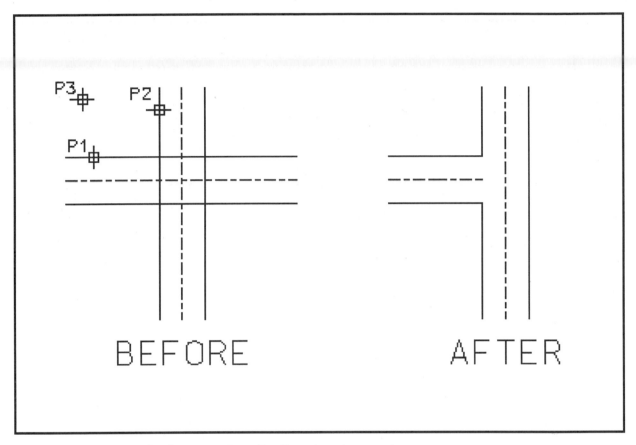

FIGURE 5–81   Example of using an Open Tee Cross Joint command.

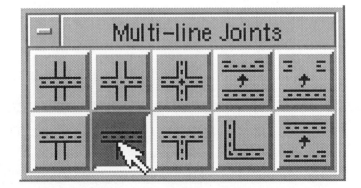

FIGURE 5–82   Clicking the Open Tee Joint icon from the Multi-line Joints palette.

The prompts are identical to the Closed Cross Joint command.

Merged Tee Joint

The Merged Tee Joint command is similar to Open Tee Joint, except the center line of the first multi-line is extended to the center line of the intersecting multi-line, as shown in Figure 5–83. To invoke the command, click the Merged Tee Joint icon in the Multi-line Joints sub-palette (see Figure 5–84).

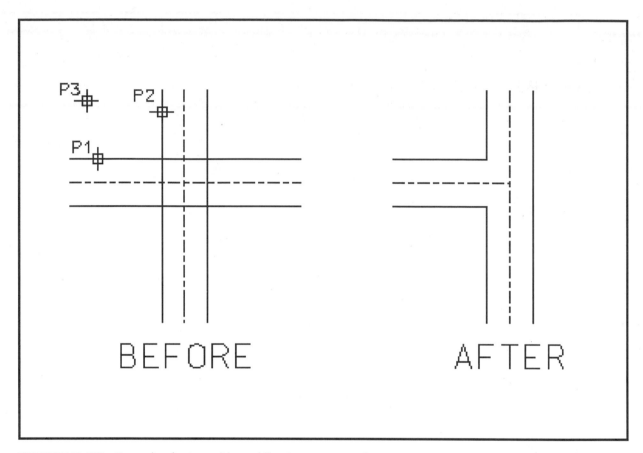

FIGURE 5–83   Example of using a Merged Tee Joint command.

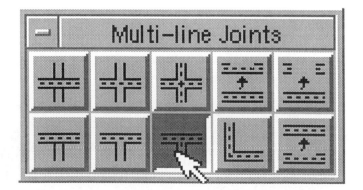

FIGURE 5–84   Clicking the Merged Tee Joint icon from the Multi-line Joints palette.

The prompts are identical to the Closed Cross Joint command.

Cornered Joint

The Cornered Joint command lengthens or shortens each of the two multi-lines you select as necessary to create a clean intersection, as shown in Figure 5–85. To invoke the command, click the Cornered Joint icon in the Multi-line Joints sub-palette (see Figure 5–86).

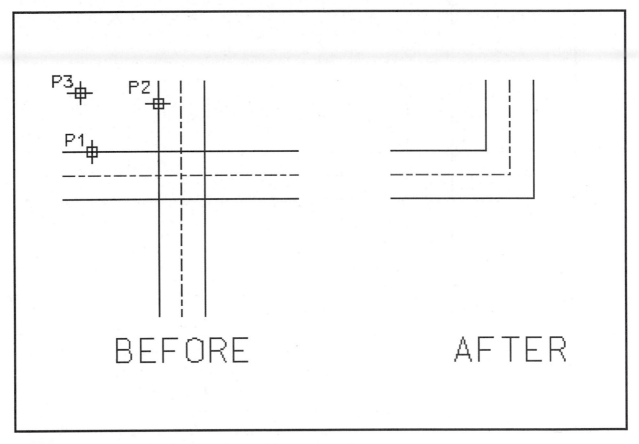

FIGURE 5–85   Example of using a Cornered Joint command.

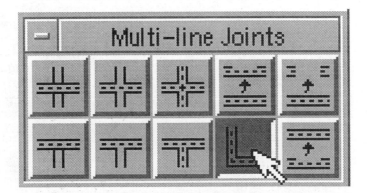

FIGURE 5–86   Clicking the Cornered Joint icon from the Multi-line Joints palette.

The prompts are identical to the Closed Cross Joint command.

Cut Single Component Line

The Cut Single Component Line command cuts a hole in the line you select in a multi-line from the first data point to the second data point, as shown in Figure 5–87. To invoke the command, click the Cut Single Component Line icon in the Multi-line Joints sub-palette (see Figure 5–88).

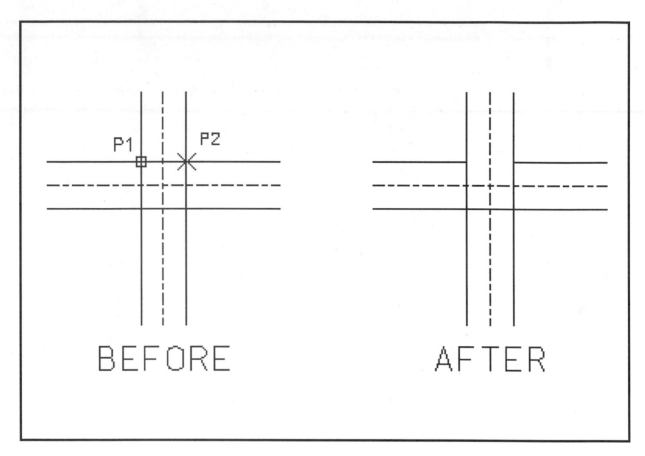

FIGURE 5–87   Example of using a Cut Single Component Line command.

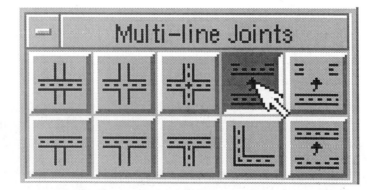

FIGURE 5–88   Clicking the Cut Single Component Line icon from the Multi-line Joints palette.

The prompts are identical to the Closed Cross Joint command.

Cut All Component Lines

The Cut All Component Lines command cuts a hole in the multi-line you select from the first data point to the second data point, as shown in Figure 5–89. To invoke the command, click the Cut All Component Lines icon in the Multi-line Joints sub-palette (see Figure 5–90).

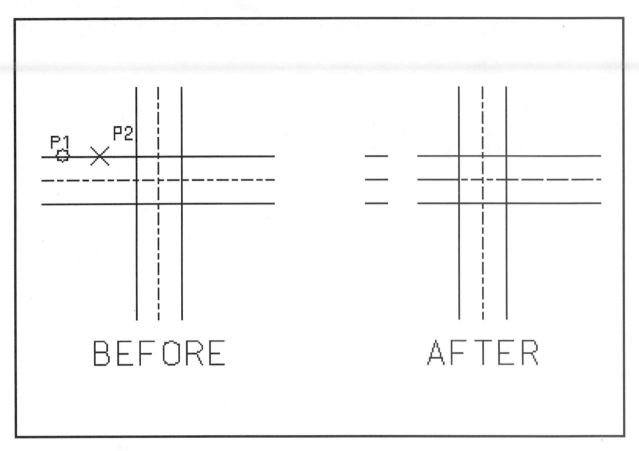

FIGURE 5–89   Example of using a Cut All Component Lines command.

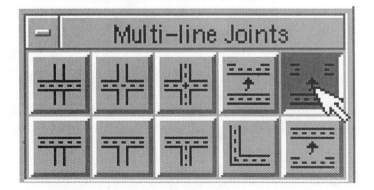

FIGURE 5–90   Clicking the Cut All Component Lines icon from the Multi-line Joints palette.

The prompts are similar to the Closed Cross Joint command.

Uncut Component Lines

The Uncut Component Lines command provides a special undo command for multi-lines. With it you can undo a cut in one line of a multi-line. Identify one end of the cut with a data point, then accept it with a second data point, as shown in Figure 5–91. To invoke the command, click the Uncut Component Lines icon in the Multi-line Joints sub-palette (see Figure 5–92).

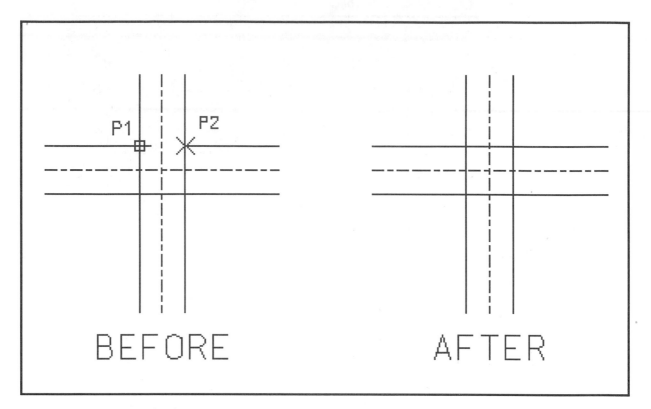

FIGURE 5–91   Example of using a Uncut Component Lines command.

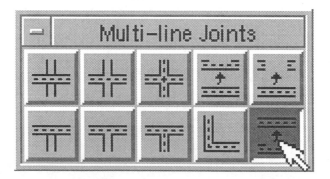

FIGURE 5–92   Clicking the Uncut Component Lines icon from the Multi-line Joints palette.

> **NOTE:** Place the first data point right at one end of the cut you want to close. If you get a message in the Command Window saying the element was not found, try another data point. It often fails to find the cut on the first attempt.

EXERCISES

Exercises 5–1 through 5–7

Use precision key-ins and appropriate grid spacing to draw the objects. Use the Array (Rectangular and Polar), fence manipulation and extend line commands to your best advantage.

Exercise 5–1

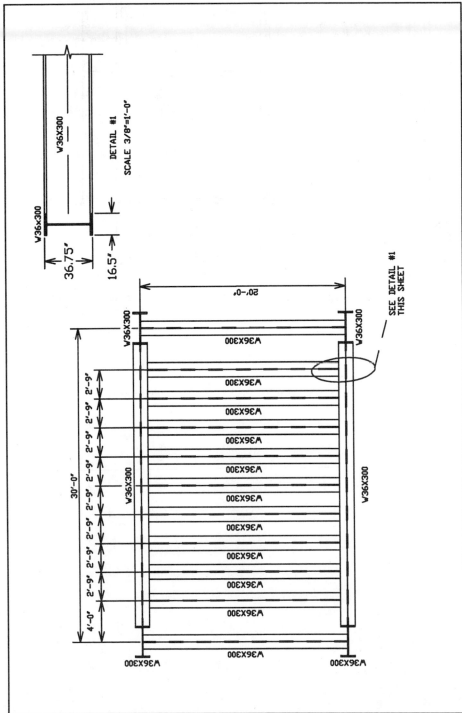

Exercise 5–2

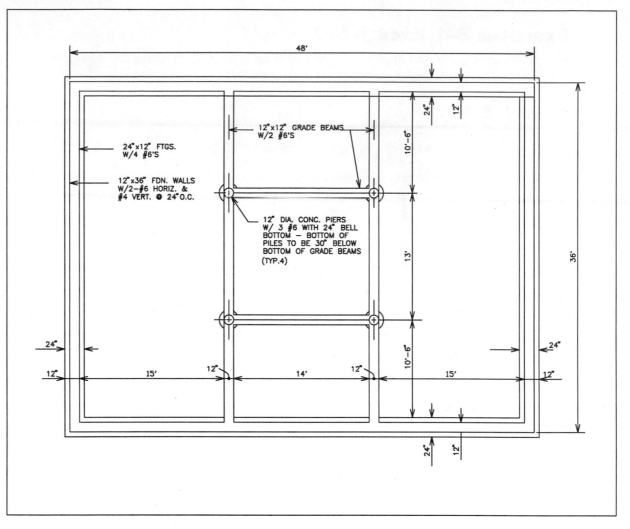

Exercise 5–3

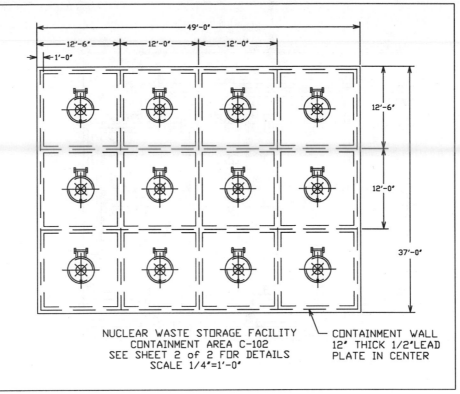

NUCLEAR WASTE STORAGE FACILITY
CONTAINMENT AREA C-102
SEE SHEET 2 of 2 FOR DETAILS
SCALE 1/4"=1'-0"

CONTAINMENT WALL
12" THICK 1/2"LEAD
PLATE IN CENTER

Exercise 5–4

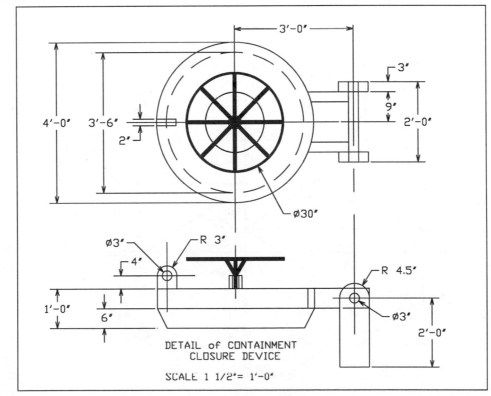

DETAIL of CONTAINMENT
CLOSURE DEVICE

SCALE 1 1/2"= 1'-0"

Exercise 5–5

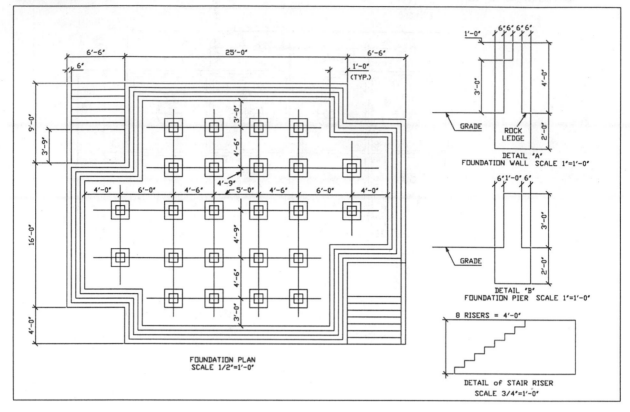

FOUNDATION PLAN
SCALE 1/2"=1'-0"

DETAIL 'A'
FOUNDATION WALL SCALE 1"=1'-0"

DETAIL 'B'
FOUNDATION PIER SCALE 1"=1'-0"

8 RISERS = 4'-0"

DETAIL of STAIR RISER
SCALE 3/4"=1'-0"

Exercise 5–6

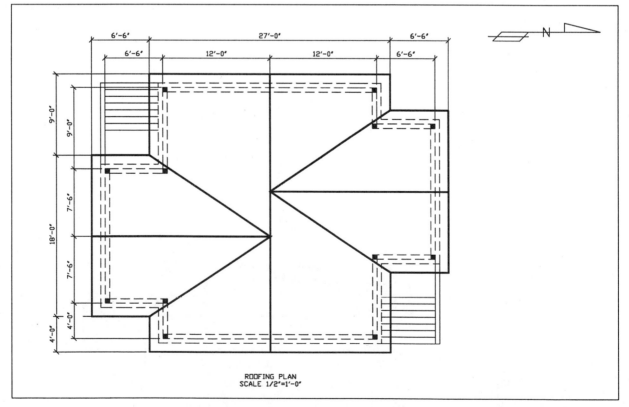

ROOFING PLAN
SCALE 1/2"=1'-0"

Exercise 5-7

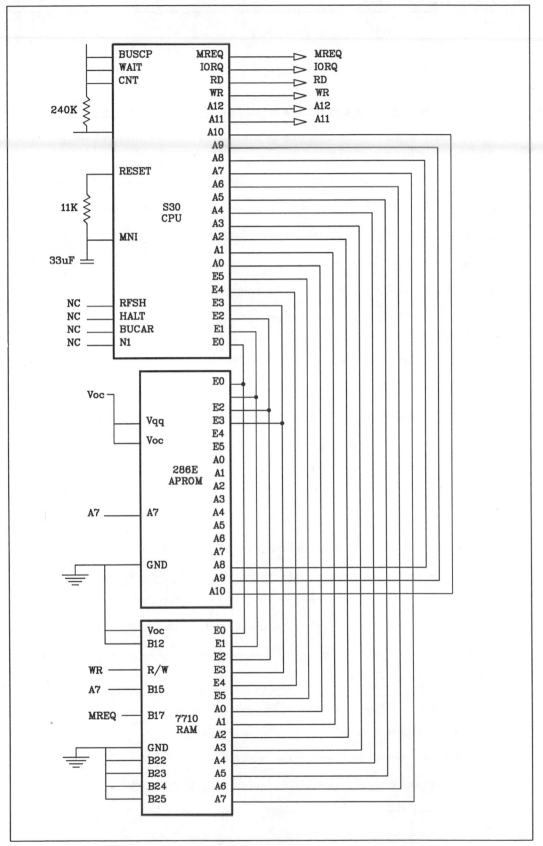

REVIEW QUESTIONS

Write your answers in the spaces provided:

1. To place natural fractions in the one-character position, turn ON the _____ toggle button.

2. The place Fitted command fits the text between two _____ .

3. When you place a text above a line by Place Text Above command, the distance between the line and the text is controlled by _____ .

4. Explain briefly when will you use Inter-character Spacing attribute in placing text.

   _____

5. At what circumstance will you use the Match Text Attributes command?

   _____

6. What would you key-in to set the Tag Increment to 5? _____

7. To determine the text attributes of an existing text in a design file, invoke the _____ command.

8. Explain briefly the purpose of placing nodes in a design file.

   _____

9. Explain briefly the different options available in using the Extend Line command.

   _____

10. List the element types that can be modified by Modify Element command.

    _____

    _____

11. List the commands that are available to modify an arc.

    _____

    _____

12. Explain the difference between creating a chain by manually and automatically.

    _____

    _____

13. To drop several complex groups invoke the _____ .

14. Explain briefly the purpose of defining tags.

    _____

15. List the steps involved in generating a template and report files.

    _____

    _____

PROJECT EXERCISE

In this project you apply MicroStation concepts and skills discussed in chapters 1 through 5 to create the structural steel plan as shown in Figure P5–1.

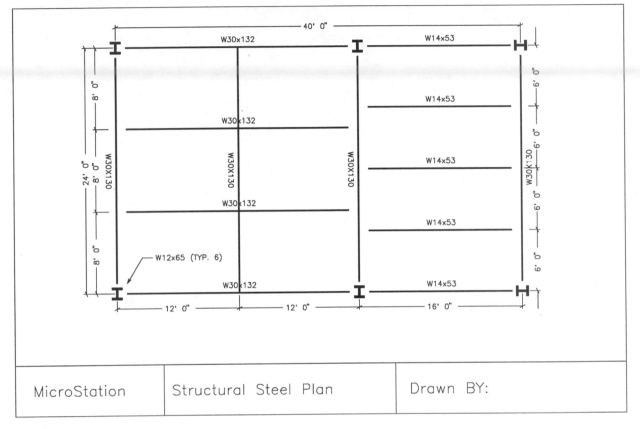

FIGURE P5–1   Completed Project Design.

> **NOTE:** The step-by-step instructions for this project are designed to provide practice in the concepts presented in chapters 1 through 5. It is not necessarily the most efficient way to draw the design.

The new concepts introduced in this project are:

- Using views
- Fence manipulations
- Element selection
- Placing Text—Above and Below a line

GETTING STARTED

STEP 1:   Create a new design file named CH5.DGN using the SEED2D.DGN seed file from the MicroStation Manager dialog box if you just started MicroStation, or from the New option in the File pull-down menu of the MicroStation Command Window.

STEP 2:   Set the design's working units as shown in Figure P5–2.

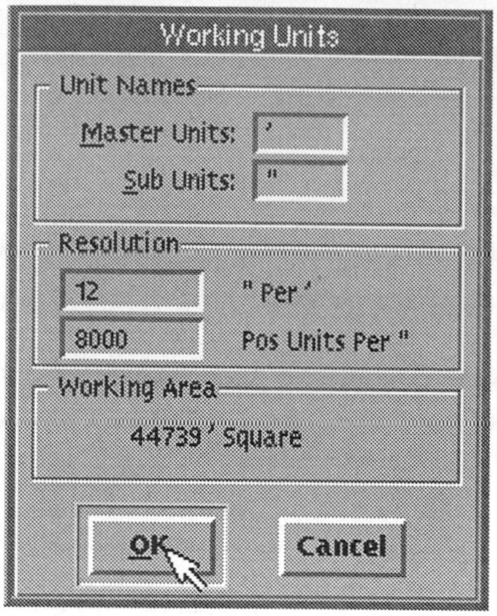

FIGURE P5–2   Working Units dialog box.

STEP 3:   Open the Grid Settings box from the Settings pull-down menu and set the grid unit to 6 in., Grid Reference to 1 ft and set the Grid Lock to ON.

STEP 4:   Set the active level to 1, color to white, line weight to 2 and the line style to 0.

STEP 5:   If it is not already open, open the Tool Settings Box.

STEP 6:   Invoke Save Settings command from the File pull-down menu to save the settings.

STEP 7:   Invoke the place block command to place a 60′ wide by 45′ border with the lower-left corner at coordinates 0,0.

STEP 8:   Invoke the Fit command and place a data point anywhere in the view. You will see the border as shown in Figure P5–3.

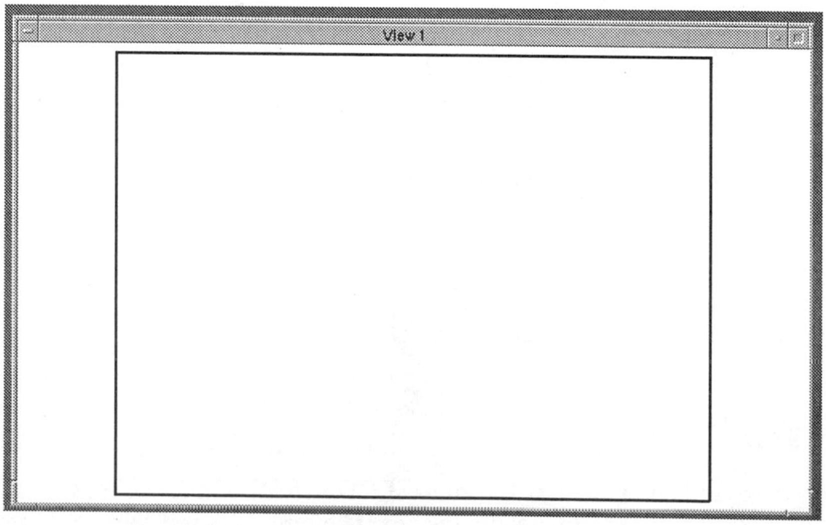

FIGURE P5–3   Border for the Project Design.

Draw the Columns

Draw the cross sections of the six columns (the heavier line weight objects shaped like the capital letter I as shown in Figure P5–1).

STEP 9:   If View 2 is not already open, turn ON the toggle button for View 2 from Open/Close sub-menu of the View pull-down menu.

STEP 10:   Invoke the Window Area command to display an area 2′ × 2′ in View 2. Invoke Window Center command to center the View 2 about XY=10,12.

STEP 11:   Set the active level to 2, color to blue, line weight to 4 and the line style to 0.

STEP 12:   Invoke Save Settings command from the File pull-down menu to save the settings.

STEP 13:   Invoke Place Line command to draw the steel column using the dimensions as shown in Figure P5–4 in View 2 (Make sure the Grid Lock is set to ON). Do not place the dimensions or text shown in the figure.

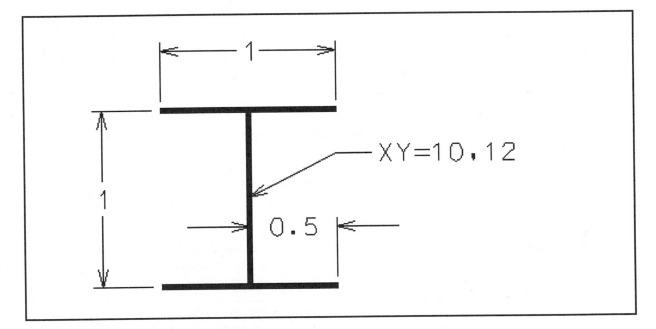

FIGURE P5–4   Placing lines to draw the steel columns.

STEP 14:   Invoke the Place Fence Block command and place a fence around the column you just drew. Place the first fence block data point just below and to the left of the column in View 2. Place the second fence block data point just above and to the right of the block.

STEP 15:   Invoke the Copy command from the Manipulate Element sub-palette. In the tool settings box, set the Use Fence toggle button to ON and select Inside from the Fence Lock options menu. MicroStation prompts:

> *Define Origin* (Place a data point.)
> *Define Distance* (Key-in **DL=24** and press ⏎.)
> *Define Distance* (Key-in **DL=16** and press ⏎.)
> *Define Distance* (Click the Reset button.)

STEP 16:   To display all three columns, invoke the Fit command and place a data point in View 1. If View 2 is on top of View 1, click anywhere on the View 1 border to pop it to the top of the stack. Your View 1 should now be similar to Figure P5–5.

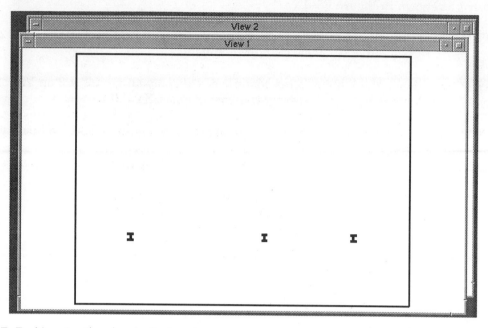

FIGURE P5–5   View 1 with columns displayed.

STEP 17:   Invoke the Place Fence Block command to remove the fence—but do not place another fence.

STEP 18:   Invoke the Element Selection command from the Main palette. While holding down the Data button, drag a selection rectangle over the right-hand column, then release the Data button. All elements in the column should now be selected.

STEP 19:   Invoke the Rotate command from the Manipulate Element sub-palette. In the tool settings box, set the By Active Angle toggle button to ON, key-in **90** in the By Active Angle edit field and press **TAB** key. MicroStation prompts:

> *Accept/Reject (Select next input)* (Click the Data button over the center of the column. Grid lock should force the screen pointer to the exact center.)

STEP 20:   Place a data point anywhere on the view to remove the selection handles.

STEP 21:   Invoke the Update command and place a data point anywhere in View 1.

STEP 22:   Invoke the Place Fence Block command and place a fence around all three of the columns.

STEP 23:   Invoke the Copy command from the Manipulate Element sub-palette. In the tool settings box, set the Use Fence toggle button to ON and select Inside from the Fence Lock options menu. MicroStation prompts:

> *Define Origin* (Place a data point.)
> *Define Distance* (Key-in **DL=0,24** and press **ENTER**.)
> *Define Distance* (Click the Reset button.)

The design should be similar to Figure P5–6.

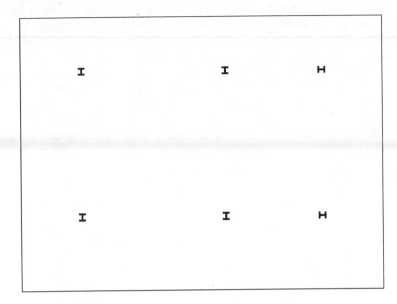

FIGURE P5–6   View 1 with columns copied.

STEP 24: Invoke the Place Fence Block command to remove the fence—but do not place another fence.

Place the Outside Structural Members

STEP 25: Set the active level to 3, color to green, line weight to 2 and the line style to 0.

STEP 26: Place a block by placing one corner in the exact center of lower left column and the other corner in the exact center of the diagonally opposite column. Your design should now be similar to Figure P5–7.

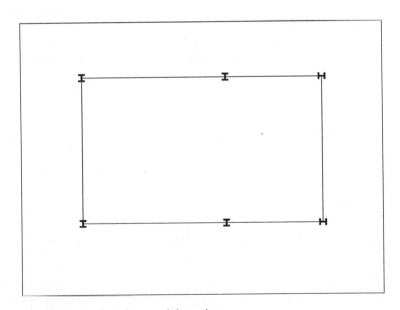

FIGURE P5–7   View 1 with block placed around the columns.

STEP 27:   Use the Partial Delete command from the Modify Element sub-palette to cut out (1′) the part of the block that overlaps and to leave a gap for each column. Make sure Grid lock is set to ON before you invoke the Partial Delete command.

> **NOTE:** The first cut requires three data points (start of cut, cut direction, and end of cut) because as the block is a closed shape. The remaining cuts for columns only require two data points each (the cut start and the end of cut) because the element is no longer a closed shape.

Your design should now be similar to Figure P5–8.

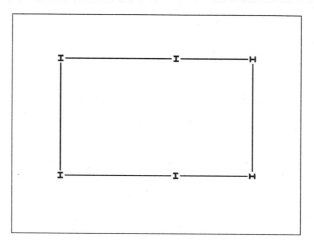

FIGURE P5–8   Modified block leaving a gap for each column.

Place the Interior Structural Members

STEP 28:   Invoke the Parallel command from the Manipulate Element sub-palette. In the Tool settings box, set the Distance and Make Copy toggle buttons to ON. Key-in **12** in the Distance edit field and press the [TAB] key. Identify the left most vertical line and place two data points to place two parallel lines at a distance of 12 feet. Click the Reset button to terminate the command sequence. Your design should now be similar to Figure P5–9.

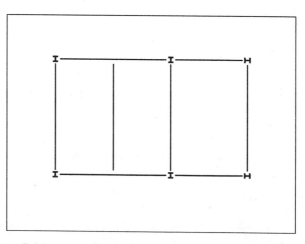

FIGURE P5–9   Place two parallel lines at a distance of 12 feet.

STEP 29: The first copy (the one that does not end at columns) must be extended until each end touches the horizontal line above and below it. Invoke the Extend Element to Intersection command from the Modify Element sub-palette. Identify the vertical line near the top of the line that does not end at columns and the horizontal line close to the end point of the vertical line. Place another data point to initiate the extension. Repeat the procedure to extend line at the bottom end of the vertical line. Your design should now be similar to Figure P5–10.

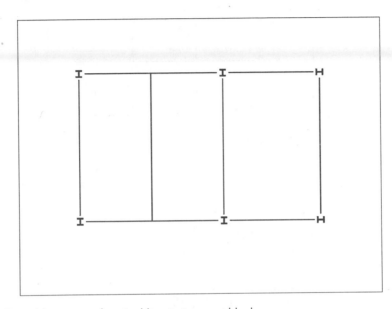

FIGURE P5–10   Extend first copy of vertical line to intersect block.

STEP 30: Invoke the Parallel command from the Manipulate Element sub-palette. In the Tool settings box, set the Distance and Make Copy toggle buttons to ON. Key-in **8** in the Distance edit field and press the ⌨ key. Identify the horizontal line labelled as Line A (see Figure P5–11) and place two data points below Line A to place two parallel lines at a distance of 8 feet. Click the Reset button to terminate the command sequence.

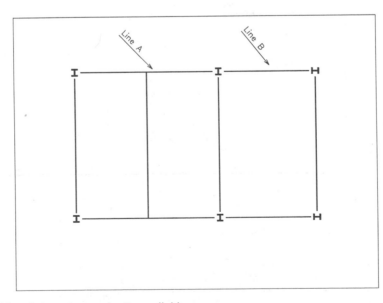

FIGURE P5–11   Identify Line A to make 2 parallel lines.

STEP 31: Change the Distance from 8 to 6 in the Distance edit field. Identify the horizontal line labelled as Line B (see Figure P5–11) and place three data points below Line B to place three parallel lines at a distance of 6 feet. Click the Reset button to terminate the command sequence. Your design should now be similar to Figure P5–12.

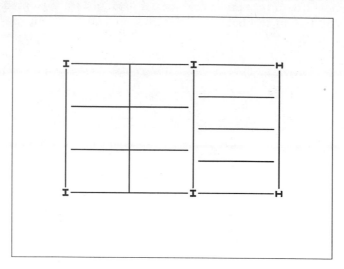

FIGURE P5–12 Line B completed with 3 parallel lines.

Place Text

Place text at appropriate places as shown in Figure P5–13.

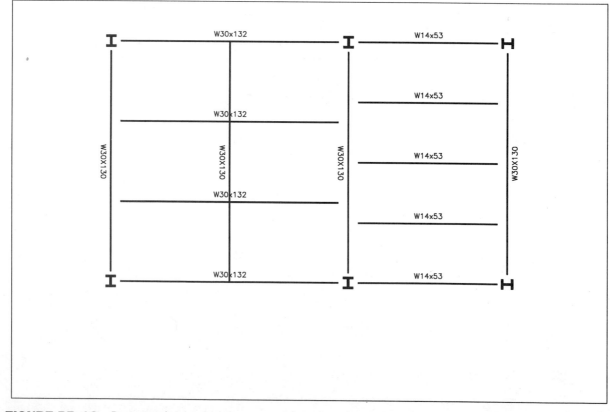

FIGURE P5–13 Design with text placed.

STEP 32: Open the Text settings box from the Element pull-down menu. Set the font to the Engineering font (3), the text Height and Width to .5, the Line Spacing to .5 and Text String Justification to Center.

STEP 33: Set the active level to 4, color to white, line weight to 0 and the line style to 0.

STEP 34: Invoke Save Settings command from the File pull-down menu to save the settings.

STEP 35: Invoke the Place Text command from the Main palette, and select Above Ele from the Method option menu in the Tool settings box.

STEP 36: In the Text Editor box, type the text string for each location and identify the horizontal line at the place where the text is to be placed above the line (see Figure P5–13).

> *NOTE:* To place text on the side of the vertical lines, select Below Ele from the Method option menu in the Tool Settings box.

Your design should now be similar to Figure P5–13.

Place the Dimensions

STEP 37: Set the active level to 5, color to red, line weight to 0 and the line style to 0. Add the dimensions using Linear Dimensioning commands as shown in Figure P5–14.

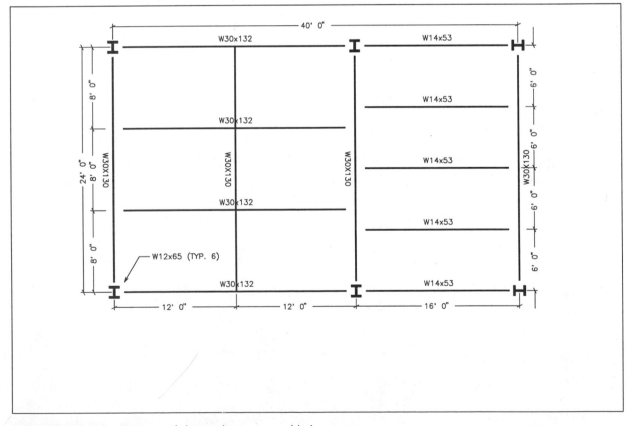

FIGURE P5–14   Design with linear dimensions added.

STEP 38: Set the active level to 1, color to white, line weight to 2 and the line style to 0. Create a title block as shown in Figure P5–15.

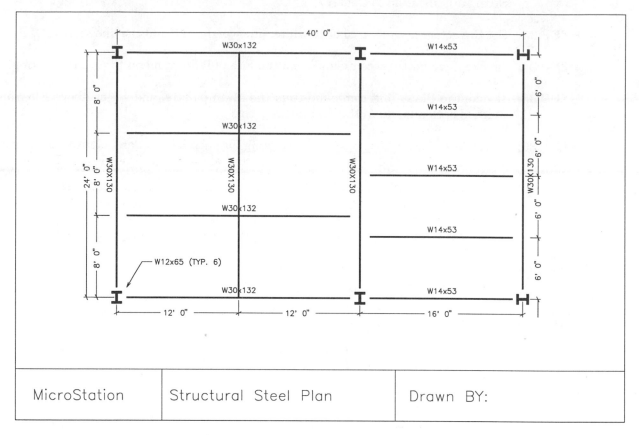

FIGURE P5–15 Completed design with border and title block.

STEP 39: Invoke Save Settings command from the File pull-down menu to save the settings.

STEP 40: If you are finished with MicroStation, exit the design file.

CHAPTER

6

PLOTTING

One task has not changed much in the transition from board drafting to CAD, and that is obtaining a hardcopy. The term *hardcopy* describes a tangible reproduction of a screen image. The hardcopy is usually a reproducible medium from which prints are made and it can take many forms, including slides, videotape, prints or plots. This chapter describes the most commonly used process for getting a hardcopy: plotting.

After completing this chapter, you will know:

- How the plotting process works.
- What components are involved in the process.
- How to create a plot file.
- How to create a hardcopy.

AN OVERVIEW OF THE PLOTTING PROCESS

In manual drafting, if you need your design to be done in two different scales, you have to physically draw the design for different scales. Whereas in CAD, with minor modifications, you can plot the same design in different scale factors on different size paper.

To plot a design with MicroStation you need to carry out a three-step process:

1. Set up the view to be plotted or place a fence around the part of the design to be plotted.
2. Use the Preview Plot dialog box to preview the plot and create a plot file.
3. Send the plot file to the plotter.

MicroStation lets you get a hardcopy of your design file by creating a "Plot file" and sending the file to a plotting device to create a hardcopy.

The Plot File describes all the elements in the plot area in a language the plotting device can understand, and provides commands to control the plotting device. It is separate from your design file, and contains the design as it existed when the plot file was created. If you make changes to the design after creating the plot file and want to plot the new design, you must create a new plot file.

MicroStation stores plot files in the directory path contained in the MS_PLTFILES configuration variable. By default, that path is <disk>:\USTATION\OUT\PLOT. Replace <disk> with the letter of the disk that contains the MicroStation program. (See Chapter 11 for detailed explanation for configuration variables.)

MicroStation uses view attribute settings (including those for reference files) to produce a WYSIWYG (what-you-see-is-what-you-get) plot of a selected view or the area defined by a fence. Everything you see in the view is plotted, except the grid display.

Plotting Devices (printers and plotters) put the information contained in the plot file on the hardcopy page. MicroStation supports many types and models of plotting devices. There are electrostatic plotters that can only provide shades of gray and more expensive models that can plot in color. Pen plotters use ink pens contained in a moveable rack. A mechanical control mechanism selects pens and moves them across the page under program control.

MicroStation provides a **Plotter Configuration File** for each supported plotting device. The information contained in this file (combined with the information you supply through the Preview Plot dialog box) tells MicroStation how to create the plot file and send it to the plotting device.

The path and name of the default plotter configuration file is contained in the MS_PLTR configuration variable. The default path is <device>:\USTATION\OUT\PLOT\. Replace <device> with the letter of the disk containing the MicroStation program.

The plotter configuration file name usually consists of the device model number and .PLT as the extension. MicroStation provides two plotter configuration files for most plotting devices, one for English measurement units and one for Metric units.

See Table 6–1 for the list of the supported plotters and corresponding sample plotter configuration files supplied with the MicroStation program Version 5.

Table 6–1.   Supported Plotters and Corresponding Sample Plotter Configuration Files.

SUPPORTED PLOTTERS	PLOTTER CONFIGURATION FILES
Calcomp 906	cal906.plt
Calcomp 907	cal104x.plt, cal524xx.plt, cal907.plt, ver8536.plt, ver8524.plt
Calcomp 960	cal960.plt
DMPL (Houston Instrument)	hidmp40.plt, hidmp56.plt, hidmp52.plt, ioline.plt
EPS	epson8.plt, epson8h.plt, epson24.plt
HP-GL	drftpro.plt, mutoh500.plt, drftmstr.plt, hp7470a.plt, hp7550a.plt, hp7580b.plt, hp7585b.plt, hp7475a.plt, hp7440a.plt
HP-GL/2	hpgl2.plt, hpljet3.plt, hpljet4.plt, hpdjet.plt, hpxl300.plt, hp650c.plt, drftprop.plt, novajet2.plt
PCL	hpljet.plt
PostScript	pscript.plt, pscriptc.plt, qms860.plt

The plotter configuration file specifies the following:

- Plotter model
- Number of pens the plotter can use
- Resolution and units of distance on the plotter
- Pen change criteria
- Name, size, offset, and number for all paper sizes
- Stroking tolerance for arcs and circles
- Border around plot and information about border comment
- Pen speeds, accelerations, and force where applicable
- Pen to element color or weight mapping
- Spacing between multiple strokes on a weighted line
- Number of strokes generated for each line weight
- The definitions for user-defined line styles (for plotting only)
- The method by which plots are generated
- Actions to be taken at plot's start, end, and on pen changes

Plotter configuration files can be edited with any text editor. For more information on the contents of these files, and changes you can make to them, consult the *MicroStation User Guide* that is furnished with MicroStation Version 5 software.

> **NOTE:** If you modify a sample plotter configuration file, it is a good idea to retain the original file and to save the modified file as a new file with a different name.

CREATING A PLOT FILE

Before you create a plot file, decide which view you want to plot, or place a fence block or shape to define the plot area. Next, make sure the view attribute settings provide the design information you want on the plot. Remember—plotting is WYSIWYG.

Open the Plotting Dialog Box

After you have the design area prepared for plotting, invoke Plot... command from the File pull-down menu. MicroStation displays the Plotting dialog box similar to the one in Figure 6–1.

The Plotting dialog box allows you to select the:

- Area to be plotted (a view or the area in a fence)
- Plotting device to use
- Page size by name
- Height, width, scale, orientation, and origin on the page
- Optional parameters (such as adding a border or plotting the fence outline)
- Name for the plot file

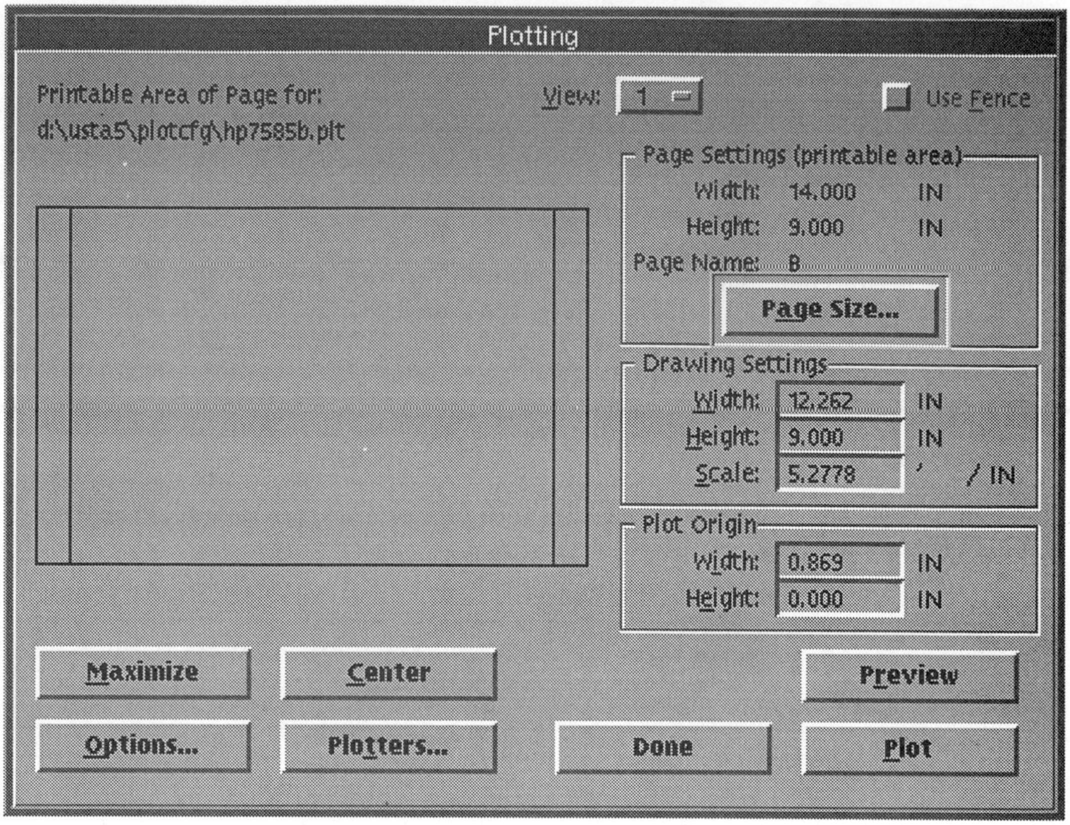

FIGURE 6–1   Plotting dialog box.

Select the Area of the Design to Plot

The upper right area of the Plotting dialog box contains the View options menu from which you select the number of the view you want to plot (closed views are shown dimmed and cannot be selected). The Use Fence toggle button, to the right of the View options menu, allows you to say if you want to plot from a fence instead of the entire view. If the button appears depressed with a dark center, MicroStation plots the fenced area. If no fence is defined, the button is dimmed.

Select a Plotter Configuration File

In the upper left of the dialog box is the name of the plotter configuration file that will be used to create the plot file. To select a different plotter configuration file, click the Plotters... button located at the bottom of the dialog box. MicroStation displays Plotter Configuration File dialog box similar to the one shown in Figure 6–2. Select the configuration file from Files list box and click OK button. MicroStation displays the name of the configuration file currently selected in the Plotting dialog box (top left).

> **NOTE:** If you change to a different plotter configuration file, the new one becomes the permanent setting, even if you exit MicroStation without selecting the Save Settings option.

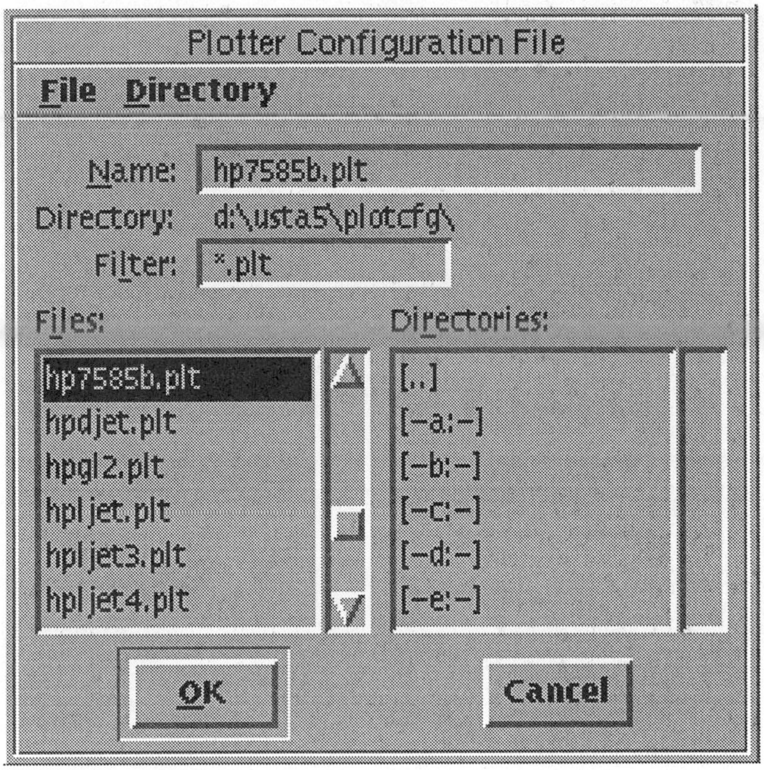

FIGURE 6-2 Plotter Configuration File dialog box.

Printable Area

Just below the plotter configuration filename is a box that indicates the usable area of the page (sheet of paper, film, or other media). Inside the box is the plot extent area denoted by a blue (dark) rectangle. If you only see one box in this area, the plot area is the same size as the maximum usable area on the page.

Selecting the Page Size

On the right side of the Plotting dialog box, and below the Use Fence toggle button, are the page size settings that are from the plotter configuration file. The page settings include the page name, dimensions of the usable area of the page, and measurement units (usually "IN" for inches or "mm" for millimeters).

To select a different page size, click the Page Size... button to open the Set Page Size dialog box similar to the one shown in Figure 6–3.

The Page Name options menu in the Set Page Size dialog box, lists the available page names in the plotter configuration file. Select any one of the available page name from the options menu. The Units section of the dialog box shows the units as set in the Resolution record in the plotter configuration file. Click the OK button to keep the changes, or click the Cancel button to close the dialog box and cancel the changes.

Page settings cannot be saved in the design file, and changes to these settings remain in effect only while the Plotting dialog box remains open.

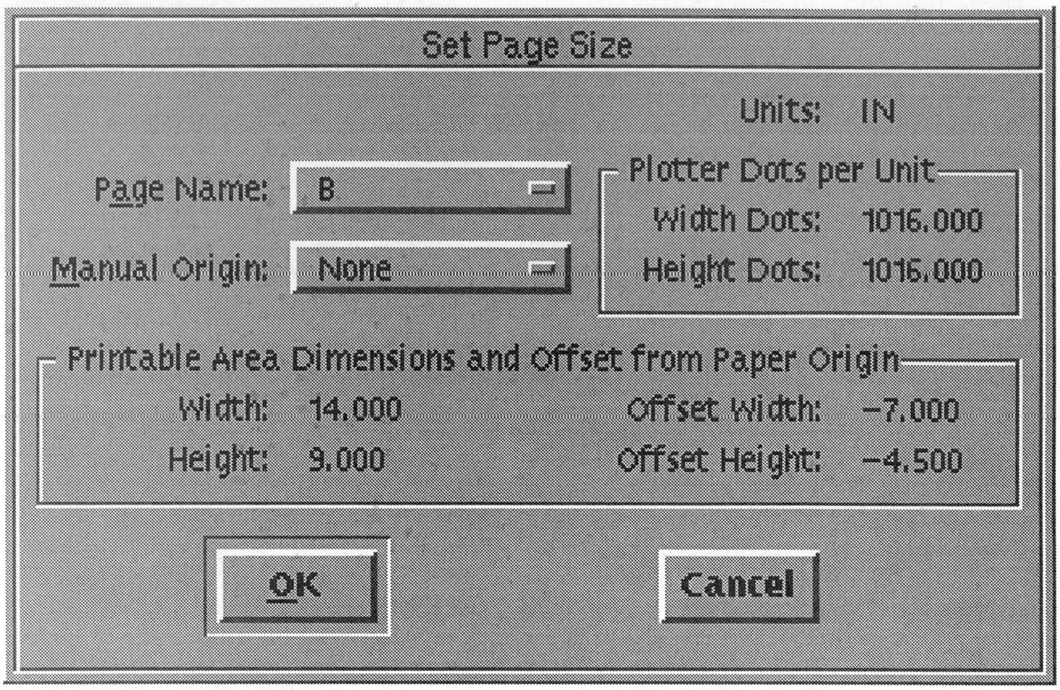

FIGURE 6-3 Set Page Size dialog box.

NOTE: On some plotters, plots are not properly generated unless the page size specified is the same as the actual size of the paper loaded in the plotter. Some plotters have one size of paper as in the case of a continuous roll type plotters, and, after the plot completes, you must trim the paper to the size you selected.

Setting the Plot Size

Below the page size information area are the Drawing Settings controls for plot width, height, and scale. You can make changes in one of the three edit fields, MicroStation reflects the corresponding changes in the remaining two edit fields. By default, MicroStation sets the size to provide the largest possible plot within the limits of the selected page. You can change the plot size by changing any of these fields, but you cannot size the drawing larger than the usable area of the page. If you need to center the plot on the selected page size, click the Center button.

The height and width are shown in plotter units (normally inches or millimeters), and the scale is shown as a ratio of design master units to page units. For example; if the Scale field says 10'/IN, the plot scale is 1"=10'.

NOTE: If you have entered a plot size smaller than the maximum size plot within the page limits, and want to return to the maximum size plot, click the Maximize button.

Setting The Plot Origin

Just below the Drawing Settings area in the Plotting dialog box is the Plot Origin area. The Width and Height settings in this area determine the bottom left corner of the plot area. The plot origin is given in page unit coordinates relative to the lower left corner of the usable area of the page. To precisely move the plot's position on the page, key in coordinates in these fields.

Click the Center button, located in the lower left area of the Preview Plot dialog box, to center the plot on the page. If you center the plot, the origin Width and Height fields show the new offset coordinates.

Click the Maximize button, to fit the selected view or fenced area into as much of the printable area as possible. The plot is centered either horizontally or vertically if it does not exactly fit the printable area, unless there is a Manual Origin, which anchors the plot at the lower left corner.

> **NOTE:** If a Manual Origin is set in the Page Settings box, the Plot Origin values are forced to zero and cannot be changed.

Setting Additional Options

The Options... button, located in the lower left corner of the Plotting dialog box, opens the Options dialog box similar to the one shown in Figure 6–4.

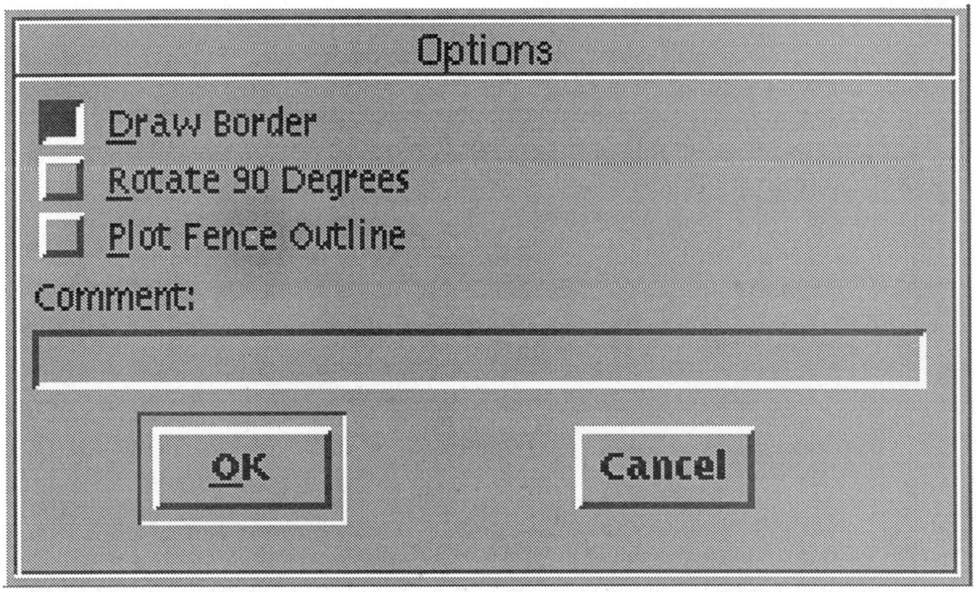

FIGURE 6–4   Options dialog box from the Plotting dialog box.

The Options dialog box contains three toggle buttons and a comment edit field.

- The **Draw Border** toggle button determines whether or not a rectangular border is drawn around the plot.
- The **Rotate 90 Degrees** toggle button determines whether or not the plot is rotated 90 degrees on the page.

■ The **Plot Fence Outline** determines whether or not the fence outline is drawn on the plot (helpful for non-rectangular fences).
■ The **Comment** edit field allows you to include a comment (40-character maximum) on the plot outside the border. (If the Draw Border toggle button is set to OFF, the comment is not plotted.)

> **NOTE:** When you open the Options dialog box, the Rotate 90 Degrees toggle button may already be set to ON. When you opened the Plotting dialog box, MicroStation calculated the largest scale plot it could fit on the page. In order to provide the largest scale, it may have rotated the plot on the page. If you change the rotation, the plot scale changes to compensate for the changed relation between the plot size and the page size.

Preview the Plot

The Preview button located in bottom right corner opens the Plot Preview window, which displays a preview image of the plot as shown in Figure 6–5. The text in the title bar is the border comment. The window displays the actual plot as it will appear on the page. While the Preview window is open, the screen cursor is inactive. To close the window and return control to the Plotting dialog box, click the Reset button or press the 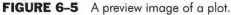 key.

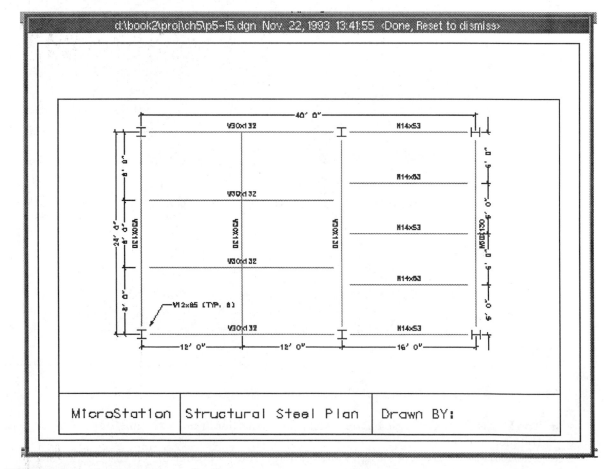

FIGURE 6–5 A preview image of a plot.

Creating a Plot File

To create a plot file, click the Plot button, located in the lower right corner of the Plotting dialog box. The Save Plot As dialog box opens similar to the one shown in Figure 6–6.

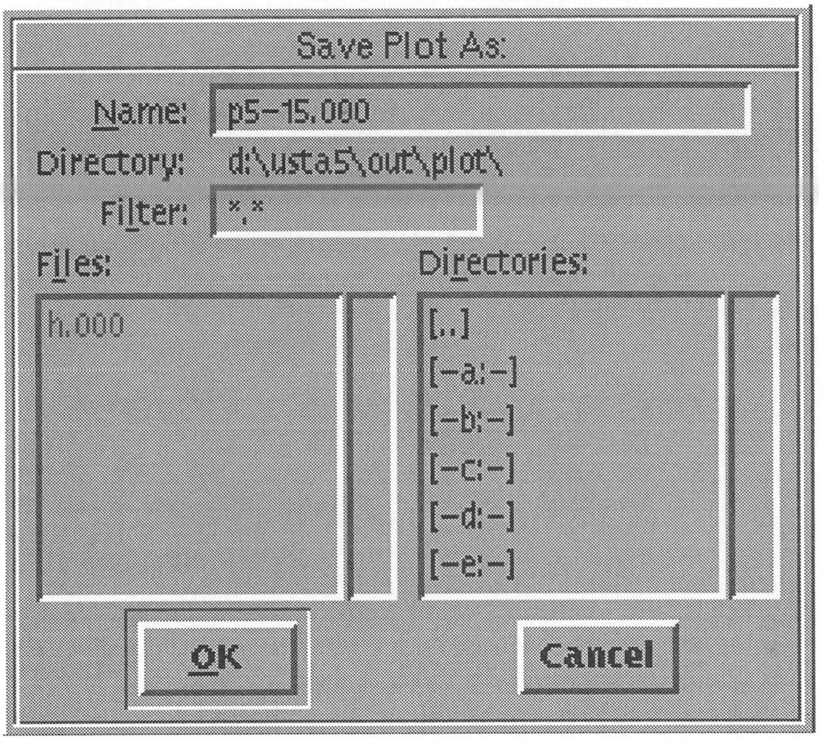

```
┌─────────────────────────────────────────────┐
│                Save Plot As:                 │
│                                              │
│     Name:   p5-15.000                        │
│  Directory: d:\usta5\out\plot\               │
│     Filter: *.*                              │
│  Files:                 Directories:         │
│  ┌──────────────┐       ┌──────────────┐     │
│  │ h.000        │       │ [..]         │     │
│  │              │       │ [-a:-]       │     │
│  │              │       │ [-b:-]       │     │
│  │              │       │ [-c:-]       │     │
│  │              │       │ [-d:-]       │     │
│  │              │       │ [-e:-]       │     │
│  └──────────────┘       └──────────────┘     │
│                                              │
│      ┌────────┐            ┌────────┐         │
│      │   OK   │            │ Cancel │         │
│      └────────┘            └────────┘         │
└─────────────────────────────────────────────┘
```

FIGURE 6–6   Save Plot As dialog box.

The default plot file name is the same as the design file name, and .000 extension is added to the file name. If necessary, change the plot file name, click the OK button to create the plot file.

> **NOTE:** If the plotter is connected to a parallel port, instead of providing a filename, you can key-in LPT1 or LPT2 (depending on which parallel port the plotter is connected). The plotter will generate a hardcopy by passing creating a plot file.

By default the plot file is saved in the <disk>:USTATION/OUT/PLOT/ directory. Replace <disk>: with the letter of the disk that contains the MicroStation program.

If the selected filename already exists, an Alert window opens. Click the OK button to overwrite the file, or click the Cancel button to return to the Save File As dialog box and enter a new filename.

> **NOTE:** If you are planning to create several plot files from your design before you plot any of them, give each plot file a different name or extension.

Close the Plotting Dialog Box

After you have completed creating the plot file, close the Plotting dialog box by clicking the Done button in the bottom right side of the dialog box.

GENERATING THE PLOT FROM THE PLOT FILE

The Plotfile utility sends the information stored in one or more plot files to the selected plotting device. It is invoked from the DOS prompt.

To start Plotfile at the DOS prompt, key-in **plotfile <plot files>** and press ⏎. Replace <plot files> with the name of the plot file or files you want to plot. If you enter more than one plot filename, separate each name with a space character. Include the path description for plot files not in the default path defined by the MS_PLTFILES configuration variable.

For example, to plot a file named plan.000 located in the default directory and a file named northelv.000 located in the c:\project directory, key-in:

C:\> **plotfile plan.000 c:\project\northelv.000** ⏎

> **NOTE:** You should run MicroStation at least once, before invoking the Plotfile utility. MicroStation program sets up the MS_PLTR and MS_PLTFILES configuration variables. MS_PLTR provides the name and path of the plot configuration file, and MS_PLTFILES provides the path to the default location of the plot files.

> **NOTE:** Additional plot control parameters can be typed with the Plotfile utility. For detailed information, consult the *MicroStation User Guide* furnished with MicroStation Version 5 software.

Printing PostScript Files

PostScript is a graphical description language much like Hwelett Packard HPGL. It gives programmers the ability to write the programs that describe and manipulate graphic objects (lines, curves, boxes, etc.), as well as text through built-in and user-defined functions. These programs are then interpreted by an output device (either hardcopy or video) to render a graphic display.

MicroStation allows you to create a PostScript file by selecting the PostScript plotter configuration file "pscript.plt" (for black & white) or "pscriptc.plt" to create Adobe EPSF (encapsulated PostScript) file.

ALTERNATE METHOD FOR PLOTTING

To plot a design file bypassing the Plotting dialog box, invoke the User command AUTOPLOT.UCM provided with MicroStation Version 5 by keying at uSTN> field **uc=autoplot** and pressing [ENTER]. MicroStation prompts:

> *Rotate/NO Rotate [1/0]* (Key-in 1 to have the plot rotate 90 degrees or 0 for no rotation.)
> *Plot size param [D,S,X,Y,M]* (To plot with default settings, key-in D, to change the scale factor key-in S, to change only X scale factor key-in X, to change only Y scale factor key-in Y or to plot to maximum size key-in M and press [ENTER].)
> *Enter page name* (Key-in one of the page names and press [ENTER].)
> *Enter border comment* (Key-in a short comment (optional) to appear outside the border of the plot.)

MicroStation creates a plot file with the same name as the design filename, and adds .000 extension to the filename.

CHAPTER

7

CELLS AND CELL LIBRARIES

Many types of drawings consist of a large number of identical symbols (for example, control valves in a P&ID drawing). MicroStation provides a powerful set of tools for placing such symbols, called cells. The tools permit you to group elements under a user-determined name and perform certain manipulation commands on the group as though they were a single element.

After completing this chapter, you will be able to:

- Create cell libraries.
- Attach cell libraries.
- Create cells.
- Select active cells.
- Place cells.
- Place line terminators.
- Place point elements, characters, and cells.
- Maintain cells and cell libraries.
- Place and maintain shared cells.

CELLS

Cells are like the variously shaped cutouts in a manual drafting template. You draw standard symbols on paper by tracing the outline of the symbol's cutout in the template. In MicroStation you do the same thing by placing a copy of a cell in your design file. Figure 7–1 shows some common uses of cells in various engineering disciplines.

Even though a cell contains separate elements, the copy you place in a design file acts like a single element when manipulated with commands such as Delete, Rotate, Array, and Mirror. When placing cells, you can change the scale and/or rotation angle of the original object(s). Cells save time by eliminating the need to draw the same thing more than once, and they also promote standardization.

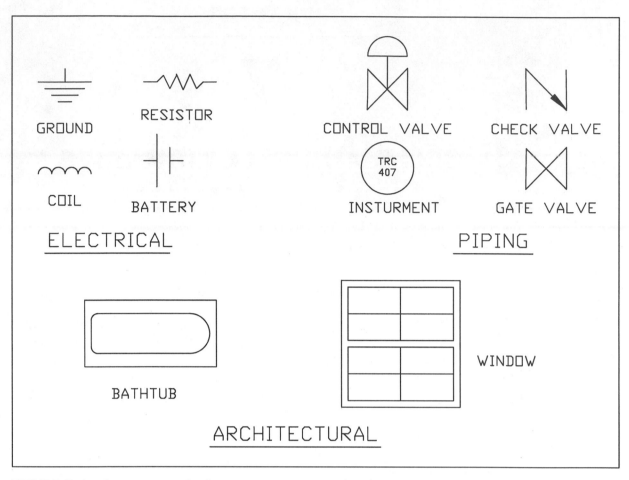

FIGURE 7–1   Common uses of cells in various engineering disciplines.

CELL LIBRARIES

If cells are like the holes in a plastic template, cell libraries are the template. A cell library is a DOS file that holds cells. Most engineering companies that use MicroStation have several cell libraries to provide standard symbols for all of their design files. Some companies also create sets of cells stored in libraries that they offer for sale.

To use the cells from a cell library you must first attach the library to your design file. Once the cell library is attached, you can access any of the cells from the cell library and place copies of them in your current design file. If you create a new cell, it is automatically placed in the library that is currently attached to your design file.

Although there is no limit to the number of cells you can store in a library, you don't want to end up with a very large, hard-to-manage library. It is advisable to create separate cell libraries for specific disciplines, such as electrical fixtures, plumbing, HVAC, and so on.

Create a New Cell Library

As mentioned earlier, you need a cell library to store cells. To create a new cell library, invoke the Cell Library settings box by selecting Cells under the Settings pull-down menu as shown in Figure 7–2.

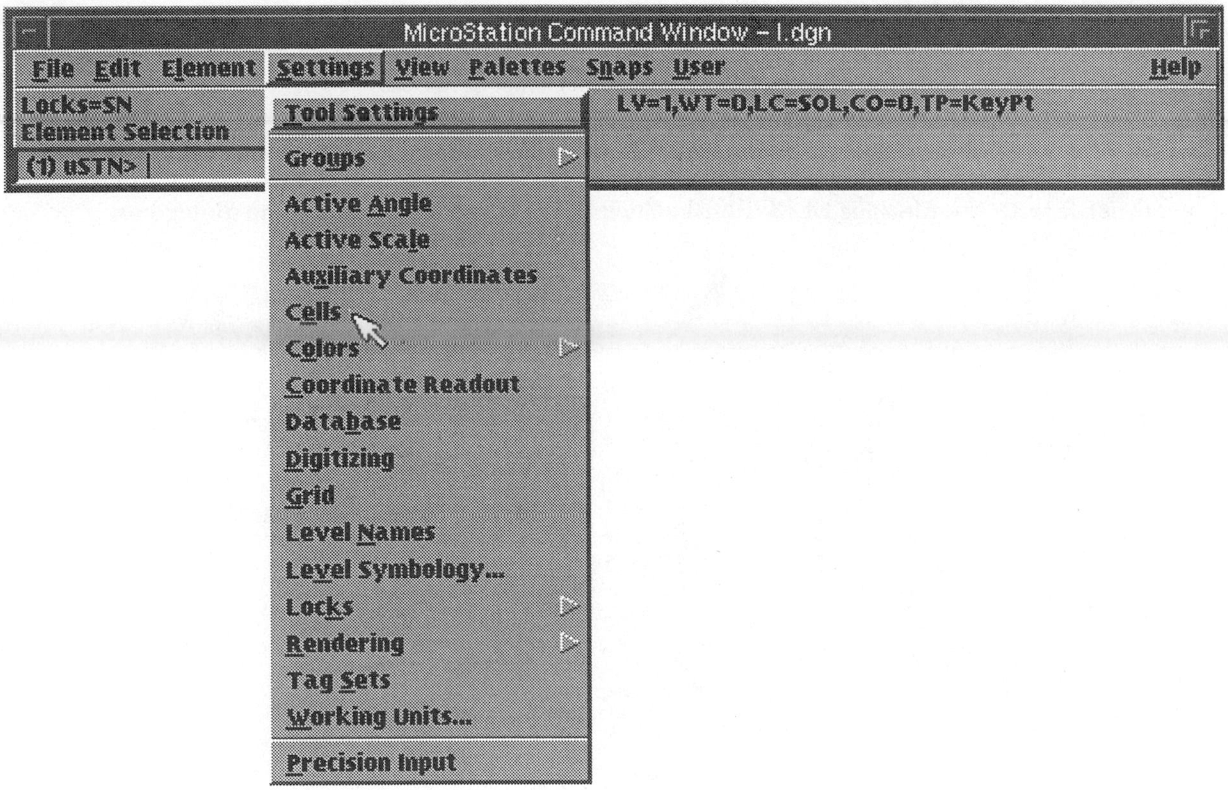

FIGURE 7-2 Invoking the Cell Library Settings box from the Settings pull-down menu in the MicroStation Command Window.

A settings box appears similar to the one shown in Figure 7–3.

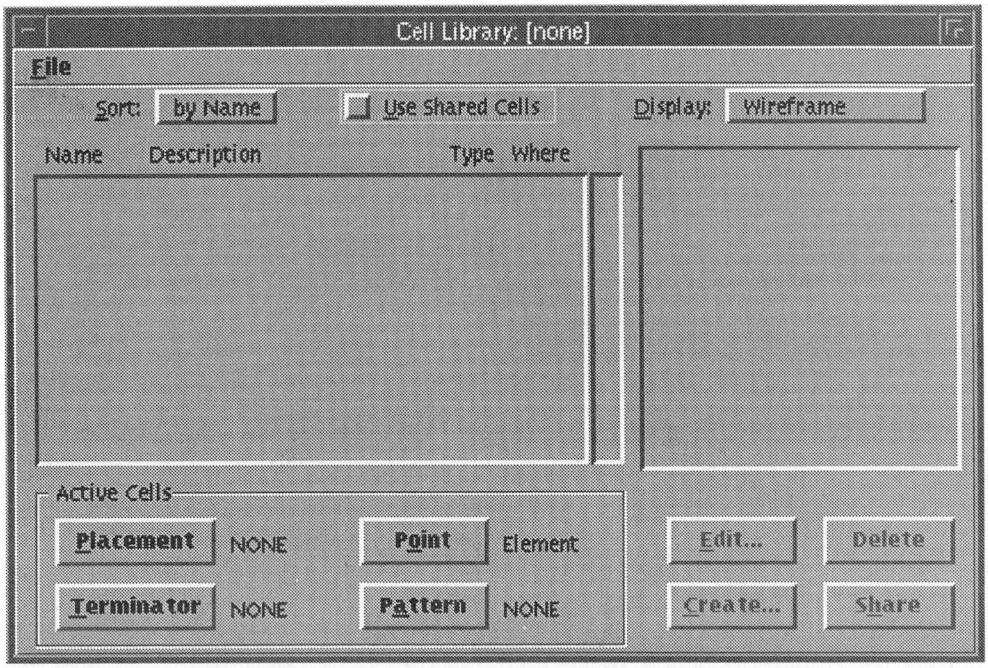

FIGURE 7-3 Cell Library Settings box.

From the File pull-down menu in the Cell Library settings box, select New. . . and a Create Cell Library dialog box similar to the one shown in Figure 7–4 appears. Select the appropriate seed file for the cell library by clicking the seed button. Select SEED2D.CEL, if you are working in a 2D design, or select SEED3D.CEL, if you are working in a 3D design. Next, click in the Name edit box and type a filename (one to eight characters long) for your new cell library. By default, MicroStation appends the extension .CEL. For instance, if you type the cell library file name ELECT, MicroStation creates a file with the file spec ELECT.CEL. Click OK or press [ENTER] to close the dialog box.

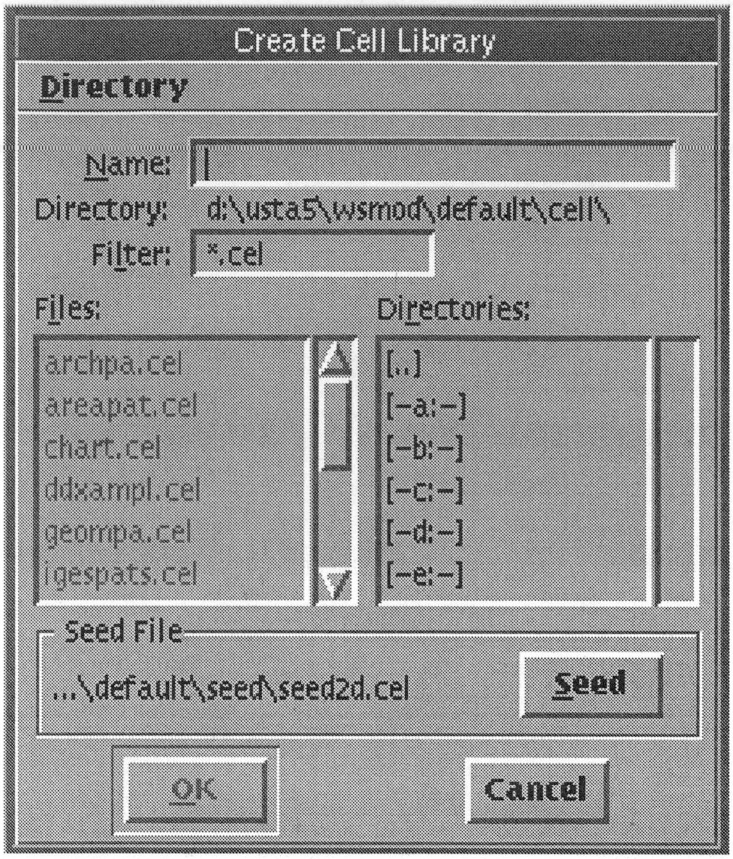

Create Cell Library

Directory

Name: | |

Directory: d:\usta5\wsmod\default\cell\

Filter: | *.cel |

Files:

Directories:
archpa.cel	[..]
areapat.cel	[-a:-]
chart.cel	[-b:-]
ddxampl.cel	[-c:-]
geompa.cel	[-d:-]
igespats.cel	[-e:-]

Seed File

...\default\seed\seed2d.cel   **Seed**

OK   **Cancel**

FIGURE 7–4 Create Cell Library Dialog box.

> **NOTE:** Before you close the dialog box, make sure the cell library file is created in the appropriate directory. If it isn't, find and select the appropriate directory from the Directories list before you key-in the file name.

When you create a new cell library, MicroStation automatically attaches it to your current design file and acknowledges the attachment with a message in the status field of the Command Window.

Your cell library is now available for use. You can start creating cells to store in your new library.

Alternate Method You can also use Create New Cell Library from the File pull-down menu of the Command Window. This is done by invoking the New. . . option under Cell Library. After that, the procedure is the same as described above.

Attach an Existing Cell Library

Let's look at how to attach an existing cell library file to your current design file. This is done by invoking the Cell Library settings box by selecting Cells under the Setting pull-down menu, as shown in Figure 7–2. A settings box will appear similar to the one shown in Figure 7–3. From the File pull-down menu in the Cell Library settings box, select Attach. . . to display the Attach Cell Library dialog box. Select the appropriate cell library file from the Files list and click the OK button to attach the library file to the current design file.

MicroStation acknowledges the attachment with a message in the status field of the Command Window. Once the cell library is attached, the Cell List in the Cell Library setting box displays the names and descriptions of the cells similar to the one shown in Figure 7–5.

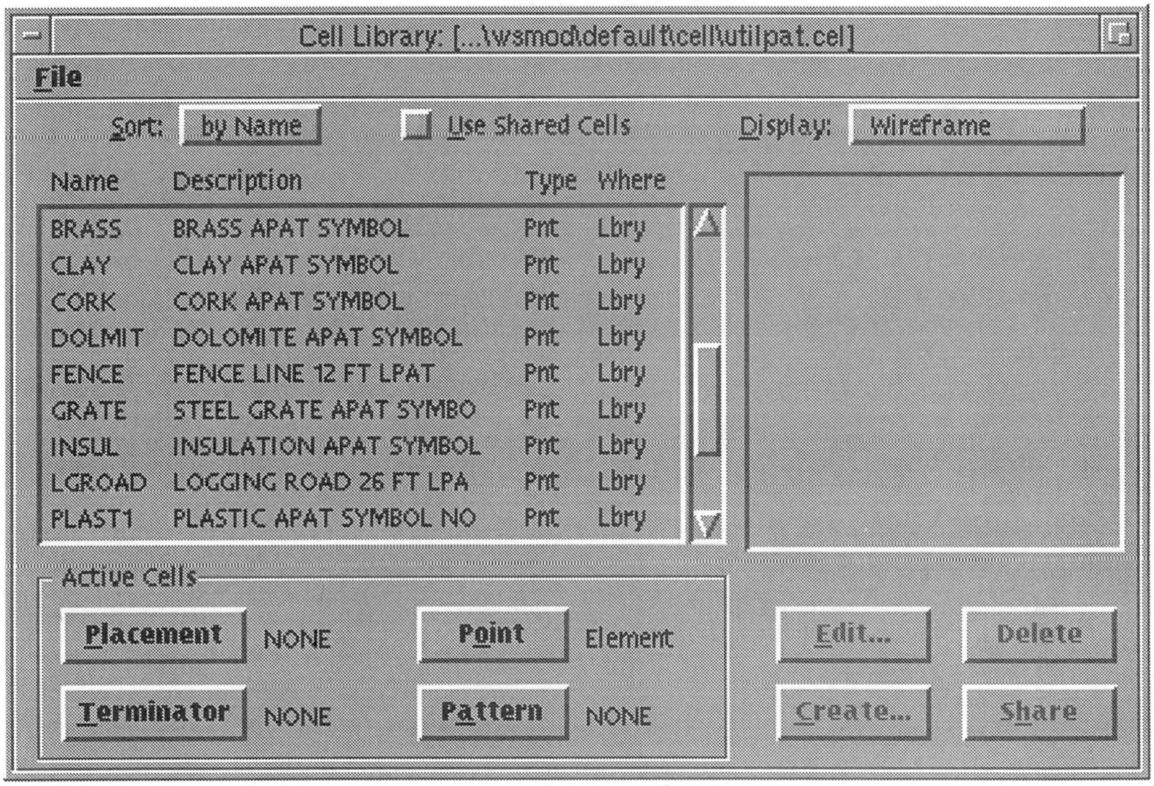

FIGURE 7–5   Listing of the Cell name and description in the Cell Library Settings box.

Alternate Attachment Methods   There are two other ways to attach a cell library.

1. You also can attach an existing Cell Library from the File pull-down menu of the Command Window. This is done by invoking the Attach. . . option under Cell Library.
2. In addition, you can attach a cell library by key-in at the uSTN> field, **RC=<file>**, and press [ENTER]. Replace <file> with the specification of the library file you want to attach.

   Example: **RC=C:\ARCH\HVAC.CEL** [ENTER]

> **NOTE:** If your cell library is in the default cell directory, you need not enter the path.

Attachment Notes Here are a few things to remember about your cell library attachment:

- The attachment is permanent as long as MicroStation can find the library file.
- You can attach only one cell library at a time. If you attach another library, the first attachment is dropped.
- When the library is attached, all the library's cells are available to you for placement, and you can store new cells in the library as well.
- There is no detach cell library command. When you attach a new one, the existing library is detached.
- In addition to the one library you can attach, MicroStation version 5.0 provides a way to have additional libraries attached to all design files using an environmental variable. (Environmental variables are discussed in Chapter 11.)

> **NOTE:** The new cells you create are stored only in the cell library that is attached to the current design file, not in the cell libraries that are attached through the environmental variable.

CREATE YOUR OWN CELLS

When you need to place copies of a symbol for which no cell currently exists, you can create your own cell (symbol), store it in the library, then use it in any design file.

Before You Start

Here are a few things to consider before starting to draw the elements that will make up your cell.

Working Units The working units in the design file you use to create the cell should be the same as the working units of the design files in which you plan to place copies of the cell. If the working units are different, you may have to scale the cell each time you place it.

Cell Elements There are no restrictions on the elements that make up the cell. All element types can be placed in a cell; they can be drawn on any level; and they can be any color, weight, and style. The elements you draw do not become a cell. The cell is made by copying your elements into the attached cell library. After you create your cell, you may delete the original elements from the design file.

Cell Rotation Always draw the object you are going to make into a cell with 0 degrees of rotation. That means it should be upright and facing to the right (see Figure 7–6).

Sticking with 0 rotation for cells makes it easier to understand what happens to the cell when it is rotated.

Steps for Creating a Cell

1. Draw the elements that will comprise the cell.
2. Place a fence around the elements and make sure the appropriate fence lock is selected.

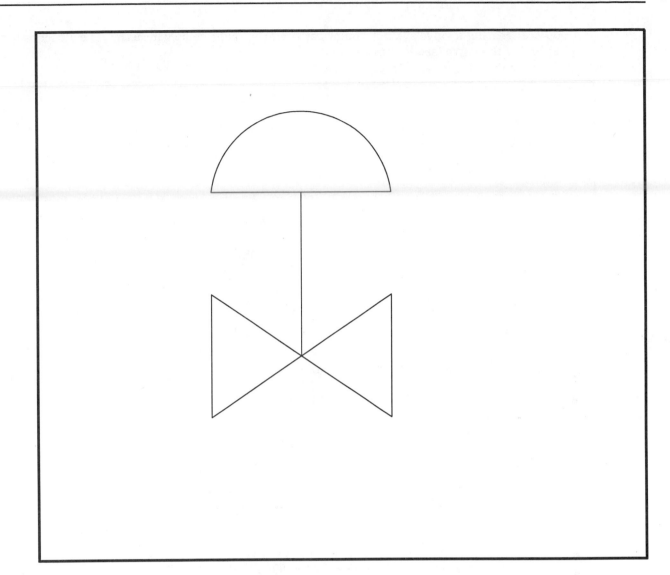

FIGURE 7–6 Example of a symbol drawn upright and facing to the right.

3. Define the cell origin clicking the Define Cell Origin icon in the Cells palette as shown in Figure 7–7, or key-in at the uSTN> field, **define cell origin** (or **def c**), and press [ENTER]. MicroStation prompts:

Define Origin (Place a data point or key-in coordinates where you want the origin to be.)

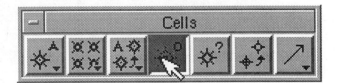

FIGURE 7–7 Invoking the Define Cell Origin command in the Cells sub-palette.

Cells are placed with a data point, which will be the cell origin. Create your origin in a logical place and, if possible, snap to an element to place it exactly where you want it. For instance, if you are creating a valve symbol, you might want the origin to be where the pipe attaches to the left end of the valve (see Figure 7–8).

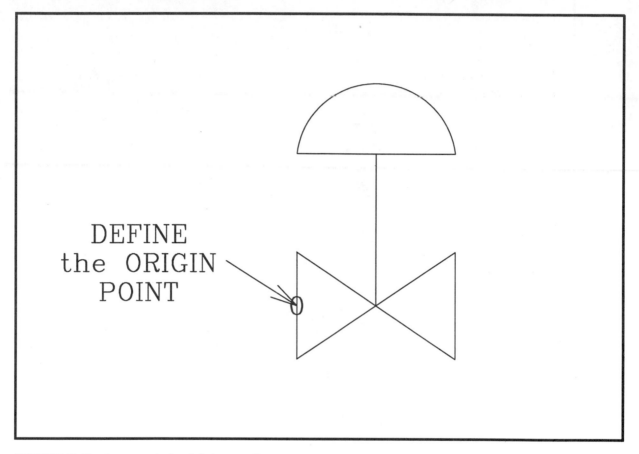

FIGURE 7–8 An example for defining a cell origin.

If you accidentally define the origin in the wrong place, just define another one. MicroStation uses the last one you defined. Each time you define an origin, the letter O appears near the point where you defined the origin. The O is not an element, it is just shown on the screen to let you know you placed an origin. Update the view and the O's disappear (but the origin is still defined).

4. If the Cell Library settings box is not already open, select it from Cells from the Settings pull-down menu. Click the create button located at the bottom right corner of the Cell Library settings box. A dialog box appears similar to the one shown in Figure 7–9.

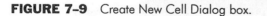

FIGURE 7–9 Create New Cell Dialog box.

5. Click in the Name field in the Create New Cell dialog box and enter a name for your cell (don't press [ENTER]). You must provide a one- to six-character alphanumeric name for your cell. In addition to letters and numbers, the name can contain dashes (-) and underscores (_), but not spaces. Help out other people who will have to use your cells by creating descriptive cell names (as well as you can in six characters).

   Good Examples: PNP is a good name for a cell that provides a PNP transistor. If the cell provides a globe valve symbol, a good name might be GLBVAL.

   Bad Examples: CELL-1 is a legal cell name but does not provide any information about the intended use of the cell. GLOBE-VALVE is an unacceptable cell name, because it contains too many characters.

6. Click on the Description field and enter a 1- to 27-character description for your cell. Use the description to describe the cell's purpose. Because cell descriptions are optional, some people do not bother to provide them. Take the time to provide a description for every cell you create. If your cell libraries contain lots of cells, the descriptions will help other people figure out what purpose you intended for the cell. It will also help you when you go back to the cell library after being away from it for a few weeks.

7. Select the appropriate cell type from the options menu. Cells that can be placed in a design come in two types—Graphic and Point. The default cell type is Graphic. Later in this chapter, we will discuss the difference between the two types and how you specify which type you want to create.

8. Click the Create button.

When you complete the procedure, the fenced elements are copied to the attached cell library, and your new cell appears in the cells list area of the Cell Library settings box (see Figure 7–10). In addition to the cell name, the cells list displays the cell description, type, and location. The cell is available for placement in the current design file and in any other design files to which your cell library is attached.

Refer to Figure 7–11 to review the steps for the creation of a cell.

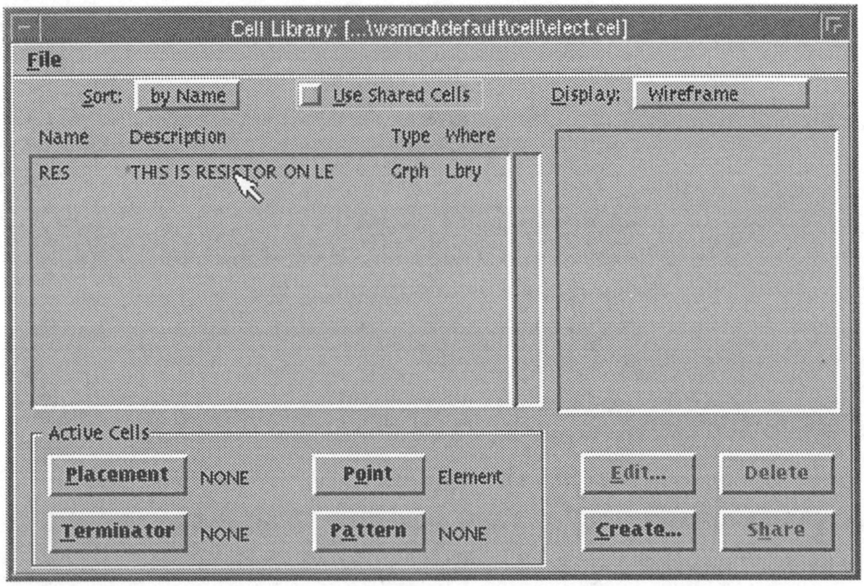

FIGURE 7-10   Displaying the name and description of the new cell in the Cell Library Settings box.

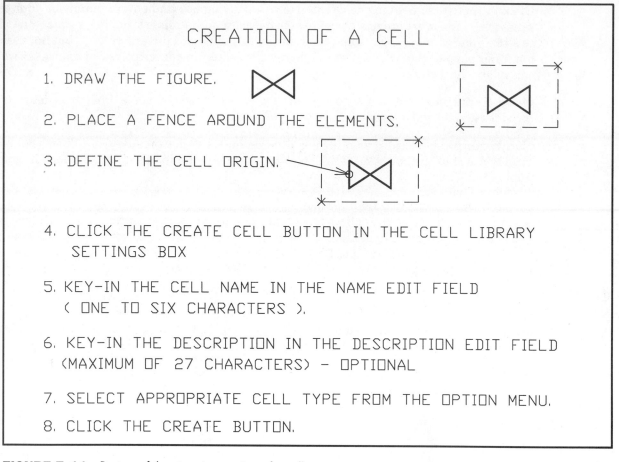

FIGURE 7–11 Review of the steps in creation of a cell.

Graphic and Point Cell Types

As mentioned earlier, two cell types, Graphic and Point, can be placed in your design. The default cell type is Graphic (also called Normal). Here are the differences between Graphic and Point cells:

A Graphic cell, when placed in a design file:

1. Keeps the symbology (color, weight, and style) of its elements.
2. Remembers the levels on which its elements were drawn. (We will learn more about this later when we discuss Relative and Absolute mode placement.)
3. Retains the keypoints of each cell element.

A Point cell, when placed in a design file:

1. Takes on current active symbology settings (color, weight, and style).
2. Places all cell elements on the current active level, regardless of what level they were drawn on.
3. Has only one keypoint—the cell's origin point. The individual cell elements do not have keypoints.

Selecting the Cell Type You can select either Graphic or Point cell type from the Create New Cell dialog box option menu when you provide the cell's name and description. The options menu has four cell types. The other two, Menu and Tutorial, do not create cells that can be placed in your design file. They are for customizing the way you use MicroStation.

ACTIVE CELLS

To place a copy of a cell in your current design file, you must first make the cell the Active Placement Cell. This is done by clicking on the cell name from the Cell List provided in the Cell Library settings box and clicking one of the four buttons provided under the Active Cell. The four types of Active Cells give you the freedom to place the cell under varying conditions in your design file.

- The Active Placement cell is used with a group of commands that place cells at a data point.
- The Active Terminator cell is used with a tool that places a cell on the end of an element.
- The Active Point cell is used with a group of commands that place cells in geometric relation to other elements.
- The Active Pattern cell is used with a group of commands that create patterns in a closed shape.

Active placement, active terminator, and active point cells are explained in detail in this chapter. Active pattern cells are explained in Chapter 8.

Alternate Methods You also can use key-in to select an active cell for each type of cell placement. At the uSTN> field, type:

> **AC=**<name> and press ⌨ to select the active Placement cell.
> **LT=**<name> and press ⌨ to select the active Terminator cell.
> **PT=**<name> and press ⌨ to select the active Point cell.
> **AP=**<name> and press ⌨ to select the active Pattern cell.

In each command replace <name> with the name of the cell you want to use.

> *Example:* **AC=COIL** ⌨

Several cell placement commands have an active cell pop-up field in their sub-palette. You can also select the active cell by keying in its name in these fields.

The Active Placement Cell

Four commands are provided to place the active Placement cell at data points in your design file. The commands are as follows:

- Place Active Cell—Places copies of the active Placement cell at data points you specify. The cell is placed at the active angle and active scale.
- Place Active Cell (Interactive)—Places copies of the Active Placement cell interactively and allows you to graphically specify the cell rotation and scale.
- Select and Place Active Cell—Lets you select a cell already placed in your design file to be the active Placement cell, then places copies at the data points you specify.
- Place Active Cell Matrix—Places a rectangular matrix (rectangular array) of the active placement cell with the lower left corner of the matrix at the data point you specify.

Place Active Cell Use the Place Active Cell command to place the active placement cell at various locations in your design file. Click on the Place Active Cell icon in the Cells palette (see Figure 7–12), or key-in at the uSTN> field, **place active cell**, and press ⌨. MicroStation prompts:

Enter Cell Origin (Place a data point where you want to place the cell.)

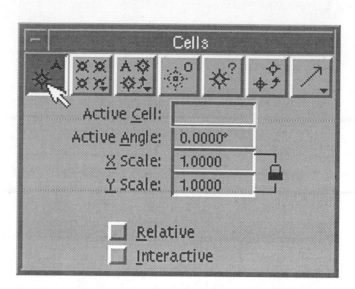

FIGURE 7–12 Invoking the Place Active Cell command from the Cells sub-palette.

Each time you place a data point, a copy of the cell will be placed such that its origin is at your data point. While this command is active, the screen cursor drags a dynamic image of the cell enclosed in a box. The cell's origin point is at the screen cursor position.

> **NOTE:** If you do not have an active cell and invoke the Place Active Cell command, MicroStation displays the message, *No Active Cell*, in the Command Window error field. You must declare an active cell before you can use this command (discussed earlier in this section).

The Place Active Cell command places the active cell at the current active angle and active scale. You can change the angle and scale any time while you are using the command, and the next cell copy you place will use your new angle and scale settings. This feature allows you to place the active cell rotated and scaled all in one operation.

You can change the angle and scale by keying-in the values in the edit box provided under the Place Active Cell icon. You can also change the settings by using the Angle and Scale settings boxes available from the Settings pull-down menu.

In addition to the edit boxes provided under the Place Active Cell icon, two toggle buttons are provided. One is for Relative placement of the cell, the other for Interactive placement of the cell.

Placing Graphic Cell in Absolute or Relative Mode MicroStation allows you to place graphic cells in Absolute or Relative mode, when you use the Place Active Cell or Select and Place Active Cell commands. (The Select and Place Active Cell command is explained later in this chapter.) The default placement mode for each command is Absolute. The difference between Absolute and Relative placement is the way the graphic cell's element levels are handled.

In Absolute placement mode, the graphic cell's elements are placed on the levels on which they were drawn originally, regardless of the active level setting. For example, if a graphic cell contains elements on levels 1 and 3, they are placed in the design file on levels 1 and 3 (see Figure 7–13a).

In Relative placement mode, the cell element on the lowest level is placed on the active level and all other cell levels are shifted by the same amount as the lowest level. For example, if the graphic cell with elements on levels 1 and 3 is placed in Relative mode, and the active level is 4, the cell elements on level one are moved to level 4 and the cell elements on level 3 are moved to level 6 (4 + 2 = 6) (see Figure 7–13b).

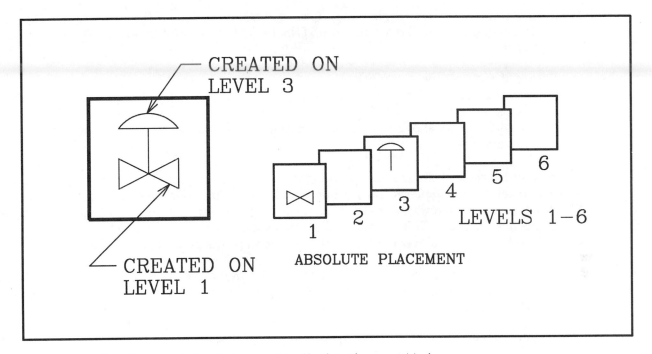

FIGURE 7–13a   An example for placing a cell by Absolute Placement Mode.

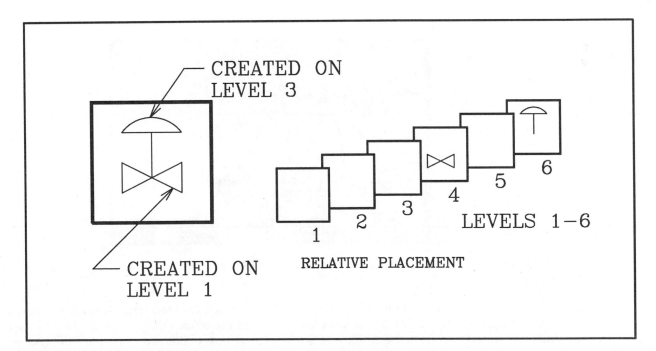

FIGURE 7–13b   An example for placing a cell by Relative Placement Mode.

If you want to place a graphic cell by Relative mode, make sure the toggle button is turned on for Relative mode.

Interactive Placement Interactive placement is helpful when you need to align your cell with existing elements, but you don't know what angle and scale to make it. You can define the angle and scale graphically as you place the cell.

Make sure the Interactive toggle button is turned ON and click on the Place Active Cell icon in the Cells sub-palette, or key-in at the uSTN> field, **Place Cell Interactive,** and press [ENTER]. MicroStation prompts:

> *Enter cell origin* (Place a data point.)
> *Enter scale or corner point* (Key-in a scale factor at the uSTN> field, or place a data point to scale the cell.)
> *Enter rotation by angle or point* (Key-in a rotation angle at the uSTN> field, or place a data point to rotate the cell.)

Select and Place Cell Often, when working in an existing design, you will need to place additional copies of a cell that was placed earlier, but is no longer your active Placement cell. The Select and Place Cell command allows you to select that cell for placement simply by clicking on a copy of the cell in the design plane. The cell you click becomes the active Placement cell and dynamic update shows it at the screen pointer position. Additional data points place copies of the cell.

To place a cell using the Select and Place Cell command, click the Select and Place Cell icon in the Cells sub-palette (see Figure 7–14), or key-in at the uSTN> field, **select cell** (or **select c**), and press [ENTER]. MicroStation prompts:

> *Identify element* (Point to the desired cell and click the Data button.)
> *Accept/Reject (Select next input)* (Place a data point to accept the cell and place a copy of it.)
> *Enter Cell Origin* (Continue placing data points to place copies of the cell, and when you finish press Reset.)

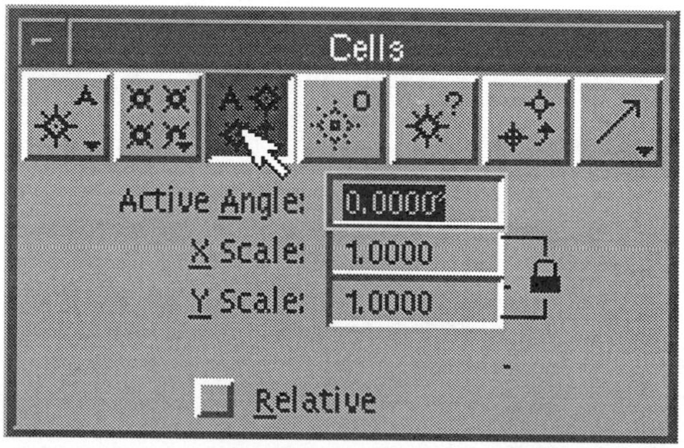

FIGURE 7–14 Invoking the Select Cell command from the Cells sub-palette.

The Select and Place Cell command places the active cell at the active angle and scale, just as the Place Active Cell command did. You can set the angle and scale from the pop-up fields that appear in the Cells sub-palette, or from the Angle and Scale settings boxes that are available from the Settings pull-down menu.

NOTE: Similar to the Place Active Cell command, you can place the cell in Relative mode by toggling the Relative button to ON.

When you click on a cell in your design file, MicroStation checks to make sure it is actually a cell. When you click the second time to indicate where you want to place a copy of the cell, MicroStation checks to see if the cell is in the currently attached cell library. If the cell is not in the currently attached library, MicroStation displays the message *Cell not found* in the error field of the Command Window, and waits for you to select another cell.

Place Active Cell Matrix Do you need to place two rectangular rows of electronic components in a circuit diagram? The Place Active Cell Matrix command can do it for you. With this command, you can place the active cell quickly in a rectangular matrix whose parameters you define (see Figure 7–15).

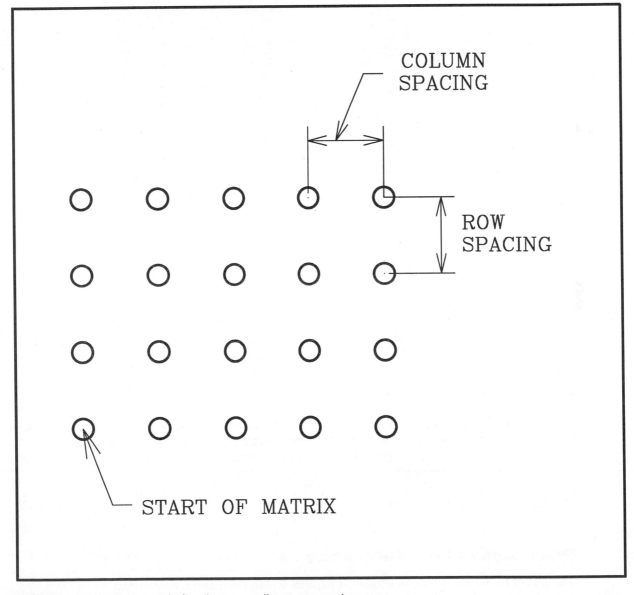

FIGURE 7–15 An example for placing a cell in a rectangular array.

The Place Active Cell Matrix command requires five parameters:

- ACTIVE CELL: The active cell name
- ROWS: The number of rows in the matrix
- COLUMNS: The number of columns in the matrix
- ROW SPACING: The space, in working units, between the rows
- COLUMN SPACING: The space, in working units, between the columns

The row and column spacing is from origin point to origin point. It is not the space between the cells.

To place an active cell in a rectangular matrix, click the Place Active Cell Matrix icon in the Cells sub-palette and enter the matrix parameters in the edit field (see Figure 7–16). MicroStation prompts:

Enter lower left corner of matrix (Place a data point.)

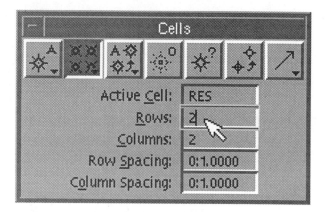

FIGURE 7–16 Invoking the Place Active Cell Matrix command from the Cells sub-palette.

The data point you place to start the matrix designates the position of the origin of the lower left cell in the matrix (see Figure 7–15).

The Place Active Cell Matrix command places each cell in the matrix at the active angle and active scale. The edit fields available in the Cells sub-palette for this command do not include angle and scale fields. You have to use the settings boxes available from the settings pull-down menu or key-in the active angle and active scale.

Alternate Method You can also place a cell matrix by key-in at the uSTN> field,

cm=*<rows>,<columns>,<row spacing>,<column spacing>,* and press ⏎. (The <rows> and <columns> designate the number of rows and columns respectively, and <row spacing> and <column spacing> designate the distance between the rows and distance between the columns respectively.)

Example: CM=3,5,4:6,8:3

Place Active Line Terminator

There will be occasions when you want to place a cell (such as an arrowhead) at the end of a line and have it rotated to match the line's rotation. This can be done by invoking the Place Active Line

Terminator command. It places the Active Terminator Cell at the end of the element you select and automatically rotates it to match the rotation of the element at the point of connection. See Figure 7–17 for examples of placing line terminators.

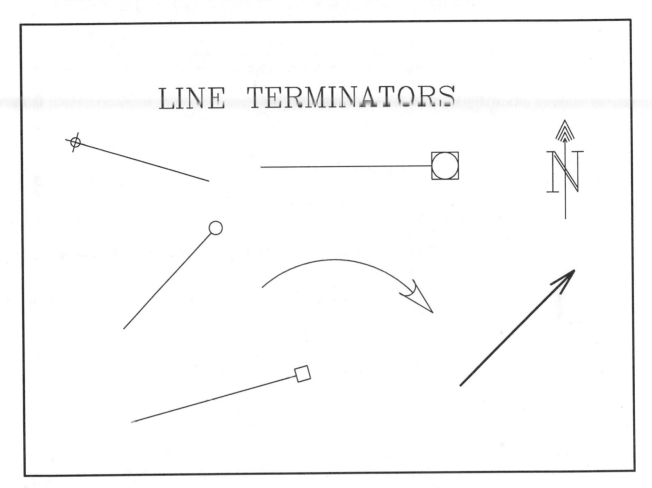

FIGURE 7–17   Examples for placing line terminators.

To place a Line Terminator, click the Place Active Line Terminator icon in the Cells sub-palette and enter the cell name in the Terminator edit box (see Figure 7–18). MicroStation prompts:

> *Identify element* (Identify the element by the data point near the end point where you want to place the Terminator.)
> *Accept/reject (Select next input)* (Click the Data button again.)

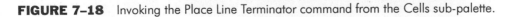

FIGURE 7–18   Invoking the Place Line Terminator command from the Cells sub-palette.

The second data point does two things; it places the Terminator cell, and it can identify the next element on which you want to place a terminator.

If your second data point does not identify another element, MicroStation displays the message, *Element not found*, in the error field of the Command Window. Ignore the message.

> **NOTE:** If you do not have an Active Cell and invoke the Place Active Line Terminator command, MicroStation displays the message, *No Active Cell*, in the Command Window error field.

> **NOTE:** Beginning users of MicroStation often select the element to place a terminator by first snapping to the element with the tentative button. That is not necessary, because MicroStation finds the end of the element automatically. Just place a data point near the end point on which you want to place the terminator.

Terminator Scale The Place Active Line Terminator command does not use the Active Scale—it has its own scale factor. If the scale factor is:

- Greater than one, the cell is scaled up.
- Equal to one, the cell is placed at its true size.
- Less than one, the cell is scaled down.

To set the Terminator Scale, key-in a scale factor in the Scale edit field in the Cells sub-palette, or key-in at the uSTN> field, **ts=**<scale> and press [ENTER]. Replace <scale> with the scale factor (example: **ts=2**).

You can change the terminator scale as often as necessary while placing Terminator cells. Each time you change it, the next Terminator cell you place is scaled to your new factor.

> **NOTE:** The Place Active Line Terminator command does not use the active angle. It rotates the cell as necessary to match the rotation of the element it terminates.

The Point Placement

MicroStation provides six point commands (invoked from the Main palette, as shown in Figure 7–19) that place a dot, character, or cell in your design file. The six commands are

Place Active Point—Places a single point at the data point you specify.

Construct Points Between Data Points—Places a set of equally spaced points between two data points.

Project Active Point Onto Element—Places a point on an element at the point on the element nearest to a data point.

Construct Active Point at Intersection—Places a point at the intersection of two elements.

Construct Points Along—Places a set of equally spaced points along an element between two data points on the element.

Construct Active Point at @Dist Along Element—Places one point at a pre-defined distance along an element from a data point.

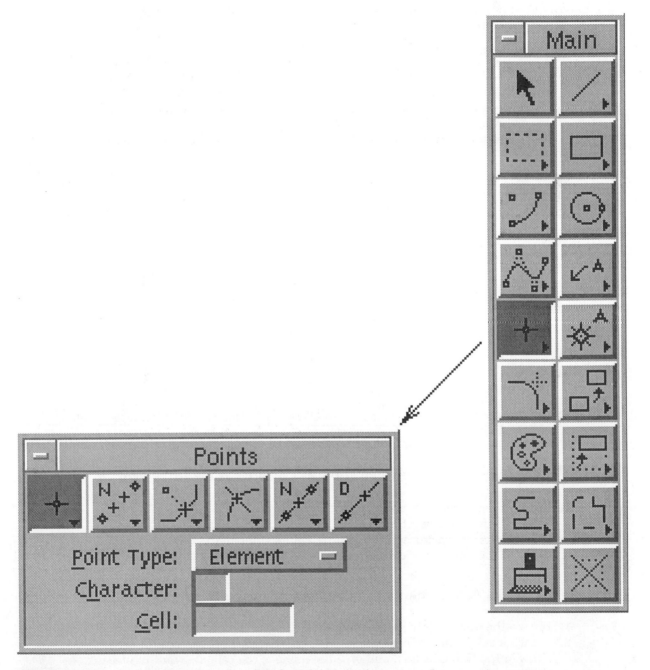

FIGURE 7-19 Invoking the Points sub-palette from the Mail palette.

Types of Points Before you use any of the point commands, you must set the type of point you want to place. An Options menu allows you to select the type of point; two edit fields for providing corresponding information are provided in the Points sub-palette, as shown in Figure 7–20. The available point types are:

Element—Places dots (0 length lines). To make these dots more noticeable, increase the active line weight before placing them.

Character—Places a text character using the currently active font. If a symbol font is active, the character point will be a symbol. Font characters are placed at the active angle rotation.

Cell—Places the currently active Point cell as the point. Point cells are placed at the active angle and active scale.

> **NOTE:** Don't confuse using a cell as the active point with point and graphic cells. You can use either a point or a graphic cell as the active point cell. The Point commands place Graphic cells in the Absolute mode only.

Select Element as Active Point To select Element as the active point, click on the Point Type options menu in the Points sub-palette and click on Element in the menu (see Figure 7–20).

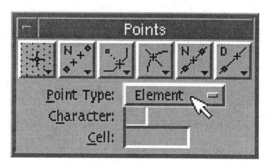

FIGURE 7–20 Displaying the selection of the Element option from the Point Type option menu.

Select Character as Active Point To select Character as the active point:

1. Invoke the appropriate point command.
2. Select the font you want to use.
3. Click in the Character edit field in the Points sub-palette and type the character you want.
4. Click on the Point Type option menu in the Points sub-palette and select Character in the menu.

Select Cell as Active Point To select a cell as the active point:

1. Invoke the appropriate point command.
2. Attach a cell library, if necessary.
3. Click in the Cell edit field and type the name of the cell you want to place.
4. Click on the Point Type option menu in the Points sub-palette and select Cell in the menu.

You can also select a cell as the Active Point from the Cell Library settings box. To do so:

1. Open the Cell Library settings box from the Settings menu.
2. Find the cell you want to use in the Cell List and highlight it by clicking with the Data button.
3. Click on the Point button (located on bottom left of the settings box).

Place Active Point The Place Active Point command places one copy of the active point (element, character, or cell) at a time. To do so, click the Place Active Point icon in the Points sub-palette (see Figure 7–21), or key-in at the uSTN> field, **place point** (or **pla poi**), and press [ENTER]. Micro-Station prompts:

> *Enter point origin* (Enter a data point to place the active point.)

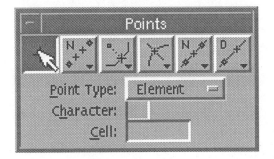

FIGURE 7–21   Invoking the Place Active Point command from the Points sub-palette.

This command remains active and you can continue placing active points.

Construct Points Between Data Points The Construct Points Between Data Points command will place a specified number of points (element, character, or cell) between two data points. The number of points placed include the two placed on your data points.

To place a series of points between two data points, click the Construct Points Between Data Points icon in the Points sub-palette (see Figure 7–22), then key-in the number of points in the edit field. Alternately, you can key-in at the uSTN> field, **construct point between** (or **con po b**), and press [ENTER]. With the key-in, you also key-in the number of points at the uSTN> field. MicroStation prompts:

> *Enter first point* (Place a data point.)
> *Enter end point* (Place a data point.)

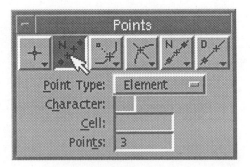

FIGURE 7–22   Invoking the Construct Points Between Data Points command from the Points sub-palette.

After you place the first set of points, you can continue placing additional sets. Each set will use the last data point of the previous set as its starting point. To start over with a first data point again, click the Reset button on your pointing device. See Figure 7–23 for an example of placing 10 points between two data points.

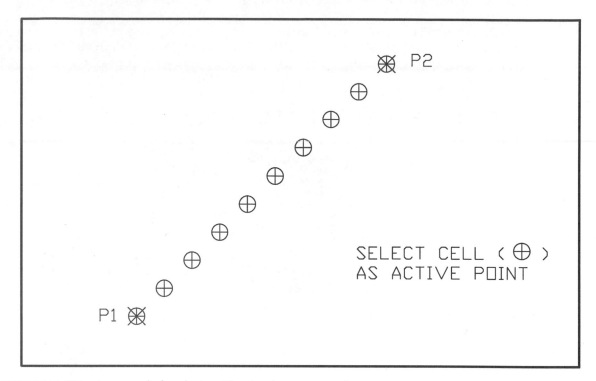

FIGURE 7–23 An example for placing 10 points between two data points.

Project Active Point Onto Element The Project Active Point Onto Element command places the active point (element, character, or cell) on the selected element at the point projected from the acceptance data point. To do so, click the Project Active Point Onto Element icon in the Points sub-palette (see Figure 7–24), or key-in at the uSTN> field, **construct point project** (or **con po p**), and press [ENTER]. MicroStation prompts:

Identify element (Click the Data button on the element onto which you want to project the active point.)
Accept/Reject (Select next input) (Place a second data point to accept the element and define the point from which the point will be projected.)

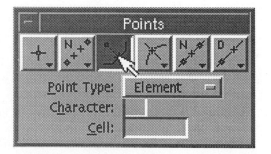

FIGURE 7–24 Invoking the Project Active Point Onto Element command from the Points sub-palette.

The second data button does two things: it accepts the element you identified, and it can identify the next element to which you want to project a point.

If your accept Data button does not identify another element, MicroStation displays the message, *Element not found*, in the error field of the Command Window. Ignore the message. See Figure 7–25 for an example of how to place an active point project onto an element.

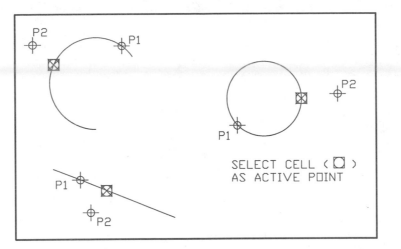

FIGURE 7–25   An example for placing an active point projected onto an element.

> **NOTE:** The only purpose of the first data point is to identify the element to which the projection will be made. There is no need to use the tentative button when identifying the element. The second data point is the one that may need precise placement.

Construct Active Point at Intersection The Construct Active Point at Intersection command places an active point (element, character, or cell) at the intersection of two elements. To do so, click the Construct Active Point at Intersection icon in the Points sub-palette (see Figure 7–26), or key-in at the uSTN> field, **construct point intersection** (or **con po i**), and press [ENTER]. Micro-Station prompts:

Select element for intersection (Click the Data button on one of the two intersecting elements.)
Select element for intersection (Click the Data button on the other intersecting element.)
Accept/Initiate intersection (Click the Data button anywhere in the view to Accept and to place the active point at the intersection.)

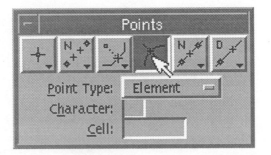

FIGURE 7–26   Invoking the Construct Active Point At Intersection command from the Points sub-palette.

The acceptance data point only initiates placement of the point; it does not identify another element. See Figure 7–27 for an example of how to place an active point at an intersection of two elements.

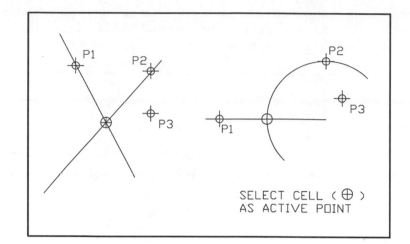

FIGURE 7–27 An example for placing an active point at an intersection of two elements.

> **NOTE:** If the two elements intersect more than once (such as a line crossing a circle), identify the two elements close to the intersection where you want the point to be placed. There is no need to use the tentative button. Just place the Data button close to the intersection.

Construct Points Along The Construct Points Along command places a set of active points (elements, characters, or cells) equally spaced along an element between two data points on the element.

To place a series of points along an element, click the Construct Active Points Along icon in the Points sub-palette (see Figure 7–28), then key-in the number of points in the edit field in the sub-palette. Alternately you can key-in at the uSTN> field, **construct points along** (or **con po a**), and press ⏎. If you key-in the command, you must also key-in the number of points at the uSTN> field. MicroStation prompts:

Identify element (Click the Data button at the point on the element where you want the set of points to start.)
Enter end point (Click the Data button at the point on the element where you want the last point in the set placed.)

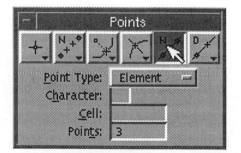

FIGURE 7–28 Invoking the Construct Active Points Along command from the Points sub-palette.

You can continue placing points along elements, and, if necesssary, you can also change the active point at any time while placing them. See Figure 7–29 for an example of how to place ten points along an element between two data points.

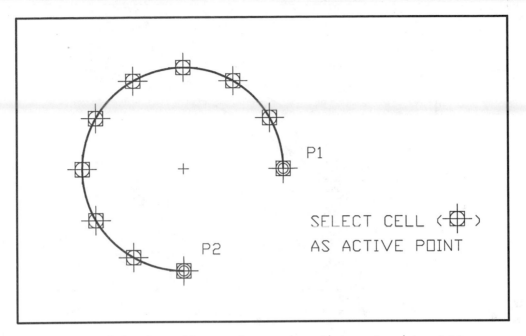

FIGURE 7–29   An example for placing 10 points along an element between two data points.

Construct Active Point at @Dist Along Element The Construct Active Point at @Dist Along Element command places the active point (element, character, or cell) at a keyed-in distance along an element from the data point that identified the element.

To place a point at a specified distance along an element, click the Construct Active Point at @Dist Along Element icon in the Points sub-palette (see Figure 7–30), then key-in the distance in the Distance edit field that appears in the sub-palette. Alternately, you can key-in at the uSTN> field, **construct point distance** (or **con po d**), and press ▨. If you invoke the command with the key-in, you must also key-in the distance at the uSTN> field. MicroStation prompts:

> *Identify element* (Click the Data button on the element at the point at which to start the distance calculation.)
> *Accept/Reject (Select next input)* (Place a data point to initiate placing the point on the element at a specified distance.)

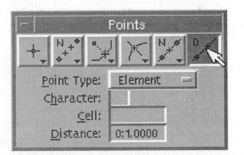

FIGURE 7–30   Invoking the Construct Active Point at @Dist Along Element command from the Points sub-palette.

You can continue selecting elements along which you want to place a point, and you can change the distance at any time while using the command. See Figure 7–31 for an example of how to place a point at a specified distance along an element.

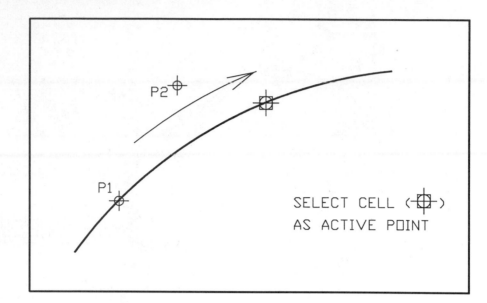

FIGURE 7–31   An example for placing a point at a specified distance along an element.

CELL HOUSEKEEPING

You have seen several commands that place copies of cells in your design file. Now let's look at additional commands that affect cells already placed in your design file. The available commands include:

Identify Cell displays the name and other related information of the selected cell.

Replace Cell replaces a cell in the design file with another cell with the same name from the currently attached cell library.

Drop Complex Status breaks up a cell into its individual elements. The elements lose their identity as a cell.

Drop Complex Status of Fence Contents breaks up all cells contained in a fence to their individual elements. The elements lose their identities as cells.

Fast Cells View speeds up view updates by displaying only a box showing the location of all cells in the view, rather than the cell elements.

Identify Cell   The Identify Cell command tells you the name of a cell in your design file and the levels the cell is on. It is useful when you want to use a cell already placed in your design file as a Terminator cell or Point cell, but you don't know the cell's name. The information is displayed in the Status field of the Command Window.

To determine the name of a cell placed in your design file, click the Identify Cell icon in the Cells sub-palette (see Figure 7–32) or key-in at the uSTN> field, **identify cell** (or **id**), and press 🔳. MicroStation prompts:

> *Identify cell* (Identify the cell with the Data button, and the information regarding the cell is displayed in the Command Window.)
> *Accept/Reject (Select next input)* (Click the Reset button.)

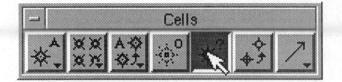

FIGURE 7–32   Invoking the Identify Cell command from the Cells sub-palette.

> **NOTE:** The first Data button causes the cell name and levels to appear in the Status field. If you select another cell with the second Data button, the information provided in the Command Window may tell you about two different cells which may be a little confusing. Clicking the Reset button after selecting the first cell avoids that confusion.

Replace Cell The Replace Cell command replaces a cell in your design file with the cell of the same name from the attached cell library. It is useful when the design of a cell is changed and there are copies of the old cell in your design file.

To replace a cell, click the Replace Cell icon in the cells sub-palette (see Figure 7–33), or key-in at the uSTN> field, **replace cell** (or **rep**), and press 🔳. MicroStation prompts:

> *Identify element* (Identify the cell with the Data button.)
> *Accept/Reject (Select next input)* (Accept with the Data button to replace the cell.)

FIGURE 7–33   Invoking the Replace Cell command from the Cells sub-palette.

The second data point also can identify another cell to be replaced.

If you need to replace a shared cell (more of this later in this chapter), identify one of them and MicroStation will replace all the instances of the shared cell with the same name instantaneously.

> **NOTE:** The replaced cell may shift position in your design file. That happens when the new cell's origin point was not defined in the same relationship to the cell elements as the old cell's origin.

Drop Complex Status The cells placed in your design file are "complex shapes" that act like one element when manipulated. If you need to change the shape of a cell in your design file, you must first "drop" the cell to break it into separate elements. The Drop Complex Status command does that for you. A dropped cell loses its identity as a cell and becomes separate, unrelated elements.

To drop complex status of a cell, click the Drop Complex Status icon in the Drop sub-palette located under the Main palette (see Figure 7–34), or key-in at the uSTN> field, **drop complex** (or **rd**), and press ⏎. MicroStation prompts:

> *Identify element* (Identify the cell you want to drop with the Data button.)
> *Accept/Reject (Select next input)* (Accept with the Data button to drop the cell.)

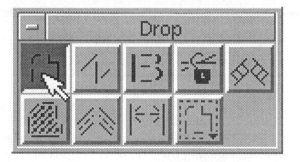

FIGURE 7–34 Invoking the Drop Complex command from the Drop sub-palette.

The second data point initiates the drop action and can also select another cell to be dropped.

Drop Complex Status of Fence Contents The Drop Complex Status of Fence Contents command breaks all the cells enclosed in a fence into separate elements. Before you select this command, place a fence and select the appropriate fence lock that encloses all the cells you want to drop.

To drop complex status of a group of cells, click on the Drop Complex Status of Fence Contents icon in the Drop sub-palette (see Figure 7–35), or key-in at the uSTN> field, **fence drop complex** (or **fen rd**), and press ⏎. MicroStation prompts:

> *Accept/Reject fence contents* (Accept with the Data button anywhere in the view to drop the cells.)

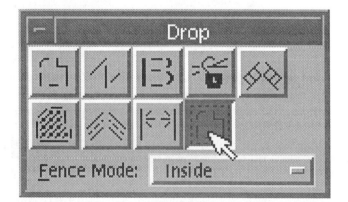

FIGURE 7–35 Invoking the Drop Complex Status of Fence Contents command from the Drop sub-palette.

All cells enclosed in the fence are broken into separate elements.

> **NOTE:** Whenever you want to create a cell that includes another existing cell, drop the cell before it is included in the creation of new cell. This prevents accidentally creating a "nested cell." A nested cell is a cell that is within another cell. Cells that contain nested cells only point to the library location of the nested cells. They do not actually store the nested cell elements with their elements. If you delete a cell from the cell library that is nested in other cells, you also delete part of all the cells that refer to it.

Fast Cells View Numerous cells in a view may cause view updates to be completed too slowly. If you see that happening, you can speed up updating by turning on the Fast Cells View attribute. When that attribute is ON for a view, a box is displayed at each cell location, rather than the cell elements. The box is the same size as the cell.

To turn on the Fast Cells View attribute:

1. Open the View Attributes setting box from the View pull-down menu in the Command Window.
2. Turn ON the Fast Cells toggle button.
3. Check the View options menu, and, if necessary, change it to the number of the view where you want the Fast Cells View attribute to be ON.
4. Click the Apply button to turn on the attribute for the selected view.
5. If you no longer need the View Attributes settings box, close it.

The Fast Cells View attribute stays ON for the selected view until you turn it OFF or exit from MicroStation. To make it permanent, select Save Settings from the File pull-down menu.

> **NOTE:** Turn OFF Fast Cells View before you plot.

LIBRARY HOUSEKEEPING

You've seen how to place cells in your design file and take care of them. Now let's look at some housekeeping commands that help you take care of the cells in the attached cell library. The discussion includes explanations of how to

- Edit a cell's name and description.
- Delete a cell from the Cell Library.
- Compress the attached Cell Library.
- Create a new version of a cell.

All these tools affect the cells in the attached library, not the cells in your design file.

Edit a Cell's Name and Description The Edit Cell Information dialog box, which is available from the Cell Library settings box, allows you to change a cell's name and description. If you need to create a new version of a cell, and you want to keep the old one around, rename it before creating the new version. If the person who designed the cell failed to provide a description, you can provide one to help other users of the cell library figure out what is in it. Following is the step-by-step procedure for renaming a cell and/or adding or changing the cell description:

1. If the Cell Library settings box is not already open, select cells from the Settings pull-down menu to open it.
2. Select the cell you want to edit from the Cells List.
3. Click the Edit button to open the Edit Cell Information dialog box (see Figure 7–36).
4. Make the necessary changes for cell name and description in the edit fields of the Edit Cell Information dialog box.
5. Click the Modify button in the Edit Cell Information dialog box to make the necessary changes.

```
┌──────────────────────────────────────────────┐
│               Edit Cell Information            │
│                                                │
│    Name:  │ RES        │                       │
│                                                │
│  Description: │ THIS IS RESISTOR ON LEFT      │ │
│                                                │
│        ┌─────────┐          ┌─────────┐        │
│        │ Modify  │          │ Cancel  │        │
│        └─────────┘          └─────────┘        │
└──────────────────────────────────────────────┘
```

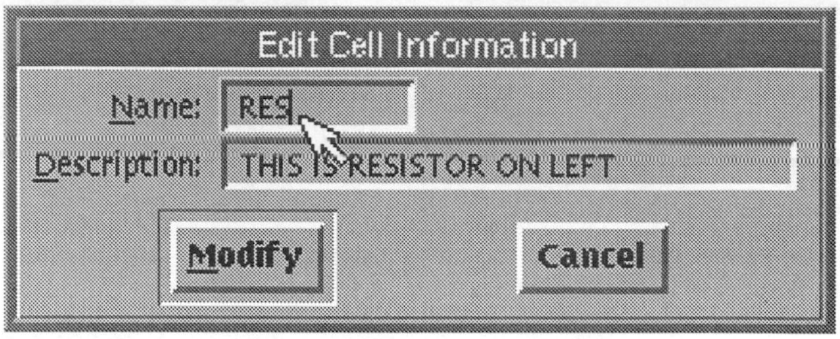

FIGURE 7–36 Edit Cell Information Dialog box.

> **NOTE:** Changing the cell name and description does not affect the cells already in the design file (or any other design file). They keep their old names.

Alternate Method To rename a cell, key-in at the uSTN> field, **CR=<old>,<new>**, and press ⏎. Replace <old> with the cell's current name and <new> with the new cell name. The key-in only changes the cell names. You cannot use a key-in to change descriptions.

Delete a Cell from the Library If a cell becomes obsolete, or if it was not drawn correctly, it can be deleted from the cell library using the Delete button in the Cell Library setting box. When you ask to delete a cell, MicroStation opens an Alert dialog box to ask you if you really want to delete the cell. Following is the step-by-step procedure for deleting a cell from the Cell Library:

1. If the Cell Library settings box is not already open, select Cells from the Settings pull-down menu to open it.
2. Select the cell you want to delete from the Cells List.
3. Click the Delete button.
4. The Alert dialog box opens to ask you if you really want to delete the cell.
5. If you really want to delete it, click the OK button. If you selected the wrong cell or change your mind, click the Cancel button.

This procedure deletes a cell from the Cell Library. It does not delete copies of the cell already placed in the design file (or any other design file).

Alternate Method To delete a cell, key-in at the uSTN> field, **CD=<name>**, and press ⏎. Replace <name> with the cell's name.

When you use the key-in to delete a cell, MicroStation does not open the Alert window to ask you if you really want to delete the cell.

> *NOTE:* The UNDO command will not undo deleting a cell from the attached library.

Compress the Attached Cell Library Deleting a cell from a cell library does not really delete it. The cell is marked as deleted and is no longer available, but its elements still take up space in the cell library file on the disk. To get rid of the no longer usable cell elements, you must compress the Cell Library with the Compress Library option in the Cell Library settings box's File pull-down menu. Following is the step-by-step procedure to compress the Cell Library:

1. If the Cell Library settings box is not already open, select Cells from the Settings pull-down menu to open it.
2. From the File pull-down menu in the Cell Library settings box, select Compress.

The attached cell library is compressed and the status message indicates that the Cell Library is compressed.

Alternate Method The option to compress the attached cell library is also available in the Cells sub-menu from the File pull-down menu in the Command Window. This method does not open the Cell Library settings box.

Create a New Version of a Cell Occasionally the need to replace a cell with an updated version of that cell will arise. The geometric layout of the object represented by the cell may have changed, or you may have discovered a mistake was made when the cell was drawn.

Following is the step-by-step procedure to create a new version of a cell:

1. Place a copy of the cell in a design file that has the same working units as the design file in which the cell was created.
2. Drop the cell.
3. Delete the old cell from the library or rename it.
4. Make the required changes to the cell elements.
5. If possible, place the cell origin at the same place it was in the old cell.
6. Create the new cell from the modified elements.
7. If you deleted the old cell, compress the library.
8. If you had already placed copies of the cell in your design files, use the Replace Cell command to replace those copies with the new version of the cell.

SHARED CELLS

Thus far, each time you placed a cell, a separate copy of the cell's elements was placed in the design file. That uses up a lot of disk space in a design file that contains many cells.

Shared cells can help with the disk space problem. Each time you place a shared cell, the placement refers back to the shared copy rather than placing more elements in your design file. No matter how many copies of a shared cell you place, only one copy is actually in your design file.

When you declare a cell to be shared, MicroStation places a copy of it in your design file. You can have the shared cell's elements stored in your design file even though no copies of the cell have ever been placed in the design plane. Later, when you use the cell placement commands, the placements refer to the locally stored cell elements, rather than the copy in the library. Shared cells can be placed even when no cell library is attached.

Let's look how you can

- Turn on the shared cell feature.
- Determine which cells are shared.
- Declare a cell to be shared.
- Place shared cells.
- Turn a shared cell into an unshared cell.
- Delete the shared cell copy from your design file.

Turn on the Shared Cell Feature The Use Shared Cells check button in the Cell Library settings box turns the shared cell feature ON or OFF. To turn on the feature, depress the button (see Figure 7–37). Each time you click the button, you toggle between using shared cells and not using them.

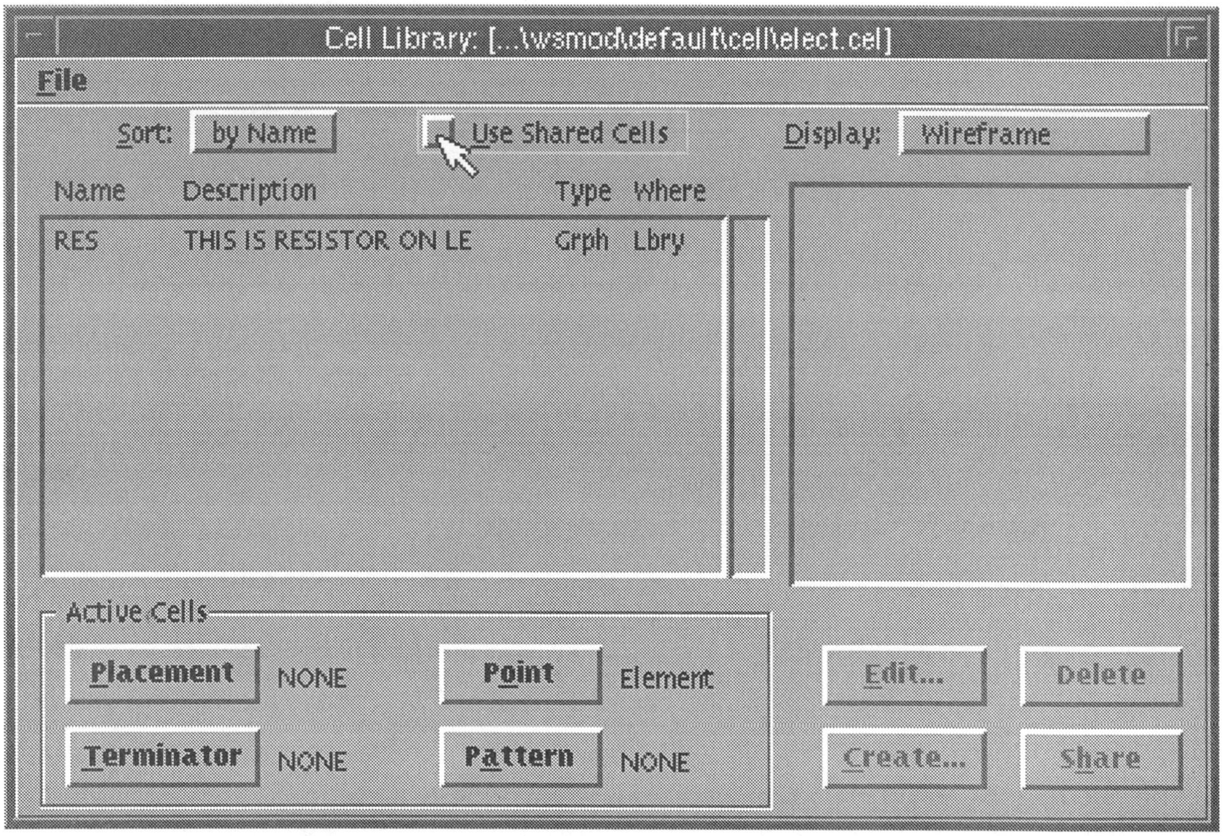

FIGURE 7–37 Displaying the status of the toggle button for the Use Shared Cells in the Cell Library Settings box.

Determine Which Cells Are Shared When the shared cells feature is ON, all shared cells in your design file show up in the Cells List in the Cell Library settings box (see Figure 7–37). You can find the shared cells by viewing the Where column in the Cells List area. Shared cells are indicated by "Shrd" in that column.

If the shared cell is also in the currently attached cell library, the list shows the shared copy in your design file—not the one in the library.

Each time you select a shared cell in your design file, the Status area of the Command Window will tell you it is a shared cell.

Declare a Cell to Be Shared Use the shared button located in the bottom right in the Cell Library settings box to place copies of the shared cells in your design file. Following is the step-by-step procedure:

1. If the Cell Library settings box is not already open, select Cells from the Settings pull-down menu to open it.
2. If the shared cells feature is not currently active, click on the Use Shared Cells button to turn it ON.
3. Select the cell you want to be shared from the Cells List.
4. Click the Shared button.

When you click the shared button, Shrd appears in the Where column of the selected cell, and a copy of the cell is placed in your current design file.

You just stored a shared copy of the cell in your design file without actually placing the cell. This is a handy way to create a seed file for a group of design files that will use the same set of cells. The procedure includes creating a new design file, attaching the cell library, and declaring all required cells shared. Then you can create new design files by copying the new seed file. Each copied file contains a copy of the elements that make up the shared cells.

Place Shared Cells When the Use Shared Cells button in the Cell Library settings box is set to ON (depressed), all cell placement tools place shared cells. Placing a cell makes the cell shared, even if you have not declared the cell to be shared previously.

The commands that place the active Placement, Terminator, and Point cells all work the same for shared cells as they do for unshared cells. The Replace Cell command automatically replaces all the copies of the shared cell when you identify one of them.

Turn a Shared Cell Into an Unshared Cell A cell that was placed shared can be turned into an unshared cell (with its own copy of the cell elements). The command that does it is only available as a key-in. Key-in at the uSTN> field, **drop sharecell** (or **dr sh**), and press [ENTER]. MicroStation prompts:

Identify element (Identify the cell with the Data button.)
Accept/Reject (Select next input) (Accept with the Data button.)

The second data point causes the cell to be made unshared and also can select another cell. If no cell is selected with the second data point, the error message, *Element not found*, appears in the Command Window. Ignore it.

> **NOTE:** Local cells cannot be turned into shared cells.

Delete the Shared Cell Copy from Your Design File The placements of shared cells can be deleted like any other element, but the actual shared cell copy takes a little more work to delete. It is done in the Cell Library settings box using the Delete cell button.

Here is the procedure for deleting the shared cell elements from your design file:

1. Either delete all placements of the shared cell, or make them into unshared cells (see above).
2. If the Cell Library settings box is not already open, select Cells from the Settings pull-down menu to open it.
3. If the Use Shared Cell button is OFF, turn it ON.
4. Select the shared cell you want to delete from the Cells List and make sure the cell has Shrd in the Where column.
5. Click the Delete button (located in the bottom right of the Cell Library Settings box).
6. The Alert dialog box opens to ask you if you really want to delete the cell. If you really want to delete it, click the OK button.

If you selected the wrong cell, click the Cancel button. This procedure deletes only the copy of the shared cell elements in your design file. It does not delete anything from the attached cell library.

> **NOTE:** If there are still any placements of the shared cell in your design file when you try to delete the shared cell, an Alert dialog box appears with a message stating that you cannot delete the cell. In this case the Alert dialog box's Cancel and OK buttons only close the box—click on either one of them.

EXERCISES

Exercises 7-1 through 7-4

Create all the Piping Flowsheet symbols shown in Figure 7–38 as cells and store it in a cell library called piping.cel. Lay out the objects shown in Exercises 7–1 through 7–4 by placing cells at appropriate places.

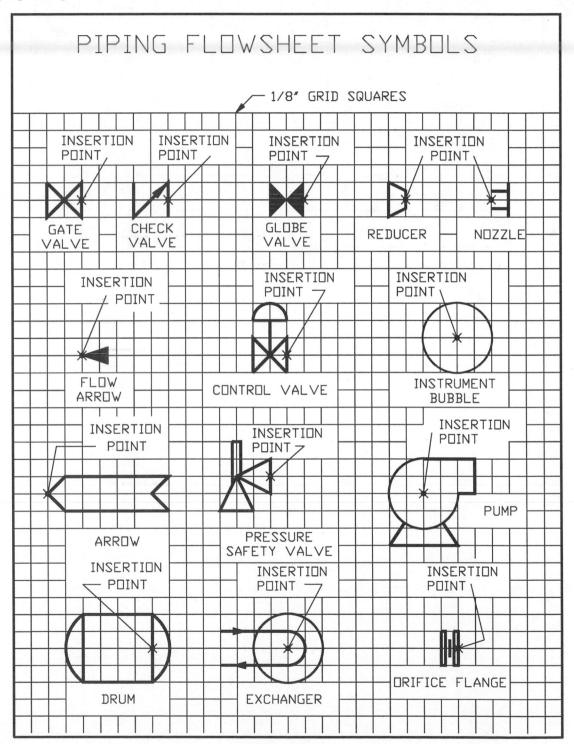

FIGURE 7-38

Exercise 7-1

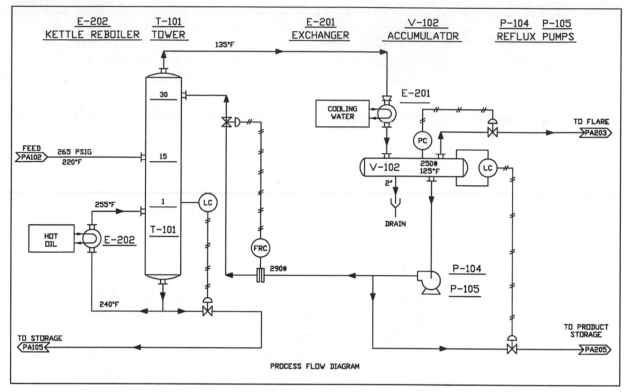

PROCESS FLOW DIAGRAM

Exercise 7-2

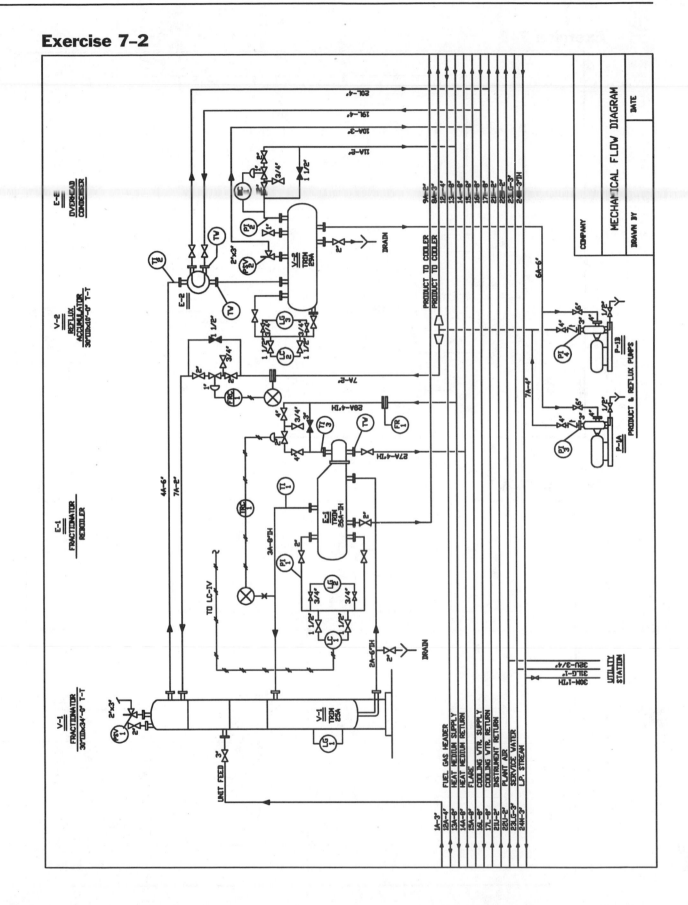

Exercise 7–3

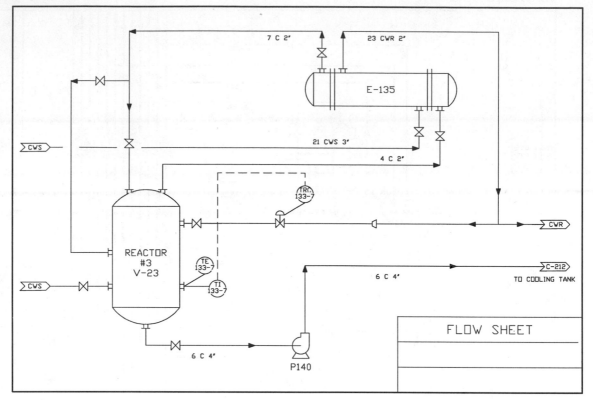

Exercise 7–4

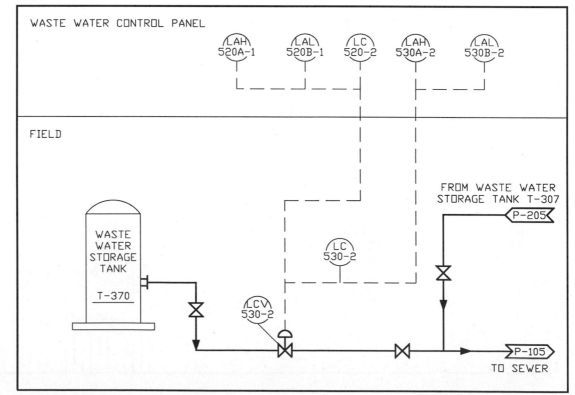

Exercises 7–5 through 7–8

Create all the Electrical symbols shown in Figure 7–39 as cells and store it in a cell library called elect.cel. Lay out the objects shown in Exercises 7–5 through 7–8 by placing cells at appropriate places.

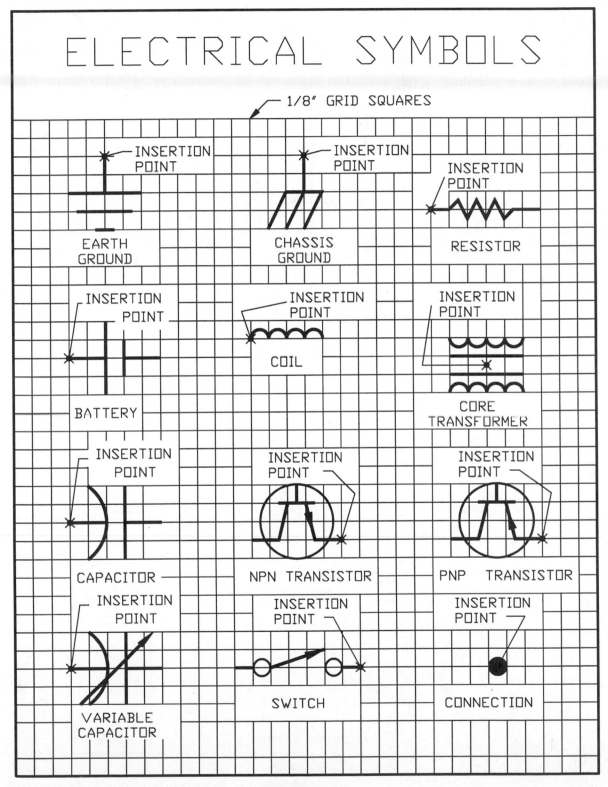

FIGURE 7–39

Exercise 7–5

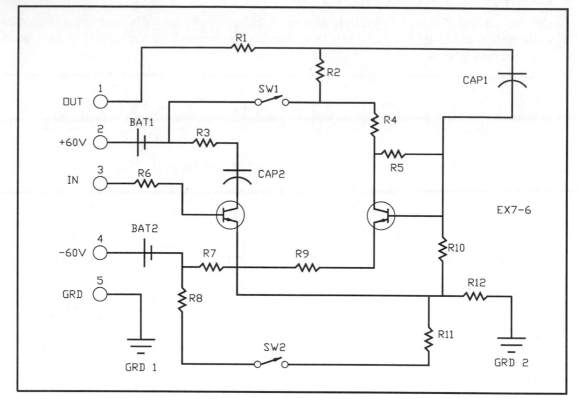

Exercise 7–6

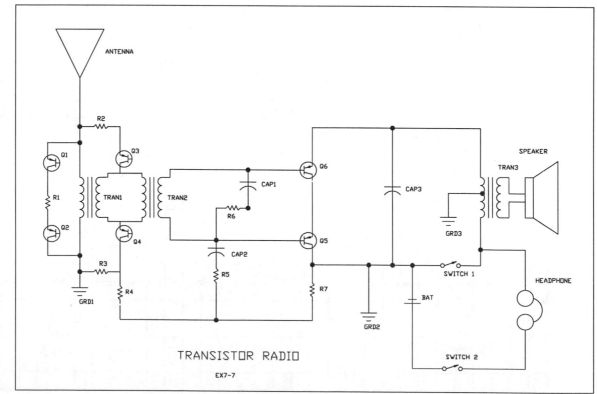

Exercise 7-7

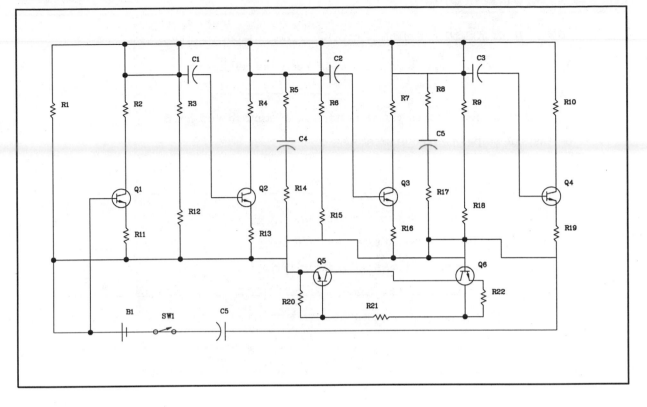

Exercise 7-8

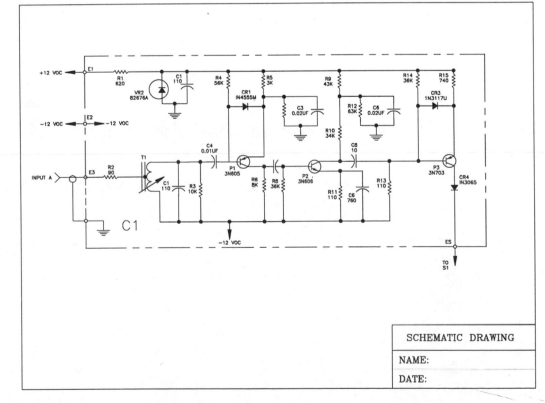

REVIEW QUESTIONS

Write your answers in the spaces provided:

1. Explain briefly the difference between a cell and cell library.

   _____

2. How many cell libraries can you attach at one time to a design file? _____

3. List the steps involved in creating a cell.

   _____

   _____

4. What is the alternate key-in AC= used for? _____

5. What is the file that has an extension of .CEL? _____

6. What does it mean to place a cell ABSOLUTE?

   _____

7. What does it mean to place a cell RELATIVE?

   _____

8. Explain briefly the differences between Graphic cell and Point cell.

   _____

   _____

9. How many cells you can store in a library? _____

10. What is the purpose of defining an active cell as a terminator?

    _____

11. What is the purpose of turning ON the Fast Cells View Attribute?

    _____

12. Explain briefly the benefits of declaring a cell as a shared cell.

    _____

    _____

PROJECT EXERCISE

In this project you apply MicroStation concepts and skills discussed in chapters 1 through 7 to create the Electrical schematic as shown in Figure P7–1.

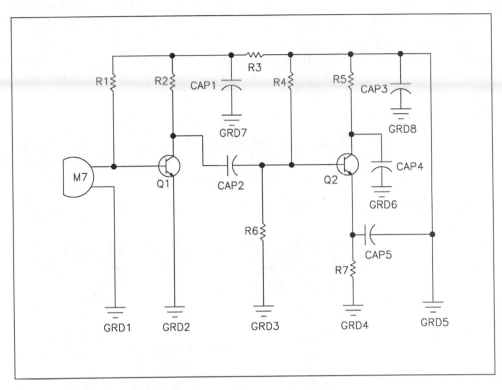

FIGURE P7–1   Completed Project Design.

To draw the schematic, you will be creating the cells as shown in Figure P7–2.

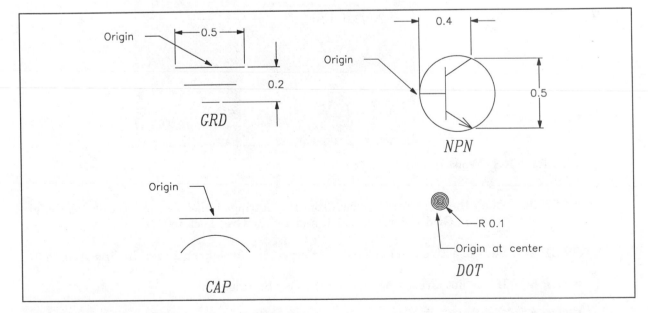

FIGURE P7–2   Creating the cells for the schematic.

> **NOTE:** The instructions for this project are designed to provide practice in the concepts presented in chapter 7. It is not necessarily the most efficient way to draw the design.

The new concepts introduced in this project are:

- Creating a Cell Library
- Creating cells and storing in the Cell Library

GETTING STARTED

STEP 1: Create a new design file named CH7.DGN using the SEED2D.DGN seed file from the MicroStation Manager dialog box if you just started MicroStation, or from the New option in the File pull-down menu of the MicroStation Command Window.

STEP 2: Set the design's working units as shown in Figure P7–3.

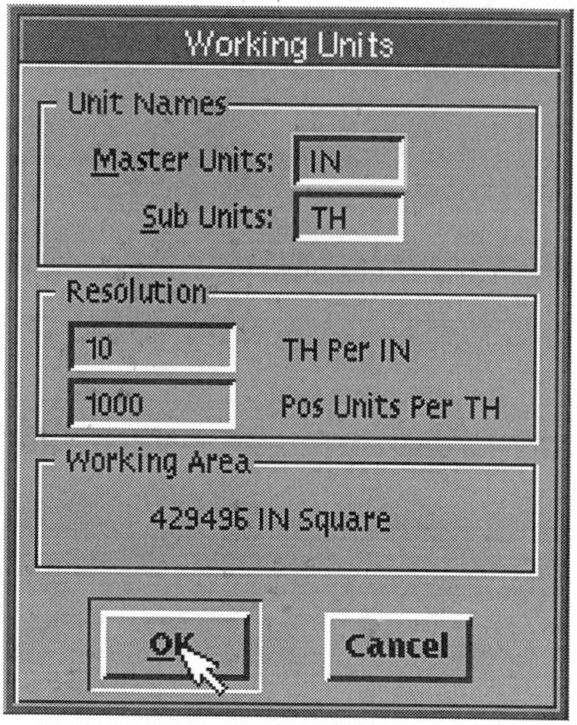

FIGURE P7–3 Working Units dialog box.

STEP 3: Open the Grid Settings box from the Settings pull-down menu and set the grid unit to .125 in., Grid Reference to 1 ft and set the Grid Lock to ON.

STEP 4: Set the active level to 1, color to green, line weight to 2 and the line style to 0.

STEP 5: If it is not already open, open the Tool Settings Box.

STEP 6: Invoke Save Settings command from the File pull-down menu to save the settings.

STEP 7: Create a new cell library file named CH7.CEL using the SEED2D.CEL seed file.

STEP 8: Using Figure P7–2 as a reference, draw the objects that are to be used to create cells. Draw all lines and the arc such that their end points are on grid. Use Place Arc by Edge to draw the arc in the capacitor. Draw the lines in the NPN Transistor first, then use Place Circle by Edge to draw the transistor circle. The Dot is a series of six parallel circles.

STEP 9: Following are the steps to create a cell called GRD to include the symbol as shown in Figure P7–2:

- Place a fence block around the GRD symbol.
- Select Inside fence contents lock.
- Invoke the Define Origin command from the Cells sub-palette.
- Place cell origin as shown in Figure P7–2 for GRD symbol.
- Click the Create Cell button in the Cell Library settings box.
- Key-in GRD in the Name edit field and press ⌨TAB key.
- Key-in Ground Symbol in the Description edit field and press ⌨TAB key.
- Select Point cell type from the option menu.
- Click the Create button or press ⌨ENTER key to create the cell. The cell is added to the cell library.

STEP 10: Create three additional cells as shown in Figure P7–2 by providing the cell names and descriptions as follows:

NPNNPN	Transistor Symbol
CAP	Capacitor Symbol
DOT	Point Symbol

STEP 11: Delete all the elements from your design.

STEP 12: Using Figure P7–1 as a reference, draw the electrical schematic diagram. Place the cells at appropriate places by using the Place Cell command.

STEP 13: Invoke Save Settings command from the File pull-down menu to save the settings.

STEP 14: If you are finished with MicroStation, exit the design file.

8

PATTERNING

•••••••••••••••••••••

For various purposes, drafters and designers use repeating patterns to fill regions in a drawing. In a cutaway (cross-sectional) view, hatch patterns help the viewer differentiate among components of an assembly and help indicate what the material is made of. In surface views, patterns depict material and add to the readability of a view. In general, patterns help drafters and designers communicate information through the drawing. Because drawing patterns is a repetitive task, it is an ideal computer-aided drafting application.

After completing this chapter, you will be able to:

- Control the display of pattern view.
- Select the area to be patterned—Element, Fence, Intersection, Union, Difference, Flood, and Points.
- Select Area Patterning—Hatch Area, Cross-hatch Area, Pattern Area.
- Select Snapping to Patterns.
- Select Associative Patterning.
- Match Pattern Attributes.
- Fill in an element.

PATTERNS VIEW ATTRIBUTE

Patterning can place so many elements in a design that view updates may start taking an unacceptable time to complete. To overcome that, MicroStation provides the pattern view attribute to turn the display of pattern elements ON and OFF.

When you need to place patterns, the first thing to do before starting is to make sure the Patterns View Attribute is set to ON for the view you are working in. If it is OFF, you will not see the patterns you place, and they will not plot. Not seeing anything happen when you place a pattern can be confusing. The old maxim, "If at first you don't succeed, try, try again," might lead to placing the pattern several times before you realize that Patterns View is set to OFF.

To determine the status of the Patterns View Attribute, invoke the View Attribute settings box from the View pull-down menu. Your screen will display a View Attributes settings box similar to the one shown in Figure 8–1. Make sure the Patterns View Attribute is turned to ON (button depressed) for the view you are working in. The view number is displayed in the View menu at the top of the settings box. If you want to apply for all the views, click All rather than Apply.

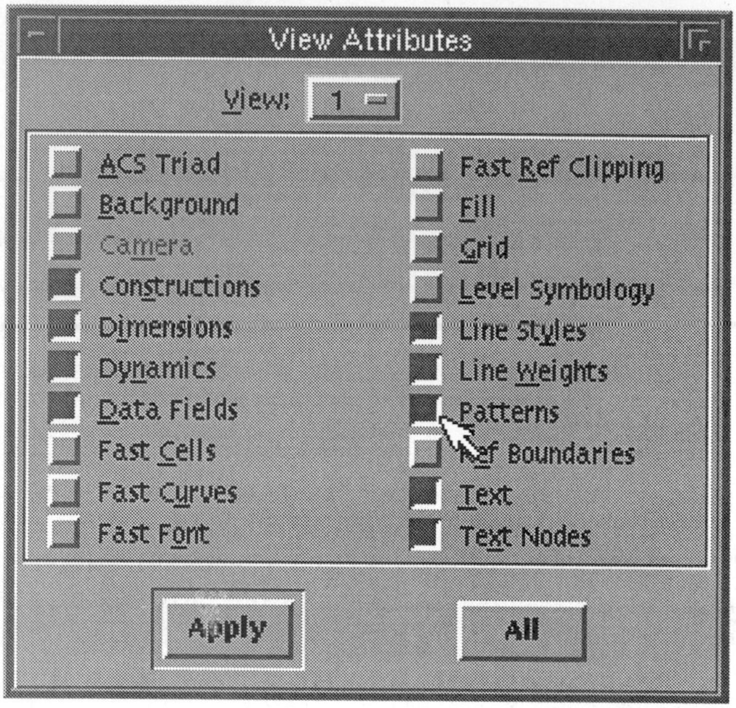

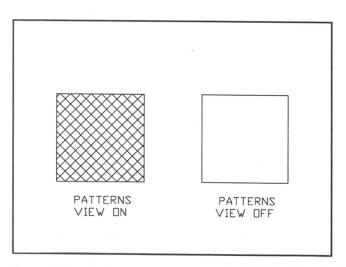

FIGURE 8–1 View Attribute Settings box pointing to the status of the Patterns display.

When you turn ON the Patterns View Attribute, the patterns you already placed will appear in the view. Of course, if you have not placed any patterns, nothing will change in the view. See Figure 8–2 for an example of a pattern display when Patterns View is ON/OFF.

FIGURE 8–2 Displaying the visibility of the patterns when the Patterns display is turned ON/OFF.

The Patterns View Attribute stays ON for the selected view until you turn it OFF or exit from MicroStation. To keep it ON permanently for the current design file, select Save Settings from the File pull-down menu.

AREA PATTERNING

MicroStation provides three sets of commands (Hatch Area, Crosshatch Area, and Pattern Area), that allow you to place patterns in the specified area or region. The commands are located in the Patterning palette (see Figure 8–3) invoked from the Palettes pull-down menu. The Hatch Area command allows you to specify a simple pattern of parallel lines at the spacing and angle desired. The Crosshatch Area command allows you to specify two groups of parallel lines at the spacing and angle desired. The Pattern Area command fills the area with tiled copies of an active pattern cell at the spacing and angle desired. Figure 8–4 shows an example of Hatch, Crosshatch, and Area Pattern.

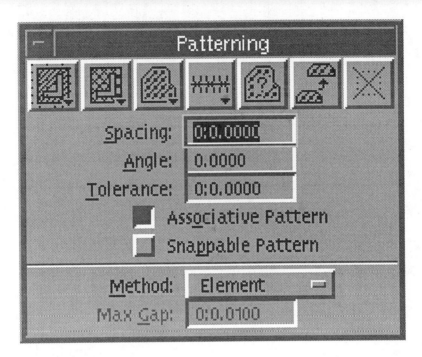

FIGURE 8–3 Patterning palette.

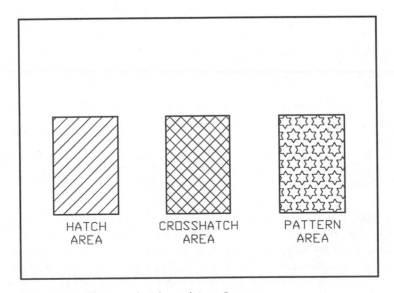

FIGURE 8–4 An example for Hatch, Crosshatch, and Area Pattern.

AREA TO BE PATTERNED

Before you can invoke one of the three commands for patterning, you have to determine the area to be patterned. There are seven different methods by which you can select the area (or region) to pattern. The option button provided in the palette, as shown in Figure 8–5, allows you to select the method by which an area will be patterned. Following are the available methods under the option button:

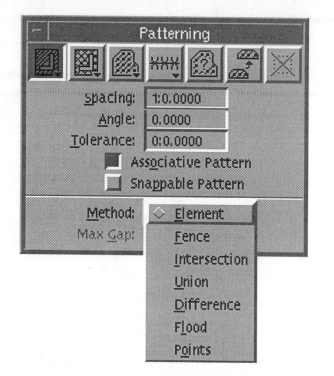

FIGURE 8–5 Listing of the various options available in the Method options menu located in the Patterning palette.

Element The element option allows you to pattern the interior of a shape, ellipse, closed b-spline curve, or between components of a multi-line. MicroStation allows you to identify only one element, and it has to be a closed element.

Fence The fence option allows you to pattern the area enclosed in a fence block or fence shape. Once the area enclosed with a fence is patterned, you can remove the fence.

Intersection The intersection option allows you to pattern a composite area formed from the area that is common to two closed elements.

Union The union option allows you to pattern a composite area formed in such a way that there is no duplication between two closed elements. The total resulting area can be equal to or less than the sum of the areas in the original closed elements.

Difference The difference option allows you to pattern a composite area formed from a closed element after removing from it any area that it has in common with a second element. If the entire area of the second element is contained in the first element, what is left is the first element minus the area of the second element. However, if only part of the area of the second element is contained within the first element, only the part that is duplicated in the two elements is subtracted.

Figure 8–6 shows examples for placing a pattern when Intersection, Union, and Difference options are selected.

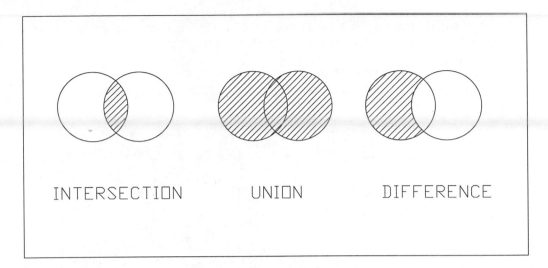

FIGURE 8–6   An example for placing a pattern when Intersection, Union, and Difference options are selected.

Flood The flood option allows you to pattern a closed area made up of one or more elements. MicroStation prompts you to pick a point inside the closed area (or region). When you place the first data point inside the area to be patterned, MicroStation searches for the elements that enclose the area and highlights pieces of the elements as it finds them.

Defining the area can take a long time when the area contains non-linear elements (such as curve strings). While MicroStation defines the area, it displays a small spinner in the Error field of the Command Window. When the spinner stops spinning, the area has been defined.

> **NOTE:** Make sure the area you select is completely enclosed by connecting or intersecting elements. If not, MicroStation may take a very long time to realize it cannot enclose the area.

Points The points option allows you to pattern a closed area defined by a set of data points. As you define the points (vertices), a temporary polygon is drawn. The polygon can be of any shape, and once you define the boundary and press Reset, MicroStation patterns the defined area.

Now let's look at how to use the three area patterning commands to pattern using each of the patterning method described above.

HATCH AREA

The Hatch Area command places a set of parallel lines in the area you select. Before you identify the area to hatch, you must tell MicroStation how far apart to place the lines and at what angle to rotate them.

To hatch an area at the desired spacing and angle, invoke the Hatch Area command from the Patterning sub-palette, or key-in at the uSTN> field, **hatch** (or **ha**), and press ⏎. MicroStation prompts depends on the patterning method you select. Whatever method you use, you must specify the line spacing in MU:SU:PU and the angle in the appropriate edit fields located in the palette. Leave the tolerance set to 0.

To hatch a closed element, click the Hatch Area icon in the Pattern palette, and select Element from the Method options menu (see Figure 8–7). MicroStation prompts:

> *Identify element* (Identify the closed element to be hatched.)
> *Accept @pattern intersection point* (Place data point to start hatching.)

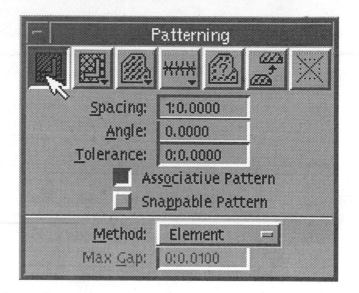

FIGURE 8–7   Invoking the Hatch Area command from the Patterning palette.

The second data point starts the hatching and defines a point through which one of the hatching lines will pass. If the second data point is placed outside the element, it defines an imaginary extension of the hatching lines. Figure 8–8 shows an example of hatching an element.

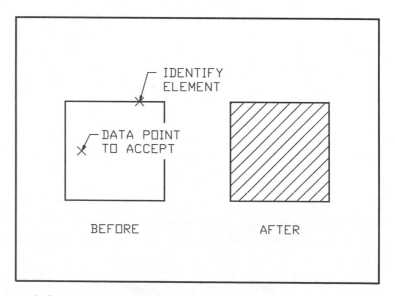

FIGURE 8–8   An example for hatching an element.

> **NOTE:** If the line spacing is 0 when you try to start the hatching, no hatching is placed, and the message, *Active pattern spacing not set*, appears in the Error field of the Command Window.

To hatch a composite area formed by the intersection of two elements, click the Hatch Area icon in the Pattern palette, and select Intersection from the Method options menu. MicroStation prompts:

Identify element (Identify one of the elements.)
Accept/Reject (Select next input) (Identify the other element.)
Accept/Reject (Select next input) (Place a data button to accept.)
Identify additional/Reset to complete (Click the Reset button to complete.)

When you identify the second element, MicroStation temporarily removes all of the elements, except the outlines of the area to be patterned. After patterning is completed, the elements reappear. Figure 8–9 shows an example of patterning the intersection of two closed elements.

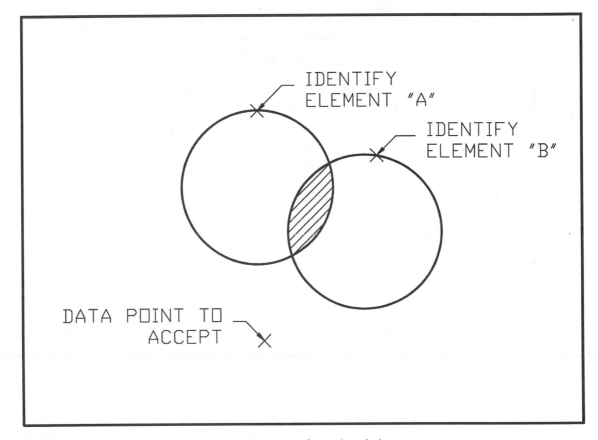

FIGURE 8–9 An example of hatching the intersection of two closed elements.

To hatch a composite area formed by the union of two elements, click the Hatch Area icon in the Pattern palette, and select Union from the Method options menu. MicroStation prompts:

Identify element (Identify one element.)
Accept/Reject (Select next input) (Identify the other element.)
Accept/Reject (Select next input) (Place a data button to accept.)
Identify additional/Reset to complete (Click the Reset button to complete.)

Figure 8–10 shows an example of hatching the union of two closed elements.

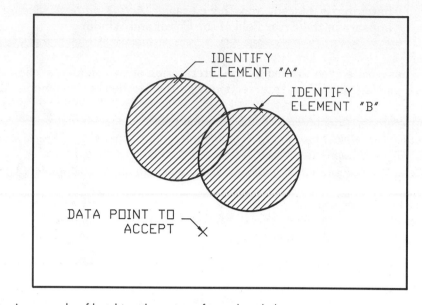

FIGURE 8–10   An example of hatching the union of two closed elements.

To hatch a composite area formed by subtracting the area of the second element from the area of the first element, click the Hatch Area icon in the Pattern palette, and select Difference from the Method options menu. MicroStation prompts:

Identify element (Identify one element.)
Accept/Reject (Select next input) (Identify the other element.)
Accept/Reject (Select next input) (Place a data button to accept.)
Identify additional/Reset to complete (Click the Reset button to complete.)

When you identify the second element, MicroStation temporarily removes all of the elements, except the outlines of the area to be patterned. After patterning is complete, the elements appear again. Figure 8–11 shows an example of hatching the difference between two elements.

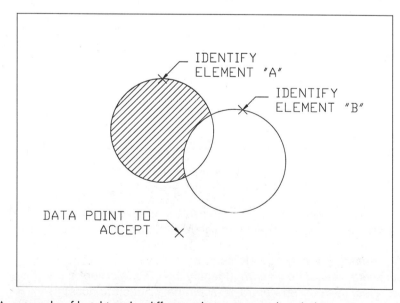

FIGURE 8–11   An example of hatching the difference between two closed elements.

To hatch a closed area formed by a group of intersecting or overlapping elements, click the Hatch Area icon in the Pattern palette, and select Flood from the Method options menu. MicroStation prompts:

Enter data point inside area (Place a data point inside the closed shape.)
Enter data point inside area (Place a data point anywhere on the screen to begin hatching.)

After you place the first data point inside the area to be patterned, MicroStation begins searching for the outline of the area. As it searches, it highlights the outline. This can be a long process for complicated outlines. Figure 8–12 shows an example of hatching using Flood method.

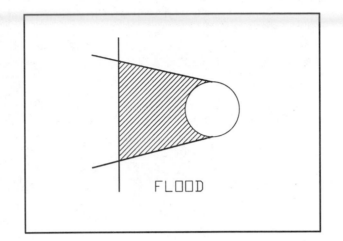

FIGURE 8–12   An example of hatching using the Flood method.

To hatch a closed area defined by a set of data points, click the Hatch Area icon in the Pattern palette, and select Points from the Method options menu. MicroStation prompts:

Enter shape vertex (Place the first data point.)
Enter shape vertex (Place data points to define the shape.)
Enter shape vertex (Press the Reset button to complete the shape and begin hatching.)

As you place the vertex points, a dynamic image appears showing the shape you are defining. The image shows you what the shape will be when you press the Reset button. This shape is not an element and it disappears when you update the screen or select another command. Figure 8–13 shows an example of defining a closed shape formed by data points.

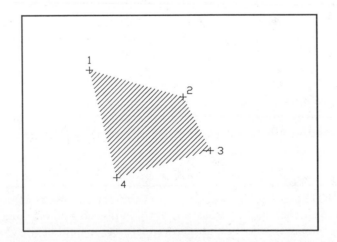

FIGURE 8–13   An example of hatching by defining a closed shape formed by data points.

CROSSHATCH AREA

The Crosshatch Area command places two sets of parallel lines in the area you select. Before you select the area to be crosshatched, you must tell MicroStation how far apart to place each set of lines and at what angle to rotate each set.

Invoke the Crosshatch Area command from the Patterning palette (see Figure 8–14) or key-in at the uSTN> field, **crosshatch** (or **cro**), and press ENTER.

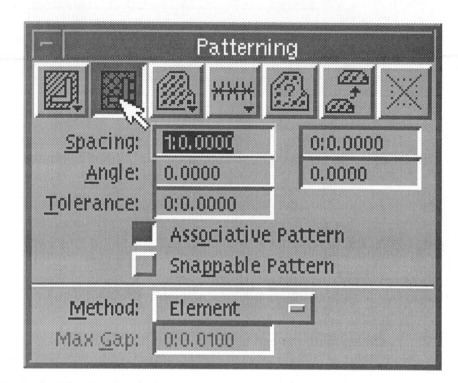

FIGURE 8–14 Invoking the Crosshatch Area command from the Patterning palette.

MicroStation prompts depend on the patterning method you select. Whatever method you use, you must specify the line spacing in MU:SU:PU and the angle for both sets of lines in the appropriate edit fields located in the palette. If you set the line spacing to 0:0:0 for the second set of lines, MicroStation sets its line spacing equal to the first set of lines. Similarly, if you set the angle to 0 for the second set of lines, MicroStation sets the angle to the complement (180 degrees) of the first set of lines. Leave tolerance set to 0.

MicroStation prompts for each cross-hatch patterning method are the same as those explained for hatch patterning method. The only difference is that you select the Crosshatch icon from the Patterning sub-palette, and you must also specify the spacing and angle of the second set of lines.

> **NOTE:** If the line spacing is set to 0 for each set of lines when you start crosshatching, no cross-hatching is placed and the message, *Active pattern spacing not set*, appears in the Error field of the Command Window.

PATTERN AREA

The Pattern Area command places copies of the Active Patterning Cell in the area you select. Copies of the cell are tiled in the selected area, and all copies are dropped so they are no longer cells. The part of each pattern element that sticks outside the pattern area is trimmed to the area boundary. Fields are provided in the palette allowing you to specify row and column spacing in working units (MU:SU:PU) and specifying a rotation angle for the pattern.

> **NOTE:** This process can be rather time-consuming, and the pattern is not displayed on the screen until the end of the process.

Invoke the Pattern Area command from the Patterning palette (see Figure 8–15) or key-in at the uSTN> field, **pattern area** (or **pat**), and press ⏎.

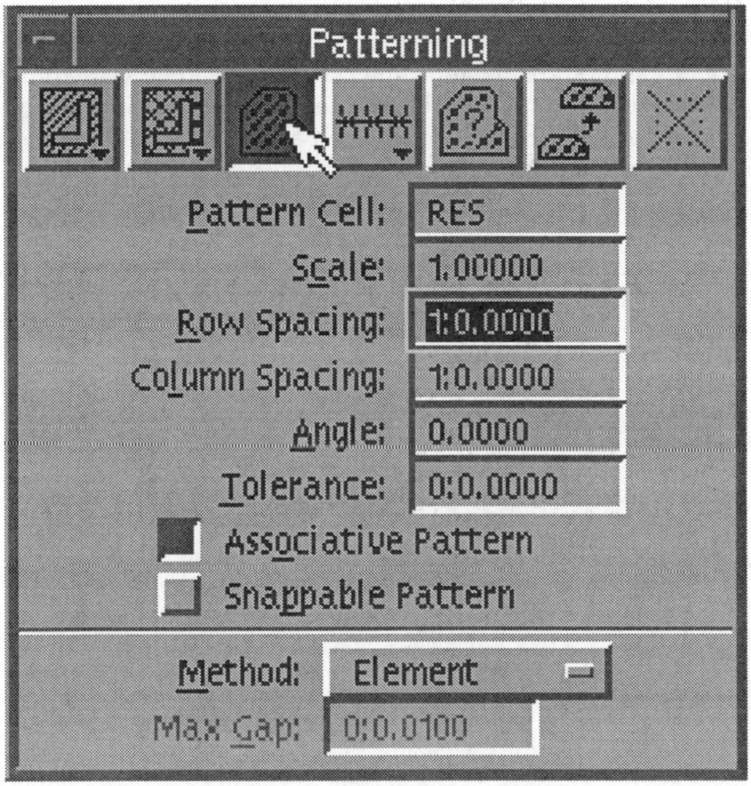

FIGURE 8–15   Invoking the Pattern Area command from the Patterning palette.

MicroStation prompts depend on the pattern method you select. Whatever method you use, you must specify the row and column spacing in MU:SU:PU and the rotation angle in the edit fields located in the palette. Leave the tolerance set to 0.

Selecting the Active Pattern Cell   Before you use the Pattern Area command, you must select a cell to be the active pattern cell. Do this by entering the name of the cell in the Edit box provided under the Pattern cell, or by selecting a cell from the Cell Library settings box. To select from the Cell Library settings box:

1. Open the Cell Library settings box from the Settings menu.
2. If no Cell Library is attached to your design file, attach one (see Chapter 7 for Cell Library attachment procedure).
3. Find the cell you want to use in the Cell List and highlight it by clicking on it with the Data button.
4. Click the Active Pattern button (located on bottom left of the settings box).

You can also select the active pattern cell by keying in at the uSTN> field, **AP**=<cell>, and pressing [ENTER]. Replace <cell> with the name of the cell you want to use for patterning.

Scaling the Pattern You may need to scale the active pattern cell, if the working units of the cell are different from the working units of your current design file. To do that, specify the appropriate scale factor in the Edit field under the Patterning Area icon or key-in at the uSTN> field, **PS**=<scale>, and press [ENTER]. Replace <scale> with your scale factor. A scale factor between 0 and 1 makes the cell smaller; a scale factor greater than 1 makes it larger.

The only problem with scaling the pattern cell is that you will not see the result of the scaling until you place the pattern. If you are not sure what scale factor to use, a good trick is to make the cell you want to place for patterning in the Active Placement Cell, then select the Place Active Cell command. Dynamic update shows an image of the cell at the screen cross-hairs point. Make changes to the Active Scale until the displayed cell is the correct size. When you have determined the correct scale factor, click the Reset button and select the Pattern Area command. Set the patterning scale to the same value as the Active Scale, and pattern your area. See Chapter 7 for a discussion of the Place Active Cell command.

Placing Area Patterns Area patterning uses the same patterning method as Hatch and Cross-hatch. MicroStation prompts are also the same as those described in the Hatch description earlier in this chapter.

SNAPPING TO PATTERNS

The Snappable Pattern button appears in the Patterning palette with each of the three pattern-ing commands. Turn the tentative snap button on to the elements. Turn the button off, and you cannot snap to any element in a pattern. The button does not change the snap setting of the patterned element.

ASSOCIATIVE PATTERNING

When one of the area patterning commands is selected in the Patterning palette, the Associative Pattern check button appears at the bottom of the palette (see Figure 8–16).

Turn this button to ON and any pattern you place using the element method is associated with the patterned element. Element manipulations affect the pattern. Element method patterns placed with the button set to OFF are not associated with the element they pattern. Any element manipulation to the element does not affect the pattern (see Figure 8–17).

> **NOTE:** The Associative Pattern check button appears in the palette with all area patterning method, but only patterns placed using the Element method can be associated with the patterned element.

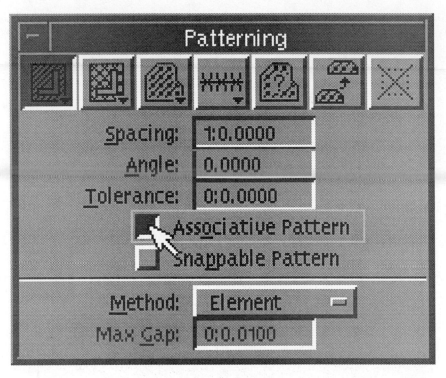

FIGURE 8-16   Displaying the status of the Associative Pattern toggle in the Patterning palette.

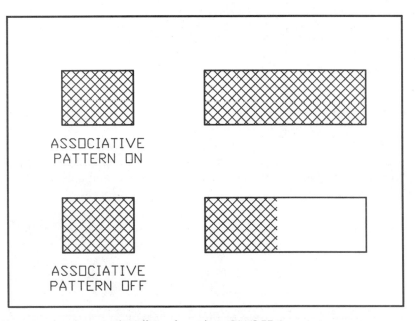

FIGURE 8-17   An example, showing the effect of toggling ON/OFF Associative pattern.

LEAVE HOLES IN YOUR PATTERN

You want to draw a wall and place a running bond brick pattern in it, but you don't want the windows to be patterned. MicroStation provides Solid and Hole Areas to do that for you. Draw the wall with Solid Area active and draw the windows with Hole Area active. Use Pattern Area with the Element Patterning method to pattern the wall, and the windows will not be patterned (see Figure 8–18).

Similarly, if you do not want to pattern text that is included in the area to be patterned (see Figure 8–19), place the text when you are in Hole Area mode.

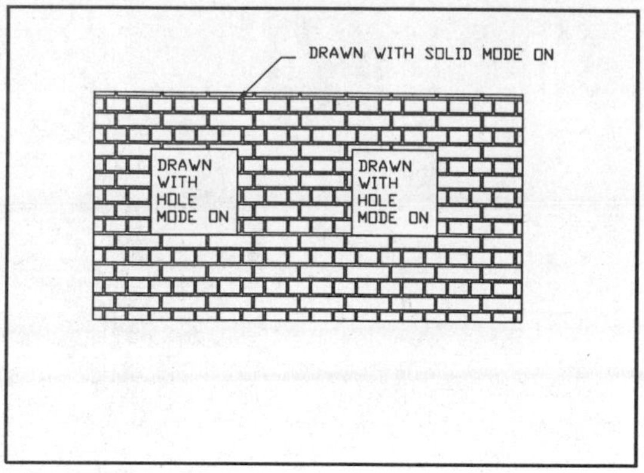

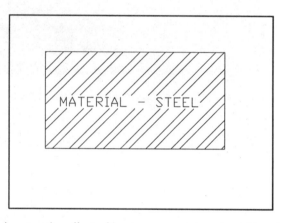

FIGURE 8–18 An example showing the effect of having an element in a hole mode in patterning.

FIGURE 8–19 An example showing the effect of having a text string placed in a hole mode in patterning.

You use a sub-palette to activate placing any closed element that can be switched between solid and hole mode (see Figure 8–20) from an Area Mode options menu in the sub-palette. To set the area mode you want to use for the element, open that options menu and select either Solid or Hole.

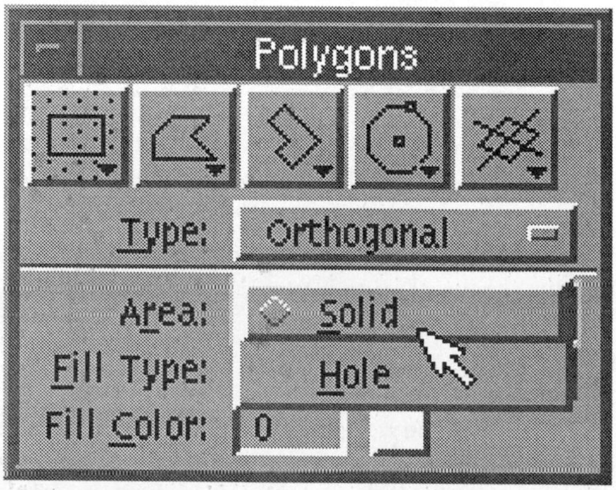

FIGURE 8–20 Polygon sub-palette displaying the option menu for the Area mode.

> **NOTE:** The only Patterning mode that recognizes Hole Area mode is Element. Fence, Intersection, Union, Difference, Flood, and Points Patterning modes all pattern right over Hole Area elements.

Change an Element's Area If you discover that you drew an element with Hole Area active, but you really needed it to be a Solid element, you can change it to Solid using the Change Element To Active Area (Solid/Hole) command.

Click the Change Element To Active Area (Solid/Hole) icon in the Change Element sub-palette (see Figure 8–21). MicroStation prompts:

Identify element (Select the element whose area you want to change.)
Accept/Reject (Select next input) (Click the Data button anywhere in the view to accept the element, or click the Reset button to reject it.)

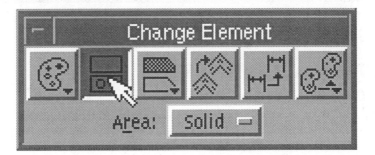

FIGURE 8–21   Invoking the Change Element To Active Area command from the Change Element sub-palette.

The second data point changes the selected element to the current active Area and can also select another element to be changed. If you invoked the command from the Change element sub-palette, before you identify the element, select the appropriate Area mode from the option button.

Alternate Method Two key-ins can also be used to change the area of an existing element. A specific key-in is provided for changing the element to each mode. Key-in at the uSTN> field, **change area solid** (or **chan a s**) and press ⏎ to change an element to Solid Area. Key-in **change area hole** (or **chan a h**), and press ⏎ to change an element to Hole area.

DELETE PATTERNS

A special delete command for patterns is provided in the Patterning palette. It deletes all elements that form a pattern, but it does not delete the element that contains the pattern.

To delete a pattern, click on the Delete Pattern icon in the Patterning palette (see Figure 8–22). MicroStation prompts:

Identify element (Click the Data button in the pattern to be deleted.)
Accept/Reject (Select next input) (Click the Data button somewhere in the view to delete the selected pattern, or click the Reset button to reject it.)

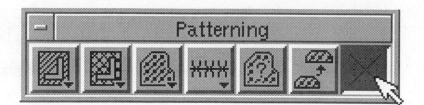

FIGURE 8–22 Invoking the Delete Pattern command from the Patterning palette.

After the first data point the pattern is highlighted, and after the second data point it is deleted. The second data point can also select another pattern to be deleted.

> **NOTE:** Patterns can contain a large number of elements. If you have deleted several, select the Compress Design option from the File pull-down menu to get back the disk space the deleted pattern elements were taking up.

MATCH PATTERN ATTRIBUTES

If you need to return to placing patterns and want to use the same pattern attributes that were used for a pattern already in your design, the Match Pattern Attributes option can quickly set them for you. The Match command sets the patterning attributes to an existing pattern that you select.

To match the attributes of an existing pattern, click the Match Pattern Attributes icon in the Patterning palette (see Figure 8–23). MicroStation prompts:

Identify element (Click the Data button on the pattern.)
Accept/Reject (Select next input) (Click the Data button somewhere in the view to match the pattern, or click the Reset button to reject it.)

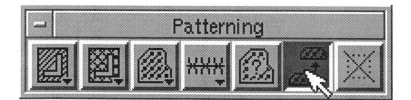

FIGURE 8–23 Invoking the Match Pattern Attributes command from the Patterning palette.

After the second data button, the Active Pattern settings are matched to those of the select pattern.

> **NOTE:** The Match Pattern Attributes command is also available in the Match palette that can be opened from the Palettes pull-down menu.

FILL AN ELEMENT

You have seen how to pattern a closed element using lines and cells. You can also fill a closed element with color. MicroStation provides three area fill placement modes:

None: The closed elements you place are not filled.

Opaque: The closed elements you place are filled, upon placement, with the Active (outline) Color.

Outlined: The closed elements you place are filled, upon placement, with the Fill Color (which can be different from the element outline).

Several commands are available for setting up area fill for closed elements. We will look at each one of them.

> **NOTE:** Some plotters cannot handle filled elements. If your plotter is one of them, your filled elements will be transparent when you plot them.

Area Fill View Attribute

The first thing to do before filling any closed elements is to make sure the Area Fill View Attribute is set to ON for the view you are working in. If it is set to OFF, all your filled elements will appear to be transparent (and they will plot that way).

To determine the status of the Area Fill View Attribute, invoke the View Attribute settings box from the View pull-down menu. Your screen displays a View Attributes settings box similar to the one shown in Figure 8–24. Make sure the Area Fill View Attribute is turned to ON (button depressed) in the view you are working in. View numbers are selected in the View options menu at the top of the settings box. If it is OFF, turn it ON, then click the Apply button to apply it to the selected view, or click the All button to apply it to all views.

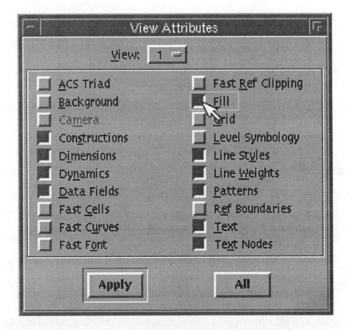

FIGURE 8–24   View Attribute Settings box pointing to the status of the Area Fill.

After you turn ON the Area Fill View Attribute, any filled or outlined elements you already placed appear filled in the view. Of course, if you have not placed any filled area, nothing changes in the view. The Area Fill View Attribute stays ON for the selected view until you turn it OFF or exit from MicroStation. To keep it ON permanently for the current design file, select Save Settings from the File pull-down menu.

Placing Elements with Area Fill

Whenever you want to place closed elements with fill color, first make sure that the appropriate option is selected for the Area Fill Type (None, Opaque, or Outline). When you use a sub-palette to start placing an element that can be filled, the fill settings fields appear in the sub-palette (see Figure 8–25).

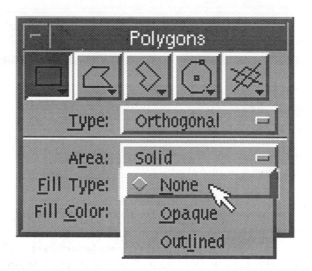

FIGURE 8–25   Polygon sub-palette displaying the option menu for the Fill Type.

Once you have set the Fill type and Fill Color, invoke the closed element placement commands and follow the prompts. All elements you place after that are filled according to the Area Fill Type you selected. Select Save Settings from the File pull-down menu to save this setting permanently for the current design file.

> **NOTE:** When either Fill or Outline is on, all closed elements you place are filled, not just the type of element you were placing when you turned on Fill or Outline.

Switching an Element Between Area Fill Modes

If you have a closed element that needs to be filled, the Change Fill command does it for you. It switches Filled and Outlined elements to None, and vice versa.

Invoke the Change Fill command from the Change Element palette (see Figure 8–26) by clicking Change Fill icon. Set the Fill Type and Fill Color in the sub-palette. MicroStation prompts:

Identify element (Identify the element to be changed.)
Accept/Reject (Select next input) (Click the Data button to accept the change, or the Reset button to reject it.)

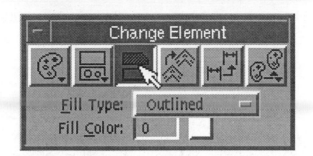

FIGURE 8-26 Invoking the Change Fill command from the Change Element sub-palette.

The second data point initiates the switch and can also select another element. If you do not select another element with the second data point, MicroStation displays the message *Element not found*, in the Error field of the Command Window. Ignore this message. Figure 8–27 shows an example of an element being switched from transparent to filled.

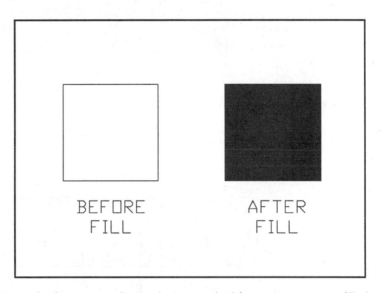

BEFORE
FILL

AFTER
FILL

FIGURE 8-27 An Example showing an element being switched from transparent to filled.

When you switch a closed element from None to Filled, the area enclosed by the element is filled with the same color as the element outline. If you want the enclosed area to be filled with a different color from the outline, set the Fill Type to outline, and select the appropriate Fill Color.

EXERCISES

Exercises 8–1 through 8–6

Lay out the views by using precision key-ins and appropriate grid spacing.

Exercise 8–1

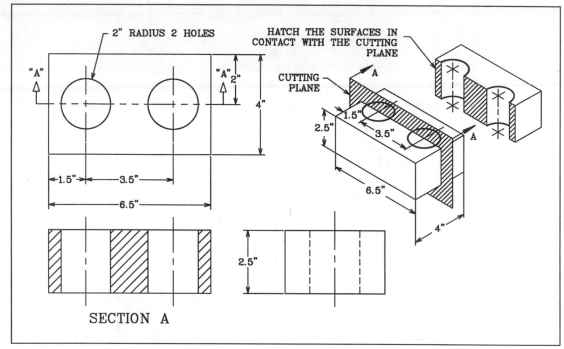

Exercise 8–2

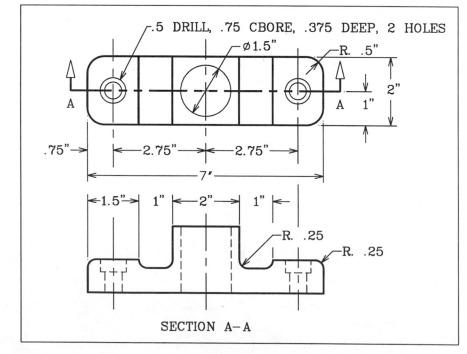

Exercise 8–3

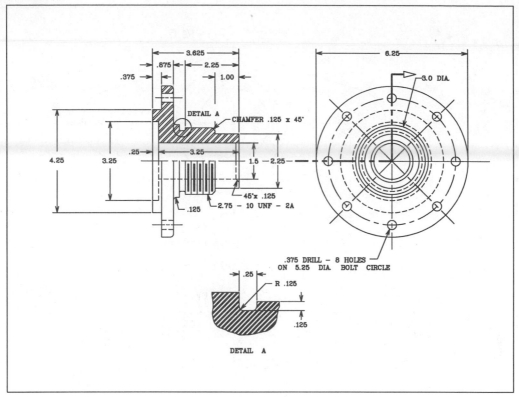

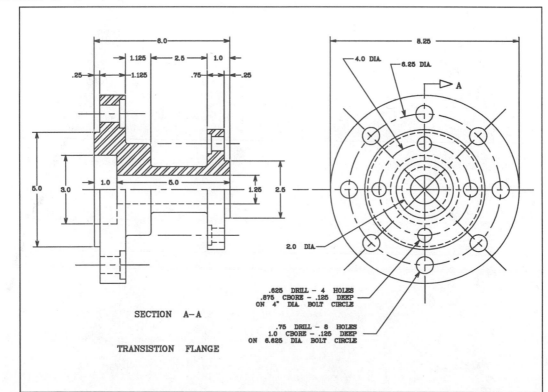

SECTION   A–A

TRANSISTION   FLANGE

Exercise 8–4

Exercise 8–5

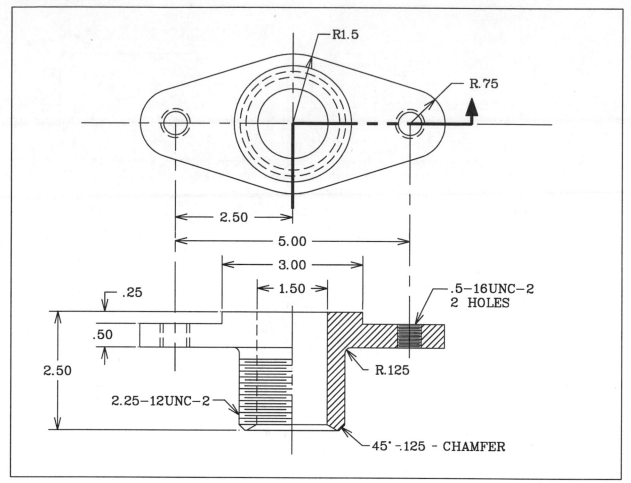

Exercise 8–6

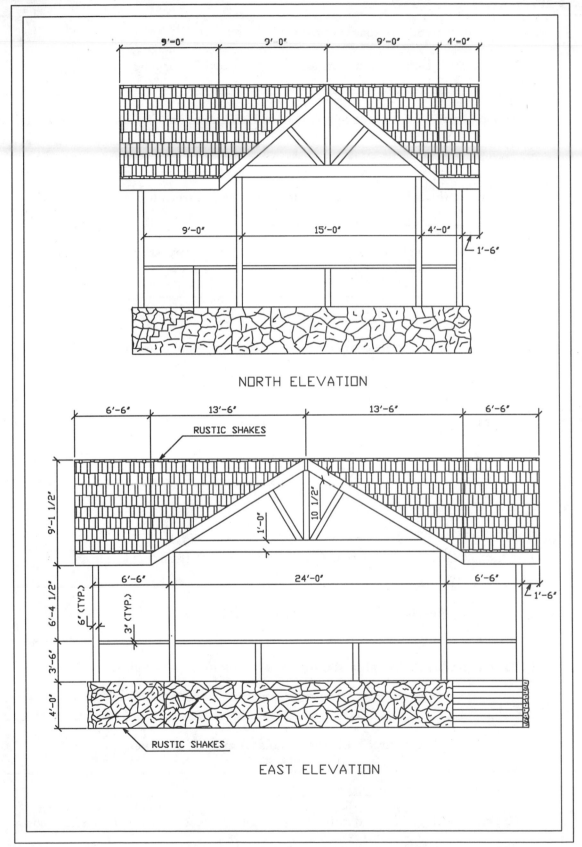

NORTH ELEVATION

EAST ELEVATION

REVIEW QUESTIONS

Write your answers in the spaces provided:

1. List the three sets of commands MicroStation provides for Area Patterning.

2. Explain briefly the difference between the Hatch Area and Crosshatch Area patterning.

3. List the methods that are available to set the area patterning.

4. Explain with illustrations the differences between Intersection, Union, and Difference options in area patterning.

5. Explain the difference between Element and Points option in area patterning.

6. What is the purpose of providing a second data point in hatching a closed element?

7. The Pattern Area command places copies of the Active Patterning _____ in the area you select.

8. The key-in PS= sets the _____.

9. The key-in PA= sets the _____.

10. What is the purpose of turning ON the Associative Pattern toggle button?

11. What is the purpose of placing elements in a Hole Area mode?

12. Explain briefly the purpose of using the Match Pattern Attributes.

13. Explain briefly the three options available for area fill placement.

14. Explain the steps involved switching an existing element between area fill modes.

PROJECT EXERCISE

In this project you apply MicroStation concepts and skills discussed in chapters 1 through 8 to create a compressor nozzle as shown in Figure P8–1.

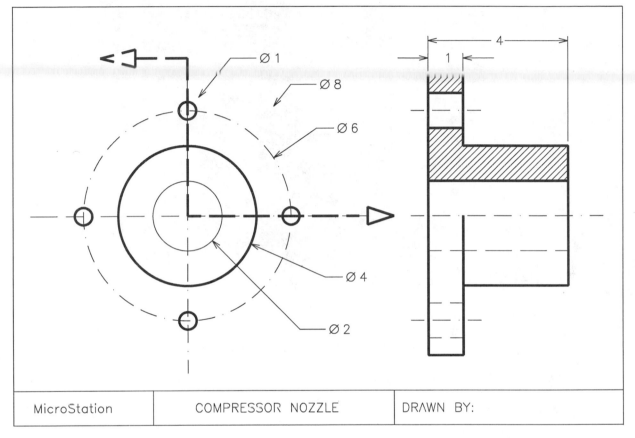

| MicroStation | COMPRESSOR NOZZLE | DRAWN BY: |

FIGURE P8–1   Completed Project Design.

> **NOTE:** The instructions for this project are designed to provide practice in the concepts presented in chapter 8. It is not necessarily the most efficient way to draw the design.

The new concepts introduced in this project are:

- Setting up the hatch parameters
- Hatch Patterning

GETTING STARTED

STEP 1:   Create a new design file named CH8.DGN using the SEED2D.DGN seed file from the MicroStation Manager dialog box if you just started MicroStation, or from the New option in the File pull-down menu of the MicroStation Command Window.

STEP 2: Set the design's working units as shown in Figure P8–2.

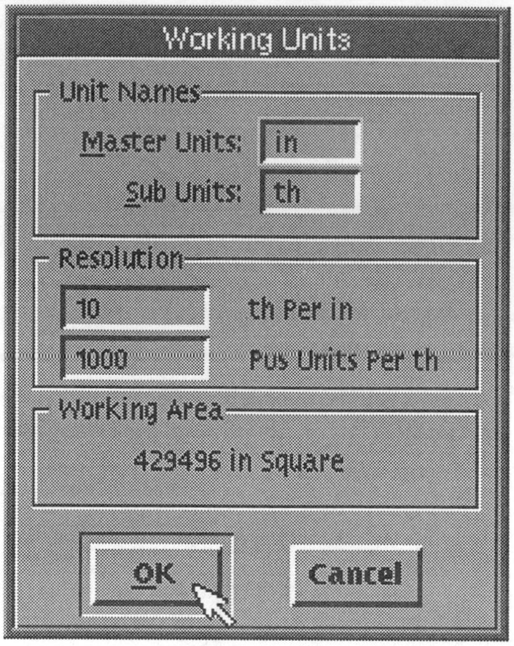

FIGURE P8–2 Working Units dialog box.

STEP 3: Open the Grid Settings box from the Settings pull-down menu and set the grid unit to 2.5 in., Grid Reference to 1 ft and set the Grid Lock to ON.

STEP 4: Set the active level to 1, color to green, line weight to 2 and the line style to 0.

STEP 5: If it is not already open, open the Tool Settings Box.

STEP 6: Invoke Save Settings command from the File pull-down menu to save the settings.

STEP 7: Draw the top and side view of the compressor nozzle as shown in Figure 8–1.

STEP 8: Invoke the Hatch Area command from the Patterning palette and set the following parameters:

Spacing:	0.125 in
Angle:	45 degrees
Associative Patterning:	ON
Method:	Flood

Hatch the top right corner of the section as shown in Figure P8–1.

STEP 9: Complete the design by placing the border and title block.

STEP 10: Invoke Save Settings command from the File pull-down menu to save the settings.

STEP 11: If you are finished with MicroStation, exit the design file.

CHAPTER

9

REFERENCE FILES

One of the most powerful time-saving features of MicroStation is its ability to view other design files while you are working in your design file. MicroStation lets you display the contents of up to 255 other design files (default is set to 32 design files) while working in your current design file. This function is in the form of reference files.

After completing this chapter, you will be able to:

- Attach a reference file.
- Move a reference file in the design plane.
- Scale your view of a reference file.
- Rotate your view of a reference file.
- Mirror your view of a reference file.
- Clip off part of your view of a reference file.
- Detach a reference file.
- Reload a reference file.

AN OVERVIEW OF REFERENCE FILES

When a design file is referenced externally in your design file, you can view and tentative point snap to all elements in the reference file, but each drawing's data is still stored and maintained in a separate design file. The only information about the referenced design file that becomes a permanent part of your design file is the name of the referenced design file and its directory path.

If necessary, you can use the regular Copy (or Fence Copy) command to copy selected elements of the reference file into your design file. Once the elements are copied into your current design file, they become part of the design file. This method is very useful if, for example, a design file that was drawn previously contains information that can be used in your current design file.

Reference files may be scaled, moved, rotated, and viewed by levels using commands that are specifically programmed to work with reference files. The reference file behaves as one element when you manipulate it with reference file manipulation commands. The only exception is the regular Copy command, in which the elements behave as individual elements. All of the manipulations are performed on your view of the referenced file, not the actual file. You cannot edit or modify the contents of a referenced file. If you need to make any changes to it, you actually have to load that file in MicroStation.

When you attach an external reference file, it is permanently attached until you detach it. When you open a design file, MicroStation automatically reloads each reference file; thus, you see the current version of each reference file when you view your design file.

EXAMPLES OF USING REFERENCE FILES

Borders and title blocks are an excellent example of design files that are useful as reference files. The entities that make up a border will use considerable space in a file and usually amount to around 40 to 50 KB. If a border and title block is drawn in each design file, it would waste a large amount of space, especially if you multiply 50 KB by 100 design files. If reference files are used correctly, they can save a lot of disk space.

Accuracy and efficient drawing time are other important design features that are enhanced through the use of reference files. As mentioned earlier, when an addition or change is made to a design file that is being used as a reference file, all the design files that use that file will reflect the modifications. For example, let's say that the name of the company is changed. Just change the company name in the title block design file, and all the design files that use title block as a reference file automatically display the new company name the next time they are accessed. (Can you imagine accessing 100 design files to correct one small detail?) Reference files save time and ensure the drawing accuracy required to produce a professional product.

When combined with the networking capability of MicroStation, external references give the project manager powerful new tools for coping with the realities of file management. The project manager can, by combining drawings through the referencing tools, see instantaneously the work of the various departments or designers working on a particular aspect of the contract. If necessary, you can overlay a drawing where appropriate, track the progress, and maintain document integrity. At the same time, departments need not lose control over individual designs and details.

Let's look at an example of this function in operation. Let's say that you are a supervisor with three designers reporting to you. All three of them are working on a project; each one is responsible for one-third of the project. As a supervisor you want to know how much progress each designer has made at the end of each day. Instead of calling up each of the three design files to see the progress, you can create a dummy design file and attach the three design files as reference files. Every day you can call up the dummy design file, and MicroStation will display the latest versions of the reference files attached to your design file. This will make your job a lot easier and give you an opportunity to put together all three pieces of the puzzle to see how they fit in the evolving design.

THE MAXIMUM NUMBER OF REFERENCES

As mentioned earlier, you can attach by default 32 reference files at any time to a design file. If necessary, you can increase this number to 255 reference files. This change is made in the Preference dialog box invoked from the User pull-down menu. The valid range is 16 to 255. MicroStation allocates approximately 0.5 KB of memory for each allowed reference file, regardless of whether an attachment actually exists. Thus, you should set the maximum no higher than necessary. A change in the Preference dialog box is not effective until the next time you start MicroStation.

ATTACHING A REFERENCE FILE

Reference files may be attached to your current design file by one of three methods. The first two methods are done with the interaction of dialog and setting boxes, the third is done via keyboard input.

Attachment From the Reference Files Settings Box Invoke the Reference Files settings box from the File pull-down menu as shown in Figure 9–1.

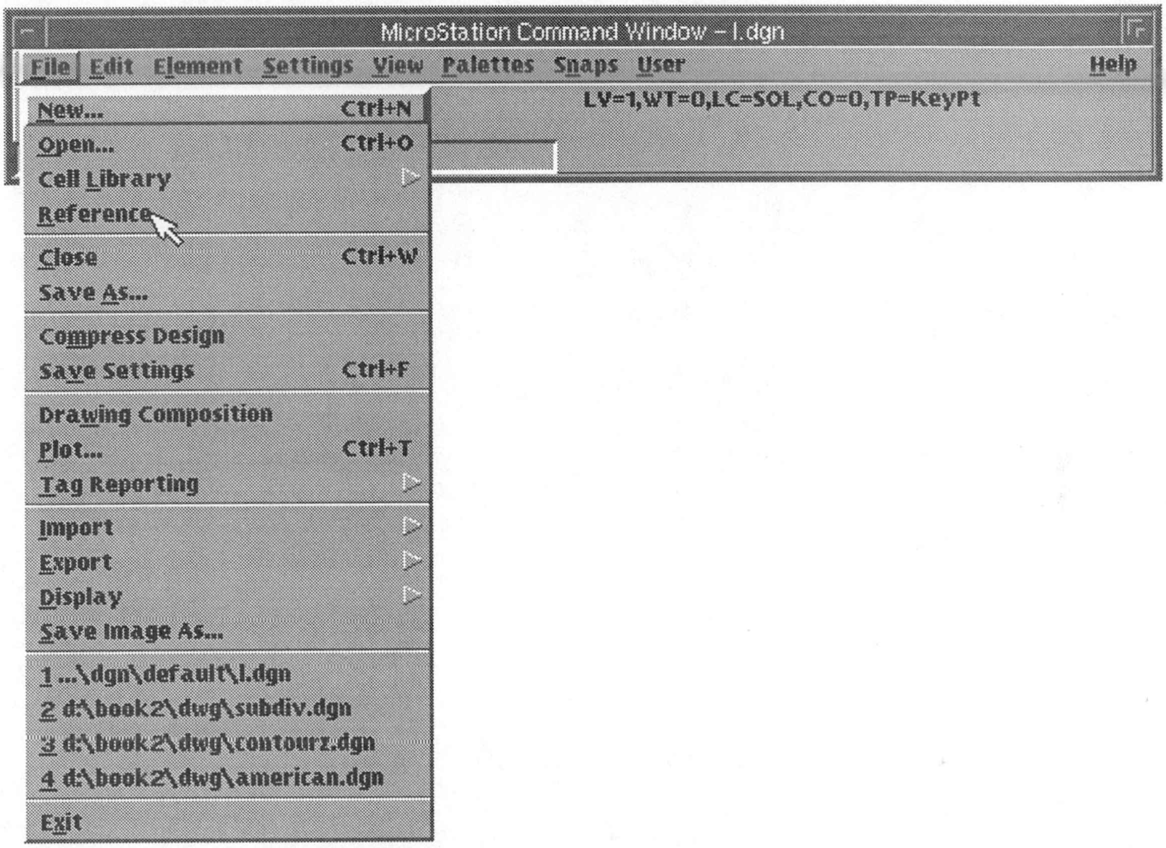

FIGURE 9–1 Invoking the Reference Files Settings box from the File pull-down located in the MicroStation Command Window.

A settings box appears similar to the one shown in Figure 9–2.

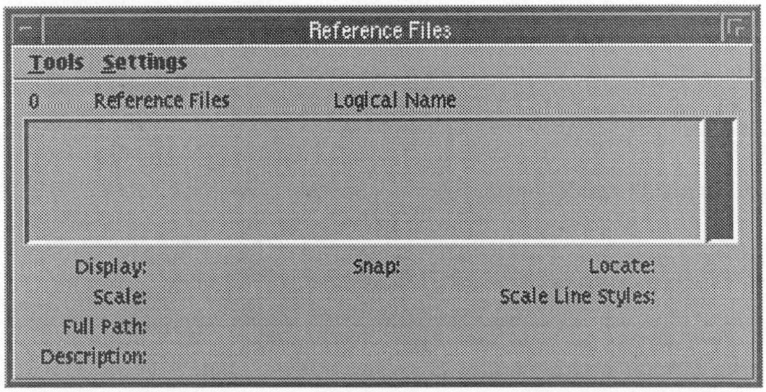

FIGURE 9–2 Reference Files Settings box.

From the Tools pull-down menu in the Reference Files settings box, select Attach... and an Attach Reference File dialog box similar to the one shown in Figure 9–3 appears. Select the appropriate design file from the Files list and click the OK button. MicroStation displays another dialog box similar to the one shown in Figure 9–4, where you can enter additional, optional information.

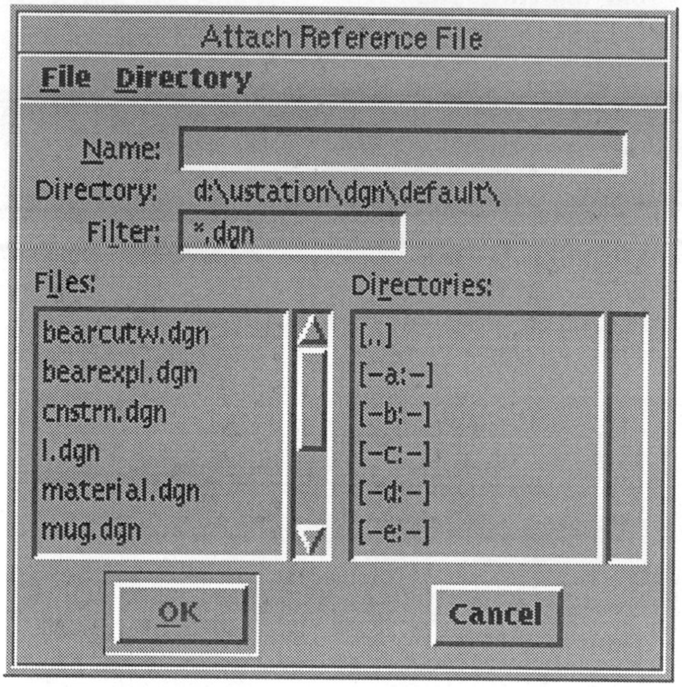

FIGURE 9–3 Attach Reference File Dialog box.

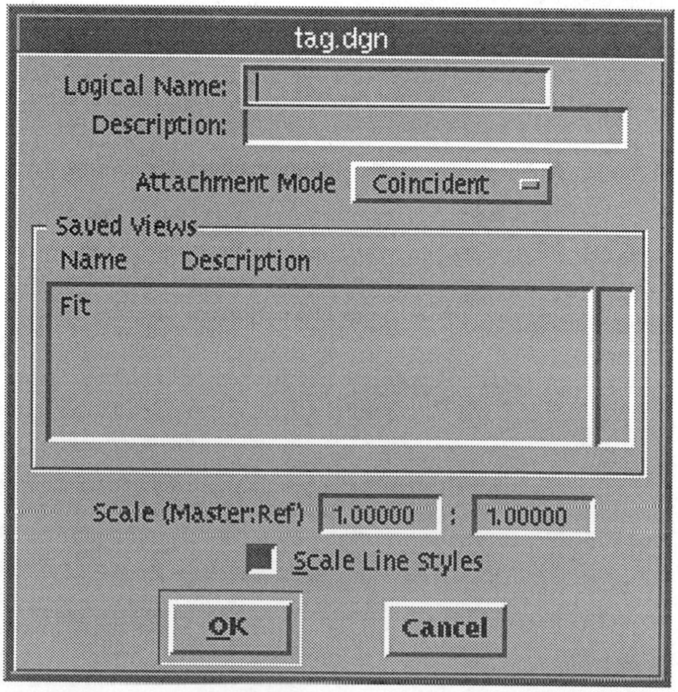

FIGURE 9–4 Optional Reference File Dialog box.

Click in the Logical Name edit field and type in a name. The logical name is a short identifier or nickname you can use later to identify the reference file being attached. The logical name is optional, unless you attach the same design file more than once to the current design file.

The next edit field is for a description. The description is optional, and can be used to describe the purpose of the attachment. If more than two or three reference files are attached, it allows you to identify the purpose of attachment quickly. The description cannot exceed 40 characters.

The final request from the reference attachment procedure is to select a named view in the dialog box from the Saved view listing (see Chapter 4 for how to Save views), as shown in Figure 9–4. A Saved view allows you to display a clipped portion of the design file. You can attach the saved view at a specified scale factor by entering the appropriate scale factor in the dialog box.

The scale factor is provided as a ratio between the master units of the active design file and the master units of the reference file. A detailed explanation is provided later in this chapter.

If you do not wish to select a saved view or the design file you are attaching does not have any saved views, click the OK button or press 🖰ENTER. MicroStation displays a message telling you the Reference File is attached in the Prompt field.

Attachment From the Reference Files Palette Invoke the Reference Files palette from Palette pull-down menu, and click the Attach Reference File icon, as shown in Figure 9–5, to open Attach Reference File dialog box (similar to the one shown in Figure 9–3). Select the appropriate design file from the Files list and click the OK button. The rest of the procedure is the same as explained in the first method.

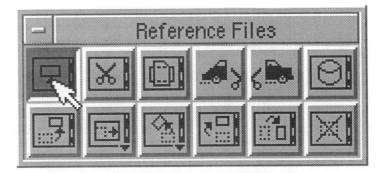

FIGURE 9–5   Invoking the Attach Reference File command from the Reference Files palette.

Attachment by Key-in Key-in at the uSTN> field, **RF=<file>**, and press 🖰ENTER. Replace <file> with the specification of the library file you want to attach, including the path.

  Example: **RF=C:\ref\border** 🖰ENTER

MicroStation displays a dialog box similar to the one shown in Figure 9–4. The rest of the procedure is the same as explained in the first method.

Figure 9–6 shows a design before and after attaching a reference file title.

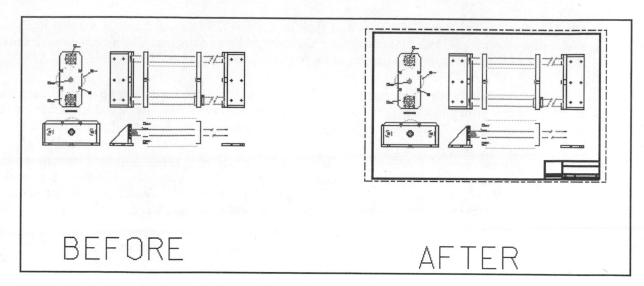

FIGURE 9–6   Design before and after attaching a reference file.

The Same File Can Be Referenced More Than Once

You can reference the same design file more than one time. The only restriction is that you must provide a unique logical name for each attachment. Though it is not required, be sure to use the description field to explain each attachment. That will save other people time in figuring out why the same file is referenced more than once.

One example of where the same design file might be referenced more than one time is when different parts of the referenced drawing are used as details in your design file.

REFERENCE FILE MANIPULATIONS

MicroStation provides a set of Manipulation commands specifically designed to manipulate reference files. As mentioned earlier, the reference file behaves as one element, and there is no way to drop it. But at the same time, Tentative Snap can snap to individual elements. The reference manipulation commands include Move, Scale, Rotate, Mirror Horizontal, Mirror Vertical, Clip Boundary, and Clip Mask. In addition, three toggle buttons are provided to toggle Snap, Display, and Locate options. First let's look at the toggle options.

To find the current status of the Display, Snap, and Locate options, highlight the reference file in the Reference File settings box. MicroStation displays the status at the bottom of the settings box, similar to the one shown in Figure 9–7. To change the status, double-click the name of the reference file in the Reference File settings box. MicroStation displays a dialog box similar to the one shown in Figure 9–8. Change the appropriate toggle settings and click the OK button to close the dialog box.

The Display toggle button controls the screen display of the specified reference file. If for some reason you don't want to display the reference file but you want to keep it attached, turn OFF the Display. When you turn the Display OFF, MicroStation does not display or plot the specified reference file.

The Locate toggle button allows you to locate elements that are displayed on your screen as a reference file and copy them into your active file using the Copy command. If you turn Locate OFF, you can see the elements on the screen display but you cannot identify the elements to use with the

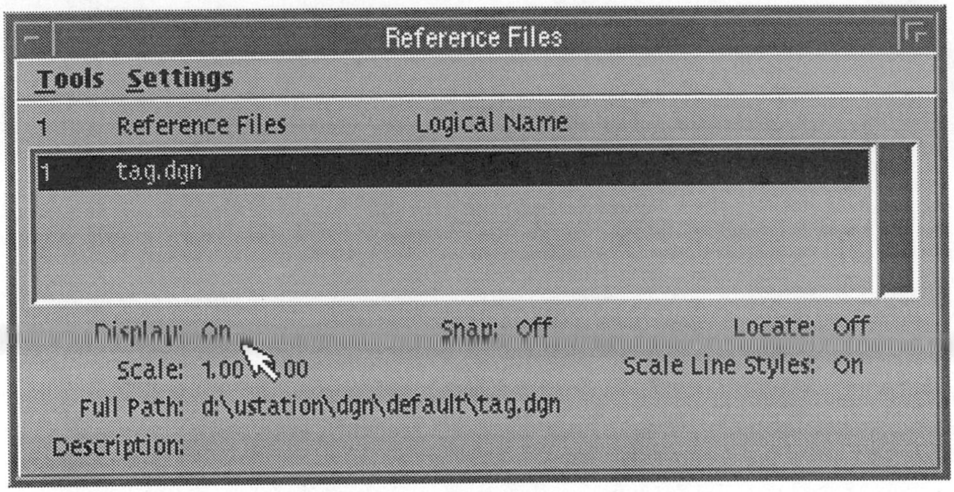

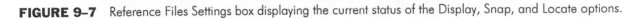

FIGURE 9–7 Reference Files Settings box displaying the current status of the Display, Snap, and Locate options.

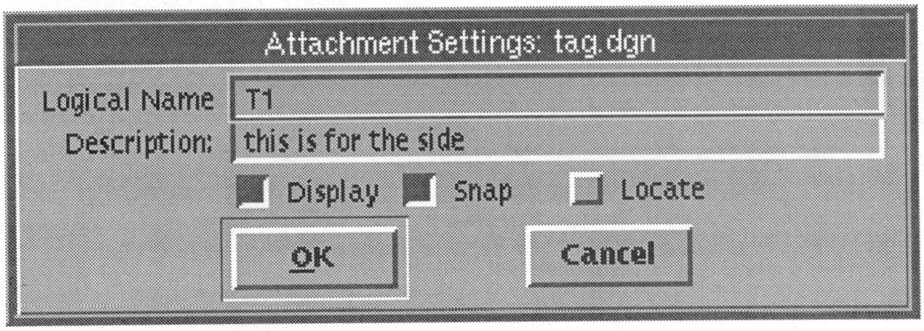

FIGURE 9–8 Attachment Settings Dialog box.

Copy command. If you turn Locate ON, you can see the elements on the screen display as well as identify for use with the Copy command.

The Snap toggle button gives you the ability to tentative point snap to any element visible in the specified reference file. If you set Snap to OFF, you can see the elements on the screen display, but you cannot tentative snap to any element in the specified reference file. On the other hand, if you set Snap to ON, you can see the elements on the screen display as well as tentative snap to any element in the specified reference file.

Move Reference File

The Move Reference File command allows you to move a reference file from one location to another. This command is useful whenever you want to reposition the reference file. Before you invoke the command, highlight the reference file by clicking the Data button in the Reference File settings box. Then invoke the Move Reference File command from the Tools pull-down menu located in the Reference File settings box or click the Move Reference File icon located in the Reference File palette, as shown in Figure 9–9. MicroStation prompts:

> *Enter point to move from* (Place a data point anywhere on the reference file.)
> *Enter point to move to* (Place a data point where you want to move the reference file in reference to the first data point.)

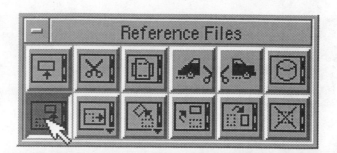

FIGURE 9–9 Invoking the Move Reference File command from the Reference Files palette.

When the file has completely finished updating, the command is complete. To move another reference file or the same file to another location, start the entire operation again. Figure 9–10 shows a view before and after moving a reference file border.

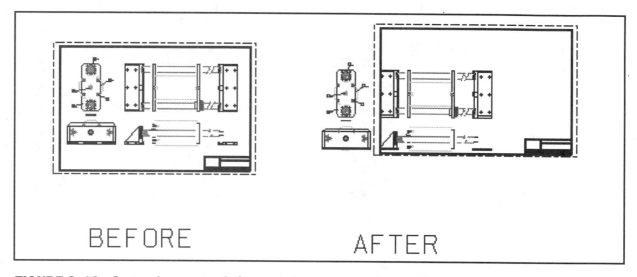

BEFORE   AFTER

FIGURE 9–10 Design shows a view before and after moving a reference file.

Scale Reference File

The Scale Reference File command allows you to enlarge or reduce a reference file. Before you invoke the command, highlight the reference file by clicking the data button in the Reference File settings box. Then invoke the Scale Reference File command from the Tools pull-down menu located in the Reference File settings box or click the Scale Reference File icon located in the Reference Files palette, as shown in Figure 9–11.

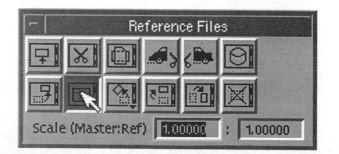

FIGURE 9–11 Invoking the Scale Reference File command from the Reference Files palette.

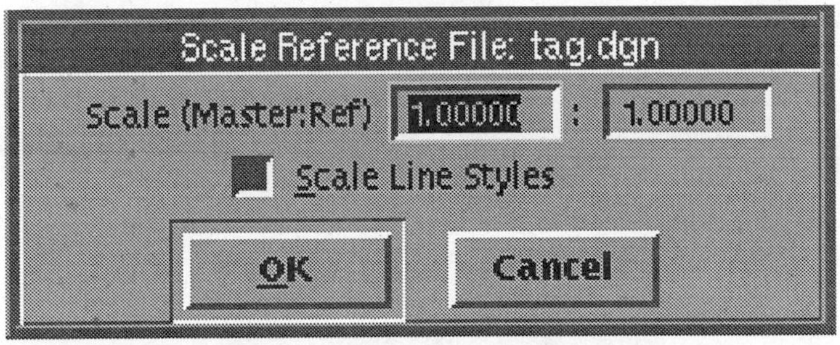

Scale Reference File: tag.dgn

Scale (Master:Ref) 1.00000 : 1.00000

☐ Scale Line Styles

OK   Cancel

FIGURE 9-12 Scale Reference Dialog box.

If you select the command from the Tools pull-down menu, MicroStation displays a dialog box similar to the one shown in Figure 9–12. Enter the scale factor in terms of a ratio of the master units of the active design file to the master units of the reference file. For example, a ratio of 3:1 scales a reference file up three times; a ratio of 1:5 scales a reference file down five times. If you make a mistake, you can always use the UNDO command to undo the last operation.

If you invoke the Scale Reference File command by clicking the Scale Reference File icon located in the Reference Files palette, key-in the scale factor provided in the Reference Files palette. Micro-Station prompts:

Enter point to scale ref file about (Place a data point from which the file will scale.)

When the file has completely finished updating, the command is complete. To scale another reference file or the same file with a different scale factor, start the entire operation again.

> **NOTE:** The scale factor ratio between the active design file and the reference file is not cumulative. For instance, if you specify a scale of 3:1 followed by 6:1, the final result will be 6:1. See Figure 9–13 before and after scaling the reference file border.

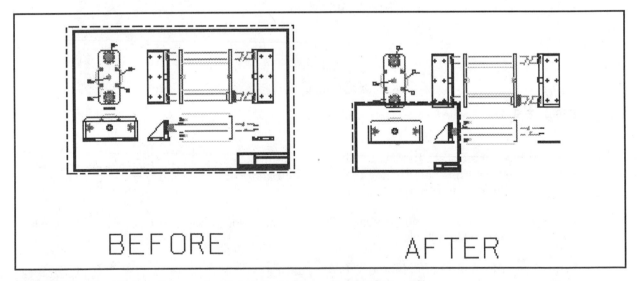

BEFORE   AFTER

FIGURE 9-13 Design shows a view before and after scaling a reference file.

Rotate Reference File

The Rotate Reference File command allows you to rotate a reference file to any angle around a pivot point. Before you invoke the command, highlight the reference file by clicking the Data button in the Reference File settings box. Then invoke the Rotate Reference File command from the Tools pull-down menu located in the Reference File settings box or click the Rotate Reference File icon located in the Reference Files palette, as shown in Figure 9–14.

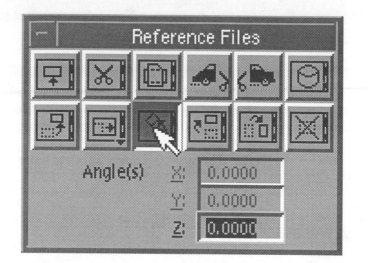

FIGURE 9–14 Invoking the Rotate Reference File command from the Reference Files palette.

If you select the command from the Tools pull-down, MicroStation displays a dialog box similar to the one shown in Figure 9–15. Key-in the rotation angle. For example, an angle of 60 degrees rotates the reference file 60 degrees counterclockwise from its current position around a pivot point. If you make a mistake, you can always use the Undo command to undo the last operation.

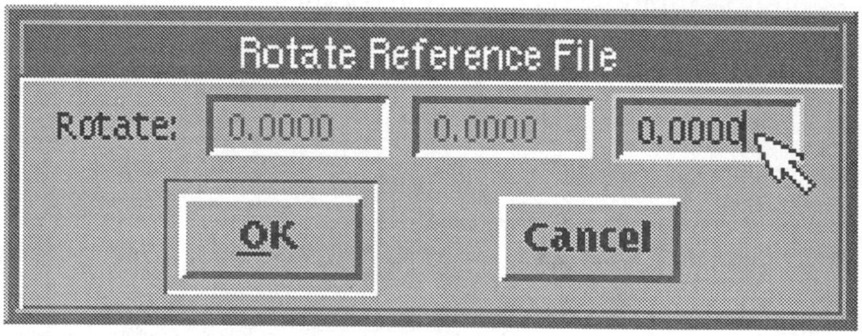

FIGURE 9–15 Rotate Reference File Dialog box.

If you invoke the Rotate Reference File command by clicking the Rotate Reference File icon located in the Reference Files palette, key-in the rotation angle in the edit box provided in the Reference File palette. MicroStation prompts:

> *Enter point to rotate ref file about* (Place a data point to define a pivot point about which the reference file will rotate.)

When the file has completely finished updating, the command is complete. To rotate another reference file or the same file to another rotate angle, start the entire operation again.

Mirror Horizontal Reference File

The Mirror Horizontal Reference File command allows you to mirror a reference file about the horizontal (or X) axis. Before you invoke the command, highlight the reference file by clicking the Data button in the Reference File settings box. Then invoke the Mirror Horizontal Reference File command from the Tools pull-down menu located in the Reference Files settings box or click the Mirror Horizontal Reference File icon located in the Reference File palette as shown in Figure 9–16. MicroStation prompts:

Enter point to mirror about (Place a data point to define the mirror axis.)

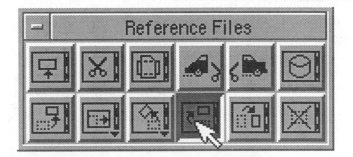

FIGURE 9–16   Invoking the Mirror Horizontal Reference File command from the Reference Files palette.

When the file has completely finished updating, the command is complete. To mirror horizontal another reference file or the same file start the entire operation again.

Mirror Vertical Reference File

The Mirror Vertical Reference File command allows you to mirror a reference file about the vertical or Y axis. Before you invoke the command, highlight the reference file by clicking the Data button in the Reference Files setting box. Then invoke the Mirror Vertical Reference File command from the Tools pull-down menu located in the Reference Files settings box or click the Mirror Vertical Reference File icon located in the Reference Files palette, as shown in Figure 9–17. MicroStation prompts:

Enter point to mirror about (Place a data point to define the mirror axis.)

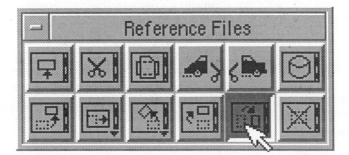

FIGURE 9–17   Invoking the Mirror Vertical Reference File command from the Reference Files palette.

When the file has completely finished updating, the command is complete. To mirror vertical another reference file start the entire operation again.

Reference Clip Boundary

The Reference Clip Boundary provides the ability to display only a desired portion of a reference file. Before you invoke the command, highlight the reference file by clicking the Data button in the Reference Files settings box. Then place a Fence Block or Fence Shape on the reference file to draw the clipping boundary. Make sure the fence defines the desired area. The clipping boundary can have up to 60 vertices. Non-rectangular clipping boundaries are displayed in a view and plotted only if Fast Reference File clipping is turned OFF for the view. The View Attributes setting box allows you to turn OFF the Fast Reference File clipping off.

Once the fence is placed, invoke the Clip Boundary command from the Tools pull-down menu located in the Reference Files settings box or click the Reference Clip Boundary icon located in the Reference Files palette, as shown in Figure 9–18. The part of the reference file enclosed within the fence will be the only part displayed when the command completes.

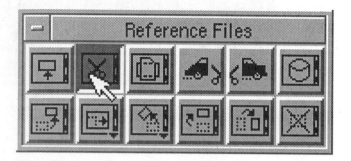

FIGURE 9–18   Invoking the Reference Clip Boundary command from the Reference Files palette.

> **NOTE:** If you make a mistake in clipping boundary, you can restore the full display of the reference file by turning the Fast Reference File clipping ON. To clip the boundary, repeat the entire procedure.

Reference Clip Mask

The Reference Clip Mask command, like the Clip Boundary command, allows you to display only a portion of a reference file. Clip Boundary displays the part inside a fence, whereas the Clip Mask command displays the part outside the fence.

Before you invoke the command, highlight the reference file by clicking the Data button in the Reference Files settings box. Then place a Fence Block or Fence Shape on the reference file to draw the clipping mask. Make sure the fence defines the desired area. The clipping mask can have up to 60 vertices. Once the fence is placed, invoke the Clip Mask command from the Tools pull-down menu located in the Reference Files settings box or click the Reference Clip Mask icon located in the Reference Files palette, as shown in Figure 9–19. The part of the reference file outside the fence is the only part displayed when the command completes.

> **NOTE:** To remove a clipping mask from a reference file use the Reference Files Clipping Boundary command to define a new clipping boundary.

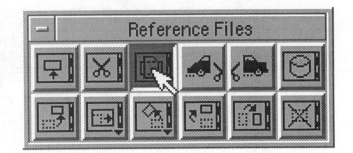

FIGURE 9-19   Invoking the Clip Mask command from the Reference Files palette.

Detaching Reference File

Whenever you no longer need the reference file, you can detach it from the current design file. Once the reference file is detached, there is no more link between the reference file and the current design file.

Before you invoke the command, highlight the reference file you want to detach by clicking the Data button on the file name in the Reference Files settings box. Then invoke the Detach command from the Tools pull-down menu located in the Reference Files settings box or click the Detach icon located in the Reference Files palette, as shown in Figure 9–20.

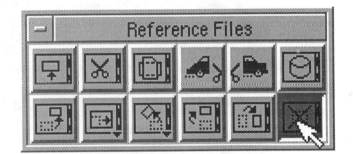

FIGURE 9-20   Invoking the Detach Reference File command from the Reference Files palette.

Reload Reference File

MicroStation reloads automatically all reference files attached to a design file only when you first open the design file. The Reload command has been provided to reread the reference file whenever it is desirable to do so while working in the design file. The Reload command is helpful, especially in a network environment, to access the latest version of the reference design file while you are working in a design to which it has been attached.

Before you invoke the command, highlight the reference file you want to reload by clicking the Data button in the Reference Files settings box. Then invoke the Reload command from the Tools pull-down menu located in the Reference Files settings box or click the Reload icon located in the Reference Files palette as shown in Figure 9–21.

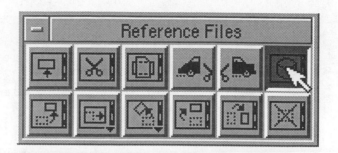

FIGURE 9–21 Invoking the Reload Reference File command from the Reference Files palette.

Levels and Level Symbology

In addition to controlling the display of the reference file, you can manipulate the display of specific levels in a reference file. To manipulate the levels, first highlight the reference file you want to manipulate by clicking the Data button in the Reference Files settings box, then invoke the Levels... command from the Settings pull-down menu located in the Reference File settings box. The Reference File Levels settings box displayed is similar to the one shown in Figure 9–22. Click on the level numbers you want to turn OFF/ON, whichever the case may be. Once the selection is completed, click the Apply button. Before you click the Apply button, make sure you have selected the appropriate view number from the options menu at the top of the settings box. Similarly, you can manipulate the Level Symbology (see Chapter 10 for a detailed explanation) in a reference file.

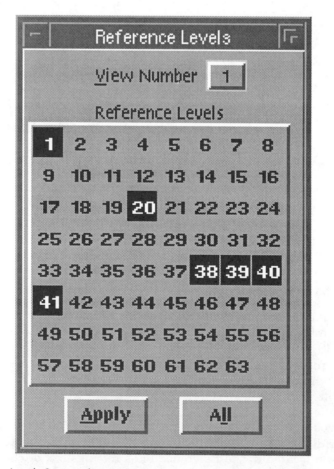

FIGURE 9–22 Reference Levels Settings box.

REVIEW QUESTIONS

Write your answers in the spaces provided:

1. List at least two benefits of using reference files.

   _____

2. By default, how many reference files can you attach to a design file?

   _____

3. What effect does attaching reference files have on a design file size?

   _____

4. List the commands that are specifically provided to manipulate reference files.

   _____

   _____

5. Explain the steps involved in attaching a reference file.

   _____

   _____

6. Explain the difference between Reference Clip Boundary command and Reference Clip Mask command.

   _____

   _____

7. List the steps involved in detaching a reference file.

   _____

   _____

10

SPECIAL FEATURES

MicroStation provides some special features that are less often used than the commands described earlier in this book, but provide added power and versatility. This chapter briefly introduces several such features. For more detailed information on each feature, consult the documentation furnished with MicroStation and the on-line help.

After completing this chapter, you will be able to:

- Create and use graphic groups.
- Select groups of elements using various selection criteria.
- Define a level symbology to help you determine what level elements are on.
- Change the highlight and vector cursor colors.
- Record and replay a series of MicroStation editing commands and cursor movements.
- Open AutoCAD drawings as MicroStation design files.
- Save MicroStation design files as AutoCAD drawings.
- Import from and export to other CAD graphic formats.
- Save and display graphic images.
- Place text from a glossary of standard terms and add text to the glossary.

GRAPHIC GROUPS

The Add To Graphic Group command allows you to group elements together so they act as if they were one element when you apply element manipulation commands with the Graphic Group Lock on. The Drop From Graphic Group command allows you to drop elements from a graphic group or drop the entire group.

As mentioned in earlier chapters, certain MicroStation commands create elements that are part of a graphic group, as follows:

The text file that is imported containing more than 128 lines, or more than 2,048 characters, is considered part of a graphic group.

The Place Text Along command makes each character a separate element and places all the characters as one graphic group.

The elements of a pattern are part of one graphic group, but the element they pattern is not part of the group.

Adding Elements to a Graphic Group

To add elements to a graphic group, click the Add To Graphic Group icon in the Chain sub-palette (see Figure 10–1), or key-in at the uSTN> field, **group all** (or **gr a**) and press [ENTER]. MicroStation prompts:

Identify element (Identify the element you want to place in a graphic group.)
Add to new group (Accept/Reject) (Identify the next element to be added to the graphic group.)

FIGURE 10–1   Invoking Add To Graphic Group command from the Chain sub-palette.

The second data point placed the first element in the graphic group and identified the next element to add into the group. Continue identifying the elements to be added to the graphic group. When all elements have been selected, click the data button one more time to add the last identified element to the group.

For example, to create a graphic group from three circles, first invoke the Add To Graphic Group command. Click on one of the circles and it is highlighted. Click on the second circle to accept the first circle and highlight the second one. Click on the third circle to accept the second circle and highlight the third one. Click somewhere in the view (not on an element) to accept the third circle. All three circles are now part of a graphic group.

In addition to creating new graphic groups, the Add To Graphic Group command can be used to add additional elements to existing graphic groups, and to move elements from one graphic group to another graphic group.

- If any elements you select after selecting the first element are part of another graphic group, they are moved from their old graphic group to the graphic group you are creating.
- If the first element you select is part of another graphic group, all elements you select are added to that graphic group, rather than creating a new group.

Manipulating Elements in a Graphic Group

The Graphic Group Lock controls the effect the element manipulation commands have on elements in a graphic group. If the lock is set to OFF, the commands only manipulate the selected element. If the lock is set to ON, all elements in the graphic group are highlighted and manipulated (even if you cannot see them in the view you are working in).

For example, if the graphic group lock is set to OFF and you select one of the elements in a graphic group to be deleted, only that element is deleted. If the lock is set to ON, all elements in the graphic group are deleted.

> **NOTE:** Only the element manipulation commands check the status of the graphic group lock. The Fence contents commands ignore the graphic group lock and manipulate the elements depending on the fence lock.

The graphic group lock is toggled ON and OFF in either the Full or Toggle Locks settings boxes (see Figure 10–2).

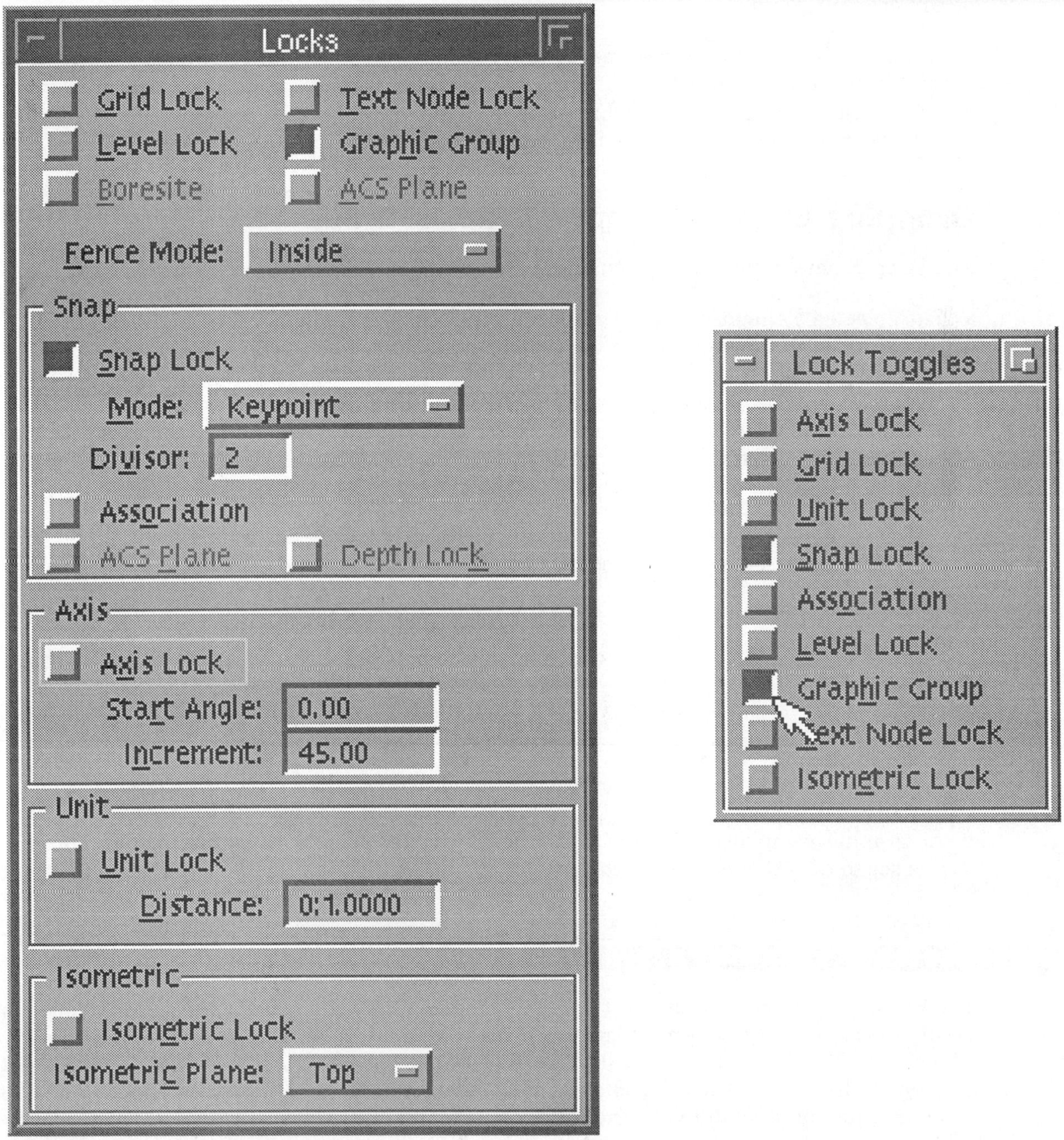

FIGURE 10–2 Full and Toggle Settings box.

> ***NOTE:*** If the graphic group lock is set to ON, you can determine if the element you select for manipulation is in a group by looking at the element type description in the status field of the Command Window. If the element is in a graphic group, the message includes "(GG)."

Copying Elements in a Graphic Group

The graphic group lock affects the way the element copy and fence contents copy commands handle elements in a graphic group. If the graphic group lock is set to OFF, the copied elements are not part of any graphic group.

- If the lock is set to ON, the element copy command copies the entire graphic group and the copies form a new graphic group.
- If the lock is ON, only the graphic group elements in the fence are copied, and the copies become a new separate graphic group.

Dropping Elements from a Graphic Group

The Drop From Graphic Group command drops:

- The selected element when the graphic group lock is set to OFF.
- All elements in the group when the graphic group lock is set to ON.

To drop elements from a graphics group, click the Drop From Graphic Group icon in the Chain sub-palette (see Figure 10–3), or key-in at the uSTN> field, **group drop** (or **gr d**) and press ⏎. MicroStation prompts:

> *Identify element* (Identify the element to drop.)
> *Accept/Reject (Select next input)* (Identify another element, place a data point anywhere in the view, or click the reject button to reject the element to drop.)

FIGURE 10–3 Invoking Drop From Graphic Group command from the Chain sub-palette.

If the graphic group lock is set to OFF, only the selected element is highlighted and dropped. If the lock is set to ON, all elements in the graphic group are highlighted and are dropped.

SELECTION BY ELEMENT TYPE

The Select By option from the Edit pull-down menu allows you to limit the selection of elements for manipulation to those that meet certain element attributes. For example, if all red ellipses on level 10 need to be changed to the color green, use the Select By settings box to select only those elements, then apply the color change to the selected elements. Handles appear on the selected elements, just as they did with the selection command described in Chapter 4. You can delete the selected elements, move them, copy them, change their attributes, and apply several other manipulation commands to them.

The Select By Settings Box

The Select By settings box contains several fields, selection menus, and options to open other settings boxes (see Figure 10–4).

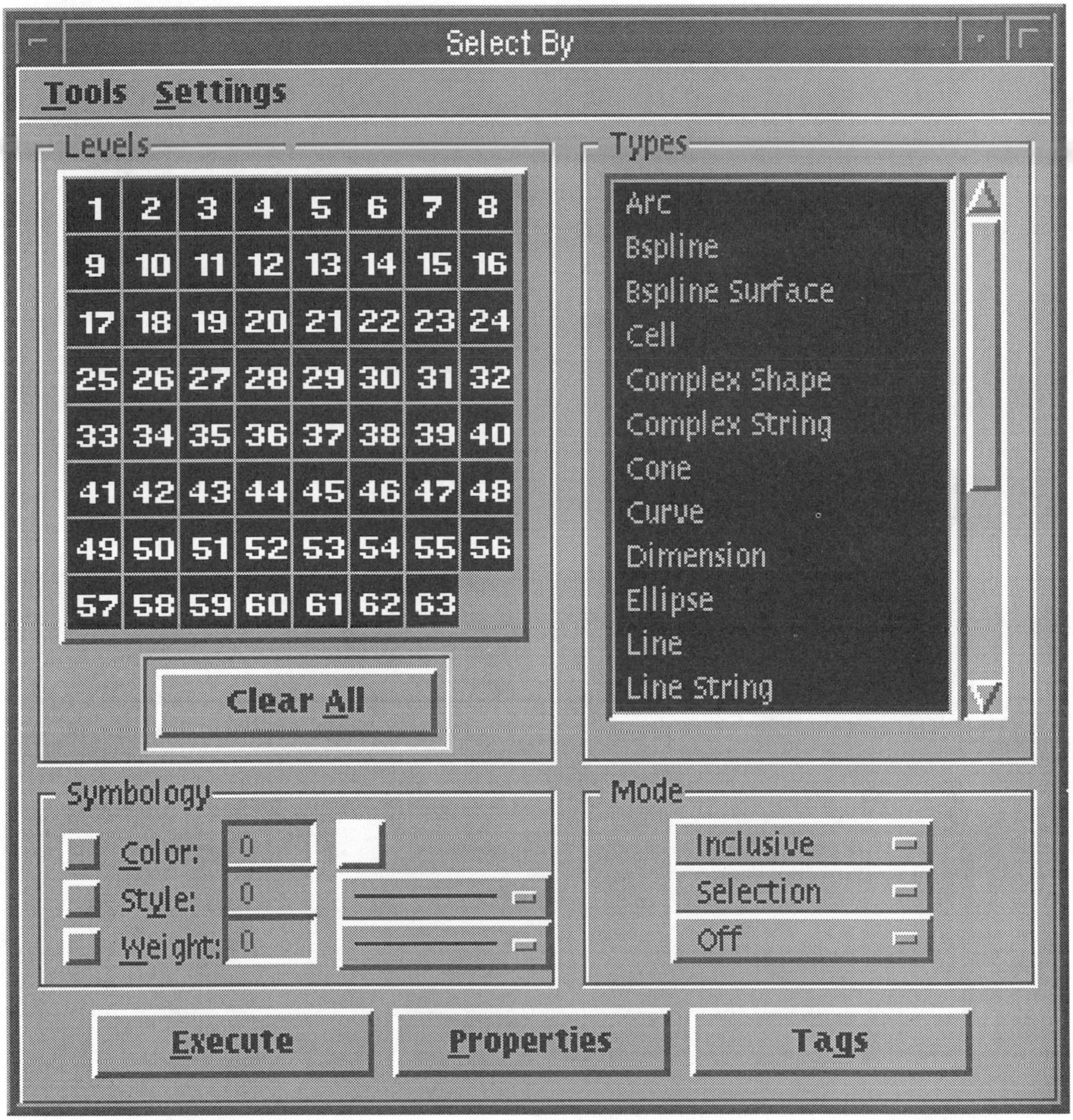

FIGURE 10–4   Select By Settings box.

The settings box is made up of the following parts:

- Selection by levels (upper left of the box).
- Selection by element types (upper right of the box).
- Selection by symbology—color, line weight, or line style (lower left of the box).

- The Mode field contains three selection menus that control the way the selection criteria is applied.
- The Properties button opens the Select By Properties settings box (see Figure 10–5) in which you can choose to select elements by property attributes (such as only filled elements) and classes (such as construction elements).

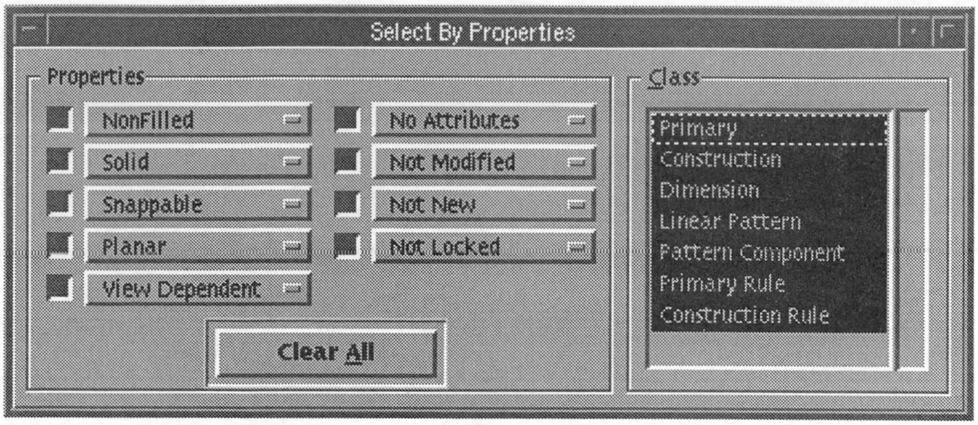

FIGURE 10–5   Select By Properties Settings box.

- The Tags button opens the Tabs settings box (see Figure 10–6) in which you can limit your selection to elements that contain only certain tags or combinations of tags.

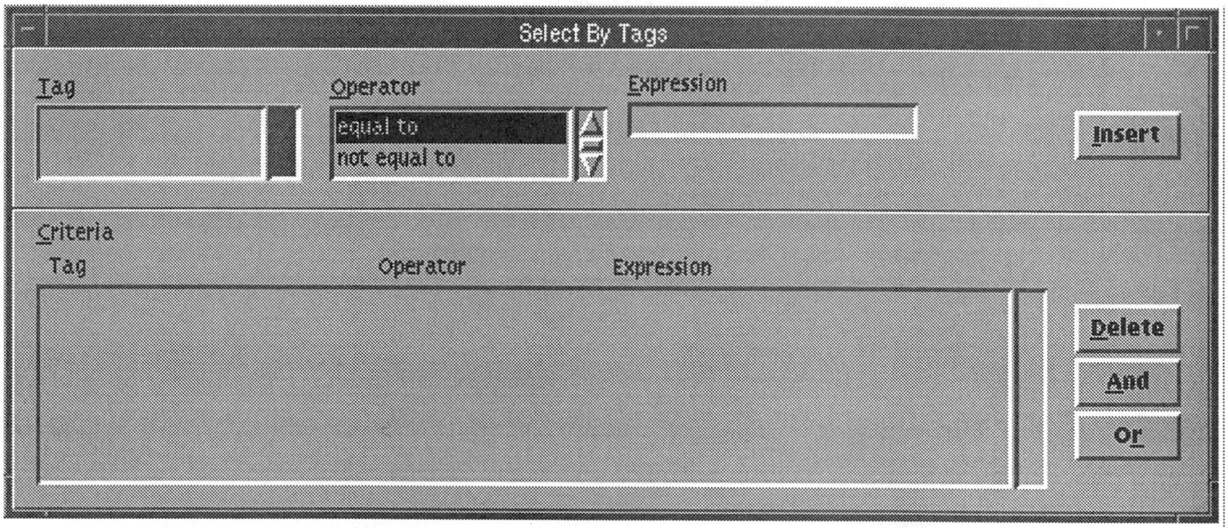

FIGURE 10–6   Select By Tags Settings box.

- The Execute button at the bottom left of the box puts into effect the selection criteria currently set in the fields.

> **NOTE:** Your selection criteria can be based on one item in one of the fields or by a combination of items in one or more fields; for example, all elements on level 10 or only ellipses on level 5 that are filled.

Selection by Level

The Levels field contains a grid of level numbers and a switch button (see Figure 10–7). If a level number is shown with a dark background, it is part of the selection criteria. A light background means the level is not part of the selection criteria.

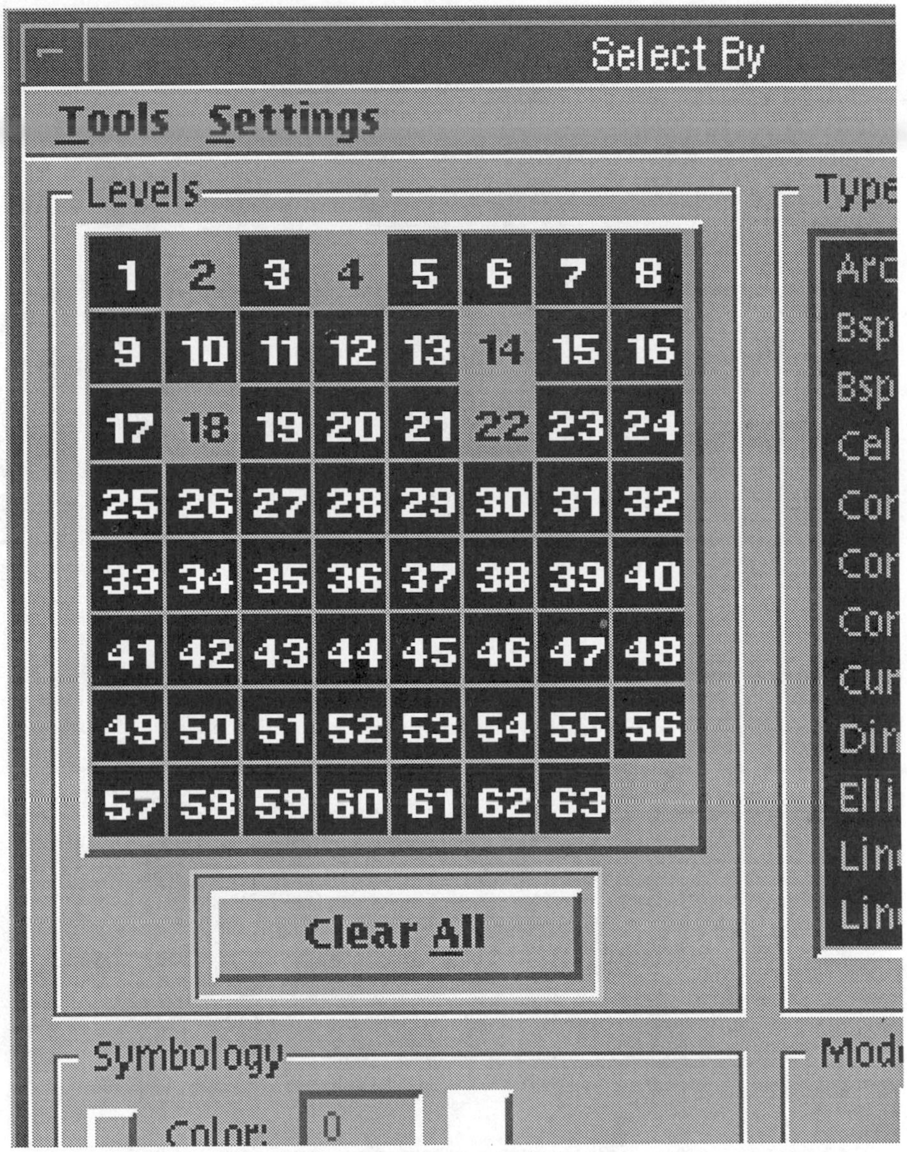

FIGURE 10–7   Displaying the Level field of the Select By Settings box.

To switch the state of a single level, click the data button on it. To change the state of a group of elements, drag the screen pointer across them while holding down the data button.

For example, if you wish to select elements on levels 10 through 15, set those six levels to a dark background and all other levels to a light background.

The option button below the level numbers field is a toggle switch that either clears all levels or selects all levels. The name of the button says what action it is going perform when you click it.

Selection by Type

The Types field contains a list of all element types (see Figure 10–8). Type names shown with a dark background are part of the selection criteria. A light background means that type is not part of the selection criteria.

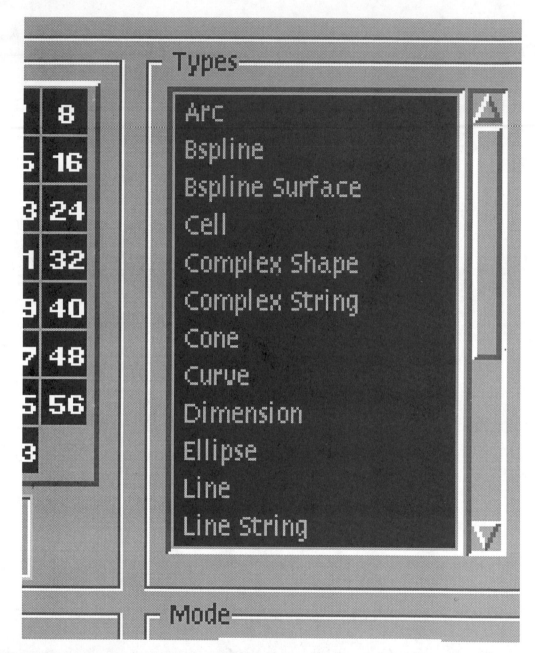

FIGURE 10–8 Displaying the Types field of the Select By Settings box.

To select a specific type and turn off all others, click the Data button on the desired type. To select additional types, hold down the [CTRL] key while clicking the Data button on type names. To select a contiguous group of types, drag the screen pointer across them while holding down the Data button. For example, to select only ellipses and lines, click the Data button on the Ellipse type, then [CTRL]-click the data button on the Line type.

Selection by Symbology

The Symbology field allows you to include element color, weight, and style in the selection criteria (see Figure 10–9). To add a symbology item to the selection criteria, turn on the button to the left of the item's name, then select a value in the menu to the right of the item's name.

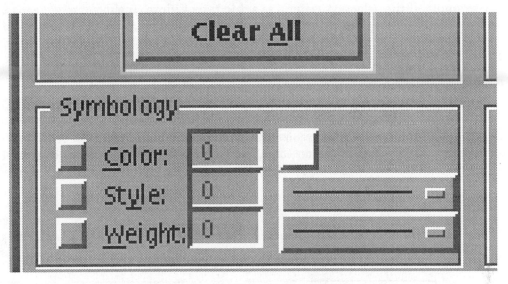

FIGURE 10–9   Displaying the Symbology field of the Select By Settings box.

For example, if the color button is set to ON, elements that are the color shown in the color field are the only ones included in the selection criteria.

Controlling the Selection Mode

The Mode field contains three option menus (see Figure 10–10) that control the way the selection criteria is applied when you click the Execute button at the bottom left of the settings box.

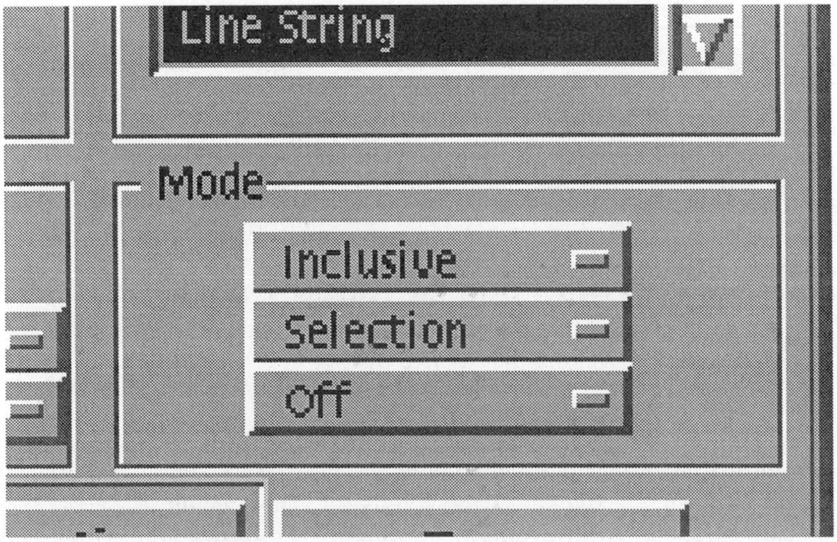

FIGURE 10–10   Displaying the Mode field of the Select By Settings box.

The first option menu located in the Mode field has two options: Inclusive and Exclusive:

Inclusive—Select only elements that meet the selection criteria.

Exclusive—Select only elements that do not meet the selection criteria.

For example, if the selection criteria is set to type Ellipse, Inclusive mode causes all ellipses to be selected, and selection in Exclusive mode causes all elements except ellipses to be selected.

The second option menu located in the Mode field has three options: Selection, Location, and Display:

Selection—Immediately select (place handles) all elements that meet the selection criteria when the Execute button is pressed.

Location—Turn on the selection criteria but do not select any elements when the Execute button is pressed. Use the Selection command in the Main palette to select elements that meet the criteria in this mode. Elements that do not meet the criteria cannot be selected.

Display—Turn on the selection criteria, and make all elements that do not meet the criteria disappear from the view when the Execute button is pressed. No handles are placed on the remaining elements, so the Selection command must be used to select from the elements that still appear in the view.

> **NOTE:** If Display mode has caused elements to disappear from the view, you must execute the criteria in Location mode, then update the view to make them reappear.

The number three option menu located in the Mode field has two options: Off and On:

OFF—When the Execute button is pressed, turns off the previously set selection criteria so it has no effect on element selection.

ON—When the Execute button is pressed, turns on the current selection criteria so it can be used.

> **NOTE:** If you close the Select By settings box with a selection criteria in effect, an Alert window appears prompting you to click OK or Cancel. OK will keep the selection criteria in effect, and Cancel will turn off the criteria.

The Select By Properties Settings Box

Use the Select By Properties settings box (see Figure 10–4) to include additional element attributes in the selection criteria. Open this box by clicking the Properties button in the Select By settings box.

On the left side of the box, select element Properties settings (see Figure 10–11). Each Property has an options menu from which you can select the property to be included in the selection criteria. To select a property, turn the toggle button to ON and then select a setting from the properties option menu. For example, the Area property options menu allows you to select one of the two available options, Solid or Hole elements.

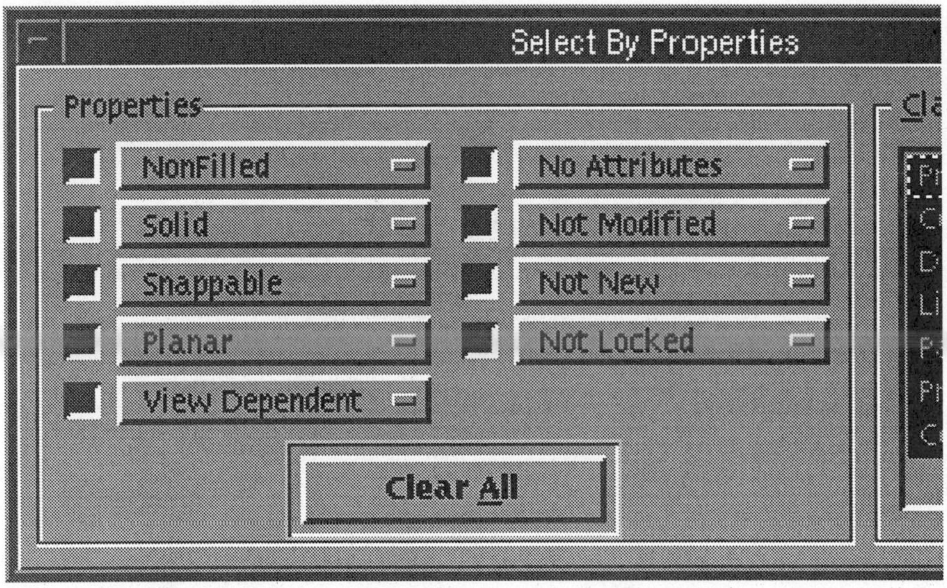

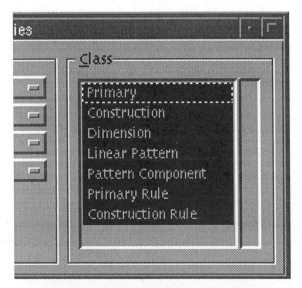

FIGURE 10–11   Displaying the Properties in the Select By Properties.

The button below the properties area is a toggle switch that turns ON or OFF all the property buttons. The name of the button says what will happen next. If it displays Select All, it will turn ON all the options in the Properties Area. If it displays Clear All, then it will turn OFF all the options in the Properties Area.

On the right side of the box is a field in which you select what class or classes of elements to include in the selection criteria (see Figure 10–12). If the class is shown with a dark background, it is included. Each name is a toggle switch. Clicking the data button on the class name adds it to or removes it from the selection criteria.

FIGURE 10–12   Displaying the Class listing in the Select By Properties.

For example, if you want to select only elements in the construction class, set the word Construction in the menu to have a dark background, and set all the others to have a light background.

The Tags Settings Box

The Tags settings box (see Figure 10–13) is used to specify criteria based on tag values. If selection criteria based on tag values are specified, elements that do not have attached tags with the specified tag name(s) will not be selected, located, or displayed.

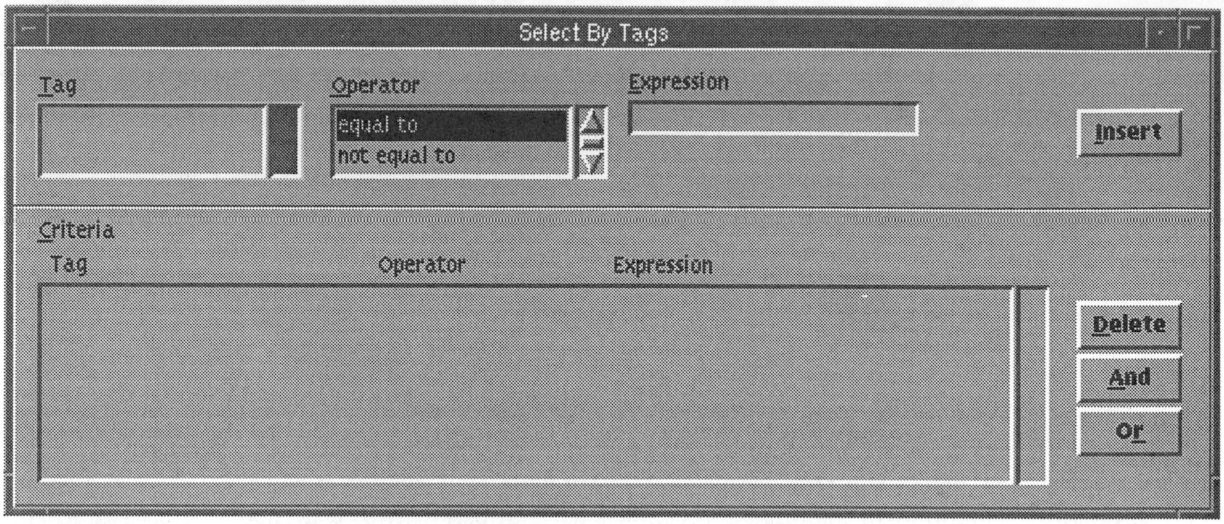

FIGURE 10–13 Select by Tags Settings box.

Selection Criteria Into Effect

Once you set all the selection criteria, click the Execute button in the Select By settings box to select the elements according to the settings. Handles appear (depending on the settings) on the selected elements. After completing the selection criteria, invoke the appropriate element manipulation command and follow the prompts.

LEVEL SYMBOLOGY

Designers often make extensive use of the sixty-three available levels to help organize the various parts of a design. For example, a plot plan may have separate levels for roadways, descriptive text, foundations, utilities, the drawing border, and title block information. An architectural plan might have the walls on one level, the dimensions on another level, electrical information on still another level, and so on. Separating parts of the design by level allows designers to turn on only the part they need to work on and allows them to plot parts of the design separately.

Keeping up with what level everything is on can be confusing. MicroStation's level symbology reduces the confusion by setting unique combinations of display color, weight, and style for each level. When level symbology is turned ON, all elements are displayed using the symbology assigned to the level the elements are on, rather than their true symbology.

For example, if level 10 symbology is set to display elements red, dashed, and weight 5, all elements on level 10 will display with that symbology, no matter what their actual color, weight, and style settings are.

The View Attributes settings box controls the display of level symbology by turning ON and OFF for selected views.

> **NOTE:** If you plot a view in which level symbology is turned on, the elements are plotted with level symbology rather than their true symbology.

The Level Symbology Settings Box

The Level Symbology settings box (see Figure 10–14) provides the options required to create or modify the level symbology. To invoke the Level Symbology settings box, select Level Symbology from the Settings pull-down menu.

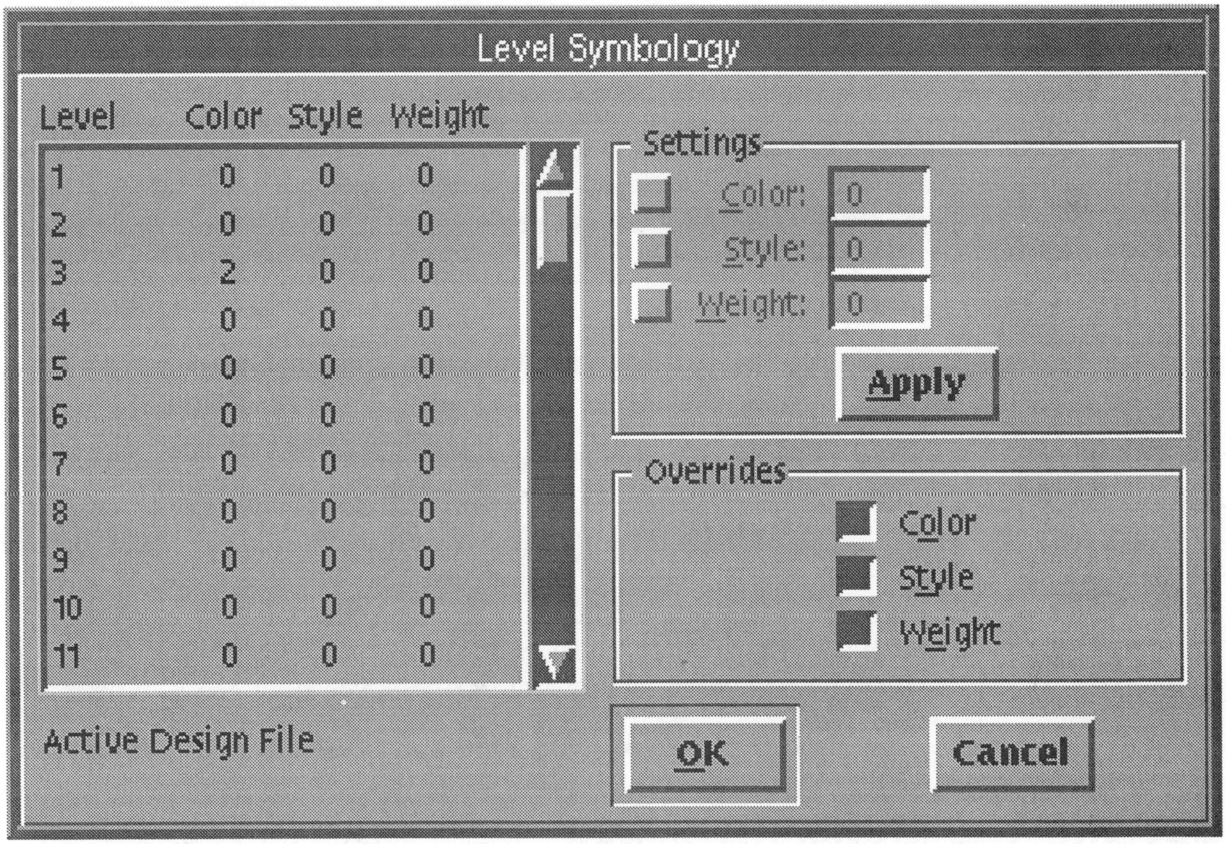

FIGURE 10–14 Level Symbology Settings box.

The Level Symbology settings box contains the following fields:

Level, Color, Style, Weight table—The table on the left side of the settings box shows the current symbology settings for each level.

Settings—The settings area on the right top of the box is where you set the symbology for each level number selected in the table.

Overrides—The overrides area determines which symbology settings are used. If the button is set to ON (appears depressed with a dark center), that symbology setting is in use. For example, if the color button is set to ON, and the style and weight buttons are set to OFF, elements on each level are displayed using the level symbology color, but each element's true style and weight are displayed.

OK and Cancel buttons—To save the level symbology settings press OK. To discard any changes you made, press Cancel. You must click one of the two buttons to close the Level Symbology settings box before you can do anything else in MicroStation.

Following is the step-by-step procedure to set up a level symbology or to modify an existing one:

1. Open the Level Symbology settings box.
2. Highlight the level by clicking with the Data button in the left side of the box.
3. Select a color, style, and/or weight from the Settings box and click the Apply button.
4. Repeat step 2 until all level symbology is set.
5. Turn on the override for each level symbology you want to use.
6. Click the OK button to save the level symbology changes.

> **NOTE:** Changes to the level symbology setup are permanent. You do not have to invoke Save settings to keep them.

Display Level Symbology

Following is the step-by-step procedure to display the level symbology attributes:

1. Open the View Attributes settings box.
2. Set the Level Symbology toggle button to ON (see Figure 10–15).
3. If you want to turn on level symbology only for one view, set the View Number to the one you want and press the Apply button.
4. If you want level symbology display to be ON for all open views, click the All button.

> **NOTE:** Any changes you make to the View Attributes are lost when you exit MicroStation, unless you Save settings from the File pull-down menu.

SETTING THE HIGHLIGHT COLOR

When you select an element for manipulation, or when you click the tentative button on an element, the element is highlighted by switching it to the color red by default. In an area containing many elements with different colors, gray highlighting can be hard to see. If you are having trouble seeing the highlighted elements, the following step-by-step procedure shows how to change the color for the highlighted element:

1. Open the Color sub-menu from the Settings pull-down menu (see Figure 10–16).
2. Select the Element Highlight Color option to open a settings box (see Figure 10–17).
3. Select one of the ten highlight colors from the Element Highlight Color options menu in the settings box.

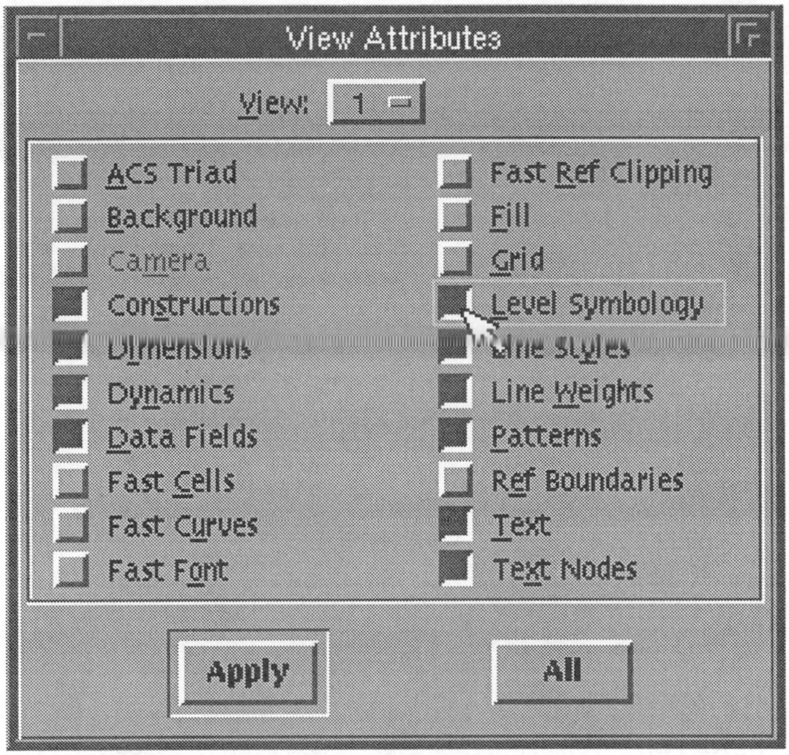

FIGURE 10–15 View Attributes Settings box displaying the status of the Level Symbology toggle.

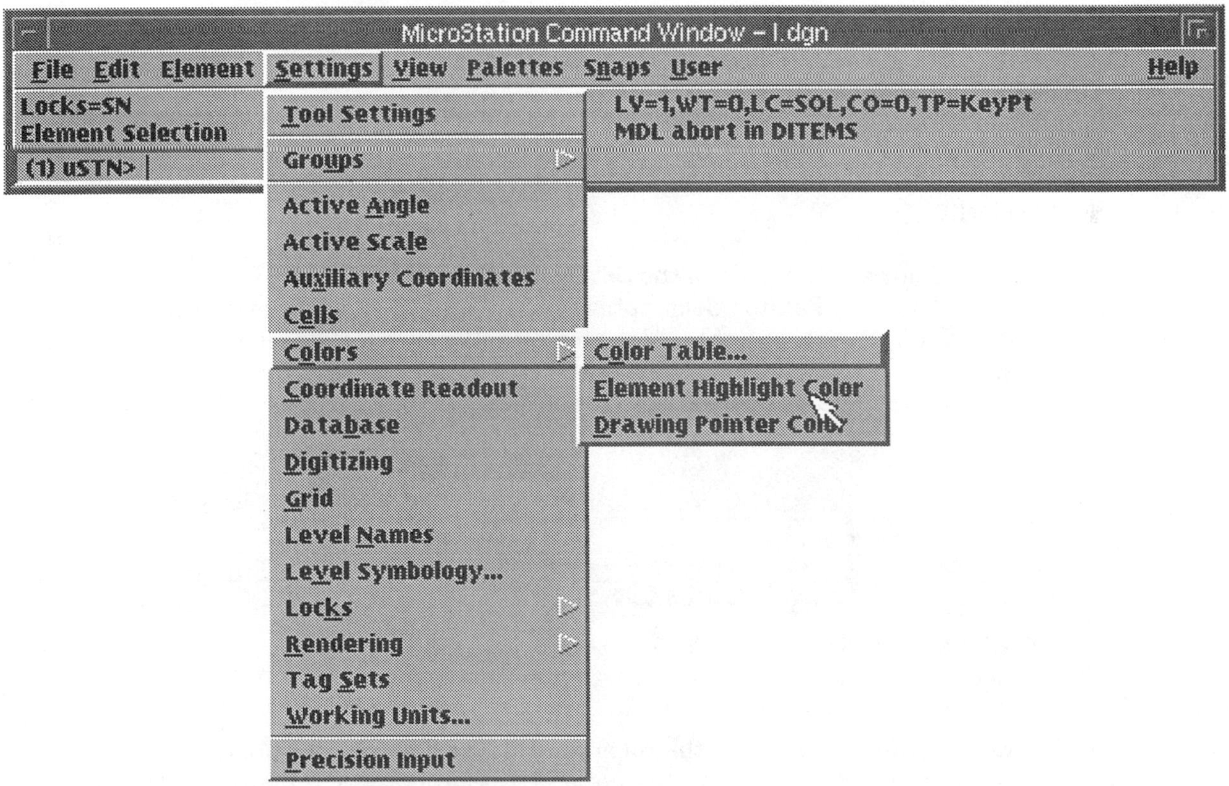

FIGURE 10–16 Invoking the Element Highlight Color Settings box from the Settings pull-down menu in the MicroStation Command Window.

FIGURE 10–17 Element Highlight Color Settings box.

All highlighting is in the color you select until you exit MicroStation. The highlight color applies only to the current design (it is not a MicroStation user preference). If you want the same highlight color to be in effect the next time you load the design file in MicroStation, select Save Settings from the File pull-down menu.

> **NOTE:** If you highlight an element that is the same color as your highlight color, you will not be able to tell if the element is highlighted. For example, if your highlight color is green and the element is green, there is no indication that the element is highlighted. Pick a color for highlighting that is not used in your design.

> **NOTE:** If you set highlighting to the same color as the view background, elements disappear when highlighted.

Setting the Drawing Pointer Color

After you place the first data point or move an element, the cursor changes to a shape of a rotated cross. By default, the rotated cross is gray, but you can change it to another color in the same way you can change the highlight color. The following step-by-step procedure shows how to change the pointer color:

1. Open the Color sub-menu from the Settings pull-down menu (see Figure 10–16).
2. Select the Drawing Pointer Color option to open a settings box (see Figure 10–18).
3. Select one of the ten possible colors from the Drawing Pointer Color options menu in the settings box.

FIGURE 10–18 Drawing Pointer Color Settings box.

The drawing pointer cursor uses the color you select until you exit MicroStation. The cursor color applies only to the current design (it is not a MicroStation user preference). If you want the same cursor color to be in effect the next time you load the design file in MicroStation, select Save Settings from the File pull-down menu.

> *NOTE:* The cursor color is also applied to the Locate Tolerance Circle that appears on the screen cursor when you select a manipulation command.

> *NOTE:* If you set pointer cursor to the same color as the view background, you will not be able to see the vector cursor or the locate tolerance circle.

RECORD AND LISTEN

The Record and Listen features of MicroStation provide a way to automate a sequence of steps in MicroStation. The Record On <filename> key-in stores all input, including pointer movements, in the file whose name you provide in <filename>. The Record Off key-in stops recording.

The Listen <filename> key-in plays back the contents of the file named in <filename>. Pointer movement is replayed during Listen, so it is critical that all windows be open in the same position they were before the recording began. Before you start recording, save settings and make a copy of your design file. Use the unaltered copy for playback. If you plan to playback the recording more than once, make another copy of the unaltered file each time, and use that copy for playback.

Record a Session

To start recording, key-in at the uSTN> field, **record on** <filename> and press ⌨. Replace <filename> with the name of the file you want to store the recording in. You can also include a directory path name.

> *Example:* **record on c:\us_demos\pla_line.rec**

After you start recording, perform all the pointer movements and command actions you want to include in the demonstration. To stop recording, key-in at the uSTN> field, **record off** and press ⌨.

Play Back a Recording

To play back the contents of a recording file, load the unaltered design file copy in MicroStation, then key-in at the uSTN> field, **listen** <filename> and press ⌨. Replace <filename> with the name of the file containing the recording. If you used a full path specification when recording, you may have to include the path.

You can pause the playback at any time by pressing ⌨+⌨. To restart the paused playback, press any key on the keyboard. To end the play back before it completes playing back all recorded information, press ⌨+⌨.

> *NOTE:* Conditions for playback must be identical to those during recording. That means all view windows and palettes must be in the same position they were when you started recording. The screen resolution must be the same as it was during recording, and the same type of pointing device must be used.

The Record and Listen commands are useful mainly in creating demonstrations for use in meetings and training. In most cases, MicroStation provides other, more efficient methods of doing repetitive tasks in a production environment. Custom seed files, reference files, cell libraries, and various grouping methods handle repetitive tasks faster than playing back a recording.

HANDLING AUTOCAD DRAWINGS IN MICROSTATION

AutoCAD is another widely used CAD package, you may occasionally need to load AutoCAD drawings in MicroStation or save a MicroStation design file as an AutoCAD drawing. For example, your customer may provide you with a plot plan drawing that was created in AutoCAD, or you may need to furnish construction detail drawings to a subcontractor in AutoCAD format.

MicroStation allows you to open AutoCAD binary format (DWG) files and save design files in AutoCAD binary format. Conversion between the two formats takes place when you open or save the files.

> **NOTE:** The methods for converting to and from AutoCAD format described here provide a quick, easy way to do the conversion, but they do not allow you to "customize" the conversion process. The Import and Export commands, described later, allow you to tell MicroStation how you want some parts of the process handled.

> **NOTE:** When you save a file using AutoCAD format, the extension is set to DWG.

Open an AutoCAD Drawing

AutoCAD drawings are opened from the MicroStation Manager dialog box or the Open dialog box (available from the File pull-down menu).

Following is the step-by-step procedure to open an AutoCAD drawing:

1. Select DWG from the Type option menu located in the Open Design File dialog box (see Figure 10–19).
2. If necessary, change the directory path using the Directories field.
3. Select the AutoCAD file you need to work on from the Files list.
4. Click OK button.

When you select an AutoCAD drawing, its contents are converted to MicroStation format, and the new design file is placed in the same directory as the AutoCAD drawing. The design file has the same name as the AutoCAD file, and its extension is DGN. When the conversion completes, the design file is opened in MicroStation. For example, if the AutoCAD drawing is C:\PROJECT\LAYOUT.DWG, the resulting design file is C:\PROJECT\LAYOUT.DGN.

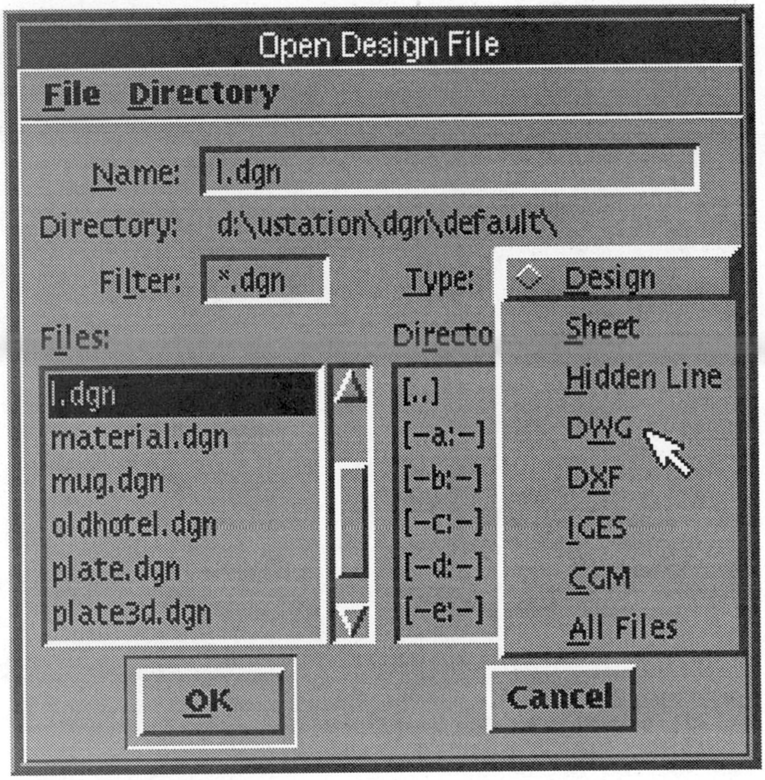

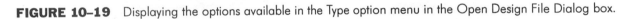

FIGURE 10–19   Displaying the options available in the Type option menu in the Open Design File Dialog box.

Save a Design File in AutoCAD Format

Following is the step-by-step procedure to save a MicroStation design file in AutoCAD format:

1. Open the Save As dialog box from the File pull-down menu.
2. Open the box's Type options menu and select DWG (see Figure 10–20).
3. If necessary, set the directory path to the directory where you want to save the drawing.
4. Key-in the file name in the Name edit field.
5. Click the OK button or press the [ENTER] key.

The contents of the design file are converted to AutoCAD format and saved on the given file name. The design file stays open in MicroStation.

If the conversion program encounters a conversion problem, it opens a DOS window to display a message describing the error.

TRANSLATE DRAWINGS BETWEEN DIFFERENT GRAPHICS FORMATS

MicroStation provides an import and export option for exchanging CAD drawings between the Intergraph Design Format System (IGDS) and other graphic formats.

Use the Import sub-menu (Figure 10–21) to import information from files that contain drawings in other graphic formats into the design file currently open in MicroStation. Use the Export sub-menu

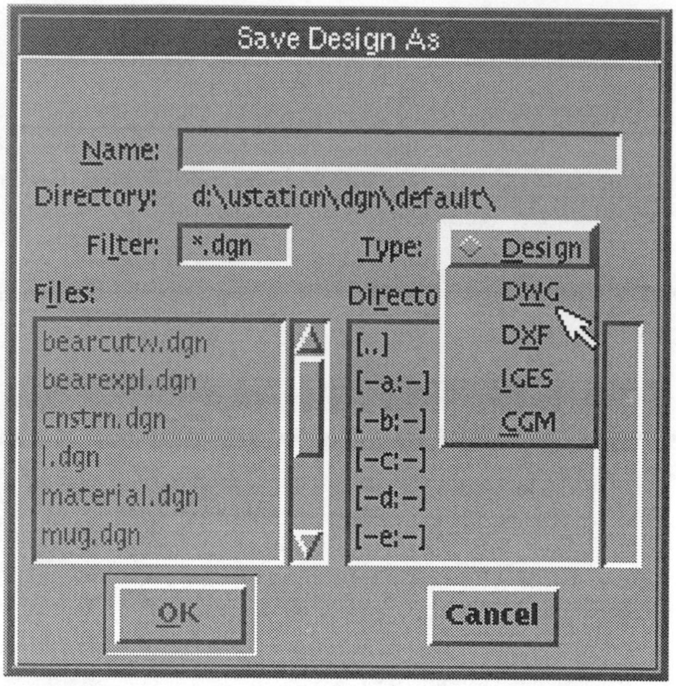

FIGURE 10–20 Displaying the options available in the Type option menu in the Save Design As Dialog box.

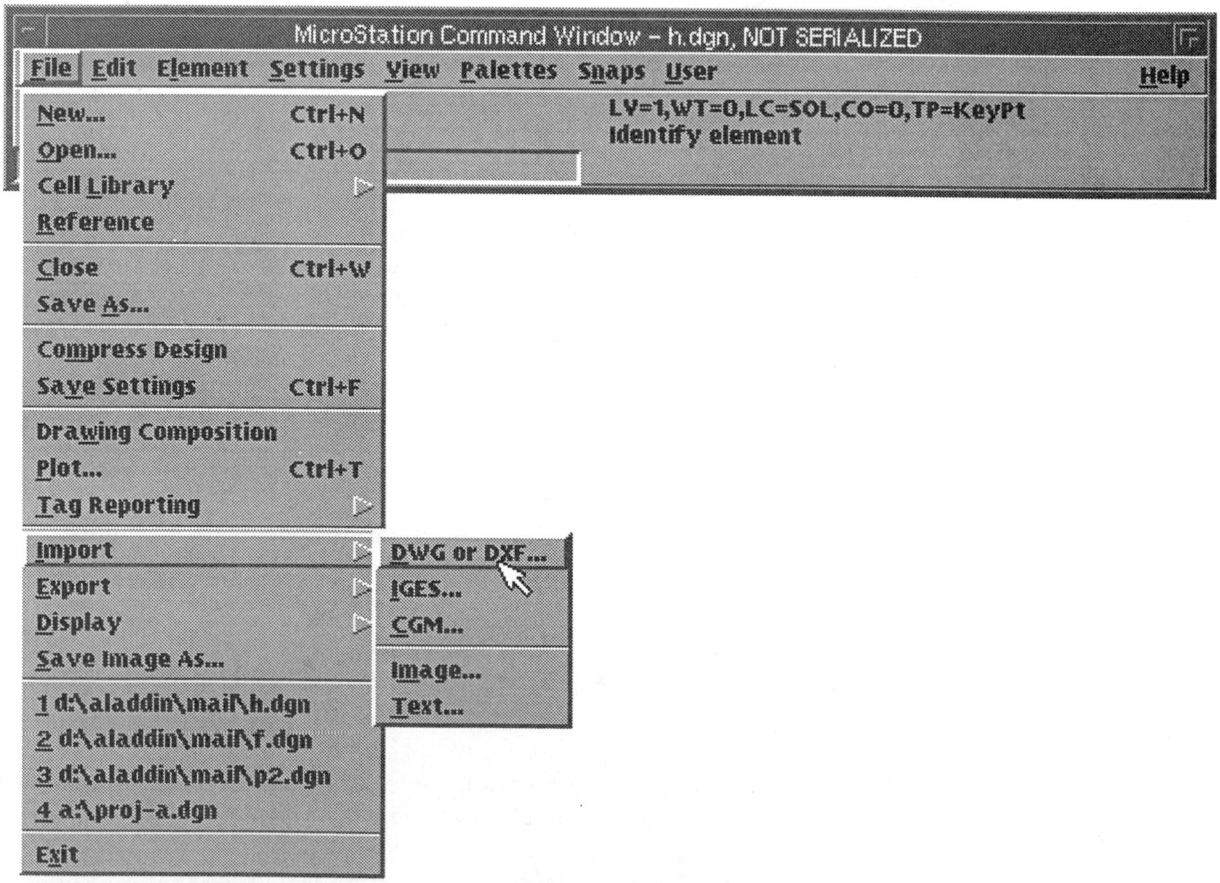

FIGURE 10–21 Displaying the different options available in the Import menu located in the File pull-down menu.

(Figure 10–22) to place copies of the elements from your design into a file using a graphic format other than IGDS.

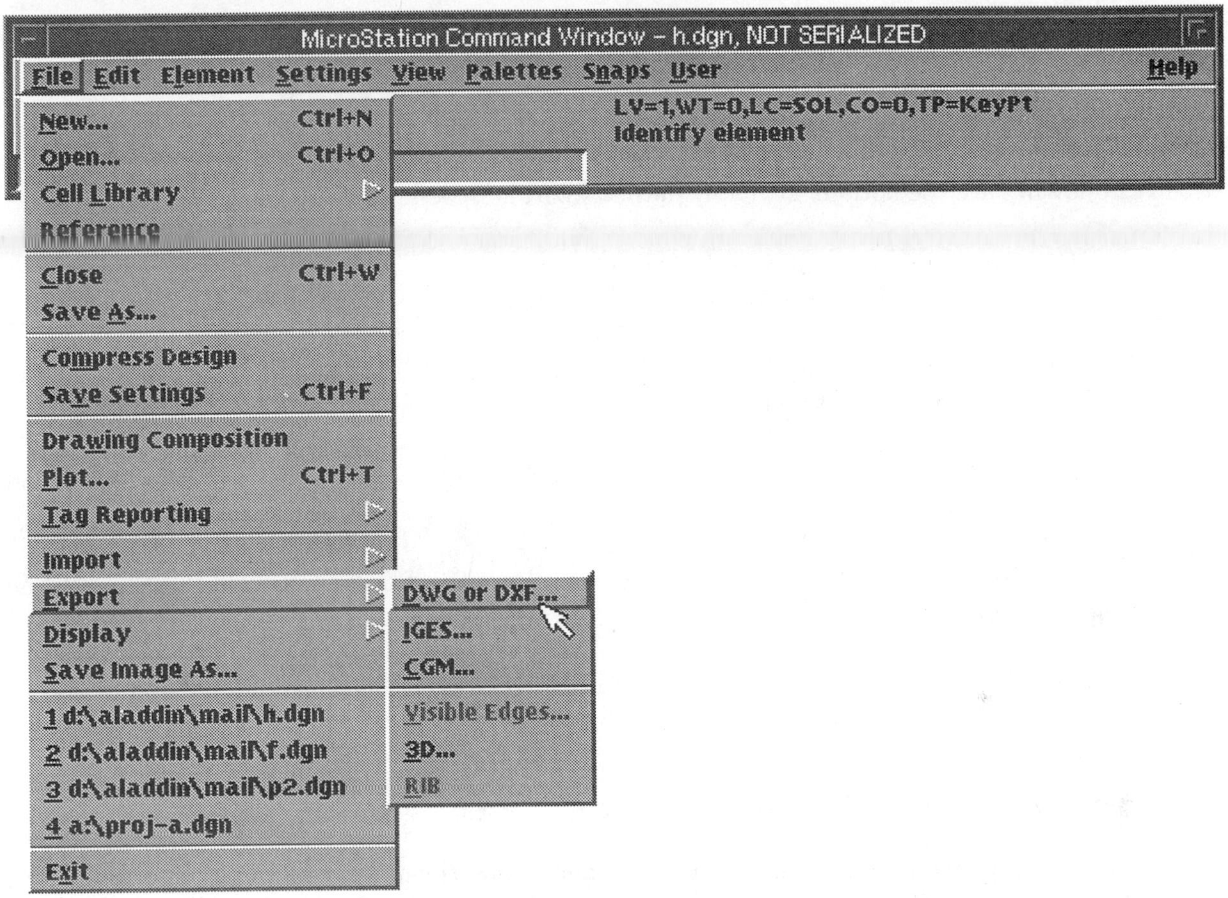

FIGURE 10–22 Displaying the different options available in the Export menu located in the File pull-down menu.

Import Formats

Following are the options available in the Import sub-menu:

DWG (AutoCAD binary drawing files)—The DWG option allows you to import AutoCAD drawings directly into MicroStation, with no intermediate translation required. DWG drawings can be added to the open design file, or, as was discussed earlier in this chapter, they can be opened directly in MicroStation.

DXF (Drawing Interchange Format)—A file exchange format created by Autodesk, Inc., that is used to exchange graphic data between many CAD and graphics applications. DWG and DXF imports are handled identically.

IGES (Initial Graphics Exchange Specification format)—A public domain, ANSI standard, neutral file format that is intended as an international standard for the exchange of product definition data between different CAD applications.

CGM (Computer Graphics Metafile format)—An ANSI standard for the exchange of picture data between different graphics software that is device- and environment-independent.

Image—Several graphic formats used by text processing and publication graphics packages.

Text—ASCII text files that were created in a text editor or word processor. Text file import is discussed in Chapter 4.

Export Formats

Following are the options available in the Export sub-menu:

CGM (Computer Graphics Metafile format)—MicroStation allows you to convert the current design file into CGM format on a given file name.

DWG (AutoCAD binary drawing files)—MicroStation allows you to convert the current design file into DWG format on a given file name.

DXF—MicroStation allows you to convert the current design file into DXF format on a given file name.

IGES—MicroStation allows you to convert the current design file into IGES format on a given file name.

2D/3D—MicroStation allows you to convert 2D designs to 3D format and vice versa.

Import/Export Settings Boxes

Select one of the Import or Export options, and, if additional information is required to perform the conversion, a settings box opens to allow you to provide the information. Which import or export format to use depends on the package used by the person you are exchanging files with. You must find a format common to MicroStation and their graphics package.

The procedures and available options vary greatly between formats. For more information on importing and exporting, refer to the documentation provided with the MicroStation.

SAVE VIEW IMAGES

The contents of any of the eight MicroStation views can be saved to several image formats that can be imported to word processing and display graphics programs.

Following is the step-by-step procedure to save a view using an image format:

1. Open the Save Image As... dialog box (shown in Figure 10–23) from the File pull-down menu.
2. Select the format you need, the number of the view to be saved as an image, and set the other required options.
3. Click the save button to open the Save Image As dialogue box.
4. Key-in the file name for the saved image and select the directory where you want to save the file, and click the OK button to save the view as an image file.

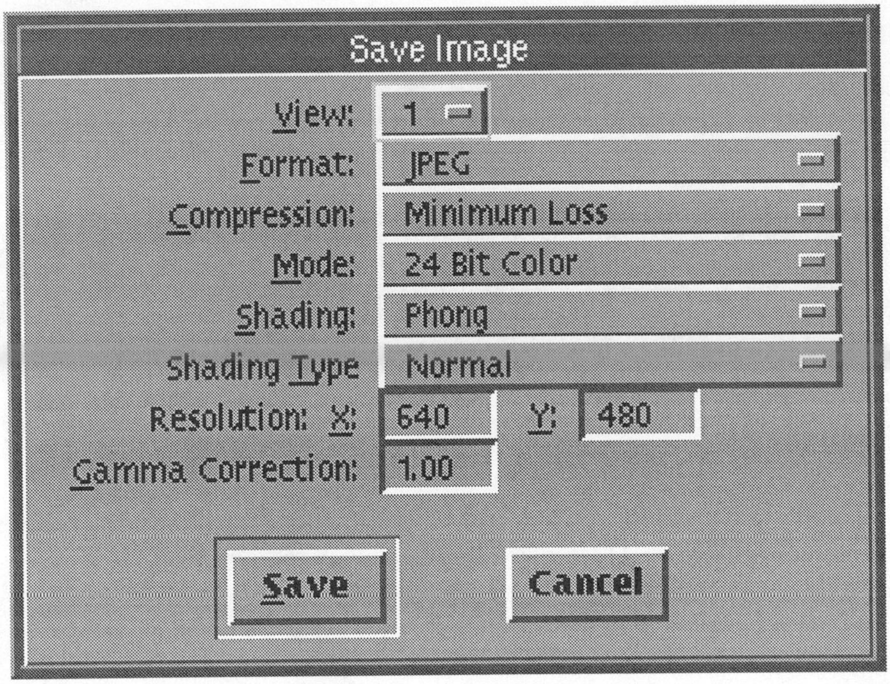

FIGURE 10-23 Save Image As... Dialog box.

DISPLAY IMAGES, MOVIES, AND TEXT

The Display sub-menu in the Files pull-down menu provides options to display an image, movie, or text in a separate window:

Image—Opens the Display Image File dialog box in which you select the image format and image file name to be displayed. The selected file is displayed in a separate window.

Movie—Opens the Movies settings box from which you can set up conditions for viewing an animated sequence in a separate window.

Text—Opens the Display Text File dialog box in which you can select a text file to be displayed in a separate window.

USING GLOSSARY TEXT

MicroStation provides a glossary file that contains commonly used text strings, each of which is identified by an abbreviation called the text-string alias. Use the Glossary settings box to place text strings, or combinations of text strings, from the glossary file into your current design file. Text placement uses the currently active text parameters (described in Chapter 4).

You can add your own text strings to the glossary file by editing it in a text editor or a word processor. The MicroStation configuration variable MS_GLOSSARY points to the location of the file, and the default file location is \USTATION\WSMOD\DEFAULT\DATA\EXAMPLE.GLS. Configuration variables are discussed in Chapter 11.

Glossary Settings Box

To open the Glossary settings box, select Glossary from the Utilities sub-menu located in the User pull-down menu (see Figure 10–24). MicroStation displays the Glossary settings box similar to the one shown in Figure 10–25.

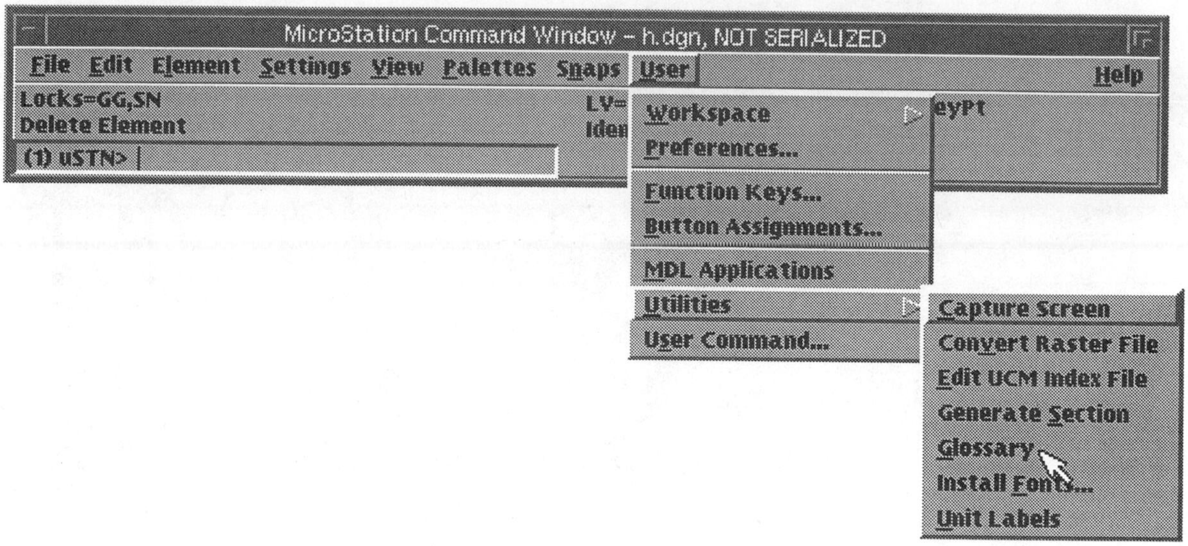

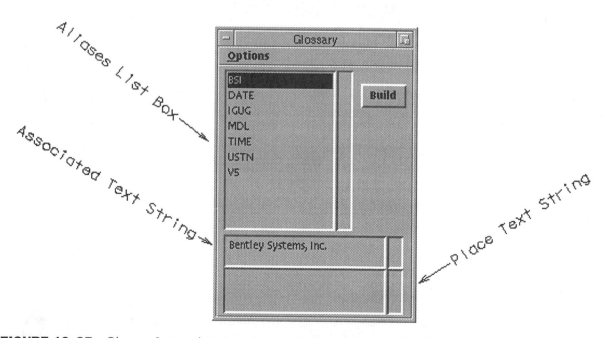

FIGURE 10–24 Invoking Glossary Settings box from the User Pull-down menu.

FIGURE 10–25 Glossary Settings box.

The Glossary settings box contains three fields.

The Aliases list box lists the aliases for all text strings in the glossary file.

The Associated Text String field displays the text string for the highlighted alias in the Aliases list box.

The Place Text field displays the text string that will be placed when you define a data point in your design.

The Options menu in the title bar of the Glossary settings box provides two sub-menus that affect text-string placement.

The Line Length sub-menu lets you control the maximum number of characters allowed in each line of text. The Custom option opens the Custom dialog box and allows you to set the line length to any number of characters. Default settings are also available (30, 40, 50, or 60 characters) in the Line Length sub-menu.

The Case sub-menu lets you control the case of the text string when you place it in your drawing. Select Default to leave the text case as it appears in the Place Text field. Select Uppercase to use all capital letters. Select Lowercase to make all letters lowercase.

Placing Glossary Text Strings

Following is the step-by-step procedure to place text strings from the Glossary in the current design file:

1. Select Utilities sub-menu from the User menu pull-down menu.
2. Select Glossary to open the Glossary settings box from the Utilities sub-menu.
3. Select the alias for the text string you want to place in the current design file.
4. MicroStation displays the text string in the Associated Text String field. If displayed text is:
   a. Not the correct text, repeat step 3.
   b. The correct text, click the Build button to place the text in the Place Text field.
5. Position the screen cursor where you want to place the text and click the data button.

Placing the text in your design clears the Place Text string in the Glossary settings box. If you need to place another copy of the same text, repeat the above procedure starting with step 3, or copy the text you already placed.

If you decide you do not want to place the text shown in the Place Text string of the Glossary settings box, click the Reset button on your pointing device to clear the text from the field.

Building Text Strings

In addition to placing one line of text string in the Place Text field, you can place multiple lines of text string from the Glossary and/or you can key-in your own text.

The first text string you place in the Place Text field must be from the glossary. After that you can place additional glossary text strings following the previous text string, and you can type text in the Place Text field. If necessary, you can even edit the text already in the field.

For example, if you want to place the date and time in your design:

1. Select the Date alias, then click the Build button to place the date text string in the Place Text field.
2. Select the Time alias, then click the Build button to add the time text string following the Date text string.

If you want only the actual date and time in the text string then:

1. Highlight and delete the lead-in text for the date.
2. Highlight and delete the lead-in text for the time.

Place the date and time in the design by placing a data point.

> **NOTE:** The example of building a text string assumes the glossary file on your system still contains the date and time strings that are in the default glossary. If your glossary file has been edited, the date and time alias fields may not exist.

Glossary File

As mentioned earlier in the discussion of the glossary, all glossary text strings are contained in a file, and, if necessary, you can add new text strings to the existing file. To add text strings and modify existing text strings, load the glossary file in a text editor or word processor.

Lines in the glossary file that start with a **#** sign are comments and do not appear as part of the glossary in MicroStation. Use them to provide notes to yourself and to other people who may edit the glossary later.

For each glossary string in the file, the text string alias is on a line by itself and the actual text string follows on the next line. For example, the alias "DATE" is followed by the date text string: "Today's date is $date."

> **NOTE:** The $ sign in the date text string ($date) tells MicroStation to replace the word date with the system date. The time string also contains "$time", which tells MicroStation to replace the word time with the system time.

Go to the end of the file to add new glossary text. Place an alias for your new text string on a line by itself and place the actual text string on the next line. The text string can be as long as required.

> **NOTE:** There is no need to place the glossary text strings in alphabetical order. MicroStation displays the aliases in ascending alphabetical order when you open the Glossary settings box.

Glossary File Location

You do not have to build your glossary in the default file that comes with MicroStation. You can create your own file and even place it in a directory path that is not part of the MicroStation directory structure.

In order for MicroStation to use your glossary file, edit the MS_GLOSSARY configuration variable to point to your file location. Include the path specification. See Chapter 11 for a detailed explanation on editing the configuration variables.

REVIEW QUESTIONS

Write your answers in the spaces provided:

1. Explain briefly the purpose of creating a graphic group.

   _____

   _____

2. List the steps in creating a graphic group.

   _____

   _____

3. Explain the purpose of the graphic group lock setting.

   _____

   _____

4. Explain briefly the purpose of element selection by element type.

   _____

   _____

5. Explain briefly the benefits of setting up a level symbology table.

   _____

   _____

6. List the steps involved in setting up a level symbology table.

   _____

   _____

7. List the steps involved in converting a MicroStation design file to AutoCAD drawing file.

   _____

   _____

11

CUSTOMIZING MICROSTATION

Off-the-shelf MicroStation is extremely powerful. But, like many popular engineering and business software programs, it does not automatically do all things for all users. It does, however, permit users to make changes and additions to the core program to suit individual needs and applications. Word processors offer a feature by which you can save a combination of many keystrokes and invoke them at any time with just a few keystrokes. This is known as a *macro*. Database management programs have their own library of user functions that can also be combined and saved as a user-named, custom designed command. These programs also allow you to create and save standard blank forms for use later to be filled out as needed. Using these features to make your copy of a generic program unique and more powerful for your particular application is known as *customizing*.

Customizing MicroStation can include several facets. After completing this chapter, you will be able to:

- Create Setting Groups and edit existing Groups.
- Provide a name for a level and group them into user-defined group names.
- Create Multi-line definitions and save them to a file.
- Create custom line styles.
- Customize User Preferences, Workspace, and Function Keys.
- Install Fonts.

SETTING GROUPS

MicroStation allows you to define a setting group with a user-specified name in three categories: Drawing (default), Scale, and Working Units. Under each setting group of the Drawing category, you can define individual group components. You can set element attributes such as color, weight, line style, level, and class, associating with a primitive command (such as place line, place text, etc.) as a part of the group component. As a group component you can also save the current Multi-line definition and active dimension settings. You can define any number of group components for each setting group.

MicroStation provides an option to save the setting groups and group components to an external file and by default the file will have an extension .STG. This file follows the same concept as the cell library. Once created, the settings file may be attached to any of your design files and activate one of the setting groups and corresponding group component. Selecting a component does the following:

All element attributes associated with the component are set as specified in the component definition.

If a key-in is defined for the component, the corresponding command is selected, letting you place an element(s) without invoking the command from a palette.

Select Settings Box

The Select Settings Box allows you to select a setting group and corresponding group component from the currently attached setting group file. The settings box also provides an option to attach another setting group file and invoke a setting group and corresponding group component. To open the Select Settings box, invoke the Select option in the Groups menu from the Settings pull-down menu of the MicroStation Command Window, or key-in at the uSTN> field, **setmgr select settings** and press ⏎. MicroStation displays a Select Settings box similar to the Figure 11–1.

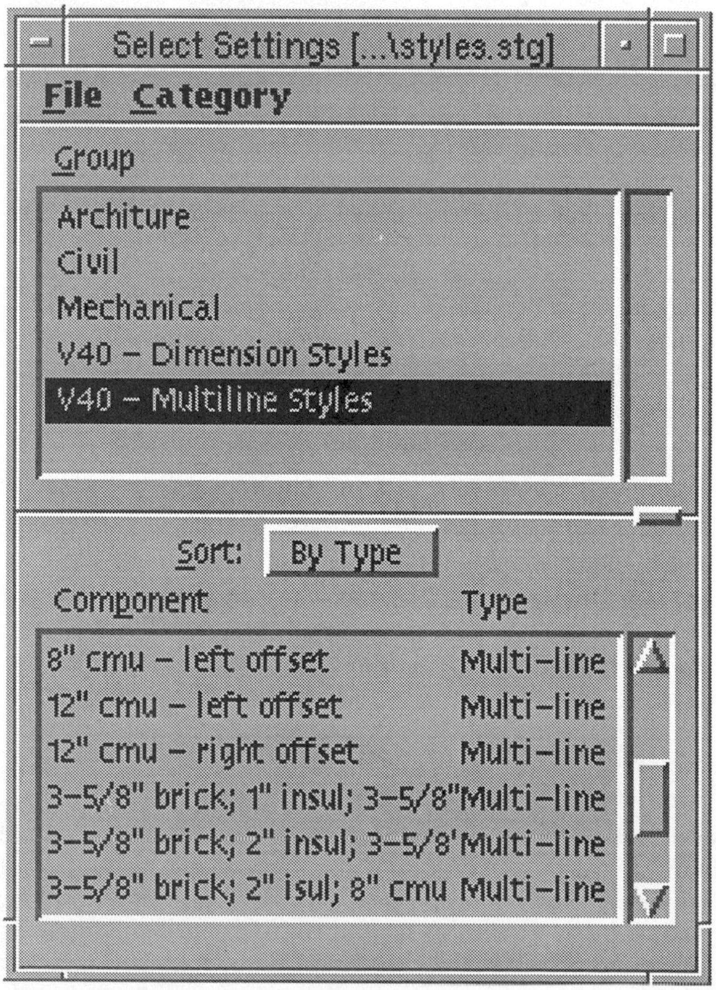

FIGURE 11–1 Select Settings box.

MicroStation displays the name of the currently opened setting group file as part of the title of the settings box. The Settings box is divided into two parts. By default, the top part lists the names of the available drawing settings groups. The bottom part of the settings box lists the name and type of each component from the selected setting group. To invoke one of the components, select the name of the component and settings associated with the component are set as specified in the definition. If a key-in is defined for the component, the corresponding tool is selected, letting you place an element(s) without using a tool palette.

To list the names of the available scale settings groups, select Scale from the Categories pull-down of the Select Settings box. MicroStation displays the Scale Settings dialog box as shown in Figure 11 2. The settings specify the relationship between plotting units and design master units. Double-click the scale setting to make its settings active and close the dialog box.

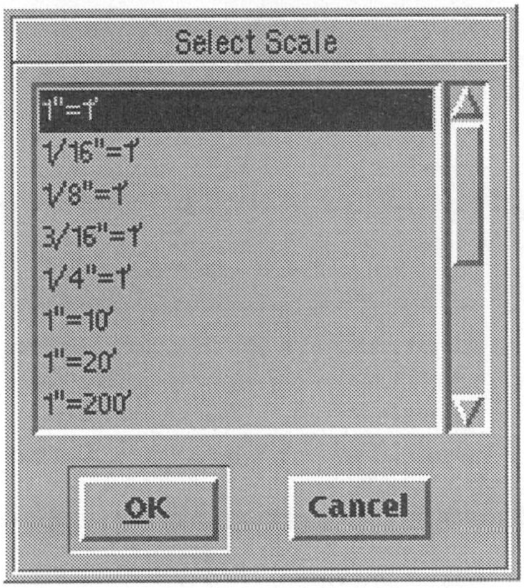

FIGURE 11-2   Scale settings box.

To list the names of the available working units settings groups, select Working Units from the Categories pull-down of the Select Settings box. MicroStation displays the Select Working Units dialog box as shown in Figure 11–3. The dialog box lists the available working units settings. To

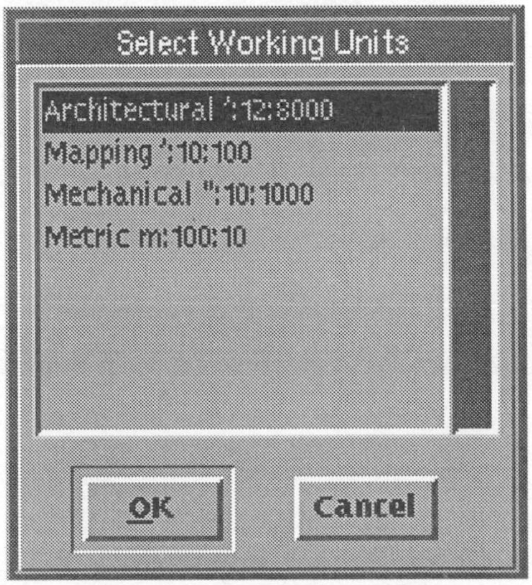

FIGURE 11-3   Select Working Units dialog box.

change the working units to one of the listed working units for the current design, double-click the working units setting to make its settings active and close the dialog box. An alert box opens for confirming the adjustment of the working units settings.

To attach an existing settings group file, invoke the Open... command from the File pull-down menu of the Select Settings box. MicroStation displays Open Existing Settings File dialog box. Select the settings group file from the list and click the OK button or press [ENTER] to attach to the current design file.

Edit Settings Box

The Edit Settings Box allows you to define, modify, and delete settings groups and group component. To open the Edit Settings box, invoke the Edit option in the Groups menu from the Settings pull-down menu of the MicroStation Command Window, or key-in at the uSTN> field, **setmgr edit settings** and press [ENTER]. MicroStation displays a edit settings box similar to the Figure 11–4.

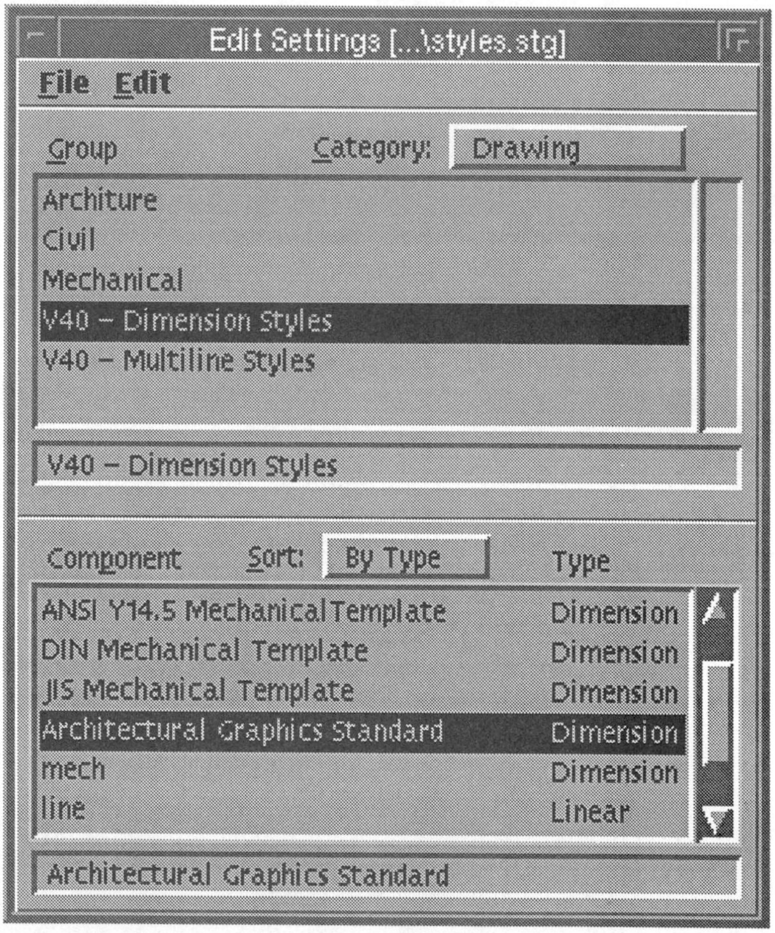

FIGURE 11–4 Edit Settings box.

MicroStation displays the name of the currently opened setting group file as part of the title of the settings box. The Settings box is divided into two parts. By default, the top part lists the names of the available drawing settings groups. The bottom part of the settings box lists the name and type of each component from the selected settings group. The Category options menu sets the category for the listing of groups in the Group list box. The Sort options menu sets the manner in which components are sorted in the Component list box By Name or By Type.

To create a new settings file, invoke the New... command from the File pull-down menu of the Edit Settings box. MicroStation displays Create Settings File dialog box to create a settings file. Key-in the name of the file, and click OK button or press [ENTER] to create a new settings file.

To attach an existing settings group file, invoke the Open... command from the File pull-down menu of the Select Settings box. MicroStation displays Open Existing Settings File dialog box to attach as existing settings file. Select the settings group file from the list and click OK button or press [ENTER] to attach to the current design file.

To create a new settings group, invoke the Group option under Create sub-menu from the Edit pull-down menu as shown in Figure 11–5. MicroStation adds a new group, called "Unnamed" to the group list box. You can change the name from "Unnamed" to any appropriate name in the name field box located just below the listing of the group names list box. The maximum number of characters for the group name cannot exceed 31.

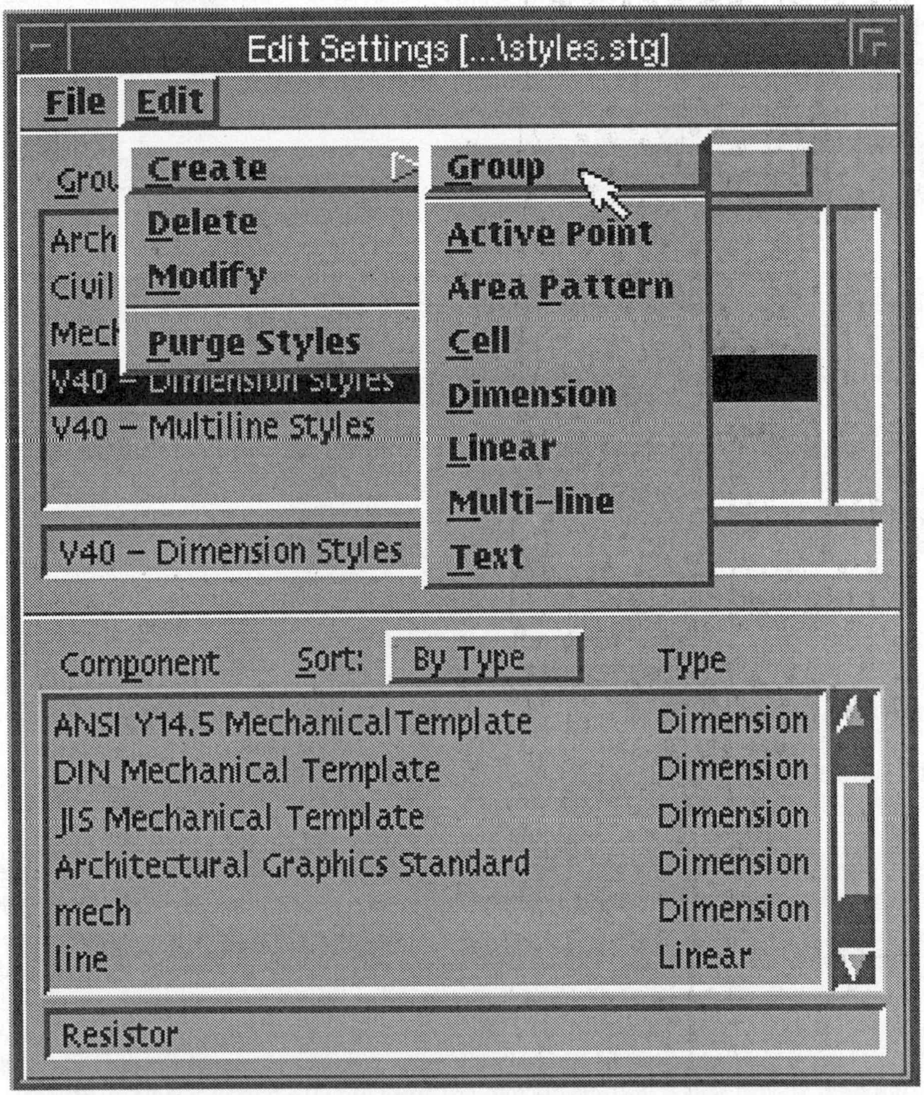

FIGURE 11–5   Invoke the Group option under Create sub-menu from the Edit pull-down menu.

To delete a selected settings group from the list of settings group, invoke the Delete option from the Edit pull-down menu. An alert box opens for confirming the deletion.

To create a new component for the selected settings group, select one of the seven component types available under Create sub-menu from the Edit pull-down menu. MicroStation adds a new component type "Unnamed" to the Components list box. You can change the name from "Unnamed" to any appropriate name in the name field box located just below the listing of the component names list box. The maximum number of characters for the group name cannot exceed 31. See Table 11–1 for the list of the component types and corresponding tools that can be used with the component type.

Table 11–1.   Component Types and Corresponding Tools

COMPONENT TYPE	TOOL
Active Point	Points Sub-palette
Area Pattern	Patterning Palette
Cell	Cells Sub-palette
Dimension	Dimensioning Palette
Linear	Lines Sub-palette
	Polygons Sub-palette
	Arcs Sub-palette
	Circles and Ellipses Sub-palette
	Curves Sub-palette
Multi-line	Key-in PLACE MLINE CONSTRAINED corresponds to the Place Multi-line tool
Text	Text Sub-palette

To modify a group component, scale settings or working units, invoke the Modify command from the Edit pull-down menu. There is a settings box for modifying each type of component.

Modify Point Component Settings box The Modify Point Component Settings box (see Figure 11–6) allows you to modify the options available related to Construct Point commands. To set the key-in that will be activated automatically when the component is selected, set the key-in toggle button to ON, and type appropriate key-in for the Construct Points command. Set the appropriate element attributes (level, color, weight, and line style) that will be activated automatically when the component is selected. Select one of the three point types, Zero-Length Line, Cell, or Character from the Type options menu. If you select Cell option, set appropriate settings in the Cell section of the Modify settings box. If you select Character option, set appropriate settings in the Character section of the Modify settings box.

Modify Area Pattern Component Settings box The Modify Area Pattern Component Settings box (see Figure 11–7) allows you to modify the options available related to Hatching and Patterning commands. To set the key-in that will be activated automatically when the component is selected, set the key-in toggle button to ON, and type appropriate key-in for the Hatching or Patterning command. Set the appropriate element attributes (level, color, weight, and line style) that will be activated automatically when the component is selected. Select one of the two pattern types, Pattern or Hatch. If you select Pattern option, set appropriate settings in the Pattern section of the Modify settings box. If you select Hatch option, set appropriate settings in the Hatch section of the Modify settings box.

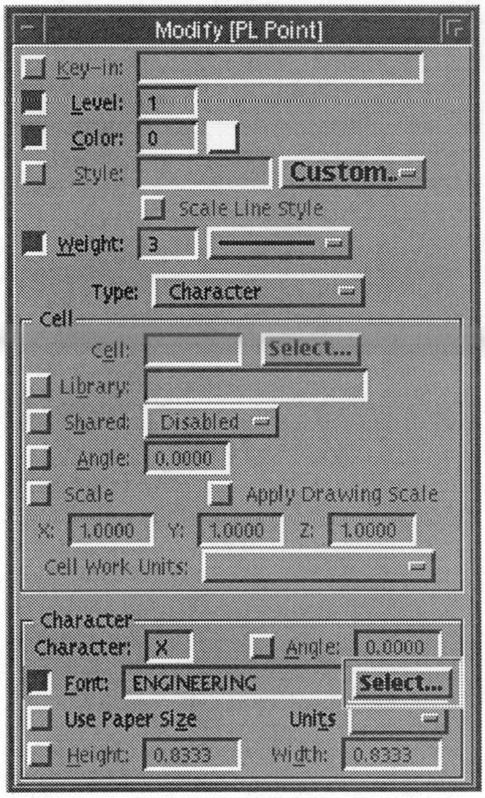

FIGURE 11–6 Modify Point Component settings box.

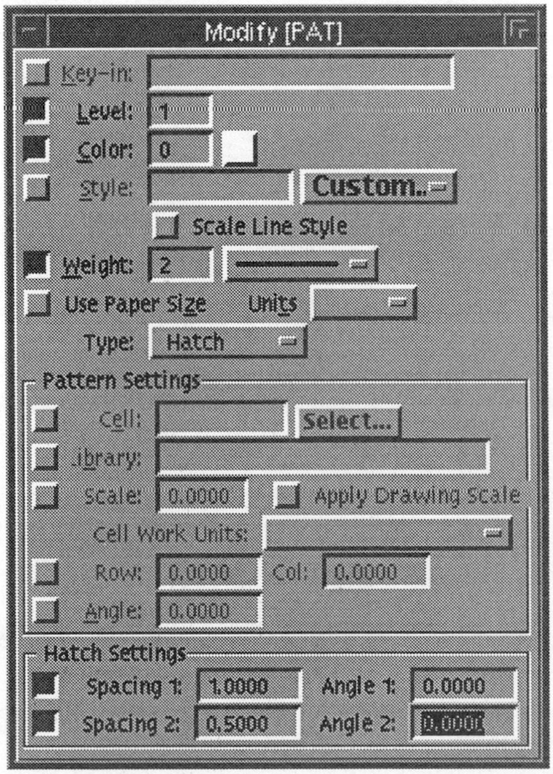

FIGURE 11–7 Modify Area Pattern Component settings box.

Modify Cell Component Settings box   The Modify Cell Component Settings box (see Figure 11–8) allows you to modify the options available related to Cell Placement commands. To set the key-in that will be activated automatically when the component is selected, set the key-in toggle button to ON, and type appropriate key-in for the Cell placement command. Set the appropriate element attributes (level, color, weight, and line style) that will be activated automatically when the component is selected. Key-in the name of the Cell Library, cell name and appropriate scale factors that will be automatically activated when the component is selected. Select one of the two cell types, Placement or Terminator from the Type options menu. If the Placement option is selected then the Cell selection will become the Active Cell when the component is selected in the Select Settings window. If the Terminator option is selected, then the Cell selection will become the Active Line Terminator.

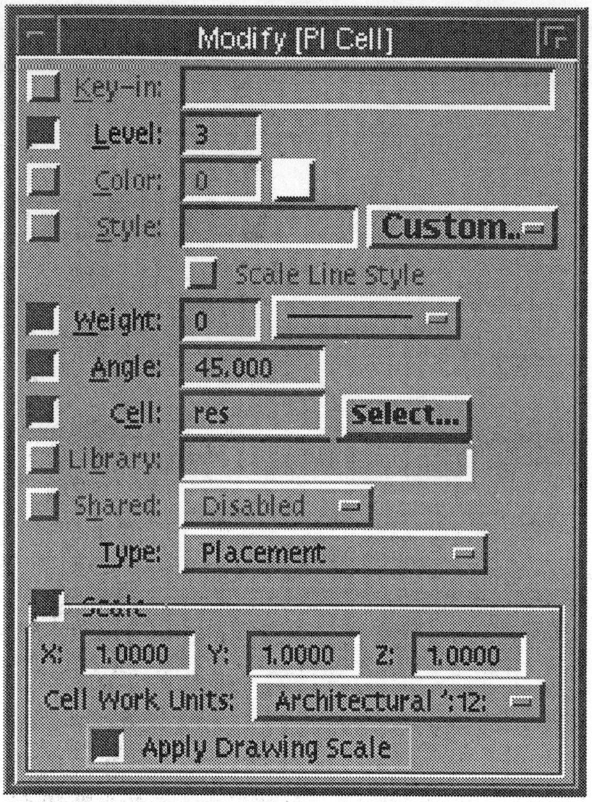

FIGURE 11–8   Modify Cell Component settings box.

> **NOTE:** The Level, Color, Style, and Weight controls can affect placement of a cell using the component only if the specified cell was created as a point cell.

Modify Dimension Component Settings box   The Modify Dimension Component Settings box (see Figure 11–9) allows you to modify the options available related to Dimension component definition. To set the key-in that will be activated automatically when the component is selected, set the key-in toggle button to ON, and type appropriate key-in for the Dimension placement command. Set the appropriate element attributes (level, color, weight, and line style) that will be activated automatically when the component is selected. The Name field shows the name with which the component's dimension settings are stored. The name is equivalent to a style name in MicroStation Version 4. Click the Get Active button to open the Save Dimension Settings dialog box, which is used to copy the active dimension settings into the component. Key-in the Name and Description with which the active dimension settings will be stored in the component. The Dimension Placement settings box and other dimension settings boxes contain controls for adjusting the active dimension settings.

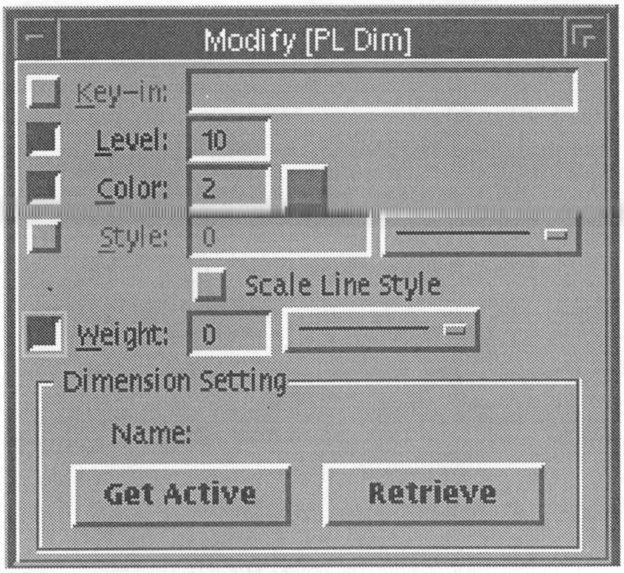

FIGURE 11–9 Modify Dimension Component settings box.

Click the Retrieve button to open the Retrieve Dimension Settings dialog box, which is used to copy previously specified dimension settings into the component.

Modify Linear Component Settings box The Modify Linear Component Settings box (see Figure 11–10) allows you to modify the options available related to Placement of Lines, Polygons, Arcs, Circles, Ellipses and Curves commands. To set the key-in that will be activated automatically when the component is selected, set the key-in toggle button to ON, and type appropriate key-in for the Linear command. Set the appropriate element attributes (level, color, weight, line style, area and fill) that will be activated automatically when the component is selected.

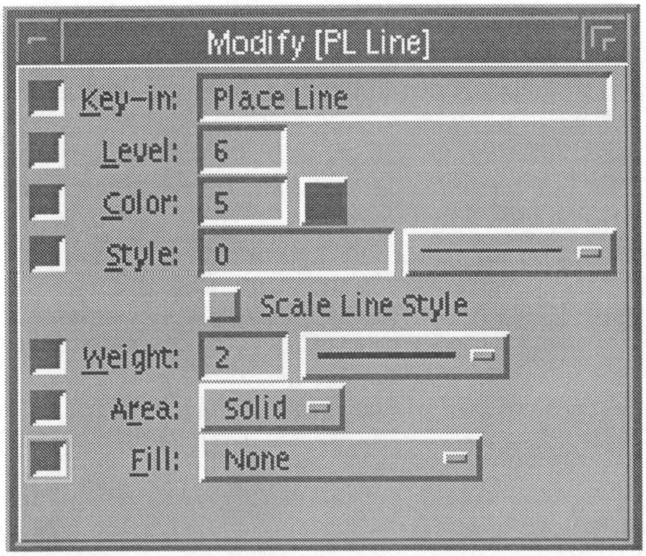

FIGURE 11–10 Modify Linear Component settings box.

Modify Multi-line Component Settings box The Modify Multi-line Component Settings box (see Figure 11–11) allows you to modify the options available related to Multi-line component definition. To set the key-in that will be activated automatically when the component is selected, set the key-in toggle button to ON, and type appropriate key-in for the Multi-line placement command. Set the appropriate element attributes (level, color, weight, and line style) that will be activated automatically when the component is selected. The Name field shows the name with which the component's multi-line definition is stored. The name is equivalent to a style name in MicroStation Version 4. Click the Get Active button to open the Save Multi-line Definition dialog box, which is used to copy the active multi-line definition into the component. Key-in the Name and Description with which the active multi-line definition will be stored in the component. The Multi-line settings box is used to define multi-lines.

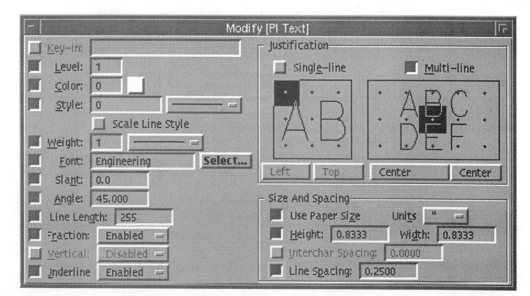

FIGURE 11–11 Modify Multi-line Component settings box.

Click the Retrieve button to open the Retrieve Multi-line Definition dialog box, which is used to copy previously specified multi-line definition into the component.

Modify Text Component Settings box The Modify Text Component Settings box (see Figure 11–12) allows you to modify the options available related to Placement of Text. To set the key-in that

FIGURE 11–12 Modify Text Component settings box.

will be activated automatically when the component is selected, set the key-in toggle button to ON, and type appropriate key-in for the place text command. Set the appropriate element attributes (level, color, weight, line style, area and fill) and text attributes (slant angle, line length, line spacing, fraction, vertical, underline, justification, font, size, and inter-character spacing) that will be activated automatically when the component is selected.

Importing Dimension and Multi-line Styles from Version 4

To import dimension and multi-line styles created with MicroStation Version 4 as a group, invoke the Import... tool from the File pull-down menu. MicroStation displays Open Existing Settings dialog box similar to the Figure 11-13. Each style that is selected from the library is converted to a component of the new group and assigned a name identical to its style name.

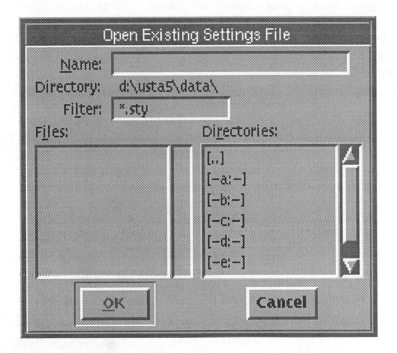

FIGURE 11-13   Open Existing Settings dialog box.

NAMING LEVELS

In Chapter 2 you were introduced to placing elements on individual levels. Each design file is provided with 63 levels and each level is assigned a number between 1 and 63 inclusive. To make a level active, key-in **LV=**<number> and press [ENTER]. You can turn ON and OFF levels by keying **ON=**<number> and **OF=**<number> respectively. Instead of keying a level number, you can assign an alphanumeric "name" which represents a level number and then substitute the "name" for the "number" when using the key-ins. By assigning a name to a level, it is easier to remember what type of elements will be placed on a specific level. Let's say you want to place dimensioning on level 10, instead of remembering level 10 for dimensioning, assign a name dim for level 10. When ever you want to place dimensioning, make sure you are in dim level by making active level by keying in **LV=dim** and press [ENTER]. It may also be helpful to assign level names if you have a need to "translate" a drawing into or out of MicroStation from or to another CAD system.

In addition to assigning a level name, MicroStation allows you to provide a group name. Under a group name you can assign a set of level names or numbers and MicroStation allows you to control the display of levels by keying in a group name for ON and OFF key-in commands. Level names and group names are analogous to the files and directories in the DOS operating system.

MicroStation provides an option to save the level name assignments and level group definitions composing the level structure to an external file. You can store any number of definitions to a single file and by default the file will have an extension .LVL. This file follows the same concept as the cell library. Once created, the level structure file may be attached to any of your design file and activate one of the definitions stored in the file.

View Levels Settings Box

The View Levels Settings Box allows you to assign level names and group names in addition to setting an active level and turn level display ON and OFF. To open the View Levels Settings box, select the Levels option from View pull-down menu in the MicroStation Command Window, or key-in at the uSTN> field, **selector level** and press [ENTER]. MicroStation displays a View Levels settings box similar to the Figure 11–14.

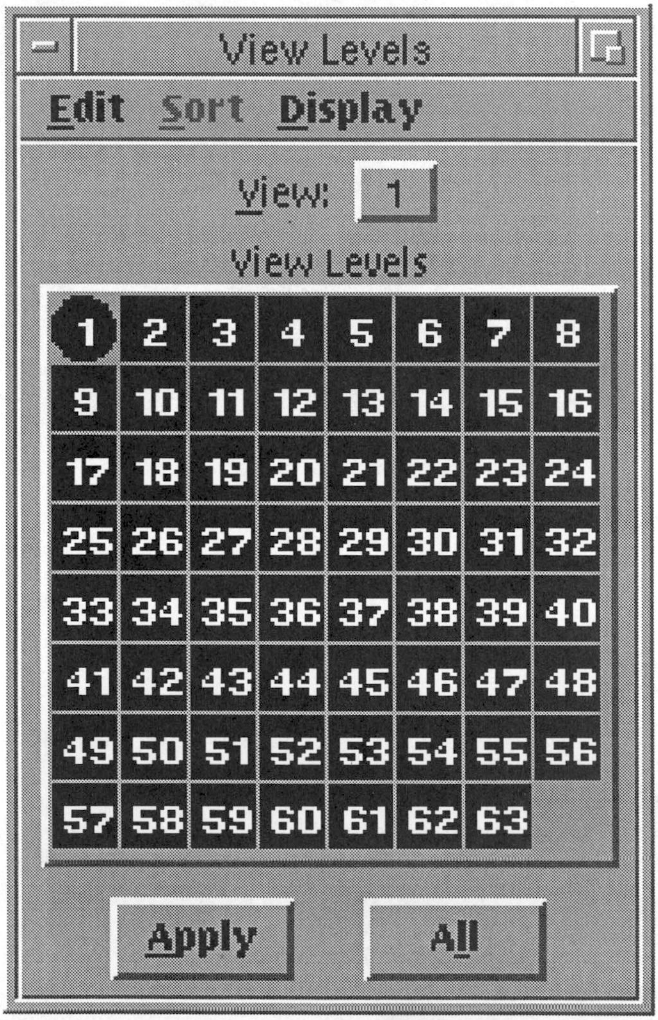

FIGURE 11–14 View Levels settings box.

Display MicroStation displays three different layouts (by level numbers, level names, or level groups) depending on the option selected from the Display pull-down menu of the View Levels settings box. By default, MicroStation displays the Level numbers layout, see Figure 11–14. See Chapter 3 for a detailed explanation for the Level numbers layout.

Level names layout displays the names of the levels similar to the one shown in Figure 11–15. The Active level name is displayed in red color. To turn ON or OFF a set of level(s), select all the level name(s) to be included (dragging or [CTRL]-clicking selects multiple levels) from Level operations layout display and click ON or OFF button. To make an active level, select a level name and click the Active button.

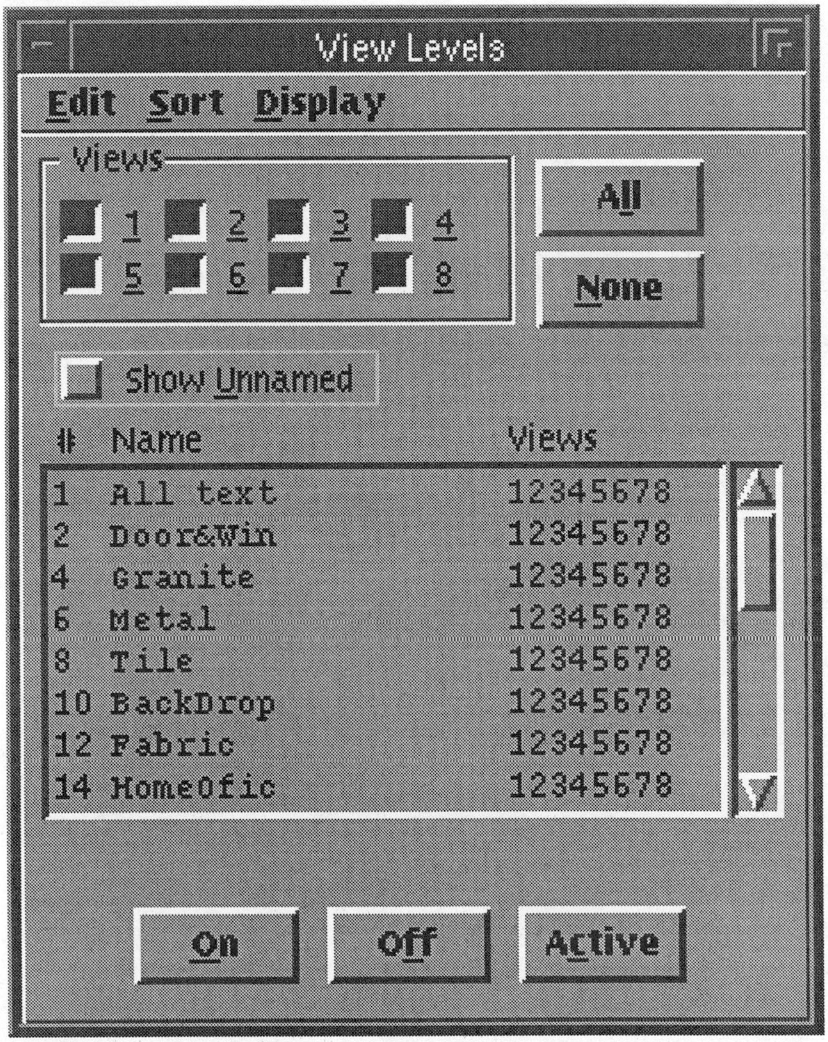

FIGURE 11–15 Level names layout displaying the names of the levels.

Level group layout lists the group names and corresponding levels similar to the one shown in Figure 11–16. The Active level name is displayed in red color. To turn ON or OFF a specific group, select the group name from the group operations layout display and click ON or OFF button. To turn ON or OFF a set of level(s), select all the level name(s) to be included (dragging or [CTRL]-clicking selects multiple levels) from a specific group name and click ON or OFF button. To make an active level, select a level name and click Active button.

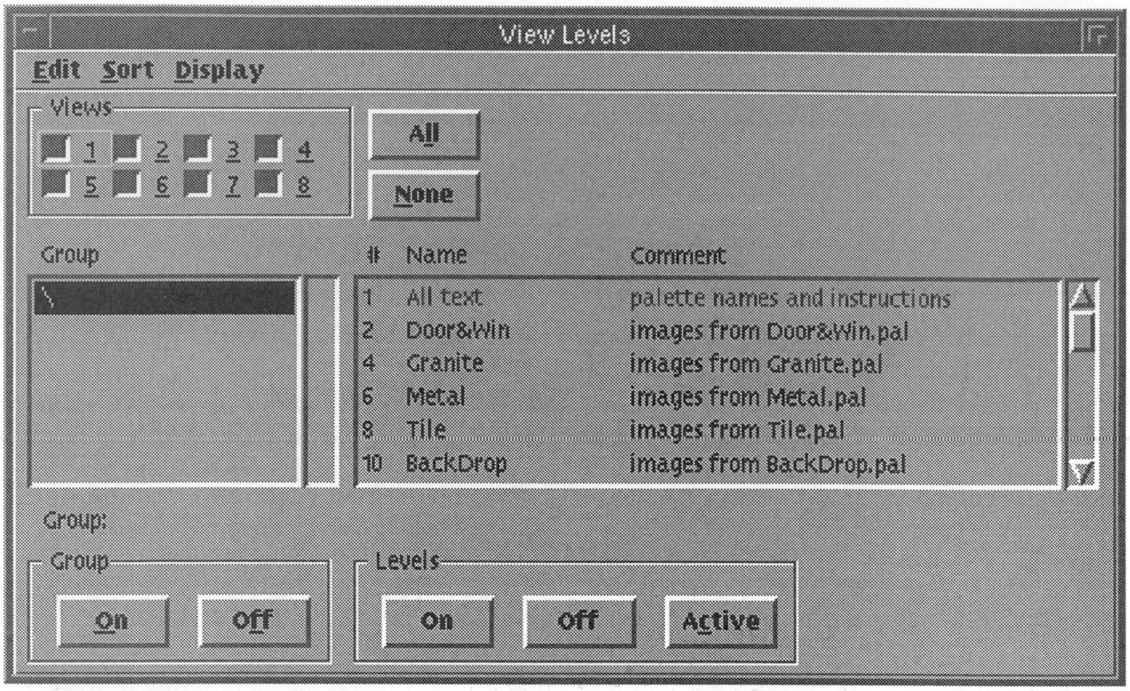

FIGURE 11-16 Level group layout lists the group names and corresponding levels.

Define Names To assign level names and group names, invoke the Define Names... dialog box from the Edit pull-down of the View Levels settings box, MicroStation displays the Level Names dialog box similar to the Figure 11-17.

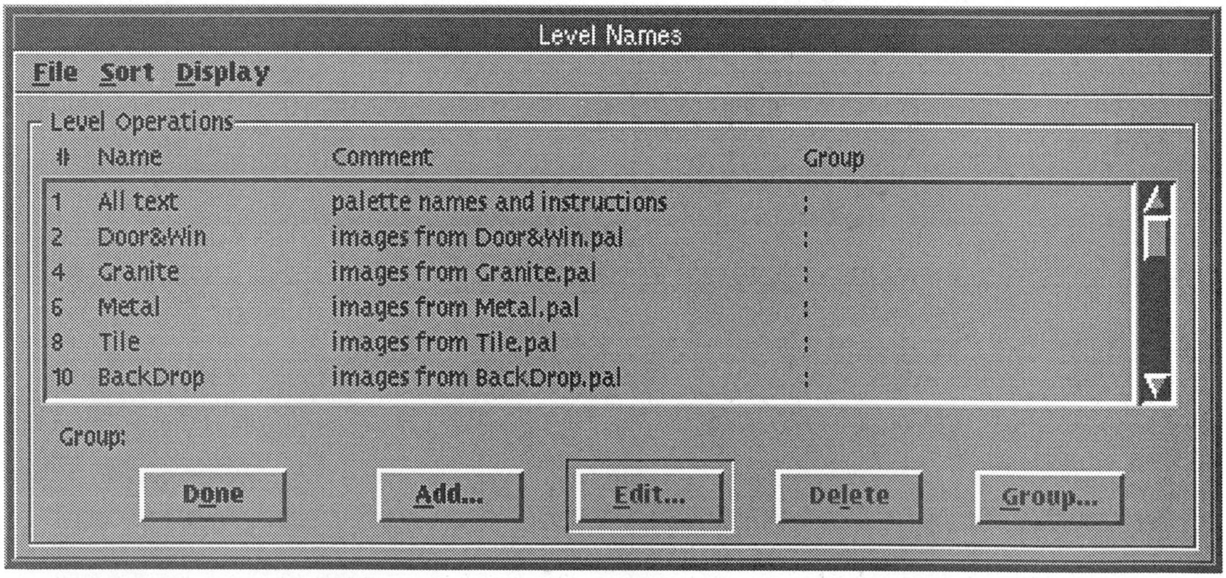

FIGURE 11-17 Level Names dialog box.

NOTE: You can also invoke the Level Names dialog box from the Settings pull-down menu of the MicroStation Command Window.

The Level Names dialog box has two alternate layouts, chosen from the Display menu as shown in Figure 11–18. Level operations layout displays all the level names assigned in the current level structure file. Level Group operations layout displays all the group names assigned in the current level structure file.

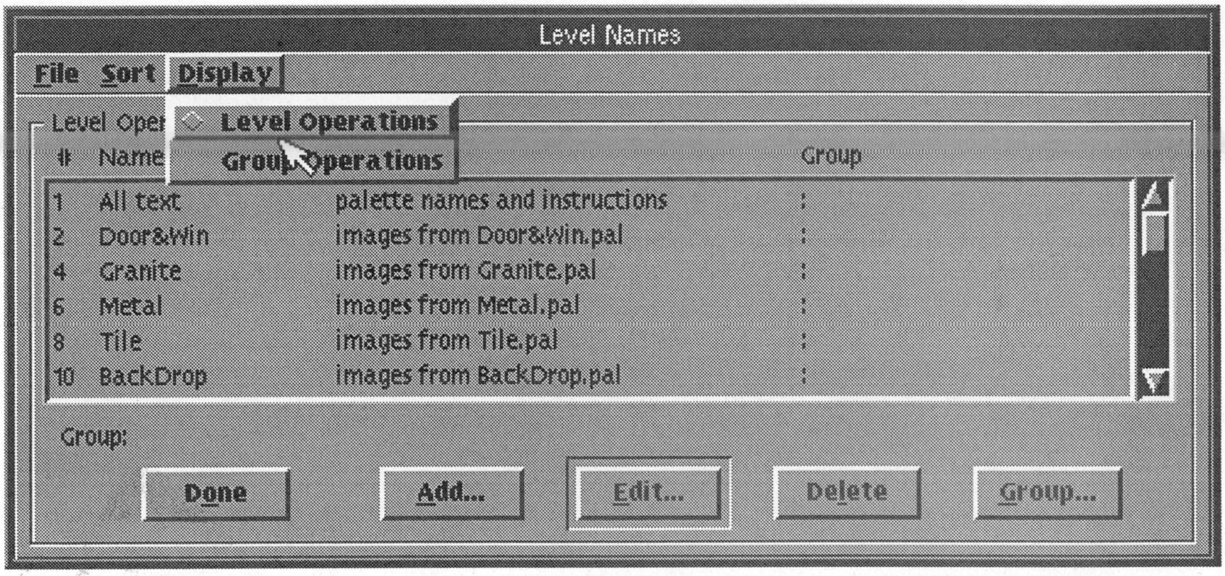

FIGURE 11–18   The Level Names dialog box has two alternate layouts chosen from the Display menu.

The Level operations layout lists the level name, comment and group affiliation (with path) for each named level as shown in Figure 11–18. The list is sorted using the criteria specified in the Sort Criteria dialog box (invoked from the Sort... pull-down menu). If a level is a member of multiple level groups, it is listed multiple times—once for each group of which it is a member. To operate on a level, you must first select it. Dragging or [CTRL]-clicking selects multiple levels.

To assign a level name, invoke the Level Name dialog box by clicking the Add... button, MicroStation displays the Level Name dialog box similar to the one shown in Figure 11–19. Key-in the level number in the Number edit field, level name in the Name edit field (maximum valid number of characters is 16) and comment in the Comment edit field (maximum valid number of characters is 32).

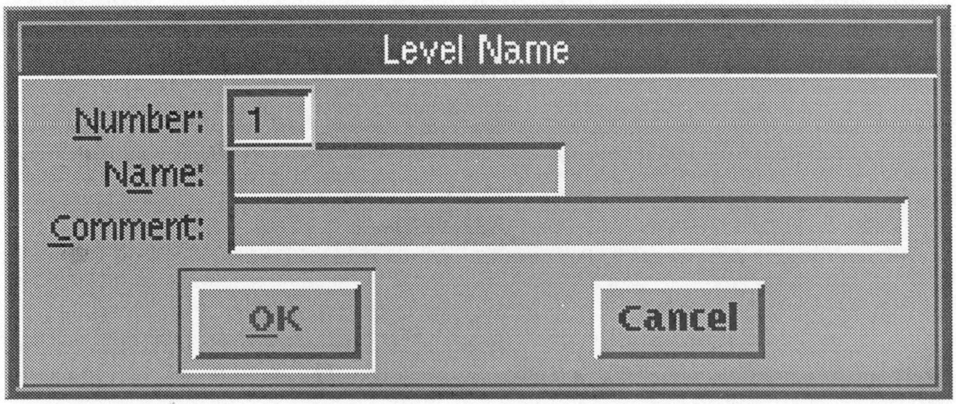

FIGURE 11–19   Level Name dialog box.

The Edit button opens the Level Name dialog box, which is used to edit the Number, Name, or Comment for the selected level. The Delete button removes the selected level from the identified group, if any. If the level is a member of only the identified group, clicking Delete discontinues the level name assignment.

The Group operations layout lists the names of level groups in a tree structure under the group listing as shown in Figure 11–20. To list the levels assigned to a group, click the group name, MicroStation lists level numbers, with corresponding level name including the comment. The list is sorted using the criteria specified in the Sort Criteria dialog box. The full path to the selected group is shown below the list box.

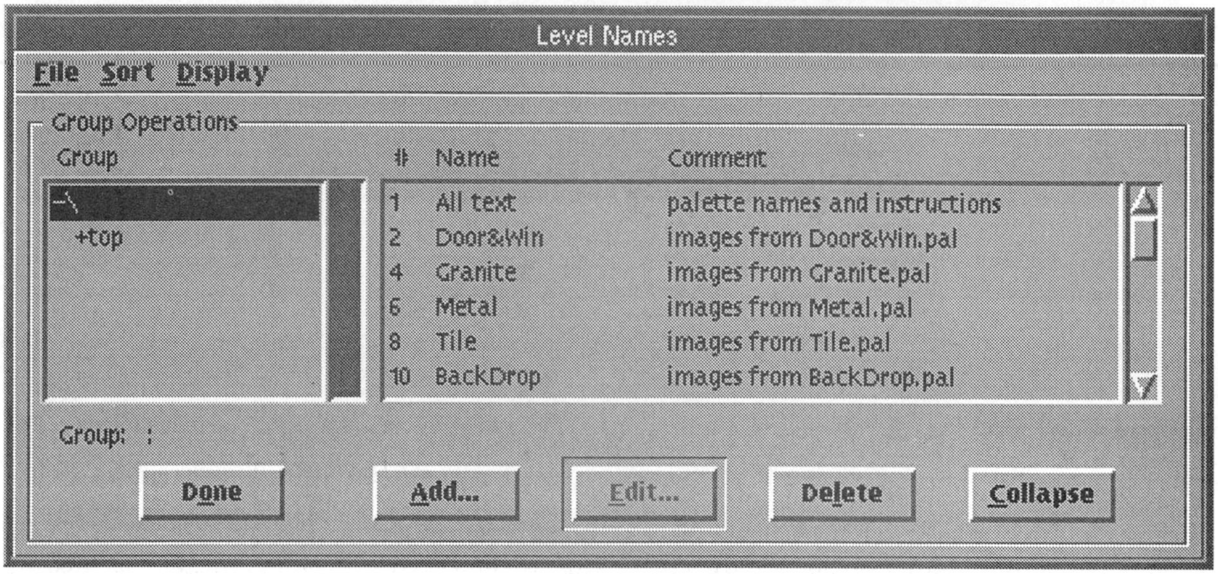

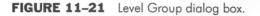

FIGURE 11–20 The Group operations layout lists the names of level groups in a tree structure.

The backslash symbol (\), indicates the "root" of the structure. Each group that has sub-groups is indicated with a symbol. The minus sign (–) indicates the group's sub-groups are listed below. The plus sign (+) indicates the group's sub-groups are not listed. Double-clicking a group name indicated with a minus or plus sign toggles the listing of its sub-groups.

To assign a group or sub-group name, invoke the Level Group dialog box by clicking the Add... button. MicroStation displays the Level Group dialog box similar to the one shown in Figure 11–21. Key-in the level group name in the Name edit field (maximum valid number of characters is 16).

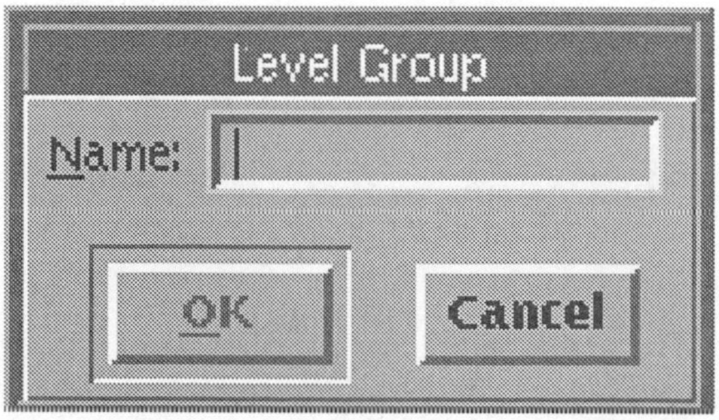

FIGURE 11–21 Level Group dialog box.

The Edit button opens the Level Group dialog box, which is used to edit the Name of the selected group. The Delete button removes the selected group and it sub-groups, if any, and discontinues component level name assignments. MicroStation displays an alert box to confirm the request.

The Collapse button toggles the listing of the selected group's sub-groups. This button is disabled (dimmed) if the selected group does not have any sub-groups.

Assigning Levels to a Group Name To assign a set of level(s) to a group name, first select all the level name(s) to be included (dragging or -clicking selects multiple levels) from Level operations layout display. Open the Select Target Group dialog box similar to the one shown in Figure 11–22 by clicking the Group... button. The Select Target Group dialog box is used to copy or move the selected level(s) to a group.

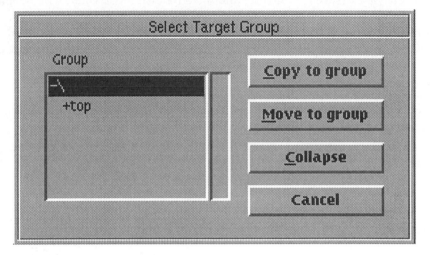

FIGURE 11–22 Select Target Group dialog box.

The dialog box lists the names of level groups in a tree structure indicated by the indenting of successive levels. The backslash symbol (\) indicates the "root" of the structure. To specify a group as the destination for the selected level(s), first click the group name. To add the level to the selected group without deleting from its present group, click the Copy to Group button. If you want to delete from the present group, if any, then click the Move to Group button. The Collapse button toggles the listing of the selected group's sub-groups. The Cancel button closes the dialog box without copying or moving the selected level(s).

Saving the Level Structure To save the current level structure, invoke the Save Level Structure dialog box by selecting Save... from the File pull-down menu of the Level Names settings box. Key-in the name of the level structure in the Name edit field and click OK button or press ⏎. The default extension for the file name is .LVL.

> **NOTE:** You can save the level structure for the active design file, by invoking the Save Settings from the File pull-down menu from the MicroStation Command Window.

Attaching Level Structure File To attach an existing level structure level, invoke the Open Level Structure dialog box by Selecting Open... from the File pull-down menu of the Level Names settings box. Select the level structure file and click OK button or press ⏎ to attach the level structure to the current design file.

Removing the Level and Group Assignment Names The Remove tool from the File pull-down menu of the Level Names settings box removes the level structure and all level name assignment from the design file. MicroStation displays an alert box to confirm the request.

To close the Level Names settings box, click the Done button or invoke the Exit tool from the File pull-down menu of the Level Names settings box. The control is passed on to View Level settings box.

MULTI-LINE DEFINITION

A *multi-line* is a special element type made up of a series of parallel lines. Depending on how it is defined, one multi-line can have up to sixteen (16) line components. Each of the components can be defined at varying distances (offsets) and have its own level, color, weight and line style.

Since a multi-line is a customized element, its components can be assigned a "style" name and can be saved and stored as part of a settings group. The Style Library concept is similar to that of the Cell Library in that it can be "attached" to any design file. The individual styles can then be made active and used as needed.

Once a multi-line is defined and made active, a multi-line can be placed in your design by using the Place Multi-line command (see Chapter 2). It is similar to a "linestring" element and it permits you to place that which identify its vertices and is terminated by pressing the RESET button. Since a multi-line is considered a "single" element, it must be edited with its own set of editing tools. These tools are called multi-line "joints" (see Chapter 5).

Multi-lines Settings Box

The Multi-lines Settings Box is used to control the active multi-line definition. A sample of the multi-line that is currently defined is displayed in the lower left corner. To open the Multi-lines Settings box, select the Multi-line option from the Element pull-down in the MicroStation Command Window, or key-in at the uSTN> field, **dialog multiline** and press [ENTER]. MicroStation displays a Multi-line settings box similar to the Figure 11–23.

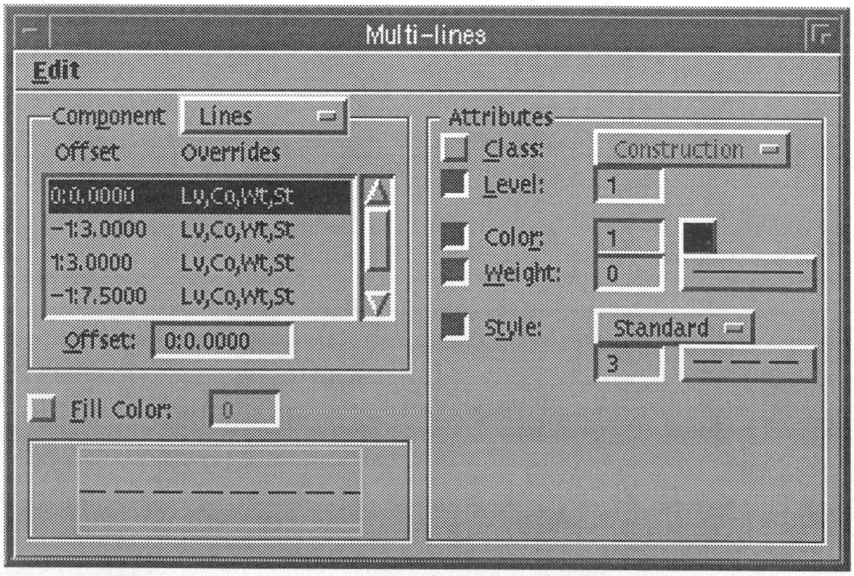

FIGURE 11–23 Multi-line settings box.

The Component option menu located in the top left-hand corner of the settings box allows you to set the component type—Lines, Start Cap, End Cap, and Joints whose attributes can be modified. The menu options in the Multi-line settings box depends on the type of the component option selected.

Lines Option The Lines option provides the controls for selecting the attributes for Line components and setting offset distances as shown in Figure 11–23. The list box lists the component lines and corresponding attribute settings in the active multi-line definition. To delete a component line from the active multi-line definition, select the component line and invoke the Delete command from the Edit pull-down menu in the Multi-line settings box. To add a component line to the active multi-line definition, invoke the Insert command from the Edit pull-down menu in the Multi-line settings box. The new component line is inserted before the selected line in the list box. To add a component line with the same attributes as the selected line to the active multi-line definition, invoke the Duplicate command from the Edit pull-down menu in the Multi-line settings box.

To set the attributes for individual component line, select the component line and set the appropriate controls for the attributes located in the top right side of the Multi-line settings box. If the toggle button to the left of a control is ON, the corresponding setting is effective for the selected component. If the toggle button is set to OFF, the active attribute setting is effective, and the control is dimmed. The controls are analogous to those in the Element Attributes settings box.

The Offset edit field sets the distance in working units (MU:SU:PU) from the work line to the selected component line. You can key-in positive or negative distance depending on the line to be placed above or below the work line.

The Fill Color toggle button when it is set to ON, the entire area between the outermost component lines of the multi-line is filled with the chosen Color.

Start Cap or End Cap Option The Start Cap or End Cap option provides the controls for specifying the appearance of the start or end cap as shown in Figure 11–24. The Line toggle button controls the

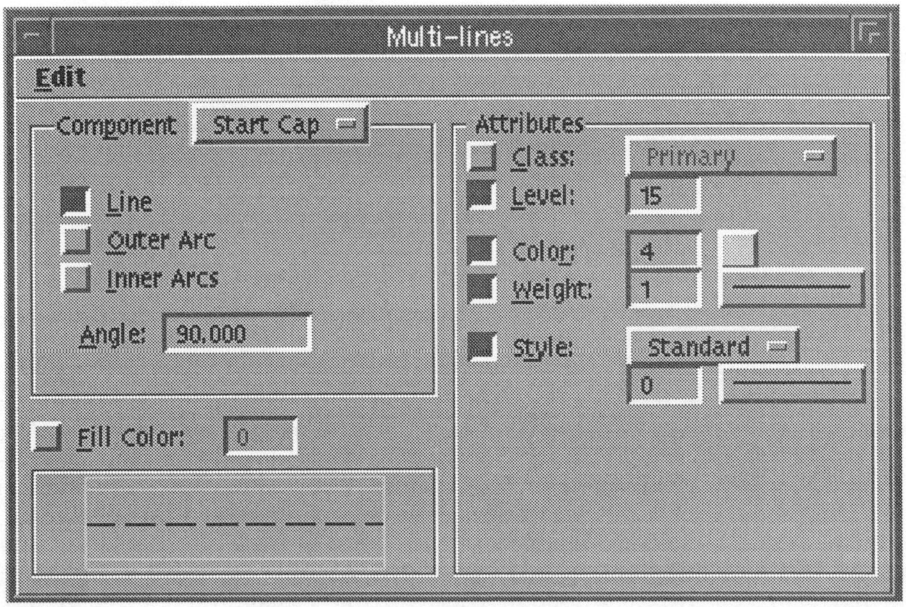

FIGURE 11–24 Start Cap or End Cap selection displaying the controls for specifying the appearance of the start or end cap.

display of the cap as a line. The Angle edit field sets the caps line angle in degrees. The Outer Arc toggle button controls the display of the cap as an arc connecting the outermost component lines. The Inner Arcs toggle button controls the display of the cap with arcs connecting pairs of inside component lines. If there is an even number of inside component lines, all are connected. If there is an odd number of inside component lines (three or more), the middle line is not connected. Controls for the attributes for the caps are located in the top right side of the Multi-line settings box. If the toggle button to the left of a control is ON, the corresponding setting is effective for the caps. If the toggle button is set to OFF, the active attribute setting is effective, and the control is dimmed. The controls are analogous to those in the Element Attributes settings box.

Joints Option The Joints option provides the only control available for specifying the appearance of the Joints as shown in Figure 11–25. If it is set to ON, the joint lines are displayed at vertices. Similar to caps, controls for the attributes for the joints are located in the top right side of the Multi-line settings box. If the toggle button to the left of a control is ON, the corresponding setting is effective for the joints. If the toggle button is set to OFF, the active attribute setting is effective, and the control is dimmed. The controls are analogous to those in the Element Attributes settings box. The Fill Color toggle button when it is set to ON, the entire area between the outermost component lines of the multi-line is filled with the chosen Color.

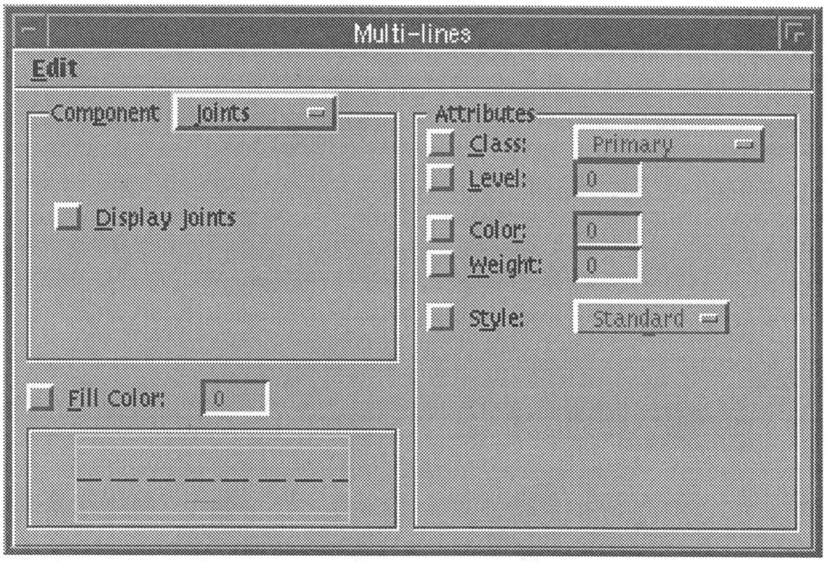

FIGURE 11–25 The Joints option selection displaying the only control available for specifying the appearance of the Joints.

You can save the Multi-line definition as a group component. For detailed explanation, see the section on Settings Group explained earlier in this chapter.

CUSTOM LINE STYLES

In versions prior to MicroStation 5.0, if you wanted to produce line work that had an appearance other than the provided line styles (LC=0...LC=7), you would have to incorporate linear patterning. Linear patterning is still available in MicroStation Version 5.0 but effectively has been replaced by the ability to create custom line styles. Any desired line work appearance that can be produced by linear patterning can be produced by a custom line style.

Custom line styles are created and stored in a Style Library (filename.RSC). The Style Library file delivered with MicroStation is called LSTYLE.RSC. The Style Library can be compared to the Cell Library concept. As with the cell library, line styles are created, stored, then recalled as needed. Once a library is created, it is "attached" to a design file and all the line styles stored in the library can be used. Only one Style Library can be attached at any time. If no style library is "attached," MicroStation's standard line styles (LC=0...LC=7) will still be available.

> **NOTE:** If you copy or move your MicroStation design from one PC to another, be sure to copy the style library as well. Your custom lines styles will not appear in your design if the style library is not present.

Let's take a short tour of the settings associated with MicroStation's custom line style feature.

Line Styles Settings Box

The Line Styles Settings Box is used to browse, activate line styles and set line style modifiers. To open the Line Styles Settings Box, select Custom option in the Line Style sub-menu from the Element pull-down menu as shown in Figure 11–26, or key-in at the uSTN> field, **Linestyle Settings** and press ⏎. MicroStation displays a Line Styles Settings Box similar to the Figure 11–27.

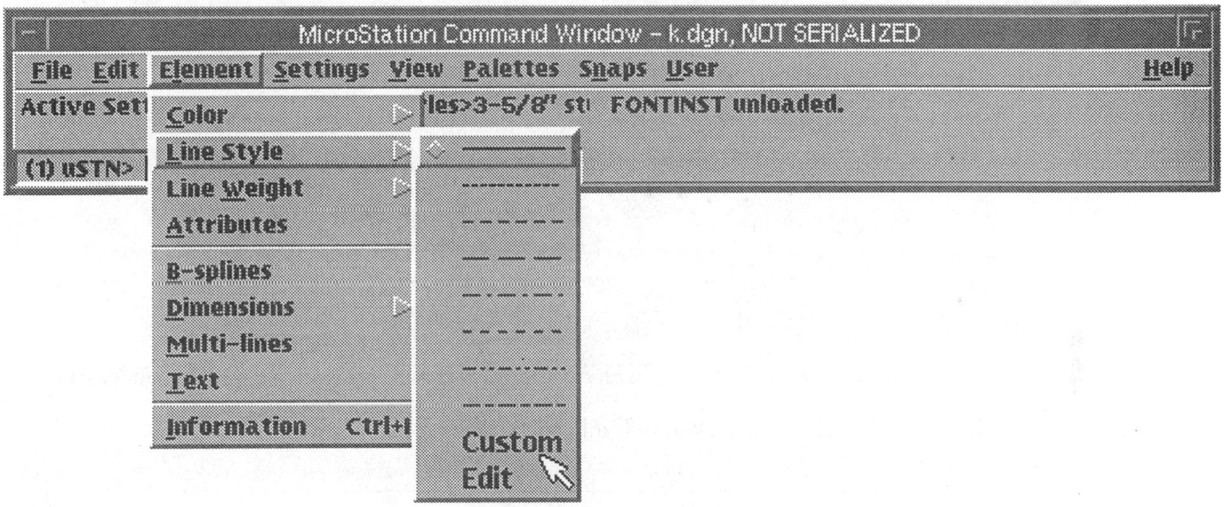

FIGURE 11–26 Invoking the Custom option in the Line Style sub-menu from the Element pull-down menu.

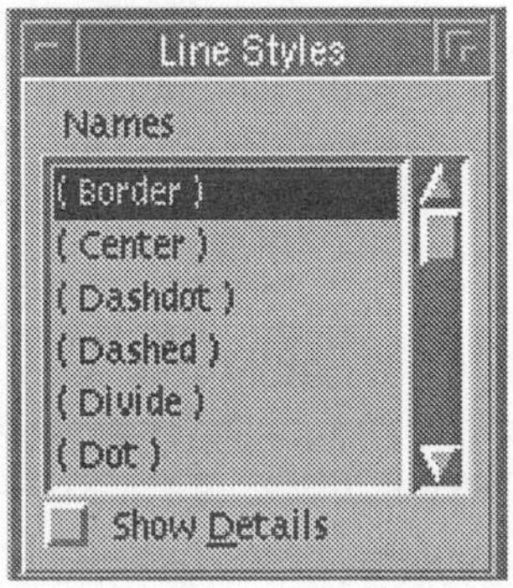

FIGURE 11–27 Line Styles settings box.

The settings box lists the names of line styles from the default line style library LSTYLE.RSC unless it is set for a different line style library. Double-clicking a line style name makes the line style the Active Line Style for element placement. To display all the attributes associated with line styles turn ON the Show Details toggle button. MicroStation displays a Line Styles settings box similar to the Figure 11–28.

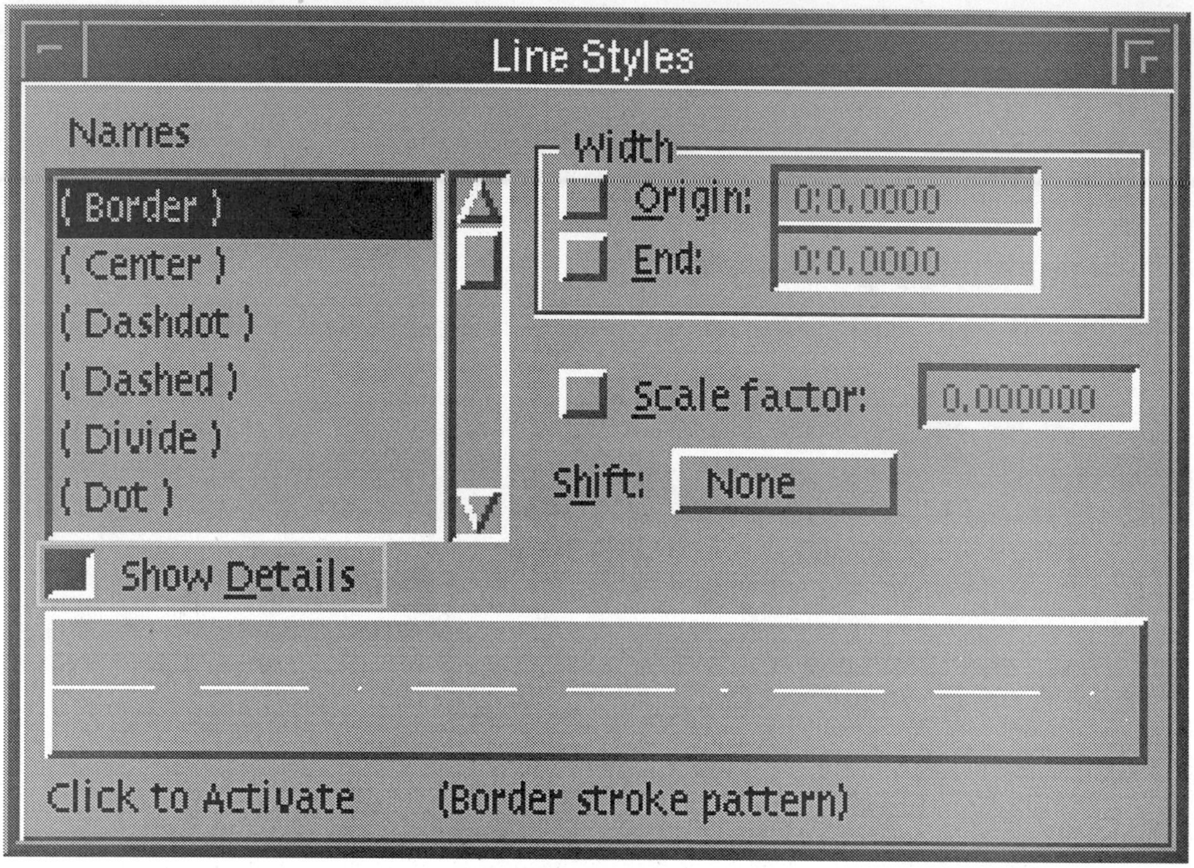

FIGURE 11–28   Line Styles settings box with additional options displayed.

At the bottom of the settings box, MicroStation shows the line style and description of the selected line style in the Names list box with active modifiers applied. Click anywhere on the sample to make the line style the Active Line Style for element placement. If necessary, you can modify the starting and ending width for the strokes as defined in the line style definition. To change the starting width turn ON the Origin toggle button and key-in the Width in Master Units in the Origin edit field. To change the ending width turn ON the End toggle button and key-in the Width in Master Units in the End edit field.

The Scale factor sets the scale to all displayable characteristics (dash length and width, point symbol size) of the Active Line Style. To change the scale factor turn ON the Scale factor toggle button and key-in the scale factor in the Scale factor edit field.

The Shift option menu sets the distance or fraction by which each stroke pattern in the Active Line Style is shifted or adjusted.

Line Style Editor Settings Box

The Line Style Editor settings box is used to define and modify line styles. To open the Line Style Editor settings box, select Edit option in the Line Style sub-menu from the Element pull-down menu, or key-in at the uSTN> field, **Linestyle Edit** and press [ENTER]. MicroStation displays a Line Style Edit settings box similar to the Figure 11-29.

Line style definitions are stored in line style libraries. The settings box lets you open and define or modify line styles in only one line style library at a time. If a line style library is open, its file specification is displayed in the title bar.

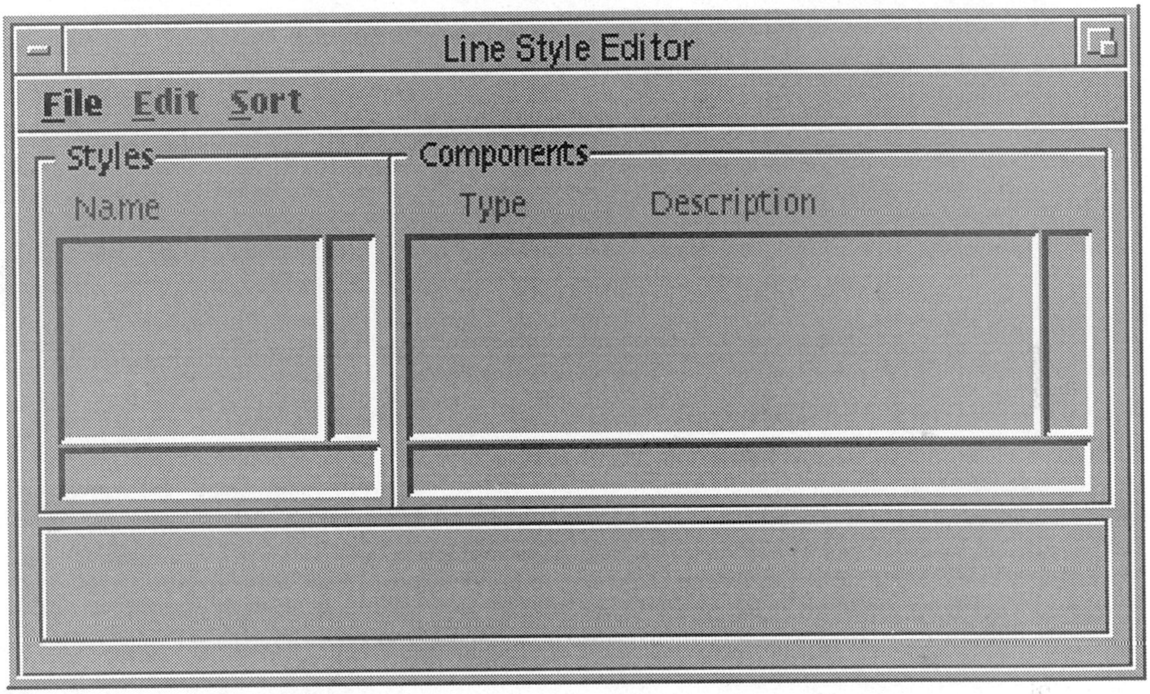

FIGURE 11-29 Line Style Edit settings box.

MicroStation lists the names of all the available line styles in the Styles list box. Selecting a name causes a sample of the line style to be displayed. Under Components list box, MicroStation lists the types and descriptions of all line styles components. If >> is displayed left of its Type, the component is directly linked to the line style whose name is selected in the Styles list box. Selecting a component causes a sample line with the component to be displayed. To modify a component, you must first select the component and make the necessary changes.

To attach an existing line style library, invoke the Open... command from the File pull-down menu of the Line Style Editor settings box. MicroStation displays Open Line Style Library dialog box. Select the line style library file from the Files list box and click OK button or press [ENTER] to attach the library to the current design file.

To create a new line style library, invoke the New... command from the File pull-down menu of the Line Style Editor settings box. MicroStation displays New Line Style Library dialog box. Key-in the name of the new line style library file in the Name edit field and click OK button or press [ENTER] to create and attach the library to the current design file.

Creating a New Line Style

To create a new line style, invoke the Name tool under the Create sub-menu from the Edit pull-down menu as shown in Figure 11–30. MicroStation adds a new line style, named "Unnamed" in the Styles list box. Unnamed is automatically selected and is linked to the component selected in the Components list box.

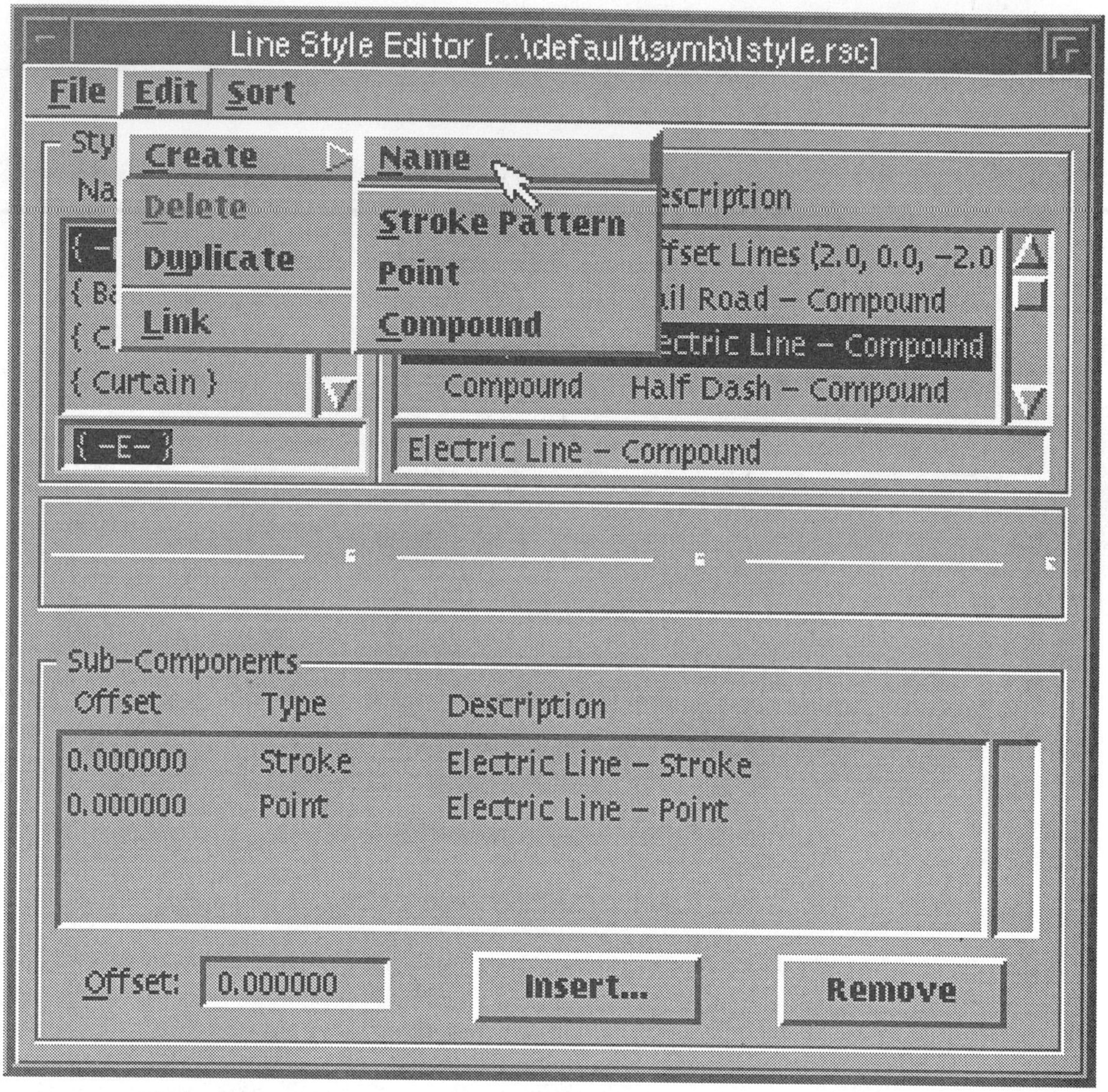

FIGURE 11–30 Invoking the Name tool under the Create sub-menu from the Edit pull-down menu.

The Link option available in the Edit pull-down menu directly links the component selected in the Components list box to the line style whose name is selected in the Styles list box. An indication of the link, >> is displayed next to the component Type.

Three tools are available in the Create sub-menu: Stroke Pattern provides controls that are used to create, modify, and delete stroke pattern line style components; Point provides controls that are used to create, modify, and delete point line style components; and Compound provides controls that are used to create, modify, and delete compound line style components.

Stroke Pattern The Stroke Pattern settings box is divided into two sections, Stroke Pattern Attributes and Stroke Patterns as shown in Figure 11–31.

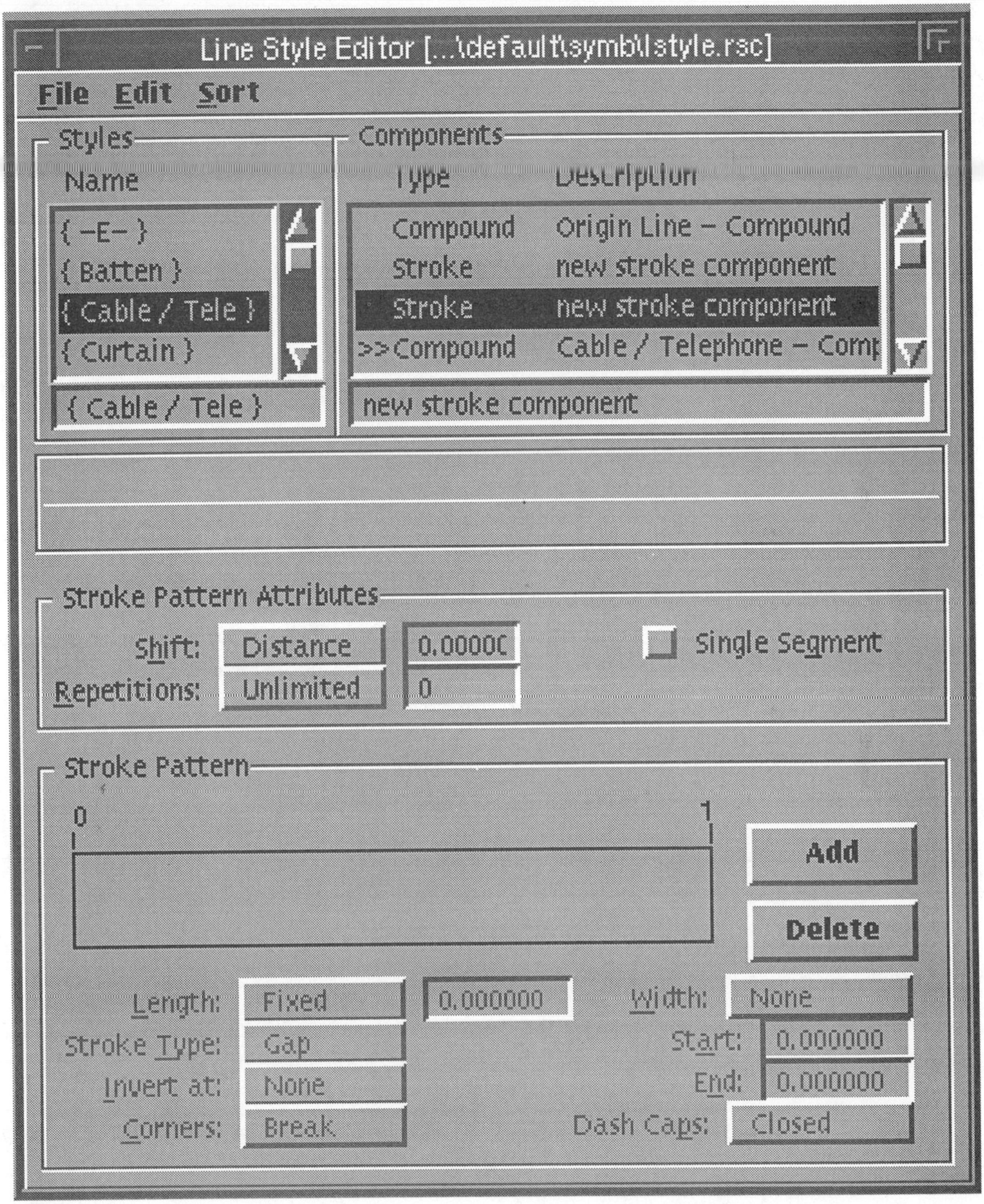

FIGURE 11–31 The Stroke Pattern settings box.

- Shift options menu sets the distance or fraction by which the stroke pattern is shifted or adjusted.

- Repetitions options menu sets the number of times the stroke pattern is repeated throughout the length of an element or element segment. The number of repetitions needs to be fixed.

- The Single Segment toggle button controls the truncation of the stroke pattern at the end of each element segment.

- Add button adds a new gap stroke at the end of the stroke pattern. The maximum number of strokes is 32. Each dash stroke is represented by a filled bar. Each gap stroke is represented by an unfilled bar. Click anywhere on the stroke for modification. The stroke is highlighted. Dragging a stroke's handle changes the stroke's length.

- Length edit field sets the selected stroke length in Master Units.

- Stroke Type option menu allows you to switch a highlighted stroke from gap to dash or vice versa.

- Corners option menu controls the behavior of the selected stroke when it extends farther than an element vertex.

- Width option menu controls the effect of width settings on the selected dash stroke.

- Dash Caps option menu sets the type of end cap on the selected dash stroke when displayed with width.

Point The Point settings provides controls (see Figure 11–32) that are used to create, modify, and delete point line style components.

- Base Stroke Pattern... button opens the Base Stroke Pattern dialog box, which is used to select the stroke pattern component on which the selected point symbol component is based.

- Length edit field sets the selected stroke length in Master Units.

- Origin toggle button selects the origin (first vertex of an element) with which a symbol can be associated.

- Vertex toggle button selects the internal vertices (of an element) with which a single symbol can be associated.

- End toggle button selects the end (last vertex of an element) with which a symbol can be associated.

> **NOTE:** If a symbol is associated with either origin, vertex, or last vertex of an element, the symbol is displayed (below left of the settings box), and the controls used to adjust the related settings (below right of the settings box), are enabled.

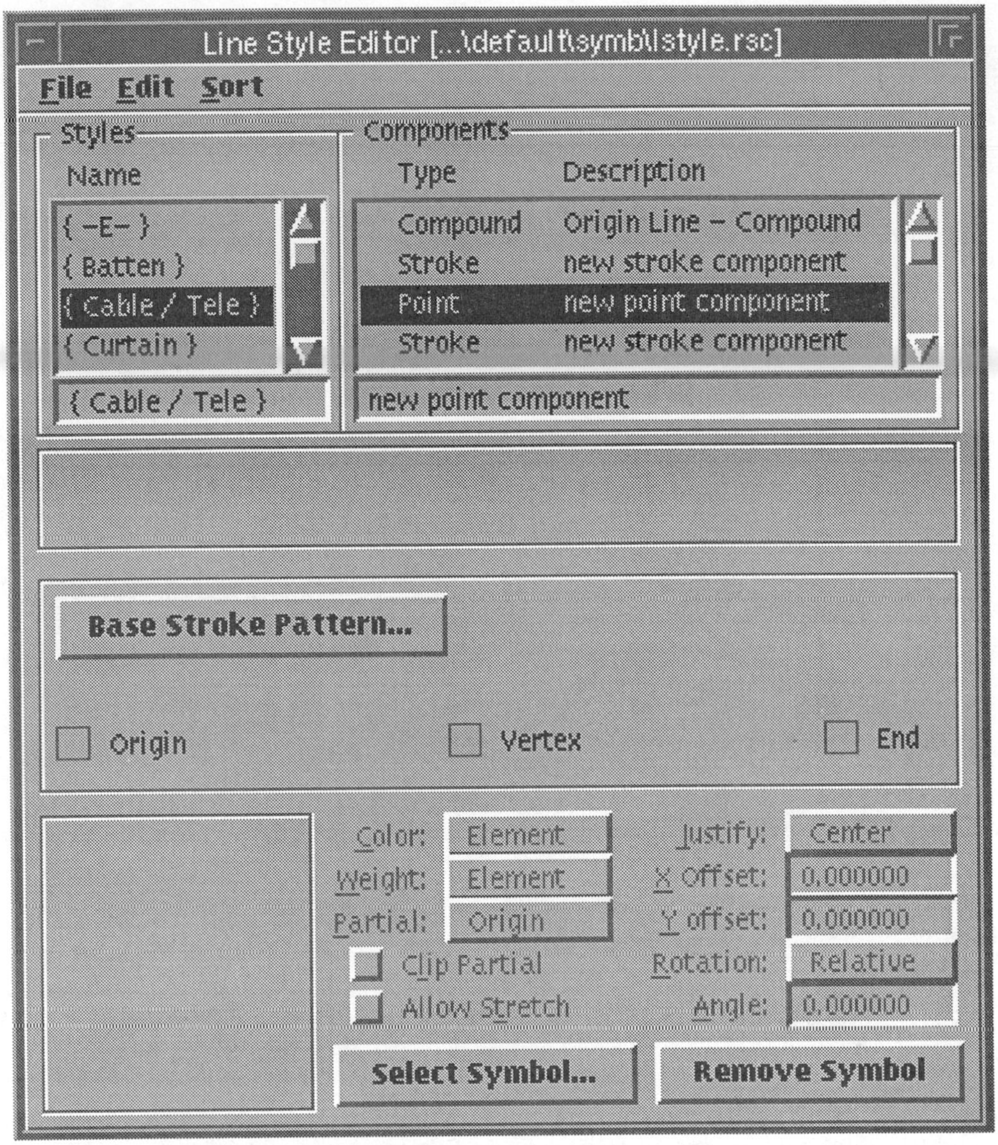

FIGURE 11–32   Point settings box.

Compound   The Compound settings provides controls (see Figure 11–33) that are used to create, modify, and delete compound line style components.

- Sub-Components list box lists the offsets, types, and descriptions of all sub-components of the compound component selected in the Components list box.

- Offset edit field sets the distance, in master units measured perpendicular from the work line, by which the selected component is displayed parallel to the work line. If Offset is set to zero, the selected component is displayed on the work line.

- Insert... button opens the Select Component dialog box, which is used to select a sub-component to insert in the compound component selected in the Components list box.

- Remove button removes the sub-component selected in the Sub-Components list box from the compound component selected in the Components list box.

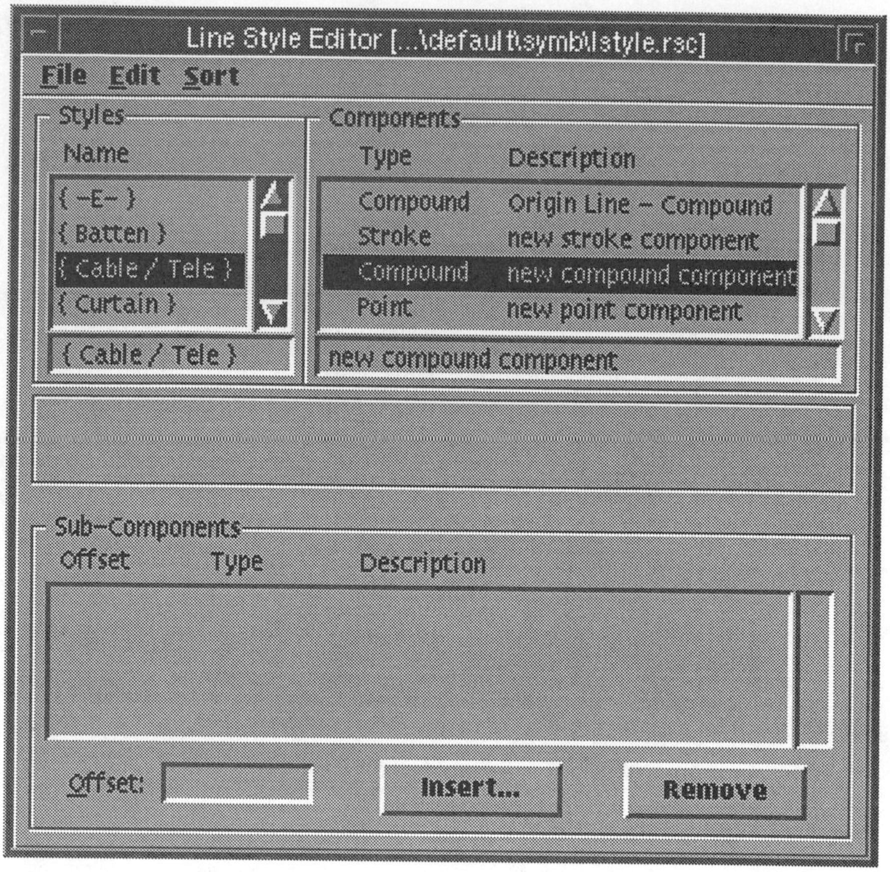

FIGURE 11–33 Compound settings box.

Saving a Line Style The Save command under the File pull-down menu in the Line Style Editor Settings Box saves new or modified line styles in the open line style library.

Following is the step-by-step procedure to a create a line style called FLOWARR, consisting of a straight 1.5″ long line segment followed by a filled arrowhead (.1″ wide, .125″ long):

STEP 1: Open the Line Style Editor Settings Box.

STEP 2: Create a new line style library called HARNESS.RSC

STEP 3: Invoke the Name tool under the Create sub-menu from the Edit pull-down menu. MicroStation adds a new line style, named "Unnamed" in the Styles list box. Change the "Unnamed" to "FLOWARR" in the edit field located under the name list.

STEP 4: Select the Stroke Pattern option from the Create sub-menu from the Edit pull-down menu. The description "new stroke component" will be added to the list. Change the description to read "LINE CODE FOR FLOW ARROW" in the edit field located under the description list.

STEP 5: Select the Link option from the Edit pull-down menu. This establishes a relationship between the new line style name and the new component.

STEP 6: In the Stroke Pattern Attributes section of the settings box, set the Shift Distance to 0.0 and the Repetitions value to Unlimited.

STEP 7: Click the Add button to add a new gap stroke.

STEP 8: Select Fixed in the Length option menu and key-in 1.5 in the Length edit field. Set the Stroke Type option menu to Dash, Invert to option menu to None, and Corners option menu to Break. The characteristics of the stroke pattern will change to reflect these settings.

STEP 9: Click the Add button to add a new gap stroke at the end of the stroke pattern.

STEP 10: Place a data point anywhere in the new stroke pattern. The stroke is highlighted.

STEP 11: Select Fixed in the Length option menu and key-in 0.125 in the Length edit field. Set the Stroke Type option menu to Dash, Invert to option menu to None, Corners option menu to Break, Width option menu to Full, set the Start Width value to .1, End Width value to 0.0 and Dash Caps option menu to Closed. The characteristics of the stroke pattern will change to reflect these settings (see Figure 11–34).

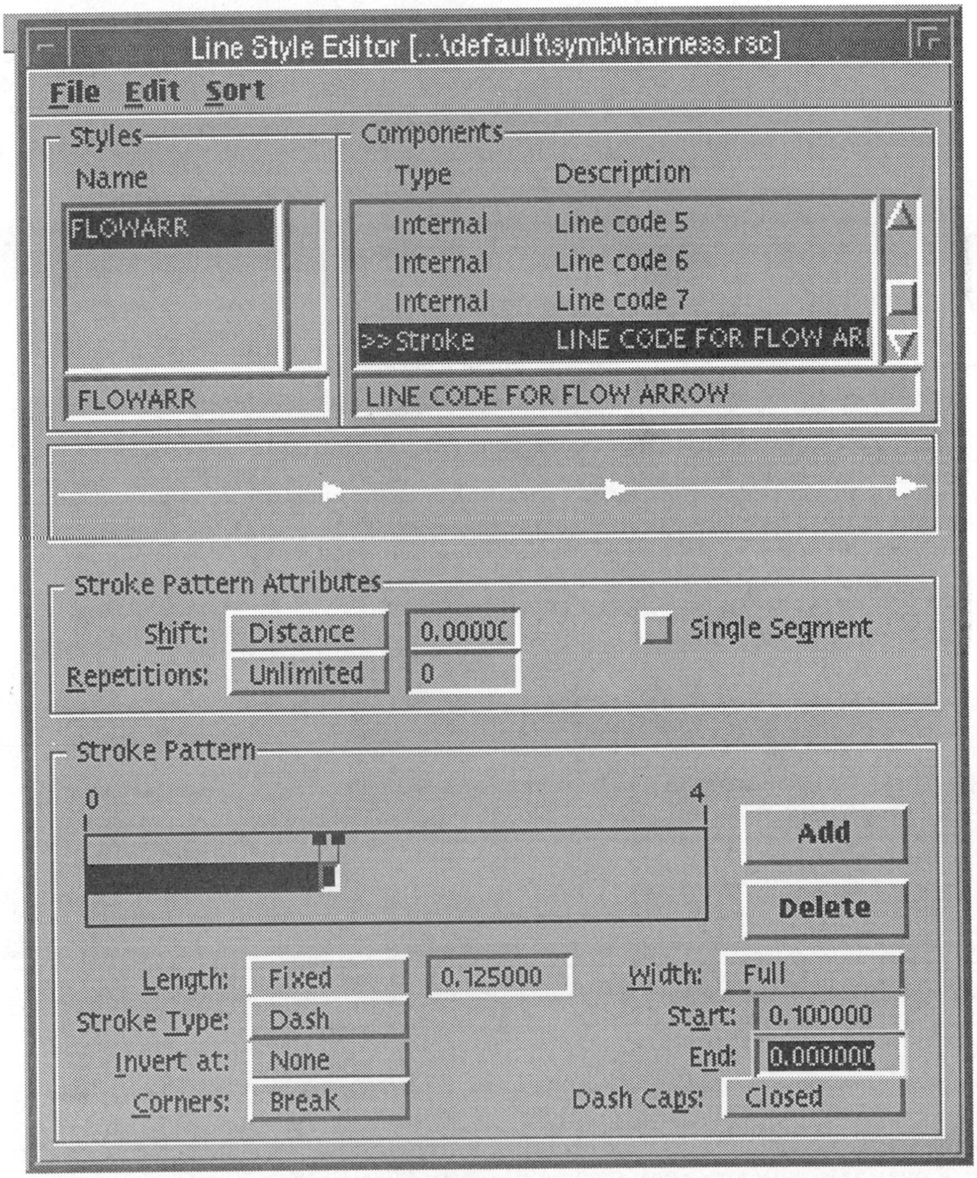

FIGURE 11–34 Displaying the new line type in the settings box..

STEP 12: Save the newly created line style by invoking the Save command under the File pull-down menu in the Line Style Editor Settings Box.

STEP 13: Close the Line Style Editor Settings Box.

STEP 14: Test the newly created line style by setting the active line style to FLOWARR.

USER PREFERENCES

PREFERENCES are comprised of all of the settings that control the way MicroStation operates and the way its palettes and tools appear on the screen. Instead of being a set of characteristics saved with each design file, preferences are saved within a configuration file that is automatically read and loaded each time MicroStation is activated.

The Preferences dialog box is used to control the settings of the preferences. To open the Preferences dialog box, select the Preferences... tool from the User pull-down menu in the MicroStation Command Window, or key-in at the uSTN> field, **dialog userpref** and press [ENTER]. MicroStation displays a Preferences dialog box similar to the Figure 11–35.

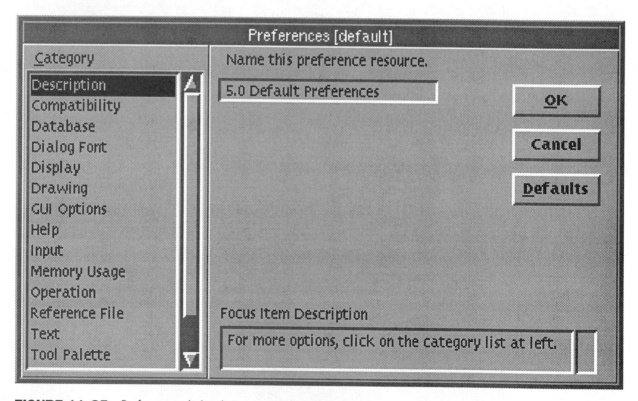

FIGURE 11–35 Preferences dialog box.

User preferences are divided into categories. The Category list box lists all the available categories. Selecting a category causes the appropriate controls to be displayed to the right of the category list. Each category controls a specific aspect of MicroStation's appearance or operation. Following is the list of available categories that control the way MicroStation operates and the way its palettes and tools appear on the screen:

DESCRIPTION This contains an editable field that identifies the currently loaded user preference file. If you choose, you could describe your own title that identifies your own configuration or workspace.

COMPATIBILITY As new versions of MicroStation have become available, new element types and features have been added. Some Version 5.0 elements cannot be read by earlier versions of MicroStation or IGDS. Toggles are provided to improve this compatibility.

DATABASE Contains the controls for setting preferences related to operation of element tags and the database interface.

DIALOG FONT Contains the controls for adjusting the dialog, border and sidebar title text sizes displayed on the screen. Adjust these settings to make the title text easier to read.

DISPLAY Contains the controls for setting preferences that affect how MicroStation displays a design.

DRAWING Contains the controls that are used to set preferences related to drawing a design.

GUI OPTIONS Graphic User Interface Options allows the user to select between the OSF Motif or Windows appearance of the MicroStation Command Window. These options also permit the user to adjust the color and appearance of MicroStation's background, windows, palettes, setting boxes and on-line help.

HELP Contains the controls for setting preferences that relate to the appearance of the on-line help system.

INPUT Contains the controls that are used to set preferences for keyed input and pointer drag operations.

MEMORY USAGE Contains the controls for setting preferences that affect how MicroStation uses system's memory (RAM).

OPERATION Contains the controls that are used to set preferences related to element selection and identification, the drawing pointer, and level identification.

REFERENCE FILE Contains the controls that are used to set preferences related to Reference Files.

TEXT Contains the controls that are used to set preferences related to Text Placement and Manipulation.

TOOL PALETTE Contains the controls that are used to set preferences for the operation of tool palettes.

TRANSLATION (Character Set) Contains the controls that are used to identify and select a character translation table, which converts "external" ASCII characters to the form of ASCII used internally by MicroStation.

WINDOW Contains the controls for setting preferences related to MicroStation windows.

Click OK button to accept changes made to preferences for all categories and close the dialog box.

WORKSPACE

A WORKSPACE is a customized drafting environment that permits the user to setup MicroStation for specific purposes. You can set up as many workspaces as you need. A workspace consists of "components" and "configuration files" for both the user and the project.

Before you create a workspace, make necessary adjustments to the user configuration variables and their respective directory path. The Configuration Variables dialog box is used to modify the settings of the configuration variables. To open the Configuration Variables dialog box, select Modify User Configuration... in the Workspace sub-menu tool from the User pull-down menu. MicroStation displays a Configuration Variables dialog box similar to the Figure 11–36.

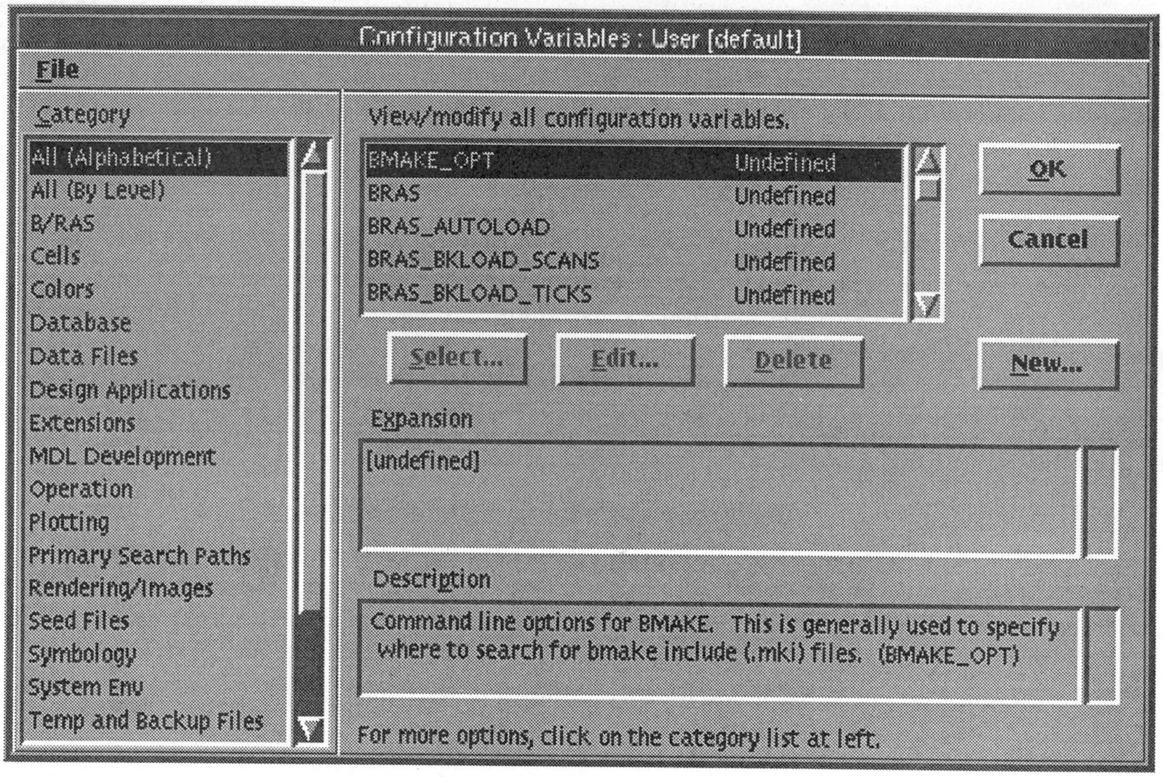

FIGURE 11–36 Configuration Variables dialog box.

Make the necessary changes to the variables in the dialog box. See Table 11–2 for the list of configuration variables available in MicroStation.

Click OK button to accept changes made to configuration variables and close the dialog box.

Similarly, make the necessary changes to the configuration variables for a specific project and save the changes to a given file name. By default, the file will have an extension .PCF (project configuration file). To open the Configuration Variables dialog box to set up for a project, select Modify Project Configuration... in the Workspace sub-menu tool from the User pull-down menu. MicroStation displays a Configuration Variables dialog box similar to the Figure 11–37.

Make the necessary changes to the variables in the dialog box. Click OK button to accept changes made to configuration variables and close the dialog box.

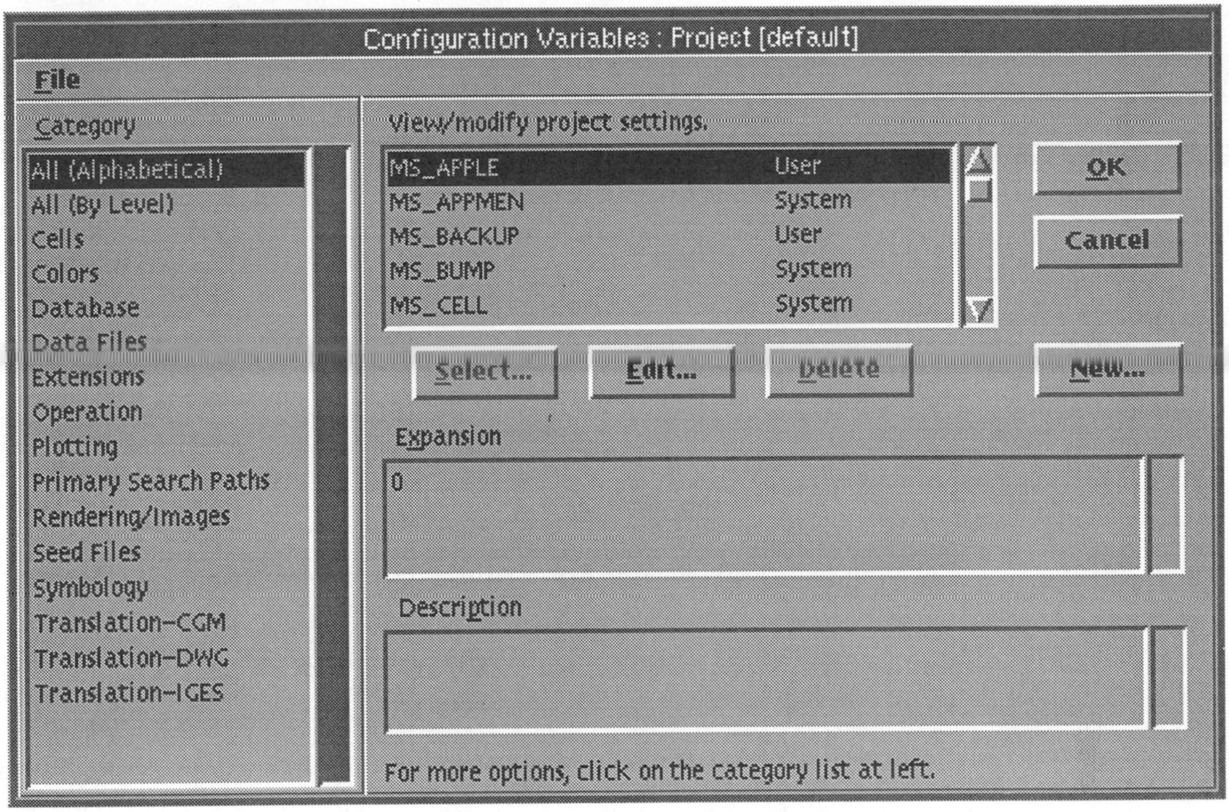

FIGURE 11–37 Configuration Variables dialog box displaying additional options.

If necessary, make modifications to the user interface. This can be done by invoking the Modify User Interface settings box, which is used to customize the user interface—menus, palettes, and dialog boxes (including settings boxes). To open the Modify User Interface Settings box, select Modify User Interface in the Workspace sub-menu tool from the User pull-down menu. MicroStation displays a User Interface settings box similar to the Figure 11–38.

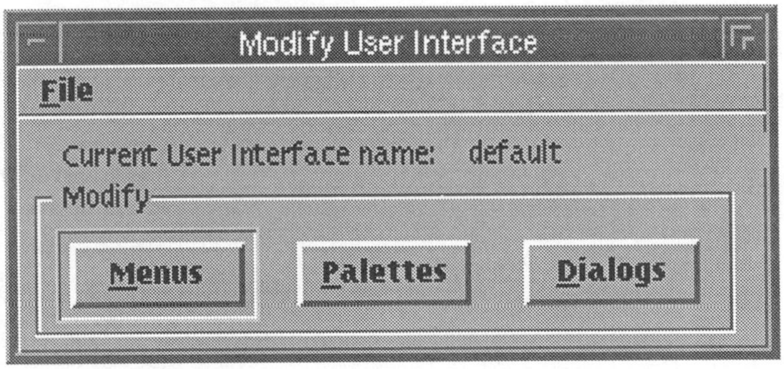

FIGURE 11–38 User Interface settings box.

Make the necessary changes to the interface, and save the changes to a given name.

Make any adjustment you wish to make to the User Preferences. The changes you make in the User Preferences dialog box will become part of the workspace. Refer to the section on User Preferences explained earlier in this chapter.

Table 11–2.   List of Configuration Variables

CATEGORY	VARIABLE	DESCRIPTION
B/RAS	BRAS	Directory containing the "bras.rsc" resource file.
	BRAS_RASTER	Default directory for the Load and Preview dialog boxes when no other raster file is loaded.
	BRAS_FILTER	Filter Default filter (e.g. "*.*") for Load and Preview dialog boxes.
	BRAS_MAX_SCAN	The maximum number of scan lines a raster file can have.
	BRAS_MAX_X	The maximum scan line length (pixels) a raster file can have.
	BRAS_MAX_FG_ RUNS	Maximum number of foreground run lengths per scan line in a raster file.
	BRAS_BKLOAD_ TICKS	Background Load Ticks Time (in MicroStation timer ticks) between background loading time slices.
	BRAS_BKLOAD_ SCANS	Number of raster scan lines loaded for each time slice of BRAS fast loading.
Cells	MS_CELL	Director Search path(s) for cell libraries.
	MS_CELLLIST	List of cell libraries to be searched for cells not found in the current library.
	MS_MENU	Cell library file containing menu cells.
	MS_TUTLIB	Library Cell library containing tutorial cells.
Colors	MS_DEFCTBL	Default Color Table Default color table if design file has none.
	MS_RMENCTBL	Right Menu Color Table Default menu colors (dialog boxes, borders, etc.) for right screen—specifies a color table (.tbl) file.
	MS_LMENCTBL	Color Table Default menu colors (dialog boxes, borders, etc.) for left screen—specifies a color table (.tbl) file.
Database	MS_DBASE	Search path(s) for database files.
	MS_SERVER	MDL application to load the database interface software.
	MS_DBEXT	The database interface "server" application.

Table 11–2.   List of Configuration Variables *(continued)*

CATEGORY	VARIABLE	DESCRIPTION
Database *(continued)*	MS_LINKTYPE	User data linkage types recognized by the database interface software. See MS_LINKTYPE.
	MS_TAGREPORTS	Output directory for tag reports.
	MS_TAGTEMPLATES	Directory containing tag report templates.
Data Files	MS_SETTINGS	Open settings file.
	MS_SETTINGSDIR	Directory containing settings files.
	MS_LEVELNAMES	Directory containing level structure files.
	MS_GLOSSARY	List of files for use with the Glossary settings box (see Utilities > Glossary).
Design Apps.	MS_DGNAPPS	List of MDL applications to load automatically when a design file is opened.
MDL Develop.	MS_DBGSOURCE	Location of source code for MDL applications (used by MDL debugger).
	MS_MDLTRACE	Additional debugging print statements when debugging MDL applications.
	MS_DBGOUT	Output of MDL debugger.
	MS_DEBUGFAULT	If set, automatically invokes the debugger when a fault is detected while an MDL application is active.
	MS_DEBUG	If set to an integer with bit 1 on, do not time out.
Operation	MS_FKEYMNU	Open function key menu file.
	MS_SYSTEM	If set, MicroStation allows the user to escape to the operating system.
	MS_APPMEN	Location of application and sidebar menus.
	MS_TRAP	Set to "NONE," "MDL," or "ALL" (default).
Plotting	MS_PLTFILES	Directory for plotting output files.
	MS_PLTR	Name of plotter configuration file.
Primary Search	MS_DEF	Search path(s) for design files.
	MS_DESIGNFILTER	File filter for opening and creating design files.
	MS_RFDIR	Search path(s) for reference files.
	MS_MDLAPPS	Search path(s) for MDL applications displayed in the MDL dialog box.

Table 11–2. List of Configuration Variables *(continued)*

CATEGORY	VARIABLE	DESCRIPTION
Primary Search *(continued)*	MS_MDL	Search path(s) for MDL applications or external programs loaded by MDL applications.
	MS_RSRCPATH	Search path(s) for resource files loaded by MDL applications.
Rendering	MS_MATERIAL	Search path(s) for material palettes.
	MS_PATTERN	Search path(s) for pattern maps.
	MS_BUMP	Search path(s) for bump maps.
	MS_IMAGE	Search path(s) for images.
	MS_IMAGEOUT	Directory in which created image files are stored.
	MS_SHADOWMAP	Directory where shadow maps will be read from and written to.
Seed Files	MS_SEEDFILES	Search path(s) for all seed files.
	MS_DESIGNSEED	Default seed file.
	MS_CELLSEED	Default seed cell library.
	MS_SHEETSEED	Seed sheet file drawing composition, DWG import, and IGES import.
	MS_TRANSEED	Default seed file for DWG, CGM, and IGES translations.
Symbology	MS_SYMBRSRC	List of symbology resource files—last one in list has highest priority.
System Environment	MS	The MicroStation root installation directory used by MDL sample "make" files.
	MS_CONFIG	Main MicroStation configuration file—sets up all configuration variables.
	MS_EDG	Directories used by EDG (not MicroStation).
	MDL_COMP	Command Text string to be inserted at the beginning of the command line by the MDL compiler (used to specify where to search for include files).
	RSC_COMP	Text string to be inserted at the beginning of the command line by the resource compiler (used to specify where to search for included files).
	BMAKE_OPT	Command line options for BMAKE. Used to search for bmake include (.mki) files.

Table 11–2. List of Configuration Variables (continued)

CATEGORY	VARIABLE	DESCRIPTION
System Environment (continued)	MS_ DEBUGMDLHEAP	If set (to the base name of an MDL application or "ALL"), use extended malloc for debugging.
Temp and Backup Files	MS_BACKUP	Default directory for backup files.
	MS_TMP	Directory for temporary files created and deleted by MicroStation.
	MS_SCR	Directory for scratch files created by MicroStation.
Translation	MS_CGMIN	CGM Input Directory for CGM translations.
	MS_CGMOUT	Output directory for CGM translations.
	MS_CGMLOG	Output directory for CGM log files.
	MS_CGMTABLES	Directory containing the CGM translation tables.
	MS_CGMINSET	Settings file for the CGMIN application.
	MS_CGMOUTSET	Settings file for the CGMOUT application.
	MS_DWGIN	Input directory for DWG translations.
	MS_DWGOUT	Output directory for DWG translations.
	MS_DWGLOG	Output directory for DWG log files.
	MS_DWGTABLES	Directory containing the DWG translation tables.
	MS_DWGINSET	Settings file for the DWGIN application.
	MS_DWGOUTSET	Settings file for the DWGOUT application.
	MS_IGESIN	Input directory for IGES translations.
	MS_IGESOUT	Output directory for IGES translations.
	MS_IGESLOG	Output directory for IGES log files.
	MS_IGESINSET	Settings file for IGES import.
	MS_IGESOUTSET	Settings file for IGES export.
User Commands	MS_UCM	Search path(s) for user commands.
	MS_INIT	Name of user command to be executed at startup.
	MS_EXITUC	Name of user command to be executed at exit.
	MS_NEWFILE	Name of user command to be executed when a new file is opened.

Table 11–2. List of Configuration Variables *(concluded)*

CATEGORY	VARIABLE	DESCRIPTION
User Commands *(continued)*	MS_APP	Apps from "TSK" state Search path(s) of applications started from "TSK" statements in user commands.
Uncategorized	MS_BANNER	Text file to be displayed in MicroStation's startup banner dialog.
	MS_CMDWINDRSC	Command Window resource file. Default is used if undefined.
	MS_CODESET	AMDL application for handling multi-byte character sets.
	MS_DATA	Directory for data files created or used by MicroStation.
	MS_DEFCHARTRAN	Default character translation table.
	MS_DEMOONLY	If set, MicroStation runs in demonstration mode only.
	MS_DGNOUT	Directory containing design files created as a result of "on-the-fly" translation from other file formats.
	MS_EXE	Directory containing the MicroStation executable program.
	MS_GUIHAND	Identifies auxiliary handlers.
	MS_HELPPATH	Path to help files.
	MS_INITAPPS	List of initial startup MDL applications.
	MS_RIGHTLOGICKB	Right to Left Character If set, type from right to left. Used for foreign language support.
	MS_RSRC	Main MicroStation resource file. Typically set to "ustation.rsc."
	MS_RSRVCLRS	Number of colors MicroStation does not use.
	MS_TUT_UCMS	Directory containing user commands that drive tutorials.
	MS_UNDO	If set, overrides the user preference Undo Buffer.
	MS_USERLICENSE	File containing MicroStation license information.
	MS_WINDOWMGR	Tells MicroStation which window manager is in use ("MOTIF" or "OPENLOOK"). MicroStation can usually infer this.
	WRK_DD_IGDS	Directory for IGDS user commands.

Create a new Workspace Invoke the Create Workspace dialog box by selecting Create Workspace... tool in the Workspace sub-menu from the User pull-down menu. MicroStation displays a Create Workspace dialog box similar to the Figure 11–39.

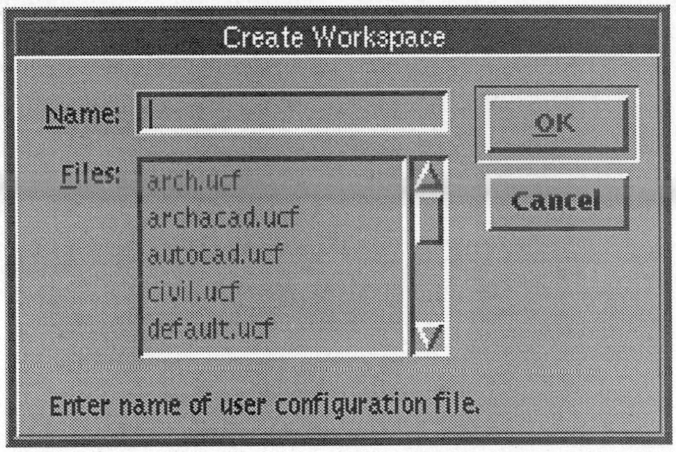

FIGURE 11–39   Create Workspace dialog box.

Key-in the name of the file in the Name edit field and press [ENTER]. MicroStation by default, adds the file extension .UCF. MicroStation displays another dialog box similar to the Figure 11–40.

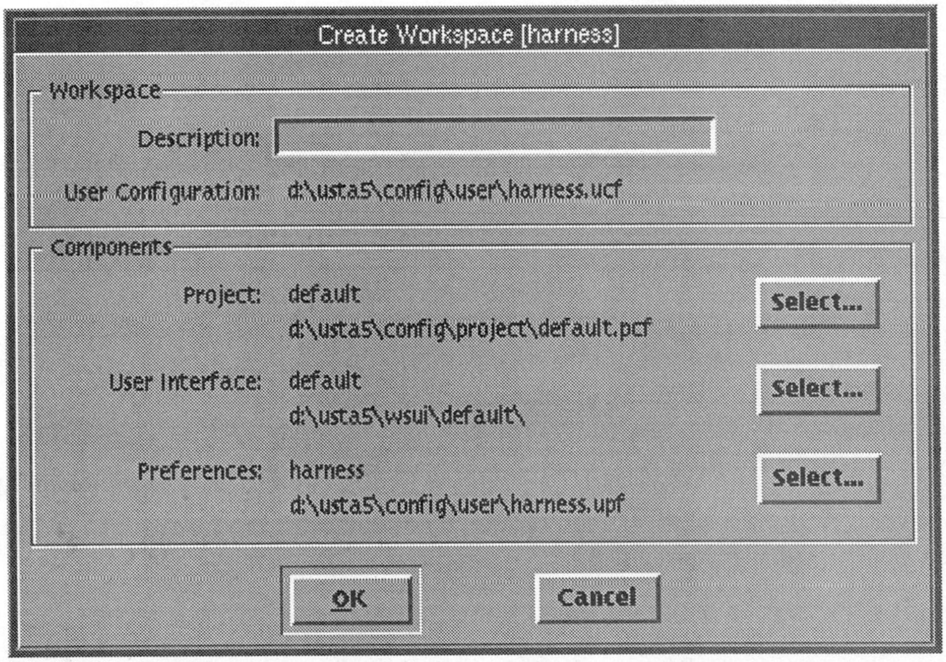

FIGURE 11–40   Create Workspace sub-dialog box.

Key-in the description (up to 32 characters) in the Description edit field. Make necessary changes to the path for the location of the Project configuration file (.pcf), user interface and preferences configuration file (.ucf) by clicking the appropriate Select... button and a corresponding File dialog box will be displayed. Select the appropriate filename from the Files list box. Click the OK button to accept changes and close the dialog box. MicroStation creates a workspace on a given filename.

Selecting a Default Workspace The Default Workspace dialog box is used to select a default workspace. The default workspace is the workspace that is used if no other workspace is specified when MicroStation is started, not the workspace named "default". Invoke the Default Workspace dialog box by selecting Default Workspace... tool in the Workspace sub-menu from the User pull-down menu. MicroStation displays a Default Workspace dialog box similar to the Figure 11–41.

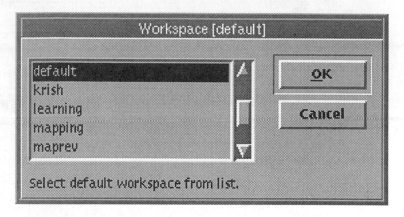

FIGURE 11–41 Default Workspace dialog box.

The Workspace list box lists the available workspaces. Select the workspace that you wish to select from the list box and click the OK button to close the dialog box. MicroStation program has seven configured workspaces (Arch, AutoCAD, Civil, Default, Learning, Mapping, and Mechdrft) that are available to use in Version 5.

> **NOTE:** You must exit MicroStation and restart to make a change take effect in the default workspace.

FUNCTION KEYS

Each personal computer keyboard has a special set of keys called *function keys*. MicroStation has a utility that assign menu action strings to the various function keys ([F1] through [F12]). Once the assignment is made, then all you have to do is select the function key and the menu action string is activated.

There are only twelve (12) functions on the keyboard, but MicroStation allows you to assign up to 96 function key assignments by combining a function key with the [SHIFT], [ALT] and/or [CTRL] key. So in essence, you can assign the [F1] with the following combinations:

[F1]

[SHIFT] + [F1]

[ALT] + [F1]

[CTRL] + [F1]

[SHIFT] + [ALT] + [F1]

[SHIFT] + [ALT] + [F1]

[ALT] + [CTRL] + [F1]

[SHIFT] + [ALT] + [CTRL] + [F1]

Function key assignments are stored in a special ASCII file and by default the extension for the function key file is .MNU. This file follows the same concept as the cell library file. Once created, the function key file may be attached to any of your design files to activate the function keys. The default function key menu file is called "funckey.mnu". It is stored under the /USTATION/MENUS/ directory.

The Function Keys dialog box is used to edit, save, and open function key menus. A function key menu contains assignments of menu action strings to function key combinations. To open the Function Key dialog box, select Function Keys... from the User pull-down menu. MicroStation displays a Function Keys dialog box similar to the Figure 11–42.

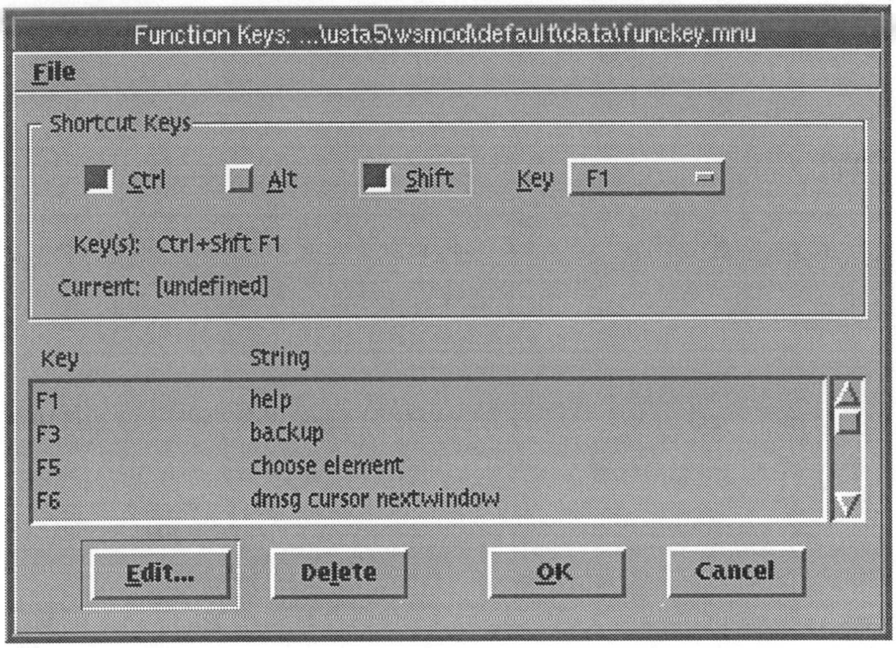

FIGURE 11–42 Function Keys dialog box.

The title bar identifies the open function key menu. The list box lists currently defined function key combinations and their definitions. You can click on any list box entry to select a currently defined function key combination for editing.

> **NOTE:** You can also select a function key combination with any modifier by simply pressing the desired keys on the keyboard to change or to create a new definition.

The Shortcut keys section contains controls that are used to select a function key definition to change or to create a new one. Turn ON the appropriate toggle buttons for ⌨CTRL⌨, ⌨ALT⌨, and/or ⌨SHIFT⌨ modifiers and select the function key from the Key option menu to change or to create a new definition.

You can also select a function key combination with any modifier by simply pressing the desired keys on the keyboard to change or to create a new definition.

Edit button opens the Edit Key Definition dialog box similar to the Figure 11–43, which is used to edit the current definition or create a new definition using the controls in the Shortcut Keys section of the Function Keys dialog box. Key-in the action string (e.g., place line) in the New edit field and click OK button accept the function key definition and close the dialog box.

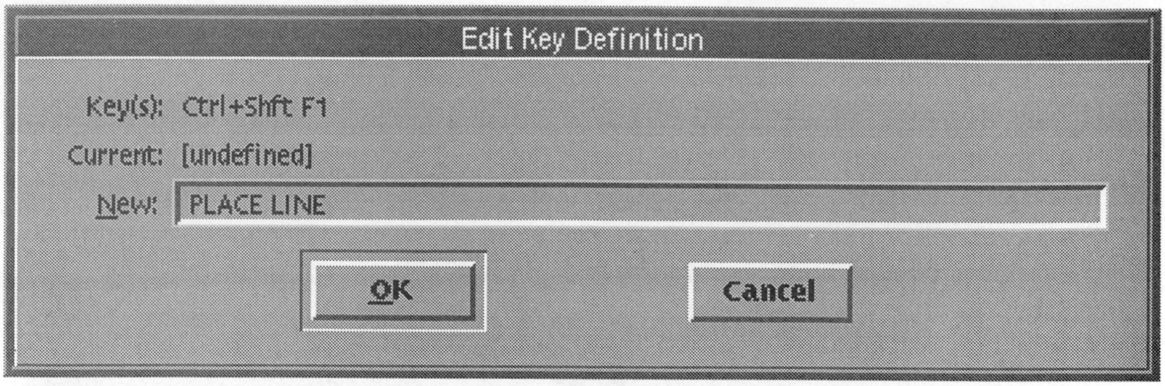

FIGURE 11–43 Edit Key Definition dialog box.

The Delete button deletes the definition of the selected function key combination.

Click the OK button to accept the changes to function key definitions for the current session and close the dialog box. To save them for your next session, you must save the function key definitions to a file. Invoke the Save command from the File pull-down menu of the Function Key dialog box to save the function key defintions. To save the function key definitions to a different file name, invoke the Save As... command from the File pull-down menu. MicroStation displays the Save Function Key As dialog box. Key-in the new file name in the Name edit field and click OK button to close the dialog box.

INSTALLING FONTS

Each time a design file is displayed, a font resource file is used that contains font definitions. Provided the font resource file name has not been changed during workspace definitions, MicroStation, by default, uses a resource file called FONT.RSC. MicroStation allow you to add new fonts to the font resource file by using the utility called Font Installer.

Font Installer dialog box is used to insert new fonts into the font library and to rename and renumber fonts. To open the Font Installer dialog box, select Font Installer... in the Utilities sub-menu tool from the User pull-down menu. MicroStation displays a Font Installer dialog box similar to the Figure 11–44.

The Open... button located beneath the Source File list box opens the Open Source Font File dialog box similar to the Figure 11–45. The Type option menu sets the file type from one of the following:

Font Cell Library—MicroStation font cell library, a standard cell library that contains cells that define the characters and symbols in a traditional MicroStation font and the font's attributes.

Font Library—MicroStation Version 5 font library.

uSTN V4/IGDS Fontlib—Version 4.1 or earlier (or IGDS) font library.

PS Type-1—PostScript Type 1 (uncompressed only).

Shape Files (AutoCAD)—AutoCAD shape files (.SHX files).

TrueType

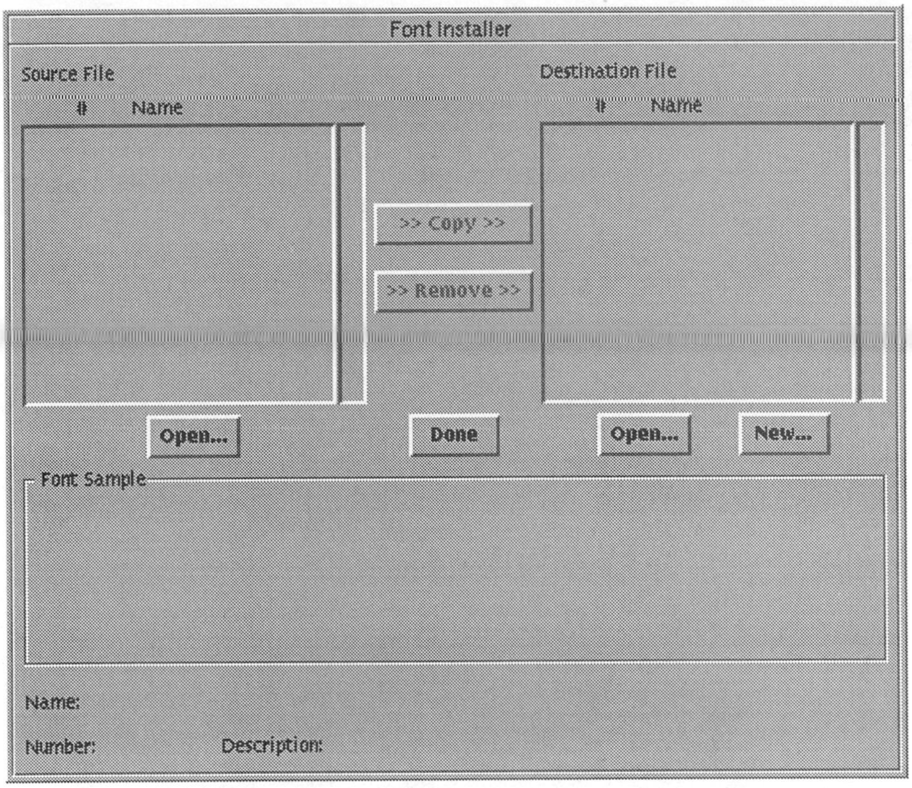

FIGURE 11–44 Font Installer dialog box.

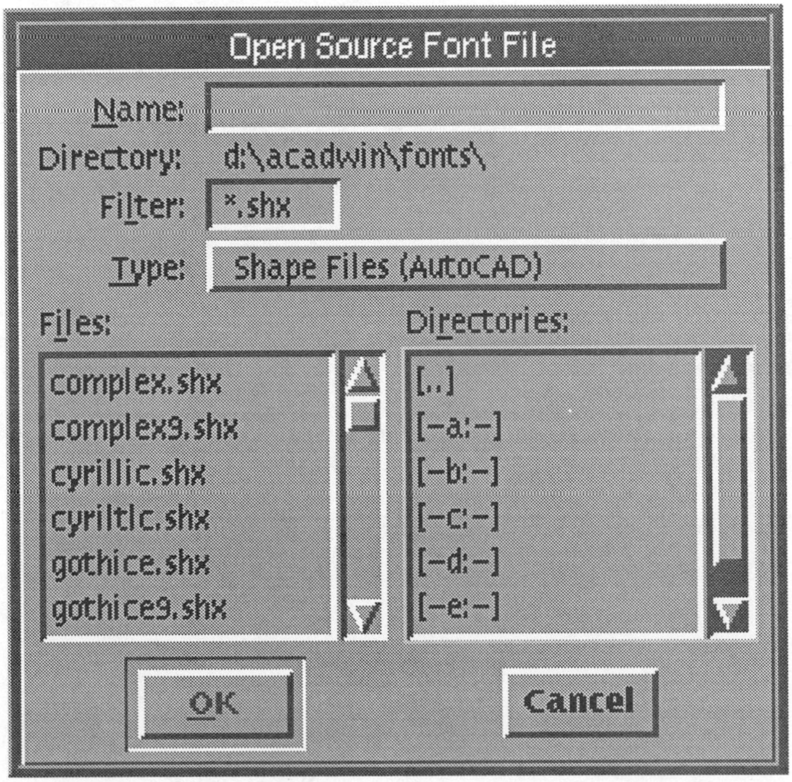

FIGURE 11–45 Open Source Font File dialog box.

Select the source font file and click OK button to close the dialog box. The source font is listed in the Source File list box.

The Open... button located beneath the Destination File list box opens the Open Destination Font File dialog box similar to the Figure 11–46. Select the font library from the Files list box as the destination for the new font insertion and click the OK button to close the dialog box. The destination file list box lists the fonts contained in the font file that is open as the destination for font insertion operation.

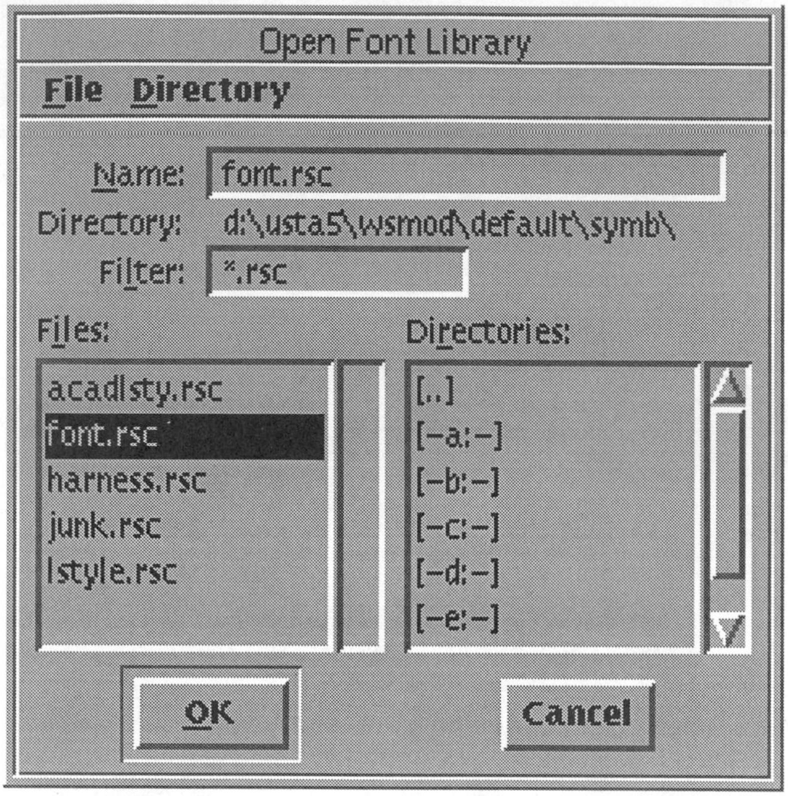

FIGURE 11–46 Open Destination Font File dialog box.

The >>Copy>> button inserts the font selected in the Source File list box into the destination font library. If a font with the same name already exists in the destination font library, it is replaced by the selected font.

The >>Remove>> button removes the font selected in the Destination File list box from the Destination font library.

Click the Done button to close the Font Installer dialog box.

12

USER COMMANDS

The purpose of this chapter is to give you a basic understanding of one of MicroStation's programming features, the User Command. Throughout this chapter, the term "UCM" refers to User Command.

WHAT IS A USER COMMAND?

A user command is an ASCII text file that groups together "statements" that are executed while in a MicroStation design file. A UCM is similar to a macro. The coded statements of a UCM follow the rules that are part of the MicroStation User Command Language. This language provides an interface consisting of a set of commands and instructions used to automate a task or set of tasks. These instructions are arranged in a logical order that imitates the steps that would be followed if you were performing MicroStation tasks manually. The coded statements are performed one after the other until all have been executed or until a condition is met that causes the UCM to exit.

GETTING STARTED

To be successful in writing a UCM, it will be helpful if you have at least a basic understanding of MicroStation and some knowledge of an ASCII text editor such as the DOS 5.0 or DOS 6.0 EDIT program. As with any programming language, it is best to organize yourself by defining what your UCM is going to do before you actually begin to write it. For example, before you manually draw a line or place text using MicroStation, there are certain parameters (level, color, weight, etc.) you need to set first. The same is true for writing a UCM.

The types of operations you can perform with UCMs include:

1. Repetitive MicroStation operations.
2. Setting element attributes such as level, color, line style, weight, rotation angle, scale, text attributes, etc.
3. Prompting the CAD operator for information, then having the user command instruct Micro-Station to draw or manipulate elements based on that information.
4. Reading and storing data from MicroStation.
5. Mathematical calculations.

MicroStation's developers have provided a source for acquiring previously written user commands. If you have access to a modem, you can obtain copies of UCMs through the MicroStation Information Center (MIC). The MIC bulletin board can be reached at 205/730-8786. Set your modem to 300–2400 baud, 8 bits, no parity. Files containing UCMs may be downloaded to your PC.

WHERE DO YOU STORE USER COMMANDS?

Each time MicroStation is activated, a series of macros are executed that define MicroStation environment variables. These macros are defined in a file called MSDIRS.CFG, which is located in the \CONFIG\SYSTEM\ sub-directory of the main MicroStation directory. The system variable MS_UCM used within this configuration file defines the path for user commands.

As delivered, MicroStation has one location (path) defined in the system variable MS_UCM. The following line is an excerpt from the MSDIRS.CFG file:

    MS_UCM   : $(MSDIR)ucm/   # User commands.

where $(MSDIR) is your main MicroStation directory

For the purpose of this chapter, add an additional path to the configuration file. Create a directory called HARNESS in the root directory (MD HARNESS) and include the path in the MSDIRS.CFG file. Use the DOS EDIT program provided in the DOS 5.0 (or as explained in the next section) to add the following statement to the MSDIRS.CFG file. Enter the statement exactly as shown. Notice the direction of the "slash" [/] character.

    MS_UCM   >   C:/HARNESS/   # new user commands

Once you have added this statement, save your changes to the MSDIRS.CFG file. All you have to do from now on is store your practice UCMs under the \HARNESS\ directory. You need not provide the path whenever you invoke any of the user commands located in the HARNESS directory.

If you activate a UCM and MicroStation returns a *File not found* message, go back and review your MSDIRS.CFG file. Usually this message occurs when your UCM is not located in a directory specified by one of the MS_UCM variables.

HOW DO YOU ACTIVATE A USER COMMAND?

Before you can activate a UCM, you must open a design file. Having done this, the simplest way to activate a UCM is by using the standard key-in method. Key-in at the uSTN> field, **UC=<name>**, and press [ENTER]. Specify the name of the UCM file for <name>. For example, to activate a UCM file <SETLEVEL>, key-in at the uSTN> field, **UC=SETLEVEL**, and press [ENTER]. Notice that there are no spaces between the **"UC="** and the filename.

You can also activate a UCM through the User Command dialog box (see Fig. 12–1), invoked from the Microstation User pull-down menu. Invoke the UCM from a list of UCMs displayed in the Files list box. If you plan to customize MicroStation by using UCMs, you can assign UCMs to your function keys, a matrix menu, or a User Command Index. More on the User Command Index later in this chapter.

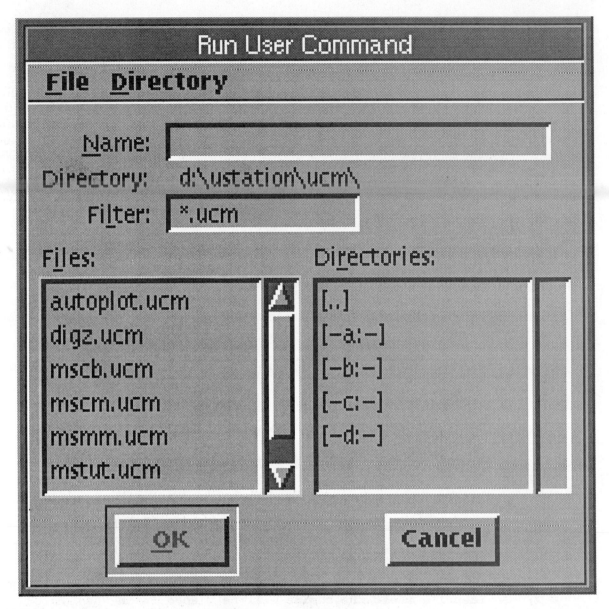

FIGURE 12–1 User Command Dialog Box.

HOW DO YOU CREATE A USER COMMAND?

The EDIT program is a utility delivered with DOS version 5.0 or later. It provides a full screen text-file editor, which may be used for generating notes, memos, letters, and other types of ASCII files. It can also be used for creating user commands.

To activate the DOS editor, change to the proper directory (CD\HARNESS), type EDIT followed by a filename, then press the ⏎ key. If the filename you enter has not been used before, EDIT will display a blank screen. If the filename has already been created, and it is an ASCII file, the contents of the file will be displayed.

Once the editor is activated, you will notice a menu bar located at the top of the screen. This menu bar contains all of the options available to you while using the EDIT program. Notice that one of the letters of each of the options is capitalized. To activate any of these options, hold the [ALT] key on your keyboard and press the appropriate capitalized letter of the option you wish to use. Press the [ESC] key on your keyboard if you wish to cancel a menu bar selection.

Once you have entered all the lines of text or code that you need, you must SAVE the file and its contents. A simple way to do this is to hold the [ALT] key, and press the letter [F] and then letter [X] key on your keyboard for Exit. If the file has not been saved before, it will be saved immediately and return to your DOS prompt. If the file has been saved before, you will be prompted <yes> or <no> to save your changes. If you answer Y, your file will be saved and you will return to your DOS prompt.

Refer to your DOS manual for an explanation of the options provided with the EDIT program.

Example 1

The following statements make up a "working" UCM. The statements may appear confusing at first; all of the parts are explained later in this chapter. Comments (characters that follow a semicolon) have been added to some of the lines that indicate where in the chapter you can get additional information.

Enter the following statements and save the file under MULTICOP.UCM in the HARNESS directory.

```
;***************

;  C:\HARNESS\MULTICOP.UCM -- September 1993 -- Tony Kendrick

;

;  This user command will permit you to create multiple copies of

;  a selected element. The type of elements you can copy are

;  lines, text, cells, shapes, etc. Once you identify an element,

;  you will be prompted to enter a number that represents the

;  number of copies to be made of the selected element.

;  To identify where the copies will be placed in the design

;  file, the user will be prompted to:

;  Enter an X and Y distance (delta distance separated by commas)

;  or Place a Data Point that identifies the distance and

;  direction of the copies.

;  Once the copies are made, the user will be prompted if any

;  other elements are to be copied. If yes, the process is

;  repeated. If no, the user command is exited.

;

;***************

   KEY    'NOECHO'                          ;see Controlling MicroStation

                                            ;Message Output.
```

```
START:                                          ;see Using Labels
    CMD     CPELE                               ;see CMD Operator and Syntax
    MSG     'PRSelect Element with a DATA'      ;see Communicating with
                                                ;the User.
    MSG     'CFMULTICOPY User Command'
    MSG     'ERRESET to Exit'
GETNXT:
    GET     P,DATAP,R,EXITUC                    ;see Receiving Data From The
                                                ;User
    GO      START                               ;see The GO Operator and
                                                ;Syntext -- Unconditional Branch.
DATAP:
    PNT                                         ;see PNT Operator.
TSTDAT:
    TST     RELERR,NE,25,SAVPNT                 ;see the TXT Operator and
                                                ;Syntax -- Conditional Branch.
    GO      GETNXT
SAVPNT:
    SET     I2=XUR                              ;see The SET Operator, Storing
                                                ;Data -- What is a Register?
                                                ;and Storing Point Data.
    SET     I3=YUR
    SET     R0=1
    MSG     'PRAccept/Reject'
    GET     P,ACCEPT,R,EXITUC
    GO      TSTDAT
ACCEPT:
    MSG     'PRKey In Quantity'
    MSG     'ERRESET to EXIT'
    GETP    ,START,R,EXITUC
    SET     R1=KEY                              ;see Storing Data -- What Is A
                                                ;Register?
    MSG     'PREnter Delta X, Delta Y or Show Point'
    GET     K,DELTA
    SET     I4=XUR
```

```
        SET    I5=YUR

        SET    I0=I4-I2                        ;see Performing Mathematical
                                               ;Calculations.

        SET    I1=I5-I3

        GO     POINT

DELTA:

        CVT    I0=KEY                          ;see Performing Conversions
                                               ;(CVT Operator).

POINT:

        SET    XUR=I2+I0

        SET    YUR=I3+I1

        PNT    XUR,YUR                         ;see Point Operator.

        SET    I2=XUR

        SET    I3=YUR

        TST    R0,GE,R1,AGAIN

        SET    R0=R0+1

        SET    MSG='PRPlacing copy #'+R0       ;see Storing and Combining
                                               ;Messages.

        MSG    MSG

        GO     POINT

AGAIN:

        MSG    'PRCopy any other elements?'

        MSG    'ER[Data pnt]-NO  [Reset]-YES'

        GET    P,START,R,EXITUC

        GO     AGAIN

EXITUC:                                        ;see How to Exit A UCM
                                               ;Gracefully.

        MSG    'PRTHATS ALL FOLKS!!'

        MSG    'ER '

        MSG    'CF '

        CMD    NULCMD

        KEY    'ECHO'

        END
```

USER COMMAND NAMING STRUCTURE

You must be aware of a few rules when assigning a name to a UCM.

1. As with any filename you create on a DOS-based personal computer, you are limited to eight characters. You may use fewer than eight characters, but no more.
2. The filename extension .UCM must be used for all user commands. This is the default extension name MicroStation looks for to recognize UCM files.
3. Character case is arbitrary. Uppercase and lowercase characters will be converted by DOS to uppercase.
4. The use of special characters, such as the dash (-), percent sign (%), and so on, is allowed. A blank space (space bar) within the filename is not allowed. The asterisk (*) should not be used since it could be confusing when using other DOS commands.
5. Attempt to add some intelligence to the filename whenever possible. For example, assign the filename CL.UCM or CLINE.UCM for a UCM that sets parameters for centerline linework parameters.

THE BODY OF A USER COMMAND—UNDERSTANDING STATEMENTS

A UCM statement consists of one of the commands provided by the User Command Language. Keep the following rules in mind as you enter each statement in your UCM.

1. You may use either uppercase or lowercase characters.
2. Each statement must contain only one command or "operator."
3. A statement beginning with a semicolon is considered a "comment."
4. Each character in a statement is positioned in "columns." The left-most position is considered column 1. "Labels" begin in column 1. Statements may begin in any column; however, you may choose to use a ⌨TAB to make the UCM more readable or divide the UCM into segments.
5. The last statement of ALL user commands must contain the END operator.

The Importance of Comments

The signature of a truly good user command programmer is the use of comments within the UCM. However, comments are optional. A comment is an internal form of documentation that provides a brief description of what the UCM can be expected to do. Although UCMs are fairly simple to read once you understand the components and commands, comments provide an additional dimension that others (non-programmers) can use to understand the purpose of the command simply by reading it.

Any time you want to add a comment to a UCM, simply place a semicolon (;), then type in your comment. MicroStation will treat the characters that follow a semicolon as a non-active part of the UCM. The following is an example of how comments may be used at the beginning of your UCM.

```
;***************
;  C:\HARNESS\SAMPLE.UCM -- September 1993 -- Tony Kendrick
;
;  This is a sample UCM that will set the appropriate parameters
;  for drawing a centerline used at XYZ Company.
;
;***************
```

Notice that all of the statements begin with the semicolon character. Some lines have no characters following the semicolon in order to make the comment section more readable.

Using Operators and Operands

An operator is a command that tells the UCM what to do. It sets up the action of the statement and serves the same purpose as a verb in a sentence. An operand, on the other hand, follows an operator and accepts the action. The operator is similar to the noun of a sentence: "Do this to or with *that*."

The most commonly used operators within a UCM include the following:

1. MSG
2. GET
3. GO
4. KEY
5. PNT
6. CMD
7. RST
8. END

Using Labels

An important part of a UCM is a label. A label is a group of characters used to control the "flow" of the UCM. It may be positioned on the same line as any other statement, but will be more readable if it is on a line by itself. The following rules must be applied for all labels:

1. Try to assign a meaningful name to your labels, something that makes sense.
2. Place the first character of your label in column 1.
3. Make sure your label always ends with a colon (:).
4. Your labels may be up to six characters long.
5. Any alphanumeric character (A–Z and 0–9) may be used, but the first character must always be a letter.
6. Do not use any special characters (!, #, $, %, etc.) or blank spaces within the label..
7. Each label used within a UCM must be unique.

Valid examples:

```
START:
POINT1:
A:
EXITUC:
```

Invalid examples:

```
BEGIN      (no colon)
PNT 1:     (space)
A&B:       (special character)
1A:        (number as first character)
```

How to Exit a UCM Gracefully

As mentioned earlier, the last statement of every UCM must contain the END operator. However, you may use a short group of statements that will allow the UCM to exit gracefully. To do so, you will need to use the EXITUC: label.

If you use the EXITUC: label, and when MicroStation encounters an error within your UCM during its execution, control of the UCM is sent automatically to the EXITUC: label, and all statements located after the label are executed. As an added bonus, a helpful error message will be displayed on the screen that identifies the statement line number that has a syntax problem. Then you can go to that line number within the UCM and make the necessary corrections.

> **NOTE:** Using the EXITUC: label will not ensure that problems with the UCM logic will be identified.

If the UCM has a successful termination (all lines within the body of UCM are executed), you will not see any error messages. Without the EXITUC: label, an erroneous termination may leave you without a clue about what might be wrong.

The following example contains statements for a routine way to end a user command.

```
EXITUC:

    MSG     'PRUCM Exited'

    END
```

Notice that the "E" in EXITUC: is in column 1 and that the last statement is the END operator. We will discuss the MSG operator in the next section.

COMMUNICATING WITH THE USER

During the normal operation of MicroStation, some messages automatically appear within the MicroStation Command Window. For example, whenever you press the tentative data button, the coordinates of that particular point are displayed in the upper left message field. When you select a command from the menu or from a palette, the name of that command is displayed in the command field. If you delete an element, a message is displayed that prompts you to Accept/Reject the selected element. UCMs use these same fields to display messages. The UCM writer has complete control over message placement and therefore can communicate with the user.

A total of six fields are available for such communications purposes. They are identified within the UCM by means of the MSG operator. A field abbreviation (operand) and subsequent message follow the operator. The operand field abbreviations include the following:

Abbreviation	Field Name
ST	Status
MS	Message
CF	Command
PR	Prompt
ER	Error
uSTN	The MicroStation key-in field uSTN> is reserved for input from the user.

MSG Operator and Syntax

The MSG operator is required to send messages to the various fields described above. Each field serves as an operand and immediately follows the MSG operator. As previously outlined, an abbreviation is provided that distinguishes the various fields.

The following statements show the proper syntax for each type of message field. Notice the use of the apostrophe ['] before the abbreviation and after the message, and also notice that the messages begin immediately after the two-letter abbreviation. (You can leave blank spaces after the abbreviation if you wish.)

```
MSG     'STThis is my Status field'        ;upper left field

MSG     'MSThis is my Ustation Message field'        ;upper right
                                                       ;field

MSG     'CFThis is my Command field'        ;center left field

MSG     'PRThis is my Prompt field'         ;center right field

MSG     'ERThis is my Error field'          ;bottom right field
```

For an illustration of message fields, see Example 2.

Clearing Messages

After a UCM has finished processing, the message will remain on the screen until some basic MicroStation operation is performed. So as not to confuse the user once the UCM has finished processing, it is a good practice to clear some or all message fields. A reasonable place to do this is at the end of the UCM. You could include the following statements after the EXITUC: label or simply leave a blank space after the two-letter abbreviation.

```
EXITUC:
    MSG     'PRUser command complete'        ;display uc complete
                                             ;message in prompt field.

    MSG     'ER '                            ;blank out error message
                                             ;field.

    MSG     'ST '                            ;blank out status message
                                             ;field.

    END
```

Controlling MicroStation Message Output During the course of a normal MicroStation session, certain MicroStation messages will appear in the various message fields. Sometimes this is not desirable and may even interfere with the messages you are trying to display with your UCM. One way to suppress these MicroStation messages is to use the NOECHO key-in.

For example, key-in at the uSTN> field, NOECHO, and press ⏎. All of MicroStation's normal message fields will be cleared and suppressed. To restore the display normally seen in these fields, key-in at the uSTN> field, ECHO, and press ⏎.

To incorporate message suppression into your UCM, add the following statement at or near the top of your UCM.

```
KEY    'NOECHO'                        ;inhibit normal MicroStation
                                       ;messages.
```

If you suppress messages with your UCM, it is good practice to "restore" the message capability before exiting your UCM so that MicroStation will display messages as usual. Add the following statement at or near the bottom of your UCM.

```
KEY    'ECHO'                          ;restore MicroStation message
                                       ;fields to original state.
```

The KEY operator is explained in detail later in this chapter.

Storing and Combining Messages

Inside a UCM, it is possible to store a message in a special storage place or register called MSG; then, later, the message can be displayed. To store the message, you must use the SET operator. You also must identify the message field abbreviation where the message will be displayed.

> **NOTE:** Though it is easy to confuse the two, be aware that there is a MSG operand and a MSG register. The following statements show how to store a message and then recall it. (The lines containing dots [.] represent statements you can add later.)

```
SET    MSG='STHello world'             ;message stored in MSG register.
       .
       .
MSG    MSG                             ;display stored message in
                                       ;status field (ST).
```

For an illustration of message fields, see Example 3. For a detailed explanation of the SET operator, see the section on Storing Data.

Example 2

Practice makes perfect. Use your text editor (EDIT program) and create the following UCMs to practice the various components described above. Refer back to the previous sections if necessary, and read the comments included within each UCM. Be sure to store your UCMs in the appropriate directory. Open a design file and try them out once you are finished.

```
;***************
;  C:\HARNESS\SHOWMSGS.UCM -- September 1993 -- Tony Kendrick
;
; This UCM demonstrates how to assign messages to screen message
; fields in the MicroStation Command Window.
;***************
;
    KEY     'NOECHO'                          ;inhibit Ustation message
                                              ;capability.
START:
    MSG     'CFThis is my Command Field'      ;center left field.
    MSG     'PRThis is my Prompt Field'       ;center right field.
    MSG     'ERThis is my Error Field'        ;bottom right field.
    MSG     'STThis is my Status field'       ;upper left field.
    MSG     'MSThis is my Ustation Message field'
                                              ;upper right field.
EXITUC:
    KEY     'ECHO'                            ;restore Ustation message
                                              ;capability.

    END
```

Example 3

```
;***************
;  C:\HARNESS\STORMSG.UCM -- September 1993 -- Tony Kendrick
;
; This UCM demonstrates how to store messages. It will prompt
; the user to press the RESET button. Once the RESET button is
; pressed, the message "Hello World" will display in the
; field.
;***************
    KEY     'NOECHO'                          ;inhibit Ustation message
                                              ;capability.
START:
    MSG     'PRPress RESET to continue'       ;message displayed in
                                              ;prompt field.
```

```
    SET    MSG='STHello World'          ;message stored in MSG register.
    GET    R,SHOMSG                     ;get RESET from user in order
                                        ;to continue.

SHOMSG:
    MSG    MSG                          ;display stored message in
                                        ;status field (ST).

EXITUC:
    MSG    'PRUCM Complete'
    KEY    'ECHO'                       ;restore Ustation message
                                        ;capability.

    END
```

EXERCISE

Exercise 12–1

Create a UCM named MESSAGE.UCM that displays:
  your name in the Status Field (ST),
  your address in the Command Field (CF)
  your birthday in the Message Field (MS)

Also include the NOECHO and ECHO key-ins.

RECEIVING DATA FROM THE USER

As mentioned earlier, the UCM communicates with the user through messages. In this section you will see what the UCM does with the data once it receives or "gets" it.

Since data usually is received from the keyboard or from one of MicroStation's cursor or mouse device buttons (command, data, or reset buttons), the UCM must be told what to do with this data once it receives it. This is where the GET operator comes in. The GET operator interprets the data and then "branches" to a label statement.

The proper syntax for the GET operator is as follows:

```
GET   KEYWORDa,LABELa,...KEYWORD,LABEL
```

where **KEYWORD** is one of the following:

  K—a key-in from the keyboard (key-in data)

  P—a data point from the pointing device (data button)

R—a reset/reject response from the pointing device (reset button)

M—a menu or function key selection (however, the user must set a bit in the TCB variable OUTFLG)

C—an unattached cursor button

T—a tutorial block selection (tutorials were used primarily before MicroStation version 4.0)

and where **LABEL** is a label statement.

To illustrate this prompting and branching process, let's look at the following statements. Notice the statement beginning with the GET operator. For a complete example, see Example 4.

```
START:
    MSG    'PRKey-in a coord or Data point its location'
    MSG    'ERPress RESET to EXIT'
    GET    K,MYKEY,P,MYPNT,R,EXITUC
    .
MYKEY:
    .
MYPNT:
    .
EXITUC:
    MSG    'PRUCM exited'
    MSG    'ER '
    END
```

As you can see in the second line, the user is prompted to provide coordinate information by either a key-in or by placing a data point. Line 3 prompts the user to press the reset button to exit the UCM.

The GET statement in line 4 interprets the input (key-in or point data or reset), then branches to the proper label.

1. If the GET statement "gets" a key-in (K), then control is transferred to the MYKEY label.
2. If the GET statement "gets" a data point (P), then control is transferred to the MYPNT label.
3. If the UCM receives a reset button (R), the UCM branches to the EXITUC label and the statements following the label are performed.

Using the GET Operator Alone

If you use the GET operator alone within a statement, the UCM will "suspend" itself until an input is received from the user. Since you are not providing a KEYWORD, the UCM simply proceeds to the next line once input is received.

One of the places where you may want to use the GET operator in a statement by itself is during the UCM "debugging" process. You can insert debugging messages within your UCM and the GET operator stops the UCM so you can read these messages. Without a way to stop the UCM, these messages are simply over-written by messages that appear later in the UCM.

Example 4

Use your text editor to create the following UCM to practice using the GET operator and branching to labels.

```
;***************

;   C:\HARNESS\GET.UCM -- September 1993 -- Tony Kendrick

;   This UCM demonstrates the GET operator and the "branching" feature.

;   Appropriate messages are displayed, based on the type of input

;   received.

;

;***************

;

START:

    MSG    'PRKey-in a coord or Data point its location'

    MSG    'ERPress RESET to EXIT'

    GET    K,MYKEY,P,MYPNT,R,EXITUC

                                           ;if key-in is received, branch

                                           ;to MYKEY label, if point is

                                           ;received, branch to MYPNT

                                           ;label, if RESET is received,

                                           ;branch to EXITUC label.

MYKEY:

    MSG    'PRKeyboard input received'

MYPNT:

    MSG    'PRData point input received'

EXITUC:

    MSG    'PRReset button input received -- UCM exited'

    MSG    'ER '

    END
```

Example 5

```
;**************
;  C:\HARNESS\MYNAME.UCM -- September 1993 -- Tony Kendrick
;  This UCM prompts the user to key-in his/her name. The key-in
;  is stored and added to the prompt (PR) message field. The
;  message is displayed and the UCM is suspended by the GET
;  operator. Once any additional user input is received
;  (such as an ENTER key or data or reset button), the UCM
;  will proceed to the next statement.
;**************
;
START:
    MSG    'PRKey-in your name'              ;prompt the user to key-in
                                             ;his/her name.

    MSG    'ERor Press RESET to EXIT'        ;or press the reset button
                                             ;to exit the UCM.

    GET    K,MYNAME,R,EXITUC                 ;if a key-in is received,
                                             ;branch to the MYNAME
                                             ;label; if a RESET is
                                             ;received, branch to the
                                             ;EXITUC label.

    GO     START                             ;if any other input is
                                             ;received, such as a data
                                             ;point, branch to the
                                             ;START label

MYPNT:
    SET    MSG='PRMy name is '+KEY           ;we will discuss the SET
                                             ;and MSG operators
                                             ;in the next section.

    MSG    MSG

    GET                                      ;use the GET operator
                                             ;alone to suspend the
                                             ;UCM until "any" input is
                                             ;received from the
                                             ;user -- ENTER, data point
                                             ;or RESET may be entered.
                                             ;The UCM will then proceed
                                             ;to the next statement.
```

```
EXITUC:

MSG     'PRUCM exited'

MSG     'ER '

END
```

STORING DATA—WHAT IS A REGISTER?

A register (or operand) is a temporary storage place for data received from the user. Registers are similar to mailboxes. Each time a keystroke, or group of keystrokes, is entered at the keyboard, those keystrokes are stored temporarily in a register called KEY, or they can be instructed to be stored in a semipermanent alphanumeric register. Whenever the user presses the data button, the point information (X,Y, and Z screen coordinates) can be stored in a temporary point register. If the chosen register already has something stored there, the current contents are discarded and the new data takes its place.

Be aware that there are different types of registers because data comes in different formats. Besides having keyboard character data and point data, there are also registers for storing integers, real numbers, messages, view numbers, errors, and so forth. It is up to you to select the proper register when storing specific types of data. This section discusses how to match the two.

Each register is identified within the UCM by an abbreviated name. This abbreviated name is similar to a mailbox address and tells the UCM what address to use. This is done by using the SET operator. More on this later.

Since some types of data are more common than others, registers are divided into two groups—general purpose and special purpose. Note that some of the register names are described as a range. The "R" register is described as R0 through R31. This means that there are 32 individual "R" registers available (R0, R1, R2,...R31).

General Purpose Registers

A general purpose register is used when you want to store data as described in Table 12–1.

Table 12–1.

REGISTER NAME (OPERAND)	DESCRIPTION OF REGISTER CONTENTS
R0–R31	Integers (zero through 31)
I0–I15	Double precision integers (zero through 15)
A0–A15	Double precision floating point numbers (zero through 15)
C0–C15	Characters (zero through 15)
N0–N15	Number of characters in C0–C15 (zero through 15)
MSG	Messages
M0	Number of characters in MSG (zero only)

Special Purpose Registers

A special purpose register is used when you want to store data as described in Table 12–2.

Table 12–2.

REGISTER NAME (OPERAND)	DESCRIPTION OF REGISTER CONTENTS
KEY	Operator key-in
K0	Number of characters in operator key-in (zero only)
XUR,YUR,ZUR	Screen UOR (units of resolution) coordinates
ERR	Errors
XDT,YDT	Digitizer tablet coordinates

The SET Operator and Syntax

The SET operator is used each time you want to store a value in a register. The values can be either alphanumeric or numeric. An abbreviated register name always follows the SET operator. An equal sign (=) always follows the register name. A second register name follows the equal sign. The data is passed from operand2 to operand1. The SET statement has the following form:

```
SET   operand1 = operand2
```

where **operand** is one of the abbreviated names of a register.

Using the SET operator, it is also possible to combine, or add, the values of two registers and store the result. The values can be either numeric or alphanumeric. Later we will see how to add words together to build sentences that can be displayed as messages. The syntax of the SET statement that combines data is as follows:

```
SET   operand1 = operand2 + operand3
```

where **operand** is one of the abbreviated names of a register.

The following two statements show the proper syntax for storing data in a register (operand) using the SET operator:

```
SET    R0=1              ;the contents of R0 is set to
                         ;equal 1
SET    R1=R0+2           ;add 2 to R0 and store the
                         ;result in R1
                         ;R1 now equal 3
```

Storing Numbers—R0–R31, I0–I15, A0–A15 MicroStation has several registers available for storing numbers that fall within specific ranges. These include integers and floating point numbers. An integer is a number that has no fraction or decimal. It is a whole number. A floating point number has a decimal value or fraction.

Small Integers (R0–R31)—Use "R" registers to store small integers ranging from –32767 to 32767. These registers are ideally used for counting or looping.

Double precision integers (I0–I15)—Use "I" registers to store very large integers such as X and Y UOR (unit of resolution) coordinate values. UOR values range from –2147483647 to 2147483647. These values represent the minimum and maximum XY coordinates in UORs of a design file.

Floating point (A0–A15)—Use "A" registers to store numbers that have a decimal value, such as the actual "calculated" XY coordinates of data point.

Storing Alphanumeric Data—C0–C15, N0–N15

Alphanumeric data is represented by any character shown on the keyboard (A through Z as well as 0 through 9, plus any of the special characters !,@,#,$, etc.).

Characters (C0–C15)—Use the "C" registers to store up to 40 alphanumeric characters. The "C" registers are ideal for storing character data that will make up a message or will be used for text placement within a design file.

Character counting (N0–N15)—The "N" register corresponds to the number of characters contained in the "C" register.

Storing Messages—MSG, M0

Message data is made up of the same characters as alphanumeric data.

Prompts (MSG)—Up to 42 characters may be stored in the MSG register. The first two characters define the message field in which the message will be displayed on the screen (PR, ER, ST, etc.). The actual message is made up of the last 40 characters.

> **NOTE:** Do not confuse the MSG register with the MSG operand. The MSG operand instructs the UCM to display a message to the screen. The MSG register is the actual "mailbox" that contains character data that will be displayed.

Character counting (M0)—The M0 register corresponds to the number of characters contained in the MSG register.

Storing Errors—ERR

To confirm that an error is present during the execution of a UCM, an error may be stored as error data. This error data may then be tested by the UCM and the UCM exited if necessary.

Error data (ERR)—Use the ERR register to store an integer value. If the value in the ERR register is set to 0, then no error is present.

Storing Point Information—XUR, YUR, ZUR

Each time MicroStation's data button is pressed by the user, point information is stored in point registers. Each point represents the intersection of the X, Y, and Z coordinates within a design file. (The Z coordinate is present only in a 3D design file.)

This point information is always stored in UORs (units of resolution). A UOR is MicroStation's smallest unit of measure and is always an integer. Since a design file measures approximately 4.2 billion UORs in the X, Y, and Z directions, there are 4.2 billion possible XYZ coordinate combinations. There are three registers that may be used for storing UOR coordinates:

XUR, YUR, ZUR

The contents of the XUR, YUR, and ZUR registers remain only until the next data point is selected. The new data point information replaces the old contents. If you plan on storing more than one point, it will be necessary to "transfer" the point information to another register. The "I" registers work very well for this purpose—see Example 6.

Storing Digitizer Coordinates—XDT, YDT If MicroStation is configured to operate with a digitizer, the X and Y coordinates of a digitizer input point may be stored in the following registers:

XDT, YDT

These registers contain the coordinate values that represent the last input point from a digitizer. The register values are integers ranging from 0 through 65535. The values are sent to the XDT and YDT registers from an "unattached" cursor button.

Storing Keyboard Input and Building Messages—KEY, NUM, K0 Keystrokes are stored in a user command's KEY register each time an [ENTER] key is pressed. Up to 42 characters can be stored at a time. The NUM register contains the number of keystrokes from the keyboard. If the user keys-in "ABCDEF" and presses [ENTER], the KEY register contains "ABCDEF" and the NUM register contains a value equal to six characters.

Since the KEY register can only hold the "current" group of characters temporarily, it will be necessary to "transfer" the contents of the KEY register to another alphanumeric register. The "C" register is ideal for storing character (alphanumeric) data. Once this is done, the UCM is ready to accept and store another key-in from the user.

Once characters are stored in a "C" register permanently, the contents can be manipulated to build new messages. For example, contents can be added together or stacked end to end. These new messages can then be stored in the MSG and displayed in a prompt field on the screen.

The K0 register contains a value equal to the number of alphanumeric characters contained in the KEY register. Since the KEY register cannot contain more than 42 characters, the K0 register's value cannot exceed 42. The K0 register, however, can be set to allow accessibility to only some of the characters stored in KEY.

Example 7 will show you how to store key-ins. Example 8 will explain how to count characters received by a key-in.

Example 6

```
;***************
;  C:\HARNESS\STOREPNT.UCM -- September 1993 -- Tony Kendrick
;  This UCM demonstrates how to store point information.
;***************
;
START:
    MSG    'PRPlace 1st Data point'        ;prompt user for 1st data
                                           ;point location or
```

```
    MSG    'ERor RESET to EXIT'              ;to press RESET to end
                                             ;UCM.
    GET    P,PNT1,R,EXITUC                   ;if UCM receives "point"
                                             ;info, branch to
                                             ;PNT1 label or if UCM
                                             ;receives a RESET,
                                             ;branch to EXITUC label.
    GO  START                                ;if any other input is
                                             ;received, branch to the
                                             ;START label.
;Store the first point's information
PNT1:
    SET    I0=XUR                            ;store X UOR point info in the
                                             ;I0 register.
    SET    I1=YUR                            ;store Y UOR point info in the
                                             ;I1 register.
    SET    I2=ZUR                            ;store Z UOR point info (if
                                             ;any) in the I2
                                             ;register.

NEXT:
    MSG    'PRPlace 2nd Data point'          ;prompt user for 2nd data point
                                             ;location.
    MSG    'ERor RESET to re-do 1st'         ;to press RESET to re-enter 1st
                                             ;data point.
    GET    P,PNT2,R,START                    ;if UCM receives "point" info,
                                             ;branch to PNT2 label.
    GO     NEXT
;Store the second point's information
PNT2:
    SET    I3=XUR                            ;store X UOR point info in the
                                             ;I3 register.
    SET    I4=YUR                            ;store Y UOR point info in the
                                             ;I4 register.
    SET    I5=ZUR                            ;store Z UOR point info (if
                                             ;any) in the I5 register.
```

```
EXITUC:

    MSG     'PRPoints 1 and 2 Stored'

    MSG     'ERUCM Complete'

    END
```

Example 7

```
;***************

;   C:\HARNESS\STOREKEY.UCM -- September 1993 -- Tony Kendrick

;   This UCM demonstrates how to store keyboard input and

;   build messages. Prompt user for name information, then

;   display a message to the screen in the prompt field.

;***************

START:

    MSG     'PREnter your LAST name'          ;prompt the user for last
                                              ;name.

    MSG     'ERor RESET to EXIT'              ;prompt the user for a
                                              ;RESET to exit the UCM.

    GET     K,LNAME,R,EXITUC                  ;if a key-in is received,
                                              ;branch to LNAME
                                              ;label or if a RESET is
                                              ;received, exit the
                                              ;UCM.

    GO      START                             ;if any other input is
                                              ;received, branch to
                                              ;the START label.

LNAME:

    SET     C0=KEY                            ;store KEY register
                                              ;contents in C0 register.

NEXT:

    MSG     'PREnter your FIRST name'         ;prompt the user for first
                                              ;name.

    MSG     'ERor RESET to re-do LAST name'   ;prompt user for RESET to
                                              ;re-enter last name.

    GET     K,FNAME,R,START                   ;if a key-in is received,
```

```
                                                    ;branch to FNAME
                                                    ;label or if a RESET is
                                                    ;received, branch to
                                                    ;START label.
           GO      NEXT                             ;if any other input is
                                                    ;received, branch to
                                                    ;the NEXT label.

FNAME:
           SET   C1=KEY                             ;store KEY register
                                                    ;contents in C1 register.

           SET   MSG='PRHello. My name is '        ;store message characters
                                                    ;MSG register and
                                                    ;set it up to display in
                                                    ;the prompt 'PR' field.

           SET   MSG=MSG + C1                       ;add contents of A1
                                                    ;register (first name) to
                                                    ;contents of MSG register.

           SET   MSG=MSG + ' '                      ;add a blank space to the
                                                    ;contents of the
                                                    ;MSG register.

           SET   MSG=MSG + C0                       ;add contents of A0
                                                    ;register (last name) to
                                                    ;contents of the MSG
                                                    ;register.

           MSG   MSG                                ;use MSG operand to
                                                    ;display contents of
                                                    ;MSG register.

      EXITUC:

           MSG   'ER '                              ;cancel or blank out last
                                                    ;error field 'ER' prompt.

           END
```

Even though the UCM prompted the user for last name first and first name last, the resulting message displayed in the prompt field will be:

"Hello. My name is First Last"

Example 8

```
;***************
;  C:\HARNESS\COUNTKEY.UCM -- September 1993 -- Tony Kendrick
;  This UCM demonstrates how to count "key" input.
;  The keystrokes representing the name Tony Kendrick are stored
;  in the KEY register. The 1st four characters are extracted
;  and combined with a message.
;***************
;
START:
    SET    KEY='Tony Kendrick'              ;store characters 'Tony
                                            ;Kendrick' in KEY
                                            ;register.
    SET    K0=4                             ;make only 4 characters
                                            ;accessible from
                                            ;KEY register.
    SET    C0=KEY                           ;store 4 characters of KEY
                                            ;register in C0 register.
    SET    MSG='PRHello, '                  ;store prompt field message in
                                            ;MSG register
    SET    MSG= MSG + C0                     ;add the 4 characters in C0 to
                                            ;MSG register
    MSG    MSG                              ;tell MSG operator to display
                                            ;MSG register on screen.
    EXITUC:
    END
```

EXERCISE

Exercise 12–2

Write a UCM named SHOWPNT.UCM that prompts the user to place a data point. Store the XY point data in registers I0 and I1. Practice combining the contents of a register (I0 and I1) with messages in the status field.

ACTIVATING KEY-INS

The KEY operator provides a means of sending "hard-coded" keyboard input to MicroStation through the UCM. The key-in that is sent is contained in the operand that follows the KEY operator. After the contents of the operand are "keyed-in," the KEY operator automatically sends a carriage return from the keyboard to MicroStation.

The following is the proper syntax for the KEY operator.

```
KEY   operand
```

where **operand** represents the characters, or register contents that serve as the key-in.

Setting Parameters

As mentioned in earlier chapters, MicroStation uses a variety of key-ins to set drawing parameters such as:

LV=1

CO=2

WT=3

You can send these "hard-coded" key-ins to MicroStation through a UCM by using the KEY operator. The following short UCM shows the application:

```
START:
    KEY     'LV=1'                      ;set the active level to 1.
    KEY     'CO=2'                      ;set the active color to 2.
    KEY     'WT=3'                      ;set the active weight to 3.
    KEY     'TX=.125'                   ;set the active text size to
                                        ;.125.
    KEY     'AA=0'                      ;set the active angle to zero.
EXITUC:
    END
```

Notice that the actual MicroStation key-in is enclosed by single quotation marks [']. Any characters that follow the KEY operand and are surrounded by a single quotation mark will be activated by the UCM. It is also possible to send the contents of a register to MicroStation as a key-in.

Activating MicroStation Commands

MicroStation consists of more than 250 commands. Some of these commands generate elements and some manipulate elements. Each command may be activated by a key-in that is available in two different formats: the "verb noun" format or the "primitive" format. The "primitive" format originated during the early VAX-based Intergraph days. Either form may be used with the KEY operator within a MicroStation UCM. See Appendix D for a list of key-in commands and Appendix F for a list of primitive commands.

For example, to activate the Place Line command, include the following statement in a UCM:

```
KEY    'PLACE LINE'                        ;verb noun form of the place line
                                           ;command
```

or

```
KEY    '/PLINE'                            ;primitive form of the place line
                                           ;command
```

Notice that, as with all other key-ins, the MicroStation command is enclosed within single quotation marks [']. Also notice that the primitive format of the commands has a slash [/].

The CMD Operator and Syntax

It can be argued that activating a command within a UCM can be done much more efficiently if the CMD operator is used. It is true that if a UCM is going to be designed to operate in both the VAX-based Intergraph platform as well as the PC-based MicroStation platform, the CMD operator and the primitive format of a command must be used.

The proper syntax for the CMD operator is as follows:

```
CMD    PLINE                               ;VAX Intergraph / MicroStation
                                           ;primitive
                                           ;for place line.
CMD    PTEXT                               ;primitive command for place text
```

See Example 10 for an illustration of command activation.

PLACING MICROSTATION POINTS

Once MicroStation point data is stored, the UCM will use the information to place or manipulate elements within the design file. The PNT operator is used to send a data point to MicroStation. The PNT operator has 13 operands associated with it. The first six operands may be used to send point information to MicroStation when placing new elements into the design file. The last seven operands may be used to help identify element search criteria when manipulating elements. The LOCELE (locate element) command is used in conjunction with this search criteria. See the section on Locating Elements for more detail about using specific search criteria. The proper syntax for the PNT operator is as follows:

```
PNT    operand1,operand2,operand3,...,operand13
```

where   **operand1** = X UOR value
        operand2 = Y UOR value
        operand3 = Z UOR value

operand4 = view number
operand5 = XDT value
operand6 = YDT value
operand7....operand13 = bit settings for element search criteria

See Example 10 for an illustration of point placement within a UCM.

Example 9

```
;***************
;  C:\HARNESS\TEXTSZ.UCM -- September 1993 -- Tony Kendrick
;
;  This UCM demonstrates the use of the KEY operator and
;  KEY register (operand). It will show how to add to or build
;  a key-in, then activate the key-in.
;
;***************
    KEY    'NOECHO'                      ;inhibit MicroStation messages.
START:
    MSG    'PREnter a TEXT SIZE'         ;prompt user for a text size,
    MSG    'ERor RESET to EXIT'          ;or press RESET to Exit UCM.
    GET    K,TSIZE,R,EXITUC              ;if a key-in is received,
                                         ;branch to TSIZE label.
                                         ;if a Reset is received,
                                         ;branch to the EXITUC label.
    GO     START                         ;if any other input is
                                         ;received, branch to
                                         ;the START label.

TSIZE:
    SET    C0=KEY                         ;store the contents of the KEY
                                         ;register in the C0 register.
    SET    KEY='TX='+C0                  ;set up the KEY register to
                                         ;hold the MicroStation 'TX='
                                         ;key-in plus the contents
                                         ;of C0 register.
    KEY    KEY                            ;use the KEY operand to
                                         ;activate the contents
                                         ;of the KEY register.
```

```
EXITUC:
    SET   MSG='PRText Size =' + C0           ;set up the MSG register to
                                             ;display in the prompt field
                                             ;(PR) a message describing the
                                             ;current text size parameter.
    MSG   MSG                                 ;use the MSG operator to
                                             ;display the current contents
                                             ;of the MSG register.
    MSG   'ER '                               ;clear the error message field.
    KEY   'ECHO'                              ;display MicroStation messages.
    END
```

Example 10

```
;--------------------------------------------------------------------------
;   C:\HARNESS\BLKCIRC.UCM -- September 1993 -- Tony Kendrick
;
;   This UCM demonstrates how to activate MicroStation commands
;   by using a key-in and by using the CMD operator. During the
;   process, the UCM will prompt the user for data point input,
;   store that data point information, draw a block element, and
;   then draw a circular element around the block.
;
;**************
    KEY   'NOECHO'                            ;inhibit MicroStation messages.
START:
    MSG   'PRData point - LL corner'          ;prompt user for the lower
                                             ;left corner of the block.
    MSG   'ERor RESET to Exit'                ;prompt user for a RESET to
                                             ;exit the UCM.
    GET   P,LLPNT,R,EXITUC                    ;if point is received, branch
                                             ;to LLPNT label.
                                             ;if reset is received, branch
                                             ;to EXITUC label.
    GO    START                               ;for any other type of input
```

```
                                              ;received, branch to the START
                                              ;label.

    LLPNT:
        SET    I0=XUR                         ;store 1st point X UOR
                                              ;coordinate value in
                                              ;I0 register.
        SET    I1=YUR                         ;store 1st point Y UOR
                                              ;coordinate value in
                                              ;I1 register.

    NEXT:
        MSG    'PRData Point - UR corner'
        MSG    'ERor RESET to re-do LL corner'
        GET    P,URPNT,R,START
        GO     NEXT
    URPNT:
        SET    I2=XUR                         ;store 2nd point X UOR
                                              ;coordinate value in
                                              ;I2 register.
        SET    I3=YUR                         ;store 2nd point Y UOR
                                              ;coordinate value in
                                              ;I3 register.
        KEY    'PLACE BLOCK'                  ;activate Place Block command
                                              ;by key-in.
        PNT    I0,I1                          ;use PNT operator to place X &
                                              ;Y coords of 1st point.
        PNT    I2,I3                          ;use PNT operator to place X &
                                              ;Y coords of 2nd point.
        CMD    PCIRD                          ;activate Place Circle by
                                              ;Diameter by CMD operator.
        PNT    I0,I1                          ;use PNT operator to place X &
                                              ;Y coords of 1st point.
        PNT    I2,I3                          ;use PNT operator to place X &
                                              ;Y coords of 2nd point.
    EXITUC:
        MSG    'PRUCM Complete'
        MSG    'ER '
```

```
CMD    NULCMD                        ;null command -- no command is
                                     ;active

KEY    'ECHO'                        ;enable MicroStation messages
END
```

EXERCISE

Exercise 12–3

Write a UCM named PLACNAME.UCM that prompts the user for a name and a data point. Next, activate the MicroStation PLACE TEXT command. Combine the key-in with a hard-coded key-in and place the resulting text string within the design file at the location of the data point.

TESTING CONDITIONS WITHIN THE USER COMMAND

As mentioned earlier, the GET operator permits control of the UCM to be transferred to various labels based on the type of data received. Transferring control is called "branching." Next, we will discover how it is possible to branch to various labels when certain conditions are met.

The TST Operator and Syntax—Conditional Branch

A conditional branch occurs when two values are tested against each other. The first value in the comparison will be stored in a register. The second value may be in the form of a number or character string or may be contained in a second register. The TST operator is used to actuate the comparison. If the test finds that a certain condition is true, execution control of the UCM is transferred to a specified label. If the tested condition is NOT true, the UCM proceeds to the next statement below the TST statement. The proper syntax for the TST operator statement is as follows:

```
TST    value1, keyword, value2, label
```

where

value1	is the contents of a register
value2	is a number, character string, or second register
keyword	is one of the following:
EQ	equal to
NE	not equal to
LT	less than
GT	greater than
LE	less than or equal to
GT	greater than or equal to
MT	match

Testing Conditions Using RELERR

RELERR is a register that contains a value that represents the status of a previously executed command. If the value of RELERR equals 0, the command was executed successfully. If the value of RELERR does not equal 0, the UCM will proceed to the next statement. A MicroStation command for which this is particularly applicable and commonly used is LOCELE (locate element).

RELERR is used with the TST operator in a statement with the following syntax:

```
TST  RELERR EQ 0,label
```

where

> **0** (zero) represents a successful command execution
> **label** instructs the UCM where to branch

The GO Operator and Syntax—Unconditional Branch

An unconditional branch occurs when control is transferred and no test occurs. The GO operator provides a means of forcing such a branch. The following statement shows the proper syntax:

```
GO  label
```

Example 11

```
;***************

;   C:\HARNESS\LVLSET.UCM -- September 1993 -- Tony Kendrick

;   This UCM demonstrates how to test the conditions or contents

;   of registers and how to perform conditional and unconditional

;   branching. This UCM requests that the user enter a level

;   number. The selection is tested and the UCM branches to a

;   specific label. The statements located beneath the label are

;   executed. In this case, the UCM sets parameters for different

;   levels.

;***************

;

START:

    KEY    'NOECHO'                          ;inhibit MicroStation
                                             ;messages.

      MSG    'PRKey-in a Level number (1,2,3)'        ;key-in a level value
                                                      ;(1, 2, or 3).

      MSG    'ERor RESET to Exit'            ;or press RESET to exit
                                             ;the UCM.
```

```
        GET    K,LVLNUM,R,EXITUC           ;if a key-in is received,
                                           ;branch to LVLNUM label.
                                           ;if a RESET is received,
                                           ;branch to the EXITUC label.
        GO     START                       ;if any other input is
                                           ;received, branch to
                                           ;the START label.

LVLNUM:
        SET    C0 = KEY                     ;store key-in value in
                                           ;alphanumeric "C"
                                           ;register.

        MSG    'PR '                        ;clear the prompt message
                                           ;field.

        MSG    'ER '                        ;clear the error message
                                           ;field.

        TST    C0 EQ '1',LVL1               ;test the value in C0.
                                           ;if the condition is true,
                                           ;branch to LVL1 label.

        TST    C0 EQ '2',LVL2               ;test the value in C0.
        TST    C0 EQ '3',LVL3               ;test the value in C0.
        GO     ERROR                        ;if the condition is false,
                                           ;branch to ERROR label.

LVL1:
        MSG    'STLevel set to 1'           ;display message in status
                                           ;field.

        KEY    'LV=1'                       ;activate the MicroStation
                                           ;level parameter key-in.

        KEY    'WT=0'                       ;activate the weight parameter
                                           ;key-in.

        KEY    'CO=2'                       ;activate the color parameter
                                           ;key-in.

        KEY    'LC=0'                       ;activate the linecode
                                           ;parameter key-in.

        KEY    'TX=.0125'                   ;activate the text size
                                           ;parameter key-in.
```

```
        GO      EXITUC                          ;all parameters are set, branch
                                                ;to the EXITUC label.

LVL2:
        MSG     'STLevel set to 2'
        KEY     'LV=2'
        KEY     'WT=1'
        KEY     'CO=3'
        KEY     'LC=2'
        GO      EXITUC
LVL3:
        MSG     'STLevel set to 3'
        KEY     'LV=3'
        KEY     'WT=1'
        KEY     'CO=4'
        KEY     'LC=4'
        GO      EXITUC
ERROR:
        MSG     'PRTry again - Y or N'          ;value entered is out of range.
        SET     MSG='ERLevel '+KEY              ;prompt the user to try again.
        SET     MSG=MSG+' out of range'
        MSG     MSG
        GET     K,ANSWER                        ;receive key-in from user.
        GO      ERROR                           ;if any other input is
                                                ;received, branch to the
                                                ;ERROR label.

ANSWER:
        TST     KEY EQ 'Y',START                ;test to see if key-in equals
                                                ;uppercase 'Y'.
                                                ;if the condition of the test
                                                ;is true, branch to the START
                                                ;label.

        TST     KEY EQ 'y',START                ;test to see if key-in equals
                                                ;lowercase 'y'.

        MSG     'PRNo new level set '
        MSG     'ER '
```

```
EXITUC:

  KEY    'ECHO'                          ;display MicroStation messages.

  KEY    'LV=$'                          ;display current MicroStation
                                         ;parameters.


  END
```

EXERCISE

Exercise 12–4

Write a UCM named CHOICE.UCM that prompts the user for two separate data points. Store the XY coordinate values for point 1 in registers I0 and I1. Store the values for point 2 in registers I2 and I3. Next, display a message asking the user to choose between drawing a line or drawing a circle between the two points. Assign an option number (1 or 2) that identifies the two choices.

"Test" the key-in response from the user (1 for draw line or 2 for draw circle) and branch to an appropriate label. Under the appropriate label, activate the PLACE LINE or PLACE CIRCLE DIAMETER command, then draw the appropriate element between the two stored points.

PERFORMING MATHEMATICAL CALCULATIONS

Performing calculations within a UCM is no different than performing them by hand or with a calculator. However, there are some rules that you need to be aware of. As you learned earlier, the SET operator is used to "copy" the value stored in the register on the right of the equal sign to the register on the left of the equal sign.

As mentioned earlier, the SET statement has the following form:

```
SET   register1 = register2
```

In this part of the chapter you will learn that it is possible to combine or mathematically manipulate the data stored in registers on the right of the equal sign then store the result in the register located on the left of the equal sign. The syntax of the SET statement that manipulates data is as follows:

```
SET   register1 = register2 keyword register3
```

where **keyword** equals one of the following:

+   addition or combining of data
−   subtraction
*   multiplication
/   division

Performing Algebraic Functions (+, –, *, /)

When performing basic algebra by hand, the correct result is obtained by building a formula that follows certain syntax rules. The proper placement of parentheses helps control the result. For example, the result of the formula ((a+b)*c) is not the same as the formula (a+(b*c)).

Within UCMs, combining functions within the same statement and using parentheses are NOT allowed. Instead, a single SET statement is used to formulate a single function. The result of the function is stored and then "passed" to the next SET statement.

Performing Conversions (CVT Operator)

Point information can be received from the user in two different formats—units of resolution (UORs) or working units (WUs). When a UCM receives point data from a data point, it has the design file's UOR format. These coordinates may be stored in floating point "A" registers. When a UCM receives point data in the form of a key-in or literal ASCII coordinate string, it has the design file's WU format. These values may be stored in "C" registers.

When a UCM places a point using the PNT command, the point data must be in the UOR format. The CVT operator is available to convert WU format point values into UOR point values. The CVT operator has the following syntax:

```
CVT  UOR registers = X Y coordinate string (in WUs)
```

where **UOR** registers are sequential "A" registers.

It is important to understand that the value to the right of the equal sign is the value to be converted. The result will be stored in "sequential" registers identified to the left of the equal sign.

```
SET    C0='12345.67,98765.43'      ;hard-coded XY coordinate
                                    ;stored in C0 register.
CVT    A0=C0                        ;X coordinate (12345.67) stored
                                    ;in A0 register.
                                    ;Y coordinate (98765.43) will
                                    ;be automatically assigned to
                                    ;the A1 register by
                                    ;MicroStation.
```

Global Origin

The global origin of a design file is the location of a "known" X Y coordinate within the design file's design plane or drawing area. All other X Y coordinates are based on and measured from this global origin. The X and Y values of the global origin for each design file are stored in UORs in the GOXUOR and GOYUOR terminal control block variables. These values are defined when the global origin is defined (GO=X,Y where X and Y are working units or real-world coordinates).

If you are converting a string from working units to UORs, you must "add" the X and Y global origin values to the X and Y coordinate values. If you do not, you will not acquire the "actual" (real-world) coordinates of the point. By "adding" the global origin values, you will make the coordinates consistent with the coordinates found within the design plane. Without it, the coordinates may "shift" off of the design plane.

> **NOTE:** If you are converting from UORs to working units, you must "subtract" the X and Y global origin values from the X and Y coordinate values.

The following are examples of working units:

Working Units to UORs

```
SET    C0='12345.67,98765.43'        ;hardcoded XY coordinate stored
                                     ;in C0 register.

CVT    A0=C0                         ;XUR coordinate stored in A0
                                     ;register.
                                     ;YUR coordinate will be
                                     ;automatically assigned to the
                                     ;A1 register by MicroStation.

SET    I0=A0+GOXUOR                  ;add the X global origin value
                                     ;to the XUR stored in A0, then
                                     ;transfer the result to I0.

SET    I1=A1+GOYUOR                  ;add the Y global origin value
                                     ;to the YUR stored in A1, then
                                     ;transfer the result to I1.
```

UORs to Working Units

```
SET    A0=I0-GOXUOR                  ;subtract the X global origin
                                     ;value from the XUR stored in
                                     ;I0, then transfer the result
                                     ;to A0.

SET    A1=I1-GOYUOR                  ;subtract the Y global origin
                                     ;value from the YUR stored in
                                     ;I1, then transfer the result
                                     ;to A1.

CVT    C0=A0,A1                      ;convert the XUR and YUR
                                     ;coordinates stored in the
                                     ;A0 and A1 registers and
                                     ;transfer the resulting string
                                     ;into the C0 register.
```

Calculating Square Roots (SQR)

Square roots can be calculated using the SQR operator. The syntax for the SQR operator is as follows:

```
SQR   register1,register2
```

where

register1 is a floating point register ("A") that will contain the result
register2 is a numeric value

Performing Trigonometric Functions (SCS, ATN Operators)

The SCS operator is used to calculate the unknown sine and cosine values for a known angle. The following identifies the syntax for the SCS operator:

```
SCS   register1,register2,register3
```

where

register1 will contain the resulting sine of the provided angle
register2 will contain the resulting cosine of the provided angle
register3 contains the angle (in degrees); it may be a literal value rather than a value contained in a register

> **NOTE:** It is desirable to use floating point ("A") registers.

The ATN operator is available for calculating an unknown angle (arc tangent) when the sine and cosine values are known. The following identifies the syntax for the ATN operator:

```
ATN   register1,register2,register3
```

where

register1 will contain the resulting angle (in degrees)
registers 1 and 2 will contain the values for an angle's sine and cosine, respectively

> **NOTE:** It is desirable to use floating point ("A") registers.

Example 12

```
;**************

;   C:\HARNESS\FORMULA.UCM -- September 1993 -- Tony Kenrick

;   This UCM prompts the user for 3 separate values. The formula

;   ((a+b)*c) is used to determine the end result. All values
```

```
;   received from the keyboard are stored as real numbers (decimal)
;   in real number "A" registers.
;***************
START:
    MSG     'PREnter 1st number'            ;prompt user for 1st number.
    MSG     'ERor RESET to EXIT'            ;prompt user for RESET to exit
                                            ;the UCM.
    GET     K,VALUE1,R,EXITUC               ;if it is key-in, branch to
                                            ;VALUE1 label or reset button
                                            ;branch to EXITUC label.
    GO      START                           ;go to START label if input
                                            ;other than key-in or reset.
VALUE1:
    SET     A0=KEY                          ;store key-in value in A0
                                            ;register
NEXT2:
    MSG     'PREnter 2nd number'
    MSG     'ERor RESET to re-enter 1st'
    GET     K,VALUE2,R,START
    GO      NEXT2
VALUE2:
    SET     A1=KEY                          ;store key-in value in A1
                                            ;register.
NEXT3:
    MSG     'PREnter 3rd number'
    MSG     'ERor RESET to re-enter 2nd'
    GET     K,VALUE3,R,NEXT2
    GO      NEXT2
VALUE3:
    SET     A2=KEY                          ;store key-in value in A2
                                            ;register.
;This section sets up the desired formula -- ((a+b)*c)
    SET     A3=A0+A1                        ;add together the values in A0
                                            ;and A1 and store the result in
                                            ;A3 register.
```

```
        SET    A3=A3*A2                    ;take the result of A3 (from
                                           ;the statement above) and
                                           ;multiply it by the contents of
                                           ;A2. Store the new result in
                                           ;A3.

    ;This section displays the values entered, the end result, then
    ;exits the UCM.
    EXITUC:
        SET    MSG='PRValues are: '+ A0    ;set up the message prompt
                                           ;field (PR) to display
        SET    MSG=MSG + ','               ;the key-in values.
        SET    MSG=MSG + A1
        SET    MSG=MSG + ','
        SET    MSG=MSG + A2
        MSG    MSG                         ;display the message in the PR
                                           ;field.
        SET    MSG='ER((a+b)*c)='+A3       ;set up the message error
                                           ;field (ER) to display the
                                           ;result of the formula.
        MSG    MSG                         ;use the MSG operator to
                                           ;display the contents of the
                                           ;MSG operand.

        END
```

Example 13

```
;***************
;   C:\HARNESS\SQR.UCM -- September 1993 -- Tony Kendrick
;
;   This UCM demonstrates the SQR operator. It prompts the user
;   to key-in a value, then calculates the square root of the
;   value.
;***************
;
```

```
START:
    MSG     'PREnter a value'                   ;prompt user to key-in a
                                                ;value.

    MSG     'ERor RESET to Exit'                ;and prompt user to press
                                                ;reset to exit.

    GET     K,VALUE,R,EXITUC                    ;if it is key-in, branch to
                                                ;VALUE label or reset button
                                                ;branch to the EXITUC label.

    GO      START                               ;go to START label if input
                                                ;other than key-in
                                                ;or reset is received.

VALUE:
    SET     A0=KEY                              ;store key-in value in A0
                                                ;register.

    SQR     A1,A0                               ;use SQR operator and store
                                                ;values in A0 and
                                                ;A1 registers.

    SET     MSG='PRSquare root = '+A1           ;display message
    MSG     MSG
EXITUC:
    MSG     'ERUC finished'
    END
```

Example 14

```
;***************
;   C:\HARNESS\SCS.UCM -- September 1993 -- Tony Kendrick
;
;   This UCM demonstrates the SCS operator. It prompts the
;   user to key-in an angle, then calculates the Sine/Cosine
;   values of the angle.
;***************
;
START:
    MSG     'PREnter an Angle'                  ;prompt user to key-in an
                                                ;angle.
```

```
        MSG    'ERor RESET to Exit'        ;or prompt user to reset to
                                           ;exit UCM.
        GET    K,ANGLE,R,EXITUC            ;if key-in is received, branch
                                           ;to ANGLE label or if reset
                                           ;is received, branch to EXITUC
                                           ;label.
    GO     START
ANGLE:
    SET    A0=KEY                          ;store key-in value in A0
                                           ;register.

DOIT:
    SCS    A1,A2,A0                        ;calculate the sine/cosine of
                                           ;angle and store the results
                                           ;in registers A1 and A2.
    SET    MSG='PRSIN='+A1                 ;display SINE/COSINE value.
    SET    MSG=MSG+' COSINE='
    SET    MSG=MSG+A2
    MSG    MSG
EXITUC:
    MSG    'ER '
    END
```

Example 15

```
;***************
;   C:\HARNESS\ATN.UCM -- September 1993 -- Tony Kendrick
;
;   This UCM demonstrates the ATN operator. It prompts the user
;   to key-in a value for SINE and COSINE. It then calcualtes
;   the arc tangent angle.
;***************
;
START:
    MSG    'PREnter a value for SINE'      ;prompt user for value.
    MSG    'ERor RESET to Exit'            ;prompt user for reset to exit.
```

```
        GET    K,SINEV,R,EXITUC                ;if key-in is received,
                                               ;branch to the SINEV
                                               ;label or if reset is
                                               ;received, branch to the
                                               ;EXITUC label.
        GO     START
SINEV:
        SET    A1=KEY                          ;store key-in value in A1
                                               ;register.
NEXT:
        MSG    'PREnter a value for COSINE'
        MSG    'ERor RESET to Exit'
        GET    K,COSINE,R,EXITUC
        GO     NEXT
COSINE:
        SET    A2=KEY
DOIT:
        ATN    A0,A1,A2                        ;calculate arc tangent
                                               ;angle and store result in
                                               ;A0 register.
        SET    MSG='PRArc Tangent Angle = '+A0 ;display result
        MSG    MSG
EXITUC:
        MSG    'ER '
        END
```

EXERCISE

Exercise 12–5

Write a UCM named MATH.UCM that prompts the user for two separate values. Store the values in the A0 and A1 registers. Next, prompt the user to key-in a function (+, −, *, /). Store the response in the C0 register. "Test" the contents of the C0 register and branch to an appropriate label such as ADD:, SUB:, MULT:, DIV:. Under each label, write a formula that will perform the proper mathematical function. For example, under the ADD: label, add A0 and A1 together. Display the result.

THE DESIGN FILE AND ELEMENT TYPES

MicroStation is delivered with a series of prototype design files called seed files. Whether you use one of the delivered seed design files or create your own for your own specific project is entirely up to you. Each design file, however, is made up of a series of common parts or elements; some are graphic, some non-graphic. As elements are placed in the design file, they are arranged sequentially and assigned a position number. As existing elements are manipulated, MicroStation changes their order. MicroStation keeps track of these elements for you.

Each graphic element in a design file also is identified by MicroStation by an element "type" assignment. These element types are in the form of a type number. For example, MicroStation understands a line to be a "type 3" element, an arc as a "type 16" element or a text string as a "type 17." A list of element types is provided in Appendix G.

Three types of non-graphic elements must exist at the top of the sequential list of elements in a design file. These elements (type 9, 8, and 10) make up the "design file header." Each design file MUST have these elements. The "type 9" consists of the design file's parameter settings and terminal control block variables. These settings are updated each time the FILE DESIGN command is activated. The "type 8" element is a carryover from the early VAX-based Intergraph days and is not used by MicroStation. The "type 10" element is used to store level symbology information.

The last element in each design is followed by an "end of file" (EOF) marker. As new elements are added to a drawing, they are placed at the EOF.

MICROSTATION VARIABLES

A series of MicroStation variables are stored internally with each design file. These variables are stored in the memory region of MicroStation and are collectively named the Terminal Control Block (TCB). The TCB variables store information about current design file parameters, view configuration, the most recently placed or manipulated elements, saved point information, and so forth. These design file parameters are stored in a special element, called a "type 9 element." This type 9 element is updated with the most current TCB variables each time the FILE DESIGN command is activated.

Three main variable types are available for use within a UCM; UCM registers, TCB variables, and DGNBUF variables. Each of these is assigned several different names by MicroStation so that it can be retrieved in a different format. The available formats include integer, double-precision floating point, ASCII, and byte.

TCB variables can be accessed or modified with a UCM. However, care should be taken when modifying parameters that could otherwise be modified by using MicroStation commands or key-ins (such as **LV=**). If a MicroStation parameter is set inadvertently to an invalid setting (such as **LV=0**), the integrity of the next element placed within the design file may be in jeopardy.

The UCM writer should be aware that the TCB variables available in one version of MicroStation may not be available in another version of MicroStation (version 3.x versus version 5.0). As MicroStation options are enhanced, TCB variables are also enhanced.

DGNBUF Variables

DGNBUF variables contain information about a selected element. If this variable information is modified, the selected element's parameters also are modified. DGNBUF variables are identified by a two-character prefix followed by an associated element type. For example, the DGNBUF variable LN.BEG identifies the beginning coordinate of a selected line.

For a complete listing of Terminal control block variables refer to the *MicroStation Reference Guide*.

OUTFLG Variable

OUTFLG is a TCB variable used to set or clear output flags within a UCM. It is normally used when the user wishes to provide a means of selecting a command from a menu while the UCM is executing. Normally, a UCM will terminate when a menu command is selected. If this is not desirable, a bit in OUTFLG that tells MicroStation not to terminate must be set. Do this by setting bit 3 (starting with bit 0) and use the menu (M) keyword with the GET operator. Care must be taken when setting this bit. If it is set improperly, there may be a problem exiting the UCM. Be sure to "clear" bit 3 in OUTFLG before the UCM exits.

The syntax used to set bit 3 in OUTFLG is:

```
SET  OUTFLG = OUTFLG!8
```

LOCATING ELEMENTS

What is the purpose of "locating" elements? This question can be answered by an example. Suppose you want your UCM to manipulate (copy, delete, move, and so forth) an element, but only if the element is of a specific type and has specific parameters (level, color, weight, class, and so forth). These specific parameters represent the search criteria needed to locate or reject an element within a UCM.

PNT Operator

Earlier in this chapter, the PNT operator and its operands were described. We also briefly introduced the LOCELE command (locate element). The LOCELE command loads a selected element into the DGNBUF variable so that information about the element can be retrieved. These two items (PNT operator and LOCELE command) may be used within a UCM to help locate design file elements.

As you know, the PNT operator has 13 operands associated with it. The first six operands are used to send point data to MicroStation. This point data is used when defining X, Y, and Z coordinate information. The last seven operands may be used to help identify element search criteria when manipulating or locating elements using the LOCELE command. The values contained by these operands help MicroStation scan the selected element, but the "bits" of the specific operands must be set so that the UCM will know what to search for. If the search criteria are not met, the selected element is rejected by the UCM.

When setting search criteria, the syntax for the PNT operator statement is

```
PNT<space>,,,,,,operand7,operand8,operand9,...operand13
```

> **NOTE:** A <space> or ⌨TAB may be placed after the PNT operator to improve readability. There are six commas [,] placed immediately after this blank space. These commas tell the UCM not to use ("skip") the first six operands.

Using operands 7 through 13 will require "setting" bits. Setting bits requires some knowledge of binary numbers or at least the values they represent. Table 12–3 shows bit settings for bits 0 (zero) through 15:

Table 12–3. Bit Set List (Decimal equivalents)

Bit 0 = 1	Bit 8 = 256
Bit 1 = 2	Bit 9 = 512
Bit 2 = 4	Bit 10 = 1024
Bit 3 = 8	Bit 11 = 2048
Bit 4 = 16	Bit 12 = 4096
Bit 5 = 32	Bit 13 = 8192
Bit 6 = 64	Bit 14 = 16384
Bit 7 = 128	Bit 15 = 32768

The following is a list describing the last seven operands of the PNT operator. Refer to Table 12–3 for values that set the appropriate bits.

operand 7 and 8—Element "type" Search
Group 1—Types 1 through 16 are set and assigned in operand 7.

Group 2—Types 17 through 32 are set and assigned in operand 8.

Values of 0 in operand 7 and 8 mean "use all element types."

Example: PNT<space>,,,,,,12,1
This allows you to search for element types 3 (lines), 4 (linestrings) and 17 (text).

The value (12) set in operand 7 is derived by adding together the values found in Table 12–3. Add bit 3 (representing type 3) and bit 4 (representing type 4) together: 4 + 8 = 12.

The value (1) set in operand 8 also is derived from a value found in bit 0 (representing type 17 in group 2) from Table 12–3.

operand 9—Level Selection
This operand allows you to search for elements on a specific level. If the value is set to 0, all levels are searched. If it is set to 10, only level 10 is searched.

Example: PNT<space>,,,,,,,12,1,10
This allows you to search for element types 3, 4, and 17 on level 10.

operand 10—Scanning Mode
This operand allows the scanning of elements to take place in one of two modes: "nested" or "unnested." Since elements can be either complex (cells, chains, etc.) or simple (lines, arcs, etc.), the mode in which they are scanned needs to be set. Nest mode does not recognize component elements of complex elements; the header of the element is used. Unnest modes permits the search to recognize the component elements of complex elements. Simple elements are recognized in either mode.

Example: `PNT<space>,,,,,,8192,,10,1`

This allows you to search for element type 14 (complex shape or bit value 13) on level 10, in "nest" mode.

operand 11—Class Selection

MicroStation elements can come in several different classes. Each class corresponds to a specified bit (see Table 12–3). Class 0 elements are associated with bit 0, class 1 elements are associated with bit 1, and so on. To search for a specific class element, set the bit to the appropriate bit value or values.

Example: `PNT<space>,,,,,,4,,10,,1`

This allows you to search for element type 3 (line or bit 2) on level 10, class 0 (primary or bit 0).

operands 12 and 13—Property Selection

MicroStation elements come with specific properties. Operand 12 is used to show the value that each property being tested must have. Operand 13 indicates which property is to be checked.

Example: `PNT<space>,,,,,,4,,10,,,512,8714`

This allows you to search for element type 3 (line or bit 2) on level 10, and search for elements that are both new and planar. In operand 13, set bit 9 and 13 (512 + 8192 = 8704). Operand 12 has the corresponding bit 9 set to ON (512)—(0 = OFF, 1 = ON).

Element Pointers and the Working Window

As elements are added to a design file, they are always appended to the end of the file. Their location in the design file is maintained by two TCB variables that indicate the "block" (sector) of the element and the "byte offset" of the element into the block. The TCB variables DFSECT (design file sector) and DFBYTE (design file byte offset) always point to the end of the design file. Care must be taken NOT to change the values in DFSECT and DFBYTE, because invalid values will corrupt your design file.

A feature that may be included within a UCM is a "working window." This feature allows the UCM to begin its search for elements at a specific location determined by the "currently selected" element within the design file. This is helpful when you are adding new elements to a design file and you plan to manipulate those elements. In essence, you can isolate the new elements from the old elements.

File pointers can be used to tell MicroStation where to search or scan for these new elements. This scanning process is controlled by setting the TCB variables WWSECT (working window sector location) and WWBYTE (working window byte offset).

Before you can set WWSECT and WWBYTE, the element to be manipulated must be loaded into DGNBUF. This is accomplished by using the LOCELE command. The block (sector) and byte information for DGNBUF is located in the TCB variables CUREBL (current element block) and CUREBY (current element block offset). The information in CUREBL can be transferred to WWSECT; and the information in CUREBY is then transferred to WWBYTE.

Example 16

```
;***************
;  C:\HARNESS\LOCATE.UCM -- September 1993 -- Tony Kendrick
;  This UCM is an example of how to use the LOCELE command
;  to locate a type 3 (line) element that is on level 10.
;  This UCM will search only for line elements meeting this
;  criterion. Any other elements with different search
;  criteria are to be disregarded. If a line element is found,
;  the UCM will change its color to 3.
;***************
;
START:
    MSG    'PRData pnt a line'          ;prompt user to data pnt a
                                        ;"line".

    MSG    'ERor Reset to Exit'         ;or RESET to exit the UCM.
    GET    P,PNT1,R,EXITUC              ;if a data pnt is received,
                                        ;branch to PNT1 label
                                        ;or if a RESET is received,
                                        ;branch to the EXITUC label.

    GO     START                        ;if any other response is
                                        ;received, branch to the
                                        ;START label.


PNT1:
    CMD    LOCELE                        ;activate the LOCATE ELEMENT
                                        ;command.

    PNT    ,,,,,,4,,10                   ;highlight only type 3 elements
                                        ;located on level 10.

    TST    RELERR EQ 0,FOUND             ;test the condition of the
                                        ;RELERR TCB variable.
                                        ;if RELERR equals 0, branch to
                                        ;the FOUND label.
                                        ;if RELERR does not equal 0, go
                                        ;to next statement.
    GO     START                        ;RELERR does not equal 0,
                                        ;branch to the START label.
```

```
FOUND:
    SET    I0=XUR                        ;store the X UOR coordinate of
                                         ;the data pnt in I0.

    SET    I1=YUR                        ;store the Y UOR coordinate of
                                         ;the data pnt in I1.

    KEY    'CO=3'                        ;set the active color parameter
                                         ;to 3.

    KEY    'CHANGE COLOR'                ;activate the change element
                                         ;color command.

    PNT    I0,I1                         ;use the PNT operator to send a
                                         ;data pnt.

    PNT    I0,I1                         ;send a second data pnt to
;change the line's color.
EXITUC:
    MSG    'PRLine found, color changed' ;tell the user that the
                                         ;search was successful

    MSG    'ER '

    END
```

Example 17

```
;***************
;
;  C:\HARNESS\NUMBER.UCM -- September 1993 -- Tony Kendrick
;  This UCM is an example of how to use the working window
;  feature.
;
;  --------------------------------------------------------------------
;
START:
    KEY    'NOECHO'                      ;inhibit messages.
    MSG    'PREnter a Number'            ;prompt user to key-in a number.
    MSG    'ERor RESET to Exit'          ;or press RESET to exit UCM.
    MSG    'CF '
    SET    I8 = 0                        ;set I8 register to 0.
    GET    K,KEY,R,EXITUC                ;if a key-in is received,
```

```
                                              ;branch to KEY label
                                              ;or if RESET is received,
                                              ;branch to EXITUC label.
        GO    START                           ;if any other input is received
                                              ;branch to the START label.

KEY:
    SET   R0 = KEY                            ;store number (integer) in
                                              ;register R0.

    SET   I11 = CHWID                         ;store TCB variable CHWID (text
                                              ;character width) in register
                                              ;I11.

    SET   I12 = EU.UOR                        ;store TCB variable EU.UOR
                                              ;(working units) in I12.

    SET   I13 = I11/I12                       ;set up point data for circle
                                              ;radius.

    SET   I13 = I13/76
    SET   KEY = R0                            ;store key-in in KEY register.
    SET   I8 = R0                             ;reset key in value to zero.
    MSG   'PRData Pnt Location for number'    ;prompt user for point to
                                              ;place number.

    MSG   'ERor RESET to enter new number'    ;or reset to get new number.
    GET   P,PNT1,R,START                      ;if point is received, branch
                                              ;to PNT1 label or if reset is
                                              ;received, branch back to the
                                              ;START label.
        GO    KEY                             ;if any other input is
                                              ;received, branch to the KEY
                                              ;label.

NEXT:
    SET   I0 = XUR                            ;store X UOR coordinate in I0
                                              ;register.

    SET   I1 = YUR                            ;store Y UOR coordinate in I1
                                              ;register.

    SET   MSG = 'STLast Number Used='+I8      ;tell user last number used.
    MSG   MSG                                 ;display message.
```

```
        SET    I9 = 1                          ;set up counter for next number
                                               ;to be placed.

        SET    I8 = I8 + I9                    ;add counter increment to key-
                                               ;in value.

        SET    KEY = I8                        ;store number to be placed in
                                               ;KEY register.
PNT1:
        SET    I0 = XUR                        ;store X UOR coordinate in I0
                                               ;register.

        SET    I1 = YUR                        ;store Y UOR coordinate in I1
                                               ;register.

        SET    I14 = DFSECT                    ;store end of file pointer
                                               ;(sector - block).

        SET    I15 = DFBYTE                    ;store end of file pointer
                                               ;(byte).

        CMD    TXJS7                           ;activate center-center text
                                               ;justification.

        CMD    PTEXT                           ;activate place text command

        KEY    KEY                             ;key-in contents of KEY
                                               ;register.

        PNT    I0,I1                           ;place text string at data
                                               ;point location.

        SET    KEY = I13                       ;set up value identifying
                                               ;circle radius.

        CMD    PCIRR                           ;activate place circle by
                                               ;radius command.

        KEY    KEY                             ;key-in radius diameter.

        SET    I7 = 0                          ;set radius key-in equal to 0.

        SET    KEY = I7                        ;set contents of KEY register
                                               ;to 0.

        PNT    I0,I1                           ;place circle by radius at data
                                               ;point location.

        MSG    'ER '

        MSG    'PRProcessing'

        MSG    'CFBuilding Single Graphic Group'
```

```
    SET    WWSECT = I14                        ;set up working window at last
                                               ;element location.

    SET    WWBYTE = I15
    CMD    ADDGG                               ;activate add to graphic group
                                               ;command.

    PNT    I0,I1                               ;add text string (number) to
                                               ;graphic group.

    PNT    I0,I1                               ;accept text string and add
                                               ;circle to graphic group.

    PNT    I0,I1                               ;accept circle to graphic group.
    RST                                        ;activate MicroStation reset
                                               ;button.

PNT2:
    MSG    'PRReset to enter next number'      ;allow user to press RESET
                                               ;to enter a new number.

    MSG    'ERor DP location for next number'  ;or simply to place
                                               ;another data point
                                               ;in order to use next sequential
                                               ;number.

    MSG    'CFGraphic Group Complete'
    SET    KEY = I8                            ;store number value in KEY
                                               ;register.

    GET    R,START,P,NEXT                      ;if reset is received, branch
                                               ;to START label
                                               ;or if data point is received,
                                               ;branch to the NEXT label.

    GO     PNT2                                ;if any other input is
                                               ;received, branch to the
                                               ;PNT2 label.

EXITUC:
    MSG    'PRUC - COMPLETE'
    MSG    'ER '
    SET    WWSECT = 4                          ;reset working window location
                                               ;(sector block).

    SET    WWBYTE = 0                          ;reset working window location
                                               ;(byte).

    CMD    NULCMD                              ;activate the NULL command.
    KEY    'ECHO'                              ;allow MicroStation messages.
    END
```

USER COMMAND INDEX

A User Command Index is a MicroStation file that is used to store a collection of user commands. The UCMs stored in this file are activated from the MicroStation command menu. You can store up to 999 UCM's in the index file.

The concept of a User Command Index is similar to that of a MicroStation Cell Library. Like the library, the UCM Index is an external file that must be "attached" to a design file. The key-in that can be used to make this attachment is

    OX=<filename.NDX>

where <filename.NDX> is the desired User Command Index file

Following are the steps to create a User Command Index:

1. Select the "User" option from the Command Window pull-down menus.
2. Select the "Utility" option.
3. Select the Edit UCM Index File option and MicroStation will display the Edit UCM Command Index File dialog box as shown in Figure 12–2.

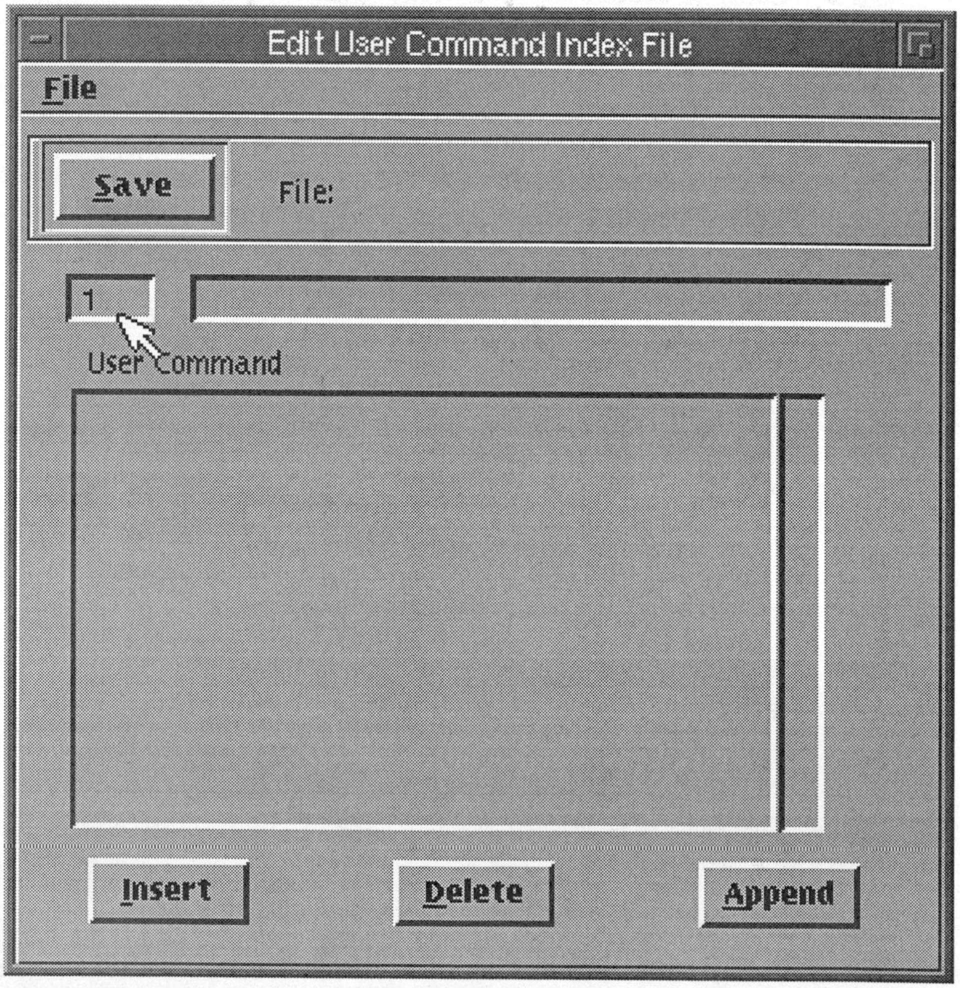

FIGURE 12–2 Edit UCM Command Index File Dialog Box.

4. Key-in the number and filename, including the path in the edit fields provided in the top of the dialog box.
5. Click the Append button.
6. You may click the Insert button if you wish to alter the order of your UCM's.
7. Once you have finished adding UCM's to the list, click the Save button and MicroStation displays Save UCM index file dialog box. Key-in the name of the file in which you want to save the index file. By default, MicroStation appends .NDX as the file extension.
8. Click the dialog box.

INTRODUCTION TO MDL

MicroStation version 4.0 has a set of application development tools along with the graphics software and utilities. The collective name for this set of tools is MicroStation Development Language or MDL. MDL is responsible for the smooth operation of most of the commands, tool palettes, and dialog boxes that you see and use within MicroStation. Prior to MDL, most of the complicated tasks performed by MicroStation were developed by using a combination of user commands and the MicroStation Customer Support Library (MicroCSL). Unlike user commands and MicroCSL, MDL provides tools for the programmer to "build" custom applications that act and appear as an extension of MicroStation.

To customize or enhance MicroStation through MDL, the programmer must have a working knowledge of the C programming language as well as extensive experience with MicroStation. Also, the programmer should have a thorough understanding of design file and element formats.

It is not the intention of this book to teach you how to develop applications using MDL. We will, however, discuss how to activate some of the applications delivered with MicroStation version 5.0. A complete description of MDL, along with its development tools and file structure, is found in the *MDL Reference Manual and User's Guide* accompanying your MicroStation software.

What Is MDL?

MDL is composed of a set of compilers, linkers, function libraries, and resource managers used to create applications that interface with MicroStation. MDL is not necessarily a replacement for user commands and MicroCSL. User commands will still be used to perform relatively simple tasks. Though it may not be desirable to recreate old applications, MDL should be used for future MicroStation software development.

File Types Associated with MDL

There are several types of files associated with MDL application development. All of them are necessary because the development of an application is a "building-block" process. The MDL development tools (MCOMP, RCOMP, MLINK, RLIB) take files of a specific type, process them, and yield subsequent files. Each file type is represented by a unique file extension. The end result is an MDL application. Table 12–4 shows a list of the files you may encounter:

Table 12–4.

TYPE	FILE EXTENSION	CONTENTS
header file	.h	definitions that need to be included in other source files
resource source file	.r	source code
source code file	.mc	MDL program source code
resource file	.rsc	compiled resources
library file	.ml	MDL object file
object file	.mo	complied MDL source code
program file	.mp	a complete MDL program
make file	.mke	contains instructions on how to create an application from the different parts
application file	.ma	an MDL program file plus its associated compiled resource files

The .h, .r, and .mc files are created by the programmer. The rest are created by the various MDL development tools:

.mo	generated from the .mc file by MCOMP
.mp	generated from .mo and .ml file from MLINK
.ml	generated from .mo by MLIB
.rsc	generated from .r file by RCOMP
.ma	generated from .mp and .rsc files by RLIB. This is the actual application that is activated within MicroStation.

The available MDL development tools are

mcomp	compiles MDL source code files into MDL object files
mlink	links MDL object files and libraries into MDL program resource files
mlib	creates and manages libraries of MDL object files
rcomp	compiles MDL source files into MDL resource files
rlib	creates and manages libraries of MDL resource files
bmake	automates the MDL development process

Where Do You Store MDL Files?

Each time MicroStation is activated, a series of macros are executed that define MicroStation environment variables. These macros are defined in a file called MSDIRS.CFG, which is located in the \CONFIG\SYSTEM\ sub-directory of the main MicroStation directory. The system variable used within this configuration file to define the path for MDL applications is called MS_MDL.

As delivered, MicroStation has three separate locations (paths) defined as the system variable MS_MDL. The following lines are an excerpt from the MSDIRS.CFG file:

```
MS_MDL  :  $(MSDIR)mdlapps/              # MDL applications

MS_MDL  <  $(MSDIR)mdlsys/required/      # System required MDL applications

MS_MDL  <  $(MSDIR)mdlsys/asneeded/      # System as needed MDL applications
```

where $(MSDIR) is your main MicroStation directory

Notice that these three locations permit the separation of MDL applications into categories of use. It is under one of these three directories that you place any of the MDL application files (.ma). If desired, you may add an additional path to the configuration file. For example:

```
MS_MDL  <  C:/HARNESS/MDL/             # new MDL applications
```

Activating an MDL Application

Once MicroStation has been properly configured and MDL applications have been placed in the necessary directory that matches the configuration, it is a simple task to activate them. You have two ways to do it:

1. Use the MDL Application dialog box
2. Use the MicroStation key-in
   MDL LOAD <filename>
   where <filename> is the MDL application name

Following are the steps to invoke the MDL application from the MDL Application dialog box:

1. Select the "User" option from the MicroStation Command Window, then select the "MDL Applications" option. MicroStation displays the MDL Application dialog box similar to the one shown in Figure 12–3.

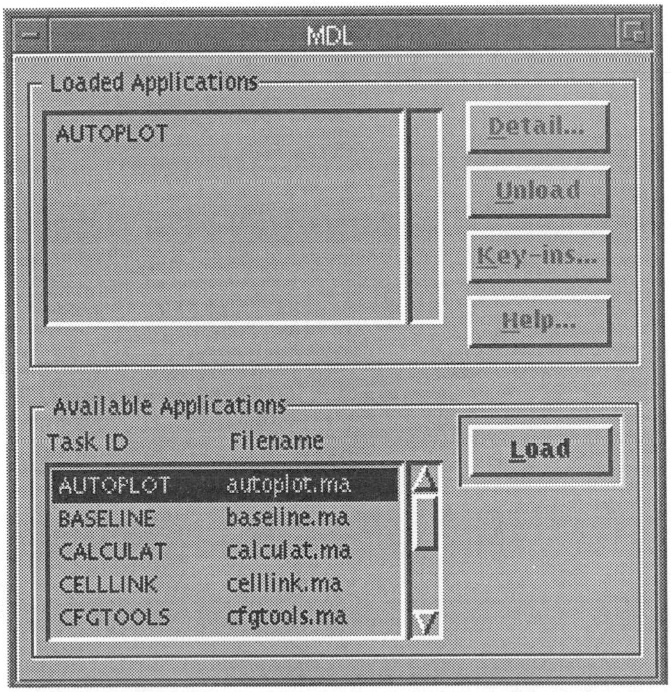

FIGURE 12–3 MDL Application Dialog Box.

2. A list of available MDL applications will appear in the lower section of the dialog box. You may scroll up or down within the list to find the application you want to load.
3. Select the file you want to load from the list with a data button, then select the "Load" button. You may also double-click on the filename to load the application.
4. Follow the prompts for the operation of the MDL application.

CHAPTER

13

3D DESIGN AND RENDERING

· · · · · · · · · · · · · · · · ·

WHAT IS 3D?

In 2D drawings you have been working with two axes, X and Y. In 3D drawings, in addition to the X and Y axes, you will be working on the Z axis as shown in Figure 13–1. Plan views, sections, and elevations represent only two dimensions. Isometric, perspective, and axonometric drawings, on the other hand, represent all three dimensions. For example, to create three views of a cube, the cube is simply drawn as a square with thickness. This is referred to as extruded 2D. Only objects that are extrudable can be drawn by this method. Any other views are achieved by simply rotating the viewpoint or the object, just as if one were physically holding the cube. You can also can get an isometric or perspective view by simply changing the viewpoint.

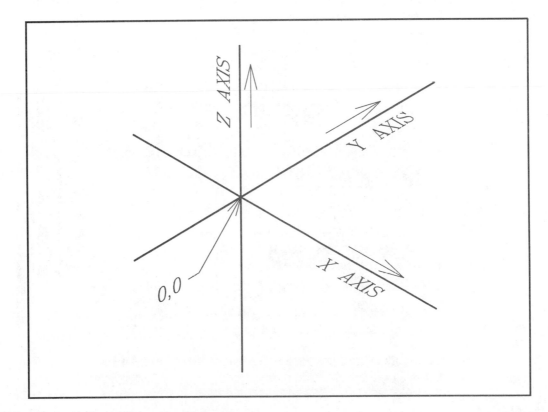

FIGURE 13–1 X, Y, and Z Axes for 3D Design.

Drawing objects in 3D provides three major advantages:

1. An object can be drawn once and then can be viewed and plotted from any angle.
2. A 3D object holds mathematical information, which can be used in engineering analysis such as finite element analysis and computer numerical control (CNC) machinery.
3. Shading can be added for visualization.

This chapter provides an overview of the tools and specific commands available for 3D design.

CREATING A 3D DESIGN FILE

The procedure for creating a new 3D design file is similar to creating a new 2D design file except you have to use a seed file that is specifically designed for 3D design. The same holds good for cell libraries. Invoke New... command from the File pull-down menu. The Create Design File dialog box opens. Click the Seed button, MicroStation displays a list of seed files available as shown in Figure 13–2. Select one of the 3D seed files from the Files list box and click the OK button. MicroStation by default highlights the name of the file you just created in the Files list box in the Create Design dialog box. To open the new design file, click the OK button and your screen will look similar to the one shown in Figure 13–3. By default, MicroStation displays four view windows and each view window is set for one of the four standard view orientations. As part of the title of the view window, MicroStation displays the name of the view being displayed.

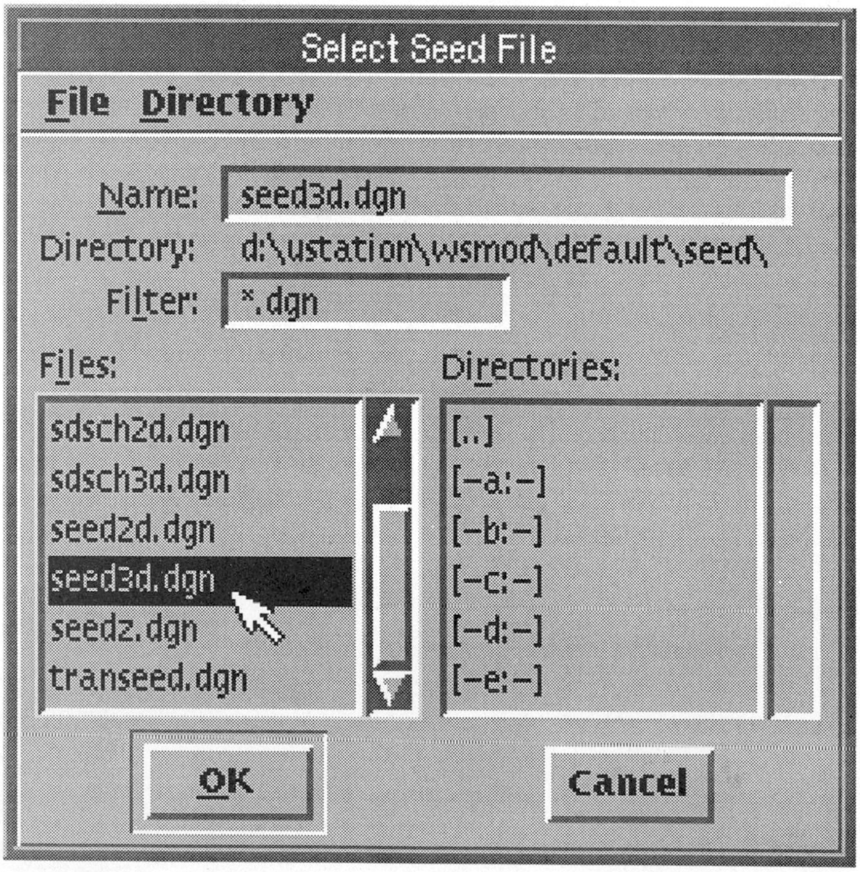

FIGURE 13–2 Select Seed File dialog box.

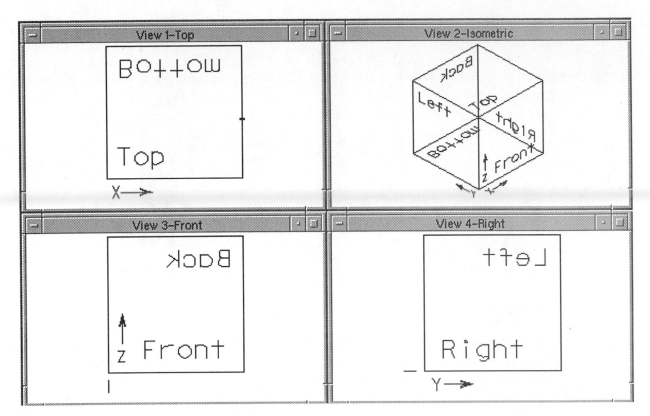

FIGURE 13–3   MicroStation Screen Display.

> **NOTE:** The elements you see displayed when you start a new design are construction elements. They will not plot. You can turn off the display of the construction elements by setting the Constructions toggle button to OFF in the View Attributes settings box.

VIEW ROTATION

There are seven standard view orientations defined in MicroStation. You can set the view orientation in any view window with the View Orientation (VI=) command. Key-in at uSTN> field, **VI=**<name of the view> and press ⏎. <name of the view> can be any one of the standard view orientations (TOP, BOTTOM, FRONT, BACK, RIGHT, LEFT, and ISO) or saved view. You can also rotate a view by clicking Change View Rotation icon in the 3D View Control sub-palette as shown in Figure 13–4, or key-in at the uSTN> field, **dialog viewrotation** and press ⏎. MicroStation displays the View Rotation settings box similar to the Figure 13–5.

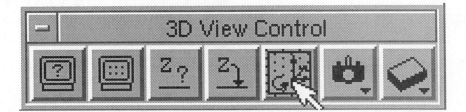

FIGURE 13–4   Invoking the Change View Rotation icon in the 3D View Control sub-palette.

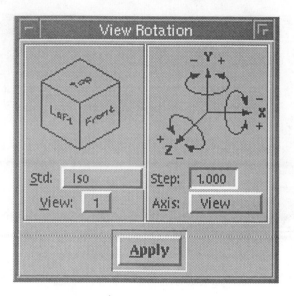

FIGURE 13–5 View Rotation settings box.

The view to be manipulated is selected in the View option menu. Key-in the rotation increment in degrees in the Step edit field. Click the "+" control to rotate the view in the positive direction by the Step amount around the specified Axis. Click the "–" to rotate the view in the negative direction by the Step amount around the specified Axis. Click the Apply button to rotate the selected view to the specified rotation.

In addition, you can also rotate the views to one of the standard view rotations by invoking the appropriate view rotation tools from View pull-down as shown in Figure 13–6.

FIGURE 13–6 View rotation tools from View pull-down.

Rotate View by Key-in You can also rotate a view by key-in at uSTN> field, by Absolute as well as Relative. In the case of Absolute View rotation, the view is rotated by the specified angles from a known starting point (0 degrees). For TOP view the absolute rotation angle is 0,0,0. To rotate the view by Absolute, key-in at uSTN> field, **rotate view absolute** <x,y,z> and press 🔳. MicroStation prompts:

Select a view (Place a data point anywhere in the view.)

For example, if you key-in rotate view absolute 0,0,0 and press 🔳, the resulting view will be a TOP view, no matter how the view is presently oriented.

In the case of Relative View rotation, the view is rotated by the specified angle relative to existing orientation. To rotate the view by Relative, key-in at uSTN> field, **rotate view relative** <x,y,z> or **rv=**<x,y,z> and press 🔳. MicroStation prompts:

Select a view (Place a data point anywhere in the view.)

The rotation will be performed about the X-axis, then the Y-axis, and the Z-axis. This key-in follows what is commonly called the "Right-Hand-Rule". For example, if you key-in a positive X rotation and point your right thumb in the view's positive X direction then the way your fingers curl is the direction of the rotation. The ISO view produced by the VI= key-in shows the TOP, FRONT, and LEFT faces (LEFT-OUT ISO). If you display the TOP, FRONT, and RIGHT orthographic views, it may be appropriate to have the ISO view (RIGHT-OUT VIEW) display the corresponding views. To display ISO view from left-out to right-out (see Figure 13–7), key-in:

RV=0,0,-90 🔳 (and place a data point in the ISO view)
RV=0,-54.7356,0 🔳 (and place a data point in the ISO view)
RV=-54.7356,0,0 🔳 (and place a data point in the ISO view)

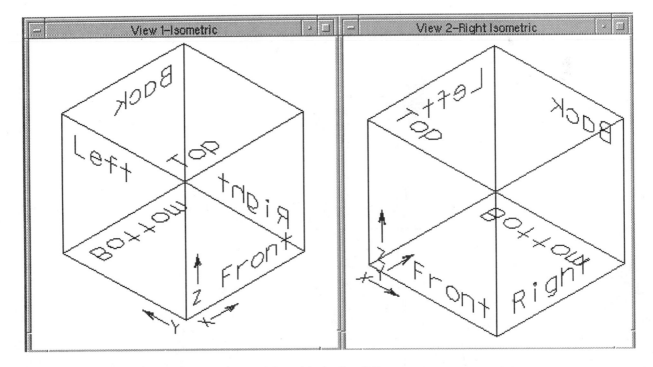

FIGURE 13–7 Views displaying Left-Out ISO and Right-Out ISO.

Rotate View by Points The Rotate view by Points command uses three data points to rotate a view so that the plane defined by these points is parallel to the screen. To rotate a view by points command, invoke the Points commands under Rotation sub-menu in the View pull-down menu or key-in at the uSTN> field, **rotate 3pts** and press ⏎. MicroStation prompts:

Enter first point @x axis origin (Place a data point for X-axis origin.)
Enter second point on x axis (Place a data point to define the positive x-axis direction.)
Enter point define y axis (Place a data point to define the XY plane to be rotated and the direction of the positive Y-axis.)
Select view(s) for rotation (Place a data point to identify the view(s) to be rotated.)

DESIGN CUBE

Whenever you start a new two-dimensional design, you get a design plane—the electronic equivalent of a sheet of paper on a drafting table. The two-dimensional design plane is a large, flat plane covered with an invisible matrix grid consisting of 4,294,967,296 (2^{32}) positional units (UOR) along the X and Y axis. In three-dimensional design, you use that same XY-plane plus a third dimension Z axis. The Z axis is the depth in the direction perpendicular to the XY-plane. The volume defined by X, Y, and Z is called the Design Cube. Similar to design plane, the design cube is covered with an invisible matrix grid consisting of 4,294,967,296 (2^{32}) positional units along each of the X, Y, and Z axes. The Global Origin (0,0,0) is at the very center of the design cube, see Figure 13–8. If necessary, you can move the Global Origin by keying at uSTN> field, **GO=<world units>** and pressing ⏎.

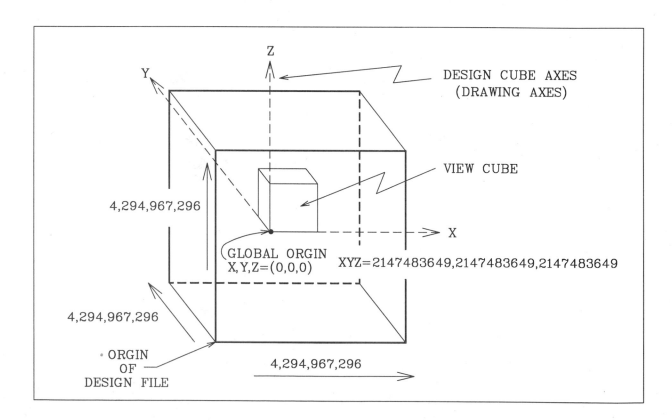

FIGURE 13–8 Design Cube.

DISPLAY DEPTH

Display depth enables you to display a portion of your design rather than the entire thing. The ability to look at a portion of the entire depth in a design comes in handy—especially if the design is complicated. Display depth settings define the front and back clipping planes for elements displayed in a view and is set for each view. Elements not contained in the display depth do not show up on the screen. If you need to work with an element outside the display depth, you must change the display depth to include the element.

Setting the Display Depth Graphically To set the display depth graphically, click the Set Display Depth icon in the 3D View Control sub-palette as shown in Figure 13–9, MicroStation prompts:

Select view for display depth (Place a data point in a view where you want to set the display depth.)
Define front clipping plane (Place a data point in any view where you can identify the front clipping plane.)
Define back clipping plane (Place a data point in any view where you can identify the back clipping plane.)

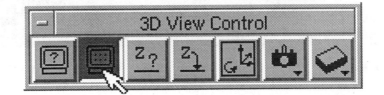

FIGURE 13–9 Invoking the Set Display Depth tool in the 3D View Control sub-palette.

> **NOTE:** When you are setting up the display depth, you will notice dashed lines, in all views, indicating the viewing parameters of the selected view. Both the display volume of the view and the active depth plane are dynamically displayed, with different style dashed lines.

In Figure 13–10, the display depth is set in such a way that only the square box is displayed but not the circles.

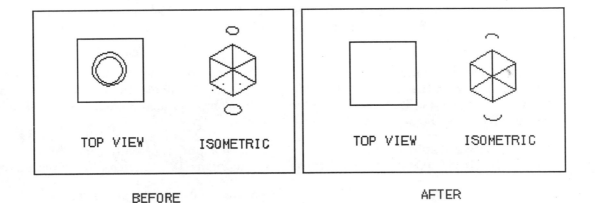

BEFORE   AFTER

FIGURE 13–10 An Example in setting up the Display Depth.

Setting the Display Depth by Key-in The most commonly used method in setting up the display depth is by key-in. At uSTN> field, key-in **DP=<front,back>** and press ⏎ to set the display depth by absolute. The <front,back> are the distances in MU:SU:PU, along the view z-axis from the global origin to the desired front and back clipping planes. MicroStation prompts:

Select the view(s) (Identify the views with a data point to set the display depth.)

To set the display depth by relative, key-in at uSTN> field, **DD=<front,back>** and press ⏎. The <front,back> are the distances in MU:SU:PU, and adds the keyed in values to the current display depth settings.

To determine the current setting for display depth, click the Show Display Depth icon in 3D View Control sub-palette as shown in Figure 13–11, or key-in at uSTN> field, **DP=$** and press ⏎. MicroStation prompts:

Select a view (Place a data point anywhere in the view.)

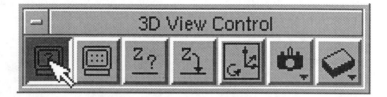

FIGURE 13–11   Invoking the Show Display Depth tool in 3D View Control sub-palette.

MicroStation displays the current setting in the Status area of the MicroStation Command Window.

Fitting Display Depth to Design File Elements A fast way to display the entire design is to invoke the Fit command and select the appropriate view. In two-dimensional design, the Fit command adjusts the view window to include all elements in the design file. Similarly, in three-dimensional design, the Fit command adjusts both the view window and the display depth to include all the elements in the design file. Fit command automatically resets the display depth to the required amount to display the entire design file.

ACTIVE DEPTH

MicroStation has a feature that allows you to place an element in front of or behind the XY plane (front and back views), to the left or right of the YZ plane (right and left views), and above or below the XY plane (top and bottom views). This can be done by setting up the Active Depth. Active depth is a plane, parallel to the screen in each view, where elements will be placed by default. Each view has its own active depth plane, which you can change at any time.

Elements are placed at the active depth if you don't tentative snap to an existing element, or use a precision input. In the top and bottom views (XY plane), the depth value is along its Z axis. In the front and back views (XZ plane), the depth value is along its Y axis. And in the case of right and left views (YZ plane), the depth value is along its X axis.

Setting Active Depth Graphically To set the active depth graphically, click the Set Active Depth icon in the 3D View Control sub-palette as shown in Figure 13–12. MicroStation prompts:

Select view (Place a data point in a view where you want to set the active depth.)
Enter active depth point (Place a data point in a different view where you can identify the location
    for the setting up the active depth.)

FIGURE 13-12 Invoking the Set Active Depth tool in the 3D View Control sub-palette.

> **NOTE:** When you are setting up the active depth, you will notice dashed lines, in all views, indicating the viewing parameters of the selected view. Both the display volume of the view and the active depth plane are dynamically displayed, with different style dashed lines.

Setting Up Active Depth by Key-in The most commonly used method in setting up the active depth is by key-in. At uSTN> field, key-in **AZ**=<depth> and press [ENTER] to set the active depth by Absolute. The <depth> is the distance in MU:SU:PU, along the view Z-axis from the global origin to the desired active depth. MicroStation prompts:

Select the view(s) (Identify the views with a data point to set the active depth.)

To set the active depth by Relative, key-in at uSTN> field, **DZ**=<depth> and press [ENTER]. The <depth> the distance in MU:SU:PU, and adds the keyed in value to the current active depth setting.

> **NOTE:** If you set the active depth outside the range of the display depth, then MicroStation displays the message in the error field:
>
> *Active depth set to display depth*
>
> Active depth is set to the closest value to the display depth.
>
> Let's say the current display depth is set to 100,450 and you set the active depth to 525, then MicroStation sets the active depth to the closest value, in this case the active depth is set to 450. Make sure that MicroStation sets the value for active depth to the intended value. If necessary, change the display depth and then set the active depth.

To determine the current setting for active depth, click the Show Active Depth icon in 3D View Control sub-palette as shown in Figure 13–13, or key-in at uSTN> field, **AZ=$** and press [ENTER]. MicroStation prompts:

Select a view (Place a data point anywhere in the view.)

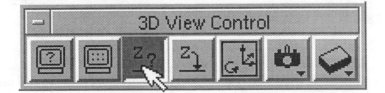

FIGURE 13-13 Invoking the Show Active Depth tool in 3D View Control sub-palette.

MicroStation displays the current setting in the Status area of the MicroStation Command Window.

> **NOTE:** Before you place elements, make sure you are working at the appropriate active depth and display depth.

Boresite Lock

The Boresite Lock controls the manipulation of the elements at different depths. If Boresite lock is set to ON, you can identify or snap to elements at any depth in the view. Elements being moved or copied will remain at their original depths. If it is set to OFF, you can identify only those elements at or very near, the active depth of a view. You can toggle ON or OFF for Boresite lock from the Toggle Settings box, as shown in Figure 13–14.

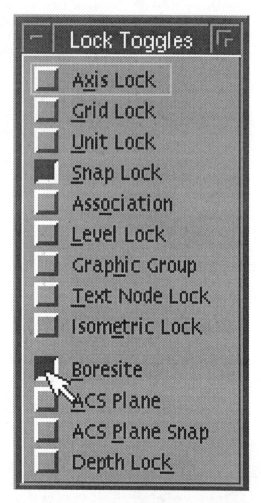

FIGURE 13–14 Toggle Settings box.

> **NOTE:** Tentative points override Boresite lock. You can tentative snap to elements at any depth regardless of the Boresite lock setting.

PRECISION INPUTS

When MicroStation prompts for the location of a point, in addition to providing the data point with your pointing device, you can use precision input commands that allow you to place data points precisely. Similar to two-dimensional placement commands, three-dimensional commands also allow you to key-in by coordinates. MicroStation provides two type of coordinate systems for three-dimensional design: Drawing coordinate system and View coordinate system.

Drawing Coordinate System The Drawing coordinate system is the model coordinate system fixed relative to the design cube, as shown in Figure 13–15. For example, in the TOP view, X is to the right, Y is up, and Z is out of the screen (right-hand rule). In the RIGHT view, Y is to the right, Z is up and X is out of the screen, etc. Following are the two key-ins available for drawing coordinate system:

XY=<X,Y,Z>
DL=<delta_x,delta_y,delta_z>

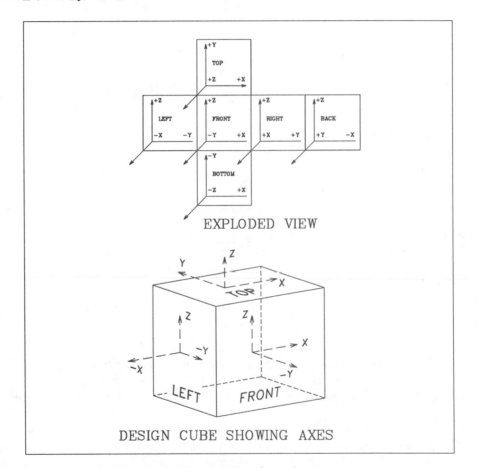

FIGURE 13–15 Design Cube Showing the Drawing Coordinate System.

The XY= key-in places a data point measured from the global origin of the drawing coordinate system. The <X,Y,Z> are the X, Y, and Z values of the coordinates. The view being used at the time has no effect on them.

The DL= places a data point to a distance along the drawing axes from a previous data (relative) or tentative point. The <delta_x,delta_y,delta_z> are the relative coordinates in the X, Y, and Z axes relative to the previous data point or tentative point.

View Coordinate System The View coordinate system is used to input data relative to the screen, where X is to the right, Y is up, and Z comes directly out from the screen in all views as shown in Figure 13–16. View coordinate system is view dependent and depends on the orientation of the view for their direction. Following are the two key-ins available for view coordinate system:

DX=<delta_x,delta_y,delta_z>
DI=<distance,direction>

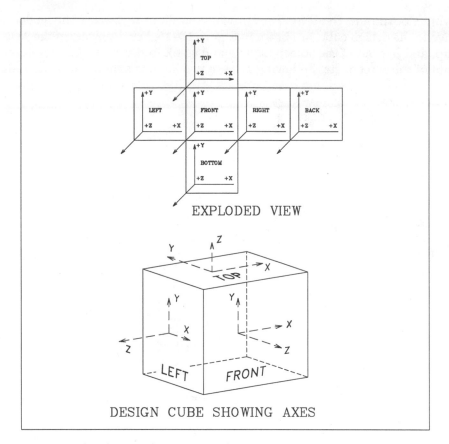

FIGURE 13–16 Design Cube Showing the View Coordinate System.

The DX= key-in places a data point to a distance from the previous data or tentative point (relative) in the same view where the previous point was defined. The <delta_x,delta_y,delta_z> are the relative coordinates in the X, Y, and Z axes relative to the previous data point or tentative point.

The DI= key-in places a data point a certain distance and direction from a previous data or tentative point (relative polar) in the same view where the previous point was defined. The <distance,direction> are specified in relation to the last specified position or point. The distance is specified in current working units (MU:SU:PU), and the direction is specified as an angle in degrees relative to the X-axis.

> **NOTE:** With key-in precision inputs, MicroStation assumes that the view you want to use is the one that you last worked in—that is, the view in which the last tentative or data point was placed. The easiest way to make a view current is to place a tentative point and then press Reset button. Updating a view is also another method of telling MicroStation that the selected view is the last worked in view.

AUXILIARY COORDINATE SYSTEMS (ACS)

MicroStation provides you a set of tools to define an infinite set of user-defined coordinate systems called Auxiliary Coordinate Systems. The Auxiliary coordinate systems allow the user to change the location and orientation of the X,Y, and Z axes to reduce the calculations needed to create 3D objects. You can redefine the origin in your drawing, and establish positive X and the positive Y axes. New users think of a coordinate system simply as the direction of positive X and positive Y. But once the directions X and Y are defined, the direction of Z will be defined as well. Thus, the user only has to be concerned with X and Y. For example, if a sloped roof of a house is drawn in detail using the Drawing coordinate system, each end point of each element on the inclined roof plane must be calculated. On the other hand, if the Auxiliary coordinate system is set to the same plane as the roof, each object can be drawn as if it were in the plan view. You can define any number of Auxiliary coordinate systems, assigning each a user-determined name. But, at any given time only one Auxiliary coordinate system is current with the default system.

MicroStation provides a visual reminder of how the ACS axes are orientated, and where the current ACS origin is located. The X, Y, and Z axis directions are displayed using arrows labeled appropriately. The display of the ACS axes is controlled by turning ON/OFF of the ACS Triad in the View Attributes settings box as shown in Figure 13–17.

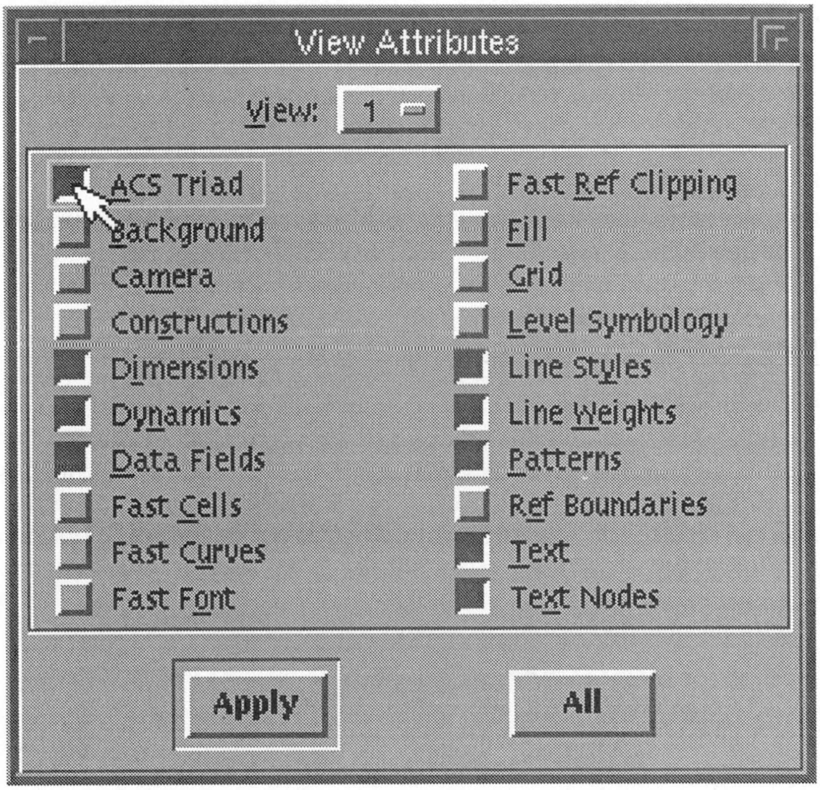

FIGURE 13–17 View Attributes settings box.

MicroStation provides you with three types of coordinate systems for defining an ACS: Rectangular, Cylindrical, and Spherical coordinate systems.

Rectangular Coordinate System The Rectangular coordinate system is the same one that is available for design cube and is also the default type to define an ACS.

Cylindrical Coordinate System The Cylindrical coordinate system is another three-dimensional variant of the polar format. It describes a point by its distance from the origin, its angle in the XY plane from X axis, and its Z value. For example, to specify a point at a distance of 4.5 units from the origin, at an angle of 35 degrees relative to X axis (in the XY plane), and with a Z coordinate of 7.5 units, you would enter: 4.5,35,7.5.

Spherical Coordinate System The Spherical coordinate system is another three-dimensional variant of the polar format. It describes a point by its distant from the current origin, its angle in the XY plane, and its angle up from the XY plane. For example, to specify a point at a distance of 7 units from the origin, at an angle of 60 degrees from the X axis (in the XY plane) and at an angle 45 degrees up from the XY plane, you would enter: 7,60,45.

Precision Input Key-in Similar to the key-ins available for drawing and view coordinates, MicroStation provides key-ins to input the coordinate in reference to the Auxiliary coordinate system. Following are the two key-ins available for Auxiliary coordinate system:

> **AX**=<X,Y,Z>
> **AD**=<delta_x,delta_y,delta_z>

The AX= key-in places a data point measured from the ACS origin and is equivalent key-in to XY=. The <X,Y,Z> are the X, Y, and Z values of the coordinates.

The AD= places a data point to a distance along the drawing axes from a previous data (relative) or tentative point and is equivalent key-in to DL=. The <delta_x,delta_y,delta_z> are the relative coordinates in the X, Y, and Z axes relative to the previous data point or tentative point.

Defining ACS

MicroStation provides you with three different tools to define an ACS. The tools are available in the ACS palette invoked from the Palettes pull-down menu. Before you select one of the three tools, select the coordinate system that you wish to use with the new ACS from the Type option menu in the ACS palette. In addition, you can also control turning ON/OFF toggle buttons for two locks in the ACS palette related to ACS. When ACS Plane Lock is set to ON, each data point is forced to lie on the Active ACS's XY plane (Z=0). When ACS Plane Snap Lock is set to ON, each tentative point is forced to lie on the Active ACS's XY plane (Z=0).

Defining ACS by Aligning With an Element This option lets you define an ACS by identifying an element, where the XY plane of the ACS is parallel to the plane of the selected planar element. The origin of the ACS is at the point of identification of the element. Upon definition, the ACS becomes the Active ACS.

To define an ACS aligned with an element, click the Define ACS (Aligned with Element) icon in the ACS palette as shown in Figure 13–18 or key-in at the uSTN> field, **define acs element** and press ENTER. MicroStation prompts:

> *Identify element* (Identify the element with which to align the ACS and define the ACS origin.)
> *Accept/Reject (Select next input)* (Place a data point to accept the element for defining an ACS.)

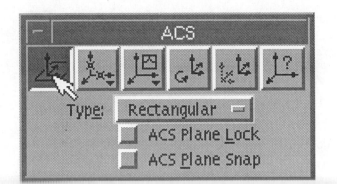

FIGURE 13–18 Invoking the Define ACS (Aligned with Element) tool in the ACS palette.

Defining ACS by Points This option is the easiest and most often used option for controlling the orientation of the ACS. This option allows the user to place three data points to define the origin and the directions of the positive X and Y axes. The origin point acts as a base for the ACS rotation, and when a point is selected to define the direction of the positive X Axis, the direction of the Y Axis is limited because it is always perpendicular to the X Axis. When the X and Y axes are defined, the Z Axis is automatically placed perpendicular to the XY plane. Upon definition, the ACS becomes the Active ACS.

To define an ACS by Points, click the Define ACS (By Points) icon in the ACS palette as shown in Figure 13–19, or key-in at the uSTN> field, **define acs points** and press ⏎. MicroStation prompts:

> *Enter first point @x axis origin* (Place a data point to define the origin.)
> *Enter second point on x axis* (Place a data point to define the direction of the positive X axis, which extends from the origin through this point.)
> *Enter point to define y axis* (Place a data point to define the direction of the positive Y axis.)

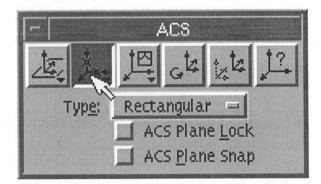

FIGURE 13–19 Invoking the Define ACS (By Points) tool in the ACS palette.

Defining ACS by Aligning With a View In this option, the ACS takes the orientation of the selected View. That is, the ACS axes align exactly with those of the View selected. Upon definition, the ACS becomes the Active ACS.

To define an ACS by aligning with a View, click the Define ACS (Aligned with View) icon in the ACS palette as shown in Figure 13–20, or key-in at the uSTN> field, **define acs view** and press ⏎. MicroStation prompts:

> *Select source view* (Place a data point to select the view with which the ACS is to be aligned and define the ACS origin.)

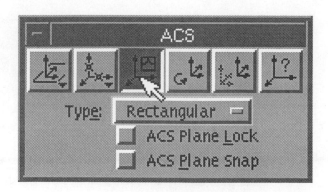

FIGURE 13–20 Invoking the Define ACS (Aligned with View) tool in the ACS palette.

Rotate Active ACS This tool is used to rotate the Active ACS. The origin of the ACS is not moved. To rotate active ACS, click the Rotate Active ACS icon in the ACS palette as shown in Figure 13–21. MicroStation displays a Rotate Active ACS dialog box as shown in Figure 13–22. Key-in the rotation angles, in degrees, from left to right, for the X, Y, and Z axes. Click Absolute button to rotate the ACS in relation to unrotated (top) orientation. Click Relative button to rotate the ACS in relation to current orientation. When you are finished, click the Done button to close the Rotate Active ACS dialog box.

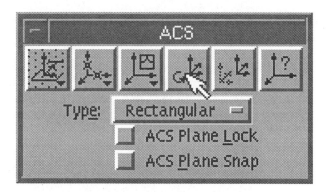

FIGURE 13–21 Invoking the Rotate Active ACS tool in the ACS palette.

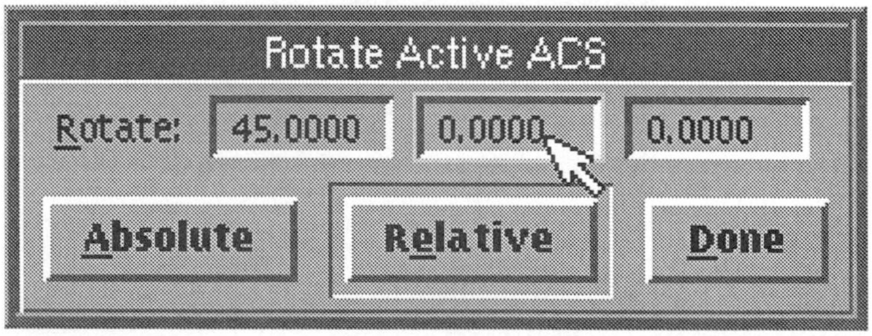

Rotate Active ACS

Rotate: | 45.0000 | 0.0000 | 0.0000 |

Absolute   Relative   Done

FIGURE 13–22 Rotate Active ACS dialog box.

Move ACS This option allows you to move the origin of the Active ACS, leaving the directions of the X, Y, and Z axes unchanged. To Move an ACS, click the Move ACS icon in the ACS palette as shown in Figure 13–23, or key-in at the uSTN> field, **move acs** and press [ENTER]. MicroStation prompts:

Define origin (Place a data point to define the new origin.)

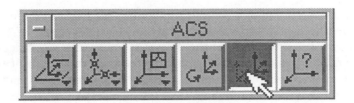

FIGURE 13–23   Invoking the Move ACS tool in the ACS palette.

Select ACS   This option allows you to identify an ACS for attachment as the Active ACS from the saved ACS in each view. To select an ACS, click the Select ACS icon in the ACS palette as shown in Figure 13–24, or key-in at the uSTN> field, **attach acs** and press [ENTER]. MicroStation prompts:

Select auxiliary system @origin   (Identify the ACS at the origin from the coordinate triad displayed.)

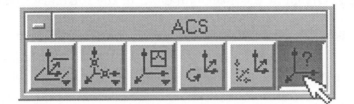

FIGURE 13–24   Invoking the Select ACS tool in the ACS palette.

Saving ACS   You can define any number of ACSs in a design file. Of these, only one can be active at any time. Whenever you define an ACS, you can save them for future use. The Auxiliary Coordinate Systems settings box is used to name, save, attach, or delete an ACS.

The Auxiliary Coordinate Systems settings box is invoked by selecting Auxiliary Coordinates option in the Settings pull-down menu. MicroStation displays the settings box similar to the one shown in Figure 13–25.

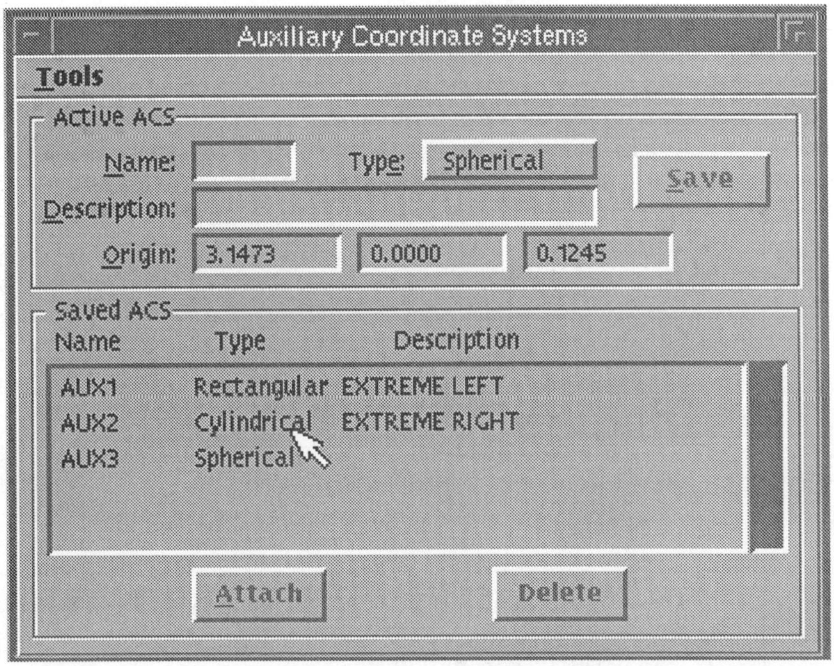

FIGURE 13–25   Auxiliary Coordinate Systems Settings box.

Key-in the Name for the active ACS in the Name edit field. The name is limited to six characters. Select the coordinate system that you wish to save with active ACS from the Type option menu. Key-in the description (optional) of the active ACS in the Description edit field. The description is limited to 27 characters. If necessary, you can change the origin of the active ACS by keying the coordinates in the Origin edit field. Click the Save button to save the active ACS for future attachment. MicroStation will display the name of the ACS, type, and description in the Saved ACS list box.

To attach an ACS as an active ACS, select the name of the ACS from the Saved ACS list box, and click the Attach button. To delete an ACS, first highlight the ACS in the Saved ACS list box, and click the Delete button.

> **NOTE:** All the tools that are available in the ACS palette are also available in the Tools pull-down of the Auxiliary Coordinate Systems settings box.

3D PRIMITIVES

MicroStation provides a set of tools to place simple 3D elements that can be used as the basic building blocks that make up the model. The primitive commands include slab, sphere, cylinder, cone, torus, and wedge.

Place Slab The Place Slab command is used to place a volume of projection with a rectangular cross-section. To place a slab, click the Place Slab icon from the 3D Primitives sub-palette as shown in Figure 13–26, or key-in at the uSTN> field, **place slab** and press [ENTER]. Select the type of surface you wish to place the slab from the Type option menu in the sub-palette. Surface (not capped) option is considered to be open at the base and top, whereas the solid (capped) option is considered to completely enclose a volume. The Axis option menu in the sub-palette sets, or "constraints," the direction in which the height is projected relative to the view or design file axes. If set to Screen X, Screen Y, or Screen Z, the height is projected with the selected screen (view) axis. If set to Drawing X, Drawing Y, or Drawing Z, the height is projected with the selected design file axis. In addition, you can turn ON the toggle buttons for Orthogonal, Length, Width, and Height in the sub-palette. If the orthogonal is set to ON, the edges are placed orthogonally. If you turn on the constraints for Length, Width, and Height, make sure to key-in appropriate values in the edit fields. MicroStation prompts:

Enter start point (Place a data point or key-in coordinates to define the origin.)
Define Length (Place a data point or key-in coordinates to define the length and rotation angle, if Length constraint is set to ON, this data point defines the rotation angle.)
Define Width (Place a data point or key-in coordinates to define the width, if Width constraint is set to ON, this data point accepts the width.)
Define Height (Place a data point or key-in coordinates to define the height, if Height constraint is set to ON, this data point provides the direction.)

> **NOTE:** To place a volume of projection with a non-rectangular cross-section, use the Construct Surface or Solid of Projection tool in the 3D Free-form Surfaces sub-palette.

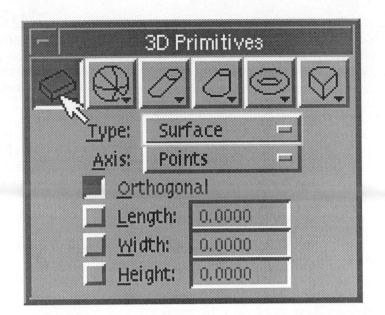

FIGURE 13–26   Invoking the Place Slab command from the 3D Primitives sub-palette.

Place Sphere   The Place Sphere command is used to place a sphere in which all surface points are equidistant from the center. To place a sphere, click the Place Sphere icon from the 3D Primitives sub-palette as shown in Figure 13–27, or key-in at the uSTN> field, **place sphere** and press [ENTER]. If necessary, turn ON the Radius constraint, and key-in the radius in the Radius edit field. The Axis option menu in the sub-palette sets, or constraints, the direction of the sphere's axis relative to the view or design file axes. If set to Screen X, Screen Y, or Screen Z, the sphere's axis is set with the selected screen (view) axis. If set to Drawing X, Drawing Y, or Drawing Z, the sphere's axis is with the selected design file axis. MicroStation prompts:

> *Enter center point* (Place a data point or key-in coordinates to define the sphere's center.)
> *Define radius and axis* (Place a data point or key-in coordinates to define the radius, if Radius is
>   set to ON, then the data point accepts the sphere.)

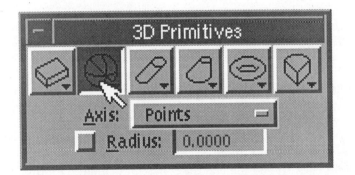

FIGURE 13–27   Invoking the Place Sphere command from the 3D Primitives sub-palette.

> **NOTE:** To place a volume of revolution with a non-circular cross-section, use the Construct Surface or Solid of Projection tool in the 3D Free-form Surfaces sub-palette.

Place Cylinder The Place Cylinder command is used to create a cylinder of equal radius on each end and similar to an extruded circle. To place a cylinder, click the Place Cylinder icon from the 3D Primitives sub-palette as shown in Figure 13–28, or key-in at the uSTN> field, **place cylinder** and press [ENTER]. Select the type of surface you wish to place the cylinder from the Type option menu in the sub-palette. The Axis option menu in the sub-palette sets, or constraints, the direction of the cylinder's axis, or height relative to the view or design file axes. If set to Screen X, Screen Y, or Screen Z, the direction of the cylinder's axis, or height set with the selected screen (view) axis. If set to Drawing X, Drawing Y, or Drawing Z, the direction of the cylinder's axis, or height set with the selected design file axis. In addition, you can turn ON the toggle buttons for Orthogonal, Radius, and Height in the sub-palette. If the orthogonal is set to ON, the cylinder is a right cylinder. If you turn on the constraints for Radius, and Height, make sure to key-in appropriate values in the edit fields. MicroStation prompts:

Enter center point (Place a data point or key-in coordinates to define the center of the base.)
Define radius (Place a data point or key-in coordinates to define the radius, if Radius set to ON, then the data point accepts the base.)
Define height (Place a data point or key-in coordinates to define the height, if Height set to ON, then the data point accepts the cylinder.)

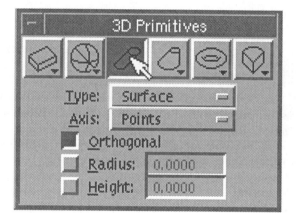

FIGURE 13–28   Invoking the Place Cylinder command from the 3D Primitives sub-palette.

Place Cone The Place Cone command is used to create a cone of unequal radius on each end. To place a cone, click the Place Cone icon from the 3D Primitives sub-palette as shown in Figure 13–29, or key-in at the uSTN> field, **place cone** and press [ENTER]. Select the type of surface you wish to place the cone from the Type option menu in the sub-palette. The Axis option menu in the sub-palette sets, or constraints, the direction of the cone's axis, or height relative to the view or design file axes. If set to Screen X, Screen Y, or Screen Z, the direction of the cone's axis, or height set with the selected screen (view) axis. If set to Drawing X, Drawing Y, or Drawing Z, the direction of the cone's axis, or height sets with the selected design file axis. In addition, you can turn ON the toggle buttons for Orthogonal, Top Radius, Base Radius, and Height in the sub-palette. If the orthogonal is set to ON, the cone is a right cone. If you turn on the constraints for Top Radius, Base Radius, and Height, make sure to key-in appropriate values in the edit fields. MicroStation prompts:

Enter center point (Place a data point or key-in coordinates to define the center of the base.)
Define radius (Place a data point or key-in coordinates to define the base radius. If Base Radius set to ON, then the data point accepts the base.)
Define height (Place a data point or key-in coordinates to define the height and top's center. If Height set to ON, then the data point defines the top's center; if Orthogonal is set to ON, then the data point defines the height only.)

Define top radius (Place a data point or key-in coordinates to define the top radius. If top Radius set to ON, then the data point accepts the cone.)

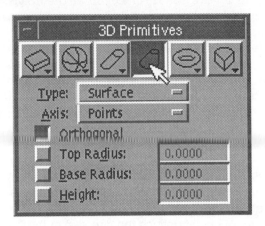

FIGURE 13–29 Invoking the Place Cone command from the 3D Primitives sub-palette.

Place Torus The Place Torus command is used to create a solid or surface with a donut like shape. To place a torus, click the Place Torus icon from the 3D Primitives sub-palette as shown in Figure 13–30, or key-in at the uSTN> field, **place torus** and press ⏎. Select the type of surface you wish to place the torus from the Type option menu in the sub-palette. The Axis option menu in the sub-palette sets, or constraints, the direction of the axis of revolution relative to the view or design file axes. If set to Screen X, Screen Y, or Screen Z, the axis or revolution is set with the selected screen (view) axis. If set to Drawing X, Drawing Y, or Drawing Z, the axis of revolution is set with the selected design file axis. In addition, you can turn ON the toggle buttons for Primary Radius, Secondary Radius and Angle in the sub-palette. If you turn on the constraints for Primary Radius, Secondary Radius and Angle, make sure to key-in appropriate values in the edit fields. MicroStation prompts:

Enter start point (Place a data point or key-in coordinates to define the start point.)

Define center point (Place a data point or key-in coordinates to define the center point, primary radius, and start angle. If Primary Radius is set to ON, then the data point defines the center and start angle.)

Define angle and secondary radius (Place a data point or key-in coordinates to define the secondary radius and sweep angle. If Secondary Radius is set to ON, then the data point defines sweep angle; if Angle is set to ON, then the data point defines secondary radius; and if both Secondary Radius and Angle is set to ON, then the data point defines the direction of the sweep angle rotation.)

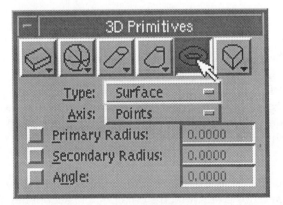

FIGURE 13–30 Invoking the Place Torus command from the 3D Primitives sub-palette.

Place Wedge The Place Wedge command is used to create a wedge—a volume of revolution with a rectangular cross-section. To place a wedge, click the Place Wedge icon from the 3D Primitives sub-palette as shown in Figure 13–31, or key-in at the uSTN> field, **place wedge** and press ⏎. Select the type of surface you wish to place the torus from the Type option menu in the sub-palette. The Axis option menu in the sub-palette sets, or constraints, the direction of the axis of revolution relative to the view or design file axes. If set to Screen X, Screen Y, or Screen Z, the axis or revolution is set with the selected screen (view) axis. If set to Drawing X, Drawing Y, or Drawing Z, the axis of revolution is set with the selected design file axis. In addition, you can turn ON the toggle buttons for Radius, Angle, and Height in the sub-palette. If you turn on the constraints for Radius, Angle, and Height, make sure to key-in appropriate values in the edit fields. MicroStation prompts:

Enter start point (Place a data point or key-in coordinates to define the start point.)
Define center point (Place a data point or key-in coordinates to define the center and the start angle. If Radius is set to ON, then the data point defines the start angle.)
Define angle (Place a data point or key-in coordinates to define the sweep angle. If Angle is set to ON, then the data point defines the direction of the rotation.)
Define height (Place a data point or key-in coordinates to define the height. If Height is set to ON, then the data point defines whether the wedge is projected up or down from the start plane.)

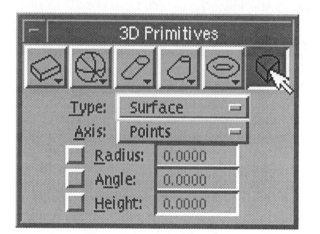

FIGURE 13–31 Invoking the Place Wedge command from the 3D Primitives sub-palette.

CHANGING THE STATUS—SOLID OR SURFACE

The Change to Active Solid or Surface Status tool is used to change an element to the active type—Surface or Solid. To change the status, click the Change to Active Solid or Surface Status icon from the Modify 3D Surfaces sub-palette as shown in Figure 13–32, or key-in at the uSTN> field, **change surface cap** and press ⏎. Select the type of surface you wish to change the status from the Type option menu in the sub-palette. The Tolerance option is used only for B-spline surfaces, in which case two trimmed planes are added as the caps to form the solid. MicroStation prompts:

Identify element (Identify the element to change the status.)
Accept, change cap/Reject (Place a data point to accept the change in status or click the Reject button to reject the operation.)

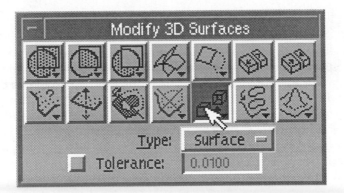

FIGURE 13–32 Invoking the Change to Active Solid or Surface Status tool from the Modify 3D Surfaces sub-palette.

PROJECTED SURFACES

The Construct Surface or Solid of Projection tool is used to create a unique three-dimensional objects from two-dimensional elements. Line, line string, arc, ellipse, complex chain, complex shape, or b-spline curve are the elements that can be projected to a defined distance. Surfaces formed between the original boundary element and its projection are indicated by straight lines connecting the keypoints. To project a boundary element, click the Construct Surface or Solid of Projection icon from the 3D Free-form Surfaces sub-palette as shown in Figure 13–33, or key-in at the uSTN> field, **construct surface projection** and press [ENTER]. Select the type of surface you wish to project from the Type option menu in the sub-palette. In addition, you can turn ON the toggle buttons for Orthogonal, Distance, Spin Angle, X Scale, and Y Scale in the sub-palette. If the orthogonal is set to ON, the boundary element is projected orthogonally. If you turn on the constraints for Distance, Spin Angle, X Scale, and Y Scale, make sure to key-in appropriate values in the edit fields. MicroStation prompts:

Identify element (Identify the boundary element.)
Define height (Place a data point to define the height. If Height is set to ON, then the data point provides the direction.)

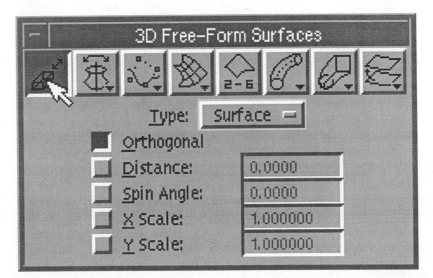

FIGURE 13–33 Invoking the Construct Surface or Solid of Projection tool from the 3D Free-form Surfaces sub-palette.

SURFACE OF REVOLUTION

The Construct Surface or Solid of Revolution tool is used to create a unique three-dimensional surface or solid of revolution that is generated by rotating a boundary element about an axis of revolution. Line, line string, arc, ellipse, shape, complex chain, complex shape, or b-spline curve are the elements that can be used in creating a three-dimensional surface or solid. Surfaces created by the boundary element, as it is rotated, are indicated by arcs connecting the keypoints. To create three-dimensional surface or solid of revolution, click the Construct Surface or Solid of Revolution icon from the 3D Free-form Surfaces sub-palette as shown in Figure 13–34, or key-in at the uSTN> field, **construct surface revolution** and press [ENTER]. Select the type of surface you wish to project from the Type option menu in the sub-palette. The Axis option menu in the sub-palette sets or constraints the direction of the axis of revolution relative to the view or design file axes. If set to Screen X, Screen Y, or Screen Z, the axis or revolution is set with the selected screen (view) axis. If set to Drawing X, Drawing Y, or Drawing Z, the axis of revolution is set with the selected design file axis. In addition, you can turn ON the toggle button Angle in the sub-palette. If you turn on the constraints for Angle make sure to key-in appropriate value in the edit field. MicroStation prompts:

Identify element (Identify the boundary element.)
Define axis of revolution (Place a data point or key-in coordinates. If Axis is set to Points, this data point defines one point on the axis of revolution and subsequently MicroStation prompts you for a second data point. If not, this data point defines the axis of revolution.)
Accept, continue surface/reset to complete (Place additional data points to continue, and/or press Reset button to terminate the sequence.)

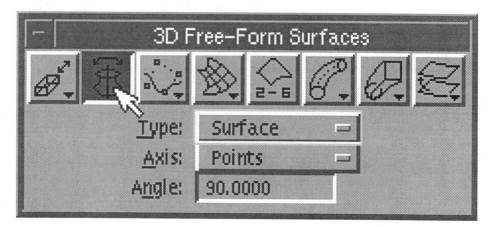

FIGURE 13–34 Invoking the Construct Surface or Solid of Revolution tool from the 3D Free-form Surfaces sub-palette.

PLACING 2D ELEMENTS

Any two-dimensional elements (such as blocks, circles, etc.) that you place with data points without snapping to existing elements will be placed at the active depth of the view. Also, they will be parallel to the screen. Elements that require less than three data points to define (such as blocks, circle with radius, circle with diameter/center, polygons) take their orientation from the view being used. The points only determine their dimensions not their orientation. Elements that require three or more data points required (shapes, circle by edge, ellipses, rotated blocks) to describe them also provides their planar orientation. Once the first three points have been specified, any further points will fall on the same plane.

CREATING COMPOSITE SOLIDS

MicroStation provides three tools that can create a new composite solid by combining two solids by Boolean operations. There are three basic Boolean operations that can be performed in MicroStation. They are as follows:

> Union
> Intersection
> Difference

Union Operation

The union is the process of creating a new composite solid from two solids. The union operation joins the original solids in such a way that there is no duplication of volume. Therefore, the total resulting volume can be equal or less than the sum of the volumes in the original solids. The parts of the solids left are determined by their surface normal orientations. These can be changed with the Change Surface Normal tool.

To create a composite solid by union operation, click the Construct Union Between Surfaces icon from the Modify 3D Surfaces sub-palette as shown in Figure 13–35, or key-in at the uSTN> field, **boolean surface union** and press ⏎. MicroStation prompts:

Identify first surface (Identify the first element for union.)
Accept/Reject (Click the Data button to accept the first element for union or Reject the selection.)
Identify second surface (Identify the second element for union.)
Accept/Reject (Click the Data button to accept the second element for union or Reject the selection.)
Accept/Reject (Click the Data button to accept the union or reject the union operation.)

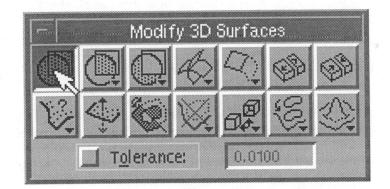

FIGURE 13–35   Invoking the Construct Union Between Surfaces tool from the Modify 3D Surfaces sub-palette.

See Figure 13–36 for an example in creating a composite solid by joining two cylinders using the Construct Union Between Surfaces tool.

Intersection Operation

The intersection is the process of forming a composite solid from only the volume that is common to two solids. The part of each solid that remains is determined by the surface normal orientations. These can be changed with the Change Surface Normal tool.

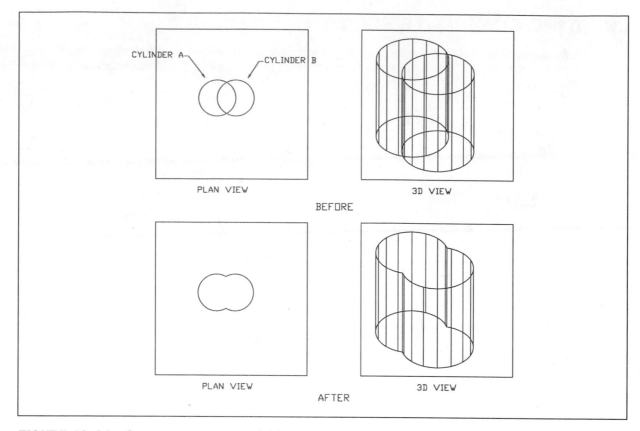

FIGURE 13–36 Creating a composite solid by joining two cylinders using the Construct Union Between Surfaces tool.

To create a composite solid by intersection operation, click the Construct Intersection Between Surfaces icon from the Modify 3D Surfaces sub-palette as shown in Figure 13–37, or key-in at the uSTN> field, **boolean surface intersect** and press [ENTER]. MicroStation prompts:

Identify first surface (Identify the first element for intersection operation.)
Accept/Reject (Click the Data button to accept the first element for intersection or Reject the selection.)
Identify second surface (Identify the second element for intersection operation.)
Accept/Reject (Click the Data button to accept the second element for intersection or Reject the selection.)
Accept/Reject (Click the Data button to accept the intersection or reject the intersection operation.)

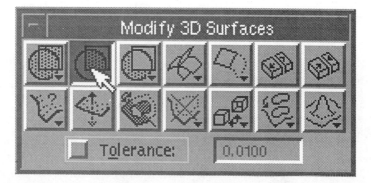

FIGURE 13–37 Invoking the Construct Intersection Between Surfaces tool from the Modify 3D Surfaces.

See Figure 13–38 for an example in creating a composite solid by joining two cylinders using the Construct Intersection Between Surfaces tool.

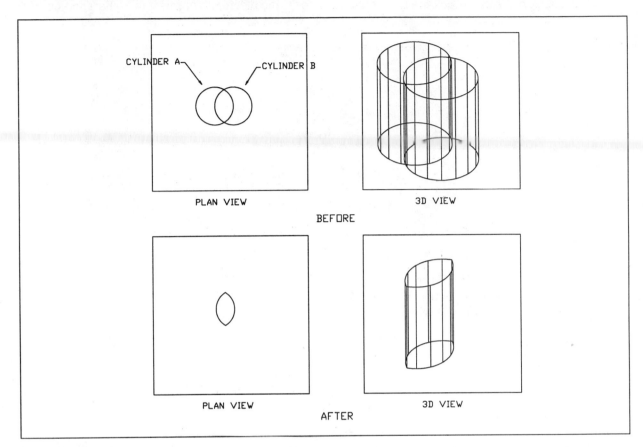

FIGURE 13–38 Creating a composite solid by intersecting two cylinders using the Construct Intersection Between Surfaces tool.

Difference Operation

The difference is the process of forming a composite solid from starting with solid and removing from it any volume that it has in common with a second object. If the entire volume of the second solid is contained in the first solid, then what is left is the first solid minus the volume of the second solid. However, if only part of the volume of the second solid is contained within the first solid, then only that part that is duplicated in the two solids is subtracted. The part of each solid that remains is determined by the surface normal orientations. These can be changed with the Change Surface Normal tool.

To create a composite solid by difference operation, click the Construct Difference Between Surfaces icon from the Modify 3D Surfaces sub-palette as shown in Figure 13–39, or key-in at the uSTN> field, **boolean surface difference** and press ⏎. MicroStation prompts:

> *Identify first surface* (Identify the first element for difference operation.)
> *Accept/Reject* (Click the Data button to accept the first element for difference or Reject the selection.)
> *Identify second surface* (Identify the second element for difference operation.)

Accept/Reject (Click the Data button to accept the second element for difference or Reject the selection.)

Accept/Reject (Click the Data button to accept the difference or reject the difference operation.)

FIGURE 13–39 Invoking the Construct Difference Between Surfaces tool from the Modify 3D Surfaces sub-palette.

See Figure 13–40 for an example in creating a composite solid by joining two cylinders using the Construct Difference Between Surfaces tool.

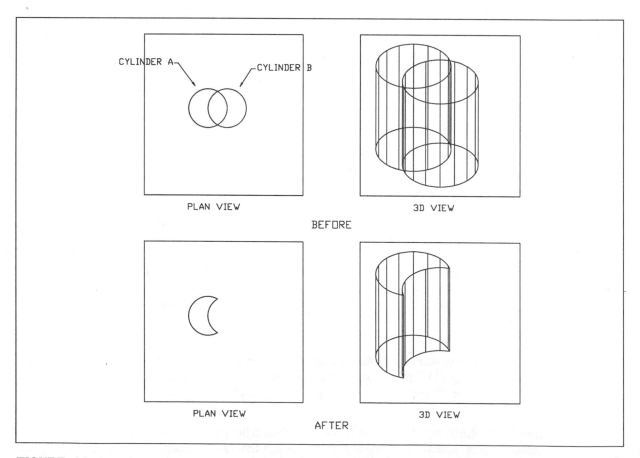

FIGURE 13–40 Creating a composite solid by subtracting Cylinder B from Cylinder A using the Construct Difference Between Surfaces tool.

CHANGE SURFACE NORMAL

The Change Surface Normal tool is used to change the surface normal direction for a surface. This tool is useful to control the way the elements are treated while performing the Boolean operations. To change the surface normal of an element, click the Change Surface Normal icon from the Modify 3D Surfaces sub-palette as shown in Figure 13–41, or key-in at the uSTN> field, **change surface normal** and press [ENTER]. MicroStation prompts:

Identify element (Identify the element, surface normals are displayed.)
Reverse normals, or RESET (Click the Accept button to accept the change in the normal
    direction.)

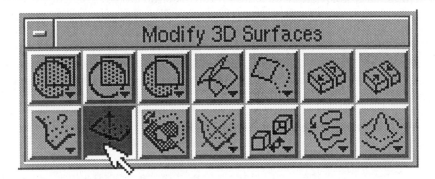

FIGURE 13–41   Invoking the Change Surface Normal tool from the Modify 3D Surfaces sub-palette.

TRIM SURFACE

The trim surface tool is used to trim two elements to their common intersection, or trim just one element. To trim the surface, click the Trim Surface icon from the Modify 3D Surfaces sub-palette as shown in Figure 13–42, or key-in at the uSTN> field, **trim surface** and press [ENTER]. Following are the three options available in the Truncate option menu:

Both—Both surfaces are trimmed to their common intersection.

Single—The first surface identified is trimmed to its intersection with the second element.

None—Neither surface is trimmed. This option is used to construct a curve along the intersection.

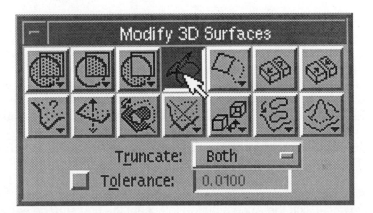

FIGURE 13–42   Invoking the Trim Surface tool from the Modify 3D Surfaces sub-palette.

The default option is Both. MicroStation prompts:

Identify first surface (Identify the first surface.)
Identify second surface (Identify the second surface.)
Accept/Reject (Click the Accept button to accept the trim or reject to cancel the operation.)

CONSTRUCT FILLET BETWEEN SURFACES

The Construct Fillet Between Surfaces tool is used to construct a 3D fillet between two surfaces. The fillet is placed by sweeping an arc with a specified radius (constant radius), or two arcs with different radii (variable radius), along the common intersection curve. The fillet is created in the area pointed to by the surface normals of both surfaces. To fillet between surfaces, click the Construct Fillet Between Surfaces icon from the Fillet Surfaces sub-palette as shown in Figure 13–43, or key-in at the uSTN> field, **fillet surface** and press [ENTER]. Select one of the two options available (Constant Radius and Variable Radius) from the Define By option menu. Truncate option menu sets the truncation at the point of tangency with the fillet. Key-in the fillet radius in the Radius edit field. MicroStation prompts:

Identify first surface (Identify the first surface.)
Accept/Reject (Click the Accept button to accept the first surface selection.)
Identify second surface (Identify the second surface.)
Accept/Reject (Click the Accept button to accept the second surface selection.)
Accept/Reject (Click the Accept button to accept the fillet or reject to cancel the operation.)

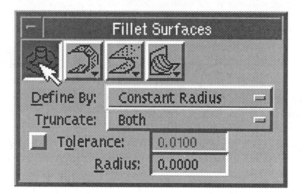

FIGURE 13–43 Invoking the Construct Fillet Between Surfaces tool from the Fillet Surfaces sub-palette.

CONSTRUCT CHAMFER BETWEEN SURFACES

The Construct Chamfer Between Surfaces tool is used to construct a 3D chamfer between two surfaces by a specified length, along the common intersection curve. The chamfer is created in the area pointed to by the surface normals of both surfaces. To chamfer between surfaces, click the Construct chamfer Between Surfaces icon from the Fillet Surfaces sub-palette as shown in Figure 13–44, or key-in at the uSTN> field, **chamfer surface** and press [ENTER]. Truncate option menu sets the truncation at the point of intersection with the chamfer. Key-in chamfer length in the Chamfer Length edit field. MicroStation prompts:

Identify first surface (Identify the first surface.)
Accept/Reject (Click the Accept button to accept the first surface selection.)
Identify second surface (Identify the second surface.)

Accept/Reject (Click the Accept button to accept the second surface selection.)
Accept/Reject (Click the Accept button to accept the chamfer or reject to cancel the operation.)

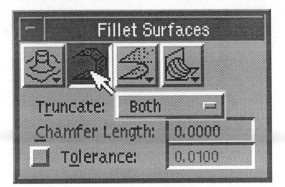

FIGURE 13-44 Invoking the Construct Chamfer Between Surfaces tool from the Fillet Surfaces sub-palette.

PLACING TEXT

MicroStation provides two options to place text in a 3D design; placing text (view-dependent) in such a way that it appears planar to the screen in the view the data point is placed, rotated in the other views or placing text (view-independent) in such a way that it appears planar to the screen in all views.

To place text (view-dependent), click the Place text icon in the Text sub-palette and select By Origin from the Method option menu and follow the prompts. To place text (view-independent), click the Place Text icon in the Text sub-palette and select View Ind from the Method option menu and follow the prompts. Setting up the text parameters is done the same way as in the 2D design.

FENCE MANIPULATIONS

Fences are used in a three-dimensional design in much the same way as they are used in a two-dimensional design. The difference is that a three-dimensional fence defines a volume. The volume is defined by the fenced area and display depth of the view the fence is placed in. The fence lock options work the same way as in a two-dimensional design.

CELL CREATION AND PLACEMENT

The procedure for creating and placing cells in 3D design is the same as in 2D design. Before you create a 3D cell, make sure the display depth is set to include all elements to be used in the cell and the origin is defined at appropriate active depth. If a normal cell was created in the TOP view and then placed in the FRONT view it will appear as it did in the TOP and rotated in other views. In other words, the normal cell is placed as view-dependent. Whereas, a point cell when placed will appear planar to the screen in all views. A point cell is placed view-independent.

You can attach a 2D cell library to a 3D design file, but the cells will have no depth and will be placed at the active depth of the view you are working in. However, you cannot create 3D cells and store them in a 2D cell library.

> **NOTE:** You cannot attach a 3D cell library to a 2D design file.

DIMENSIONING

The procedure for dimensioning setup and placing dimensions in 3D design is similar to 2D design. The main difference is that, you have to consider on which plane you want the dimensioning to be located. Before you place dimensions in a 3D design, make sure the appropriate option is selected from the Alignment option menu in the Linear dimension sub-palette. The View measurement axis measures the projection of the element along the view's horizonal or vertical axis. The True measurement axis measures the actual distance between two points, not the projected distance. And Drawing measurement axis measures the projection of an element along the design cube coordinate system's axis.

RENDERING

Shading or Rendering can turn your 3D model into a realistic (eye-catching) image. MicroStation's rendering options gives you complete control over the appearance of your final images. You can add lights and control lighting in your design and also define the reflective qualities of individual surfaces in your design, makings objects dull or shiny. In MicroStation Version 5, you can create the rendered image of your three-dimensional model entirely within MicroStation. This section provides an overview of the various options available for rendering. Refer to the *MicroStation Reference Guide* for a detailed explanation of various options.

Setting Up Cameras

In establishing a viewing position in MicroStation, the assumption you must make is as if you were looking through a camera to see the image. By default, MicroStation places the camera at right to a view's XY plane. If necessary, you can move or reposition the camera to view the model from a different viewing angle. To enable/disable the default camera setting, click the Camera Setting icon in the 3D View Control sub-palette and select Turn On/Turn Off setting from Camera Settings option menu as shown in Figure 13–45. The Set Up option provided in the Camera Settings options menu is used to set the target, position, and clipping planes for a view camera and turn on the camera for the view. The Move Camera option is used to move the camera without moving the camera target and Move Target option is used to move the target without moving the camera. Just like with a regular camera you are able to change lenses, MicroStation also provides seven standard lenses, Fisheye, Extra Wide, Wide, Normal, Portrait, Telephoto, and Telescopic. Each has a different viewing angle and focal length, simulating real-life lenses. You can select one of the seven standard lenses from the Lens settings box invoked from the Camera sub-menu of the View pull-down menu.

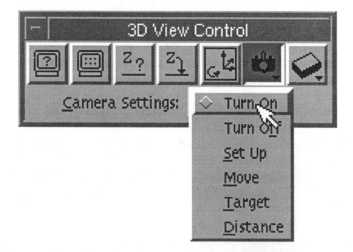

FIGURE 13–45 Invoking the Camera Setting tool in the 3D View Control sub-palette and select Turn On/Turn Off setting from Camera Settings option menu.

Placement of Light Sources

In addition to setting the camera angle, equally important is the lighting setup to produce a high-quality rendered image. MicroStation allows you to use four types of lighting:

Ambient Lighting
Flashbulb Lighting
Solar Lighting
Source Lighting includes Point, Spot, and Distant.

Ambient Lighting is a uniform light that surrounds your model. Flashbulb light is a localized intense light that appears to emanate from the camera position. Solar light is the light provided by sun light. By defining your location on the earth in latitude, longitude, day, month, and time you can simulate lighting for most exterior architectural projects. Ambient, Flashbulb, and Solar lighting is set in the Global settings box invoked from the Rendering sub-menu of the Settings pull-down menu.

Source lighting is achieved by placing light sources in the form of cells. MicroStation program comes with three light source cells (point lights—PNTLT; spot lights—SPOTLT; and distant lights—DISTLT) provided in the LIGHTING.CEL cell library.

Point light can be thought of as a ball of light. It radiates beams of light in all directions. These lights also have more natural characteristics. Their brilliance may be diminished as the light moves away from its source. An object that is near a point light will appear brighter. An object that is farther away will appear darker.

Spot lights are very much like the kind of spotlight you might be accustomed to seeing at a theater or auditorium. Spot lights produce a cone of light toward a target that you specify.

Distant light gives of a fairly straight beam of light that radiates in one direction and its brilliance remains constant, so that an object close to the light will receive as much light as a distant object.

Before you place the light cells, set up the settings in the Source Lighting settings box invoked from the Rendering sub-menu of the Settings pull-down menu. Invoke the Place New Light tool from the Tools pull-down menu in the Settings box to place a light.

Rendering Options

MicroStation provides seven different tools to render a view. Depending on the needs, and availability of the hardware, you can choose one of the seven tools to render the model. To render a view, click the render view icon from the 3D View Control sub-palette and select one of the seven tools available from the Render Mode option menu as shown in Figure 13–46.

Wiremesh option display is similar to the default wireframe display in that makes all elements are transparent and do not obscure other elements.

Hidden Line option displays only parts of elements that would actually be visible are displayed.

Filled Hidden Line option display is identical to a hidden line option display except that the polygons are filled with the element color.

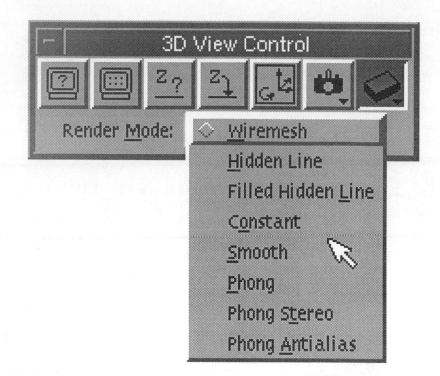

FIGURE 13–46 Invoking the Render View tool from the 3D View Control sub-palette and selecting one of the seven tools available from the Render Mode option menu.

Constant shaded option displays each element as one or more polygons filled with a single (constant) color. The color is computed once for each polygon from the element color, material characteristics, and lighting configurations.

Smooth shaded option displays the appearance of curved surfaces more realisticly than in constant shaded models because polygon color is computed at polygon boundaries and color is blended across polygon interiors.

Phong shaded option recomputes the color of each pixel. Phong shading is useful for producing high-quality images when speed is not critical and very exact lighting effects are desire.

Phong Stereo shading option displays two smooth rendered images on the screen. First, an image from the perspective of the right eye is displayed. Next, the system superimposes an image from the perspective of the left eye. The images are separated by color coding. To view the image in stereo, you have to use the colored glasses that are provided with MicroStation program.

DRAWING COMPOSITION

One of MicroStation's useful features is the ability to compose multiple views (standard and saved) on a drawing sheet. This will allow you to plot multiple views on one sheet of paper—what-you-see-is-what-you-get (WYSIWYG). The Drawing Composition settings box automates the process of attaching the views of the model. The views are attached as reference files. An attached view in a sheet file can be any standard (TOP, BOTTOM, RIGHT, LEFT, FRONT, BACK, and ISO), fitted view, or any saved view of a model file. Standard views can be clipped or set to display only certain levels. An attached view of the model file can be attached in any position at any scale. MicroStation provides a tool that allows you to group a set of views. A group of attached views can be moved, scaled, or detached as one. If necessary, you can remove or add a view to a group. In addition, MicroStation provides a tool that allows you to attach a view by folding an attached view about an orthogonal axis or a line defined by two data points. A folded view is automatically aligned and grouped with the attached view from which it is folded.

The Drawing Composition settings box is invoked from the File pull-down menu of the MicroStation Command Window. MicroStation displays the settings box similar to the Figure 13–47.

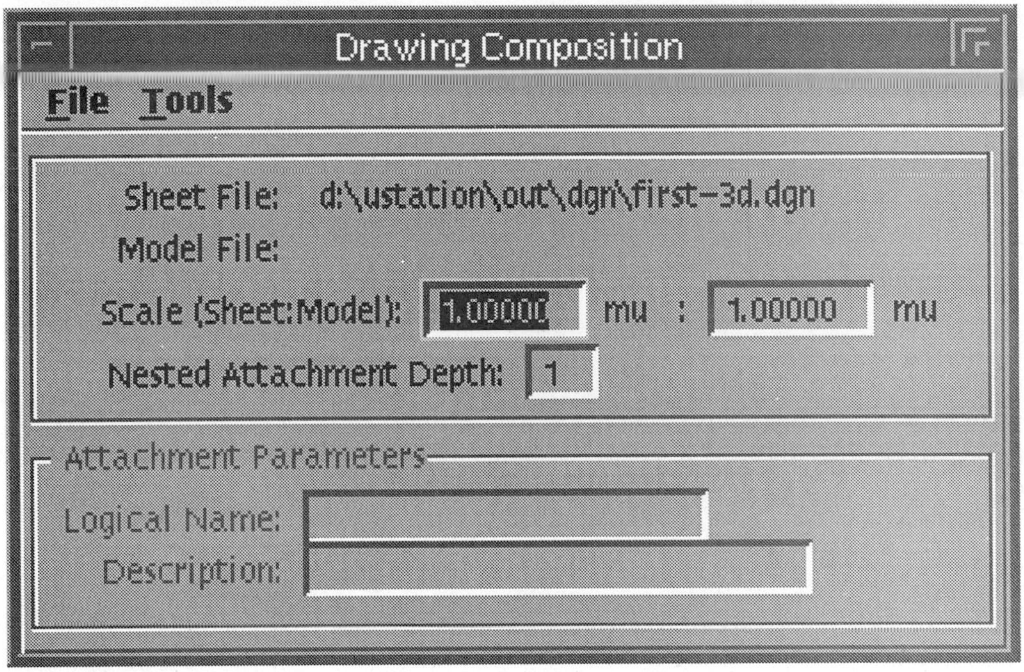

FIGURE 13–47 Drawing Composition Settings box.

MicroStation, by default displays the current design file as the name of the sheet file. To create a new sheet file, invoke the New... command from the File pull-down menu of the Drawing Composition settings box and MicroStation opens the Create Sheet File dialog box. The default sheet seed file is SEED.SHT. Select the appropriate seed file by clicking the Seed button, enter a name for your new sheet file in the Name edit field, and click OK. Following are the seed sheet files delivered with MicroStation program:

Seed File	Drawing Size
Seed.sht	11 × 17
Seedas.sht	A (horizontal orientation)
Seedav.sht	A (vertical orientation)
Seedb.sht	B
Seedc.sht	C
Seedd.sht	D
Seede.sht	E
Seedf.sht	F

To open an existing sheet file, invoke the Open... command from the File pull-down menu and select Sheet option. MicroStation opens the Open Sheet File dialog box. Select the sheet file from the files list box to make it as the active sheet file and click the OK button.

To open a design file to place the views on the active sheet file, select the Open... command from the File pull-down menu of the Drawing Composition settings box and select Model option. MicroStation opens the Open Model File dialog box. Select the Model file from the files list box to attach as the reference file to the active sheet file and click the OK button.

The Scale edit field sets the ratio of the master units in the sheet file to the master units in the model file.

The Nested Attachment Depth displays the number of levels of reference file attachments that are recognized. Model design files can have their own reference file attachments, which, in turn can have more reference file attachments, and so on.

To attach a standard view, select the name of the view from the Attached Standard sub-menu from the Tools pull-down menu. MicroStation prompts:

> *Identify view center* (Place a data point to position the view and attach it to the sheet file.)

To attach a saved view, select Attached Saved view... from the Tools pull-down menu. MicroStation open the Select Saved view dialog box. Select the saved view to attach by selecting its name and click the OK button. MicroStation prompts:

> *Identify view center* (Place a data point to position the view and attach it to the sheet file.)

To attach a copy of a view, select Attach Copy from the Tools pull-down menu. MicroStation prompts:

> *Identify attachment to copy* (Identify an element in the view to be copied.)
> *Accept/Copy attachment* (Place a data point to place the copy of the view.)

To attach a view of the model with the coordinates of the design plane aligned with those of the sheet file, select Attach Coincident from the Tools pull-down menu. MicroStation prompts:

> *Accept to attach coincident* (Place a data point to accept for attachment.)

The view is attached without any rotation, scaling, or offset.

To attach a view of the model by folding it orthogonally about the edge of an attached view, select Orthogonal option from the Attach Folded sub-menu from the Tools pull-down menu. Micro-Station prompts:

> *Identify principle attachment* (Identify an element in an attached view from which to fold the new attached view.)
> *Accept @fold line* (Identify the edge of the attached view about which the new attached view is to be folded.)
> *Identify view center* (Place a data point to position the view.)
> *Identify fold line* (Continue identifying the fold line to place additional views or press Reset button to terminate the command sequence.)

The attached view is automatically aligned with the attached view from which it was folded.

To attach a view of the model by folding it from an attached view about a line defined by two data points, select About Line option from the Attach Folded sub-menu from the Tools pull-down menu. MicroStation prompts:

> *Identify principle attachment* (Identify an element in an attached view from which to fold the new attached view.)
> *Accept at fold line end point* (Place a data point to define one endpoint of the line about which the new attached view will be folded.)
> *Identify fold line end point* (Place a data point to define other endpoint of the line about which the new attached view will be folded.)
> *Identify fold line end point* (Continue identifying the fold line to place additional views or press Reset button to terminate the command sequence.)

The options available under Clip are the same options available in reference file display. For detailed explanation of the options available for clipping, see Chapter 9.

The Group option in the Tools pull-down menu allows you to add or remove attached view to or from a group.

The Move option in the Tools pull-down menu allows you to move an attached view of the model file, a group of views or all attached views.

The Scale option in the Tools pull-down menu allows you to scale (Master Scale:Reference Scale) of an attached view of the model file, a group of views or all attached views.

To Detach a single attached view of the model file, a group of attached views, or all attached views, invoke the Detach option from the Tools pull-down menu. MicorStation prompts:

> *Identify the reference file(s) to detach* (Identify an element in the attached view.)

Once you set up all the views, add any annotations, and title block information. Invoke the Plot... command to create a plot file.

EXERCISES

Exercises 13–1 through 13–5

Lay out the objects shown in 3D form. Create the design to the given dimensions.

Exercise 13–1

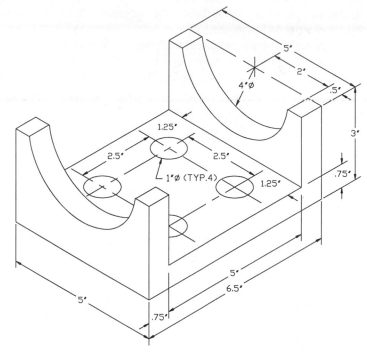

Exercise 13–2

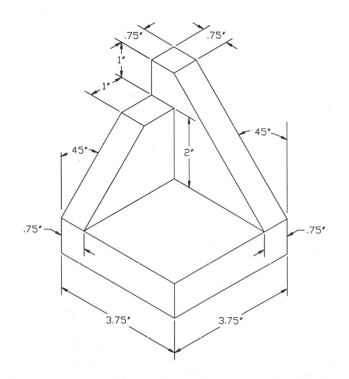

Exercise 13–3

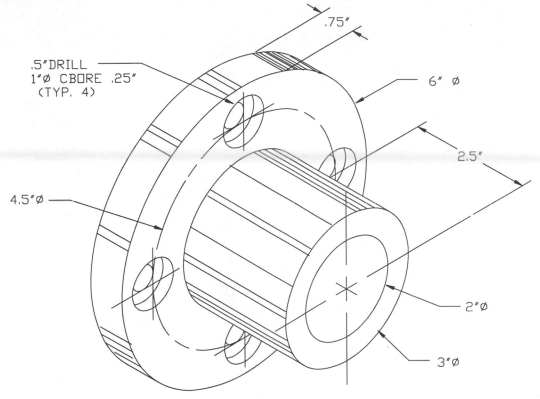

.5"DRILL
1"∅ CBORE .25"
(TYP. 4)

.75"

6" ∅

2.5"

4.5"∅

2"∅

3"∅

Exercise 13–4

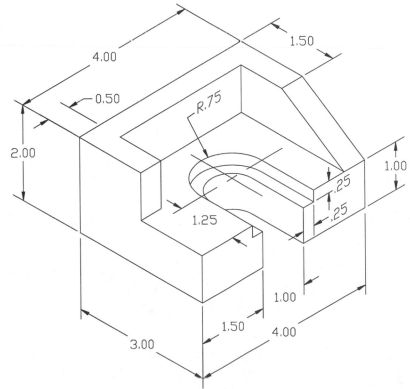

4.00

1.50

0.50

R.75

2.00

1.00

.25

.25

1.25

1.00

3.00

1.50

4.00

Exercise 13–5

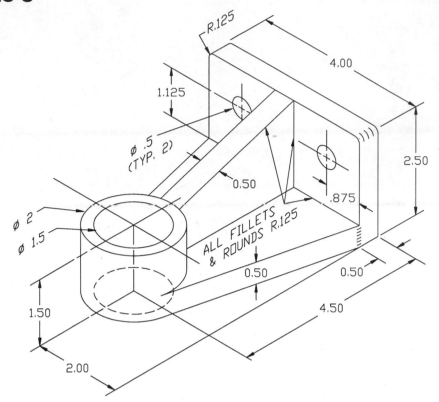

A

MICROSTATION COMMAND WINDOW PULL-DOWN MENU LAYOUT AND PALETTES

(See tear-out sheet in back of book.)

APPENDIX

B

TABLET MENU

(See figure on following page.)

TO ATTACH MENU, KEY-IN AT <STN> FIELD, AM=50MENU,CM AND PRESS ENTER. FOLLOW THE PROMPTS.

ENTER POINT #2

ORIGIN (AM=50MENU,CM)

C

DOS AND FILE HANDLING

▪ ▪ ▪ ▪ ▪ ▪ ▪ ▪ ▪ ▪ ▪ ▪ ▪ ▪ ▪ ▪ ▪ ▪ ▪ ▪

This section of the appendix briefly explains the DOS-related features, commands, and terms that are useful to the operator in using the MicroStation program.

DISKS

Floppy disks are the media on which software is stored. The software is in the form of files. Once properly formatted, a floppy disk is simply addressed by the name of the drive in which it is inserted.

Usually floppy disk drives are labeled drive A and (if there is a second floppy drive) drive B. Important uses of the floppy disk are:

1. Safe backup storage of files.
2. Transfer of files from one computer to another.
3. Temporary repository of files for support or editing without copying them onto the fixed disk.

The fixed disk (or hard disk drive), like floppy disks, stores software in the form of files. Like its name says, it is fixed and not removable for the purpose of transferring files to another computer. The main advantage is in its large capacity, being equal to that of hundreds of floppy disks. Fixed drives are usually labeled drive C and (if a second fixed drive is installed) drive D. The fixed drive is where the main MicroStation program files are stored. Because of the risk of fixed disk failure (beyond recoverability of files), all important files on a fixed disk should also be stored on backup floppy disks or backup tapes. These backup files are not the same as the files that are created automatically by some programs and have the file extension of .BAK. Backup files that are copied to floppy disks for purpose of safekeeping usually have the same name and file extension as the file they back up.

FILES

File specifications (or filespecs) include the drive label, the filename, and an optional extension. The directory path is sometimes included when accessing a file. The drive label and directory path do not always have to be included, as will be explained later.

A file contains data and is stored under a particular filename. The data on the file may be a simple two-line batch file, a ten-page letter, or a large, encrypted and compiled executable program like MicroStation's MGDS.EXE file or one of your larger design files with the file extension of .DGN. When DOS commands operate on a file, they usually operate on the whole file as a unit. Programs like MicroStation, line editors, word processors, and data base manipulators (which are all program files themselves) create or open data files, edit, and close them. Being able to create files and knowing how and when to address them are skills necessary to do advanced file editing and manipulating.

DRIVES AND DIRECTORIES

Drives and directories are established for the purpose of storing files. The combination of a floppy drive and a fixed drive is like a warehouse with a railroad loading dock attached. DOS is the warehouse manager, and does the following when properly instructed by the user:

1. Handles the files into and out of storage;
2. Takes you to a program file that can operate on a data file (reading, editing, and printing are all done by using a program file);
3. Takes you to a data file and opens it for you to read, edit, or print a copy of the file; and
4. Closes the file when you are through and takes you to another set of program and data files.

The main warehouse is the fixed drive. You may have the manager, DOS, store all the files in the open space, known as the root directory. But when enough files start to fill the root directory, it becomes unwieldy. Just listing all the files causes the screen to fill and scroll making it difficult to locate and identify particular files. Therefore, DOS can create storerooms in the warehouse called sub-directories, which conveniently allow you to store groups of related files apart from other groups of files. A sub-directory may even have its own sub-sub-directories, like storerooms within the storerooms in the warehouse.

It is advisable to keep the root directory (the area of the warehouse outside of all storerooms) as free as possible. Only the needed DOS command files and batch files (to be explained later) should be stored in the root directory. All other data and program files should be stored in sub-directories created especially for them. It is also advisable to use short names for the sub-directories. They will have to be keyed-in from the keyboard as part of the path to the files. Keep them as short as possible and still have them identifiable. If you have created a directory named User-Com you will be surprised how quickly you will get tired of keying-in "User-Com", or even "User", every time you key-in the path to your file. You will soon get used to remembering that "UC" or just "U" is the name of the directory that your files are stored in and is much easier to key-in. However, if most of your file manipulations are done with the help of a Utility program such as Norton Utilities™, PCTOOLS™, or XTREE™, then longer, more recognizable directory names are easily accessed without the burden of keying-in.

The floppy drive is like the railroad loading dock. The disk inserted in the drive is like a railroad car parked at the loading dock. It is accessible through the label for the drive it is in.

It is possible, though not as commonly done as on the fixed drive, to create sub-directories on the floppy disk while it is parked in the floppy drive. These sub-directories are like storerooms and rooms in the main warehouse. They stay with that diskette and when it leaves the dock (the floppy drive) the sub-directories go with it. A new car (floppy diskette) brings its own rooms (sub-directories) with it if they have been created previously by DOS.

As an experienced MicroStation operator, you will soon learn your way around drives and directories in order to get to appropriate files. The most common arrangement is to have the computer start up (boot up) with the floppy drive door open. The computer, after memory check, looks at drive A (floppy) first, finds it inaccessible, redirects itself to the fixed drive, looking for the disk operating system on a file called COMMAND.COM. When the boot up is complete, you are automatically logged on to the fixed drive (usually labeled C) and a C:\> or C> prompt appears. Failure to keep the A drive (floppy) open during boot up will cause a message to appear regarding a "nonsystem disk...". However, if the A drive contains a diskette with the COMMAND.COM file on it, an A:> or A> prompt would appear, indicating that you were "logged on" to the A drive. This would be your current drive until you invoked the DOS command to change drives.

Should the "non-system disk..." message appear, simply open the floppy drive door and press any key. The redirection to drive C should proceed without further problems.

CHANGING DRIVES

To change from one drive to another simply enter the new drive letter followed by a colon. For example, while on drive A the prompt reads:

    A>

After keying-in **C:** the prompt reads:

    A>C:

After pressing the ⌷ENTER key, the prompt reads:

    C>

You are now logged on to drive C. It is your current drive. Reversing the above: C>A: produces A> and logs you back on to drive A, the floppy drive.

LOGGING ON TO A DRIVE AND DIRECTORY

The importance of being logged on to a particular drive and directory depends on the type of file you are operating with. As mentioned before, some files just contain data to be operated upon by other programs. These data files are letters, designs, or lists of items such as a phone list or bill of materials. Other files are, of course, the programs themselves.

If you decide to delve into customizing MicroStation, one of the first files you become involved with is the MENU file (with the extension .MNU). It is an excellent example of a file that, while being created or edited is a data file, but when completed becomes a program file. The student should note with care which drive and directory he/she is currently logged onto and which drive and sub-directory the program and data files are on at the time a command is invoked. It is possible that four different locations (drives and directories) could be involved at the same time during one command.

As mentioned previously, diskettes and fixed disks are addressed through their drive label. To access or operate on a file stored on a floppy disk in drive A (and drive A is not the current drive) the user must prefix the file specification with "A:" For example:

    *C>***TYPE A:MYNEW.UCM**

In order for the DOS command called TYPE to operate on the file called MYNEW.UCM, you must address MYNEW.UCM through its drive label, followed by a colon if you are not logged onto drive A. If you are logged onto drive A you may address the file without using the drive label prefix as follows:

    *A:>***TYPE MYNEW.UCM**

Three things must be taken into consideration concerning drives when operating on files:

1. **Current Drive**—You need to know which drive you are presently logged onto.
2. **Source and Target Drives**—You need to know the drive(s) where the source file and the target are. For instance, in using the DOS COPY command, the *source* is where the file is stored before the command is used and the *target* is where the new copy of the file will reside.
3. **Internal or External DOS Command**—It is advisable to study the list of the particular DOS commands you will be using in order to know if they are internal or external commands. For example, the DOS commands COPY and TYPE are internal commands. They reside within the COMMAND.COM program file and can be invoked from any directory while logged on any drive because COMMAND.COM was loaded into RAM when the computer was booted up.

FIRST THE RULE

The DOS command PRINT is an external command. It requires access to the program file called PRINT.COM. In versions of DOS prior to 3.0, it can only be invoked when the directory that it is stored on is the current directory of its drive. The commands with the extension of .COM, .EXE, and .BAT are accessed in a similar manner.

In DOS version 3.0 and later, accessing files on drives other than the current one can be done in an easier fashion than before. If the computer environment has previously been setup with a PATH to the .COM, .EXE, or .BAT file, then they can be invoked from another directory than their own. For example, PRINT.COM is on the directory named DOSX. When the computer is booted up enter the following:

PATH=\DOSX

Then while in the USTATION directory you may simply enter:

PRINT MYNEW.MNU

and DOS will go to the DOSX and use the PRINT command to print the file on the USTATION directory named MYNEW.MNU.

The "PATH=" entry is best included in the AUTOEXEC.BAT file.

By studying carefully and understanding the following examples, the novice can apply the same approach to other file handling procedures and programs, including his/her own custom programs that involve file handling. Even the moderately experienced DOS user can get into some procedure habits that might be improved upon.

EXAMPLE NO. 1:

Objective: *Print the file named MYNEW.UCM*
Current drive: **A**
Current directory: *Root directory (of Drive A)*
Drive where MYNEW.UCM is stored: **C**
Directory where MYNEW.UCM is stored: **\USER**
Drive where PRINT.COM is stored: **C**
Directory where PRINT.COM is stored: **\DOS**

Entering the following will work under one condition:

*A>***C:PRINT C:\USER\MYNEW.UCM**

Even though the path to the file is correct, the path to the DOS command PRINT will work only if, when you changed from drive C, the current directory on drive C was \DOS (in older versions of DOS) or the PATH= \DOS\ has been entered previously. Otherwise, if you had been in the root directory or in the \USER directory when you left drive C (by entering A: to get to drive A), then the path "C:" to PRINT.COM would not work.

EXAMPLE NO. 2:

Objective: *Print the file named MYNEW.UCM*
Current drive: **C** *(Changed from Example No. 1)*
Current directory:**\USER** *(Changed from Example No. 1)*
Drive where MYNEW.UCM is stored: **C**
Directory where MYNEW.UCM is stored: **\USER**
Drive where PRINT.COM is stored: **C**
Directory where PRINT.COM is stored: **\DOS**

ENTRY NO. 1:

*C>***CD\DOS**

This logs you onto the DOS directory where the program file called PRINT.COM is stored. It is an EXTERNAL DOS command.

ENTRY NO. 2:

*C>***PRINT \USER\MYNEW.UCM**

This will work now.

Review Files may be accessed through their paths no matter which drive and directory you are logged onto. The drive label and/or directory path may be omitted when you are logged onto the same drive and/or directory as the file you are accessing.

Internal DOS commands may be invoked from any drive and directory. But not at all times—while a program is running, DOS may or may not be accessible, depending on the program.

External DOS commands requires one of three things: One option is to be logged on to the same directory as the DOS program file for that command. Another option, if you are on another drive, then the drive on which the DOS command program file is stored must have as its current directory the one on which the DOS program file is stored (this applies to older versions of DOS with or without the PATH= entry). The third option is to have entered a "PATH=" command so that DOS will seek out the .COM, .EXE, or .BAT file from any directory.

NOW THE EXCEPTION—PATH

The following example is a method of using external DOS commands from a directory other than the one on which they are stored. This shows how to set up a PATH to their directory. Care must be taken in doing this. If the computer environment has already had a PATH set up to include other directories, then arbitrarily using the DOS command called PATH might nullify the other preset paths. It is best to include the path to external DOS commands with the path to other necessary directories in the PATH command in the AUTOEXEC.BAT file as mentioned previously. An example would be as follows:

Objective: *Provide access to files in the USTATION directory, certain digitizer files in the DIGI directory, and to the EXTERNAL DOS commands in the DOSX directory.*

Context: **PATH=C:\USTATION;\DIGI;\DOSX;**

Because the DOS command PATH is an INTERNAL command, the above can be entered from any directory or drive.

> **NOTE:** In using the above setting, it should be noted that duplicate filenames in different directories might cause a problem. Under the circumstances this is not likely, but if a design were named PRINT.DGN, then trying to use the DOS command named PRINT from some other directory that DOSX might try to access the PRINT.DGN file instead of the PRINT.COM file. Because of the different extensions, this may not happen, but extension differences may not prevent DOS from trying to use a wrong file in other cases. When DOS looks for a file by the PATH route, it looks in the directories in the order that they are placed after the PATH command. In the above example, the USTATION directory will be searched first, the DIGI second, and the DOSX last.

DIRECTORY COMMANDS

While logged onto the root directory of Drive C, the prompt should show only the C or C:\ without any sub-directory name displayed. It would be advisable to key-in **CD** to be sure that you are on the ROOT DIRECTORY. Depending on the boot up parameters for the prompt, it is possible for you to be logged on a sub-directory and not have it show in the prompt area. Under certain prompt parameter settings, if you were logged onto the sub-directory named USTATION on Drive C, the prompt might display "C:\USTATION".

Making Directories

You may use the MKDIR or MD command to create a new directory as a branch of any directory including the root directory. A sub-directory called MENU is created as follows:

*C:\\>***MD\MENU**

This creates a sub-directory to the root directory. This only creates the sub-directory, and does not log you onto it. Another command is used for that purpose.

> **NOTE:** Note the use of the "\" (backslash) for specifying a directory. Any time you are logged onto a directory other than the root directory or the one whose path you wish to specify, you must prefix the name of the target directory with the "\" symbol. The root directory is the "NO NAME" directory, therefore when specifying a path to it from some other directory, you must use the "\" symbol without a directory name.

For simplicity, from here on, directories and sub-directories will primarily be referred to as just directories. The distinction between directories and sub-directories is primarily technical and not critical as long as one learns the correct path to any file.

Searching Directories

It is useful to be able to display on the screen a list of all the files that are stored on a directory. This is accomplished using the DOS command called DIRECTORY or DIR. This command will display the files and also any directories created as a part of the particular directory you are searching. A search of the root directory can be entered as follows:

*C:\>***DIR**

The following might be displayed:

```
Volume in drive C has no label
Directory of C:\
COMMAND  COM      23456      1-23-93
DOS              <DIR>       1-23-93
AUTOEXEC BAT        128      2-13-93
USTATION BAT         28      3-21-93
USTATION         <DIR>       3-21-93
PIPESTAR         <DIR>       4-12-93
SIDEKICK         <DIR>       4-30-93
```

After having used the MD\MENU command the DIR command would display:

```
Volume in drive C has no label
Directory of C:\
COMMAND  COM      23456      1-23-93
DOS              <DIR>       1-23-93
AUTOEXEC BAT        128      2-13-93
USTATION BAT         28      3-21-93
USTATION         <DIR>       3-21-93
PIPESTAR         <DIR>       4-12-93
SIDEKICK         <DIR>       4-30-93
MENU             <DIR>       (the current date is displayed)
```

An additional convenience of the DIR command is to be able to list the files across the screen in a wide fashion. This is done by adding a "/W" to the DIR command:

*C:\>***DIR/W**

The display would be as follows:

```
Volume in drive C has no label
Directory of C:\
COMMAND COM    [DOS]    AUTOEXEC BAT    USTATION BAT
[USTATION]    [PIPESTAR]    [SIDEKICK]    [MENU]
```

The sizes and dates of files are not displayed when the "/W" parameter is added to the DIR command. Another handy feature is the "/P" either with or without the "/W" following the DIR command. "/P" causes the scrolling to pause each time the screen is filled with a display of the list of files and directories. Of course, it is only needed when the list is larger than the screen can display.

When a directory has been created, there are two unnamed hidden files created at the same time. Their presence is indicated by the "." and the ".." symbols displayed when the DIR command is used.

These are of no special concern to the average operator. An effort to delete them, however, might play havoc with DOS so they are best left alone.

Changing Directories

Logging on to another directory on the same drive is done by using the DOS command called CHDIR or CD. It requires the "\" (backslash) prefix in the following manner:

> *C:\>***CD\MENU**

This will log you on to the directory called MENU. In the later version of DOS, logging on to (or accessing) another directory from the root directory can be done without the backslash as follows:

> *C:\>***CD MENU**

If the prompt parameter "PG" (which causes the current directory with the ">" following it) is to be included in the prompt area, the display will read:

> *C:\MENU>*

Getting Back to the Root Directory

Because the root directory has no name, enter the following:

> *C>***CD**

This will return you to the root directory.

Drive and Directory Specifiers

It is possible (but not advisable at this time) to create a sub-directory inside the MENU directory. It may be done in three different ways depending upon which is the current drive and directory. This example is for the purpose of illustrating the use of the ":" symbol for the drive specifier and the "\" symbol for the directory specifier.

EXAMPLE NO. 3:

> Objective: *Create a sub-directory named USERMENU to the directory named "MENU" which is itself a sub-directory of the root directory of drive C.*
> Current Drive: **A** *(Same as Example No. 1)*
> Current directory: *(Root of A) (Same as Example No. 1)*

Enter the following:

> *A>***MD C:\MENU\USERMENU**

EXAMPLE NO. 4:

> Objective: *(Same as Example No. 3)*
> Current Drive: **C** *(Changed from Example No. 3)*
> Current directory: *(Root of C) (Changed from Example No. 3)*

Enter the following:

    *C>***MD \MENU\USERMENU**

FORMATING THE DISK

Before you can write information onto a new disk, you must prepare the diskette so that you can store information. This can be done by a program called FORMAT.COM. The formatting program is located on your DOS directory. You only need to format a disk once. Log on to the directory that has the FORMAT program or if you have a path for the directory that has the FORMAT program, then you can type the command at any DOS prompt.

EXAMPLE NO. 5:

    Current Drive: **C**
    Current Directory: *Root directory*
    Drive where FORMAT.COM is stored: **C:**
    Disk to be formatted is in drive A

A suggested sequence would be as follows:

    *C:***format a:**

Following message will appear:

    Insert new diskette for drive A:
    and strike ENTER when ready

Insert a new diskette and press [ENTER].

You will see the message:

    Formatting...

After a few minutes, the clanking sound stops and the following message appears:

    Format complete
    Format another (Y/N):

If you want to format another disk, take out the newly formatted disk and replace it with another new disk. Then press the [Y] key and the [ENTER] key. If you do not want to format another disk, press [N] and [ENTER] to terminate the program. Remember, you only have to format a disk once, even if you erase the information on it.

> **NOTE:** To format a low density diskette (360KB), you have to add switch /4 to the format command as shown below:
>
>   *c:>***format a:/4**

COPYING FILES

It is sometimes necessary to copy files from one location to another. The only case where a file can be copied to its same drive and directory is if the name is changed in the process. This would produce two identical files with different names.

An example of a need to copy a file would be if you created a custom menu on a directory containing a word processing program, and wanted to transfer it to the USTATION directory for use in MicroStation. This is not the most efficient way to write and test programs, but it does illustrate the DOS command called COPY.

EXAMPLE NO. 6:

> Objective: *Copy the file named TRIAL.MNU from the directory called WRDPRCSR to the directory called USTATION*
> Current Drive: **C**
> Current Directory: *Root directory*

A suggested sequence would be as follows:

> *C>***COPY \WRDPRCSR\TRIAL.MNU \USTATION\TRIAL.MNU**

EXAMPLE NO. 7:

> Objective: *(Same as Example No. 6)*
> Current Drive: **C**
> Current Directory: **\WRDPRCSR**

A suggested sequence would be as follows:

> *C>***COPY TRIAL.MNU \USTATION\TRIAL.MNU**

EXAMPLE NO. 8:

> Objective: *(Same as Example No. 6)*
> Current Drive: **C**
> Current Directory: **B\USTATION**

A suggested sequence would be as follows:

> *C>***COPY \WRDPRCSR\TRIAL.MNU**

Note the permissible omission of the target altogether.

Copying Between Drives

Another common need for copying files is from floppy drives to fixed drives (or vice versa). This method also facilitates transferring files from one computer station to another.

EXAMPLE NO. 9:

Objective: *Copy the file named TRIAL.MNU from a floppy disk in Drive A to the USTATION directory on the fixed drive.*
Current Drive: **C**
Current Directory: *Root directory*

A suggested sequence would be as follows:

*C>***COPY A:TRIAL.MNU \USTATION\TRIAL.MNU**

EXAMPLE NO. 10:

Objective: *(Same as Example No. 9)*
Current Drive: **A**
Current Directory: *Root directory*

A suggested sequence would be as follows:

*A>***COPY TRIAL.MNU C:\USTATION\TRIAL.MNU**

EXAMPLE NO. 11:

Objective: *(Same as Example No. 9)*
Current Drive: **C**
Current Directory: **USTATION**

A suggested sequence would be as follows:

*C>***COPY A:TRIAL.MN**

EXAMPLE NO. 12:   (Use of the global symbol "*")

Objective: *Copy all files with the file EXTENSION of .MNU from Drive A to the USTATION directory on Drive C.*
Current Drive: **C**
Current Directory: **USTATION**

A suggested sequence would be as follows:

*C>***COPY A:*.MNU**

EXAMPLE NO. 13: (Use of the global symbol "*")

Objective: *Copy all files on Drive A to the USTATION directory on Drive C.*
Current Drive: **C**
Current Directory: **USTATION**

A suggested sequence would be as follows:

*C>***COPY A:*.***
or
*C>***COPY A:.**

As you can see, like in programming, DOS commands can be made easier with a little planning.

DELETE A FILE OR GROUP OF FILES

The storage space on a disk is limited, all of it may eventually be occupied by files. Therefore, it is sometimes necessary to delete files you no longer need. The built-in command ERASE and its shorter form DEL can delete a single file or a group of files. Both commands do exactly the same thing and work the same way. You can use whichever command you prefer.

EXAMPLE NO. 14:

Objective: *Delete the file XMPL.BAK.*
Current Drive: **C**
Current Directory: *Root directory*
Drive where XMPL.BAK is stored: **C**
Directory where XMPL.BAK is stored: **\USTATION\DGN**
    (Note that \DGN\ is a sub-directory of \USTATION\)

A suggested sequence would be as follows to delete the file XMPL.BAK

*A:\>***ERASE C:\USTATION\DGN\XMPL.BAK**

EXAMPLE NO. 15:

Objective: *Delete all the files with extension .BAK in drive A.*
Current Drive: **C**
Current Directory: *Root directory*

A suggested sequence would be as follows to delete the files:

*C:\>***erase a:*.BAK**

EXAMPLE NO. 16:

Objective: *Delete all the files in the directory DGN.*
Current Drive: **C**
Current Directory: **c:\dgn**

A suggested sequence would be as follows to delete the files:

*C:\dgn>***erase *.***
or
*C:\dgn>***erase .**

The following message will appear:

Are you sure (Y/N)?

You must answer ⌨ if you want DOS to continue. Otherwise, the operation is terminated without further action.

DOS REFERENCE BOOKS

A variety of books are available that discuss the MS DOS operating system. Read any one of the available books for detailed information about the operating system and system management.

D

KEY-IN COMMANDS

TOOL NAME	KEY-IN
Add to Graphic Group	GROUP ADD
Attach Active Entity	ATTACH AE
Attach Active Entity to Fence Contents	FENCE ATTACH
Attach Displayable Attributes	ATTACH DA
Attach Reference File	REFERENCE ATTACH (RF=)
Automatic Create Complex Chain	CREATE CHAIN AUTOMATIC
Automatic Create Complex Shape	CREATE SHAPE AUTOMATIC
Automatic Fill in Enter Data Fields	EDIT AUTO
B-spline Polygon Display On/Off	MDL LOAD SPLINES; CHANGE BSPLINE POLYGON
Chamfer	CHAMFER
Change B-spline Surface to Active U-Order	MDL LOAD SPLINES;CHANGE BSPLINE UORDER
Change B-spline Surface to Active U-Rules	MDL LOAD SPLINES; CHANGE BSPLINE URULES
Change B-spline Surface to Active V-Order	MDL LOAD SPLINES; CHANGE BSPLINE VORDER
Change B-spline Surface to Active V-Rules	MDL LOAD SPLINES; CHANGE BSPLINE VRULES
Change B-spline to Active Order	MDL LOAD SPLINES; CHANGE BSPLINE ORDER
Change Element to Active Class	CHANGE CLASS
Change Element to Active Color	CHANGE COLOR
Change Element to Active Level	CHANGE LEVEL
Change Element to Active Line Style	CHANGE STYLE
Change Element to Active Line Weight	CHANGE WEIGHT
Change Element to Active Symbol	CHANGE SYMBOLOGY
Change Fence Contents to Active Color	FENCE CHANGE COLOR
Change Fence Contents to Active Level	FENCE CHANGE LEVEL
Change Fence Contents to Active Style	FENCE CHANGE STYLE
Change Fence Contents to Active Symbology	FENCE CHANGE SYMBOLOGY
Change Fence Contents to Active Weight	FENCE CHANGE WEIGHT
Change Fill	CHANGE FILL
Change Text to Active Attributes	MODIFY TEXT
Circular Fillet (No Truncation)	FILLET NOMODIFY

TOOL NAME	KEY-IN
Circular Fillet and Truncate Both	FILLET MODIFY
Circular Fillet and Truncate Single	FILLET SINGLE
Closed Cross Joint	MDL LOAD CUTTER; JOIN CROSS CLOSED
Closed Tee Joint	MDL LOAD CUTTER,JOIN TEE CLOSED
Complete Cycle Linear Pattern	PATTERN LINE SCALE
Construct Active Point at Distance Along an Element	CONSTRUCT POINT DISTANCE
Construct Active Point at Intersection	CONSTRUCT POINT INTERSECTION
Construct Active Points Between Data Points	CONSTRUCT POINT BETWEEN
Construct Angle Bisector	CONSTRUCT BISECTOR ANGLE
Construct Arc Tangent to Three Elements	CONSTRUCT TANGENT ARC 3
Construct B-spline Curve by Least Squares	MDL LOAD SPLINES; CONSTRUCT BSPLINE CURVE LEAST SQUARE
Construct B-spline Curve by Points	MDL LOAD SPLINES; CONSTRUCT BSPLINE CURVE POINTS
Construct B-spline Curve by Poles	MDL LOAD SPLINES; CONSTRUCT BSPLINE CURVE POLES
Construct B-spline Surface by Cross-Section	MDL LOAD SPINES; CONSTRUCT BSPLINE SURFACE CROSS
Construct B-spline Surface by Edges	MDL LOAD SPLINES; CONSTRUCT BSPLINE SURFACE EDGE
Construct B-spline Surface by Least Squares	MDL LOAD SPLINES; CONSTRUCT BSPLINE SURFACE LEAST SQUARE
Construct B-spline Surface by Points	MDL LOAD SPLINES; CONSTRUCT BSPLINE SURFACE POINTS
Construct B-spline Surface by Poles	MDL LOAD SPLINES; CONSTRUCT BSPLINE SURFACE POLES
Construct B-spline Surface by Skin	MDL LOAD SPLINES; CONSTRUCT BSPLINE SURFACE SKIN
Construct B-spline Surface by Tube	MDL LOAD SPLINES; CONSTRUCT BSPLINE SURFACE TUBE
Construct B-spline Surface of Projection	MDL LOAD SPLINES; CONSTRUCT BSPLINE SURFACE PROJECTION
Construct B-spline Surface of Revolution	MDL LOAD SPLINES; CONSTRUCT BSPLINE SURFACE REVOLUTION
Construct Circle Tangent to Element	CONSTRUCT TANGENT CIRCLE 1
Construct Circle Tangent to Three Elements	CONSTRUCT TANGENT CIRCLE 3
Construct Line at Active Angle from Point (key-in)	CONSTRUCT LINE AA 4
Construct Line at Active Angle from Point	CONSTRUCT LINE AA 3
Construct Line at Active Angle to Point (key-in)	CONSTRUCT LINE AA 2
Construct Line at Active Angle to Point	CONSTRUCT LINE AA 1
Construct Line Bisector	CONSTRUCT BISECTOR LINE
Construct Line Tangent to Two Elements	CONSTRUCT TANGENT BETWEEN
Construct Minimum Distance Line	CONSTRUCT LINE MINIMUM
Construct Perpendicular from Element	CONSTRUCT PERPENDICULAR FROM
Construct Perpendicular to Element	CONSTRUCT PERPENDICULAR TO
Construct Points Along Element	CONSTRUCT POINT ALONG
Construct Surface/Solid of Projection	SURFACE PROJECTION
Construct Surface/Solid of Revolution	SURFACE REVOLUTION
Construct Tangent Arc by Keyed-in Radius	CONSTRUCT TANGENT ARC 1

TOOL NAME	KEY-IN
Construct Tangent from Element	CONSTRUCT TANGENT FROM
Construct Tangent to Circular Element and Perpendicular to Linear Element	CONSTRUCT TANGENT PERPENDICULAR
Construct Tangent to Element	CONSTRUCT TANGENT TO
Convert Element to B-spline (Copy)	MDL LOAD SPLINES; CONSTRUCT BSPLINE CONVERT COPY
Convert Element to B-spline Original	MDL LOAD SPLINES; CONSTRUCT BSPLINE CONVERT ORIGINAL
Copy Fence Content	FENCE COPY
Copy Parallel by Distance	COPY PARALLEL DISTANCE
Copy Parallel by Key-in	COPY PARALLEL KEYIN
Corner Joint	MDL LOAD CUTTER; JOIN CORNER
Create Complex Chain	CREATE CHAIN MANUAL
Create Complex Shape	CREATE SHAPE MANUAL
Crosshatch Element Area	CROSSHATCH
Cut All Component Lines	MDL LOAD CUTTER; CUT ALL
Cut Single Component Line	MDL LOAD CUTTER; CUT SINGLE
Define ACS (Aligned with Element)	DEFINE ACS ELEMENT
Define ACS (Aligned with View)	DEFINE ACS VIEW
Define ACS (By Points)	DEFINE ACS POINTS
Define Active Entity Graphically	DEFINE AE
Define Cell Origin	DEFINE CELL ORIGIN
Define Reference File Back Clipping Plane	REFERENCE CLIP BACK
Define Reference File Clipping Boundary	REFERENCE CLIP BOUNDARY
Define Reference Clipping Mask	REFERENCE CLIP MASK
Define Reference File Front Clipping Plane	REFERENCE CLIP FRONT
Define True North	DEFINE NORTH
Delete Element	DELETE ELEMENT
Delete Fence Contents	FENCE DELETE
Delete Part of Element	DELETE PARTIAL
Delete Vertex	DELETE VERTEX
Detach Database Linkage	DETACH
Detach Database Linkage from Fence Contents	FENCE DETACH
Detach Reference File	REFERENCE DETACH
Dimension Angle Between Lines	DIMENSION ANGLE LINES
Dimension Angle from X-Axis	DIMENSION ANGLE X
Dimension Angle from Y-Axis	DIMENSION ANGLE Y
Dimension Angle Location	DIMENSION ANGLE LOCATION
Dimension Angle Size	DIMENSION ANGLE SIZE
Dimension Arc Location	DIMENSION ARC LOCATION
Dimension Arc Size	DIMENSION ARC SIZE
Dimension Diameter (Extended leader)	DIMENSION DIAMETER EXTENDED
Dimension Diameter Parallel	DIMENSION DIAMETER PARALLEL
Dimension Diameter Perpendicular	DIMENSION DIAMETER PERPENDICULAR
Dimension Diameter	DIMENSION DIAMETER
Dimension Element	DIMENSION ELEMENT
Dimension Location (Stacked)	DIMENSION LOCATION STACKED
Dimension Location	DIMENSION LOCATION SINGLE
Dimension Ordinates	DIMENSION ORDINATE
Dimension Radius (Extended Leader)	DIMENSION RADIUS EXTENDED

TOOL NAME	KEY-IN
Dimension Radius	DIMENSION RADIUS
Dimension Size (Custom)	DIMENSION LINEAR
Dimension Size with Arrow	DIMENSION SIZE ARROW
Dimension Size with Strokes	DIMENSION SIZE STROKE
Display Attributes of Text Element	IDENTIFY TEXT
Drop Association	DROP ASSOCIATION
Drop Complex Status	DROP COMPLEX
Drop Complex Status of Fence Contents	FENCE DROP
Drop Dimension	DROP DIMENSION
Drop from Graphic Group	GROUP DROP
Drop Line String/Shape Status	DROP STRING
Drop Text	DROP TEXT
Edit Text	EDIT TEXT
Element Selection	CHOOSE ELEMENT
Extend 2 Elements to Intersection	EXTEND ELEMENT 2
Extend Element to Intersection	EXTEND ELEMENT INTERSECTION
Extend Line By Key-in	EXTEND LINE KEYIN
Extend Element to Intersection	EXTEND ELEMENT INTERSECTION
Extend Line by Key-in	EXTEND LINE KEYIN
Extend Line	EXTEND LINE DISTANCE
Extract Bspline Surface Boundary	MDL LOAD SPLINES; EXTRACT BSPLINE SURFACE BOUNDARY
Fence Stretch	FENCE STRETCH
Fill in Single Enter Data Field	EDIT SINGLE
Freeze Element	FREEZE
Freeze Elements in Fence	FENCE FREEZE
Generate Report Table	FENCE REPORT
Global Origin	ACTIVE ORIGIN (GO=)
Group Holes	GROUP HOLES
Hatch Element Area	HATCH
Horizontal Parabola (No Truncation)	PLACE PARABOLA HORIZONTAL NOMODIFY
Horizontal Parabola and Truncate Both	PLACE PARABOLA HORIZONTAL MODIFY
Identify Cell	IDENTIFY CELL
Impose Bspline Surface Boundary	MDL LOAD SPLINES; IMPOSE BSPLINE SURFACE BOUNDARY
Insert Vertex	INSERT VERTEX
Label Line	LABEL LINE
Load Displayable Attributes	LOAD DA
Load Displayable Attributes to Fence Contents	FENCE LOAD
Match Pattern Attributes	ACTIVE PATTERN MATCH
Match Text Attributes	ACTIVE TEXT
Measure Angle Between Lines	MEASURE ANGLE
Measure Area	MEASURE AREA
Measure Area of Element	MEASURE AREA ELEMENT
Measure Distance Along Element	MEASURE DISTANCE ALONG
Measure Distance Between Points	MEASURE DISTANCE POINTS

TOOL NAME	KEY-IN
Measure Minimum Distance Between Elements	MEASURE DISTANCE MINIMUM
Measure Perpendicular Distance From Element	MEASURE DISTANCE PERPENDICULAR
Measure Radius	MEASURE RADIUS
Merged Cross Joint	MDL LOAD CUTTER; JOIN CROSS MERGE
Merged Tee Joint	MDL LOAD CUTTER; JOIN TEE MERGE
Mirror Element About Horizontal (Copy)	MIRROR COPY HORIZONTAL
Mirror Element About Horizontal (Original)	MIRROR ORIGINAL HORIZONTAL
Mirror Element About Line Copy	MIRROR COPY LINE
Mirror Element About Line (Ordinal)	MIRROR ORIGINAL LINE
Mirror Element About Vertical (Copy)	MIRROR COPY VERTICAL
Mirror Element About Vertical (Original)	MIRROR ORIGINAL VERTICAL
Mirror Fence Contents About Horizontal (Copy)	FENCE MIRROR COPY HORIZONTAL
Mirror Fence Contents About Horizontal (Original)	FENCE MIRROR ORIGINAL HORIZONTAL
Mirror Fence Contents About Line (Copy)	FENCE MIRROR COPY LINE
Mirror Fence Contents About Line (Original)	FENCE MIRROR ORIGINAL LINE
Mirror Fence Contents About Vertical (Copy)	FENCE MIRROR COPY VERTICAL
Mirror Fence Contents About Vertical (Original)	FENCE MIRROR ORIGINAL VERTICAL
Mirror Reference File About Horizontal	REFERENCE MIRROR HORIZONTAL
Mirror Fence About Vertical	REFERENCE MIRROR VERTICAL
Modify Arc Angle	MODIFY ARC ANGLE
Modify Arc Axis	MODIFY ARC AXIS
Modify Arc Radius	MODIFY ARC RADIUS
Modify Element	MODIFY ELEMENT
Modify Fence	MODIFY FENCE
Move ACS	MOVE ACS
Move Element	MOVE ELEMENT
Move Fence Block/Shape	MOVE FENCE
Move Fence Contents	FENCE MOVE
Move Reference File	REFERENCE MOVE
Multi-Cycle Segment Linear Pattern	PATTERN LINE MULTIPLE
Open Cross Joint	MDL LOAD CUTTER; JOIN CROSS OPEN
Open Tee Joint	MDL LOAD CUTTER; JOIN TEE OPEN
Pattern Element Area	PATTERN AREA ELEMENT
Pattern Fence Area	PATTERN AREA FENCE
Place Active Cell (Interactive)	PLACE CELL INTERACTIVE ABSOLUTE
Place Active Cell	PLACE CELL ABSOLUTE
Place Active Cell Matrix	MATRIX CELL (CM=)
Place Active Cell Relative (Interactive)	PLACE CELL INTERACTIVE RELATIVE
Place Active Cell Relative	PLACE CELL RELATIVE
Place Active Line Terminator	PLACE TERMINATOR
Place Active Point	PLACE POINT
Place Arc by Center	PLACE ARC CENTER
Place Arc by Edge	PLACE ARC EDGE
Place Arc by Keyed-in Radius	PLACE ARC RADIUS
Place B-spline Curve by Least Squares	MDL LOAD SPLINES; PLACE BSPLINE CURVE LEASTSQUARE

TOOL NAME	KEY-IN
Place B-spline Curve by Points	MDL LOAD SPLINES; PLACE BSPLINE CURVE POINTS
Place B-spline Curve by Poles	MDL LOAD SPLINES; PLACE BSPLINE CURVE POLES
Place B-spline Surface by Least Squares	MDL LOAD SPLINES; PLACE BSPLINE SURFACE LEASTSQUARES
Place B-spline Surface by Points	MDL LOAD SPLINES; PLACE BSPLINE SURFACE POINTS
Place B-spline Surface by Poles	MDL LOAD SPLINES; PLACE BSPLINE SURFACE POLES
Place Block	PLACE BLOCK ORTHOGONAL
Place Center Mark	DIMENSION CENTER MARK
Place Circle by Center	PLACE CIRCLE CENTER
Place Circle by Diameter	PLACE CIRCLE DIAMETER
Place Circle by Edge	PLACE CIRCLE EDGE
Place Circle by Keyed-in Radius	PLACE CIRCLE RADIUS
Place Circumscribed Polygon	PLACE POLYGON CIRCUMSCRIBED
Place Ellipse by Center and Edge	PLACE ELLIPSE CENTER
Place Ellipse by Edge Points	PLACE ELLIPSE EDGE
Place Fence Block	PLACE FENCE BLOCK
Place Fence Shape	PLACE FENCE SHAPE
Place Fitted Text	PLACE TEXT FITTED
Place Fitted View Independent Text	PLACE TEXT VI
Place Half Ellipse	PLACE ELLIPSE HALF
Place Helix	MDL LOAD SPLINES; PLACE HELIX
Place Inscribed Polygon	PLACE POLYGON INSCRIBED
Place Isometric Block	PLACE BLOCK ISOMETRIC
Place Isometric Circle	PLACE CIRCLE ISOMETRIC
Place Line at Active Angle	PLACE LINE ANGLE
Place Line	PLACE LINE
Place Line String	PLACE LSTRING POINT
Place Multi-line	PLACE MLINE
Place Note	PLACE NOTE
Place Orthogonal Shape	PLACE SHAPE ORTHOGONAL
Place Parabola by End Points	MDL LOAD SPLINES; PLACE PARABOLA ENDPOINTS
Place Point Curve	PLACE CURVE POINT
Place Polygon by Edge	PLACE POLYGON EDGE
Place Quarter Ellipse	PLACE ELLIPSE QUARTER
Place Right Cone	PLACE CONE RIGHT
Place Right Cone by Keyed-in Radius	PLACE CONE RADIUS
Place Right Cylinder	PLACE CYLINDER RIGHT
Place Right Cylinder by Keyed-in Radius	PLACE CYLINDER RADIUS
Place Rotated Block	PLACE BLOCK ROTATED
Place Shape	PLACE SHAPE
Place Skewed Cone	PLACE CONE SKEWED
Place Skewed Cylinder	PLACE CYLINDER SKEWED
Place Slab	PLACE SLAB
Place Space Curve	PLACE CURVE SPACE
Place Space Line String	PLACE LSTRING SPACE
Place Sphere	PLACE SPHERE

TOOL NAME	KEY-IN
Place Spiral By End Points	MDL LOAD SPLINES; PLACE SPIRAL ENDPOINTS
Place Spiral By Length	MDL LOAD SPLINES; PLACE SPIRAL LENGTH
Place Spiral by Sweep Angle	MDL LOAD SPLINES; PLACE SPIRAL ANGLE
Place Stream Curve	PLACE CURVE STREAM
Place Stream Line String	PLACE LSTRING STREAM
Place Text Above Element	PLACE TEXT ABOVE
Place Text Along Element	PLACE TEXT ALONG
Place Text Below Element	PLACE TEXT BELOW
Place Text Node	PLACE NODE
Place Text On Element	PLACE TEXT ON
Place Text	PLACE NODE VIEW
Place View Independent Text Node	PLACE NODE VIEW
Place View Independent Text	PLACE TEXT VI
Polar Array	ARRAY POLAR
Polar Array Fence Contents	FENCE ARRAY POLAR
Project Active Point Onto Element	CONSTRUCT POINT PROJECT
Rectangular Array	ARRAY RECTANGULAR
Rectangular Array Fence Contents	FENCE ARRAY RECTANGULAR
Reload Reference File	REFERENCE RELOAD
Replace Cell	REPLACE CELL
Review Database Attributes of Element	REVIEW
Rotate ACS Absolute	ROTATE ACS ABSOLUTE
Rotate ACS Relative	ROTATE ACS RELATIVE
Rotate Element Active Angle Copy	ROTATE COPY
Rotate Element Active Angle Original	ROTATE ORIGINAL
Rotate Fence Contents by Active Angle (Copy)	FENCE ROTATE COPY
Rotate Fence Contents by Active Angle (Original)	FENCE ROTATE ORIGINAL
Rotate Reference File	REFERENCE ROTATE
Scale Element (Copy)	SCALE COPY
Scale Element (Original)	SCALE ORIGINAL
Scale Fence Contents (Copy)	FENCE SCALE COPY
Scale Fence Contents (Original)	FENCE SCALE ORIGINAL
Scale Reference File	REFERENCE SCALE
Select ACS	ATTACH ACS
Select and Place Cell	SELECT CELL ABSOLUTE
Select and Place Cell (Relative)	SELECT CELL RELATIVE
Set Active Depth	DEPTH ACTIVE
Show Active Depth	SHOW DEPTH ACTIVE
Show Active Entity	SHOW AE
Show Linkage Mode	ACTIVE LINKAGE
Show Pattern Attributes	SHOW PATTERN
Single Cycle Segment Linear Pattern	PATTERN LINE SINGLE
Spin Element (Copy)	SPIN COPY
Spin Element (Original)	SPIN ORIGINAL
Spin Fence Contents (Copy)	FENCE SPIN COPY

TOOL NAME	KEY-IN
Spin Fence Contents (Original)	FENCE SPIN ORIGINAL
Symmetric Parabola (No Truncation)	PLACE PARABOLA NOMODIFY
Symmetric Parabola and Truncate Both	PLACE PARABOLA MODIFY
Thaw Element	THAW
Thaw Elements in Fence	FENCE THAW
Truncated Cycle Linear Pattern	PATTERN LINE ELEMENT
Uncut Component Lines	MDL LOAD CUTTER; UNCUT

E

ALTERNATE KEY-INS

• •

AA=ACTIVE ANGLE	set active angle
AC=ACTIVE CELL	set active cell; place absolute
AD=POINT ACSDELTA	data point—delta ACS
AE=ACTIVE ENTITY	define active entity
AM=ATTACH MENU	activate menu
AP=ACTIVE PATTERN CELL	set active pattern cell
AR=ACTIVE RCELL	set active cell; place relative
AS=ACTIVE SCALE	set active scale factors
AT=TUTORIAL	activate tutorial
AX=POINT ACSABSOLUTE	data point absolute ACS
AZ=ACTIVE ZDEPTH ABSOLUTE	set active depth
CC=CREATE CELL	create cell
CD=DELETE CELL	delete cell from cell library
CM=MATRIX CELL	place active cell matrix
CO=ACTIVE COLOR	set active color
CR=RENAME CELL	rename cell
CT=ATTACH COLORTABLE	attach color table
DA=ACTIVE DATYPE	set active displayable attribute type
DB=ACTIVE DATABASE	attach control file to design file
DD=SET DDEPTH RELATIVE	set display depth (relative)
DF=SHOW FONT	open Fonts settings box
DI=POINT DISTANCE	data point—distance, direction
DL=POINT DELTA	data point—delta coordinates
DP=DEPTH DISPLAY	set display depth
DR=TYPE	display text file
DS=SEARCH	specify fence filter
DV=VIEW	delete saved view
DX=POINT VDELTA	data point—delta view coordinates
DZ=ZDEPTH RELATIVE	set active depth (relative)
EL=ELEMENT LIST	create element list file
FF=FENCE FILE	copy fence contents to design file
FI=FIND	set database row as active entity
FT=ACTIVE FONT	set active font
GO=ACTIVE ORIGIN	Global Origin
GR=ACTIVE GRIDREF	set grid reference spacing
GU=ACTIVE GRIDUNIT	set horizontal grid spacing
KY=ACTIVE KEYPNT	set Snap divisor

LC=ACTIVE STYLE	set active line style
LD=DIMENSION LEVEL	set dimension level
LL=ACTIVE LINE LENGTH	set active text line length
LS=ACTIVE LINE SPACE	set active text node line spacing
LT=ACTIVE TERMINATOR	set active terminator
LV=ACTIVE LEVEL	set active level
NN=ACTIVE NODE	set active text node number
OF=SET LEVELS <level list> OFF	set level display off
ON=SET LEVELS <level list> ON	set level display on
OX=ACTIVE INDEX	retrieve user command index
PA=ACTIVE PATTERN ANGLE	set active pattern angle
PD=ACTIVE PATTERN DELTA	set active pattern delta (distance)
PS=ACTIVE PATTERN SCALE	set active pattern scale
PT=ACTIVE POINT	set active point
PX=DELETE ACS	delete ACS
RA=ACTIVE REVIEW	set attribute review selection criteria
RC=ATTACH LIBRARY	open cell library
RD=NEWFILE	open design file
RF=REFERENCE ATTACH	attach reference file
RS=ACTIVE REPORT	name report table
RV=ROTATE VIEW	rotate view (relative)
RX=ATTACH ACS	select ACS
SD=ACTIVE STREAM DELTA	set active stream delta
SF=FENCE SEPARATE	move fence contents to design file
ST=ACTIVE STREAM TOLERANCE	set active stream tolerance
SV=SAVE VIEW	save view
SX=SAVE ACS	save auxiliary coordinate system
TB=ACTIVE TAB	set tab spacing for importing text
TH=ACTIVE TXHEIGHT	set active text height
TI=ACTIVE TAG	set copy and increment value
TS=ACTIVE TSCALE	set active terminator scale
TV=DIMENSION TOLERANCE	set dimension tolerance limits
TW=ACTIVE TXWIDTH	set active text width
TX=ACTIVE TXSIZE	set active text size (height/width)
UC=USERCOMMAND	activate user command
UCC=UCC	compile user command
UCI=UCI	user command index
UR=ACTIVE UNITROUND	set unit distance
VI=VIEW	attach named view
WO=WINDOW ORIGIN	Window Orgin
WT=ACTIVE WEIGHT	set active line weight
XD=EXCHANGEFILE	open design file; keep view config.
XS=ACTIVE XSCALE	set active X scale
XY=POINT ABSOLUTE	data point absolute coordinates
YS=ACTIVE YSCALE	set active Y scale
ZS=ACTIVE ZSCALE	set active Z scale

PRIMITIVE COMMANDS

. . . .

NAME OF THE COMMAND	PRIMITIVE COMMAND
ACTIVE ANGLE PT2	/ACTAN2
ACTIVE ANGLE PT3	/ACTAN3
ACTIVE CAPMODE OFF	/WOCMDE
ACTIVE CAPMODE ON	/CAPMDE
ACTIVE SCALE DISTANCE	/ACTSCA
ACTIVE SCALE DISTANCE	/ACTSCA
ACTIVE TNJ CB	/TJST#
ACTIVE TNJ CC	/TJST7
ACTIVE TNJ CT	/TJST6
ACTIVE TNJ LB	/TJST2
ACTIVE TNJ LC	/TJST]
ACTIVE TNJ LMB	/TJST5
ACTIVE TNJ LMC	/TJST4
ACTIVE TNJ LMT	/TJST3
ACTIVE TNJ LT	/TJSTO
ACTIVE TNJ RB	/TJST14
ACTIVE TNJ RC	/TJST13
ACTIVE TNJ RMB	/TJSTl 1
ACTIVE TNJ RMC	/TJST 1 0
ACTIVE TNJ RMT	/TJST9
ACTIVE TNJ RT	/TJSTl 2
ACTIVE TXHEIGHT PT2	/TXTHGT
ACTIVE TXJ CB	/TXJS8
ACTIVE TXJ CC	/TXJS7
ACTIVE TXJ CT	/TXjs6
ACTIVE TXJ LB	/TXJSZ
ACTIVE TXJ LC	/TXJSl
ACTIVE TXJ LT	/TXJSO
ACTIVE TXJ RB	/TXJS14
ACTIVE TXJ RC	/TXJS13
ACTIVE TXJ RT	/TXJSlz
ACTIVE TXWIDTH PT2	/TXTWDT
ALIGN	/ALIGN
ATTACH AE	/ATCPTO

NAME OF THE COMMAND	PRIMITIVE COMMAND
CHANGE COLOR	/CELECR
CHANGE STYLE	/CELELS
CHANGE SYMBOLOGY	/CELESY
CHANGE WEIGHT	/CELEWT
CONSTRUCT BISECTOR ANGLE	/ANGBIS
CONSTRUCT BISECTOR LINE	/PERBIS
CONSTRUCT LINE AA 1	/CNSAA1
CONSTRUCT LINE AA 2	/CNSAA2
CONSTRUCT LINE AA 3	/CNSAA3
CONSTRUCT LINE AA 4	/CNSAA4
CONSTRUCT LINE MINIMUM	/MDL2EL
CONSTRUCT POINTALONG	/NPAE
CONSTRUCT POINT BETWEEN	/NPNTS
CONSTRUCT POINT DISTANCE	/PPAE
CONSTRUCT POINT	/CNSINT
CONSTRUCT POINT PROJECT	/PRJPNT
CONSTRUCT TANGENT ARC 1	/PTARCC
CONSTRUCT TANGENT ARC 3	/ATN3EL
CONSTRUCT TANGENT BETWEEN	/LTZELP
CONSTRUCT TANGENT CIRCLE 1	/CTN1EL
CONSTRUCT TANGENT CIRCLE 3	/CTN3EL
CONSTRUCT TANGENT FROM	/PTFROM
CONSTRUCT TANGENT	/LNTNNR
CONSTRUCT TANGENT TO	/PITO
COPY ED	/EDCOPY
COPYELEMENT	/CPELE
COPY PARALLEL DISTANCE	/CPYPP
COPY PARALLEL KEYIN	/CPYPK
COPY VIEW	/COPY
CREATE CHAIN MANUAL	/CONNST
CREATE SHPAE MANUAL	/CPXSHP
DEFINE ACS ELEMENT	/AUXELE
DEFINE ACS POINTS	/AUX3PT
DEFINE ACS VIEW	/AUXVW
DEFINE AE	/DEFPTO
DEFINE CELL ORIGIN	/DOCELL
DELETE ELEMENT	/DLELEM
DELETE PARTIAL	/DLPELE
DELETE VERTEX	/DVERTX
DEPTH ACTIVE PRIMITIVE	/ADEPTH
DEPTH DISPLAY PRIMITIVE	/DDEPTH
DIMENSION ANGLE LINES	/ANGLIN
DIMENSION ANGLE LOCATION	/PITLOC
DIMENSION ANGLE SIZE	/PTSIZ
DIMENSION ARC LOCATION	/ARCLOC
DIMENSION ARC SIZE	/ARCSIZ
DIMENSION AXIS DRAING	/ACTAXD
DIMENSION AXIS TRUE	/ACTAXP
DIMENSION AXIS VIEW	/ACTAXV
DIMENSION DIMAETER PARALLEL	/DIAPAR

NAME OF THE COMMAND	PRIMITIVE COMMAND
DIMENSION DIAMETER PERPENDICULAR	/DIAPER
DIMENSION DIAMETER POINT	/DIACIR
DIMENSION FILE ACTIVE	/MEAACT
DIMENSION FILE REFERENCE	/MEAREF
DIMENSION JUSTIFICATION CENTER	/JUSC
DIMENSION JUSTIFICATION LEFT	/JUSL
DIMENSION JUSTIFICATION RIGHT	/JUSR
DIMENSION LOCATION SINGLE	/LOCSNG
DIMENSION LOCATION STACKED	/LOCSTK
DIMENSION PLACEMENT AUTO	/ADMAUT
DIMENSION PLACEMENT AUTO	/PADMAU
DIMENSION RADIUS POINT	/RADRAD
DIMENSION SIZE ARROW	/SIZARW
DIMENSION SIZE STROKE	/SIZOBL
DIMENSION UNITS DEGREES	/UNITDG
DIMENSION UNITS LENGTH	/UNITLN
DIMENSION WITNESS OFF	/WITLOF
DIMENSION WITNESS ON	/WITLON
DROP COMPLEX	/DRCMPX
EDIT AUTO	/EDAUTO
EDIT SINGLE	/EDSING
EDIT TEXT	/EDTEXT
EXTEND ELEMENT 2	/EXLIN2
EXTEND ELEMENT INTERSECTION	/EXLNIN
EXTEND LINE DISTANCE	/EXLIN
EXTEND LINE KEYIN	/EXLINK
FENCE ATTACH	/AAEFCN
FENCE CHANGE STYLE	/CFNCLS
FENCE CHANGE SYMBOLOGY	/CFNCSY
FENCE COPY	/CPFNCC
FENCE DELETE	/DLFNCC
FENCE DETACH	/RATFCN
FENCE LOCATE	/FNCLOC
FENCE MIRROR COPY HORIZONTAL	/MHCPFC
FENCE MIRROR COPY LINE	/MLCPFC
FENCE MIRROR COPY VERTICAL	/MVCPFC
FENCE MIRROR ORIGINAL HORIZONTAL	/MFHRIZ
FENCE MIRROR ORIGINAL LINE	/MFLINE
FENCE MIRROR ORIGINAL	/MFVERT
FENCE MOVE	/MVFNCC
FENCE REPORT	/RPTACT
FENCE ROTATE COPY	/RTCPFC
FENCE ROTATE ORIGINAL	/RFNCC
FENCE SCALE COPY	/SCCPFC
FENCE SCALE ORIGINAL	/SCFNCC
FENCE TRANSFORM	/TRSFCC
FENCE WSET ADD	/ADWSFN
FENCE WSET COPY	/ADWSFC
FILEDESIGN	/FILDGN

NAME OF THE COMMAND	PRIMITIVE COMMAND
FILLET MODIFY	/PFILTM
FILLET NOMODIFY	/PFILTN
FILLET SINGLE	/FILTRM
FIT ACTIVE	/FIT1
GROUP ADD	/ADDGG
GROUP DROP	/DRFGG
IDENTIFY CELL	/IDCELL
IDENTIFY TEXT	/TXNODA
INCREMENT ED	/CIDATA
INCREMENT TEXT	/CITEXT
INSERT VERTEX	/IVERTX
JUSTIFY CENTER	/EDCJST
JUSTIFY LEFT	/EDLJST
JUSTIFY RIGHT	/EDRJST
LABEL LINE	/LABLN
LABEL LINE	/LBLINE
LOCELE	/LOCELE
LOCK ACS [OFF|ON|TOGGLE]	/CPLOCK
LOCKANGLE [OFF|ON|TOGGLE]	/ANGLLK
LOCK AXIS [OFF|ON|TOGGLE]	/AXLKFF
LOCK BORESITE [OFF|ON|TOGGLE]	/BORSIT
LOCK FENCE CLIP	/CLIP
LOCK FENCE INSIDE	/INSIDE
LOCK FENCE OVERLAP	/OVRLAP
LOCK GGROUP [OFF|ON|TOGGLE]	/GGLOCK
LOCK GRID [OFF|ON|TOGGLE]	/GRIDLK
LOCK SCALE [OFF|ON|TOGGLE]	/SCALLK
LOCK SNAP KEYPOINT	/KEYSNP
LOCK SNAP [OFF|ON]	/SNPOFF
LOCK SNAP PROJECT	/SNAPLK
LOCK TEXTNODE [OFF|ON]	/TXTNLK
LOCK UNIT [OFF|ON]	/UNITLK
MEASURE ANGLE	/LINANG
MEASURE AREA	/AREAPT
MEASURE AREA ELEMENT	/AREAEL
MEASURE DISTANCE ALONG	/MDAE
MEASURE DISTANCE PERPENDICULAR	/PRPND
MEASURE DISTANCE POINTS	/PERIM
MEASURE RADIUS	/RADIUS
MIRROR COPY HORIZONTAL	/MHCPEL
MIRROR COPY LINE	/MLCPEL
MIRROR COPY VERTICAL	/MVCPEL
MIRROR ORIGINAL HORIZONTAL	/MEHRIZ
MIRROR ORIGINAL LINE	/MELINE
MIRROR ORIGINAL VERTICAL	/MEVERT
MODIFY ARC ANGLE	/MDARCA

NAME OF THE COMMAND	PRIMITIVE COMMAND
MODIFY ARC AXIS	/MDARCX
MODIFY ARC RADIUS	/MDARCR
MODIFY ELEMENT	/MDELE
MODIFY FENCE	/MDFNC
MODIFY TEXT	/TXNODC
MOVE ACS	/AUXORC
MOVE ELEMENT	/MVELEM
MOVE FENCE	/MVFNC
NULL	/NULCMD
PLACE ARC CENTER	/PARCC
PLACE ARC EDGE	/PARCE
PLACE ARC RADIUS	/PARCR
PLACE ARC TANGENT	/PTARCC
PLACE BLOCK ORTHOGONAL	/PBLOCK
PLACE BLOCK ROTATED	/PRBLOC
PLACE CELL ABSOLUTE	/PACELL
PLACE CELL ABSOLUTE TMATRX	/PACMTX
PLACE CELL RELATIVE	/PACELR
PLACE CELL RELATIVE TMATRX	/PACRMX
PLACE CIRCLE CENTER	/PCIRC
PLACE CIRCLE DIAMETER	/PCIRD
PLACE CIRCLE EDGE	/PCIRE
PLACE CIRCLE RADIUS	/PCIRR
PLACE CONE RADIUS	/PRCONR
PLACE CONE RIGHT	/PRCONE
PLACE CONE SKEWED	/PCONE
PLACE CURVE POINT	/PPTCRV
PLACE CURVE SPACE	/PSPCRV
PLACE CURVE STREAM	/PSTCRV
PLACE CYLINDER RADIUS	/PRCYLR
PLACE CYLINDER RIGHT	/PRCYL
PLACE CYLINDER SKEWED	/PCYLIN
PLACE ELLIPSE CENTER	/PELL1
PLACE ELLIPSE EDGE	/PELL2
PLACE ELLIPSE HALF	/PPELL1
PLACE ELLIPSE QUARTER	/PPELL2
PLACE FENCE BLOCK	/PFENCB
PLACE FENCE SHAPE	/PFENCE
PLACE LINE	/PLINE
PLACE LINE ANGLE	/PLINAA
PLACE LSTRING POINT	/PPTLST
PLACE LSTRING SPACE	/PSPLST
PLACE LSTRING STREAM	/PSTLST
PLACE NODE	/PTEXTN
PLACE NODE TMATRX	/PTNMTX
PLACE NOTE VIEW	/PVITXN
PLACE PARABOLA HORIZONTAL MODIFY	/PPARMD
PLACE PARABOLA HORIZONTAL NOMODIFY	/PPARNM
PLACE POINT	/PLPNT

NAME OF THE COMMAND	PRIMITIVE COMMAND
PLACE POINT STRING	/PDPTST
PLACE POINT STRING DISJOINT	/PCPTST
PLACE SHAPE	/PSHAPE
PLACE SHAPE ORTHOGONAL	/POSHAP
PLACE TERMINATOR	/PTERM
PLACE TEXT	/PTEXT
PLACE TEXT ABOVE	/PTXTA
PLACE TEXT ALONG	/PTAE
PLACE TEXT BELOW	/PTXTB
PLACE TEXT FITTED	/PFTEXT
PLACE TEXT FVI	/PVIFTX
PLACE TEXT ON	/PTOE
PLACE TEXT TMATRX	/PTXMTX
PLACE TEXT VI	/PVITXT
REFERENCE CLIP BACK	/RFCBCK
REFERENCE CLIP BOUNDARY	/RFCBND
REFERENCE CLIP FRONT	/RFCFRO
REFERENCE DETACH	/RFDTCH
REFERENCE DISPLAY OFF	/RFDISO
REFERENCE DISPLAY ON	/RFDIS1
REFERENCE LEVELS OFF	/RFLEVO
REFERENCE LEVELS ON	/RFLEV1
REFERENCE LOCATE OFF	/RFLOCO
REFERENCE LOCATE ON	/RFLOC1
REFERENCE MOVE	/RFMOVE
REFERENCE ROTATE	/RFROT
REFERENCE SCALE	/RFSCAL
REFERENCE SNAP OFF	/RFSNPO
REFERENCE SNAP ON	/RFSNP1
REPLACE CELL	/RPCELL
REVIEW	/RVWATR
ROTATE 3PTS	/VIEWPL
ROTATE COPY	/RTCPEL
ROTATE ORIGINAL	/ROTELE
ROTATE VIEW POINTS	/VIEWPL
ROTATE VMATRX	/VMATRX
SCALE COPY	/SCCPEL
SCALE ORIGINAL	/SCAELE
SELECT CELL ABSOLUTE	/PSCELL
SELECT CELL ABSOLUTE MATRX	/PSCMTX
SELECT CELL RELATIVE	/PSCELR
SELECT CELL RELATIVE TMATRX	/PSCRMX
SET CONSTRUCT [OFF|ON|TOGGLE]	/CONST1
SET CURVES [FAST|SLOW|OFF|ON|TOGGLE]	/FCURV1
SET DELETE [OFF|PN|TOGGLE]	/DLENSW
SET DIMENSION [OFF|PN|TOGGLE]	/DIMEN1
SET DYNAMIC [FAST|SLOW|OFF|ON|TOGGLE]	/DRAG
SET ED [OFF|ON|TOGGLE]	/UNDLI1
SSET FONT [FAST|SLOW|OFF|ON|TOGGLE]	/FFONT1

NAME OF THE COMMAND	**PRIMITIVE COMMAND**
SET GRID [OFF | ON | TOGGLE]	/GRID1
SET NODES [OFF | ON | TOGGLE]	/TXNOD1
SET PATTERN [OFF | ON | TOGGLE]	/PATRN1
SET TEXT [OFF | ON | TOGGLE]	/TEEXT1
SET TPMODE ACSDELTA	/AXDTEN
SET TPMODE ACSLOCATE	/AXXTEN
SET TPMODE DELTA	/MDELTA
SET TPMODE DISTANCE	/MANGL2
SET TPMODE LOCATE	/LOCATE
SET TPMODE VDELTA	/MDLTVW
SET WEIGHT [OFF | ON]	/DWGHT1
SHOW HEADER	/HEADER
SURFACE PROJECTION	/PRJELE
SURFACE REVOLUTION	/SURREV
SWAP SCREEN	/SWAP
TRANSFORM	/TRSELE
UPDATE1...UPDATE8	/UPDATE
UPDATE BOTH	/UPDBTH
UPDATE LEFT	/UPDAT2
UPDATE RIGHT	/UPDAT1
UPDATE VIEW	/UPDATV
VIEW OFF	/VIEWOF
WINDOW AREA	/WINDA1
WINDOW CENTER	/WINDC1
WINDOW VOLUME	/WINVOL
WSET ADD	/ADWSEL
WSET COPY	/ADWSEC
WSET DROP	/WSDROP
ZOOM IN 2	/HALF1
ZOOM OUT 2	/DOUBL1

TYPE	ELEMENT
1	CELL DEFINITION HEADER
2	CELL PLACEMENT HEADER
3	LINE
4	LINE STRING
5	GROUP DATA
6	SHAPE
7	TEXT NODE
8	DIGITIZER SETUP DATA
9	DESIGN FILE HEADER
10	LEVEL SYMBOLOGY
11	CURVE STRING
12	COMPLEX STRING
13	CONIC
14	COMPLEX SHAPE
15	ELLIPSE
16	ARC
17	TEXT
18	SURFACE (3D)
19	SOLID (3D)
21	B-SPLINE POLE ELEMENT
22	POINT STRING
23	CIRCULAR TRUNCATED CONE (3D)
24	B-SPLINE HEADER (3D)
25	B-SPLINE SURFACE BOUNDARY (3D)
26	B-SPLINE KNOT ELEMENT
27	B-SPLINE CURVE HEADER
28	B-SPLINE WEIGHT FACTOR ELEMENT

APPENDIX

H

SEED FILES

Name of the Seed File	Working Units			View Attributes	Text Parameters
	MU	SU	RESULTION		
USTATION/WSMOD/DEFAULT/ SEED/SCHEM2D.DGN	MM	TH	1MM=100TH 1TH=1000PU	SEE NOTE 1	TX=0.5000 LS=0.0500
USTATION/WSMOD/DEFAULT/ SEED/SCHEM3D.DGN	MM	TH	1MM=100TH 1TH=1000PU	SEE NOTE 1 GRID DISPLAY OFF	TX=0.0100 LS=0.0500
USTATION/WSMOD/DEFAULT/ SEED/SDSCH2D.DGN	IN	TH	1IN=10TH 1TH=1000PU	SEE NOTE 1 GRID DISP. OFF	TX=6.0000 LS=0.5000
USTATION/WSMOD/DEFAULT/ SEED/SDSCH3D.DGN	IN	TH	1MM=100TH 1TH=1000PU	SEE NOTE 1 GRID DISP. OFF	TX=0.1250 LS=0.5000
USTATION/WSMOD/DEFAULT/ SEED/SEED2D.DGN	MU	SU	1MU=10TH 1SU=1000PU	SEE NOTE 1	TX=1.0000 LS=0.5000
USTATION/WSMOD/DEFAULT/ SEED/SEED3D.DGN	MU	SU	1MU=10TH 1SU=1000PU	SEE NOTE 1 GRID DISP. OFF	TX=0.1250 LS=0.5000
USTATION/WSMOD/DEFAULT/ SEED/SEEDZ.DGN	MU	SU	1MU=10TH 1SU=1000PU	SEE NOTE 1 GRID DISP. OFF	TX=0.1250 LS=0.5000
USTATION/WSMOD/DEFAULT/ SEED/TRANSEED.DGN	MU	SU	1MU=10TH 1SU=1000PU	SEE NOTE 1	TX=1.0000 LS=0.5000
USTATION/WSMOD/ARCH/ SEED/ARCHSEED.DGN	'	"	1'=12" 1"=8000PU	SEE NOTE 1 FILL DISP. ON	TX=1.0000 LS=0.5000
USTATION/WSMOD/ARCH/ SEED/SDARCH2D.DGN	'	"	1'=12" 1"=8000PU	SEE NOTE 1	TX=0:9000 LS=0.3000
USTATION/WSMOD/ARCH/ SEED/SDARCH3D.DGN	'	"	1'=12" 1"=8000PU	SEE NOTE 1 GRID DISP. OFF	TX=1.0000 LS=0.3000
USTATION/WSMOD/CIVIL/ SEED/CIV2D.DGN	FT	TH	1'=10TH 1TH=100PU	SEE NOTE 1	TX=1:5000 LS=5:0000
USTATION/WSMOD/CIVIL/ SEED/CIV3D.DGN	FT	TH	1'=10TH 1TH=100PU	SEE NOTE 1 GRID DISP. OFF	TX=25.4 LS=25.4
USTATION/WSMOD/MAPPING/ SEED/MAP2D.DGN	FT	TH	1'=10TH 1TH=100PU	SEE NOTE 1	TX=2:5.00 LS=5:0.00
USTATION/WSMOD/MAPPING/ SEED/MAP3D.DGN	FT	TH	1'=10TH 1TH=100PU	SEE NOTE 1	TX=2:5.00 LS=5:0.00
USTATION/WSMOD/MAPPING/ SEED/SDMAP2D.DGN	FT	TH	1'=10TH 1TH=100PU	SEE NOTE 1 GRID DISP. OFF	TX=1.0000 LS=0.5000
USTATION/WSMOD/MAPPING/ SEED/SDMAP3D.DGN	FT	TH	1'=10TH 1TH=100PU	SEE NOTE 1 GRID DISP. OFF	TX=1.000 LS=5:000

SEED FILES *(concluded)*

Name of the Seed File	Working Units			View Attributes	Text Parameters
	MU	**SU**	**RESULTION**		
USTATION/WSMOD/MAPPING/ SEED/SDMAPM2D.DGN	M	MM	1M=1000MM 1MM=10PU	SEE NOTE 1 GRID DISP. OFF	TX=2.0000 LS=3.0002
USTATION/WSMOD/MAPPING/ SEED/SDMAPM3D.DGN	M	MM	1M=1000MM 1MM=10PU	SEE NOTE 1 GRID DISP. OFF	TX=6.0000 LS=3.0001
USTATION/WSMOD/MECHDRAF/ SEED/MECHDET.DGN	IN	TH	1IN=1000TH 1TH=254PU	SEE NOTE 1 GRID & NODES DISP. OFF	TX=0.0047 LS=0.0295
USTATION/WSMOD/MECHDRAF/ SEED/MECHDETM.DGN	MM		1MM=1000 1=100PU	SEE NOTE 1 GRID DISP. OFF	TX=0.0300 LS=0.0150
USTATION/WSMOD/MECHDRAF/ SEED/MECHLAY.DGN	IN	TH	1IN=1000TH 1TH=254PU	SEE NOTE 1 GRID & NODES DISP. OFF	TX=0.0047 LS=0.0295
USTATION/WSMOD/MECHDRAF/ SEED/MECHLAYM.DGN	MM		1MM=1000 1=100PU	SEE NOTE 1 GRID DISP. OFF	TX=0.0300 LS=0.0150
USTATION/WSMOD/MECHDRAF/ SEED/SDMECH2D.DGN	IN	TH	1IN=1000TH 1TH=254PU	SEE NOTE 1 GRID DISP. OFF	TX=2.0000 LS=0.5000
USTATION/WSMOD/MECHDRAF/ SEED/SDMECH3D.DGN	IN	TH	1IN=1000 1TH=254PU	SEE NOTE 1 GRID DISP. OFF	TX=0.1000 LS=0.0295
USTATION/WSMOD/MECHDRAF/ SEED/SDMENG2D.DGN	MM	SU	1MM=1000SU 1SU=100PU	SEE NOTE 1 GRID DISP. OFF	TX=2.0000 LS=0.0500
USTATION/WSMOD/MECHDRAF/ SEED/SDMENG3D.DGN	MM	SU	1MM=1000SU 1SU=100PU	SEE NOTE 1 GRID DISP. OFF	TX=0.0100 LS=0.0500

NOTE 1: Following are the Display Attributes turned on by default unless noted differently in the table:

    CONSTRUCTIONS
    DIMENSIONS
    DYNAMICS
    DATA FIELDS
    GRID
    LINE STYLES
    LINE WEIGHTS
    PATTERNS
    TEXT
    TEXT NODES

INDEX